Operational Research '72

Operational Research '72

Proceedings of the Sixth IFORS International Conference
on Operational Research

Dublin, Ireland, August 21-25, 1972

Actes de la Sixième IFORS Conférence Internationale
de Recherche Opérationnelle

Dublin, Irlande, 21-25 août, 1972

Edited by

MICEAL ROSS

Economic and Social Research Institute, Dublin, Ireland

1973

NORTH-HOLLAND PUBLISHING COMPANY, AMSTERDAM • LONDON
AMERICAN ELSEVIER PUBLISHING COMPANY, INC. — NEW YORK

Library of Congress Catalog Card Number 72–93497
North-Holland ISBN 0 7204 2081 4
American Elsevier ISBN 0 444 10512 3

Published by:

NORTH-HOLLAND PUBLISHING COMPANY—AMSTERDAM
NORTH-HOLLAND PUBLISHING COMPANY, LTD.—LONDON

Sole distributors for the U.S.A. and Canada:

AMERICAN ELSEVIER PUBLISHING COMPANY, INC.
52 VANDERBILT AVENUE, NEW YORK, N.Y. 10017

PRINTED IN THE NETHERLANDS

To the memory of Paul Naor of Israel
who was killed in an air crash
while flying to a meeting of the
Programming Committee, and in whose memory
Meeting No. 10 at the Conference was also dedicated.

Also to the memory of J. Walsh
former president of ORSA
who died at the Conference.

PLAN OF THE CONFERENCE

Plan de la conférence

MICEAL ROSS

Economic and Social Research Institute, Dublin, Ireland

During the banquet speech at the 1969 Venice conference the retiring President of IFORS, A.M. Lee, spoke of the need for an optimal form of conference and sought support for an experimental structure. He promised that in 1972 the organisers would "stage a different form of conference — one centred on working groups and discussion of major problem areas. Few papers will be prepared and presented and the volume of 'Proceedings' will be primarily a record of the conclusions of the working groups" in the hope that this would prove a better medium for the dissemination of information among delegates.

The programme committee saw in these remarks a challenge to its powers of innovation — a challenge they readily accepted. Indeed they went further and sought to enhance the value of the conference to delegates by ensuring that papers dealt mainly with solving actual problems. As the chairman, Heiner Müller-Merbach, put it, this was "not due to any disregard for theoretical work but rather occasioned by the great disparity between the enormous number of really beautiful theoretical developments reported compared to the paucity of original and exemplary applications, notwithstanding the very many problems of public interest currently awaiting the insights of Operations Research".

Given the pragmatic orientation and experimental nature of the conference some brief comments on the novel aspects of the structure are in order.

The conference was characterised by four simultaneous streams. The mainstream was made up of three highlight papers, the "statement of the problem" by the chairman of each of the eight workshop groups, two papers read by representatives of Allied organisations, eight state-of-the-art sessions consisting of a central paper and two discussants, and finally the eight reports on the workshop groups. A second stream consisted of the twenty-eight national contributions. A third stream was comprised of the meeting of the individual workshops while the fourth stream was devoted to the discussion forum.

The highlight papers were designed to alert OR practitioners to some of the challenging problems of international and national concern to which Operations Research could be usefully applied. The three speakers from the UK, the US and the USSR presented a remarkably unified approach, given their varied backgrounds and spoke of the problems of suboptimisation in national planning. In particular they dwelt on the conflicts between growth and environmental preservation and the needs for interdisciplinary cooperation in achieving a solution. The Russian paper is, in addition, an extremely valuable and vivid statement of the position of OR in that country and the first contribution of the USSR to an IFORS conference.

As already indicated the workshop groups played an important role in the conference. Their objective was to provide an opportunity for delegates to get together in discussion and to think through one of eight management problems of current interest selected on the grounds that they had not been adequately structured as yet. The role of chairman was to guide in formulating the problem by making an introductory statement at a mainstream session early in the conference; to act as moderator during the discussion and to lead the group through an orderly investigation aimed at suggesting a solution, or an approach to a solution. In particular he was required to obtain an informed consensus first approximation solution to be reported back at a mainstream session on the last day of the conference.

Each workshop group was provided with a designated work area and left to organise their time as they wished. Management decision makers, familiar with the problem area in the Irish context or elsewhere, were invited to participate. Conference delegates could join in in various ways: either as full-time "committed" members of a particular workshop, part-time in a "specialised consultative capacity," or on an occasional "quasi-dilettante" basis. Arrangements were made to publish each day the following day's work schedule with details of any special help a workshop might require in the form of "expert opinion" on particular aspects of their problem. Some groups found it helpful to form subgroups to make a more intensive examination of special aspects of the problem under consideration.

Feedback from the conference demonstrates the great popularity of these workshops, and many delegates were enthusiastically in favour of developing and extending the method for future conferences. The active participation of delegates in the discussion lent these activities a greater value than the more passive reception of state-of-the-art papers.

It was left to the workshop to decide what form the report should take. Accordingly a wide variety of formats was employed. No attempt was made to impose any uniformity on them subsequently which may account for some slight uneveness in their presentation.

It had been hoped to publish all eight reports. However, the groups studying supranational problems* found their discussions too controversial to provide a synthesis. A detailed report was not supplied by the workshop on education. The delegates attending this popular workshop were convinced of the great merits of the experiment for those who took part, but were less convinced of the value of attempting to condense this experience into a report for the conference. Accordingly no report was presented. The chairman did, however, provide an unusual feedback by asking one of the guests at the workshop to report on her experience. This, together with the chairman's comments on the experiment, will serve to provide some general impression of the topics treated by the participants.

Since the Venice meeting the cause of multidimensional cooperation on an interdisciplinary and international scale was furthered by the creation of FIACC – the Five** International Associations Coordinating Committee – in 1970, following a proposal by Professor Victor Broida of Paris – Past President of IFAC. These five associations have agreed to cooperate in their planning and in carrying out certain activities. As a practical demonstration of this solidarity Dr. Zemanek, President of IFIP, and Dr. Cuénod, Treasurer of IFAC accepted invitations to speak on developments in their fields.

The eight state-of-the-art papers are a regular feature of the conferences and need no introduction. The role of discussants was to complement the presentation of the main speaker where necessary. Only seven are reproduced here since the text of the eight was unavailable from the speaker concerned.

The member societies of IFORS were invited to select a paper or papers for the "National Contributions" session, on the grounds that they were in a better position than the programme committee to review the work going on in their own country and to select the papers likely to prove of greatest

---

* These were mainly studying the application of computer technology for development, the creation and support of professional managerial cadres in developing nations and the problems of world population growth.
** i.e. IFORS, AICA (Association Internationale due Calcul Analogique), IFAC, (International Federation of Automatic Control), IMEKO (International Measurement Confederation) and IFIP (International Federation for Information Processing).

international interest. Large societies were invited to contribute two papers (France, Germany, India and Japan) or three in the case of UK and USA. The procedure for selection was left to each national society though a preference was indicated for selection on a competitive basis. In furtherence of the general aims of the conference the national societies were asked to submit, as far as possible, recent unpublished specific applications which displayed a good balance between theory and practice. "Blanket" review papers were not favoured. The quality of the papers published in this section is a clear demonstration of great cooperation between the member societies and the programming committee and an ample vindication of the approach.

It was not possible for the US Societies to follow this procedure by reason of their size and dispersed nature. Accordingly, the three papers from the USA have been grouped into a separate section in the published proceedings as they differ considerably in content from the other national contributions.

In recognition of the fact that there is more to a conference than a series of formal papers the "discussion forum" was devised so as to facilitate the delegates in developing a web of informal direct contact with people sharing their particular interests. The "forum" consisted of a number of booths equipped to accomodate small groups. In addition two lecture rooms were available for those topics for which a large attendance was anticipated. In keeping with the purposes of the experiment only a proportion of forum time was scheduled in advance of the conference. The remainder could be reserved by giving the forum manager notice by lunch time of the previous day. This was to ensure their receiving adequate advance publicity in the forum bulletin for the day concerned. These proceedings contain a report on this experiment, given by the manager, R.H.W. Johnston.

Acknowledgements

The manifest success of the conference was due to the work of two committees which had the active support of the Council of IFORS. Their work began immediately after the Fifth International Conference in Venice in 1969. The three years of effort they put into the preparation were rewarded by the presence of 480 delegates from 28 different countries and their achievements testified to by the material recorded in this volume.

Under the chairmanship of H. Müller-Merbach of Germany the programme committee comprised:

R.H.W. Johnston, Deputy Chairman – Ireland,   E. Johnsen – Denmark,
B.M. Brough – UK,   G. Morgenthaler – USA,
F.G. Foster – Ireland,   A. Stravs – Switserland.

The eighth member, Paul Naor of Israel, died in an aircrash while travelling to a meeting of the programme committee. In acknowledgement of his work for the conference meeting number 10 was dedicated to his memory.

Under the chairmanship of F.J. Ridgway the Irish committee responsible for local arrangements comprised:

D. O.Byrne (Secretary),	J.M. Lynch,
T. Forsyth (Treasurer),	J. McGilligan,
M. Flinter,	S. O'Carrol,
M.A. Foley,	W.P. O'Grady,
D.M. Kennedy,	M. Ross.

In the second half of the period this committee benefitted greatly from the experience and dedication of Miss T. Higgins who became full time conference organiser and head of the Conference Secretariat.

Both committees profitted considerably from the experience of the two IFORS officers who were ex officio members of the programme committee.

A. Jensen, Denmark – President,
A.M. Lee, U.K. – Immediate Past President,

while the advice of the IFORS Secretary, Mrs. M. Kinnaird, and the Treasurer, R.H. Colcutt, was invaluable.

For my part, as editor of the proceedings, I should like to record my thanks to John Lawrence and Einar Frederiksson for their helpful advice. Because of space constraints I found it necessary to ask some contributors to shorten their contributions. I would like to express my gratitude to the many authors who responded so readily to my request and who were so prompt and courteous in their dealings with me. Finally, I would like to thank the Director and Council of the Economic and Social Research Institute in Dublin who graciously released me from other duties to enable me to devote more time to the production of these proceedings.

Fé rath Dé go rabh siad uilig.

CONTENTS

PART I

OPENING OF CONFERENCE

Ouverture de la Conférence

Chairman: F.J. RIDGWAY (Ireland)

Opening Address
E.H. CHILDERS, An Tanaiste (the Deputy Prime Minister) and Minister for Health of the Republic of Ireland

Presidential Address
A. JENSEN, President of IFORS

Welcome from Host Society
J.P. HYLAND, President of OR Society of Ireland

M. Ross, ed., OR '72. North-Holland Publishing Company (1973)

OPERATIONAL RESEARCH AND THE POLITICIAN

Recherche opérationnelle et le politicien

ERSKINE H. CHILDERS

An Tanaiste (Deputy Prime Minister) and Minister for Health, Republic of Ireland

Some years ago mathematics was largely associated with statistics in relation to decision making. We appreciated then the value of providing good information enabling good projections to be made and telling us of trends and matters relating to economic and social progress and the development of our health and social welfare services. For example, it was interesting for us in this country to study in great detail the life expectancy tables. From these we could compare the level of health in this country in so far as was possible as a result of examining the findings of insurance companies all over the world as to the length of time a male or female child was likely to live from birth onwards. We found that we are among the top ten countries of the world in relation to life expectancy. Also we were checking the gradual reduction 'of infantile mortality – the deaths of infants of under one year – another very good way of checking the comparative excellence of health services. Of course in relation to these matters there were other social trends and social factors to be taken into account.

In some cases the statistics have proved unreliable. I hope that your operational research discussions can help in bringing mathematics to bear in a more effective way to correct inaccuracies. For example, a great many countries have found that it is almost impossible to check accurately the growth of the population. We have, indeed, found this ourselves in our own country quite recently when we underestimated the number of children that were going to be born even in a period of five years. This is an example where statistics, and even Operational Research, often fail in their objective because the factors to be calculated and assessed vary themselves and change without anyone being able to predict how they will change as the years go by.

Operations Research activities can be valuable in many respects. When speaking of the statistical element we have also found them of great value in relation to psychiatric medicine. We're trying to estimate the various factors in relation to social and economic conditions and the age groupings of those who are afflicted with mental illness either severe illness or less severe trouble. The decisions made were rational at the time if short of being truly scientifically calculated.

Decision-making following a statistical analysis and without the benefit of the kind of Operational Research undertakings which you examine has tended to be time-consuming. I think that is one of the realities we have to face. Governments at large and wide are frequently slow in giving directions as a result of information which they are given and which seems absolutely definite. For example, I should think it is true to say that no government has ever supplied the right number of police at the right moment to deal with an ever increasing amount of crime in both rich and poor countries. It's one example of the inevitable slowness of governments. Governments in some instances tend to ignore the advice they receive or to delay in making their decisions.

I notice from reading statistics in a very wide field of governmental activities we have at last given up using averages and all you gentlemen will know how deadly averages can be when presented in a simple form. I notice from the operations of our own Economic and Social Research Institute that if averages are given they are always further analysed because nothing can be more dangerous than for a government to act simply as a result of simple averages being given in relation to almost any activity.

Again decision making by governments, or by local authorities, or by state companies sometimes has to be based on intuition; sometimes have to be pragmatic in character because of the human situations involved. No government however desirous they might be of wishing to take advice from operational research conclusions could afford to ignore the purely human values that have to be considered when they make their decisions. In some cases we in our country have been able to make decisions that were simple and pragmatic — such as the decision we made as far back as 1952 when we were one of the first countries in Europe to provide very special capital grants for industries in remote rural areas. Now we have had the level of what could be described as operational research, through a very extensive and detailed programme of industrial planning on a regional basis and planned for the whole of our country that was recently presented to us by one of our great state companies — the Industrial Development Authority.

And then again I think it is true to say that sometimes governments have to act on the basis almost of hunch as to when they are to take action, when they are to change the laws, when they are to announce certain directions. We must have regard to this element in decision-making when securing a consensus of opinion for conclusions which we have made and for the decisions we want to take in relation to acting on a report based on operational research. All of you will realise how difficult it is to quantify the result of any government action in relation to the reactions of the people when the act is passed or when the decision is taken.

And I suppose that all the delegates here can be offered a challenge as to how, for example, through operational research you could present a case using first class public relations to arrest the appalling tide of inflation that continues to sweep over the most modern countries where the great majority of the population have been well educated. There is an example where emotional feeling seems entirely indifferent to operational research conclusions which could result in the ending of inflation without any disadvantage to the workers or to those receiving low salaries. And this indeed is a challenge to all those who consider operational research – how they can make it live in the minds of the ordinary people watching their television sets. Because I think I am right, ladies and gentlemen, in saying this, that in Europe since World War II there have only been four countries that were able to maintain the rules and guidelines to avoid inflation from 1949 onwards. Some of them succeeded in doing for a period of ten or twelve years, others for a longer period and at the end of the period every single country in Europe had broken the rules designed to restrain inflation. They were not able to present to their people the kind of conclusion, that can be derived from elaborate operational research, which will excite the hearts of those employed in industry and trades so that they would accept rules which would mean that if their wages and salaries, whether calculated by job evaluation or by any other method, would rise in such a way there would not be an increase in the cost of living which would wipe out from one half to two-thirds of all the extra incomes which they were receiving. I mention this in passing because I always think of any operation, such as operational research, as being connected eventually with public relations – with appealing to people's minds and hearts, appealing to their commonsense in regard to the ability of the government to implement the schemes proposed.

And then of course I should point out in relation to consensus that there is no such thing as operational research when applied to decisions of democratic countries as to how people are to vote. You have the extraordinary fact that in countries with highly educated populations only a 5%, 3% or 1% change of vote will put out of office the government of the day. And if the government wishes to maintain stability why then it must be careful when it takes decisions to take account of the human factor because otherwise in a great many countries of Europe you could see changes of government occurring every three months, with eventually disastrous results, as ministers would be quite incapable, if in office for so short a period, of even understanding the nature of operational research and all that it implies.

But we do recognise that as the practical problems of governments grow and as government becomes more complex, as business and industry proliferate, that we must pay more attention to scientifically produced decisions, scientifically drafted programmes. That we recognise. And we recognised it first in this country in 1958 when there was presented to the government the first economic programme. It fell far short of the kind of programme that you, ladies and gentlemen, could design today. But nevertheless it was the first economic programme presented. This programme had excellent results because all over the country and in all departments of State, and in all local authorities, people began to think scientifically about how they could plan in order to make available more economic resources, in order to establish more industries, and in order to use surplus profits and the taxation placed thereon, for the benefit of social progress.

The question that, therefore, lies before you is: can complex data when scientifically assessed provide pointers that perhaps give governments a choice of options, gives state companies a choice of options, gives private companies a choice of options in regard to the decisions they are going to take? Can a model of a complex scientific type be provided in which all the implications are assessed? And can the model be of a kind so that there can be experimentation in some cases before a real life situation can be faced and the final decisions taken? The operational research experts answer 'yes' to this problem and you are dealing with these sort of matters at your international conference.

Operational research has made obviously great strides in the last years and this can be well demonstrated by the number and variety of papers which are going to be read at this conference. The conference objective, I understand, is to demonstrate the capacity of operational research to make a significant contribution to the solution of current problems at national level, at international level, at local authority level and at individual firm level.

Indeed you have many challenges before you. If you could apply operational research to the problems in relation to international monetary exchange and convince the governments concerned of the rightness of your decision-making, why then it would be a great help. If you could apply operational research as to how we are going to prevent many of the poor countries growing poorer while the rich countries get richer. And if you could provide such convincing models of economic programming as would reverse that trend you would be able to make a contribution to world civilisation that would be of great importance.

Obviously you have to face prejudice of every kind in everything you do. And this introduction of operational research into the field of authority, of management, obviously cannot be achieved overnight. You must expect a degree of immobility to which I have already referred, a degree of criticism. Mathematical analysis is not understood by many people. You've got to convince those who do not understand the nature of your work. You have got to make them feel part of a living process, something of value to the future of humanity. And these techniques must prove worthwhile and convincing.

I suppose one of the best means by which you can expand operational research is to prove that problems have been solved and that operational research was a vital part of the process. In this way you will be able to convince people that they should engage in these kinds of projections. I mention this because in my experience as minister for twenty years in charge of five departments I have always found that public relations in relation to complicated procedures, in relation to scientific advances, in thought and in determining policies are vital to the success of any operation.

Now we in our country have an operational research unit — not what you might describe as of full magnitude — but an important operational research unit which applies to the public services as a whole. I am very glad to tell you that, as minister with long experience, I was the first minister to apply operational research methods in this country in 1951 in the Department of Posts and Telegraphs. I well remember, as a result of our operational research that we got rid of 120 unnecessary forms used in the Post Office department and in the telephone service and simplified many of the procedures. We did much other work in increasing the productivity of the telephone service.

I suppose that perhaps the most interesting piece of operational research in which I was interested was the introduction of work study and operational research methods in the whole of our forestry operation. We were the first country in Europe to have a complete bonus payment system in relation to the production of forestry — from the draining of the land, to the fencing of the land, to the planting of the trees, to the cleaning of the young saplings, to the pruning of the trees, the thinning of the trees and the replanting. We were the first country to have a complete and elaborate system involving operational research in that regard. The interesting thing about it was that the elderly Englishman who came over to do this work had never looked at a tree in his life before with a view to operational research. He had been engaged in matters purely of an entirely different kind. He wandered through the forests and he talked with the foresters. He was able to succeed in this most difficult project. When you consider all the different varieties of soil, the different slopes on the mountains, the different climatic conditions, the great number of species of trees that had to be planted, the variations of the soil that had to be drained, you will agree that to present a code in relation to operational research covering such a complex field was a matter of great triumph for him.

Now again operational research applies to the Department of Health and to our hospital and health services. I am glad to see that you are going to hear about our ambulance services and the operational research being conducted in this most complicated field. It involved deciding what is the optimum method of centring the position of ambulances and of their utilisation under radio control, bearing in mind the inevitable growth in the number of motor accidents, the scattered nature of our rural population and the need to bring all serious ambulance cases to a multidiscipline hospital rather than to the nearest district hospital. All this is complicated. Very important work has already been done on it and we are indebted to the experts in this field.

I welcome the inclusion in your workshop sessions of studies in relation to our health and social welfare systems. Many problems arise in relation to health and hospital services including the evaluation of output. This is a difficult matter because always the care of the patient and the humane attitude towards the patient has to be considered in all matters, in all questions and in all suggestions that might lead to greater efficiency.

Every Minister for Health in Europe faces a frightening problem of hospital cost – we no less than other countries. Hospital costs have virtually doubled in five years. It is difficult to see any levelling off in this increase in cost, because in Northern Europe, roughly speaking 2.5% more people every year enter for a period, short or long, an acute care hospital. So we do expect some results from operational research in relation to hospital management. Indeed results have been secured already in a number of countries and I have started an operational research unit in my own department which will begin its real work when we have completed the reorganisation of our hospital and health administration services. This reorganisation will be completed by October.

It is probable that with the preoccupation of governments with economic and social research that operational research will become more extensive and will make a greater contribution to human wellbeing. This field is full of great challenges for people with imagination and people with scientific capacity.

The governments must commit themselves to the welfare of their communities, to the maintenance of employment and the ordered development of social services of one kind or another. Indeed, we in this country are one of a number of countries in Europe who believe in private enterprise working hand-in-hand with government intervention, or what might be described as socialism — although that word has been defined in so many ways that one hardly dares to use it. It is quite certain that with the problems affecting pollution, affecting the growth of the whole world system government intervention and international intervention are bound to grow with the complexity of the whole of life around us. For this reason your operational research activities should become more and more important.

I hope this conference will be of great value. I hope it will stimulate further investigation in regard to the scientific handling of many problems. And, ladies and gentlemen, I hope you will enjoy yourselves. I hope you will find some relaxation in the peace of our countryside around the city of Dublin. You will find the Wicklow Mountains most beautiful. One of the most beautiful parts of this earth can be found only twenty minutes from the city. I hope you will visit our mountainland and see some of our ancient monuments while you are here. May I conclude again by welcoming you to this sixth international conference on operational research.

M. Ross, ed., OR '72. North-Holland Publishing Company (1973)

2

IFORS – MELTING POT FOR PROGRESS

IFORS – creuset pour le progrès

ARNE JENSEN

The Technical University of Denmark, Lyngby, Denmark

In this century we have concentrated very much on studying the flow of people, materials and money. Only during the past 10 years have we come to realize the enormous significance of the information flow for the changing equilibrium within areas. The reduction of delays in communication have created an entirely new situation – both for large organizations and for individuals as such. The speed of this development has weakened the individual's influence over the establishment of rules so that this legitimate demands for a stable life are not adequately fulfilled.

So far, I believe we have to admit that we have not yet learned to master the organization and control of the information systems in such a way that they fulfill not only the wishes of the group for higher standards of living and social welfare, but also the individual's wish for some freedom in his activities.

All over the world we have to look at our organizations and ask ourselves whether they fit into the modern world and are able to implement our original goals in an adequate way.

The explosion in education and science during the post-war period has quite naturally caused an explosion within the international organizations covering the different scientific fields. Thus when we look ahead to the next 15 years we begin to realize the immense need that an immense number of scientists will have for the exchange of information, not only through periodicals, books, and cassettes – but also by face-to-face meetings with colleagues.

It is our task in the Federation to make this exchange possible, and since the future requirements are expected to be ten times their present level, something has to be done about it. Every individual scientist in the whole wide world needs this personal contact. Each individual is carrying a bit of information about the problems prevailing within his particular group, and we have to realize that in future the formulation of problems may be more important than their solution.

Compared with problem solving, problem formulation requires an even greater creativity on the part of the scientist and a closer link between science and its environment. The priority to be afforded to particular problems varies a lot from one corner of the world to another. Therefore, we need to stimulate and organize activities at the regional level and in specialized subjects in between our International Meetings.

At the FIACC meetings — the annual meeting between representatives from the five international federations covering information processing, automatic control, measurement, analog computation, and operations research — we have realized the need for and discussed the possibility of establishing regional meetings in some parts of the world which would stimulate further progress and greater activity in our sciences. We have also discussed new solutions to facilitate the communication process and have already benefited greatly from our getting together.

Every year these five sister federations sponsor and give international recognition to between 20 and 30 local meetings each with 500—1,000 participants. I think that one of the main tasks of IFORS and its sister federations during the coming years, will be to stimulate local and regional activities in such a way that we get the best material from these activities presented at the international meetings.

I have recently participated in a meeting on operations research and information processing in Buenos Aires attended by 600 participants, at which many very good papers from the Ibero-American world were presented. However, due to travel costs involved and, I think, the language barriers we do not see sufficient papers representing this region at the international conferences. Thus our international meetings are not sufficiently representative of activities all over the world.

We need fresh thinking within our organization on contact between scientists and, as you have already observed, this meeting in Dublin has been organized in an untraditional way in the hope that by experimenting we will get ideas for new trends.

During the last decade we have observed that the traditional freedom of science to choose its field for research and its methodology has been changed by manipulations – due to the great economic requirements necessary to carry these two goals through and to inform the public about the results.

The conflict between the individual scientist's desire for absolute freedom and the limited resources available is still unsolved.

Furthermore, it is possible for forces outside – and, I am afraid to say, also inside – the universities and research laboratories to diminish these two high goals by the choice of the individuals to carry through the work. If you do not want to face the truth in a given situation, then do not start a research project on it, and do not hire people with those type of interests. If, unfortunately, you already have some researchers in that area, then do not give them adequate resources.

We always have the lack of funds as an excuse, and this excuse also gives you the possibility to exert influence on the information presented concerning the state of the art. I do not say it is always so, and I do not say that pressure groups always succeed. But I do say that when we talk about scientific freedom in the future, we need to look not only at the working conditions of the individual scientist, but also at the system as a whole.

In future we are going to become responsible for a great part of the development of fields which earlier were considered to be technical economics and parts of econometrics. This has already been emerged from our discussions with our sister federations. On several occasions they have asked us to assume responsibility for activities in this economic and planning sector which has been initiated inside their organizations.

In our own science – operations research – we also have to follow up developments in our environment and try to adapt our federation to these changes. In practice we are covering more and more subjects and, for example, now extend over the entire area of management science.

I think it should also be clear to the users that this is so. Even in the IFORS statutes, it should be clear that management science is a part of operations research – and some would say vice versa. It should be natural that management sciences groups work together with operations research groups inside the same overall organization. I hope that our next President will be able to change IFORS to IFORMS.

In the future we have to complete our task in the implementation of science and technology in the developing areas of the world in order to narrow the disparities in living standards, be they economic, social or cultural which may exist between different societies or between different individuals in the same society.

The freedom of individuals and groups to give all what they have in them of creativity and productivity for the benefit of mankind should be assured to the extent it does not interfere with the same right possessed by other human beings.

We, as producers and users of science, are going to have greater responsibility for world problems of development.

In the past, science was always paid for by the rich with the result that the problems of the poorer groups received a lower priority – not only from the individual scientist, but also from the system as such.

In the future this weakness in the organization of science has to be changed. Scientific circles have always been a melting-pot for new ideas and new developments for the benefit of mankind. Students all over the world demand that greater social responsibility be employed in the production and use of science.

The activities behind the Limits to Growth Study, and the so called Rome Club, show that scientists also are aware of their responsibility. But to give this awareness sufficient quality and effect, this has to be expanded to an overall, general policy in the scientific world when we plan the use of scientific resources.

With the young generation behind us, we have the best of hope that in the future our science is going to be even more truly a melting-pot for new developments – for the benefit of mankind.

Let us devote this meeting on operations research to

PROGRESS AND HARMONY FOR MANKIND.

M. Ross, ed., OR '72. North-Holland Publishing Company (1973)

3

IRELAND AND OPERATIONAL RESEARCH

L'Irlande et la recherche opérationnelle

JOHN P. HYLAND

Hyland Associates, Dublin, Ireland

A dhaoine uaisle, thar cheann Cumann na hÉireann um Taighde Gníomhaíochta fearaim fíor-chaoin fáilte rómhaibh uilig. Is cúis mór-áthais dúinne gur toghadh Baile Átha Cliath mar ionad don Chruinniú seo agus go bhfuil in ár measc inniu an oiread seo de theachtaí as gach áird sa domhan. Tá súil againn go mbainfidh sibh sár-leas agus sár-taithneamh as gnó na chruinnithe agus as bhúr gcuaird ar an chathair agus an tír seo.

* * *

This year the Operational Research Society, the first of its kind, celebrates the twenty-fifth anniversary of its founding in 1947, a date which may be said to mark the emergency of operational research as a separate inter-disciplinary (should I say super-disciplinary?) professional activity in its own right. Some eleven or twelve years passed before its first organisational acceptance in Ireland. This occurred at Aer Lingus in 1957 with the appointment of an executive with specific responsibility for OR.

There had been of course, as elsewhere, some early studies carried out by individuals in this country, which would now be properly regarded as OR. For example, a model developed in the early fifties by the Irish Meteorological Service for predicting the incidence and minimising the development of potato blight is still being used today and some early applications of queueing theory date from the same time.

The focus provided by Aer Lingus, however, led to the purposive training of a small number of graduates in the field of OR. Most of these were sent to the United States to attend special courses. About the same time other Irish graduates working or studying abroad moved into this field and acquired valuable training and experience, some of them with the intention of return-ing to Ireland when the practice of OR became more established here.

Thus from 1959 to 1964 there began to emerge a small band of profession-ally qualified OR personnel, some with considerable experience. They were rather scattered however and only one major group developed, namely at Aer Lingus. Companies then actively supporting OR activity included Bord na Mona (the Irish Peat Development Board), Esso Ireland Ltd., Cement Ltd., as well as Aer Lingus. Some projects were also undertaken by foreign consult-ancies. Progress was slow, however, and due to a severe shortage of trained and qualified men in many areas of management and the emergence of auto-matic data processing, some OR personnel found themselves moving into functional roles in these areas — a trend which has since continued.

By 1964 there was a sufficient nucleus of people available to establish a national OR Society, which was constituted in December of that year with about twenty members. Largely because of an association with AGIFORS through Aer Lingus, but also through personal contacts, two national observ-ers had attended the IFORS Triennial Conference in Oslo in 1963. In 1965 OECD selected Ireland for a pilot venture into the promotion of the use of OR in the public service. This had the support of IFORS and our Society's participation led to a closer association and finally to membership at Boston in 1966.

In 1967 the Society began to pay particular attention to bringing about the provision of specialised professional training in OR in this country. Its first task was to specify the scope and depth of training needed, the qualifica-tions for entry and the preferred institutional arrangements. It had reached conclusions on these matters by 1968. Before making submissions to the authorities for the necessary support and funds it established a joint working committee with industry, the public services and the universities to determine how many graduates from the programme would be employed on OR work in Ireland.

As a result of the recommendations of this committee, the University of Dublin decided to add a curriculum in OR to that of the Department of Statistics under Professor Foster and it now offers a Master's Degree in Statis-tics and Operational Research, based on one calendar year of academic and project work. This programme is in its second year and produces about a dozen graduates annually.

Membership of the Society has expanded from the initial twenty members to about ninety this year. We have two grades of membership, full members having training and practical experience to a professional level. About fifty members are in this class. We have therefore secured a reasonable rate of growth and this should accelerate in the next five years as a result of the improved facilities for training and a delayed but now expanding demand.

While much of our resources in the past three years have been devoted to the organisation of this Conference we have maintained the activities of the society in other directions. In November 1971 we held our first National Conference, which some eighty people attended over a period of three days. This was a major success and we believe that the current and future level of professional activity will support an annual conference on this scale.

In parallel with these developments, and due to varying influences, there was an irregular but continuing growth in the application of OR and in the number of establishments pursuing projects either with their own staff or through consultants. OR staff were and continue to be located in Management Services or Computer Departments or, in the more technically oriented companies, in the Research and Development Department. Frequently, only one or two men are involved, although some of the larger enterprises have organisationally separate OR groups. The distinctive role of OR has in some cases been blurred by a contemporaneous growth in the deployment of personnel from other disciplines (for example, economics, industrial engineering) and functional specialisations (for example, marketing, systems analysis, urban and regional planning, business administration), which have adopted parts of the established methodology of OR, and their involvement in assignments of a kindred nature. However, there is now emerging a better appreciation of the true function of the professional OR man in problem solving in relation to what he can achieve in comparison with other specialists.

Probably the most significant progress in the past five years has been the large-scale development of OR in banking and the public administration. These centre around the Bank of Ireland Group and the Department of Finance.

In the latter case the OR Group provides a central service to all government departments and is involved currently in such areas as the Departments of Justice, Local Government, Posts and Telegraphs and the Forestry Division of the Department of Lands. Other projects have been carried out over a longer period in the Departments of Education and Labour, chiefly in connection with manpower problems.

It is very gratifying that the use of OR specialists is now an established policy in the public service. Following a substantial success at the tactical level of decision-making, there will be greater inclination to apply OR to the major strategic, environmental and political problems in due course.

In industry the size of Irish enterprises is, in general, quite small and application of OR is mainly confined to about twenty-five or thirty of the largest organisations. Virtually all the work is directed towards specific current problems and little has been published in the way of radically new theoretical advances. Until quite recently we have lacked the necessary fusion between the academic and industrial worlds which would most likely engender such developments.

The fairly rapid promotion of the OR specialist into a functional management role continues to be a significant feature. With the increasing availability of qualified personnel we have or can look forward to the situation where they will undertake projects serving functional managers who were formerly working as OR specialists. This should materially reduce the age-old problem of communication between specialist and manager.

To sum up then, OR in Ireland started somewhat late and without the high level of scientific and institutional resources of the leading industrial nations or the organisational stimulus of the second world war. Once started, we have made reasonable progress and we now have a base on which we can build more confidently and more extensively. We have learned that we have special problems but that we can resolve them by the exercise of appropriate initiatives and properly directed effort. Speaking biblically, we can look forward to seven years of plenty.

PART II

HIGHLIGHT PAPERS

Grands Points

Chairman: A.M. LEE (United Kingdom)

4

THE CRITICAL PATH TO GROWTH

Le chemin critique de la croissance

SIR CHARLES GOODEVE

Tavistock Institute of Human Relations, London, England

Abstract. Growth has for long been accepted as one of the major objectives of most people. Recently it has been challenged from a number of directions and the challengers have been counter-challenged. The inadequacy of scientific evidence lays the field open to much controversy, but the questions which have been brought into prominence are of great importance and demand answers. These answers in turn require knowledge associated with many branches of the physical, biological and social sciences. The techniques of OR can be and are being used to assemble and blend the evidence. These techniques can also show up the gaps and the obstacles in the paths to progress. This area offers a tremendous opportunity for OR workers, whose experience in clarifying objectives, in avoiding subjective judgements, and in analysing complex data should serve them in good stead.

The first IFORS conference was held in Oxford in 1957. Its major task was to prescribe the objective and the functions of this branch of science and to establish its disciplines. One of these functions was to form a bridgehead between the natural and the social sciences; there was a large and growing gap between the two.

One can look back over these fifteen years with satisfaction in regard to the development and use of OR techniques to assist in decision making by management both in industry and government, but only with disappointment in the use of these techniques in the application of social science knowledge generally. Today we see economists in disarray and seeking refuge by hiding from the growing problems of society. We see our precious 'freedom of choice' so badly abused that the press and many responsible public figures are reacting and pressing for more controls, for more powers to the centre, for a move towards dictatorship. We have recently seen in Britain the law-lords joining the many politicians who do not accept the basic laws of economics. To all this has been added the spread of the anti-growth movement. All these phenomena are hardly surprising in view of our failure to advance our knowledge of how society works or could work, or even to make more widely known what knowledge we have.

The minister, Mr. Childers, suggested that, on this international occassion, we in the OR world should resolve to re-examine this challenge. He put this challenge very forcibly and backed it with numerous examples. Many of us are envious of our Irish colleagues in their having such a well-informed and forward looking Deputy Prime Minister.

Perhaps the most noticeable example is this current controversy related to growth. Here the issues are not only technological, i.e. based on the physical and biological sciences but also social and political. Indeed the latter two with their much less rigid disciplines of logic are tending to overwhelm the more rigid disciplines of the natural sciences. The objectives of the group are seldom specifically clarified. Worse still the facts are selected or distorted to support objectives believed in by individuals prominent in the controversy. The controversy is likely thus to lie in the objectives rather than in the actions. Very often it is simply in the meaning of words.

One of the cardinal principles of OR is that a group should be helped to ascertain its objectives and should not have its objectives imposed upon it. By definition, the objectives of a group are the things the members of a group want. Their choice of these may of course be influenced by persuasive individuals.

If you accept this as the basic method of clarifying objectives, it is not difficult to find a definition for the word 'growth' in the context of the current controversies.

Growth is an increase in the satisfaction of all people's wants.

This is a less precise but also less controversial meaning of the word than that used by many. But it is a much more satisfactory one because it refers not just to material wants but rather to a whole package of wants (including psychological) that form the basis of human behaviour. This package includes the wanting of children or at least of the actions that lead to children. It also includes the wanting to continue to live and thus it involves the growth of population. It implies a degree of equality of satisfaction between people.

Growth as defined here is difficult to measure but it is not impossible. Opinion surveys or even migration can be useful. A theoretical method was described in the concluding paper to the second IFORS conference. This measures the *expected* satisfaction or 'eudemony' of one geographic or social state compared with another by observing the net migration between the two.

Much more needs to be said. People's wants differ and worse still, the satisfaction of one person's or one group's wants puts restraints or limits on the satisfaction of other persons' or group's wants.

To OR people this is a typical case of multiple and divergent objectives, not one to be solved by propaganda but by careful analysis and the presentation to the group or the world of a balanced picture. What do we get instead? A highly exaggerated presentation of doom by many people, including ecologists, which has generated a vigorous defensive reaction from many economists, scientists, industrialists and others. The whole subject has become polarized, with most people taking up a position either for or against growth; there are few people in mid-position, keen to analyse and to seek a balance. The exaggeration of the anti-growth people is perhaps due to the difficulties of alerting the public to real risks in the face of the fact that people by and large *want* growth, want it very strongly. Threats of curtailment are resented. But is exaggeration the best method of getting an idea across? No scientist likes it but it may be necessary in order to produce an impact.

Many OR people will have read the book 'The limits to growth', a report to the Club of Rome by Dennis L. Meadows and others [1], which followed 'World dynamics' by J.W. Forrester [2]. This book starts in a moderate key but almost immediately descends into extravagances of 'catastrophes' or of 'collapse of society' which can only be avoided by restraining growth, even of things that people want most. The computer, which to an OR man is a basic tool or 'ploughshare', is used by Forrester and Meadows as a 'sword' to alert people to a danger which may or may not face us sooner than we think. It must be very difficult to get people worried about the hothouse effect of a rise in the carbon dioxide in the atmosphere, when they have suffered the discomfort of a 1972 so-called 'summer'. It also must be very difficult to get people worried about limitations to resources which are unlikely to come in in the lives of anyone living today. The future often ranks low in people's thoughts and ecologists have done a service if only by bringing it more into prominence.

This whole subject area is too big, too complex and too important to treat properly in this opening paper. There are hundreds of people in it already. What can we as OR people contribute? The answers are manifold but I can only pick a few problems where OR techniques should prove useful. I am glad that President Charles J. Hitch will be dealing more fully with other examples in the next high-light paper.

The first problem is the balancing or the realignment of objectives in the package of wants referred to a moment ago. Objectives are related to motivations which are forces and these usually pull in different directions. Through analysis one can find whether the objectives are realignable or whether they can only be resolved by compromise. For example an objective of satisfaction some time in the future is often in the opposite direction to satisfaction today, an 'either/or' situation. People differ widely in the relative importance they put on the future but they would have less problem in deciding the best balance if they knew how these two objectives were related. Employees sometimes object if their employers make and retain a profit but don't realize that their security for the future depends very much on profits.

Much has been written on the factors which affect population growth but it is still one of the most unpredictable characteristics of society. Many of the factors can be measured with substantial accuracy, but other factors such as education, degree of affluence or poverty, of religion, ethics, etc. are only vaguely understood and indeed are controversial. This is a very serious problem and every scientific approach should be used. At the moment population growth is greatest in those countries which do not have the technical skill and the resources to feed and clothe themselves properly. Yet most of the education or propaganda for control is in the countries that *can* feed themselves. Perhaps this will right itself. People want children to give them support and companionship in ill-health or old age but this need diminishes with growth as defined here. In deciding to have more children the danger to these children of dying by starvation or of violence can perhaps come more on to the scales.

This situation of local overpopulation formerly was solved by mass migration but the acceptability of this cure is on the decline as the infra-structure of a receiving country plays a greater and greater part in its eudemony. The indigenous population of a country claim an ownership right to their infra-structure and sharing it with newcomers does not accord with their own desire for growth. Currently there exists a poor substitute for migration in the form of so-called 'aid' but nevertheless the economic gap between the rich and the poor nations continues to grow. One can tear down Meadows' exponential growth of population as much as one wishes but we are still left with this problem of imbalance and one which is already with us.

A third problem is that of establishing indices of urgency or priorities for the many problems brought into the open by ecologists. What do we need to worry about and how much do we need to worry? What aspects should we tackle first and how urgent are they? We need a worry, or urgency, index.

To illustrate this let us look again at the growth of CO_2 in the atmosphere through the burning of fossil fuel. The CO_2 content is not difficult to measure but its effect on the climate is very uncertain. Any model must take into account the relative cloud cover over the globe between day and night, the dynamics of the oceans and their ability to absorb CO_2, plus many other factors. Much work is being done on this and we can focus attention on the possible consequences and remedies. Nobody is going to worry much about a small rise in average temperature and anyway it is almost impossible to isolate a change due to CO_2 from those due to other more natural causes. Indeed there is growing evidence that natural and so far unlocated causes are at the moment producing a cooling effect which may continue for 50 years or so. So we have got some time before we need to start worrying and well before then our children or grand-children are likely to know whether there is a need to worry or not. In the past, drastic climatic changes have required thousands of years.

Any index of urgency is likely to be dominated by a quantity which is a ratio between the predicted time (in the denominator) of a given change and the time required to take action to prevent that change having serious consequences. A second important part of this index would be the cost/benefit ratio of the action and its effect. So long as the combined ratio is well less than unity there is little need for worry. This appears to be the case in regard to CO_2 but numerous people would be happier if they knew that a close watch was being kept on the Antarctic ice-cap, the melting of which would lead to a rise in the level of the oceans. Indeed such a rise might occur through causes unconnected with CO_2.

Similarly indices of urgency should be established for the non-renewability of resources. This would include the effects of the automatic negative feedback of the price mechanism, the omission of which by Meadows has hardly attracted support from economists. It would also include the fact that searches for more reserves are strongly held back by the commercial disadvantages of diverting effort today to find resources unlikely to be wanted for 20, let alone 50, years hence; discount cash flow calculations here act as a deterrent to expenditure for the future.

This suggestion of an index of urgency, a 'worry index', needs much more refining. Its evaluation falls right in the middle of the OR area. It needs a model to establish and quantify effects, it needs methods of resolving multiple and conflicting objectives and it needs the presentation of results in order to get commitments.

I come now to my fourth and by far the most important example of a problem area where OR techniques should be able to help, an area that has been hinted at in the opening two paragraphs and one which led to the choice of title for this paper. The paths leading to growth as defined above have many obstacles to surmount and man's ability so to surmount them is dependent upon his knowledge, including, I repeat, the distribution of knowledge. The increase in knowledge in the physical and biological areas is to some extent keeping pace with man's problems that are arising in growth; indeed the pace of growth is set by such increases in knowledge and by its dissemination.

But physical and biological growth has led to a shrinkage of this 'one earth' of ours. The advances of technology, of transportation, of communication, of commerce, even of medicine have vastly increased the interdependence of one person on another or of one group on another. One person's decisions and actions are more and more likely to restrain the choices open to others. Man is an emotional animal and he resents restraints, particularly when he misunderstands or does not accept some of the reasons for them. This resentment is the basic cause of conflict and conflict can escalate rapidly to the point where its wasteful aspects vastly overshadow its benefits. The scientific analysis of social conflict is in its very early stages but some things are known. Like an epidemic, conflict can feed on itself and grow with astonishing speed. 'Explosive' is a better adjective than 'exponential'. More important is that the background of interdependence, restraints, stress and ignorance is with us today; it is not just a problem for our children. Conflict or its threat is not only the earliest but the biggest obstacle to growth. It is the manifestation of the shrinking earth with its pressures of populations, of resources, of pollution.

The critical path to growth is one which surmounts or avoids this obstacle of conflict.

The problem of setting out a network to find or build this path is one for all of us to try to solve. Its solution will make handleable most of the physical and biological limits to growth and will prevent or at least modify the 'catastrophes' predicted by the anti-growth ecologists. Failure to find a solution leaves open the expectation of sudden bursts of conflict which could exceed these predictions. Our worry index here has a high positive value.

You might say that the finding of this critical path is the job of the social scientist and with that I would agree. Unfortunately the area of applied social sciences is so fraught with difficulties and dangers that most social scientists withdraw from the arena of public discussion or activity. Bolder ones like Professor Steven Rose mix up their objectives, which are usually political, with their analyses. Some go even further and claim that it is not good social science unless the objectives are the 'right' ones.

A study of the social sciences and of the associated methods of working have convinced me that our best hope is that social scientists and OR people should work together on this problem. I don't underestimate the difficulties in this. Anyone going from the physical through OR to the social sciences is struck by many differences, the complexity of the subject, the absence of attention to laws and principles, the concentration on pushing out the frontiers of each specialized subject, the small part that the experiment can play — one could go on at length. The problems get worse when one attempts to apply the subject. Political and ethical problems are bound to interfere with action. Communication becomes a severe problem. It doesn't matter if a man-in-the-street believes in perpetual motion but, if he is a citizen, it does matter if he believes he can consume more of the national cake without leaving less for others or believes that a government or an industry can control prices without control of costs. How can one communicate a truth, once found, to those who need to know, when one is faced with a multitude of pens, all writing different and incompatible things — it is hardly any wonder that the sword has become mightier than the pen. What is written or spoken, or let us say believed, is chosen not by reason but by the degree of comfort it gives to the recipient.

Despite all these difficulties we have managed to start a small unit at the Tavistock Institute of Human Relations in London which is applying social science and OR to the analysis of wasteful conflict. Resources are low but confidence in achieving something useful is high. We have already got a long way in extracting from the vast literature certain key laws and principles which have a high validity and are relevant to conflict. We are now exploring the problems of communication of these to part of the citizenship and of observing the results.

Pat Rivett and David Hertz have both expressed a worry that OR has pushed its frontiers nearly to the limit. Anyone feeling like this should look beside him at this vast area of applied social science which needs his help.

References

[1] D.L. Meadows et al., Limits to growth (Universe Books, New York, 1972).
[2] J.W. Forrester, World dynamics (Wright–Allen Press, Cambridge, Mass., 1971).

M. Ross, ed., OR '72. North-Holland Publishing Company (1973)

5

THE ENVIRONMENT:
A NEW CHALLENGE FOR OPERATIONS RESEARCH

L'environment: un défi nouveau pour la recherche opérationnelle

CHARLES J. HITCH

President University of California, Berkeley, California, U.S.A.

Abstract. The principal lessons of the application of the planning-programming-budgeting system to military problems were (1) the necessity for clarification of objectives and criteria, and (2) the rather limited problem areas which are susceptible, in the present state of the OR art, to successful applications. Attempts to apply PPBS to broad problems of conventional or limited war or to research have been disappointing. Similarly, the attempt of the Johnson Administration in 1965 to extend PPBS techniques to a wide range of ill-defined and poorly structured civilian problems has done much to discredit them. There is now, however, tremendous interest in air and water pollution and related problems of population and technology which appear similar in important respects to the more tractable military problems. Objectives appear amenable to classification; economic criteria are clearly applicable; and we know or think we can learn how to structure the important relationships. There are enemies, more akin to nature and therefore with reactions to our strategies more predictable than those of enemy governments; neutrals with the same incentives as neutrals in war to sit out conflicts and let others bear the costs; and active and potential allies. Formidable difficulties – all inter-related – include the intensity of political interactions, disincentives built into economic systems, and the overzealousness of friends demanding immediate and total victory.

During the period beginning with World War II and continuing until recently most of the effort of American operations researchers has been focused on military applications. This has been particularly true of large, organized, persistent team efforts, represented by my old organization, the Rand Corporation, where several hundred professionals have labored continuously for over two decades to improve the design and use of military systems. During the 1960's operations researchers and systems analysts attempted with moderate and at least transient success to install in the American Defense Department a comprehensive planning-programming-budgeting system (PPBS) designed to rationalize military planning in the United States and to facilitate the application to military planning of systematic quantitative analysis.

There is no question that this effort has paid some high dividends. It has produced successes as well as failures. You are familiar with the achievements of the early OR teams in improving naval, air, and ground operations, both in the British and American forces, during World War II. I am convinced that the deployed strategic nuclear forces of the two great nuclear powers — deplorable and threatening as they are — are far more stable and less threatening than they would have been without the contributions of civilian analysts. Missiles are now hardened or hidden beneath the sea; bombers and bombs are fail-safe. It would be hard to ask for a more significant pay-off.

But if there have been successes, there have also been failures. We have learned that some military problems are tractable: easy to structure, with definable and acceptable criteria of performance, and with empirical data available that are sufficiently reliable and adequate for computation and solution. We have learned that other problems, while apparently intractable at first because deficient in one or more of these respects, become tractable with the exercise of sufficient effort, time, and intellectual ingenuity. Still others have so far defied attempts at solution: they remain intractable. It is a fair assessment, I think, that OR has contributed little in the area of limited and particularly guerrilla warfare — a better rifle, perhaps, a more efficient air-to-ground weapon or two, more economical transportation and supply systems — small contributions when contrasted with those flowing from the psychological insights and political skills of a Mao or a Ho Chi Minh. We haven't learned how to structure limited war problems, to define criteria, or to get the data we need. I think it is also fair to say that, despite much effort, we have contributed little to the better use of our research and development resources, except perhaps in the final prototype production stage of development. The pervasive uncertainties of the process have turned out to be too subtle for our tools.

We have also learned that even in some cases where the problems have proved tractable and the solutions satisfactory from the analyst's point of view, political considerations (in the broad sense of 'political') have thwarted their adoption. And that this can be true even in military organizations where command is supposed, somewhat naively, to flow exclusively from the top down. Some solutions, no matter how strongly buttressed by logic, are simply unacceptable to the uniformed military – inconsistent with tradition or with the real or imagined interests of a proud Service. Powerful congressmen have convictions which are not necessarily based on analysis, and can exert influence to protect the well-being of their constituents. Allied governments must be listened to and placated. The Defense Department may have assigned non-military objectives which conflict with simple military objectives. Certain solutions (for example, air raid shelters) may be taboo because of deep-seated popular emotional resistance, no matter how cost-effective.

Operations researchers and others who have observed the successes have long been intrigued with the possibility of applying the same techniques to the civilian economy and government. Some of the wartime practitioners, notably P.M.S. Blackett in Britain and Philip Morse in the U.S., returned to civilian life hoping for, expecting, and encouraging large-scale industrial applications. There have been many attempts at civilian applications during the past two decades, both by those calling themselves operations researchers and by economists who have developed the parallel and merging discipline called 'cost-benefit' analysis. In 1965 President Lyndon Johnson issued an Executive Order calling on all departments of the Federal Government to adopt and adapt the Pentagon's PPBS techniques in their planning and budgeting. In 1966 I was so bold and foolish as to attempt to devise a PPBS system for the Department of State!

While we have undoubtedly had some successes in civilian applications as in military, several comments are in order. First, the initial military successes during World War II were misleading easy. Most involved improving *operations* which (a) used new technologies which had never been applied in combat before, so that large ('order of magnitude') improvements were not hard to find, and (b) could be implemented by command decision, so that the 'political' obstacles were minimal.

By contrast, in civilian industry, the same or similar operations had typically undergone years of test and trial and adaptation under the spur of the profit motive, and had either become so efficient that large improvements were not possible without technological advances, or so encrusted by tradition that political obstacles were maximal. Similarly in civilian government political obstacles were generally much greater than in the military, even the peacetime military.

Second, early attempts at civilian applications were, by and large, on a small scale, and usually the work of individual practitioners. Given the scale and complexity of the problems, the effort was ludicrously small and discontinuous. There was nothing remotely comparable to a Rand Corporation or an Institute for Defense Analyses to provide multidisciplinary teams or, even more important, the kind of institutional continuity necessary to permit a cumulative learning process over a period of time.

Third, the best that can be said for President Johnson's 1965 Executive Order is that it was well-intentioned but hopelessly premature. The skilled and trained manpower did not then and does not now exist to apply our techniques across the board of civilian government. What manpower did exist has been spread so thin, much of it over precisely the kinds of problems which were found intractable in the military, that the result has been disillusionment and some cynicism.

What we need, I think, is a broad new focus for our interests and talents, and a most promising one has emerged — the tremendous international concern over the prospects of 'Spaceship Earth', over air and water pollution and the related problems of population, economic growth, and technology. It would be hard to imagine a greater or more significant intellectual challenge to operations researchers, systems analysts, and cost-benefit economists. And moreover, the problems look to me more like those which we found tractable in military applications than like those which we found intractable. Consider:

(1) They have a high technological content. This is always helpful. Many of our practitioners are scientists and engineers who understand the technological aspects much better than do the politicians and businessmen. And as we have seen, new technologies and processes, where experience is no guide and there is no encrustation of tradition, afford us great opportunities. There are order of magnitude differences in alternative courses of action.

(2) The problems appear to be *relatively* easy to structure, more analogous to the problem of sea warfare or nuclear exchange than to those of counter-insurgency.

(3) While the criterion problem is formidable, it is much less so than in many other civilian problems, e.g., those of education or the urban crisis, and I think we know how to go about it. We can classify the objectives, and are learning how to measure some of them. The economic criterion: to maximize objectives for given costs, or minimize costs for given objectives, is clearly applicable.

(4) Many data exist, many more are becoming available, and only cost considerations are preventing us from obtaining more. We have much to learn about the sources of air pollution, but we know a great deal. We know even more about the sources of water pollution. Our population statistics are imperfect but the best we have in any field. Our greatest gaps are in the effects of pollutants.

In one respect environmental problems are likely to be more tractable than most military problems: we are playing a game not against an intelligent opponent, but essentially against nature, and despite progress in psychology and game theory in recent decades, inanimate nature remains more predictable than people. Of course, the *behavior* of people is critically important in both environmental problems and in military problems. Many *want* to go on driving or selling powerful smelly cars. One of the great and most hotly disputed unknowns is the effect of living standards and food supplies on birthrates.

Is our experience with military problems relevant and transferable to this civilian application? Some is and some is not. Clearly our analytical and computational techniques, our 'bag of tricks', are applicable in both areas. That is not what I want to talk about. I want to consider the similarities and differences in the general character of the problems involved, and their significance for our approach to the problems. I will emphasize first the similarities, and conclude with some important differences.

In both military problems and environmental problems the choice of the right *criterion* or value system for distinguishing better from worse alternatives is fundamental. Choosing the wrong criterion is equivalent to asking the wrong question. I recall that Rand began analyzing strategic nuclear bombing as a transportation problem, and came up with some remarkably wrong answers, recommending bombers and base systems to minimize transportation costs to target. The breakthrough consisted in recognizing that it wasn't a transportation problem but a gaming problem, in which the objective is deterrence and the critical capability not a first-strike but a second-strike capability. Then everything began to fall into place and the answers came out completely different.

This is far from the only example of the use of highly sophisticated OR techniques in conjunction with a casually selected and very imperfect criterion. We learned with experience to devote at least as much care and thought to objectives as to means. In the words of Alain Enthoven, the first Assistant Secretary of Defense: 'Systems analysis is a cycle of definition of objectives, design of alternative systems to achieve those objectives, evaluation of the alternatives in terms of their effectiveness and costs, a questioning of the objectives and a questioning of the other assumptions underlying the analysis, the opening of new alternatives, the establishment of new objectives, etc.' [1].

It is not at all clear that we are using the right objectives and criteria in environmental problems, or, and this is closely related, correctly defining the variables and the boundaries of the system. In fact, some very bright and imaginative people are convinced we are not, because we are sub-optimizing at too low a level, ignoring higher level objectives and their interrelations.

The OR world, as you know, tends to split into sub-optimizers and grand optimizers. The trouble with sub-optimizing is that, while relatively easy to accomplish, it may give results inconsistent with higher level objectives. For example, a fine new transport aircraft may provide a much more efficient means of moving troops and equipment to trouble spots around the globe, but tempt some future President into adventurism. For example, replacing fossil fuel plants with nuclear plants may cut down sulphur emissions dramatically, but add to formidable problems of nuclear waste disposal. The trouble with grand optimizing is that it is so difficult to accomplish that the analyst gets lost in the complexities, or aggregates to the point where he loses his head in the clouds.

I think both grand optimizing and sub-optimizing have their places. I have always maintained that most of the useful work of operations researchers will be at fairly low levels of sub-optimizing, but that the analyst should at least learn enough about the problem at the next higher level to avoid gross inconsistency and error. Sometimes more than that is called for and possible. But I doubt that in our time we will simultaneously solve all the problems of the U.S. Government or any major department in one grand optimization.

In recent months J.W. Forrester, Donella and Dennis Meadows and their associates have attempted to do even more than that with the whole range of pollution, population, and growth problems [2]. Forrester presents a simple simulation model of the *world*, consisting of five first order differential equations in five highly aggregated state variables*. He also includes auxiliary variables, which he calls 'quality of life' as his measures of performance — what I have been calling 'criteria'.

The results are unmitigated disaster for the world, and soon! Nothing seems to help — not industrial growth in the underdeveloped world, not measures to mitigate pollution, not a green revolution in agriculture, nothing! Pollution overwhelms us, food supplies fail, and eventually Malthus' 'positive checks' come into play to decimate the population by famine and disease. A nuclear exchange looks almost inviting by contrast.

I certainly have no quarrel with the Forrester/Meadows objective. We must attempt some grand optimizing here. But their first effort seems to me to be completely unpersuasive and not a useful policy tool. They seem to be guilty of the charge frequently and rightly leveled at my economics profession: casual empiricism. Their model structuring is equally casual. I am skeptical both of their parameters and of the relations explicitly included (and those

---

* The Meadows' book does not include a detailed description of their model; it is apparently similar to Forrester's but has more than five state variables.

not included) in their differential equations. They prove only that if you put Malthusian assumptions in such a model you get a Malthusian answer.

In fact, Forrester is straight Malthus. The world read it all more than 150 years ago. Malthus called it 'geometric' growth instead of exponential growth, but he meant precisely the same thing. Forrester makes the Malthusian assumptions a little more precise, but they are the same assumptions. The quantity of natural resources is fixed and the productivity of industry based on them decreases with time. Agricultural productivity may be increased only by increasing capital investment in agriculture. Pollution output is a linear function of GNP. Birth rate increases strongly with increasing food per capita.

Malthus' predictions have by and large not been borne out during the past 150 years, except in some underdeveloped parts of the world. Wherever nations have had economic and educational systems which have permitted technological advances, both industrial and agricultural productivity have increased steadily and dramatically despite the pressure of a rapidly growing population on available land. What Malthus did not foresee, and what Forrester leaves out of his equations, is a constantly adjusting powerful technology which, in addition to pushing up productivity in both industry and agriculture, develops substitutes for each and every limited resource as it begins to become scarce.

Robert Boyd of the University of California at Davis has done some interesting experimenting with the Forrester model to test its sensitivity, and specifically to make it reflect the views of the people he calls technological optimists [3]. He introduces a constant for rate of increase of technology. He introduces an assumption that as quality of life declines society will invest more technology to improve that quality, and that the investment will be effective. He tries to reflect in a reasonable way the technological optimist's faith that we can find a substitute for any diminishing natural resource. And he changes the birth rate assumptions so that birth rate is unaffected by food per capita, and more strongly reduced than Forrester assumes by an increase in the standard of living.

The result is a complete reversal of Forrester's conclusions. Instead of disaster, a utopian equilibrium is reached with low pollution levels, stable population, and steadily rising living standards.

I find Boyd's conclusions no more convincing than Forrester/Meadows'. Neither does he. The fact that Malthusianism failed to manifest itself during the past 150 years doesn't mean that it won't during the next 150, or 50. Exponential growth obviously has a limit. And we know now that the limit may not be imposed by 'land' in the dictionary sense. Actually, Malthus and the 19th century political economists meant by 'land' any finite limited resource, but most of their attention was directed to land and exhaustible minerals. Perhaps air and water will impose earlier and more severe constraints on growth. And it may be harder in the case of air to use the price system as effectively as it has worked in the case of land and minerals to damp down demand for the scarce resource and stimulate the development of substitutes.

In any event, we must devise better models with a larger number of disaggregated state variables which will allow experts in various fields to provide inputs which rise above the level of casual empiricism. Then we might have a model which would provide useful guidance for operations researchers working on all those essential sub-optimizations.

In military applications at every level — from the grand optimization of strategic nuclear exchanges to the performance specifications of new aircraft and missiles — we have wrestled with the question 'How much is enough?'. Operations researchers have done yeoman work, not always accepted, in estimating the cost and effectiveness of increases in performance of various kinds. Many of the notorious cost-overruns, delays, and failures in military development programs have been the consequence of demanding too much too soon, or in wrong combinations, and arbitrarily, in defiance in the almost universal law of diminishing returns. In offensive nuclear systems, what constitutes 'overkill'?

The question 'How much is enough?' and the law of diminishing returns follow us with a vengeance into the morass of pollution. The Council on Environmental Quality once estimated that the cost of removing 90—95% of all pollutants from U.S. waters would be approximately $60 billion; of removing 95—99%, twice that much or $120 billion; and of 'ecological perfection', perhaps $300 billion. How far do we go, and at what cost to other high priority needs? It is apparent that one of the perils of the pollution business, not unknown in the military business, is the overzealousness of friends demanding immediate and total victory.

Enough of similarities and analogies. There are also highly significant differences, which make the job of the OR practitioner in environmental problems a different kind of job.

Most importantly, and obviously, the political aspects of civilian decision making, and not least in this area, are central and crucial. They cannot be disposed of in asides or mere qualifications. The question confronting the analyst, as Charles Schultze so well states it, is: 'How can systematic analysis be effectively applied to governmental decisions that are reached through the essentially political process of advocacy, bargaining, and negotiated solutions?' [4].

Ernst and Ernst have made a number of technically excellent cost effectiveness studies of air pollution control strategies in American cities. They discovered, for example, in Kansas City [5], that to require each pollution source to reduce its emissions of suspended particulates by one-half (an eminently reasonable and 'fair' performance specification) would cost $26.4 million, whereas a 'least cost' strategy, i.e. minimizing cost for the whole area but requiring some polluters to reduce more than others, would achieve virtually the same results in terms of reduction by one-half of all particulates for the city, at a cost of only $7.5 million.

But this, of course, involves different performance requirements for different sources. It is not manifestly 'fair', however cheap. For example, it prescribed a 97% cut for nonferrous foundries, but only 38% for chemical plants. Not too surprisingly, the report was not well received. The Wall Street Journal carried a story on it under the headline 'Sometimes the facts aren't what people really want to hear'. Political feasibility is going to be a much more severe test in the pollution-population area than it ever was in the military. It has somehow to be incorporated in the structure of the analysis, rather than discovered as an unhappy surprise after the analysis has been completed and published.

One aspect of politics is particularly troublesome when we are dealing with pollution problems: governmental jurisdictions are not geographically coextensive with the problems. The natural area for dealing with water pollution is the watershed, but watersheds typically include many local and state governments and frequently several national governments. The same difficulty arises in connection with air pollution and airsheds, if one can legitimately use that term. And some of the most threatening ecological problems – the genetic effects of radioactivity, the poisoning of the oceans, possible disastrous alterations in the earth's climate from discharging CO_2 or aerosols into the atmosphere or water vapors into the stratosphere – are problems for every nation, for literally the whole world. 'Command system' solutions won't do because there is no command system.

In military problems neutrals are sometimes a nuisance. 'Neutrals' in pollution and population control, who stand aside and above the battle, can thwart the best efforts of governments which seek constructive solutions. In fact, neutralism can take quite aggressive forms. One Latin American country is actively encouraging the construction of new industrial plants by those who want to avoid the costs of mandatory pollution controls in their home countries.

Finally, there is another consequence of the lack of an adequate 'command system' which distinguishes this whole area from that of military applications: a great deal more reliance must be placed on designing appropriate incentives and avoiding perverse incentives. Let me say that I think that in military applications one of our failures was our inability to make effective use of incentives. Perhaps because a command system theoretically existed operations researchers relied too exclusively upon it. We never provided a Service or a Command with incentives to be cost effective. We never succeeded, although we tried, in providing defense contractors with effective incentives to economize or even to submit realistic cost estimates. In fact, we still make it worth their while, perversely, to underestimate costs at every stage of development and procurement.

I am completely convinced that in the environmental area our whole emphasis must be reversed and primary reliance placed on the design of appropriate incentives. I think this would be true even if governmental areas corresponded geographically with problem areas: their lack of correspondence makes it imperative. We have no serious problems with the depletion of minerals because we have a price system which provides powerful incentives to economize and find substitutes for whatever mineral becomes scarce. The price system does not work in the case of air and water pollution because of externalities, i.e. costs or benefits which accrue not to the person or firm responsible, but to others. We must learn how to tax pollutants so that those responsible pay the costs.

Walter Heller, former Chairman of the Council of Economic Advisors, cites four persuasive arguments for preferring taxes and user charges to direct regulation [6]. The regulatory powers are slow and cumbersome, as well as diverse. Regulators bend more readily than tax collectors and a healthier atmosphere results when energies are devoted to reducing taxes rather than to out-manuevering the regulators. A proportional or progressive penalty can accomplish any desired level of pollution abatement more cheaply than regulation. And by leaving discretion in the hands of the individual polluter the tax approach does not require as much centralized information.

Political requirements as well as considerations of efficiency will often call for decentralized incentive programs. But the design of such programs, linking cost benefit analysis to techniques of regulation and control, will require all the skills we have learned to muster and some skills we have not yet learned. It will also require that new mixes of talents be brought together, perhaps in one or more environmental Rand's. The contributions of scientists and engineers are, of course, indispensable, but so are those of legal experts, economists, political scientists, and psychologists who can build into both the analyses and the controls the behavior responses of individuals, business organizations, governmental bureaucracies, and political instrumentalities. As the work goes forward we must be as sensitive as the multi-national firms have learned to be to the differences between one culture or political situation and another in the characteristics of a viable solution. What may be very workable in the institutional environment of the United States or Western Europe may not work, at least in the same form, in some other countries.

In all probability we will have to approach solutions by stages, with pilot experiments on a small scale to test the potency of incentives and controls. Where agreements between national governments are necessary, to share costs or to create supra-national monitoring and control agencies, the work of design and the task of institution building will have to go hand in hand.

This sounds hard. It is hard. But stakes are enormous. If we can internalize external costs, technology can be bent to our will and may yet save Spaceship Earth.

References

[1] A. Enthoven, Operations research at the national policy level, unpublished transcript of an address at the Operations Evaluation Group Vicennial Conf. Washington, May 1962.
[2] J.W. Forrester, World dynamics (Wright–Allen Press, Cambridge, 1971); D.L. Meadows et al., Limits to growth (Universe Books, New York, 1972).
[3] R. Boyd, World dynamics: a note, unpublished paper (1972).
[4] C. Schultze, The politics and economics of public spending (The Brookings Institution, 1968) p. 103.
[5] Ernst and Ernst, A cost–effectiveness study of air pollution abatement in the greater Kansas City area, submitted to the Kansas City, Kansas – Kansas City, Missouri Air Pollution Abatement Conf. July 1969.
[6] W.W. Heller, Coming to terms with growth and the environment, a paper prepared for the Forum on Energy, Economic Growth, and the Environment, Resources for the Future, Washington, April 1971.

M. Ross, ed., OR '72. North-Holland Publishing Company (1973)

6

OPERATIONS RESEARCH IN THE U.S.S.R.
DEVELOPMENT AND PERSPECTIVES

Recherche opérationnelle en U.R.S.S.
évolution et perspectives

NIKITA N. MOISEEV

Academy of Sciences of the U.S.S.R. Moscow, U.S.S.R.

Abstract. This paper traces the distinctive evolution of OR in the USSR where the writings of the mathematician Tchebischeff resulted in an unusually close union between mathematics and engineering. Modern OR dates to three developments in the late thirties — work on the determination of the extreme of functions defined on given sets, on control theory and on the evaluation of technological efficiency. The first, associated with Kantorovitch, gave rise to mathematical programming and optimal economic planning. Control theory began with a realisation of the importance of stability but gradually came to consider multicriteria systems, optimal control and non-stationary processes. Under Ventsel the evaluation of efficiency paved the way for the development of game theory. The blending of these three strands in the mid-fifties promoted the rapid growth of OR. Of particular importance was the work of Mikhalevitch on sequential analysis and indeterminacies, and Zhuravlev's concept of the "near optimal" algorithm. These led to a recognition of the limitations of mathematical formalism and the growth of the theory of expertise with its interest in intermediary goals, non-formal aggregation (and decomposition) and the analysis of experts' reports. Gradual qualitative changes have led to a systems orientation and the promising development of imitator systems in recent years.

This is the first time that a representative of the Soviet Union has addressed a meeting of this Congress as a member of the IFORS, the organisation whose general activities at both practical and conceptual level can, under certain conditions, play an important role in the evolution of human society. The role of this scientific discipline in the Soviet Union is growing from one decade to the next, its methods are being successfully developed, its field of application is being constantly enlarged. Because of the language difficulties, very few in the West are aware of this activity. So I would like to devote my paper to an analysis of the principal directions developed by the specialists of my country. Essentially, I will talk about a number of ideas which gave rise to the theory of operations research, which determined its progress, and which, it seems, will exert a decisive influence on the perspectives of its development in the near future.

I should like to apologise in advance for the subjectivity of my analysis. One cannot be a specialist on every problem at once. One of the well-known maxims of Kozma Proutkov, the Russian writer, is: "If you do not know the language of the Iroquois, do not talk about it". This advice causes me to forgo completely any discussion of queuing theory.

1. The influence of Tchebischeff

The history of the appearance and development of operations research in the Soviet Union shows many distinctive features when compared with the analogous processes which were taking place in other countries with a high scientific potential.

The formation of the mathematical idea and the orientation of Russian mathematicians were enormously influenced by the ideas of one of the greatest mathematicians of the 19th century P.L. Tchebischeff who said in the middle of the last century: "Mathematics was created and developed under the influence of the essential general objective of all human activity: to use the means at hand in such a way as to obtain the greatest profit".

We owe to P.L. Tchebischeff a very clear understanding of the orientation of mathematics. It is precisely because of this that in Russia the gap between mathematicians and engineers has never been as great as in the West. It is also for this reason that first-class mathematicians and applied scientists with professional competence in mathematics could participate from the start in the formation of the theory of operations research. The very understanding of the new scientific discipline took on a wider dimension on this account. In the preface to his superb work "An Introduction to the Theory of Operations Research", J.B. Guermeyer says: "By an operation... we mean a set of actions, of measures directed towards the attainment of a certain goal". I merely add that among these operations we see particularly a set of actions designed to reveal the aim of another operation.

This very wide understanding of the meaning of operations makes it possible to attract and gather into an inseparable whole certain areas which could have been considered as autonomous scientific disciplines.

Operations research is a non-mathematical discipline because very few actions can be studied on the basis of solution of particular mathematical problems. At the same time, mathematics and the mathematical mode of thought have played an important part in its evolution.

2. Mathematical programming

The beginning of operations research in the Soviet Union dates back, probably to the end of the 1930's when three areas appeared which gave rise to the formation of its mathematical approach, ideas and concepts. These were the problems of the determination of the extreme of functions defined on given sets, quality control theory and the problem of the evaluation of technological efficiency.

In the late 1930's Professor L.V. Kantorovitch, a young mathematician from Leningrad, began to study a new class of mathematical problems: the determination of the extreme of a linear form defined on a simplex. Thus was laid the foundation-stone of linear programming, a chapter of mathematics which fate has made one of the principal tools of operations research.

Wartime conditions greatly slowed down the development of the new theory as well as its use in the solving of practical problems. After the war, in the late 1940's and the early 1950's, the situation began to change very rapidly. The economy became the principal source of new problems. The ideas and methods of L.V. Kantorovitch gained solid backing and evolved rapidly. In conjunction with the great Soviet economists, Novogilov and Nemtchinov, L.V. Kantorovitch created the concept of optimal planning which played an important part in the development of the principles of economic planning in the socialist state. The development of optimal planning methods acted, among others, as a very important stimulus to the progress of operations research methods.

Optimisation problems made their appearance in the 18th century and the study of them is now more than 200 years old. The key idea, which inspired the development of the theory throughout this long history, was very simple. Let $f(x)$ be a required solution: a function reaching the extreme (value) of the functional $I(f(x))$, then the variation of this solution must inevitably cancel out. These classical ideas of analysis were shown to have little application to the solution of problems aiming at the determination of the extremes of functions and functionals defined on sets of sufficiently arbitrary form. But it

happens that conditions which are equally simple and obvious can be constructed, but in terms of possible direction cones.

Let us denote by K_{x_0} the totality of all the directions coming from the
point x_0 and along which the function $I(x)$ decreases and by $\hat{K}_{x_0}$ interior of
the admissible set. For the point x_0 to give the extreme of the function $I(x)$,
it is necessary and sufficient that the intersection be

$$K_{x_0} \cap \hat{K}_{x_0} = \emptyset \tag{1}$$

that is, empty.

Despite the fact that this affirmation is evident and trivial, it has become a
source of profound theoretical explorations. Condition (1) holds for functional spaces of a general form and, consequently, has made it possible to
construct very general mathematical theories. Despite the fact that condition
(1) is well known to specialists in topology and functional analysis, at least
since M.G. Kreine's work on the theory of cones, it was first used for the
construction of the necessary conditions for an extreme by the Soviet
mathematicians A.A. Milioutine and A.I. Doubovitski. These ideas were used
as the basis of many studies both of a theoretical and an applied nature. They
were developed intensively in Kiev (Cybernetics Institute of Ukrainian Academy of Sciences), in Moscow (Central Institute of Economics and Mathematics and the Calculation Centre of the USSR Academy of Sciences), in
Novosibirsk (Institutes of Economics and Mathematics of the Siberian branch
of the Academy of Sciences) and in many other cities and organisations in the
Soviet Union. It is impossible to list the names of the specialists who have
contributed to the theory and practice of mathematical programming. However I think it is necessary to single out the names of Drs. V.N. Pchenitchni
and I.M. Ermoliev, disciples of Professor V.S. Mikhalevitch, who succeeded
in combining a high level of competence in general explorations theory with
the pragmatism and clear understanding of the meaning of the problems of
operations research theory which are necessary in order to use mathematical
programming successfully and who, on that account, exerted a great influence
on the fate of operations research in the USSR.

3. Control theory

The second source, which provided material for the formation of operations research theory, its concepts and ideas, is control theory. The 1920's
and 30's saw the formation of a new discipline: automatic control theory.

The study of the classical heritage of the 19th century and of the works of the engineers, Vichnegradski, Stodolla and the others, resulted in the formation of the principal and necessary conditions for the functioning of a control system: its stability. The principle of reaction as a means of bringing about the stable functioning of a technical system and as an indispensable element of any control system began to be clearly understood. After the classic works of Van der Paul and Bogolioubov, Mendelchtam and Papaleksi, Nyquist and many others it was found that engineering practice had a sufficiently solid basis to make possible studies of complicated technological systems embodying stationary, or approximately stationary, processes.

The realisation that stability is one of the principal criteria for the evaluation of technical systems constitutes an important stage in the formation of the fundamental principles of control theory. During the years before the war the problem of the stability of technical systems was one of the principal sources which inspired the creative efforts of engineers and mathematicians working in the field of control theory. I would like to draw your attention particularly to the fact that from the bases of classical control theory emerged some new ideas which had decisive repercussions on the formation of the essential tools of operations research theory during the 1950's.

Let us point out first of all that the problem of stability can take the form of an optimisation problem. In fact, the movement will be stable if the feedback operator ensures that the functional be at a maximum:

$$I = \begin{cases} \infty \text{ if the movement is stable,} \\ 0 \text{ if the movement is not stable.} \end{cases}$$

However, this criterion does not generally give the only solution, that is to say, it does not determine in a unequivocal manner the structure of the feedback (or the control impulses) which brings about the stable functioning of a technological item. This means that the engineer engaged in solving a study problem can make this same system satisfy certain supplementary requirements apart from ensuring the stability of his control system. So it was that the concept of quality control appeared at the end of the 1930's. The engineer can study the possibilities of a system controlling a technological item (an aeroplane for example) which he has to perfect and can construct the system in such a way that its movement will be stable and that at the same time, overloading, for example, will not exceed the admissible limits in the case of random disturbances.

But if the concept of quality control exists, then it is natural that the logical development of this point of view should result in the creation of control systems possessing a maximum quality, and being optimal in one sense or another. So, in the late 1930's, two typical operations research problems came into being within control theory: multicriteria systems and optimal control.

To use the language of modern operations research theory one could say that at the period engineers were already attempting to solve the problem of the choice of optimal strategy according to two criteria: stability I_1 and quality control I_2.

However, as so often happens, the attachment to fixed norms prevented automatic control theory specialists at that time from realising that the problems they had before them and the problems peculiar to operations research theory can be formulated in the same language and studied with the help of the same methods.

Gradually optimisation problems have begun to play an ever-increasing role in the creation of control systems.

When we pass on to the study of non-stationary processes or processes whose active characteristic time is compatible with the characteristic time of transitory processes, these become the central problems of all operations research theory.

In the mid-1940's, certain countries began to develop missile technology very rapidly, and this became an important factor in accelerating the evolution of optimisation ideas and procedures. During that period it was thought that the evolution of dynamic systems control theory should be a simple combination of the classic methods developed in automatic control theory, and the methods of the calculus of variations. But the problem turned out to be much more difficult. It was quickly realised that the practical problems of control theory are not related to the problems of classical calculus of variations and that adequate procedures for solving them quite simply do not exist.

The first concrete presentation of the contents of control theory, one of the principal branches of modern operations research theory, in the Soviet Union and, perhaps, in the whole world, appeared in the book by D.E. Okhotchimski. Because of the war, this work was not published until 1946. In studying the problem of the vertical takeoff of a rocket, the author of this work was able to formulate it in the language used by modern optimal control theory and proposed an original solution to it. The number of similar problems being presented by technology mounted very rapidly. However, the absence of one unique framework held back the creation of the new scientific theory, each problem being solved by specific methods. This framework was not created until the fifties and was named the maximum principle of

L.S. Pontryagin. So, in the mid-1950's work by mathematicians, technicians, economists and engineers, resulted in numerous effective studies of the problems of the determination of the extremes of functions and functionals defined on certain sets, including closed sets, which had appeared in conjunction with economic problems just as much as in the study of dynamic technical processes. These efforts played an important part in the progress of operations research theory itself, in the evolution of its concepts and methods, as well as in practical applications.

4. Evaluation of technological efficiency

If the work done on mathematical programming and automatic control (including optimal automatic control theory) created the mathematical apparatus of operations research theory, then its ideology, its conceptions were defined by research in the field of quality (efficiency) evaluation of technical means. Research of this kind was already being carried out in the Soviet Union in the 1930's.

I leave to the historians of science the responsibility of finding out who first used the term "efficiency". For my part, I think it is quite incontestable that this area was strongly influenced by the late Professor D.A. Ventsel. Unfortunately, Professor D.A. Ventsel left very few written works. But a very large number of his pupils, direct and indirect, have assimilated the principles and the ideas without which it is impossible to imagine the development of the theory of operations research.

The author of this paper had the good fortune to be among those who were able to associate with Professor D.A. Ventsel and to participate in the discussion of problems concerning the evaluation of the quality of technical decisions. Among the qualities of this admirable man we can single out his ability to understand profoundly the possibilities and place of the exact sciences and his freedom from illusions about the potentialities of rigorous mathematical methods. He formulated all the essential characteristics involved in making of complicated decisions, to the analysis of which operations research devotes its efforts, practically in their present form i.e. multiple criteria, the presence of indeterminacies, the impossibility of formalising what are perhaps the most important stages of projects and the role of information. It was just at this time the process of creating technological constriction came to be viewed as an inevitable conflict which makes the realization of contradictory demands utterly impossible.

Moreover, this system greatly facilitated the absorption of game theory into operations research theory. In turn the development of the Soviet school of game theory is due to the practical use of its ideas in operations research theory.

Game theory is being developed successfully in the USSR at present. Its success is due to the Moscow and Leningrad schools. The classic areas of game theory, in particular, are being developed in Leningrad under the direction of Professor N.N. Vorobiev. The different problems of operations research theory are considered as examples illustrating the theory.

In Moscow the fate of game theory was somewhat different. Professor J.B. Guermeyer and his disciples approached the problems of game theory through concrete problems arising in operations research. The necessity to consider an operation as a conflict situation brought with it the need to study many new non-classical problems of game theory. As a result, Professor J.B. Guermeyer laid the foundations of the theory of games with non-conflicting interests.

5. Sequential analysis

The theory of operations research as a new and autonomous scientific discipline was formed as a blending of the ideas and concepts of the theory of efficiency and the mathematical methods of optimal control theory and mathematical programming. From the mid-1950's the term "operations research" or "theory of operations research" became quite current and the intensity of the explorations began to increase rapidly. Not only did new fields of application appear, but also new scientific ideas and directions.

I would like to emphasize two important ideas put forward in the late 1950's. The first concerns the possibility of using Wald's methods, in the theory of decision-making and, especially, in optimisation. Wald, a well-known American mathematician, whose works are concerned with statistics, created the concept of sequential analysis. It is not difficult to demonstrate that his concept can be recast in the language of optimisation methods. Let us suppose that we wish to determine the extreme value of the function $f(x)$ defined on a set M. Let us then suppose that we will be able to divide this subset into M_1 and M_2 and to observe that M_2 does not contain an optimal x. Then that allows us to study the optimisation problem only on a set narrower than $M_1 \in M$. In the general case, we can only obtain the estimate of the extreme value (or its probability). Then, at the following stage, if we can manage to split the set M, between M_{11} and M_{12} by one procedure or another and to obtain corresponding estimates, we must also take into consideration the estimation of set M_2. There may be cases when we will have to return to the analysis of set M_2. On the basis of this scheme we can obtain a series of efficient algorithms for the solution of complicated optimisation problems. Noting that the determination of $f(x)$ for a concrete x can be treated as experience, we can, to describe the procedure of sequential analysis, retain the terminology used in Wald's well-known work.

Towards the end of the fifties, the professor V.S. Mikhalevitch proposed a general schema for the formation of similar procedures for the sequential analysis of variants and a number of schemes for the solution of concrete optimization problems. When we learned of the existence of Bellman's works (written before Mikhalevitch's works), we realised that dynamic programming is one of the special cases of sequential analysis. Similarly, from Mikhalevitch's general scheme we derive the well-known method of branches and bounds described in the literature which appeared after Mikhalevitch's work. Moreover, that does not exhaust the possibilities of sequential analysis which can be applied to the analysis of the problem of decision-making in circumstances where there is a plurality of criteria.

Today the problem of optimisation of projects has assumed very great importance. This problem has many different aspects. But it is our concern to examine one of these aspects more closely, that of operations research. Every project, whether it be a system of planning models, a commercial aeroplane or a project on the use of water for irrigation, industry of pisciculture, always has the same peculiarity. It must meet several different and often contradictory requirements. The problem of the choice of parameters for a project inevitably comes up against the difficulties of "vectorial optimisation". Mikhalevitch's schema allows us to construct the procedure for determining a domain in criteria space which may be called minimal in a completely natural way. Within this domain, we have no reason for preferring one choice of parameter to another. This domain may also be called: the domain of total indetermination of our desires.

The subsequent analysis immediately calls for the application of other procedures. Optimisation methods must give way to gaming methods or to the introduction of the hypotheses: of the principle of quaranteed result or of the function of risk.

V.S. Mikhalevitch's schema can also be used for the processing of information obtained as a result of expert appraisal.

6. The "near-optimal" algorithm

The second idea is that of the "near-optimal" algorithm. It was proposed by Professor Y.I. Youravlev. This idea can be explained in a schematic manner as follows. The analysis of the alternatives in the case of decision-making procedures very often necessitates the classification of a large number of variants. The designation problem is to be found in the same class of examples.

From the point of view of pure mathematician the problem does not exist because there is always a solution. However the fact that this solution exists does not help us. In order to find the exact solution to a problem concerning the drawing up of a timetable including 10,000 jobs we would have to run a very modern machine for a time equal to that which has elapsed since the appearance of our galaxy. This is why in principle we cannot do without heuristic methods which would diminish the expenditure of machine time. But the tragedy of this situation lies in what follows. In practice each heuristic method has a counter-example which reduced its application to a classification of all the variants. In what way can these methods be chosen and evaluated?

However, if we are going to analyse the different methods, then for "good" methods the number of counter-examples will be reduced. If you like, they will constitute a certain pathology. Now let us suppose that the proportion of pathological cases will decrease according as the number of problems to be solved with the help of this algorithm increases. We can therefore say that this algorithm is sufficiently good. Then using such and such an index we can choose the best algorithm from among those which are "good". These ideas have served as a basis for a number of original studies which were not of a purely practical nature. The methods of Professor Y.I. Youravlev have proved very efficient for problems of diagnosis by tests, of recognition of images, and in recent times they are becoming one of the most efficient means of processing expert evaluations.

7. Non-formal methods

The development of mathematical methods and the increase in the power of computers makes it possible to enlarge considerably the sphere of problems to be resolved. But it is not mathematics which constitute the instrument of analysis in operations research theory. With rigorous mathematical methods it is possible to solve only relatively simple problems. I have just quoted examples of what is in fact a simple problem concerning a timetable the exact solution of which cannot be worked out within a reasonable time. This is not a weakness of calculating technique. Even machines with hypothetical power will need thousands and thousands of years to be able to solve such problems in an exact manner. The fact that the future of operations research as an applied science is determined to a large extent by our ability to succeed in uniting mathematical formalism and the non-formal faculty of thought using the profound possibilities of the human brain was not understood at once. It is only gradually that specialists have come to understand that this fact is not due to the weakness of mathematics or of calculating techniques. In reality, this fact reflects the complexity of the real world in which we live. Mathematical procedures constitute only one way of knowing the truth. Realisation of this has considerably strengthened the positions of our science and its role in the solving of applied problems.

At present more and more efforts are being made to find procedures making it possible to combine in a rational manner mathematical formalism and non-formal methods which make use of intuition, associations, and quite simply, man's natural talent. The heuristic principle, the method of intermediary goals, non-formal aggregation and, of course, the organisation and processing of experts' reports — all these are links in the same chain.

In the course of the last decade the theory of expertise developed very rapidly. Beginning with isolated rules, principles which mark the appearance of a new scientific discipline now began to emerge. The most important one is probably the principle of the decomposition of a complex problem into a number of simple problems, a principle which lies at the root of all the procedures for organising complex expert opinions. In Russia this principle was formulated by G.S. Pospelov who, when studying the problems of budget allocation, proposed the said method of solution matrices. V.M. Glouchkov proposed an interesting method for organising expert appraisal of technological forecasts and of the evaluation of projects. Now that many works have been published, it is interesting to point out certain parallels between the works of Soviet and American specialists. However, the works of Soviet specialists include some ideas which have no counterpart in the works of western specialists.

There are above all the ideas of Professor Y.I. Youravlev based on the methods of diagnosis by tests. The following are the stages in the organisation and processing of the experts' evaluations according to Youravlev's schema:

(a) Establishment of an information table, that is, a description (with the help of experts) of known "similar" or "related" situations.

(b) Choice of the best algorithm in the given class of algorithms, that is, an algorithm which, according to the information table, makes the minimum number of errors.

(c) Use of the chosen algorithm to solve problems of recognition (and in particular of classification) in the table of data proposed by the experts or obtained through experiment.

"The consensus of opinions" among the experts is one of the difficult problems of the theory of expert opinions. Many procedures of all kinds have been proposed. Among these are very important procedures linked to the arrival and analysis of additional information, that is, informing the experts. But situations exist in which the very wide supplementary information of the experts is not sufficient and their opinions are divergent. These situations have been a subject of discussion for a long time. Several procedures for treating them mathematically have been and are at present being proposed. Professor J.B. Guermeyer has observed that this situation is typical of decisionmaking in conditions of indeterminacy. Many important facts result from it – and, in particular, the possibility of using the principle of guaranteed strategy.

8. Systems

According as operations research develops the problems to be solved are not simply becoming more complicated. In the last 15 years we can see that qualitative changes have been taking place in the work of operations research specialists. Gradually we have been passing from the study of isolated problems, even very complicated ones, to the study of systems. Analysis is becoming more and more oriented towards operations which put into effect the actions with a precise aim which make up complicated social, socioeconomic and economic systems.

The theory of operations research is in fact becoming the basis of a new technology of systems projects of similar complexity.

In order to characterise this class of problems I would like to inform you about two projects which are being discussed with the participation of the Calculation Centre of the USSR Academy of Sciences.

(a) Project for the development (and administration) of Western Siberia, a region which is rich in gas and petroleum. This region, covering 1.5 million square kilometres, is practically deserted, marshy and partly wooded and it seems that it contains the richest gas and petrol deposits in the whole world. How can the prospecting, production, transport and processing of these riches be organised in the most rational way? How can the problem of peopling this region be solved in a reasonable manner, that is to say, what solutions can be found for the most complex social problems on territory so ill-adapted for human life? Finally, how can the related problems – the exploitation of rich forests, the exploitation of the great Siberian rivers which teem with wild life etc. – be solved?

(b) Project for using the water resources of the rivers flowing into the Sea of Azov. The rivers Kuban and Don and their tributaries cross very rich and fertile areas of the Soviet Union which are inhabited by tens of millions of people. The waters of these rivers are necessary for agriculture. They are necessary for the industry of the Donetz basin, the third largest industrial region in the country. They are necessary for man's relaxation. They must be fit for drinking. They are necessary for the Sea of Azov which is rich in fish and they must be at once fresh and unpolluted. How can the different variants of the projects for these systems be evaluated? We must learn to reconcile different, and often contradictory, requirements. We must also realise that natural resources and human destinies are at stake and that these cannot be measured either in dollars or in rubles.

The evolution of scientific and technological progress will place before humanity the necessity to create even more complicated projects. Humanity is now in a position to use a certain amount of energy on a world scale. That is to say that in the near future we can expect to see projects not only on regional scale, but on world scale.

The execution of projects of this magnitude is no longer possible using the traditional procedures of engineers and economists. In these conditions particular importance attaches to the participation of operations research specialists in the projects, that is, human action oriented towards a precise goal. Complicated systems projects now constitute a stage in the development of the science of operations research. One of the special features of this operations research lies in the fact that the first phase of actions directed towards a precise goal consists in pointing out the vector of the goals, the conditions and the criteria.

9. Simulation

What are the means which permit operations research theory to take an active part in the creation of projects as complicated as these? They are above all its basic methods, i.e. the ability to approach the analysis of complex operations which has been built up over several decades. But methods alone are not sufficient. Procedures are needed which make it possible to analyse and compare the variants. These procedures already exist but they are not yet perfect. To be more precise, we have now arrived at an understanding of how to construct these procedures.

At the outset operations research theory dealt with isolated models which made it possible to reduce operations research to a mathematical problem. Later we learned how to combine the mathematical model with the experts and, finally, in the last few years we have seen the appearance of a new and sufficiently general approach which has been named in the Soviet Union imitator systems.

In Russia what we call an imitator system is any system which includes the following elements at least:

(a) Systems of models. It is impossible to describe the functioning of the Siberian oil-bearing complex with a single model. We must have a model of the subterranean hydrodynamics and models describing the transport and refining of the petroleum as well as many other models.

(b) Experts and procedures. One of the ideas of the imitator systems is to replace the classification of all possible variants by the analysis of certain variants chosen (proposed) by the experts. Consequently, the experts and the rules of their behaviour constitute a biological element inseparable from the system.

(c) Language. The experts are generally not mathematicians and can belong to various professions. So specialists in hydrology and hydro-technology, agronomists, doctors etc. participate in projects on the use and filtering of water. It is therefore necessary to have a language which is sufficiently simple and sufficiently easily learned by all the experts and by the electronic machine since the latter will have to receive the experts' instructions.

When approaching work on the water use project we wanted to use the "Dynamo" language proposed by Forrester. But it proved to be a very primitive language. Now an idea exists for a language which can be expanded. It is possible that this language will be based on the "Dynamo" language.

(d) Operational system. It must control the functioning of the whole imitator system and must be linked to the operational system which controls the calculating complex. It must have several languages. Besides the language used by the experts who are not mathematicians, it must control the models which are recorded according to their nature in one of the universal languages, Cobol or any other simulation language.

10. Conclusion

In this paper I have attempted to give an account of the history of the ideas of operations research in the Soviet Union not only up to the present day, but also a little way into the future.

I have a very firm conviction – if you like, it is a simple hypothesis – that the future of operations research theory is closely linked to the creation of imitator systems. But this affirmation is far from being an alternative to the traditional areas of this science. On the contrary, the effect of the functioning of imitator systems will be determined first of all by the level of our mastery of graphical solutions, mathematical programming, problems of queuing theory and other classical divisions of operations research.

The understanding of any theory consists not only in seeing what is before our eyes, but also in seeing a little further ahead. When we do this, then the horizons which open before our science seem marvellous to us. Marvellous, too, seems the place which it must occupy in the development of humanity. Because our occupation is the study of means of action directed towards very precise goals, including actions necessary for determining the goals.

PART III

GUEST PAPERS

Contribution d'invités

Chairman: B.P. BANERJEE (India)
Vice President of IFORS

Papers presented by

H. ZEMANEK (Austria) President of IFIP

M. CUÉNOD (Switzerland) Treasurer of IFAC

M. Ross, ed., OR '72. North-Holland Publishing Company (1973)

7

FORMAL DEFINITION AND GENERALIZED ARCHITECTURE

Définition formelle et architecture généralisée

HEINZ ZEMANEK

University of Technology, Vienna, Austria

Abstract. Formalization is a requirement for any exact science and for its technical application. The terms and the ideas of algebra and of algorithm were introduced more than a thousand years ago – the computer extends the need over many other fields.

In particular, there is a requirement at the next level: in order to talk about programming languages one needs a meta-language, and this language must be formalized, too. Examples of such meta-languages are the Backus Normal Form and the Vienna Definition Language. The first step of generalization is to extend the formal description to programming systems including operating systems and application programs. Formal definition becomes for algorithmic structures what the drawing is for hardware structures; it means reduction to the essential, precise instruction for the execution, and a yardstick for the completed object.

Formal definition, furthermore, permits transition to a higher design. In the early period, more complex structures in technology are constructed by combining elements. In the advanced period, the complex structure is formally designed from top to bottom, the elements are a function of the whole. This principle is called architectural construction and it is already applied in computer construction. A second step of generalization yields architectural design of systems and, in a third, entities such as factories and enterprises, but also governments and whole countries become the subject of architecture.

However, formal definition can never cover the entire real world. There are philosophical reasons why there will always remain a gap between the constructed system and real life – a task for man in the future.

1. Formalization

There is no better means of communication than good, spoken, natural language. It is strange, therefore, that mathematics and science had to develop formal, constructed, artificial languages before they became successful. The explanation lies in the character of the objects described. There is an important difference between live structures, for which natural language has developed and remains ideal, and constructs, for which constructed languages must be created.

The more complicated constructs have systems character; live structures are always both complex and have systems character. In this respect a system is a structure composed of interconnected and interdependent elements with a substructure. Conforming to certain rules these elements exchange material, energy or information and change their state. A particular system during a particular period of time is described by the flow of material, energy or information, and by the sequence of states. One can speak of a flow of events, of a history. The system as such is characterized by the sets of possible states and possible flows, by its behaviour. The rules of behaviour, therefore, are essential to the description: they show the difference between live objects and constructs. As a first approximation one could say that the living object exists before we discover the rules while the construct comes into existence in conformity with the pre-established rules. In the first case, the rules are and remain an approximation, in the second case the rules are the definition of the object. The better the definition, in the constructed case, the better, the clearer, and the more reliable is the object. The formal language compresses the pre-assumptions into a few axioms, while all derivations can be made free from error, ambiguity and objection. Of course, the technical realization afterwards will not be as ideal as the formal definition, but usually technology can keep the deviations within agreed and acceptable tolerances.

The computer has made all of this more distinct and more important; for the computer is the perfect means for executing formal rules, primarily within a symbolic system. Since symbols can operate effectors, the computer can control material systems; since symbols can be derived via artificial sensory organs from reality, any kind of automatic system can be run by computer control – provided the rules are formalized.

The constructed languages of the computer, normally called programming languages, appear in a new light in this view. They are not simply special computer forms of the algebraic rules developed since the invention of algebra, they are general attempts to create the formal means of description for the different systems realized and controlled by computers. The algebraic languages were only the first family. The Babylonian confusion in the field of programming languages which looks so hopeless in our days is nothing but a transition from algebraic description, typically by a differential equation, to more general philosophies of description and to more general constructed languages. These latter will not only include what algebra offers but also aim at optimal control of the system — optimal in a very pragmatic, economic sense. This will mean formalization of many more fields, fields which so far have remained informal, mostly with good reason. Legal wording is a typical, but not unique example: for many centuries lawyers have conserved language logic and quasi-formal expressions; the computer will oblige them to apply formal logic and formal expressions, to formalize many of their systems, if not all.

The problems of Operations Research range from logics and algebra to law, from fields formalized since centuries ago to fields to be formalized* during the next hundred years. In general, however, formalization is common to Operations Research, automatic control and information processing — and it has been practized since their beginnings. However, I wish now to describe certain new lines of thinking which have evolved in the field of information processing and which very probably will spread into most fields where computers are applied, certainly with different speeds and different importances. What I mean by new lines of thinking is a little more than formalization: it is the organization of formalized structures as closed entities, without interconnecting parts in natural language; it is the creation of formally defined systems, a generalization of the classical programming languages.

This implies far more than may appear — it is the transition from equations and systems of equations in the hands of the mathematically trained specialist to a self-contained and man-independent set of mathematical, logical, and time-frame relations, capable of simulating and even controlling a system. The main problem in this transition is the meaning of the processed information, because in the automatic system there is no human being watching the conservation of sense in the actions, in the operation of a system. The set of relations exceeds the domain of algebra; one has to do with languages.

2. Semiotics, the theory of language

An investigation in depth would call for a long chapter on *semiotics*, the theory of language [1,2] setting out how it was developed from a behaviouristic into a logical theory by the philosophical school of empiricism. For our

---

* Not everything, by the way, must be formalized; there are fields which we may not be able to cover by formal methods and there may be fields which we should not try to formalize — but this is the subject of a paper on the limitations of science and technology.

rather summary treatment a few notions and a few classifications of semiotics will suffice.

Semiotics distinguishes three levels of investigation of increasing coverage and difficulty, i.e. *syntactics, semantics and pragmatics.*

Syntactics is the study of the relationships between the signs and on the level of signs: the rules of construction of words, sentences and texts – but without any references to the meaning and the use of the signs, words, sentences and texts.

Semantics is the study of the relationships between the signs and the objects to which the signs refer, the relationship between the level of description and the level of described objects: the rules of verification of the meaning of the signs, words, sentences and texts – but without any reference to the use and the user.

Pragmatics, finally, is the study of the use and the user of the signs, words, sentences, texts and the language and including both generalities like history and specialities like individual habits or cases.

Either natural or constructed languages can be studied; some parts of the theory will be common to both, some will be different. The set of rules controlling the production of well-formed words or sentences is called the *syntax* of the language; in the case of a constructed language, the syntax will be as precise as we know it from algebra, it will be very clear and free of exceptions, so that automatic checking for syntactical correctness is possible, and also automatic production of texts and automatic parsing (taking the text apart into the syntactic elements). The rules for verification and the establishment of the meaning, however, are quite another problem and no general solution is in sight.

Semiotics also has other principles of classification. Important for our purposes is the distinction of description levels. If we speak about language, we speak in a language, but on a higher level: we speak in a meta-language. Natural language is suited for both levels: one can speak in English about English. But there is the danger of confusion. If we say, for instance, that *language has eight letters,* we can recognize that this is a sentence about the word language and, therefore, a meta-sentence; we had better put *'language'* into quotation marks, so that any doubt is removed. In other instances the difference may be less obvious.

Another distinction in semiotics concerns the difference of description before and after the generation of the described object – the difference between describing an existing, maybe live, system and describing an object to be produced or constructed. Languages theory speaks of descriptive and normative language.

This same difference applies to many fields and also to Operations Research where research can on the one hand find out how existing, perhaps living, systems or concepts of operation can be understood and described, while on the other hand, at a systematized and parameterized second stage, one can proceed to synthesize operation systems, to simulate them and to get them applied. The languages will follow the methods: living language will be required in the first attempts at analysis, but as soon as the description has model character and at least parts in a formal language, perhaps in algebraic relations, a real synthesis will require a highly formalized language, avoiding omissions and contradictions in defined terms and relationships.

3. Automatic design

There is a further reason for formal description. Large systems can no longer be hand-made – automatic production [3] will not only be more economical, it might even be a condition for a successful production.

The contrast between manual and automatic production comes from the involvement of human intellect in the manual case: the working man, even when not an expert, not only follows the prescribed production algorithm but also can deal with unexpected events. The application of intuitive knowledge sometimes is essential but not reflected by any record; the programmer who wants to get a process under computer control asks many questions which no one who worked at the job for years previously can answer. And when finally the algorithm is programmed, it still does not contain features of the intelligence of the manual procedure.

Where only skill is involved, the algorithm may finally be improved almost to perfection; but where semantical aspects come in, the human mind can never be completely replaced by the algorithm and special care is necessary to maintain the meaning of processed information.

In the computer industry, this stage has been reached long ago. There is hardly a computer today which has not been designed with the support of design automation. This principle favours the synthesis of the whole system from a few building elements, and the repetition, the multiple application of a few elements is the basis for economic production. The syntax of the technology, the sets of combination rules, can be programmed. Iterated application of the design automation program supported by an automatically produced checklist of errors and omissions will reduce them to zero (or almost zero).

As a byproduct we get excellent, complete and error-free documentation, at no additional cost because the computer simply prints out the final result of the computer-aided design. The same information can control automatic production. In the case of the computer it began with a program for the lay-out of building elements in the rack and automatic production of the wiring diagram, and continues with automatic insertion of the building elements and automatic wiring. For hardware, it is already true that computers produce computers.

In software, in the production of computer programs, we are not yet in the same stage of development, but large programming systems are already designed with computer support and it is certain that programming systems will end up almost completely computer designed. The problem here is one of an appropriate description language – and this is taking rather more time to be generally estimated and accepted.

Developments are similar for many other industrial products. Automatic production is no longer synonymous with mass production of simple things: automatic control and information processing allow automation for complicated products in small numbers. The principle is to break down the products and the processes into small elements, to describe the combination of these elements formally and to automatically turn the description into the product on a general-purpose production line.

4. Formal definition

Mathematics was the first field where the need for formalization came up and was carried through – it was, consequently, also the first field where the need for an operational definition of the meaning of its most important terms came up and was also carried through. And the most important term of mathematics is *computation*.

The definition of a *computation* [4] was given by several authors in different ways, but a deeper investigation showed that essentially all of them are only different forms of the same notion. In terms of computer-oriented thinking, one can say that all of them conceived an *abstract machine,* defined by its *states* and by the *transition functions* which decide how a certain state changes to the next state. The abstract machine is driven by some control mechanism; the set of states which the abstract machine runs through for a given text establishes the meaning of this text, i.e. of this computation. The abstract machine defines the notion of a computable number and the notion of a decidable logical problem.

The best-known abstract machine is the *Turing Machine* [5], invented before the advent of the computer by the British mathematician A. Turing. Although hardly ever built as an actual machine, it is now commonly used in literature to define terms and concepts.

The exact description of programming languages has become increasingly a problem as languages become more machine-independent: if syntax and semantics of the language cannot be based on a specific hardware, some other kind of definition has to take its place.

The syntactic problem was resolved, when J. Backus [6,7] had the idea to describe the grammar of ALGOL by a set of *production rules,* rules which define how to construct well-formed sentences. Let me give a small example of how to define the integers and the names in a programming language. We need two kinds of characters

CHARACTER ::= DIGIT | LETTER

and we define these two by the list of them

DIGIT   ::= 0 | 1 | 2 | 3 | 4 | 5 | 6 | 7 | 8 | 9
LETTER ::= A | B | C | D | E | F | ... | Z

The number is built by attaching digits

NUMBER ::= DIGITS | NUMBER·DIGIT

while the name starts off with a letter, but can continue with letters or digits

NAME ::= LETTER | NAME·LETTER | NAME·DIGIT

With such rules the syntax of any formal language can be built up; for convenience and greater freedom, a few more notations may be added, but in principle those indicated will suffice.

The semantic problem remained open much longer. An easy way out is to map a semantically undefined language in a language, the meaning of which is considered as being defined. This is not really a solution. Some authors tried to resolve as much of the semantic problems as possible by syntactic means — such efforts were not very successful and could not be. A genuine method of definition for semantics was required. As in mathematics the definition can be based on a set of axioms from which the remainder of the meaning in the language can be derived; but this seems to work only in elegant and small systems. The better solution, we think, is to apply the concepts of computation and abstract machine. Such a method of definition was worked out in the IBM Laboratory Vienna from 1965 to 1970 for the definition of the programming language PL/I [8] and is known as the *Vienna Definition Language (VDL)* [9], while the PL/I definition as such was called *Universal Language Document (ULD)* [10].

The basic notion of the abstract machine is called an abstract object [11]. In general such an object has components which are again abstract objects. The components are designated by selectors which form a tree in the case of a compound abstract object. There is a generating and changing function which defines changes in the tree – replacements, additions and omissions. By means of predicate logic, abstract objects can be defined in terms of their properties, so that the formal definition can be kept partly in terms of properties, of classes of objects. It is possible to make statements and to give proofs concerning a class of objects before defining any particular member of the class. Processing of abstract objects can be controlled by programs which again are abstract objects, built into the over-all abstract object – the abstract language machine which defines the language. The method is very homogeneous and can be applied not only to languages, but also to programming systems, to operating systems and to hardware.

The advantages of formal definition are that the description can be reduced to the extent desired, omitting uninteresting or irrelevant details and restricting the description to the essential; the formal definition represents a precise instruction for the realization of the structure and a perfect basis for its application. In the case of a programming language, it contains the information which the compiler writer needs in order to conform to the language (so that all compilers yield programs which conform to the language definition). Finally formal definition is a yardstick for comparing the completed object with the abstract object to which it corresponds; from a formal definition one can judge whether a programming task has been executed correctly or not.

The formal definition of PL/I and several other programming languages has proved the idea to be applicable; the design of a programming language based on formal definition from the very beginning, unfortunately, has not yet been possible, and the extension of the method to operating and other programming systems has not yet been carried out.

A lot of further work must still be invested in this idea. At many universities such work has been started and there are already a number of publications dealing with definition languages and with VDL in particular.

The existence of tools for syntactic and semantic definition is a prerequisite for good design of a language or a system, but the tool does not tell how to apply the tool: the principles of design are a separate question. Here, intuitive methods are of course even more in use than in definition. The idea of developing computer families rather than a set of models of different capacities furthered the search for systematics in design and in recent years more and more publications on computer design are preparing a new period of design philosophy.

5. Generation of systems

How do systems come into existence? It is a striking and in a way disturbing fact that the class of natural systems called organisms are generated fully automatically, i.e. without human intermediate interference, while constructed systems can be produced automatically only in a very advanced state of technology. And natural automatism is basically different from technical automation.

The element of the natural organism not only carries the full information for the system in its genetic code, it even has in principle *all the properties* of the system; cells only *specialize* to form organs and effectors. The architecture of the natural system, therefore, is a genuine architecture, preconceived when the first cell of the new organism is created.

Technical construction, at least in the early stage of the game, proceeds very differently. It is building and not growing. All kinds of necessary elements are assembled, either systematically or unsystematically, more often unsystematically by a trial and error process because only in exceptional cases do we possess a theory to control the assembling. Normally we try variation after variation until the system works to satisfaction, and this is usually the satisfaction of the constructing engineer and not necessarily the satisfaction of the user.

Information processing, however, will be faster in reaching architectural design, for two reasons. First, the digitalization of computing and formal text processing allows and requires large systems built up from a few basic building blocks of logical nature. Secondly, advanced systems have several layers of software on top of hardware; then construction and their use can easily go out of control, unless architectural systematics keep the amount of construction work and the complication of application rules within reasonable limits — saving a lot of costs. This is why the ideal principle of architecture will be furthered in this field, pulling all the other application fields more or less along in its train.

Information processing will profit from the preparatory work in formal definition of its languages and systems; and since everything is (at least in principle) built up from single bits there need not be any inconsistent parts. In reality, the situation might not be that good, simply because advancement cannot proceed without respect for the past: inconsistent elements may remain for historical (i.e. economical) reasons.

Architectural design [12–15] is design from top to bottom, making every detail a function of the whole. In this view, architectural design becomes complementary to formal definition: only if the method of description provides full freedom to omit details and to speak about the wanted properties of the full system before starting any work combining the building parts, can one derive the details from the general structure.

6. Systems architecture

What makes systems architecture good architecture? I will quote here a paper by Gerrit A. Blaauw [16]: *'Good architecture is consistent. That is, with a partial knowledge of the system the remainder of the system can be predicted'*. This implies that there is quite some redundancy in the design – remarkable in a century in which everybody wants and gets too much information. Information, we know, is surprise. But good architecture avoids surprising, arbitrary design decisions. Technology obviously is aiming at natural systems the architecture of which can be predicted from partial knowledge, and this is in no way astonishing, as the computer generally makes technology more natural and more human.

Good architecture, we said, is consistent architecture. And consistency means three other properties (I quote again the paper by Blaauw): *orthogonality, propriety and generality*.

Orthogonality is the principle of keeping functions which are independent of each other separate in their specification and, consequently, separate in their realization. *Propriety* is the principle of accepting only functions which are proper to the essential requirements of the system, to avoid extraneousness. And *generality* here means the principle of using a function, if it has to be introduced, for as many purposes as possible; to introduce a concept, if it has to be introduced, in its most general form.

The consequences of consistent architecture are symmetry, transparency and compatibility. Consistency yields an inclination to open-endedness and to completeness at the same time: namely, a complete set of possibilities without elaborating the infinity of combinations. Good architecture, in other words, creates a world in which other people in turn can be creative. Good architecture is stimulating and self-teaching, because it confirms and encourages our expectations.

All this may sound rather idealistic, or even unrealistic. With all its ideal properties architectural design will not bring an ideal world; hopefully it will only reduce the complication of present-day computer hardware, operating systems, programming languages and user programming systems to an extent which will not exceed our mental and financial resources.

The transparency and compatibility of good architecture will give as much freedom as possible to the realization and production processes, and at the same time many kinds of products will interface without problems. This is a very important property, because the computer systems will be more and more interconnected, finally ending in one world-wide computer network with world-wide sub-networks, very similar to the electrical power network or to the telephone network. How does good architecture stand in these areas, by the way? Let this be a merely rhetorical question, even these relatively simple and relatively old networks do not yet meet all our expectations. The computer will have to go much further and the computer can go much further because of the incredible flexibility of information and because information is everywhere.

7. Generalized architecture

In information-processing technology, the concept of architectural design of hardware — which yields families of computers, such as the IBM/360 family — is presently being extended to operating systems, programming systems and programming languages. We will see families of such structures where the members of a family look very much alike, but are distinguished by parameters.

But the generalization of architectural design will not stop there. It will spread into the application fields of computers and automation. For operations research, the idea will appear on two levels: on the level of application — architectural design of the product which the structure studied is generating, whether material, material structures, energy, information or information structures — and secondly on the level of organization of the application — architectural design of the generating structure, of management, of operation. In this sense, many of you have practised architectural design certainly for years, even if you have never used the term *architecture,* even if you have never heard of it. I am not bringing forward an entirely new subject here, I merely want to make you aware of a fashionable vocabulary which will spread in the scientific world and to show parallel ideas in other fields.

Now, the technical product, which is the main interest of automatic control and information processing, is not the primary subject of operations research which rather is interested in how the technical product comes into existence and what kind of operations are involved in the related technical and administrative organizations. The structures usually are mixtures of constructs and live bodies where men, computers, and all other elements of an enterprise cooperate in order to achieve a certain goal.

Operations research will develop, therefore, I am sure, a new and very difficult kind of abstract architecture, a set of principles on how to design these dynamic structures, combining and optimizing mechanical and human needs and conditions − a real generalized architecture.

8. Operations research, description and design

What information-processing adds to the classic mathematical and physical methods and views is the new dimension of information. Information has a number of properties which are, at the least, uncommon. It can be distributed like material and energy − the difference is that a certain portion of material or energy can be given only once, while an item of information can be distributed to as many receivers as required, and sometimes receivers not planned by the distributor get it too. Information has become a good like material and energy, to be produced, stored, and delivered; it can be improved and corroborated, it can be useful and disastrous. To be more precise: in fact, it cannot be *produced* − what can be produced is redundancy, information can only be collected, but there is plenty of it waiting to be recorded.

It cannot be said frequently enough: the computer is not merely a calculator, the computer is the general device for the processing of any kind of information. Computer systems, consequently, are the nervous systems which interconnect the sensory organs and the effectors of any technical or scientific ensemble to a live system. We do not think of all the many forms of information which we encounter in our daily life or which occur in industry and economy. Who realizes, for instance, that the key is not only the effector for the lock, but also the information device which selects the appropriate operator? The key looks like a simple and inflexible identifier; but key systems can be extremely intelligent, and once little computers become looped into such a system, it will become flexible and live.

There is no need to continue with such examples − operations research covers most of them. From an information-processing point of view it can be said that all these systems will either be more and more computer-controlled or they will have computer-like information-processing structures built in. Architectural design, therefore, will not remain a subject for computer scientists, it will become a tool throughout technology. More and more fields will realize that what we need is not a mass of isolated, however perfect, solutions, but architecturally well-designed systems with clearly planned operations. The interdependence of all larger systems will require more and more over-all studies. While the technological environment will increase in perfection, it will be true at the same time, as professor Speiser (a former IFIP president) once formulated [17], that arbitrarily small disturbances may cause arbitrarily big breakdowns with non-zero probability in such highly interdependent systems. Systems and operations research, therefore, will become even more important than today.

Technology has improved a lot of individual features in today's towns cities and countries. Nonetheless our environment grows daily more ugly, more disorganized, more dangerous and more inacceptable. Further perfect items will not help. What we need is architectural design and philosophy, a view of the entirety — all applications of technology becoming a function of an architectural plan. This brings an important problem for operations research: how to ensure that a general plan does not remove the liberty and the initiative of the individual. Such a question goes far beyond the merely technological problems we usually see as our tasks. We have reached the point where the generalization of architectural design ends at a general systems theory and an operations concept. Both include constructed and natural systems and processes and both will not only be studied by some specialists after the fact: they will be general tools applied by everybody holding a position of leadership. Description and design will become almost identical notions, because computer programs will turn the systems description in a system operation. A dream? Maybe, but the only way to protect the world of tomorrow from chaos is to transform this dream into reality.

9. Conclusion

Operations research, automatic control and information processing are without any doubt inseparable fields having essential parts in common, overlapping in most of their interests and goals, and complementing each other in many details. Architectural design will be one of the most important common tools and since architectural design can only be based on formal definition, these two technologies deserve particular interest.

What I have tried to show is not really new for most of you, but since I see the problems very much from an information-processing point of view, I may have shown aspects which can encourage and foster your future work. At one or the other point of my paper the limitations of the formalized models may have become clear: whatever object or system we try to describe and to define formally will never be completely grasped by the formal mechanisms of information-processing. The scientific and technological methods never manage to incorporate all facets of the real world. There are philosophical reasons why a certain gap will always remain in the future between the logical model and the living environment with which the model must communicate.

Here is a task for man in which he never will be replaced by automatic devices. We have good reasons to pay more attention to the human and social aspects of our professional work. Technology is not a purpose in itself; it has to be a tool for the welfare of mankind. Optimism alone is not sufficient; we must constantly watch what we are doing, on the metalevel, on the meta-metalevel. This might be a reason for the existence of IFIP, IFAC and IFORS.

References

[1] C. Morris, Foundations of the theory of signs, International Encyclopedia of Unified Science, Vol. 1, No. 2 (Univ. of Chicago Press, Chicago, 1938).

[2] H. Zemanek, Semiotics and programming languages, ACM Commun. 9, No. 3 (1966) 139.

[3] Proc. IEEE, Spec. issue on computers in design, 60, No. 1 (1972).

[4] M. Davis, The undecidable; basic papers on undecidable propositions, unsolvable problems and computable functions (Raven Press, Hewlett, New York, 1965).

[5] A.M. Turing, On computable numbers, with an application to the Entscheidungsproblem, Proc. London Math. Soc. (Ser. 2) 42 (1936) 230; Ann. Rev. Automatic Programming 1 (1960) 230.

[6] J. Backus, The syntax and semantics of the proposed international algebraic language, Proc. Intern. Conf. Inform. Process, Paris (1959) p. 125.

[7] P. Naur, Revised report on the algorithmic language ALGOL 60, Commun. ACM 6 No. 1 (1963) 1.

[8] P. Lucas and K. Walk, On the formal description of PL/I, Ann. Rev. Automatic Programming 6 (1969) part 3.

[9] P. Wegner, The Vienna Definition Language, ACM Computing Surveys 4, No. 1 (1972) 5.

[10] K. Walk, K. Alber, M. Fleck, H. Goldmann, P. Lauer, E. Moser, P. Oliva, H. Stigleitner and G. Zeisel, Abstract syntax and interpretation of PL/I, Tech. Rept. IBM Lab. TR 25.098 (1969).

[11] H. Zemanek, Abstrakte Objekte, Elektron. Rechenanl. 10, No. 5 (1968) 208.

[12] W. Buchholz, Planning a computer system: project stretch (McGraw-Hill, New York, 1962).

[13] G.M. Amdahl, G.A. Blaauw and F.P. Brooks, Jr., Architecture of the IBM System/360, IBM J. Res. Develop. 8, No. 2 (1964) 85.

[14] G.A. Blaauw, Hardware requirements for the fourth generation, in: Fourth generation computers: user requirements and transition (Prentice Hall, New York, 1970) p. 155.

[15] E.W. Dijkstra, Hierarchical ordering of sequential processes, Acta Informatica 1 (1971) 115.

[16] G.A. Blaauw, Computer architecture, Elektron. Rechenanl. 14, No. 4 (1972) 154.

[17] A.P. Speiser, Computers and technology, in: Skylines of information processing, ed. H. Zemanek (North-Holland, Amsterdam, 1972).

IDENTIFICATION PROCEDURES FOR DYNAMIC SYSTEMS

Procédures d'identification pour les systèmes dynamiques

MICHEL CUÉNOD

Prospective Engineering Gestion, Geneva, Switzerland

Abstract. A major impact of research in system theory today comes from the development of "identification" methods. These use variations of the input and output values to determine the relations of cause and effect established by a "system".

The report surveys some of these methods and describes their application in the analysis of economic phenomena and the determination of mathematical models for the simulation of micro- and macro-economic systems. The use of these methods for the prediction and prevention of crises is outlined.

In the conclusion, some views about the overlapping fields between operation research and system theory are developed. The case for closer collaboration between the specialists of these fields is made and a guide provided as to the topics where this cooperation could be particularly profitable.

1. Introduction

The methods for the estimation and identification of the dynamic characteristic of a system through the observation of the input and output values of this system form the subject matter of an important branch of the system theory. These methods can be used not only for the study of the behaviour of physical systems, but also to analyse the cause-effect relationships within a micro- or macro-economic system, such as a plant, a town, a country, or to analyse the reaction of a biological system.

Considering only permanent states and abstracting from the development of the phenomenon over time, correlation techniques can be used for the "static identification" of the cause to effect relationship. But in general phenomena display inertia: they do not react instantly, so we need to know the dynamic response of the system, how this reaction acts as a time function.

Three different categories of approach have been developed for the "dynamic identification" of systems.

(1) Identification using input and output system, variations known as a mathematically not defined function of time.

(2) Identification with stochastic input and output, which can be characterized by their statistical properties, i.e., by spectral density, correlation function or mean square value of their fluctuations. These functions and parameters can only be estimated from samples taken from these stochastic functions.

(3) Estimation of the parameters of systems in state phase representation. This last approach is more powerful and can be used for non-linear multivariable systems but needs more sophisticated mathematical tools.

In this paper we shall only consider the first approach as being more appropriate to the needs of identification in OR problems and deal with four methods, i.e., convolution, deconvolution, parameters identification and means square value methods. But first let us define some concepts.

2. Some basic concepts in systems theory

The "step response" $\gamma(t)$ is the variation in outputs resulting from a variation in inputs according to a step function. The Laplace transform $g(s)$ of the analytical expression of the step response is the "transfer function" of the system. The step response gives concrete information about the dynamic characteristics of a system. (In practice it is only possible to observe, rather than cause, variations of the inputs and outputs during a time interval.)

"Identification" means the determination of the step response, or the transfer function of the system, based on these observations. This paper presents some identification methods for linear systems starting with single input-output systems. The approach adopted is "impulse analysis", i.e., replacing an analytical function $f(t)$ by its "distribution" namely, by a sequence $S(F)$ of numbers corresponding to the values of this function for the different units of time

$$f(t) \rightarrow S(F) = [f_0; f_1; f_2; ...; f_n; ...] ,$$

with $f_n = f(n\tau)$ and τ = time unit.

3. Identification by numerical simulation using convolution

If the step response $\gamma(t)$ of a single variable system is known, the variation $y(t)$ in output resulting from the variation $x(t)$ in input can be calculated by means of the "Duhamels integral":

$$y(t) = x_0\gamma(t) + \int_0^t \dot{x}(u)\gamma(u - t)\,\mathrm{d}u\ , \qquad \dot{x}(t) = \frac{\mathrm{d}x}{\mathrm{d}t}\ .$$

To each function $x(t), y(t), \gamma(t)$ it is possible to determine the corresponding sequence $S(x), S(y)$ and $S(\gamma)$, using the notation of the impulse analysis:

$$S(x) = [x_0; x_1; x_2; ...; x_n; ...]\ ,$$

$$S(y) = [y_0; y_1; y_2; ...; y_n; ...]\ ,$$

$$S(\gamma) = [\gamma_0; \gamma_1; \gamma_2; ...; \gamma_n; ...]\ .$$

The sequence of the derivative $S(x)$ is the "step sequence" $S_e(x)$ given by the difference of the terms before and after the considered term (with the exception of the first term):

$$S_e(x) = [x_{e0}; x_{e1}; x_{e2}; ...; x_{en}; ...]\ ,$$

with

$$x_{e0} = \tfrac{1}{2}(x_0 + x_1)\ , \qquad x_{e1} = \tfrac{1}{2}(x_0 - x_2)\ , \quad x_{e2} = \tfrac{1}{2}(x_1 - x_3)\ , \quad \text{etc.}$$

Formally, convolution can be represented by a star and defined as the "composed product" of the sequence $S(\gamma)$ by the sequence $S_e(x)$

$$S(y) = S(\gamma) * S_e(x)\ .$$

This operation is commutative.

Assuming linearity, the variation in output y (see fig. 1) is the sum of the variations resulting from the different steps $x_{e0}; x_{e1}; x_{e2}; ...$ of the input, namely,

for the 1st step: $x_0\gamma_0; x_0\gamma_1; x_0\gamma_2; ...\ ,$

for the 2nd step: $0; x_1\gamma_0; x_1\gamma_1; ...\ , \qquad \text{etc.}$

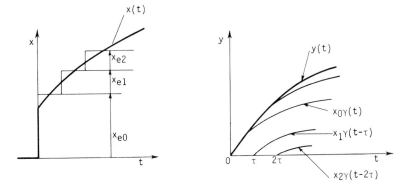

Fig. 1. Principle of the numerical convolution operation.

This leads to the following algorithm for the determination of the sequence $S(y)$:

	γ_0	γ_1	γ_2	
x_{e0}	$x_{e0}\gamma_0$	$x_{e0}\gamma_1$	$x_{e0}\gamma_2$	$\cdots$
x_{e1}	0	$x_{e1}\gamma_0$	$x_{e1}\gamma_1$	$\cdots$
x_{e2}	0	0	$x_{e2}\gamma_0$	$\cdots$
$S(y) =$	$x_{e0}\gamma_0$	$x_{e0}\gamma_1 + x_{e1}\gamma_0$	$x_{e0}\gamma_2 + x_{e1}\gamma_1 + x_{e2}\gamma_0$	$\cdots$

3.1. Numerical example

Let this result in a system with the following function:

$$g(s) = \frac{1}{(2s+1)(6s+1)} .$$

Here (see also curve 1 of fig. 2) the step response equation is given in a Laplace transform table:

$$\gamma(t) = 1 + \tfrac{1}{2}\exp\left(-\tfrac{1}{2}t\right) - \tfrac{3}{2}\exp\left(-\tfrac{1}{6}t\right) .$$

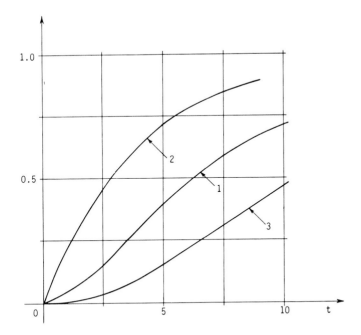

Fig. 2. Numerical example of convolution. Curve 1: step response, curve 2: variation of the input, curve 3: variation of the output.

The corresponding sequence is (with the second as time unit):

$$S(\gamma) = [0; 0.0254; 0.1158; 0.1971; 0.3076; 0.3845;$$

$$0.484; 0.544; 0.622; 0.668; ...] .$$

We assume that the variation of the input is given by an exponential curve (curve 2, fig. 2)

$$x(t) = 1 - \exp\left(-\tfrac{1}{4}t\right) .$$

The sequence is:

$$S(x) = [0; 0.2212; 0.3935; 0.5276; 0.6321; 0.7135; 0.7690; ...] .$$

The terms of the step sequence $S_e(x)$ are:

$$x_{e0} = \tfrac{1}{2}(x_0 + x_1) = \tfrac{1}{2}(0.2212) = 0.1106 ,$$

$$x_{e1} = \tfrac{1}{2}(x_2 - x_0) = \tfrac{1}{2}(0.3935) = 0.1967 ,$$

$$x_{e2} = \tfrac{1}{2}(x_3 - x_1) = \tfrac{1}{2}(0.5276 - 0.2212) = 0.1527 , \quad \text{etc.,}$$

namely:

$$S_e(x) = [0.1106; 0.1967; 0.1527; 0.1193; 0.0929; 0.0724; 0.439; ...] .$$

The sequence of the output is given by the convolution of $S_e(x)$ with $S(\gamma)$:

$$S(y) = S_e(x) * S(\gamma) .$$

$S(\gamma)$	0.0254	0.1158	0.1971	0.3076	...
$S_e(x)$					
0.1106	0.002809	0.012807	0.021799	0.034020	...
0.1967	–	0.004996	0.022777	0.038769	...
0.1527	–	–	0.003878	0.017682	...
0.1193	–	–	–	0.003030	...
.	–	–	–	–	...
.	–	–	–	–	...
$S(y) =$	0.002809	0.017803	0.04854	0.093501	...

In this particular case, the analytical expression of output variation can be calculated:

$$y(t) = 1 - \tfrac{1}{2}\exp\left(-\tfrac{1}{2}\right) - \tfrac{9}{2}\exp\left(-\tfrac{1}{6}t\right) + 4\exp\left(-\tfrac{1}{4}t\right) .$$

This function (fig. 2, curve 3) has a sequence very close to that obtained by numerical convolution:

$$S(y) = [0.0028; 0.0178; 0.0485; 0.0935; ...] .$$

The steps in identification by convolution are:
(1) Assume a step response.
(2) Apply the convolution of the sequence corresponding to this step response to the sequence corresponding to the variation of the input.

(3) Compare the result obtained with the measured variation of the output.

(4) Where distortion occurs make successive modifications to the admitted step response until calculated and measured output are sufficiently close.

Since linearity is assumed, this approach can be extended for any number of inputs and outputs. However, this "trial and error" procedure is very long and calls for a less time consuming procedure.

4. Identification by numerical deconvolution

"Deconvolution", the inverse operation to the convolution, uses input and output variations to find the sequence of the step response $\gamma(t)$. The notation for this operation is two stars or two fraction lines:

$$S(\gamma) = S(y) \overset{*}{*} S_e(x) = \frac{S(y)}{S_e(x)}.$$

This operation corresponds to the numerical solution of the Fredholm-Volterra integral equation and is performed by the following algorithm:

$$
\begin{array}{llll}
y_0 \qquad y_1 \qquad\quad y_2 & \qquad\qquad y_3 \;\ldots & \left| \begin{array}{lll} x_{e0} & x_{e1} & x_{e2} \;\cdots \end{array} \right.
\end{array}
$$

$$
\begin{array}{llll}
y_0 \quad x_{e1}\dfrac{y_0}{x_{e0}} \quad x_{e2}\dfrac{y_0}{x_{e0}} & x_{e3}\dfrac{y_0}{x_{e0}} \;\ldots & \left| \dfrac{y_0}{x_{e0}} \quad \dfrac{1}{x_{e0}}\left(y_1 - x_{e1}\dfrac{y_0}{x_{e0}}\right) \cdots \right.
\end{array}
$$

$$
0 \quad y_1 - x_{e1}\dfrac{y_0}{x_{e0}} \quad y_2 - x_{e2}\dfrac{y_0}{x_{e0}} \quad y_3 - x_{e3}\dfrac{y_0}{x_{e0}}
$$

$$
y_1 - x_{e1}\dfrac{y_0}{x_{e0}} \quad \dfrac{x_{e1}}{x_{e0}}\left(y_1 - x_{e1}\dfrac{y_0}{x_{e0}}\right) \quad \cdots
$$

$$
0 \quad \left(y_2 - x_{e2}\dfrac{y_0}{x_{e0}}\right) - \dfrac{x_{e1}}{x_{e0}}\left(y_1 - x_{e1}\dfrac{y_0}{x_{e0}}\right)
$$

$$\cdots$$

This operation is easier to perform if the sequence of the denominator starts with one, viz:

$$S_e(x) = x_{e0}[1; x'_{e1}; x'_{e2}; x'_{e3}; \ldots; x'_{en}; \ldots],$$

with

$$x'_{en} = \frac{x_{en}}{x_{e0}} \; .$$

The following algorithm can be used:

n	y	$\gamma'_n = y_n - \Sigma_n$	$\gamma_n = \dfrac{\gamma'_n}{x_{e0}}$	x'_{e1}	x'_{e2}	x'_{e3}	x'_{e4}	$\cdots$
0	y_0	$\gamma'_0 = y_0$	$\gamma_0 = \dfrac{\gamma'_0}{x_{e0}}$	$x'_{e1}\gamma'_0$	$x'_{e2}\gamma'_0$	$x'_{e3}\gamma'_0$	$x'_{e4}\gamma'_0$	$\cdots$
1	y_1	$\gamma'_1 = y_1 - \Sigma_1$	$\gamma_1 = \dfrac{\gamma'_1}{x_{e0}}$	Σ_1	$x'_{e1}\gamma'_1$	$x'_{e2}\gamma'_4$	$x'_{e3}\gamma'_1$	$\cdots$
2	y_2	$\gamma'_2 = y_2 - \Sigma_2$	$\gamma_2 = \dfrac{\gamma'_2}{x_{e0}}$		Σ_2	$x'_{e1}\gamma'_2$	$x_{e2}\gamma'_2$	$\cdots$
3	y_3	$\gamma'_3 = y_3 - \Sigma_3$	$\gamma_3 = \dfrac{\gamma'_3}{x_{e0}}$			Σ_3	$x'_{e1}\gamma'_3$	$\cdots$
4	y_4	$\gamma'_4 = y_4 - \Sigma_4$	$\gamma_4 = \dfrac{\gamma'_4}{x_{e0}}$				Σ_4	
$\vdots$	$\vdots$	$\vdots$	$\vdots$					$\vdots$

4.1. Numerical example I

Again considering the second order system represented by fig. 3 where the variations of the input x and output y have been registered and the corresponding sequence $S(x)$ and $S(y)$ are given:

$$S(x) = [0; 0.2212; 0.3935; 0.5276; 0.6321; 0.7135;$$

$$0.7690; 0.8262; 0.8647; 0.8946; ...] \; ,$$

$$S(y) = [0; 0.0028; 0.0178; 0.0485; 0.0935; 0.1493;$$

$$0.2122; 0.2787; 0.3460; 0.4120; 0.4750; ...] \; .$$

Let us also determine the step sequence $S_e(x)$:

$$S_e(x) = [0.1106; 0.1967; 0.1527; 0.1193; 0.0929;$$

$$0.0724; 0.0563; 0.0439; ...] .$$

Using the above algorithm, we obtain by deconvolution the following sequence:

$$S(\gamma) = \frac{S(y)}{S_e(x)} = [0.0369; 0.1091; 0.2975; 0.3891;$$

$$0.4731; 0.5480; 0.6138; ...] .$$

Curve 1 of fig. 3 corresponds to the exact solution and curve 2 to the solution obtained by this deconvolution. These two curves differ in the first term. Curve 2 (deconvolution) possesses some instability which is damped for higher terms. We shall come back to these two aspects of the deconvolution.

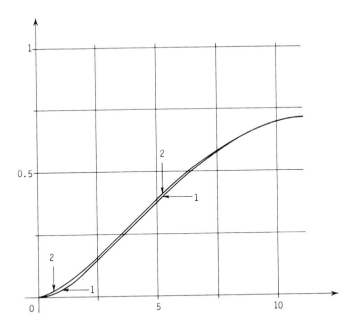

Fig. 3. Example of numerical deconvolution. Curve 1: exact step response; curve 2: step response determined by numerical deconvolution.

If we have a system with many inputs, for example, two inputs x_a and x_b and one output y, deconvolution can be used to determine the step response for each input.

We assume that we have made two tests and that we have obtained two records of x_a, x_b and y. Using superscripts (1) and (2), especially, to designate these two registrations we obtain the following system of equations:

$$S(y^{(1)}) = S_e(x_a^{(1)}) * S(\gamma_{x_a y}) + S_e(x_b^{(1)}) * S(\gamma_{x_b y}) ,$$

$$S(y^{(2)}) = S_e(x_a^{(2)}) * S(\gamma_{x_a y}) + S_e(x_b^{(2)}) * S(\gamma_{x_b y}) .$$

We solve this system with respect to the unknown sequences $S(\gamma_{x_a y})$ and $S(\gamma_{x_b y})$ and obtain:

$$S(\gamma_{x_a y}) = \frac{S_e(x_b^{(2)}) * S(y^{(1)}) - S_e(x_b^{(1)}) * S(y^{(2)})}{S_e(x_a^{(1)}) * S_e(x_b^{(2)}) - S_e(x_b^{(1)}) * S_e(x_a^{(2)})} ,$$

$$S(\gamma_{x_b y}) = \frac{S_e(x_a^{(1)}) * S(y^{(2)}) - S_e(x_a^{(2)}) * S(y^{(1)})}{S_e(x_a^{(1)}) * S_e(x_b^{(2)}) - S_e(x_b^{(1)}) * S_e(x_a^{(1)})} .$$

The approach can be extended to systems with any number of inputs and outputs.

4.2. Numerical example II

Consider a system (given by fig. 4) with the two inputs x_a and x_b, the single output y and the two following transfer functions:

$$g_{x_a y} = \frac{y}{x_a} = \frac{\dfrac{1}{sT_1(sT_2 + 1)}}{1 + \dfrac{1}{sT_1(sT_2 + 1)}} = \frac{1}{s^2 T_1 T_2 + sT_1 + 1} ,$$

$$g_{x_b y} = \frac{y}{x_b} = \frac{\dfrac{1}{sT_2 + 1}}{1 + \dfrac{1}{sT_1(sT_2 + 1)}} = \frac{sT_1}{s^2 T_1 T_2 + sT_1 + 1} .$$

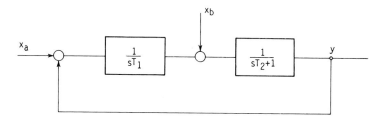

Fig. 4. Example of a feedback system with two inputs.

Assuming that $T_1 = 10$ and $T_2 = 2$ the following equation for the step responses is obtained:

$$\gamma_{x_a y} = 1 - 1.617 \exp(-0.138\ t) + 0.618 \exp(-0.362\ t)\ ,$$

$$\gamma_{x_b y} = 2.23 \exp(-0.138\ t) - \exp(-0.362\ t)\ .$$

The corresponding sequences are:

$$S(\gamma_{x_a y}) = [0;\ 0.019;\ 0.069;\ 0.137;\ 0.215;\ 0.292;\ ...]\ ,$$

$$S(\gamma_{x_b y}) = [0;\ 0.4014;\ 0.6244;\ 0.7359;\ 0.7582;\ 0.7515;\ ...]\ .$$

We assume that x_a and x_b vary as a step function with the following magnitude:

1st test: $x_a^{(1)} = 6; \quad x_b^{(1)} = 4\ ,$

2nd test: $x_a^{(2)} = 2; \quad x_b^{(2)} = 3\ .$

In that case the sequence $S_e(x_a)$ and $S_e(x_b)$ have only one term:

$$S_e(x_a^{(1)}) = [6]\ , \qquad S_e(x_b^{(1)}) = [4]\ ,$$

$$S_e(x_a^{(2)}) = [2]\ , \qquad S_e(x_b^{(2)}) = [3]\ .$$

We obtain for $S(y)$ the following sequences:

$$S(y^{(1)}) = [6]\,S(\gamma_{x_a y}) + [4]\,S(\gamma_{x_b y})$$

$$= [1.720; 2.912; 3.766; 4.323; 4.758; 5.074; ...]\ ,$$

$$S(y^{(2)}) = [2]\,S(\gamma_{x_a y}) + [3]\,S(\gamma_{x_b y})$$

$$= [1.242; 2.011; 2.482; 2.705; 2.839; 2.866; ...]\ .$$

We assume that these two sequences have been established by tests. Using the above relationship, we obtain

$$S(\gamma_{x_a y}) = \frac{[3]\,S(y^{(1)}) - [4]\,S(y^{(2)})}{[6]\,[3] - [4]\,[2]}$$

$$= [0; 0.0192; 0.0692; 0.137; 0.2149; 0.2918; 0.3758; ...]\ ,$$

$$\overset{...}{S}(\gamma_{x_b y}) = \frac{[6]\,S(y^{(2)}) - [2]\,S(y^{(1)})}{[6]\,[3] - [4]\,[2]}$$

$$= [0; 0.4012; 0.6242; 0.7360; 0.7584; 0.7048; ...]\ .$$

These two sequences are very close to the exact solution which is known in this particular case.

4.3. Remark 1: Determination of the variation of the output corresponding to any variation of the input

If the output $y(t)$ resulting from the input variation $x(t)$ of a single variable linear system has been measured, it is possible, by combining the deconvolution and the convolution operations, to determine the sequence of the output $v(t)$ for any variation $u(t)$ of the input, as shown by fig. 5 overleaf:

$$S(v) = \frac{S_e(u) * S(v)}{S_e(x)} \approx \frac{S(u) * S(y)}{S(x)}\ .$$

All things being equal, this rule enables us to predict output variation by measuring the previous behaviour of the system.

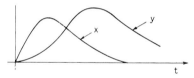 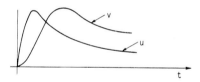

Fig. 5. Determination of the variation of the output v due to the input u from the observation of the input x and the output y.

4.4. Remark 2: Instability of the deconvolution

If the systems to be considered are strictly linear, and the precision of the computation is sufficient, the numerical convolution gives a result which is stable and coherent. But if these conditions are not fulfiled the result is affected by an error (which can be important for the first terms of the sequence given by the deconvolution) and by an increasing numerical instability which distorts the result of the computation.

The methods, developed to improve the precision of the calculation of the first terms of the deconvolution and to control or suppress this numerical instability, are beyond the range of this paper.

4.5. Remark 3: Determination of the analytical expression of the step response of the transfer function

Convolution and deconvolution, as outlined above, permit us to obtain results as a sequence of numbers. If we want analytical expression of the step response or the transfer function other methods exist to obtain the equation of a curve going through a given number of points. However, these methods are also outside the scope of this paper.

5. Identification of parameters

If, however, general considerations or experience permit us to make some assumptions about the structure of the transfer function to be identified we can avoid the stability problems associated with deconvolution. The identification procedure then consists of determining the parameter values for this structure.

In a general way, this transfer function can be written as the ratio of two polynomials of operator s.

$$g(s) = \frac{a_0 + a_1 s + \ldots + a_m s^m}{b_0 + b_1 s + \ldots + b_n s^n} \, ,$$

with the condition $n > m$. By dividing these two polynomials by s^n we obtain:

$$g(s) = \frac{\dfrac{a_0}{s^n} + \dfrac{a_1}{s^{n-1}} + \ldots + \dfrac{a_m}{s^{n-m}}}{\dfrac{b_0}{s^n} + \dfrac{b_1}{s^{n-1}} + \ldots + b_n} \, .$$

Table 1 presents as a sequence in closed form the sequence corresponding to the integration operators $1/s$, $1/s^2$, ..., $1/s^n$.

By replacing the operators $1/s$, $1/s^2$, ... in the above expression of $g(s)$ with the corresponding sequences, one obtains an expression $S(g)$ resulting from the composed quotient of two sequences:

$$g(s) = \frac{N(s)}{D(s)} \rightarrow S(g) = \frac{S(N)}{S(D)} \, .$$

Table 1
Survey of some integration operators.

$\dfrac{1}{s}$	$\dfrac{\tau}{[1;-1]}$	$\tau\,[1;1;1;1;\ldots]$
$\dfrac{1}{s^2}$	$\dfrac{\tau^2}{2}\dfrac{[0;1;1]}{[1;-1]^2}$	$\dfrac{\tau^2}{2}\,[0;1;4;9;16;\ldots]$
$\dfrac{1}{s^3}$	$\dfrac{\tau^3}{3!}\dfrac{[0;1;4;1;]}{[1;-1]^3}$	$\dfrac{\tau^3}{6}\,[0;1;8;27;32;\ldots]$
$\dfrac{1}{s^4}$	$\dfrac{\tau^4}{4!}\dfrac{[0;1;11;11;1]}{[1;-1]^4}$	$\dfrac{\tau^4}{24}\,[0;1;6;81;128;\ldots]$
$\dfrac{1}{s^5}$	$\dfrac{\tau^5}{5!}\dfrac{[0;1;26;66,26;1]}{[1;-1]^5}$	$\dfrac{\tau^5}{120}\,[0;1;12;243;512;\ldots]$
$\vdots$	$\vdots$	$\vdots$

If the input and output sequences $S(x)$ and $S(y)$ are known, we can write in impulse analysis notation:

$$S(y) = S(x) * \frac{S(N)}{S(D)} \ ,$$

viz:

$$S(y) * S(D) = S(x) * S(N) \ .$$

This equation gives the relationship that the transfer function establishes between the adjacent terms of the sequence $S(x)$ and $S(y)$.

Taking into consideration the equations for the related $m + n$ successive terms, we obtain the necessary conditions for determination of the $m + n$ unknown parameters $a_0, a_1, ..., a_m, b_0, b_1, ..., b_n$.

5.1. Example 1

Let us consider a first order differential equation:

$$T \frac{dy}{dt} + y = x \ .$$

Using the Laplace transform, this equation becomes:

$$Tsy + y = x \ ,$$

$$g(s) = \frac{y}{x} = \frac{1}{sT + 1} = \frac{\frac{1}{s}}{T + \frac{1}{s}} \ .$$

It is assumed that we have measured the variation $x(t)$ and $y(t)$ and that T is the unknown parameter to be identified.

As indicated in table 1, the integral operator $1/s$ corresponds with the sequence

$$\frac{\tau}{2} \frac{[1; 1]}{[1; -1]} \ .$$

Consequently:

$$S(g) = \frac{\dfrac{\tau}{2} \dfrac{[1;1]}{[1;-1]}}{T + \dfrac{\tau}{2} \dfrac{[1;1]}{[1;-1]}} = \frac{[1;1]}{\dfrac{2T}{\tau}[1;-1] + [1;1]} \; .$$

We assume that $\tau = 1$; this means that the parameter T is measured with τ as unit. We obtain the sum, term by term:

$$S(g) = \frac{[1;1]}{[2T+1; 1-2T]} = \frac{S(N)}{S(D)} = \frac{S(y)}{S(x)} \, ,$$

$$S(x) * [1;1] = S(y) * [2T+1; 1-2T] \; .$$

We perform these two convolutions:

	x_0	x_1	x_2	
1	x_0	x_1	x_2	...
1		x_0	x_1	...
	x_0	$x_0 + x_1$	$x_1 + x_2$ ...

	y_0	y_1	y_2
$2T+1$	$y_0(2T+1)$	$y_1(2T+1)$	$y_2(2T+1)$ ...
$-(2T-1)$		$-y_0(2T-1)$	$-y_1(2T-1)$ ...
	$y_0(2T+1)$ $y_1(2T+1) - y_0(2T-1)$	...	...

Equating the corresponding terms, we obtain the following equations:

$$x_0 + x_1 = y_1(2T+1) - y_0(2T-1) \, ,$$

$$x_1 + x_2 = y_2(2T+1) - y_1(2T-1) \, , \quad \text{etc.}$$

We obtain a considerable redundancy of equations for the unknown parameter T alone. We solve these equations with respect to T:

$$T = \frac{1}{2} \frac{x_0 + x_1 - (y_0 + y_1)}{y_1 - y_0} = \frac{x_1 + x_2 - (y_1 + y_2)}{y_2 - y_1} = \dots .$$

We assume that $T = 5$ and that the input x varies according to a unit step. We can easily determine, in this particular case, the equation of y:

$$y(t) = 1 - \exp\left(-\tfrac{1}{5}t\right) .$$

The corresponding sequences are:

$$S(x) = [1; 1; 1; 1; 1; \dots] ,$$

$$S(y) = [0; 0.1813; 0.3298; 0.4512; \dots] .$$

It is assumed that these sequences have actually been measured and that the parameter T is to be identified. Using the relationship given we obtain:

$$T = \frac{1}{2} \frac{1 + 1 - 0.1813}{0.1813} = \frac{1}{2} \frac{1.8187}{0.1813} \approx 5 ,$$

$$T = \frac{1}{2} \frac{2 - (0.1813 + 0.3298)}{0.3298 - 0.1813} = \frac{1}{2} \frac{1.4889}{0.1485} \approx 5 .$$

We obtain the result which was expected.

5.2 Example 2

We consider the second order transfer function with the parameters T_1 and T_2 to be identified:

$$g_{xy}(s) = \frac{1}{(sT_1 + 1)(sT_2 + 1)} = \frac{1}{s^2 T_1 T_2 + s(T_1 + T_2) + 1}$$

$$= \frac{\dfrac{1}{s^2}}{T_1 T_2 + \dfrac{T_1 + T_2}{s} + \dfrac{1}{s^2}} .$$

We assume again that the parameters T_1 and T_2 are measured with the unit τ, which means that we can put $\tau = 1$. From table 1 we take the sequences corresponding to the operators of integration $1/s$ and $1/s^2$:

$$S(g_{xy}) = \frac{\dfrac{1}{6}\dfrac{[1;4;1]}{[1;-1]^2}}{T_1T_2 + \dfrac{1}{2}\dfrac{[1;1]}{[1;-1]}(T_1+T_2) + \dfrac{1}{6}\dfrac{[1;4;1]}{[1;-1]^2}} = \frac{S(N)}{S(D)},$$

$$S(g_{xy}) = \frac{[1;4;1]}{6T_1T_2[1;-2;1] + 3(T_1+T_2) * [1;1] * [1;-1] + [1;4;1]},$$

$$S(g_{xy}) = \frac{[1;4;1]}{[6T_1T_2 + 3(T_1+T_2)+1; -12T_1T_2 + 4; 6T_1T_2 - 3(T_1+T_2)+1]}.$$

To simplify the notation we put: $T_1T_2 = A$ and $T_1 + T_2 = B$. It follows:

$$S(y) * [6A+4B+1; -12A+4; 6A-3B+1] = S(x) * [1;4;1].$$

After the 3rd term we obtain the following equations:

$$y_2(6A+3B+1) + y_1(-12A+4) + y_0(6A-3B+1) = (x_2+4x_1+x_0),$$

$$y_3(6A+3B+1) + y_2(-12A+4) + y_1(6A-3B+1) = (x_3+4x_2+x_1),$$

$$y_4(6A+3B+1) + y_3(-12A+4) + y_2(6A-3B+1) = (x_4+4x_3+x_2).$$

When the numerical values of the sequences $S(x)$ and $S(y)$ are known, it is possible to calculate the unknown A and B and therefore T_1 and T_2. We assume again that x varies according to an exponential function with a time constant equal to 4:

$$x = 1 - \exp\left(-\tfrac{1}{4}t\right),$$

$$S(x) = [0; 0.2212; 0.3935; 0.5276; 0.6321; 0.7135; 0.7769; 0.8262; ...].$$

In this particular case, with $T_1 = 2$ and $T_2 = 6$ it is possible to calculate the exact expression of the output variation:

$$y(t) = 1 - \tfrac{1}{2}\exp\left(-\tfrac{1}{2}t\right) - \tfrac{9}{2}\exp\left(-\tfrac{1}{6}t\right) + 4\exp\left(-\tfrac{1}{4}t\right),$$

with

$$S(y) = [0; 0.0028; 0.0128; 0.0485; 0.0935; 0.1493; 0.2122; 0.2787; ...] .$$

It must be mentioned that the error of the result using the first terms of these sequences, is relatively important because it is necessary to differentiate between very small terms; this error decreases, with higher terms; for instance, using the 2 equations given by the terms 3 to 6 and 4 to 7, we obtain the following two equations, to be solved with respect to the unknowns A and B:

$$0.1493(6A + 3B + 1) + 0.0935(-12A + 4) + 0.0485(6A - 3B + 1)$$

$$= 0.7135 + 4(0.6321) + 0.5276 ,$$

$$0.2122(6A + 3B + 1) + 0.1493(-12A + 4) + 0.0935(6A - 3B + 1)$$

$$= 0.7769 + 4(0.7135) + 0.6321 .$$

Consequently:

$$0.0648\,A + 0.3024\,B = 3.1877 ,$$

$$0.0426\,A + 0.3561\,B = 3.3601 ;$$

$$A = \frac{0.7562}{0.0648} = 11.668 , \qquad B = \frac{1.9233}{0.2392} = 8.0406 ;$$

$$T_2 = \frac{A}{T_1} = \frac{11.668}{T_1}, \qquad T_1 + \frac{11.668}{T_1} = 8.0406 ,$$

$$T_1^2 - 8.0406\,T_1 + 11.668 = 0 ,$$

$$T_1 = 1.90 , \qquad T_2 = 6.14 .$$

These values are relatively close to the exact values:

$$T_1 = 2 \quad \text{and} \quad T_2 = 6 .$$

The exactitude of this calculation could be improved by using a smaller time unit and terms of higher order.

6. Identification by the mean square value method

The identification procedure outlined above introduces considerably more equations than the number of parameters to be identified. We obtain different values for the same parameters and we can apply the statistical methods to determine the "most probable" values. Another way to obtain these "true" values is to find values which minimize the sum of the square values of the errors between the exact solution and the function with the parameters to be identified.

Using the usual notation for this kind of approach, we suppose that the following equations are given:

$$y_i = \theta_1 \varphi_1(x_i) + \theta_2 \varphi_2(x_i) + \ldots + \theta_n \varphi_n(x_i) + e_i \, ,$$

with x_i = given value of the input, φ_i = relation given with some assumption of the structure of the transfer function, θ_i = parameters to be identified, y_i = given value of the output, e_i = error.

The parameters θ_1, θ_2, ..., θ_i are to be chosen so that the sum of the squares value of e_i is minimized:

$$\sum_{i=1}^{N} e^2 \quad \text{must be minimized} \, ,$$

with $i = 1, 2, ..., N$, where N = number of observations of y.

It is convenient to introduce the matrix and vector notation, namely:

$$y = \begin{pmatrix} y_1 \\ y_2 \\ \vdots \\ y_N \end{pmatrix}, \quad e = \begin{pmatrix} e_1 \\ e_2 \\ \vdots \\ e_N \end{pmatrix}, \quad \theta = \begin{pmatrix} \theta_1 \\ \theta_2 \\ \vdots \\ \theta_N \end{pmatrix},$$

$$\phi = \begin{pmatrix} \varphi_1(x_1) & \varphi_2(x_1) & \ldots & \varphi_n(x_1) \\ \varphi_1(x_2) & \varphi_2(x_2) & \ldots & \varphi_n(x_2) \\ \vdots \\ \varphi_1(x_N) & \varphi_2(x_N) & \ldots & \varphi_n(x_N) \end{pmatrix}.$$

Using these notations the initial equation becomes:

$$y = \phi\theta + e \ ,$$

with the "error function"

$$\sum_{i=1}^{N} e_i^2 = ee' \ ,$$

where e' is the transposed matrix of e. This function is to be minimized with respect to the choice of

$$e'e = \{y - \phi\theta\}'\{y - \phi\theta\} = y'y - y'\phi\theta - \theta'\phi'y + \theta'\phi'\phi\theta.$$

If we assume that $\phi'\phi$ does not present any singularity we may write:

$$e'e = \{\theta - (\phi'\phi)^{-1}\phi'y\}\phi'\phi\{\theta - (\phi'\phi)^{-1}\phi'y\} + y'y - y'\phi(\phi'\phi)^{-1}\phi'y$$

$$\geqslant y'y - \phi'\phi(\phi'\phi)^{-1}\phi y \ .$$

We obtain equality if

$$\theta = (\phi'\phi)^{-1}\phi'y \ .$$

This is the condition which enables us to identify the vector θ.

6.1. Example

Again we assume that we have a first order transfer function

$$y_1(2T + 1) - y_0(2T - 1) = (x_0 + x_1) \ ,$$

$$y_2(2T + 1) - y_1(2T - 1) = (x_1 + x_2) \ .$$

These equations can be written in the following way:

$$y_1 - ay_0 - b(x_0 + x_1) = e_1 \ ,$$
$$y_2 - ay_1 - b(x_1 + x_2) = e_2 \ ,$$
$$\vdots$$
$$y_N - ay_{N-1} - b(x_{N-1} + x_N) = e_N \ ,$$

with

$$a = \frac{2T-1}{2T+1} \qquad \text{and} \qquad b = \frac{1}{2T+1} \ .$$

In this case:

$$y = \begin{pmatrix} -y_1 \\ -y_2 \\ \vdots \\ -y_N \end{pmatrix}, \qquad e = \begin{pmatrix} e_1 \\ e_2 \\ \vdots \\ e_N \end{pmatrix}, \qquad \theta = \begin{pmatrix} a \\ b \end{pmatrix},$$

$$\phi = \begin{pmatrix} -y_0 & -(x_0+x_1) \\ -y_1 & -(x_1+x_2) \\ \vdots & \vdots \\ -y_{N-1} & -(x_{N-1}+x_N) \end{pmatrix},$$

$$\phi'\phi = \begin{pmatrix} \sum\limits_{k=0}^{N-1} y_k^2 & \sum\limits_{k=0}^{N-1} y_k(x_{k-1}+x_k) \\ \\ \sum\limits_{k=0}^{N-1} y_k(x_{k-1}+x_k) & \sum\limits_{k=0}^{N-1} (x_{k-1}+x_k)^2 \end{pmatrix},$$

$$\phi'y = \begin{pmatrix} \sum\limits_{k=0}^{N-1} y_{k+1}y_k \\ \\ \sum\limits_{k=0}^{N-1} y_{k+1}(x_{k-1}+x_k) \end{pmatrix}.$$

We assume that $x(t)$ varies as a step function with $T = 5$; the variation of the output in that case is:

$$y = 1 - \exp\left(-\tfrac{1}{5}t\right) .$$

We obtain the following corresponding sequence (with $N = 4$)

$S(x) = [1; 1; 1; 1]$,

$S(y) = [0; 0.1813; 0.3298; 0.4512; 0.5507]$.

Consequently:

$$\phi = \begin{pmatrix} -0.1813 & -2 \\ -0.3298 & -2 \\ -0.4512 & -2 \\ -0.5507 & -2 \end{pmatrix} ,$$

$$\phi'\phi = \begin{pmatrix} -0.1813 & -0.3298 & -0.4512 & -0.5507 \\ -2 & -2 & -2 & -2 \end{pmatrix} \cdot \begin{pmatrix} -0.1813 & -2 \\ -0.3298 & -2 \\ -0.4512 & -2 \\ -0.5507 & -2 \end{pmatrix}$$

$$= \begin{pmatrix} 0.6485 & 3.0260 \\ 3.0260 & 16 \end{pmatrix} ,$$

$\Delta = 1.2193$,

$$(\phi'\phi)^{-1} = \frac{1}{1.2193} \begin{pmatrix} 16 & -3.026 \\ -3.026 & 0.6485 \end{pmatrix} = \begin{pmatrix} 13.1255 & -2.4824 \\ -2.4824 & 0.532 \end{pmatrix} ,$$

$$\phi'y = \begin{pmatrix} -0.1813 & -0.3298 & -0.4512 & -0.5507 \\ -2 & -2 & -2 & -2 \end{pmatrix} \cdot \begin{pmatrix} -0.3298 \\ -0.4512 \\ -0.5507 \\ -0.6321 \end{pmatrix}$$

$$= \begin{pmatrix} 0.8052 \\ 3.9276 \end{pmatrix} ,$$

$$(\varphi'\varphi)^{-1}\varphi'y = \begin{pmatrix} 13.1255 & -2.4824 \\ -2.4824 & 0.532 \end{pmatrix} \begin{pmatrix} 0.8052 \\ 3.9276 \end{pmatrix} = \begin{pmatrix} 0.8188 \\ 0.0906 \end{pmatrix},$$

$0.1812\,T + 0.0906 = 1$.

Therefore

$$T = \frac{1 - 0.0906}{0.1812} = 5.0187 .$$

This result is very close to the expected one:

$T = 5$.

7. Conclusion

The identification methods based on the impulse analysis, deemed to be "soft mathematics", at least make it possible to introduce experimental research into fields where tests, based on the rigours of "hard mathematics", are difficult or impossible. By measuring experimental data, these methods provide mathematical models which do not explain the facts, but rather permit simulation of these facts within prescribed limits. In the process the researcher is helped to recognise the nature of the problem. The simulation has the added attraction that it can be improved as fresh data becomes available.

The current interest in these methods has many causes: (1) "Soft mathematics" and the theory of complex systems are both relatively new fields. Computers are now available to handle the mass of data involved. (2) The analytical methods applicable to large physical systems can be extended to management systems.

Each national economy can be considered as a closed system of production, distribution, consumption of goods and services and the corresponding circuits of payment in the inverse direction. Bottlenecks and the lagged interreaction between different factors continuously threaten and upset the stability of the system. One has only to think of the sequence of time lags which intervene before an increase in salaries influences in turn the general level of prices, consumption, production and salaries.

Theoretically prices provide an auto-regulatory system which intervenes to correct an imbalance between supply and demand. In practice many factors, including State intervention, inhibit this automatic adjustment of prices. The same state intervention at different times can either remove or aggravate the imbalance. This is demonstrated by system theory — a fact which illustrates the usefulness of knowing the methods of identifying the dynamic characteristics of national subsystems in dealing with such a situation.

The application of identification methods to micro- or macro-economic systems is one way to check on traditional rules or to discover and introduce new ones. It can be combined with the more sophisticated analysis of nonlinear multivariable systems (with or without feed back), with dynamic analysis of stochastic systems and with the new approaches of heuristics.

Paradoxically it can be maintained that, the less a cause to effect relationship is evident, the more this relationship is covered with noise, the more appropriate it is to use the sophisticated methods of systems theory to discover relationships between facts which seem independent. This is specially true whenever time constants are very large or systematic tests are ruled out.

The fields of automatic control, systems theory, OR, biological and human sciences as they continue to overlap more and more are becoming increasingly difficult to delimit. While many approaches developed in one field can be applied in another it is generally in the overlapping domain that the most significant progress can be achieved. This provides a fascinating field for cooperative research between the specialists of systems theory and OR.

This collaboration is particularly necessary, for

(1) the development of a common language and symbols, to facilitate communication;

(2) the simultaneous application of different methods to the same problem to determine their possibilities and limits, advantages and disadvantages;

(3) the systematic development of impulse analysis building on the algorithms and methodology previously developed by control engineers;

(4) the common study of technico-economic problems, such as transportation, communication, utilities, water supply and industrial location.

Such systems have a considerable impact on the development of a country. Given the tools now available for data processing and system theory, the study of these problems is an exciting and necessary challenge for the young generation. May IFORS and IFAC join their efforts to promote the desire to find solution for these worldwide problems.

References

[1] A.P. Sage and J.L. Melsa, System identification (Academic Press, New York, 1970).

[2] K.J. Astrom and P. Eykhoff, System identification; a survey, presented at the IFAC Symp. on Identification and Process Parameter Estimation, Prague (1970).

[3] M. Cuénod and A.P. Sage, Comparison of some methods used for process identification, presented at the IFAC Symp. on the Problem of Identification in Automatic Control System, Prague (1967).

[4] M. Cuénod and A. Durling, A discrete-time approach for system analysis (Academic Press, New York, 1969).

[5] M. Cuénod, Introduction à l'analyse impulsionelle; principe et application (Dunod, Paris, 1970).

PART IV

THE STATE - OF - THE - ART

Etat de la technique

Reviews of

Planning under Uncertainty, D.B. HERTZ

Models for Corporate Planning, H.I. ANSOFF and R.L. HAYES

Information Systems for Decision and Control, H. WEDEKIND

General Systems Research, G. KLIR

Simulation and Validation, T. NAYLOR

Stochastic Processes, F.G. FOSTER

Behavioral Science Models, J. STRINGER

M. Ross, ed., OR '72. North-Holland Publishing Company (1973)

9

PLANNING UNDER UNCERTAINTY

Planification dans des conditions incertaines

DAVID B. HERTZ
McKinsey and Company, Inc., New York, U.S.A.

Abstract. Public and private planners must develop programs, whose outcomes are affected by the interaction of a great many variables, both controllable and uncontrollable. This paper reviews the methods that have been proposed and used in facing up to the risks imposed by uncertain and unanticipated future events. General models covering decision making under uncertainty are examined. Decision and utility analysis that have been suggested to maximize returns, minimize risks and balance pay off — uncertainty trade offs are subject to some theoretical difficulties. Adaptive planning and the retention of flexibility imply serious practical difficulties. Conventional deterministic methods do not work well in a world of uncertainty, and results are strongly sensitive to stochastic assumptions. Planning models based on analysis of risk, or on mean-variance measures, to deal with uncertainty require the use of common sense to be effective. Planners have their choice of assuming unlikely conditions of certainty and developing programs and schedules that will be robust under some alternative sets of such conditions, or accepting the inevitable facts of uncertainty a priori and attempting to produce plans that will either be optimal under the assumed uncertainty conditions, or flexible enough to meet a reasonable set of contingencies, or provide effective insurance against the hazards of the future. Or the planner may select parallel approaches to his goals, measuring their effectiveness as time unfolds. Several methods for choosing one or more of such strategies for planning under uncertainty have been proposed and what is certain is that the planner will have to use at least one of them if his programs are to have practical value to his organization.

1. Planning as engineering

Planning, using a disciplined intellectual methodology, begins with an understanding and specification of purpose and broadly envisioned end results. It develops intermediate objectives and specific targets or goals to be attained, toward the achievement of which a network of activities to be undertaken and organizational arrangements to be established are described and assigned. Defined in this way planning seems well known and well practiced throughout history in civilian and military arenas. I think one can say that modern 'planning methodology' does not offer major practical improvements in carrying out large-scale engineering type projects over that of Julius Caesar or Georges Haussmann. The latter hired and designated Deschamps as head of a planning department (Service du Plan) and laid out an action program and set of procedures for rebuilding Paris that would be acceptable to most city planning agencies today.

The methodologies and the discipline used by such planners and builders as Haussmann and Deschamps perhaps have been tightened by present day network models and computer simulations. A number of the latter are described in a recent volume edited by Schrieber [1]. But as we shall see, each step in the attempt to improve the planning process runs into problems that involve decision making under uncertainty.

2. The introduction of uncertainty – PERT and CPM

As an example of these ubiquitous paths leading to questions of risk, the arrangement and sequencing of the network of activities included in a plan to assure consistency and to develop efficient time-based flows of information and material have been developed as activity network models, such as PERT and CPM. Elmaghraby [2] gives detailed expository treatment of the functional relations defined on network models dealing with shortest path and maximum flow problems, signal flow graphs and activity networks. Early PERT models related uncertainty to the duration of activities but not to their eventuation. Clearly, since a directed sequence of activities dependent upon interrelated outcomes is involved, PERT – CPM models would not be able to deal practically with the multitude of event possibilities that could negate the basic logic of the network. Elmaghraby and others have described generalized activity networks (GERT and GAN) to represent the complex logical relationships that include the possibilities of future events occurring at various levels of probability.

In all cases, as in the network models, the planner bases his description of the proposed set of activities — including the activity of choosing from among alternatives sequentially made available by new facts — on a broad set of assumptions, some explicit and some implicit, in his formulation of the planning problem.

These assumptions include statements or private ideas about (1) objectives, (2) available feasible activity alternatives, (3) causal relationships between alternative activities and outcomes, (4) time sequencing and durations of activities, (5) resource availability, (6) organization of and communications among actors, and (7) external events that may affect the desired end results and the causal relationships among them. Thus, the meaning of these assumptions in terms of the decisions they affect and the monitoring of them on a continuous basis must be part of an effective plan. If the assumptions do not in fact hold, then the decisions that were involved in a developing, describing and implementing plan become subject to question in terms of desired end results. Contingency planning, flexibility, adaptability are all means that have been adapted by planners to face up to the universal presence of uncertainty.

3. Flexibility and adaptive planning

The roles of adaptability and flexibility in meeting the demands that uncertainty places upon a plan have been described by Meyer [3]. The potentiality of varying the outputs of a system, as assumptions are proven incorrect, by changing the variable inputs may be called flexibility, while adaptability is the possibility of varying the relatively fixed inputs as the actual situation unfolds in a different manner than the planner envisaged. Maximum flexibility is preserved when minimum effective resource expenditures are coupled with as much reversible end products or results as possible. Thus, optimum resource allocation methods and dynamic programs become a part of the planners art, as Charnes et al. [4] point out in their review of models for social and economic accounting and planning. Ackoff [5] goes further in calling for adaptive planning as the step beyond satisficing and optimizing. He says:

"Adaptive planning requires even more [understanding of an organization's behavior than does optimizing or satisficing] ... Adaptive planners must be aware of, and responsive to, values held by the organization as a whole, its parts, the individuals who make it up, and those organizations and individuals in its environment whose behavior affects the system planned for ... Thus, the understanding of collective and individual be-

havior that is required by adaptive planning is considerably greater than
that currently possessed by many corporate planners and managers."

Placing such demands upon the planner makes it clear that a large element
of the planning process involves the gathering and analysis of information
about the internal and external system being planned for. The military services, of course, provide the obvious examples of planners who try to cope
with the information requirement through intelligence operations and pre-
structured contingency plans. With the recognition of the need to provide
basic intelligence for planning in non-military systems in industrial and other
social institutions, financial and planning models based upon the use of the
calculational power of computers are becoming more widespread. Gershefski
[6] has described one such model that incorporates financial and physical
historical information about a company in an analytical deterministic model
to generate a financial outcome from a set of projected physical and financial
inputs. Gershefski [7] surveyed the field of corporate model building in the
United States in 1970, reporting that about one out of three companies
responding to a survey have, or are developing, corporate models, most of
which were non-optimizing deterministic simulations.

4. Planning as fantasy

Strange as it may seem, the practical planner lives in a fantasy world. In
setting objectives and choosing (deciding) alternatives for later action, he
plots the outlines of fictional (but possibly attainable) futures. Appropriate
planning involves a subtle, complex relationship between objectives and proposed steps to be taken, between ideas and action, between human beings and
physical artefacts, between society and its environment. Planning is a product
of the imagination more than anything else, a mapping of probabilities and
preferences onto models of social and economic relationships that are intended to provide some stochastic basis for assuming that what is projected
by the models actually might take place.

The questions that are most significant are, *first,* what is the likelihood of
specific futures, given a set of decisions? *second,* which of the futures are to
be preferred over others? *and finally,* what can be done to maximize the
probable value of the end result?

These difficult questions have surfaced gradually and become better defined as the issues of risk and uncertainty have begun to disturb the conventional, deterministic views of managers and management analysts. Knight [8]
in 1921 distinguished between the concept of decisions taken under known

frequency probabilities (risk) and those involving conjectures for which probabilities could not be stated (uncertainty). He clearly pointed to the fact that business decisions are made under conditions of uncertainty, not risk. Until recently, economic doctrine continued to accept a distinction between risk and uncertainty, but with the growing acceptance of personal probability as more realistic than frequentist, it appears no longer useful to do so, as Borch and Mossin [9] point out.

5. Uncertainty in practical economic decisions

Other than Knight's work, the economic literature prior to the pioneering work of von Neumann and Morgenstern [10] did not deal with uncertainty to any significant degree. The latter defined a set of axioms providing for the choice of a probability distribution that maximizes expected utility over a set of uncertain outcomes, to suggest that uncertainty and risk were indeed key problems for the corporate and institutional planner. But business and government continued to act in the present to affect purposefully the unknown future and to adapt to uncertainty. Inventory and quality control, preventive maintenance, insurance, risk-sharing market structures, hedging, among others, were well-established means for taking action to deal with future events that were, when desirable, at best, only likely to occur, or, at worst, when unwanted, might occur anyway.

Shewhart [11] in 1930 proposed a methodology for analyzing the controllable variations in the quality of manufactured products and relating this control to the economics of manufacture, and the risks of accepting variable results outside of control limits. He demonstrated a rational methodology for dealing with inevitable uncertainties in manufacturing — a viewpoint that was soon extended to other fields such as services. The reasoning involved in making practical descisions under uncertainty was treated comprehensively by Wald [12] in 1950 in problems of optimizing decisions in which data become available sequentially.

Economic decisions for inventory control were treated rigorously by Dvoretzky et al. [13] in 1952. They discussed the case of unknown distributions of demand and developed an optimum result for a risk function which represented the minimum present value of the expected loss as a function of initial stock, an ordering policy and the distribution of demand, yielding the socalled $(s\,S)$ model, where s is the stock level below which an order is triggered and S is the level to which the new order is intended to return the inventory. The state of research and application in inventory planning has been reviewed by Veinott [14].

Insurance is a particular case of the general problem of planning for uncertainty dealing with choice from a set of probability distributions on a space of prospects. The insurance company must plan for a continuous game of chance with its policy holders. The gains or losses incurred during a given time period may be considered random variables that are affected by choices (of premiums, types of policies, reinsurance, etc.) of the company. Specific distributions involved in the risk process and the ruin problem were developed by Cramer [15] in 1954 and related to the von Neumann – Morgenstern utility theory assumptions.

The analysis of operational problems of insurance enterprises has continued to be the object of intensive study, with planning criteria such as probability of ruin, dividend policy and utility being considered as the basis for setting premiums and designing products. Buhlmann [16] describes the insurance process as stochastic with independent increments, applying the theoretical model to premium calculations, retentions-reserves, and stability. Two important results emerge: first, that increasing wealth permits organizations to accept, and profit from, risks that individuals or institutions with less assets would not choose to bear, and secondly, that inventory and insurance are closely related – inventory being a form of insurance against specified risks – as means for planning the allocation of resources in an uncertain world.

And in another area of human enterprise, the uncertainties of research and development and their effects upon the fortunes of companies and governments made it abundantly clear that deterministic economics and single-point plans, while they might serve as pointers toward a desired direction, simply would not do as a surrogate for the rough and tumble real world. Klein [17] discusses the problems of resource allocation and tradeoffs among projects. Bobis and Atkinson [18] present a series of dynamic models in which the uncertainties involved in achieving a solution and the resultant benefits in research projects are related to the use and timing of alternative resource levels. Optimum budgets on an annual basis to maximize expected gains are suggested.

Parallel strategies, or the simultaneous pursuit of two or more distinct approaches to a task that need only be completed successfully by one, have been analyzed (in terms of the rate at which uncertainty is reduced) by Abernathy [19] and Abernathy and Rosenbloom [20]. Such strategies are suggested to maintain options while better information for decision making is obtained, hedge against failure, and stimulate competition among researchers. The selection of research projects under uncertainty as to the outcomes is discussed by Bobis and Atkinson [21], and procedures are proposed to rank projects under a set of (subjective) success criteria. Dean [22] has edited a set of papers that cover a range of topics relating to the problems of planning for and dealing with uncertainty in research and development.

Closely related to research and development are competitive strategy problems that have been explored, for example, in the contexts of bidding, exploring and exploiting mineral land rights or bidding on government contracts. Allais [23], in his classic study of mineral exploration in the Sahara in 1957, provided a study based upon estimated distributions of potential deposits and their value in a cost-benefit framework. Friedman [24] in 1956 and Hanssmann and Rivett [25] in 1959 discussed the rationale for bidding strategies that were intended to exploit, under varying assumptions, the underlying empirical structure information of the bidders' probable bids and the probable payoffs in terms of the value of the property or contract won. Rothkopf [26], in the framework of *n*-person games, and subsequently Pelto [27] have brought this early work up to date. It is agreed generally that bids on many kinds of objects are log-normally distributed, and Pelto shows that the distribution of winning bids, as related to the average bid and the number of bidders, also is a log-normal variate. Methods for efficient and effective action in the face of competitive uncertainty have been proposed on the basis of such statistical regularities.

Finally, beyond this array of approaches by the management science community to practical decision-making in concretely evidenced situations where uncertainty is clear-cut, resource allocation using various forms of programming bumped into the prickly problem of uncertainty not long after it began to be used for problems of, inter alia, process scheduling and ingredient formulation. Thus, in 1955, Dantzig [28] described methods of optimizing the expected value of an objective function (under constraints) which he termed linear programming under uncertainty, and Tintner [29] introduced applications of stochastic linear programming in which random elements are used to generate statistical distributions of the optimal solution vector and the value of the objective function from which chance constraints can be evaluated and confidence intervals established for the maximand and the optimal solution vector. In 1959, in Charnes' and Cooper's [30] 'chance-constrained programming' the decision maker prescribes a specified level that the expected frequency of forced departures from specified constraints should not exceed.

These methods generally assume normality of the random elements and the existence of feasible solutions after a deterministic equivalent has been developed [29]. Sengupta [31] replaces the normality assumption with a number of non-negative distributions, including chi-square and truncated nor-

mal. Fricks [32, 33] has prepared comprehensive surveys of current developments in stochastic, dual chance-constrained programming.

6. Probability and economic thought

Most of the analyses of and approaches to problems in the real world of
managerial uncertainty now assume that the distributions of various data,
future events and relationships needed to provide expectations and variances
of outputs can, or should be, determined by informed participants in the
decision process and that the accuracy of the distributions can be improved
by information provided to the estimators. Also, most of the approaches
cited provide the decision maker with optimized expectation of cost, utility
benefit or net gain as a figure of merit for making choices. Some additionally
give variances for these outputs, and a very few provide distributions of
outcomes.

While economics long has recognized the existence of uncertainty, without
actually incorporating its implications into the main body of theory, it is in
the last 20 years that truly substantive work has been done. Much of this
work is related directly to the issues of decision making and behavior in the
kinds of problems already discussed. The work of von Neumann and Morgenstern [10], relating probability theory to utility theory and economic choice
has led to extensive investigations of the utility functions of individuals and
groups and theories of behavior under uncertainty. Equilibrium theory (see,
for example, Fama [34]), portfolio selection, the balancing of risk prospects,
and mixed and sequential investment choices have begun to interact with
operations research models for planners in a significant way. The so-called
decision theory postulates of Savage [35] established the conditions under
which a preference ordering for a set af alternatives with subjective probabilities could be described under the Bernoulli expected monetary value principle
along with a utility function and probability distribution. Certainty equivalents to risky bets were one way of dealing with an unsure world. The significance to the planner of this intrusion of uncertainty into the world of economics is clear: What are the long-term managerial implications of decisions
made without (relatively) certain knowledge of the outcome? The broad
dimensions of this problem and its effects upon the specific processes of
decision are described by Champernowne [36] and Borch [37]. Issues relating to questions of uncertainty involved in economic planning decisions,
including national planning, have been addressed in the series of papers edited
by Borch and Mossin [9, 38].

Representative descriptions of normative rules for decision making under the expected utility hypothesis are described by Raiffa [39], Schlaifer [40], and Lindley [41]. And an early, but still pertinent, specific application of these Bayesian and expected utility approaches to the petroleum exploration industry is Grayson [42].

With respect to subjective probability, Fellner [43] discusses economic behavior along Bayesian lines, taking (in 1965) an increasingly popular position, that subjective degrees of belief should be regarded as probabilities. An elementary, but comprehensive, introduction to Bayesian statistics is provided by Schmitt [44], and Morales [45] discusses economic structural analyses in Bayesian terms.

The expected-utility and subjectivist probability viewpoints have been gaining in usage, as problems in everyday life seem to require normative rather than descriptive decision-making approaches. The issues involved in invoking personal probabilities and taking action under decision rules, where, for example, an act is defined by Savage [46] as "a function or schedule, associating a consequence for the person with each possible state of the world", give rise to a number of philosophic difficulties. Thus, these consequences are not necessarily the "real" consequences of the acts, but surface surrogates that serve suitably to distinguish among them. For this reason, among others, the planner is especially pushed toward the use of (somebody's) personal, as opposed to frequentist, probabilities. Savage has said that *every* application of the idea of probability can be viewed as an application of the preference theory. "To use the preference theory is to search for incoherence among potential decisions, of which you, the user of the theory, must then revise one or more. Accepting the inherent complexity of this requirement means behaving in accordance with the logical implications of your knowledge." Foundations for reasonable axioms of a normative theory for such action are proposed by Fishburn [47,48]. Brown [49] discusses how one may undertake to develop estimates of personal probabilities of increasing credibility.

Utility theorists are faced also with the problem of measuring risk for the decision maker who wishes to reduce, or eliminate, incoherence and inconsistency in his decisions. Utility functions evaluate risks, and Savage [46] and Arrow [50] have shown that a risk-averse utility function which is a strictly increasing function of wealth must be strictly concave, the risk-indifferent function linear, and the risk-preferent function strictly convex. One assumes that most individuals are risk-averse, but this does not necessarily hold over a wide range of corporate decisions, such as, mineral exploration, where risk-preference may be a strong element in many situations. In the analysis of preference orderings over mixtures of prospects, the variance of the random variable has been used as a measure of risk by Markowitz [51], Sharpe [52,53]. and others. (Tobin [54] discusses liquidity preference as a measure of risk aversion.) However, since utility-theory requires that an acceptable measure of risk aversion be invariant under a linear transformation, the use of variance as such a measure is not satisfactory. Arrow [50] and Pratt [55] have shown that the negative of the variance divided by the mean is a useful measure of absolute risk aversion (meaning that "fair" bets are transformed into bets that favor the decision maker) and that risk aversion which is proportional to the amount of initial wealth is the elasticity of the marginal utility of the variable [56].

Mean-variance analysis provides an "efficiency frontier" in which a combination of assets (Markowitz and Sharpe), a combination of new projects as suggested by Hertz [57], or solution procedures for interrelated risky investments as discussed by Hillier [58], are measured in terms of the expectation and variance of returns, points on the frontier being those for which no additional expectation can be obtained without increasing variance. The decision maker then can choose according to his own preferences. This frontier is not the indifference set that would be generated under the same circumstances by expected utility-theory. And furthermore, it implies a quadratic utility function that implies the absolute risk-aversion function is a strictly increasing function of wealth.

McCall [59] surveys the intrusion of probabilistic notions into classical economics and finds they are making headway. Further, he points out that some of the usual economic rules that apply under conditions of certainty, do *not* do so when the analysis of the behavior of the firm is stochastic. Thus, the setting of a control variable, such as production level, depends upon the firm's attitude toward risk, and generally would take on significantly different values for firms that are more or less risk-averting or risk-preferring.

McCall points out that "the postponement of decision making (the decision to collect more information) is in many ways the distinguishing feature of probabilistic economics", and reviews the previous applications of Markov processes and martingales (a sequence of sums of independent random variables, in which the sum at any point is a function of the values of the sequence up to that point). He shows how the properties of this particular stochastic process may be applied to optimal stopping rules, under which the decision maker need look only one period ahead to determine whether the expected gain from that next look exceeds the expected cost.

7. Probabilistic economics and behavior

In the world of real decision makers, major choices usually are made by groups, as a consequence of a sequence of choices made by individuals, each acting under his own set of preferences. (It usually has been the case that experiments demonstrate the latter to be inconsistent with the expected utility theory.) It has been clearly shown by Arrow [50] and others [39], that assumptions of rational decision making on the part of a group, such as giving positive association between individuals and the preference ordering of the group, lead either to contradictions, inconsistencies, or the imposition of a choice rather than majority rule.

Fishburn [60] has reviewed various social choice functions that are generalizations of the simple majority rule, and described the implications of various alternatives. It turns out that there is no satisfactory way to establish rules for developing a consistent utility function.

And beyond group assessment of decisions, since much of the end results of analysis of consequences of decisions under uncertainty depend upon individual assessments of probability distributions, the efficacy of the individual as an assessor must be considered a part of the planner's problem. While work in this area still is at an early stage, some of it [61] suggests that simple mechanical methods of assessment may outperform individuals. On the other hand, Raiffa [39] suggests that probability assessment by individuals may be teachable and effectively the only way to obtain necessary inputs for analysis of significant decisions.

A number of mechanisms have been described for obtaining subjective probabilities of key variables, including individual and group interview sessions [62,49]. The Delphi process, using a group of knowledgeable individuals, repeated measurement and anonymous controlled feedback of sequential group results, is intended to replace confrontation and debate and eliminate psychological factors. Dalkey and Helmer [63,64], who developed the Delphi process at the Rand Corporation, have used it largely for technological, social and environmental forecasting. The rationale for the process is that with repeated measurement the range and variance of the responses will decrease and the median will move towards the best probability estimate, which depends on there being some "true" (to the group) joint information base.

8. Planning and decision making

Elements of planning, defined here as the envisioning of a set of activities contributing to a pre-selected range of end results, are a part of all decisions. It should be apparent that planning exists and will operate at all levels of institutional activity. There is a hierarchy of decisions that lead to plans that lead to decisions that lead to plans. No matter how explicit the orders are from the top of the organization to the succeeding echelons, there is an element of planning in everyone's job. And this planning, perforce, is carried out under uncertainty. That is, even if the planner-decision maker acts as though the consequences of his alternatives were known with certainty, the world continues to unfold the future in its own way. Surely, to assume a deterministic posture is to act arrogantly – as though the projections used to take action were completely certain and the envisioned end results were *faits accomplis*. Clearly, the deterministic planner is acting contrary to any rational logic or theoretical structure – and is saved, when he is, from unpleasant consequences by the very uncertainty he has ignored.

Under these circumstances, there is a need in an institutional framework that general rules for planning under uncertainty at all levels be established. Military organizations have evolved such rules as "appraisal of the situation", and "examination of contingencies". Other institutions are beginning to see that such rules are needed, as well. The more stable and recurring the environment, the less the uncertainty, and the less rigorous the policy rules need be. Ansoff [65], Ackoff [5], and Steiner [66] all put these rules in general terms, basically taking a "control theory" stance – continuously monitoring the environment to detect gaps between projected or desired performance and actual results, and taking decisions intended to close those gaps via a plan, using models to determine what decisions would achieve an efficient directed movement of the institution. None of these corporate planning processes deals explicitly with uncertainty, but step-by-step planning is inherent in the control process, and, as Strauss [67] indicates, this is of considerable assistance in dealing with uncertainty.

Planning activities leading to decision making are found at all levels of the management ladder, but the planning horizon broadens and the consequences of the decisions increase in significance as *the decisions made at one level influence or dictate the planning of increasingly larger numbers of others*. A pyramid effect occurs, in which decisions at each hierarchical level limit the scope of plans at successively lower levels. Thus, incremental controls and "continuous" decision systems for maintaining an institution on "target" can be an effective way to plan in the face of uncertainty.

9. The compleat planner

Putting all these threads together seems now to be both the task and the goal of the institutional and corporate planner. The attempts of economists to understand the implications of uncertainty, of behaviorists to analyze the methods for assessing personal probabilities, taking their examples and problems from the operations researchers' and management scientists' attempts to build models for decision making in:

capital budgeting	insurance	inventory control
quality control	research and development	purchasing
bidding for land rights	bidding for contracts	portfolio selection

among other areas where management faces uncertainty, are proliferating and maturing, and I perhaps only have scratched the surface in this review.

These activities have led to the development of planning models going beyond feedback and control as a means of dealing with uncertainty. They permit many of the ideas to be combined in a coordinated way that provides the display of alternative outcomes or alternative futures to managers. Capital budgeting and project selection in the public and private sectors come in for increasing scrutiny. It is now understood that under uncertainty it is not possible necessarily to classify decisions as right or wrong, and procedures for optimizing decisions under the utility-theory have been formalized by Howard [68,69] among others. The approach developed by Weingartner [70] for capital budgeting of interrelated projects is extended by Byrne et al. [71,72] to include chance-constrained programming, and linear programming under uncertainty in which the tradeoffs between the value of the functional and, for example, payback constraints, are explored. Hillier [58,73] models interrelated risky investments in a portfolio to determine the mean, variance and functional form of the present value of the cash flows developed, optimizes their expected utility, and explores some methods whereby managers can establish an approximate utility function to evaluate alternatives. Näslund [74] formulates capital budgeting under risk as an insurance problem, which allows for the evaluation of some economic policies such as interest rates on the outcomes. Albach [75] formulates a specific problem of capital budgeting under uncertainty to achieve a utility scale ranking on the basis of the number of cases in which financial constraints might not be met [76].

Another approach to integrating subjective probability inputs and displaying the consequential outcomes of decisions under uncertainty for alternative plans has been that of simulation as proposed by Hess and Quigley [77] and Hertz [78] and extended to the decision tree type of decision analysis (Magee [79,80]), by Hespos and Strassman [81]. While simulation provides only estimates of distributions of outcomes rather than optimal results, these may be closer to the "real" world than those more rigorous formal manipulations of the available data can achieve. And managers can be led to understand bcth the input of simulation models and the form of the output and recognize the particular kind of an uncertain future they are up against. The integration of this approach into the planning process has been demonstrated by Adelson and Norman [82], while the implications of the several approaches are reviewed by Byrne et al. [83].

Cohen and Elton [84] and Hertz [57] extended the simulation concept to portfolios, the former for evaluating the efficiency of the portfolio and the latter to establish empirical utility project choice criteria for managers based on the initial simulation of the distributions of projected results of individual projects. Hertz argued that, unless the decision maker took into consideration the entire range of outcomes of projects, planning tools for the *identification* and *initiation* of projects would not be forthcoming. He suggests criteria of expected value and the expectations above and below some part of the tails of the distribution as effective surrogates for a corporate utility function. Wilson [85] analyzes the sufficient conditions to accept individual projects in a programmed portfolio.

The statistical input estimates to such models, whether analytical or simulational, were in large measure related to technology or capital return. Technological forecasting is the assessment of the probabilities of future technologies being transferred to specific production functions. Bright [86], Ayres [87], and Cetron [88] have presented alternative methods for projecting the development of future technologies: (1) extrapolation of historical trends, (2) future need-oriented probable developments, and (3) computer-based simulations of an assumed model of technical and social relationships. Roberts [89] has reviewed the kind of end results these methods give. Any of them can provide probabilistic estimates of some part of the future. Van Horne [90] suggests that the "rate of resolution of uncertainty" as projects are added to a firm's product mix would yield a time-related risk profile for the firm.

These developments of planning under uncertainty have begun to be utilized in the public sector in most economies, including the planning, programming and budgeting systems that have been so much in vogue the last several years. Ruefli [91] reviews the development of PPBS and proposes a goal decomposition model which permits the incorporation of non-linear or probabilistic relations in their constraints. Pouliquen [92] and Reutlinger

[93] describe the use of uncertainty analysis in project development for lesser developed countries. Siroyezhin [94] and Unčovský [95] present some of the problems of uncertainty in planned economics, and Thore [96] introduces a dynamic Leontief model with chance constraints into national planning. Upton [97] and Meyer [3] provide examples of environmental and transportation problems using models that deal with the pricing of externalities and the development of large scale public plans under uncertainty. Threads of technology forecasting, decision analysis and system simulation have been brought together by Blackman [98] in a planning structure for decisions on the initiation and support of new ventures.

Other aspects of integrating the developments of the last decade have been reported on in connection with planning systems for managerial control by Gonedes [99], and for growth planning by Larson [100] who has synthesized financing policies. Helmer [101] describes planning games that permit the appreciation of the outcomes and affect a variety of interrelated future events to simulate the decision-making processes that constitute the planning toward a preferred future.

10. Conclusions

The outcomes of programs developed and decisions taken by planners of the future in the public and private sectors will always be affected by the interaction of uncertain and sometimes unanticipated variables. Conventional deterministic economic theory and decision analyses can lead to undesirable end results. Planners have their choice of assuming unlikely conditions of certainty and developing programs and schedules that will be robust under some alternative sets of such conditions, or accepting the inevitable facts of uncertainty a priori and attempting to produce Bayesian type plans that will either (1) aim at optimality under the assumed uncertainty conditions, (2) be flexible or adaptible enough to meet a reasonable set of contingencies, or (3) provide effective insurance against the hazards of the future. Planning is a process, and a specific "plan" is only one step in preparing the way to face the unfolding future.

Planning, as a continuing process, is a connected series of resource allocations and commitments, each based upon a set of assumptions, the assumptions being that things are as they seem to be and that the results of internal and external actions will bring about changes in the state of the world within limits envisaged by the "plan" at a specific point in time. Each step in the process of deciding on an activity to which resources will be committed is essentially a micro-image of the total planning process. Therefore, the monitoring of micro- and macro-assumptions entering into the planning process is perhaps as important as the understanding of the implications of stochastic economic theory. We probably have been protected in the past by both the environment and the enterprise itself. That is, as long as many organized units of society and many individuals operated within fairly narrow decision making constraints, we could expect the outcomes – even with perhaps wrong decisions – to be robust under conditions of uncertainty and somewhere near acceptability with respect to the general welfare. But as we look around us, in both the market and planned economies, that day seems past. Therefore, we must come to grips with the essential problems of dealing with uncertainty inherent in forecasts, or projections [102], of any set of variables and taking into account the complex relationships among the many uncertain variables whose specific outcomes will determine the state of the world for enterprises, institutions and nations.

With Lucretius we may say:

"Time changes the nature of the world and all things must pass from one condition to another, and nothing continues as it was exactly; all things leave their original boundaries; nature changes all things and compels them to alter."

Planning under uncertainty is a field of immense challenge and boundless research opportunity for the operations research and management science communities; I can think of none more important.

References

[1] A.N. Schrieber, Corporate simulation models, College on Simulation and Gaming of the Inst. Mgmt. Sci., Providence, and Graduate School of Business Admin. of the Univ. of Washington, Seattle (1970).

[2] S.E. Elmaghraby, Some network models in management science (Springer, Berlin, 1970).

[3] J.R. Meyer, Techniques of transport planning (The Brookings Institution, Washington, 1971).

[4] A. Charnes, C. Colatoni, W.W. Cooper and K.O. Kortanek, Economic social and enterprise accounting and mathematical models, Accounting Rev. 47 (1972) 85.

[5] R.L. Ackoff, The concept of corporate planning (Wiley–Interscience, New York, 1970).

[6] G.W. Gershefski, Building a corporate financial model, Harv. Business Rev. 47 (1969) 61.

[7] G.W. Gershefski, Corporate models – the state of the art, Mgmt. Sci. 16 (1970) B303.

[8] F. Knight, Risk, uncertainty & profit (Houghton Mifflin, New York, 1921).

[9] K. Borch and J. Mossin, Risk and uncertainty (Macmillan, London, 1968).

[10] J. von Neumann and O. Morgenstern, Theory of games and economic behavior, 2nd ed. (Princeton Univ. Press, Princeton, 1947).

[11] W. Shewhart, Statistical method from the viewpoint of quality control (Graduate School Press, U.S. Dept. Agr., 1939).

[12] A. Wald, Statistical decision functions (Wiley, New York, 1950).

[13] A. Dvoretzky, J. Kiefer and J. Wolfowitz, The inventory problem, Econometrica 20 (1952) 187, 450.

[14] A.F. Veinott, The status of mathematical inventory theory, Mgmt. Sci. 12 (1966) 745.

[15] H. Cramer, On some questions connected with mathematical risk (Univ. of California Press, Berkeley, 1954).

[16] H. Buhlmann, Mathematical methods in risk theory (Springer, Berlin, 1970).

[17] B.H. Klein, The decision making problem in development, in: The rate and direction of inventive activity: economic and social factors (Princeton Univ. Press, Princeton, 1962).

[18] A.H. Bobis and A.C. Atkinson, Analyzing R & D investments via dynamic modeling, Chem. Eng. 77, No. 5 (1970) 133.

[19] W.J. Abernathy, Some issues concerning the effectiveness of parallel strategies in R & D projects, IEEE Trans. Eng. Mgmt. EM-18 (1971) 80.

[20] W.J. Abernathy and R.S. Rosenbloom, Parallel strategies in development projects, Mgmt. Sci. 15 (1969) B486.

[21] A.H. Bobis and A.C. Atkinson, A mathematical basis for the selection of research projects, IEEE Trans. Eng. Mgmt. EM-16 (1969) 2.

[22] B.V. Dean, Operations research in research and development (Wiley, New York, 1962).

[23] M. Allais, Method of appraising economic prospects of mining exploration over large territories, Mgmt. Sci. 3 (1957) 285.

[24] L. Friedman, A competitive bidding strategy, Opns. Res. 4 (1956) 104.

[25] F. Hanssmann and B.H.P. Rivett, Competitive bidding, Opns. Res. Q. 10 (1959) 49.

[26] M.H. Rothkopf, A model of rational competitive bidding, Mgmt. Sci. 15 (1969) 362.

[27] C.R. Pelto, The statistical structure of bidding for oil and mineral rights, J. Am. Statist. Assoc. 66 (1971) 456.

[28] G. Dantzig, Linear programming under uncertainty, Mgmt. Sci. 1 (1955) 197.

[29] M. Beckmann and H.P. Kunzi, Economic models, estimation and risk programming: essays in honor of Gerhard Tintner (Springer, Berlin, 1969). In particular see: J.K. Sengupta, Distribution problems in stochastic and chance constrained programming, p. 391; A. Charnes and W.W. Cooper, Deterministic equivalents for optimizing and satisficing under chance-constrained programming, p. 424.

[30] A. Charnes and W.W. Cooper, Chance-constrained programming, Mgmt. Sci. 6 (1959) 73.

[31] G.K. Sengupta, Distribution problems in stochastic and chance-constrained programming, in: Economic models, estimation and risk programming, eds. M. Beckmann and H.P. Kunzi (Springer, Berlin, 1969).

[32] R.E. Fricks, Probabilistic programming 1950–1963: an annotated bibliography, Case Western Reserve Univ., Cleveland, Tech. Mem. No. 155 (1969).

[33] R.E. Fricks, A research bibliography on "two-stage" probabilistic programming, 1964–1969, Case Western Reserve Univ., Cleveland, Tech. Mem. No. 160 (1969).

[34] E.F. Fama, Risk, return and equilibrium, J. Polit. Econ. 79 (1971) 30.

[35] L.J. Savage, The foundations of statistics (Wiley, New York, 1954).

[36] D.G. Champernowne, Uncertainty and estimation in economics, Vol. 3 (Oliver & Boyd, Edinburgh, 1969).

[37] K. Borch, The economics of uncertainty (Princeton Univ. Press, Princeton, 1968).

[38] K. Borch, General equilibrium in the economics of uncertainty, in: Risk and uncertainty, eds. K. Borch and J. Mossin (Macmillan, London, 1968).

[39] H. Raiffa, Decision analysis (Addison–Wesley, Reading, 1968).

[40] R. Schlaifer, Analysis of decisions under uncertainty (McGraw-Hill, New York, 1969).

[41] D.V. Lindley, Making decisions (Wiley–Interscience, New York, 1971).

[42] C.J. Grayson, Jr., Decisions under uncertainty, Harvard Business School, Cambridge (1960).

[43] W. Fellner, Probability and profit (Richard D. Irwin, Homewood, 1965).

[44] S.A. Schmitt, Measuring uncertainty (Addison–Wesley, Reading, 1969).

[45] J.A. Morales, Bayesian full information structural analysis (Springer, Berlin, 1971).

[46] L.J. Savage, Difficulties in the theory of personal probability, Phil. Sci. 34 (1967) 305.

[47] P.C. Fishburn, Decision and value theory (Wiley, New York, 1964).

[48] P.C. Fishburn, The theorem of the alternative in social choice theory, Opns. Res. 19 (1971) 1323.

[49] R.V. Brown, Research and the credibility of estimates, Harvard Univ., Boston (1969).

[50] K.J. Arrow, Essays in the theory of risk bearing (Markham, 1971).

[51] H.M. Markowitz, Portfolio selection (Wiley, New York, 1959).

[52] W.F. Sharpe, A simplified model for portfolio analysis, Mgmt. Sci. 9 (1963) 277.

[53] W F. Sharpe, Portfolio theory and capital markets (McGraw-Hill, New York, 1970).

[54] J. Tobin, Liquidity preference as behavior towards risk, Rev. Econ. Stud. 25 (1957–1958) 65.

[55] J.W. Pratt, Risk aversion in the small and in the large, Econometrica 32 (1964) 122.

[56] N.H. Hakansson, Optimal entrepreneurial decisions in a completely stochastic environment, Mgmt. Sci. 17 (1971) 427.

[57] D.B. Hertz, Investment policies that pay off, Harv. Business Rev. 46 (1968) 96.

[58] F.S. Hillier, The evaluation of risky interrelated investments (Elsevier, Amsterdam, 1969).

[59] J.J. McCall, Probabilistic microeconomics, Bell J. Econ. Mgmt. Sci. 2 (1971) 403.

[60] P.C. Fishburn, A comparative analysis of group decision methods, Behav. Sci. 16 (1971) 538.

[61] R.L. Winkler, Probabilistic prediction: some experimental results, J. Am. Statist. Assoc. 66 (1971) 675.

[62] P.E. Green, Bayesian decision theory in pricing strategy, J. Marketing 27 (1963) 5.

[63] N.C. Dalkey and O. Helmer, An experimental application of the Delphi methods to the use of experts, Rand Corp., Santa Monica (1962).

[64] N.C. Dalkey, The Delphi method: an experimental study of group opinion, Rand Corp., Santa Monica (1969).

[65] H.I. Ansoff, Corporate strategy: an analytical approach to business policy for growth and expansion (McGraw-Hill, New York, 1965).

[66] G.A. Steiner, Managerial long range planning (McGraw-Hill, New York, 1963).

[67] A. Strauss, An introduction to optimal control theory (Springer, Berlin, 1968).

[68] R.A. Howard, Proximal decision analysis, Mgmt. Sci. 17 (1971) 507.

[69] R.A. Howard, Decision analysis: applied decision theory, Stanford Res. Inst., Menlo Park (1966).

[70] H.M. Weingartner, Capital budgeting of interrelated projects: survey and synthesis, Mgmt. Sci. 12 (1966) 485.

[71] R.F. Byrne, A. Charnes, W.W. Cooper and K.O. Kortanek, A discrete probability chance-constrained capital budgeting model, Opns. Res. 6 (1969) 172, 225.

[72] R.F. Byrne, A. Charnes, W.W. Cooper and K.O. Kortanek, C^2 and LPU^2 combinations for treating different risks and uncertainties in capital budgets, in: Studies in budgeting (Elsevier, Amsterdam, 1971).

[73] F.S. Hillier, A basic approach to the evaluation of risky interrelated investments, in: Studies in budgeting, eds. R.F. Byrne et al. (Elsevier, Amsterdam, 1971).

[74] B. Näslund, A model of capital budgeting under risk, in: Studies in budgeting, eds. R.F. Byrne et al. (Elsevier, Amsterdam, 1971).

[75] H. Albach and W. Schüler, On a method of capital budgeting under uncertainty, J. Math. Phys. Sci. 4 (1970) 208.

[76] H. Laux, Expected utility maximization and capital budgeting subgoals, Unternehmensforsch. 15 (1971) 130.

[77] S.W. Hess and H.A. Quigley, Analysis of risks in investments using Monte Carlo techniques, in Chem. Eng. Symp. Ser. 42: Statistics and numerical methods in chemical engineering, Am. Inst. Chem. Engrs., New York (1963).

[78] D.B. Hertz, Risk analysis in capital investment, Harv. Business Rev. 42 (1964) 95.

[79] J.F. Magee, Decision trees for decision making, Harv. Business Rev. 42 (1964) 126.

[80] J.F. Magee, How to use decision trees in capital investment, Harv. Business Rev. 42 (1964) 79.

[81] R.F. Hespos and P.A. Strassmann, Stochastic decision trees for the analysis of investment decisions, Mgmt. Sci. 11 (1965) B244.

[82] R.M. Adelson and J.M. Norman, Operational research and decision-making, Opnl. Res. Q. 20 (1969) 399.

[83] R.F. Byrne, A. Charnes, W.W. Cooper and K.O. Kortanek, Some new approaches to risk, Accounting Rev. 18 (1968) 18.

[84] K.J. Cohen and E.J. Elton, Inter-temporal portfolio analysis based on simulation of joint returns, Mgmt. Sci. 14 (1967) 5.

[85] R. Wilson, Investment analysis under uncertainty, Mgmt. Sci. 15 (1969) B650.

[86] J.R. Bright, Technological forecasting for industry and government (Prentice Hall, Englewood Cliffs, 1968).

[87] R.U. Ayres, Technology forecasting and long range planning (McGraw-Hill, New York, 1969).

[88] M.J. Cetron, Technological forecasting (Gordon and Breach, New York, 1969).

[89] E.B. Roberts, Exploratory and normative technological forecasting: a critical appraisal, Technol. Forecasting 1 (1969) 113.

[90] J.C. van Horne, The analysis of uncertainty resolution in capital budgeting for new products, Mgmt. Sci. 15 (1969) B376.

[91] R.F. Byrne, A. Charnes, W.W. Cooper, O.A. Davis and D. Gilford, Studies in budgeting (Elsevier, Amsterdam, 1971).

[92] L.Y. Pouliquen, Risk analysis in project appraisal (Intern. Bank for Reconstr. and Develop., Washington, 1970).

[93] S. Reutlinger, Techniques for project appraisal under uncertainty (Intern. Bank for Reconstr. and Develop., Washington, 1970).

[94] I.M. Siroyezhin, Risk and uncertainty in the management of soviet firms, in: Risk and uncertainty, eds. K. Borch and J. Mossin (Macmillan, London, 1968).

[95] L. Unčovský, Some problems of risk in a socialist economy, in: Risk and uncertainty, eds. K. Borch and J. Mossin (Macmillan, London, 1968).

[96] S. Thore, A dynamic Leontief model with chance constraints, in: Risk and uncertainty, eds. K. Borch and J. Mossin (Macmillan, London, 1968).

[97] C. Upton, A model of water quality management under uncertainty, Water Resources Res. 6 (1970) 690.

[98] A.W. Blackman, Jr., The role of technological forecasting in the analysis and planning of new ventures, paper presented at Inst. Mgmt. Sci. Meeting, Houston (April 1972).

[99] N. Gonedes, Accounting for managerial control: an application of chance-constrained programming, J. Accounting Res. 8 (1970) 1.

[100] R.B. Larson, The optimal choice of corporate growth plans under risk, Case Western Reserve Univ., Cleveland, Tech. Mem. No. 225 (1971).

[101] O. Helmer, Multi purpose planning games, Inst. for the Future, Menlo Park (1971).

[102] J.C. Chambers, S.K. Mullick and D.D. Smith, How to choose the right forecasting technique, Harv. Business Rev. 49, No. 4 (1971) 45.

M. Ross, ed., OR '72. North-Holland Publishing Company (1973)

10

PLANNING UNDER UNCERTAINTY: DISCUSSANT 1

Planification dans des conditions incertaines: porte-parole 1

STOCHASTIC PROGRAMMING

PETER KALL

Institut für Operations Research, Universität Zürich, Zürich, Switzerland

The very wide, excellent survey of David B. Hertz convinced me, that there is no real possibility to enter into competition with him. Therefore, I decided to restrict myself to one special field of planning under uncertainty, namely stochastic programming. Problems of stochastic programming arise whenever some, or all, coefficients of a linear program are random variables with known probability distributions. Obviously a lot of quite different types of problems may arise and be meaningful in such situations. In fact three types have been investigated in more detail up to now. These are: distribution problems, two stage problems and chance constrained problems. In the following, I shall try to explain these problems and to give some hints to the state of the art in handling them. This shall not at all be an attempt of a complete survey. This is impossible within 10 minutes even considering that stochastic programming is a very young object of research.

1. Distribution problems

Distribution problems arise in the so-called "wait and see" case, i.e., the decision maker is allowed to wait for the actual values of the random variables and then to determine an optimal solution of the linear program. However, he is interested in knowing the probability distribution of the optimal value in advance.

One essential theoretical question is whether there is a Borel measurable function defined on the coefficient space which coincides with the optimal value whenever it exists, i.e., whether the optimal value is a random variable in the true mathematical sense. A positive answer is given to this question in the very general case by Kall [1] and Walkup and Wets [2].

Another problem is to get a finite partition of the coefficient space which allows us to calculate the distribution of the optimal value by integration over the elements of this partition and by adding all these parts. It turns out that it is quite easy to define such a partition theoretically but that this partition may be hard to handle computationally. Bereanu [3] proposed that for special cases we use decision regions, as understood in parametric programming. He supposed that these sets could be used to define the partition mentioned above in very general cases with original distributions of continuous type. But just recently it was shown by a simple counterexample, that this suggestion does not hold in general.

Therefore, we still lack efficient computational methods for solving the general distribution problem, since Monte Carlo methods cannot be regarded as efficient where large scale linear programs are involved.

2. Two stage problems

Two stage problems, as well as chance constrained problems, are of the so-called "here and now" type, i.e., the decision maker has to decide on the original decision variables before knowing the actual values of the random coefficients. The assumption of the two stage model is that there is a second stage linear program which permits, at least sometimes, compensating the violations of the original constraints occurring after the determination of the original decision variables and of the actual values of the random coefficients. The problem then is to optimize the expected sum of the original and the second stage program's objectives. This model is also known as stochastic programming with recourse.

The theory of two stage programming is very highly developed. For example Wets [2] has shown that the feasible region with respect to the original variables is convex as is the total objective. For the complete recourse case, i.e., where almost certainly any original decision allows a compensation to occur then there are convexity and differentiability results with respect to the total objective (shown by Kall [1] and Wets [4]). Furthermore, necessary and sufficient conditions for the complete recourse case were derived by Kall [1]. Due to inequalities, first proved by Madansky [5], one may generate upper and lower bounds of the optimal value of the total objective by replacing all random coefficients by their expected values and solving the resultant linear program.

Another question was whether it is reasonable from the point of view of decision theory to choose a fixed program using the original variables or whether it would not be better to look for a mixed strategy. However, Wessels [6] proved that there is always a pure strategy which is optimal and thus gave a recent justification for the two stage programming model introduced by Dantzig [7]. Further decision theoretical aspects of this model have been investigated by Marti [8].

Computational problems are by no means solved. Up to now only a few special types may be solved by efficient algorithms. For example the "discrete distribution—complete recourse" case is amenable to the application of decomposition methods. Another special type — to my knowledge due to Beale — has the following characteristics: only the right-hand side coefficients are random and equally (orthogonal) distributed and the recourse matrix consists of a positive and a negative identity matrix. (This is a very special complete recourse case). Then the problem may be reformulated as a convex quadratic program. For a similar case having exponentially distributed right-hand sides, Wets [4] proposed to truncate the Taylor series of the total objective beyond the second order term and to use this quadratic program as approximation of the original problem. Tock [9] derived error bounds for this approximation. In my opinion this approach, i.e., looking for fairly good approximating models for which efficient methods exist, could be helpful in yielding further practical results in more general cases. At the moment it seems to be hopeless to apply standard nonlinear programming methods to the general model, since the representation of the total objective and its gradient is so complicated, that it is completely inefficient to solve functional equations involving them (as required in some gradient methods) or even to evaluate them repeatedly.

3. Chance constrained problems

As mentioned above chance constrained problems are of the "here and now" type. In these models an optimal decision shall be made with respect to the objective provided the decision is feasible with at least a predefined probability given the original constraints. Examples are easy to find which show that in general the feasible region is not convex. Therefore, the specialists are concerned with trying to find conditions on distribution types and relations to the predefined probability levels asserting convexity. For discrete, normal and Cauchy distributions Marti [10] got such results. Recently Prekopa [11] found convexity theorems for a rather wide class of distributions containing more than the normal and exponential cases.

Besides the convex discrete distribution case (which leads obviously to a linear program) and some other very special cases almost no efficient methods are known. Nevertheless, the model seems to be of great practical importance and generally may not be replaced by the two stage model. This will be clear if one thinks, for example, of a diet problem: No responsible physician would agree with defining finite penalty costs for violating human helath, but physicians are very familiar with the idea of requiring certain probability levels for the success of their treatments.

References

[1] P. Kall, Qualitative Aussagen zu einigen Problemen der stochastischen Programmierung, Z. Wahrscheinlichkeitstheorie und verwandte Gebiete 6 (1966).

[2] D. Walkup and R. Wets, Stochastic programs with recourse, SIAM J. Appl. Math. 15 (1967).

[3] B. Bereanu, The distribution problem in stochastic linear programming, in: Methods of operations research, Vol.8 (A. Hain, Meisenheim).

[4] R. Wets, Programming under uncertainty: the complete problem, Z. Wahrscheinlichkeitstheorie und verwandte Gebiete 4 (1966).

[5] A. Madansky, Inequalities for stochastic linear programming problems, Mgtm. Sci. 6 (1960).

[6] H. Wessels, Stochastic programming, Statistica Neerlandica 21 (1967).

[7] G. Dantzig, Linear programming under uncertainty, Mgmt. Sci. 1 (1955).

[8] K. Marti, Entscheidungstheorie; Grundlagen der stochastischen Optimierung, Dissertation, Universität Mannheim (1970); Z. Wahrscheinlichkeitstheorie und verwandte Gebiete, to be published.

[9] H. Tock, Numerische Behandlung einiger spezieller Probleme der stochastischen Programmierung, Diplomarbeit, Universität Zürich (1968).

[10] K. Marti, Konvexitätsaussagen zum linearen stochastischen Optimierungsproblem, Z. Wahrscheinlichkeitstheorie und verwandte Gebiete 18 (1971).

[11] A. Prekopa, Logarithmic concave measures with applications to stochastic programming, Acta Sci. Math. (Szeged) 32 (1971).

M. Ross, ed., OR '72. North-Holland Publishing Company (1973)

11

PLANNING UNDER UNCERTAINTY: DISCUSSANT 2

Planification dans des conditions incertaines: porte-parole 2

NORMAN TOBIN

B.E.A., Ruislip, Middlesex, England

Dave Hertz has given us an impressive and useful tour around broad areas of the field, and his script has more references than I shall have time to read between now and the next IFORS Conference. There is little I could usefully add to most of the areas he has covered.

There is, however, one broad question I would like to put to Dave, namely, are you happy with the scene you have described? Do you feel that some of the areas you have discussed are sadly underdeveloped, or even overdeveloped? Do you see an urgent need to concentrate on particular areas, or do you feel that overall there has been a good balanced advance across the whole field? Having asked the questions, I shall give an answer of my own, but not necessarily one you will agree with.

After reading this morning's paper, we need have no doubts, even if we had any before, that a great deal of research has gone into developing and elaborating normative theories of decision making under uncertainty. On the other hand, quite a lot of work has been done by many people on descriptive theories of decision making under uncertainty. There are many, but I think particularly of Cyert and March and in particular of their book "A behavioural theory of the firm". Anyone who has spent his working life solely absorbed in the intricacies of normative decision making might be driven to despair by reading their extremely plausible account of how decisions are actually taken.

Incidentally Cyert and March have a lot to say about uncertainty *avoid-*

ance, which they see as a characteristic of all kinds of decision behaviour in the firm, from price collusion between firms to collaboration in maintenance of professional standards. It is a very rational tactic in the face of uncertainty but not one that I have seen included explicitly in any normative modelling.

A few years ago there was a meeting in Birmingham at which 3 top executives with high reputations in large organisations, one in production, one in marketing and one in finance, were asked to speak on "decision making in practice". They spoke in turn, independently, but the same message was coming out of each of them. They all signed a lot of pieces of paper, but they hardly ever took any decisions. In each case, their job was the creation and maintenance of a system of men and procedures from which decisions emerged. Implicit in most normative models and much of the general theory of decision making is this concept of an actual decision-making event. But as many people have pointed out, decision making is more commonly an evolutionary process. By the time a decision came up to any of these three men it was either easy, (being heavily weighted one way) trivial, (being evenly balanced) or a quick leap in the dark that had to be made because there was no more time to study the issues further.

Now, given that we have an immense body of normative decision theory and a fairly wide range of more or less convincing descriptive models of decision making, who is doing anything to knit these together? It seems to me that one of the outstanding problems of OR in the field of planning under uncertainty is not in the modelling of particular problems, but in the design and establishment of systems in which actual people are likely to come to better decisions, aided by the kinds of normative models that we know how to produce.

Maybe Dave Hertz or someone else knows of work in this field that I have missed, but in my view this is an area that very few people are trying to tackle systematically. For some time we have seen this gap as the problem of implementation, of how to persuade managers or planners to use the excellent models we have constructed. People like Churchman and Bavelas have shown that even in surprisingly simple situations it is extremely difficult to persuade anybody of anything. And yet some models do get used. How should we structure a normative model so as to have a high probability of having a real impact on planning decisions, when they are going to be taken not by a single planner or a coherent committee or team but in various degrees by an undefined set of people from various parts of the organisation? My own current view is that the answer will be in interactive models accessed from different sides by planners covering different aspects of the problems. They will then not only interact with the models, but with each other through the models.

There is a reference in the paper to Ackoff (p.587) and adaptive planning and the quotation demonstrates his awareness of these problems in structuring the planning in the light of actual human behaviour. In fact he is one of the people who are active in this area. Another who has devoted his main attention to it is Stafford Beer. Stafford's pronouncements on planning and control under uncertainty have a flavour of certainty that many people find unpalatable, but I feel that when we come to understand these problems better we shall find ourselves repeating much that he has been saying for a long time.

M. Ross, ed., OR '72. North-Holland Publishing Company (1973)

12

ROLE OF MODELS IN CORPORATE DECISION MAKING

Rôle des modèles dans les processus de décision globaux

H. IGOR ANSOFF and ROBERT L. HAYES

Vanderbilt University, Nashville, Tennessee, U.S.A.

Abstract*. The salient conclusions of this paper can be summarized as follows: The focus of managerial model-building activity has been on a relatively narrow segment of the total domain of model-building opportunities. Typically it is concerned with operating problems and the management of process, with problems which occur at middle management levels, which are determined by economic variables and have scalar payoff functions and quantifiable variables. This segment *does not* include managerial problems which are of highest current priority and which are most consequential to managerial decision-making. Priority areas which have received little attention from modelling are: strategic and integrative, concerned with management of managerial capability, occur at top and bottom levels of management, determined by a multi-disciplinary set of variables, have multi-dimensional payoff functions, contain non-quantifiable variables. The type of models built have been determined more by professional values and standards of the professional model builders and less by the applicability and useability of the results in decision-processes. As a result, the rate of acceptability has been low, the relationship of managers and model-builders has frequently been one of mutual distrust and suspicion. The segment has been predominantly focused on a particular step in overall decision making process, namely the evaluation of outcomes and choice of action alternatives. As a result, little attention has been paid to systems-wide modelling of the planning function. Existing planning process models have been largely derived from trial and error experience. In spite of concern with model quality, the modelling activity has contributed little to emergence of a body of theory which would provide a foundation for a science of management. Today's "management science" is primarily a collection of model libraries, richer in variety of techniques than in variety of distinctive models.

* This abstract both summarizes and presents the main conclusions of the paper.

The distinction between models and techniques for operating on models has seldom been recognized. The bulk of management science literature is concerned with techniques for manipulating models. The stock of distinctive and different models has been relatively small and static. Developments of the past few years suggest that many of the past shortcomings are being overcome. The significant trends are shift of model-builders' priorities to problems of planning and system design, interest in multi-disciplinary modelling, retreat from maximizing models to "decision support" (what if) models, improved relationships between professional planners and management scientists, advent of real-time computers.

1. Introduction

When we were invited to submit this paper, we were asked to deal with corporate *planning* models. If planning is broadly defined as decision making in advance of and in preparation for future events, then virtually all management science models have been planning models because they use future time as an ordering independent variable. Thus, an inventory control model is a planning model because it deals with future outcomes of alternative control policies.

If planning is taken, somewhat more narrowly, as decision making based on forecasts of future occurrences and events, inventory type models would not qualify because the data base typically uses past experience which is assumed to remain both secularly and statistically stable in the future. We would argue, however, that this is a limitation of past inventory model building practices and not of the inherent problem of inventory control. Inventory control models *ought* to take account of futurity such as impending obsolescence of inventories, inflation trends, variability and trends in supply prices, etc.

Finally, if planning is defined, as it frequently is, as an organization-wide social-political-cognitive dynamic process of making decisions and proposing action schedules based on forecasts of future events, an important distinctive element of decision-process modelling is introduced which until very recently had not been a major concern of management science modellers. As we hope to show, however, modelling of decision processes ("designing of planning systems") is a process which ideally should incorporate and integrate a variety of "problem models" such as inventory control or strategic portfolio selection. Again the fact that a majority of problem planning models has remained ad hoc, unintegrated in the ongoing planning systems, is due to a deficiency in the state of the art and not an inherent barrier between problem models and process models.

It is true that "planners" have historically concerned themselves with system models and management scientists with problem models; it is true that planners have frequently been "on line" participants in management and many management scientists have been "off line" arms' length contributors; it is true that emphasis on forecasted data has been much stronger among planners than management scientists; it is true that planners have done rudimentary modelling because their major concern has been with applicability rather than construction of models; it is true that management scientists have constructed models of much greater sophistication because their concern has been with scientific quality rather than applicability; it is finally true that, until a few years ago, planners and management scientists were not on speaking terms. We suggest, however, that all of these are historical facts; we suggest that recent years have shown new mutual awareness of planners and management scientists; and we finally suggest that this is a very welcome trend which augurs well for the future progress of planning practice. In keeping with this trend, in this paper we shall take planning to encompass all modelling activities which include use of forecasted occurrences in managerial decision making. We will, however, point to special issues and difficulties, such as, for example, the problem of model validation, which are brought about by this element of futurity in decision making.

2. Scope of the paper

In this paper we shall use the term *model* in a very broad sense as a description of some part of the real world which has explanatory and/or predictive powers. Models are put to two generic uses. Those who apply the scientific method use modelling as a crucial step in the chain of hypothesis formulation, model building, prediction, validation. A model which is proven valid attains the status of a theory. The net result is a better understanding of some part of the real world.

In management, models are used to gain insight into the value of action alternatives and thus provide a more explicit basis for choice than direct application of judgment and experience. The net result is a prescription for managerial action. The focus in this paper is on the latter use of models. We shall be less interested in modelling as a theory-building tool and more as a problem-solving one.

Our focus will be further limited to "corporate" problem-solving models applicable to organizations, such as the business firm, with well-defined environmental boundaries and exhibiting identifiable purposes in their activities.

Thus, "societal" models such as the French national plan, or the recent global modelling, underwritten by the Club of Rome, are beyond our perspective [1].

A major set of criteria by which a model is judged describes its *quality*. Thus a model is *non-trivial* if it permits inferences not readily perceivable by direct observation; it is *powerful* if it offers a large number of non-trivial inferences; and it is *elegant* if a minimum of carefully selected analytic tools are used to produce a model of great power. This set of criteria is the major concern of model builders whose scientific reputation, chances of promotion, and personal self-fulfillment are all highly correlated to the quality of models they build.

Another major set of criteria is the *applicability* of a model to the world of action. A model is *relevant* if it treats a problem of importance to the manager; it is *valid* if a high degree of confidence exists that inferences obtained from the model will, in fact, occur in the real world; it is *useable* if it has a high probability of being accepted as a basis for action; it is *cost-effective* if the improvement in organizational action exceeds the expense of developing and applying the model. This set of criteria is correlated with objectives and rewards of the model users, the managers.

As an inspection of the respective criteria readily reveals, the point of maximum quality does not coincide with the point of maximum applicability. As a result, the model builder's preference for quality and the manager's applicability create a dialectic tension, not unlike the tension between research/development and production usually found in the business firm.

We propose to use this tension as a major explanatory variable of the current state of modelling in purposive organizations. Historically, model quality has been a major concern of the profession of management scientists, while model applicability has been neglected and poorly explored. For this reason, our emphasis shall be on the latter.

We shall start by constructing a crude model of our own of the temporal sequence of information processing events which occur in the course of a managerial-decision process. We hope that it will be sufficiently non-trivial to permit useful inferences in two distinctive categories of modelling. The first is modelling of the management-wide activity which perceives needs, recognizes and diagnoses the problem, develops and selects new action directions, schedules these and induces others in the organization ("workers") to carry them out. Here our interest will be in *total decision process modelling*.

The second category of interest is *models of process steps* – events which occur in the course of the overall process. Here the most commonly recognized and modelled step is the choice of the preferred action alternative (commonly known as "decision modelling"). However, we propose to call attention to a number of other steps in the overall process which received varying amounts of modelling attention.

We shall construct another crude taxonomic model of managerial problem space to identify, first, the domains which have been modelled and second, those of managerial priorities. Domains of *problem-models* will be compared with domains of priorities to comment on the relevance of historical modelling activities. The problem and the process dimensions can easily be identified as orthogonal descriptors which locate a model with the managerial activity.

We shall then address the problem of model choice — the process by which a selection is made from among the multitude of available problem-solving methodologies. Our interest will be in identifying the variables affecting model choice and in examining the model builder-manager dynamics which lead to selection of a particular model.

Finally, we shall consider the important problem of validation both of the problem model itself and of the analyses performed by it. It will be apparent that, as the problems being modelled tend more toward the ill-structured end of the spectrum, the difficulties associated with validating the analytic processes performed upon models become as great as those involving the model itself.

3. Modelling of decision processes

It is commonly assumed that a management scientist's task is confined to constructing models for problems which had been previously recognized and diagnosed by others in the organization. In the world of practical decision making, this perspective is unduly narrow, like the peak of an iceberg above the water. The prior events of problem perception and recognition, as well as later events of converting the answer into action, are equally and sometimes more influential on the success of the overall decision-making process. On one hand, practicing managers are concerned with organizationally unrecognized but important problems which fall "between-chairs", and do not receive attention until a proper response is overdue. On the other hand, they are equally concerned about theoretical "solutions" that fail to produce appropriate organizational actions. Therefore, in dealing with modelling we need a broader definition of decision making. One such definition is represented by eleven problem-solving steps shown in fig. 1 [2].

Step 1 is *problem recognition* at which a manager somewhere in the

State of the art

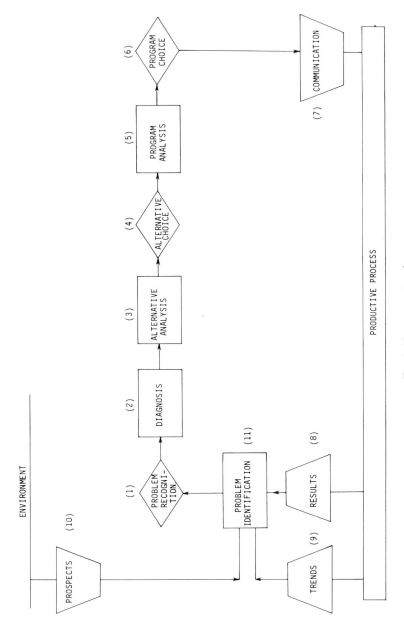

Fig. 1. Management cycle.

organization decides that there is a present or potential discrepancy between the probable and existing conditions. The desired state of the organization is that the discrepancy is important enough to require priority attention [2]. As fig. 1 indicates, this first decision step may be triggered by information from inside the organization or from the environment.

Recognition of a problem is based on symptoms such as loss of profit, concern with future profitability, perception of an exciting opportunity. Usually these symptoms, while identifying existence of *a* problem do not tell the manager what *the* problem is: where in the organization, when in time, what key variables affect its solution, etc. Therefore, a necessary step 2 is *diagnosis*. Diagnosis pinpoints the problem and, almost invariably, suggests some alternatives for solving the problem.

Step 3 is *alternative analysis*. Here additional alternatives are generated and an evaluation is made of the merits of respective alternatives. Analysis can range from use of judgment to an elaborate quantitative model of the outcomes of a number of competing alternatives.

Step 4, *alternative choice*, is separated from step 3 to indicate that identification of desirable change does not become actionable until management makes a specific commitment to them. When a single manager both performs an analysis and makes the action decision, steps 3 and 4 tend to blend. However, when separate people are involved (such as a staff analyst and line manager, or a consultant and a client) the distinction becomes of crucial importance to the success of problem-solving. It is frequently observed that, when managers fail to make explicit action decisions, problem-solving in the firm tends to be erratic and ineffectual.

Analysis and choice concern themselves with the question of *what* change should be made in the firm. The next step 5, *program analysis*, is concerned with *how*: the step-by-step actions, expenditures of money, use of people and other resources, changes in relationships and structure. Just as step 3 is a consideration of alternative "whats" and their consequences, step 5, in principle, is similarly analysis of alternative "hows". In practice, it is usual to design only one program. Step 6, *program choice*, is another step of management commitment to a particular path by which the chosen change will be implemented.

Step 7, *communication and leadership*, is concerned with communicating the chosen programs to the people who will have to carry them out and of creating positive attitudes toward this work.

The work begins, but in a real sense the problem has not been solved; it is not solved until the programs have been carried out and *measurement of results* (step 8), and *assessment of trends* (step 9) and *prospects* (step 10) have been brought together in *problem identification (step 11)* to reveal that the originally perceived deficiency no longer exists.

The eleven step process offers a widely applicable array of *information processing* steps identifiable in all decision processes, both on individual and organization-wide levels, Descriptive studies of organizational behavior have produced a fair agreement on a particular variant of fig. 1 known as an *incremental model* of decision making: the process is triggered by adverse results (step 8) and not by anticipation of the future (steps 9 and 10); problem recognition is delayed until substantial record of adversity is accumulated; diagnosis is superficial; strategy analysis involves search for familiar precedents which represent incremental departure from the previous states of the organization; strategy alternatives are generated one at a time; strategy decision is a "satisficing" one: the first alternative which restores the organization to a "level of aspiration" is accepted. Typically, this decision is based on judgment and political consensus rather than rational choice. Because the decision is incremental and familiar, no formal programming is involved; implementation is informal [3–5].

The incremental model is widely observable and has been empirically [4] tested. Some observers have claimed that the model should also be used as a *prescriptive* paradigm. ᵀn one case [3] the proponent argued that a more complex approach is inherently inapplicable in large complex organizations.

Historical evolution of decision-making in large organizations does not support this assertion. Since the beginning of this century, purposive organizations, particularly the business firms, have developed a succession of organization-wide decision routines which are complex and non-incremental. The success of these in some firms led to imitation by others, and to their codification as prescriptive decision models [6]. The principal systems models which evolved are (a) *control system* which is designed for removing an organizational deficiency (inputs 9 and 10 are suppressed) using sophisticated problem identification and diagnosis procedures; (b) *planning system* which seeks to anticipate deficiencies and/or opportunities using inputs from steps 9 and 10; and (c) *information systems* which incorporates steps 8, 9, 10, and sometimes 11, and thus provides input to the other two. All three systems are inherently non-incremental. Planning (in particular, its later stages of development: entrepreneurial-strategic PPBS) combines multiple-alternative evaluation techniques with sophisticated programming.

To our knowledge, no systematic empirical investigation has been made of the relative advantage of a formal control or information system over incremental informal decision making, although spreading usage and impressionistic comparison between firms with well-functioning systems and those without, support the value of formal systems. Recent empirical studies of the value of planning systems [7,8] *do* support the hypothesis that formal planning produces better organization results than informal incrementalism. Thus, formal systematic arrangements for non-incremental decision-making are not only inherently applicable, they also produce superior organizational results. However, the state-of-the-art of modelling of such systems is still rudimentary.

As suggested above, current system models are not the result of careful, validated modelling, but are rather an outgrowth and codification of organizational trial and error. As a result, while non-trivial, they possess very little predictive power and certainly very little elegance. They consist largely of information flow diagrams, similar to our Fig. 1, which partition the decision in sub-decisions, indicate interconnection, flows and their timing. The individual transfer functions (the boxes on fig. 1) are typically specified in terms of inputs, outputs, and the sets of variables to be included in the function. The relations between variables and algorithms for input-output transformation, are typically not specified. Because of the lack of specific transformation function, such systems models lack predictive power; it is not possible, for example, to predict the decision output of a particular change in environmental prospects, or a particular trend*.

There is a similar lack of understanding of the structure of systems. For example, information systems are typically constructed to follow the lines of organizational authority, whereas it is commonly observed that lateral communications play a major role in decision making. Another example, in design of planning systems there is a common failure to differentiate between three principal foci of authority (steps 1, 4 and 6). Systems are designed as if the alternative choice is the key point of authority, whereas observations suggest that problem identification (setting problem agenda) is the deciding point in some complex systems and that program decision is the key in others.

Nor are the process properties of modern management systems well understood. A number of questions critical to successful functioning of a system remain unanswered. For example, what is the optimal time horizon in a planning system, what is the optimal number of decision levels (the "looping problem"), what is the appropriate feedback time constant (for that matter, what is the nature of the appropriate feedback signal), what is the appropriate level of flexibility for a given system ("requisite variety" in cybernetic terms), etc.

---

* Modelling of the decision process should not be confused with total organization modelling such as industrial dynamics, which will be discussed later.

Lacking predictive power and knowledge of optimal design constants and procedures, the state-of-the-art of system modelling today is that of crude design tools for assigning responsibilities and assuring coherent and timely flows of information in complex organizations. Refinement is largely lacking to make possible deliberate tailoring of the system to a particular organization or a particular set of environmental conditions.

Contrasted with the rudimentary state of practice, the importance of complex systems for decision making has been rapidly growing since the middle 1950's, as evidenced by the rapid spread of their application not only to purposive organizations but also to governments and even the total human race. Nor is there a lack of apparently relevant technology. Servo system design theory, mathematical control theory, information science, cybernetics, and so-called general systems theory – all have high relevance to understanding and design of complex decision systems. In fact, a considerable amount of theoretical speculation is available [9], but few of the efforts have produced models which are specific enough to be applied to and tested in practical managerial activity.

One of the major reasons for the lack of this connection has been suggested by Stafford Beer [10] : a lack of access to the "board room" – lack of acceptance of management scientists by top managerial levels which have responsibilities for system-wide decisions. Repeated comments by both managers and management scientists do indeed suggest a mutual "credibility gap" which has in the past impeded the latters' acceptance by management and particularly by top management. We suggest two major reasons for the gap: the first, an interpersonal behavioral conflict between manager and decision-maker and the second, a lack of homeomorphism between the variable space of the scientist and the relevant variables in complex managerial problems.

Application of models typically involves a dyad: the *model builder* who suggests the course of action and the *manager* who selects and initiates action. Historically, the two actors typically have had different backgrounds, different motivations, different objectives [11]. The manager's objective is to produce organizational results, while the model builder typically seeks model quality. The model builder expects others to generate and to legitimize problems. He is not held responsible if a particularly pressing problem is not receiving organizational attention. On the other hand, the manager *is* responsible. He may be severely penalized failing to focus organizational attention on a critical problem, but he receives little reward for selecting an elegant solution to a problem of secondary importance.

Differences in outlook lead to differences in model preferences. The model builder's natural propensity is for models which will give the greatest latitude for application of his skills and which will produce the greatest recognition and reward for him. This is to be found in highly non-trivial, powerful, and elegant models. In application to managerial problems, these preferences become *criteria of problem choice*. The model builder seeks to work only on problems which offer opportunities for models of high quality.

However, such problems are not necessarily the most urgent or the most consequential from the manager's viewpoint. Further, he may feel that, even when working on highly relevant problems, in order to obtain quality, the model builder oversimplifies reality. A solution which is maximal within the model may be sub-maximal or even infeasible because of exclusion of important variables. Or the model may overstructure and overelaborate intuitively obvious relationships.

Thus, the model builder's desire for quality not only affects the choice of model structure and content; it also affects the choice of problems to be tackled. "Solvability" rather than importance becomes the choice criterion with the result that much of management science literature has been referred to as "solutions in search of problems". The manager's concern, on the other hand, is with "problems in search of solutions".

The model builder's search for elegance is expressed through a preference for closed-form tautological formulations which yield maximal solutions. In order to maximize, the analyst needs to abstract from the manager a scalar (or collinear) utility function. This implies a problem-solving sequence in which the model builder first interacts with the manager to define the problem and learn the objective, then he goes off on his own, usually for a protracted period of time, to build the model, gather data, verify, develop alternatives, evaluate them, and select the preferred one. Only after all this is done does he return to the decision maker with the results.

By this time a conflict has been set up. Having been left out of the solution, the manager is suspicious of the model. He has no assurance that the model is rich enough and not an emasculation of reality. But he has no ready means for reassuring himself because the model builder typically presents results in a complex, technical language of his trade, foreign and incomprehensible to the manager. An excellent example is provided in many models of risk analysis, where risk is defined in terms of mathematical variance and covariance, terms which have little to do with the manager's understanding of risk taking.

Lacking the method and language for testing the analyst's result, the manager is left to make intuitive judgments about the accuracy of the objective function; the importance of excluded variables (usually human variables); the validity of the relations in the model. Most importantly he is left to judge the usefulness of the model within the larger managerial cycle: has the proper problem been recognized, has it been suitably diagnosed, is it important relative to other problems? At the other end of the scale: is the solution implementable within the organizational culture and time and resources available?

Instead of model quality, the manager wants relevance. Triviality is of no concern, if the solution will have a major impact on organizational success. Maximality *within* the model is irrelevant if the elegant solution is not useable; richness of the model is preferred to clarity of structure and quantification of variables.

Contradictions and conflicts arising from methodological preferences of management scientists have been amplified by limitations of the variable sub-space which they are equipped to handle. Viewed from a scientific disciplinary point of view, organization is a complex economic–informational–psychological–sociological–political system. Problems encountered within the system do not map readily on the respective subsets of disciplinary variables. Some can be treated with adequate validity as pure "economic or business problems", some as "people problems", etc. A majority, particularly top management problems, are strongly influenced by more than one variable subset.

But a majority of modelling in management science has proceeded not from the imperatives of the problems but from the variable space encompassed by perspective of the model builder, who in today's prevailing culture is either an economist *or* a mathematician, *or* a psychologist, *or* a political scientist, etc. Whenever the analyst encounters a problem whose important variables are essentially uni-disciplinary, the chances are high that the model will be valid; whenever a problem is multi-disciplinary, it is likely that the model will have low validity, regardless of its quality. This difficulty was succintly described by Alfred North Whitehead when he said: "The man with a method good for purposes of his dominant interests is a pathological case in respect to his wider judgment on the coordination of this method with a more complete experience." [12] In dealing with complex multi-disciplinary problems, even if the manager and the scientist enjoy mutual acceptance and trust, no amount of access to the "board room" is likely to produce long-term benefits, simply because it will be perceived soon enough that the models do not reflect the working reality.

The bulk of theoretical attention to systems has come from scientists whose scientific biases are for mathematical, rational, cognitive, informational processes. Organizational behavior (both formal and informal) certainly contains these, but it is strongly influenced and sometimes determined by psychological—sociological—political variables. Therefore, it is not surprising that progress in development of system models has been largely confined to experiential trial and error.

This conflict of values and perceptions and lack of homeomorphism between disciplines and managerial problems has in the past substantially inhibited scientific modelling of decision processes. In part, this led to exclusion of model builders from the ranks of "planners"; in part it has caused a lack of recognition of similarity between "planning" and "modelling"; in part, it created mutual distrust and lack of appreciation between managers and management scientists. Model builders accused managers of near-sightedness, of reluctance to admit the analyst to the higher levels of management. [10] Decision makers reacted with charges that quantitative techniques are inherently inapplicable, inconsequential to esoteric planning decisions.

Recent trends promise substantial improvement of this situation [13]. One of these has been "discovery" by management scientists of planning (and systems in general) as a valid and important area for modelling attention. Another is a growing recognition that, in spite of claims to the contrary, management science has largely been uni-diciplinary and that development of multi-disciplinary modelling is needed for tackling systems modelling.

A very important development has been the emergence of a new type of working relationship. Instead of serial roles: manager poses problem, analyst solves it, manager *accepts* recommended solution (sic italics), the new arrangement is of parallel participation in which the manager and model builder interact during the solution process. The analyst's role is to construct the model and evaluate "what if" consequences, but no longer to seek maximal solutions. The manager applies decision functions to alternatives, provides judgments on certain exogenous variables, enriches the decision through his judgment and experience. Advent of real-time computer technology made it possible to involve the busy manager. It has also made possible rapid joint exploration of multiple alternatives.

The price paid by the analyst is a loss of maximality in decisions and hence lower quality of models. He gains both acceptability of his work, as well as a more satisfying working environment.

4. Modelling of steps in the decision process

The preceding section focused on modelling the decision-making process as a total system. Here we turn attention to modelling of the constituent decision blocks within the system. By contrast with modelling of the decision-process, we shall refer to this activity as *modelling of steps in the decision process*.

As discussed in the preceding section, systems modelling emerged from the urgent needs of managers with the resulting emphasis on the criterion of applicability and the sacrifice of the criterion of model quality. In modelling of decision steps the predominant initiative came not from managers but from model builders and the priorities have been in reverse. The dominating criterion, influencing the choice of situations to be modelled and types of models to be built, has been model quality. As a result, professional propensities of the model-builders, and not necessarily the real world priorities, determined choice of the steps to be modelled.

Looking at fig. 1 from this vantage point, one would predict, for example, that a political scientist, who believes in the populist theory of democratic decision making, would point to the information sub-system as the critical area for attention because, given knowledge, a political democracy would arrive at correct decisions without the benefit of externally imposed rationality [3]. His concern with the system-wide process would focus on the political variables determining conflict resolution processes.

A psychologist would likely emphasize the block dealing with communications and interpersonal influence processes in the belief that harmonious human relations are the key to effective decision making. His approach to the system would focus on "organizational development" – harmonizing of the human environment. Or the might focus on problem-solving situations in which human relations variables are dominant in the outcomes [4].

A mathematician, an economist, an engineer, or a physicist – all brought up within the tenets of Cartesian rationality – would naturally view the system problem as one of analytic-logical information transformation, subject to both exogenous and endogenous statistical uncertainties. Lack of control over and strong influence of exogenous variables would naturally lead them to an "open systems" formulation of the problem. When looking for critical links in the systems chain which need to be modelled, a natural scientist would point to alternative analysis and choice (steps 3 and 4) as the critical steps because it is the unique choice of what an organization *should* do that, according to a rationalist, sets the direction, permits unbiased communication, rallies individuals around a common course of action.

For a variety of historical reasons, scientists brought up in the Galilean–Cartesian scientific method have been the most numerous modellers of decisions with industrial psychologists and organizational psychologists being a not too distant second. Other disciplines, sociology and political science in particular, have tended to stay away from managerial modelling and concerned themselves largely with speculative theory building [15–18]. The bulk of the models of natural scientists has thus been focused on alternative selection. The underlying philosophy is that alternatives should be judged in accordance with the relative outcomes they induce in the productive processes of the firm (see bottom of fig. 1). As a result, the focus of modelling is not on how the decision is arrived at (the eleven-step chain) but rather on their resulting consequences on the "shop floor": e.g., what is the resulting output of a certain inventory reorder procedure, what is the buying response to a particular advertising campaign, what is the profitability of a particular procedure scheduling a fleet of oil barges on the Rhine, etc.

In the last thirty years, a large number of models of this type have been built. Because they yield maximizing solutions and they satisfy model builders' search for quality, "well-structured" models [19] constitute the bulk of this number, This type of model requires quantifiable variables, explicit relations among them, existence of algorithmic computational procedures for determining the "best alternatives". More critically, these also require the existence of a scalar (or collinear) utility function of managerial preference.

Most of the models thus constructed have been addressed to specific managerial decisions and have had little impact on theory building – an enlargement of general understanding of how managers and organizations behave. The reasons for this include a relatively narrow scope of the problems tackled, lack of model power, and particularly lack of elegance and "transparancy" which make possible important general inferences. This has created a peculiar paradox.

While a great deal of effort and professional attention has gone into model quality through application of sophisticated mathematical and computational techniques, the final utility of the effort must rest not on the criterion of quality but on the criterion of applicability. Put into somewhat simpler terms, thirty years of modelling efforts have added very little to the emergence of what might be called a "management science"; instead they add up to a library of models addressed to specific problem types. Thus, "management science" modelling must be judged on the extent to which it has affected managerial action. On this criterion, we would judge the success to be very modest in comparison with the amount of effort expended.

As mentioned, successes occurred in problem areas which met the requirements of the well-structured problem. This most frequently occurs in unidisciplinary problems concerned with economic use and allocation of physical and monetary resources in the firm. These are typically found at so-called "middle management" levels. Below this level at "first line supervision", "people" variables begin to dominate. Above, in "top management", problems quickly become multi-disciplinary with psychological, sociological and political importance to economic variables. Neither the interpersonal relation variables nor sociological-political variables lend themselves readily to quantification. This and the lack of homeomorphism between the natural scientists' perspective and the problem space has severely limited the number of modelling successes at both top and low level management levels. At top management success was further limited by the failure (despite many years of effort by decision theorists) to reduce the managerial utility function to a scalar (or even collinear) quantitative form, and even the failure to prove its temporal stability.

Thus success in modelling alternative selection in the total enterprise has been limited*. At one time, it appeared as if a simulation technique known as *industrial dynamics* promised an answer. While the open-system feedback philosophy of ID does indeed appear to be one of the most promising approaches to modelling of the total enterprise, the success of this particular approach has been limited. One of the reasons is that the variable space included in ID simulations has been largely limited to economic variables; another is that it assumed quantification of managerial variables which do not lend themselves to quantification (e.g., "quality of a firm"); a third is that by virtue of the particular model-building technique ("brute force" simulation of existing reality), applications of ID have shown limited power in predicting non-trivial outcomes [20]**.

Another technique which offered promise for modelling of the total enterprise is *systems analysis*. It should be pointed out that SA *is not* decision process modelling of the eleven steps of fig. 1; it is rather large scale modelling of alternative selection, steps 3 and 4 (occasionally including programming steps 5 and 6). In fact, this very limitation to rational choice has been a major deterrent to the success of SA. Typically systems analysts have failed to take specific account of the fact that *large enterprise-level choices usually involve large numbers of problem-solving participants,* with the result that the process is practically never fully rational but is rational—political—sociological—psychological. For example, difficulties encountered by PPBS in

---

* Here again practice-derived models do exist; e.g., the financial model of the firm expressed through the balance sheet and operating statement. But it has a limited scope of variables, permits a limited amount of inference, and provides little basis for generalization.

** Recent work on global modelling of global ecology does not appear to change these conclusions.

the Defense Department and other branches of the government demonstrate vividly that logical rationale becomes greatly "distorted" by political processes [21].

The content of SA is, first, a "large problem philosophy", all "important" variables must be included. (Unfortunately it is virtually impossible to find operational prescriptions on how this "importance" is to be determined.) Second, SA is an assortment of analytic techniques borrowed largely from techniques of marginal analysis used in economics. On the whole SA models tend to be rudimentary as models, through very impressive in the scope of the problems tackled and the volume of data handled. In this respect they closely resemble decision process models described earlier in this paper.

Returning to fig. 1, we have so far focused our attention on modelling alternative selection in steps 3 and 4 as practiced by natural science-based management scientists. While the bulk of the effort has been on steps 3 and 4, substantial effort and more successful applications have occurred in programming (steps 5 and 6). Here experience gave birth a long time ago to techniques of financial budgeting. Like most experience-derived techniques, budgeting has had high applicability and low quality. More recently, under pressure of industrial necessity, a variety of programming-scheduling techniques (critical path and varieties of Pert) has been developed, which are more sophisticated than budgeting. These have found applications in large project management both in industry and government. In part, the success of programming techniques was due to the relatively well-structured nature of programming problems. An important part of their success is traceable to the fact that they signalled a departure by modellers from insistence on well-structured modelling, specifically departure from insistence on a specifiable utility function.

The steps of fig. 1 which received third priority attention from modellers are encompassed by the information generation activities (steps 8, 9, 10). Trend extrapolation, commonly known as forecasting, has a long, voluminous (cf. regression analysis), and technically unexciting history since, in its various ramifications, it is little more than complex curve fitting. Prospect identification, which was triggered by increasing incidence (since early 1950's) of discontinuities in historical trends, is conceptually very complex and is currently receiving increasing emphasis. Methodologically, modelling of prospect identification is still a weak area. However, because of the nature of the underlying problem, it has so far avoided unidisciplinary distortion which has plagued alternative analysis.

Measurement of organizational performance, capacities, and capability (step 8 in fig. 1) has received less attention from management scientists than any other part of the decision process. Just as steps 9 and 10, this step is all-important to the validity of subsequent ones and yet it received little attention from modellers. The prevalent data base available today in most organizations is derived from accounting data. The shortcomings of the accounting data and its inadequacies for managerial decision making are widely recognized in business firms. And yet, curiously, there has been as little progress from the practical side (such as took place in evolution of system models) as there has been from the theoretical developments. It is only recently that concern with "human resource accounting", "social accounting", "social indicators" began to give a long overdue impetus to development in this area.

Finally, problem recognition, diagnosis, and communication (steps 1, 2 and 7) appear to have been largely neglected by management science modellers. The neglect of the latter is easy to understand because it is an interpersonal influence process and, therefore, outside the interests and competence of natural scientists. The neglect of problem finding can only be explained by the traditionally narrow view of scientific modellers described in the opening of the earlier section on systems modelling.

The focus of our remarks has been on the accomplishment of scientists trained in economics-mathematics and committed to the Galilean–Cartesian scientific method of inquiry. Their contribution to formal modelling has been predominant. It should be recognized, however, that industrial psychology has contributed important models, such as, for example, models for personnel evaluation and selection, which are widely used in practice. Psychology has also contributed a highly distinctive approach to improvement of managerial decisions through humanistic psychology which is based on existential rather than the scientific-rational philosophy of the management scientists. Group dynamics techniques, such as T-groups, have been accepted and are used as widely as the rational models which we have been discussing. However, their discussion is both beyond the scope of this paper and the competence of the authors.

5. Modelling of problems

We now turn attention away from managerial process to the problems which are handled by it. We have already had occasion to comment on one dimension of the problem space, namely, the differences among problems at different hierarchical levels in the organization. Here we deal with more fundamental differences which arise from different modes of organizational interaction with the environment. As previously, we shall briefly describe a simple model which will be used as a basis for discussion. (For a more detailed exposition of the model see [22].)

We shall concern ourselves with a class of social organizations which can be called purposive. All of these share the following characteristics:

(1) They deliver to society identifiable goods and/or services. They are rewarded for these in the form of sale price, university tuition, hospital charges, municipal water bill payment.

(2) The goods and services are the result of an internal resource conversion process: "raw materials" are taken in (untutorted student, sick patient); "value is added" to them by internal activities, and the final product is returned back to society.

(3) Because of their continuing need to replenish consumed resources, all purposive organizations need a consistently positive difference (called profit in the firm) between costs incurred and the rewards received from the environment. If the difference remains negative for an appreciable period of time, the organization withers and dies.

(4) The very fact that all members of a purposive organization engage in activities directed toward a common output suggests that they pursue common objectives. The differences among organizations, however, are very significant. In the business firm, the objectives are readily identifiable because they form the core of a common performance discipline. The focus is on the *outcome* of the activities whether it be growth, profit, or market share. The performance against these objectives is measurable in quantitative terms and is usually measured through periodic reviews. New proposals for products, markets, or organizational changes, although not as easily measurable, are weighed in terms of their potential contribution to the objectives. A series of objective-setting techniques, such as budgeting, management by objectives, and long-range planning is used in many firms. There are, of course, differences among firms in the extent to which they use the quantitative discipline of outcomes to run the business. Generally, firms that use it extensively are the more aggressive and successful ones.

Non-profit organizations resemble less aggressive firms in their common failure to use objectives as a management tool. The common agreement of the participants is not on common objectives but on the common *process* (curing patients, educating students, pursuing research excellence). Because they are process-oriented and because non-profit organizations lack quantitative measurements and techniques for evaluating outcomes, the performance discipline is usually lax and much less rigorous than in the firm. This provides latitude for individuals to pursue their individual objectives simultaneously (though not always in accord) with those of the organization.

Such purposive organizations are essentially open systems (though the degree of "openness" varies greatly) in the fact that their nature and their survival are strongly conditioned by interaction with the external environment*. They engage in this interaction by "solving problems" – removing intra-organizational dissonances which are partly due to internal political conflicts and partly due to the uncertainties and imbalances in the relation between the organization and the environment.

It is convenient, therefore, to subdivide the organizational problem space according to the condition of the *linkages* between the organization and environment. When the pattern of the linkages (the products, the customers, the technology) remains relatively stable over time, the organization can be said to be engaged in *operating behavior* (the term *competitive* applies a little better to the business firm). In this behavior, the organization seeks to fulfill its particular objectives through exploiting exchange of goods/services and rewards to the organizations. The activity has both external and internal components. Externally the business firm advertizes, sells, distributes, purchases. Internally, it produces, maintains inventories, maintains, improves and expands facilities, develops and maintains organizational capabilities, promotes harmonious work-oriented behavior of the human resource.

A second, fundamentally different mode of behavior focuses on change and maintenance of viable linkages with the environment. This we call *strategic* (in the firm *entrepreneurial*) behavior. Internally, it involves setting the organizational objectives, creating new products, developing new physical, organizational capabilities. It also involves cutting back on programs which are no longer viable environmentally. The external component deals with determining major thrusts, developing new markets, test-marketing new products, and introducing them on a large scale to the customers.

When a firm's product line is confined to a single linkage, strategic and operating behavior occur sequentially in the course of the life cycle: first, strategic (product introduction) then operating (exploitation), then again strategic (divestment). When the firm's product family consists of several different life cycles, the need to maintain a proper and harmonious balance between the strategic** and operating mode raises another problem which we

---

* This point has been largely lost on some early sociologists; e.g., Simon, Thompson, Bernard, Cyert and March, who sought to explain behavior largely in closed system terms. A present trend toward an open systems perceptive is exemplified in the recent work of Thompson, Lawrence and Lorsch and others.

** Frequently, the term "strategic" is used to apply to top management activity. Note that in our definition, strategic activity pervades the organization. (For further discussion, see [23].)

shall call *integrative*. It involves allocation of resources between strategic and operating activities, maintenance of a balanced strategic linkage portfolio, provision of an organizational framework in which the other two activities can coexist, resolving conflicts between them and assuring timely transition between the modes.

Within each major mode of organizational behavior, it is useful to distinguish two distinctive types of managerial activity: management of the process and management of the capability to support the process. Examined in the light of the taxonomic structure of table 1, historical focus has been predominantly on the *operating activities of modelling with little relative attention paid to the strategic and virtually none to the integrative.* Within the class of operating activities, the *predominant emphasis has been on modelling of the process and very little on modelling of organizational capabilities.*

The reasons for this focus are traceable to two sources. The first of these has already been explored: the previous experience, the interests, the technical equipment, and the philosophical perspective of the scientists who en-

Table 1
Managerial tasks

Mode of behavior	Management activity (planning, implementing, controlling)	
	process	capability
strategic	determination of position strategy	development of overall structure and systems for strategic process
	development, introduction, divestment of new business and products	development of capabilities and capacities for strategic process
operating	determination of competitive strategy	development of structure and systems for operating process
	exploitation of existing product-markets through purchasing, manufacturing, distribution, advertising, selling	development, maintenance, improvement of capabilities and capacities for operating process
integrative	balancing of strategic and operating activities through strategic portfolio balance	determination of overall structure and systems
	management of transfer from strategic to operating activities, resolution conflicts	development of capabilities and capacities for transfer from strategic to operating activities and for divestment activities

tered the management science model building field in the mid 1940's have been strongly homomorphic with the characteristics of the operations problems (and particularly with process management) and not with either the strategic, or the integrative ones.

The second reason lies in managerial problem priorities at the time management science was launched in the immediate post-WW II period. When management scientists first sought to apply their talents and knowledge to the business firm in the late 1940's and early 1950's, operating behavior had a dominant priority on the managerial agenda [22]. The economy was emerging from a war with a strong pent-up demand for civilian goods of any and every kind. "The name of the game" was to produce efficiently, to distribute, to sell competitively through the traditional linkage. Neither the strategic problem of linkage change, nor the integrative problem of accommodating relatively low level strategic activity among the predominant operating activities seemed of importance.

Thus at the time of its inception, management science was responsive to managerial priorities. Unfortunately, it also became a captive of these. In the past thirty years it produced an impressive volume of process management models, has witnessed successful application of many of these, and trained several generations of management scientists whose capabilities and rewards are derived from proliferation of similar models and refinement of previous ones.

In the meanwhile, the priorities of the firm and other purposive organizations have undergone a drastic change. A discussion of the underlying reasons is beyond the scope of this paper [24]. The important consequence was both a revision and an intensification of priorities. Thus, the absolute importance of operating competitive behavior did not diminish but increase. But first the strategic behavior, and more recently the integrative behavior, displaced the operating as priority items on the managerial agenda [25].

For modellers this poses a peculiar dilemma: the large literature of operations models is not obsolete to the extent it applies to the change of competitive conditions*. These models are not as well accepted as they should be and they do not adequately cover the domain of operating problems. Thus, much progress can be made in enhancing their acceptance and in developing additional ones. On the other hand, this effort would make only a modest contribution to closing the gap between the management scientist and the

---

* An example of obsolescence: production allocation and scheduling models in firms which have become multi-national which do not take account of financial, cultural, political discontinuities among production sites.

manager (particularly top manager) because the latter's highest priorities are no longer in the operating domain. The matter is complicated further by the fact that several generations of management scientists have a large vested interest in proliferating the literature on operations process management, and very few with interest, competence, and a "track" record in strategic and integrative processes or in capability modelling.

The problem is serious but not hopeless. First, comfortable living is still to be made in modelling operations management. Secondly, in this period of general social upheaval there are already foci of research which are seeking to break out of the past tradition, particularly outside the United States where the management science tradition is not ingrained. Finally, the worst outcome would not be atrophy of management science modelling but perpetuation of an unattainable yearning to gain full partnership with the manager in advancing the frontiers of management knowledge.

6. Model selection

The process of generating a decision in an ill-structured environment is a complex one. The occurrence of an event in the form of a real-world problem stimulates the development of some kind of model of that problem (M_1). The transformations effected on the actual problem to produce the abstract model are represented by T_1. Once the model has been constructed, it is the responsibility of the manager to develop a set of inputs, frequently in the form of contingency-type questions. A set of transformations, T_2, is then selected by the analyst to analyze the inputs in the context of the model. The resulting outputs are then used by management as a basis for decision-making.

An example from the operational side of the enterprise will help clarify the concept. If the problem is one of scheduling and resource allocation in an oil refinery then we can think of the transformation T_1 as the process by which materials flow diagrams and various financial and physical constraints are represented by a set of linear-forms, M_1. The inputs may consist of such questions as the effect of the addition of a new pipeline or the expansion of a refinery. The transformation T_2 might be a technique such as linear programming, and the resulting outputs may be the optimal schedules or minimum costs for a given set of inputs.

Alternatively, M_1 might consist of an industrial dynamics type of model involving various time lags and feedback loops. T_2 might then be a computer simulation in which the results of system perturbations can be explored. This second type of model, while not yielding an optimal solution, would have the advantage of being able to handle a multi-dimensional objective function.

As we have previously stated, the management activity known as planning is characteristically too complex to admit to either simple formulation or straightforward methods of attack. In order to cope with these problems, practitioners of management have developed a range of what may be called *ill-structured techniques*, which introduce partial structuring to problem-solving. When joined to the methodology of quantitative and fully analytic model building, these techniques offer a *spectrum* of *methodologies* which can be arranged in the order of increasing mathematical precision of the model using the following descriptors [2] :

(1) Variables – which can be either implicit or explicit, ordered or quantified.

(2) The relationship among variables – which is sometimes absent; sometimes consists of simple variable groupings; sometimes has qualitative and quantitative submodels; and, in its most precise form, establishes explicit fully quantitative relations among variables.

(3) The payoff function or the decision rules – which sometimes are made explicitly; sometimes expressed as a checkoff list; sometimes as a vector of quantities. and sometimes as a scalar function.

(4) The solution alternatives – sometimes single; sometimes multiple but not exhaustive; and sometimes exhaustive of all possibilities.

(5) The solution process – which may be use of judgment, or analysis, or both: and which can vary from a simple trial and error procedure to a complicated and explicit procedure for arriving at the best answer.

In the terminology suggested at the opening of this section, the choices of items one through three constitute a model, whereas items four and five describe the solution technique.

An illustrative array of alternative problem-solving methodologies is shown in table 2*. The table suggests that a model builder need not alternate between extremes of intellectual precision and intuitive judgment in his problem-solving work. It further suggests a higher level problem-solving activity which occurs every time a segment of the real world is represented through a model. This activity is *the choice of the methodology by which the problem is to be solved.* And, just as the spectrum of methodologies itself, the problem of choice from the spectrum is poorly explored. It is clear from the above discussion that there are essentially two, non-independent, choices to

---

* Table 2 represents a taxonomy of *methodologies*. A sample taxonomy of *problem classes* which can be mapped onto the methodologies is to be found in [26, chap. 15].

Table 2
Spectrum of problem structures

Attribute	Structure type							
	Unstructured	Criteria	Influence matrix	Decision flow work	Quasi analytic	Analytic heuristic	Quantitative heuristic	Algorithm
Variables	implicit ←→ identified and ordered		← implicit & explicit → ← ordered & quantified →			← explicit → ← quantified →		quantitative
Relation among variables	none	none	variables identified, sensitivity relations established	variables grouped, groups sequenced	partly explicit, quant. & analytic function	analytic	quantitative	
Payoff	none	none	non collinear vector, dimensions explicit, function implicit ← weighing or judgment →		partly explicit, quant. & analysis	vector analytic; shifting goal priorities	← scalar goal →	quantitative
Selection of alternatives	single	← require search → ← small number →			← large number →			self-generating
Selection of solution	← judgment → ← justification →	← trial and error →			judgment & analysis; simulation	analysis; heuristics; difference reduction		algorithm
Example	resolution of interpersonal conflict	R&D project selection	planning system design	strategy formulation	organization simulation	chess program	warehouse location program	linear program of distribution

be made: T_1, the transformation of the real world into an abstract model and T_2, the technique which will be used to perform any analyses on the model.

The choice of a T_1 circumscribes a set of possible M_1's and hence the range of possible T_2's. Similarly, prior selection of a computation procedure, T_2, would serve to constrain the feasible set of T_1's, a situation which frequently occurs when a model builder with too strong a disciplinary bias constructs a model based on the tools he has available to analyse it. Assuming that the choice of T_1 is to be made deliberately in some rational manner, then the criteria which underlie this choice should include the six which follows.

6.1. Availability of theory relevant to the problem situation or of previously successful models of similar situations

Theory is useful in providing a set of rules or guidelines on which to base a decision model or procedure, thus avoiding the necessity of starting from scratch each time. Most planners unfortunately find themselves in a situation in which theory is in the developmental stage and where few, if any, attempts have previously been made to construct practical models. Much of the theory and models that do exist derive from microeconomics and hence are lacking in many of non-quantitative variables essential to top management. The resulting phenomenon, alluded to earlier, has practitioners finding themselves in a leading role in developing theory. Since the typical manager may have less than an overwhelming interest in formal theory development, a strong bias is created in favor of choosing the intuitive approach with no effort being made to reap the benefits of explicit modelling.

6.2. Cost of model building and analysis

First and most obvious of these costs are the direct costs of human and financial resources committed to the modelling effort. There is also presumably an opportunity cost arising from possible alternative allocation of these same resources. Another category of cost, seldom the concern of model builders, is the possible disruptive effect of a modelling effort on the operational aspects of the enterprise. This cost may arise in two places: during the actual construction of the models and later, if some attempt at real-time validation is necessary. These last two categories have two undesirable attributes in common: a potential to be very high relative to direct costs and a strong tendency to escape measurement in most accounting/information systems.

Also to be considered is the likely cost of installing and operating the solution. Since certain classes of models give rise to varying degrees of future implementation costs, a priori constraints on these expenses might serve to limit the feasible set of model alternatives. For example, a model based on a large-scale computer simulation that would itself require continuous maintenance and upgrading might be deleted from the set of feasible alternatives on the basis of an organizational commitment to lessen reliance on such models.

6.3. Availability, quality, and cost of empirical data

Once again a comparison with operating systems reveals significantly increased difficulty in providing the data base for planning models. First, the kinds of data needed are quite different: much of it is from sources external to the firm. Such information as must be gathered from within the organization frequently is of a type normally provided by current management information systems. Examples are such items as managerial capabilities and informal organization structure, both of extreme importance in considering major departures from the present product-market-technology position.

The extreme difficulty in providing data for models of ill-structured problems (or, alternatively stated, of creating models within the constraints of available data) is dramatized in a recent survey of R & D organizations. It showed that, of the over 150 R & D project selection models appearing in the literature, fewer than 10 were actually used. Much of the failure of these models to achieve implementation could be traced to unrealistic (from the point of view of existing information systems) data requirements.

6.4. Potential for and cost of validation

As models become more realistic approximations of management problems and the organization's environment, the opportunity for hidden assumptions and implicit relationships increases, rendering the job of validation more difficult. Since planning problems typically involve distant time horizons, the opportunity for direct empirical validation is usually lacking. More will be said about this problem later.

We should point out that, with respect to its role in the model selection process, validity should not be considered a binary variable. Not only would few model builders care to judge a model as being either "valid" or "invalid" but also few managers would be willing to pay the price for an "absolutely valid" model. As the degree of validity increases, the marginal cost of improvement presumably increases. At the same time the value to the decision maker of these improvements also increases, but most likely at a decreasing rate. A measure of benefit to cost ratio would therefore presumably peak at something less than the most valid model that money can buy.

6.5. Behavioral consequences to the organization arising from use of a particular methodology

Much of what belongs under this heading has been discussed earlier; it is useful to recognize that different reward and value systems affect different organizational participants in such ways as to give rise to potential for serious conflict surrounding the selection of a particular form of model. For example, attempts to introduce planning into organizations that do not reward it specifically have frequently failed.

The cultural acceptability of models also depends to a large extent on the skill level of potential users. Corporations that have combined management education programs with attempts to implement significant modelling efforts have found the additional cost worthwhile.

A further behavioral issue that has arisen in the context of planning models is an attempt by managers to "game" the model rather than the real world. This is a satisfactory procedure provided that the model is isomorphic to the real world, but disastrous when it is not. Clearly this behavior is equally the fault of a poorly conceived reward system, a subject which itself could well be the object of modelling.

6.6. Potential benefits to the organization arising from the selection of a particular model

Benefits accruing to the users of models are highly subjective in nature. One of the most obvious would be improved decisions, to the extent that this can be measured. The trouble is, of course, that this seldom can be measured, except possibly in laboratory situations, and surrogate measures must be sought. One such measure, the number of alternatives examined, has been shown to increase through the use of formal models as compared to implicit models [27]. Similarly, the processing time associated with analyzing an alternative can usually be expected to decrease when formal models can be used in conjunction with computers. The concept of measuring the benefit of improved decisions itself suffers from the familiar malady of information shortage. Management information systems are seldom designed to provide a posteriori evaluation of either the process by which a particular model was selected or the desirable and undesirable consequences of having chosen it.

Another benefit that has often been claimed for the formal modelling process is the greater clarity with which a manager sees the problem and the interrelationships of the variables. While this makes the rather strong assumption that the manager is intimately involved in the modelling effort, it is doubtlessly true that almost any device which allows a manager to make a normally internalized process explicit will be of some benefit.

The point that we would like to make most forcefully in this section is the need for a more deliberate process of methodology selection; as scientists we characteristically behave rather unscientifically in this regard. When, as managers, we employ non-manager model builders, we frequently accept their criteria for model selection as well as allowing ourselves to be constrained by their preference for techniques.

7. Model validation

The concept of model building and model using is a general one; the steps are present whether the problem is a well-structured one, like scheduling, or an ill-structured one, such as planning. There are, however, significant differences in the difficulties of validation depending on the degree of structure in the problem. The concept of validation is best considered as one of degree as opposed to an either-or notion; it seeks to ensure that the abstraction is sufficiently accurate for the purpose at hand. In the case of T_1 we are concerned that the conversion from real world to model is accurate; with respect to T_2 we ask whether the conversion of inputs to outputs is accurate, i.e., whether we have chosen the correct technique. In the literature of the management sciences, the problem of validation of the underlying model M_1 is frequently alluded to, but the papers have for the most part dealt mainly with the development of new T_2's or the improvement of old ones.

In well-structured problems, validation is onerous but it is usually possible to generate a set of indicators yielding some assurance that no serious errors have been made. Validation of T_2 has been less of a problem; algorithms* can be proven optimal and many of the heuristic techniques can be shown to yield solutions which are improvements over established benchmarks. But too little attention has been paid to the problem of determining that the model M_1 is a good representation of the real world, i.e. that T_1 is valid. This has led to a great deal of well-deserved criticism of operations research's cavalier

---

* An algorithm is, in fact, a computational procedure (T_2) which assures that not only valid but optimal use is being made of model M_1.

attitude toward the problem, the preference of most professionals historically having been the development of T_2's. Validation of T_1 is frequently aided by the possibility of empirically testing within the reasonable time and cost constraints. Even then, however, the experimental nature of the trial may make it difficult to detect the effect of missing variables. For instance, in our scheduling example, the absence of behavioral variables may not become apparent until full-scale implementation is attempted. Nor does the normal validation procedures give any assurance that the T_1 chosen is the best available.

This examination of validation difficulties in models concerned with well structured problems only serves to highlight the even greater difficulties associated with validation of models dealing with ill-structured problems such as planning. One difficulty arising at the outset is that T_1 and T_2 are seldom made distinct in planning models. A useful first step, therefore, is to recognize the dichotomy which does exist and proceed to examine the two separate validation problems.

The most stringent tests of validity that usually can be applied are a check for internal consistency and an analysis based on past experience with this type of problem. To the extent that the problem is unique, as top management problems often are, and the model is truly powerful and non-trivial, use of the model is likely to yield outputs that defy judgment based on past experience. And since validation criteria are usually applied only at the output stage, we are seldom able to discern whether bad output is the result of a poor mapping of the real world into a model (T_1) or improper analysis on the model itself (T_2).

It is interesting to look across the spectrum of problem-solving techniques and compare various categories with respect to their potential for validation. Starting at the far left side of table 2 with the most ill-structured problems, we find that the analytic technique T_2 is seldom made explicit. The problem-solving process is usually such that analytic skill cannot be substituted for "expertise". Further, the cause of defective output is not uniquely identifiable, and since measurement problems are severe it is often even difficult to judge output as defective or to determine which of the two actions is preferred.

As we move right toward the heuristic procedures, we find T_2 becoming explicit and we begin to gain the ability to judge alternative outputs – first against each other and then against some externally derived benchmark. When we reach the far right-hand column, we find explicit techniques which are demonstrably best; i.e., given M_1 we can prove that the output is optimal in some desired sense. At all levels, however, the fact remains that the quality of the output is no better than the quality of the least of T_1 and T_2*.

References

[1] D.A. Meadows et al., The limits to growth, A report for the Club of Rome's project on the predicament of mankind (Universe Books, New York, 1972).

[2] H.I. Ansoff, Managerial problem-solving, in: Management science in planning and control, ed. J. Blood, Jr., Tech. Assoc. of the Pulp and Paper Industry, Spec. Tech. Assoc. Publ. 5 (1969).

[3] C.E. Lindblom, The science of muddling through, Public Admin. Rev. (Spring 1959).

[4] R.M. Cyert and J.G. March, The behavioral theory of the firm (Prentice Hall, Englewood Cliffs, 1963).

[5] J.G. March and H.A. Simon, Organizations (Wiley, New York, 1958).

[6] H.I. Ansoff, The evolution of corporate planning, Rep. SRI Long Range Planning Service, Palo Alto (Sept. 1967).

[7] H.I. Ansoff, G. Brandenburg, R. Radosevich and F.E. Portner, Acquisition behavior of U.S. manufacturing firms, 1946–1965 (Vanderbilt Univ. Press, Nashville, 1971).

[8] R.J. House and S. Thune, Where long range planning pays off, forthcoming.

[9] H.I. Ansoff and R.G. Brandenburg, Design of optimal business planning system: a study proposal, Cybern. of Planning and Organization (March 1967).

[10] S. Beer, Decision and control (Wiley, New York, 1966).

[11] C.W. Churchman and A.H. Schainblatt, Researcher and manager: A dialectic of implementation, Mgmt. Sci. (Feb. 1965).

[12] A.N. Whitehead, The function of reason (Beacon Press, Boston, 1958).

[13] H.I. Ansoff, Long range planning in perspective, in: Proc. 15th CIOS intern. Management Congr. (Kogakusha Corp., Tokyo, 1969).

[14] N.R. Maier, Problem solving discussions and conferences: leadership methods and skills (McGraw-Hill, New York, 1963).

[15] H.A. Simon, The new science of management decision (Harper and Row, New York, 1960).

[16] J. Thompson, Organizations in action (McGraw-Hill, New York, 1967).

[17] A. Etzioni, Modern organizations (Prentice Hall, Inglewood Cliffs, 1964).

[18] W. Bennis, Planning of change, (Holt, Rinehart and Winston, New York, 1969).

[19] H.A. Simon and A. Newell, Heuristic problem-solving: the next advance in operations research, Opnl. Res. 6, No. 1 (1958).

[20] H.I. Ansoff and D. Slevin, An appreciation of industrial dynamics, Mgmt. Sci. 14 (March 1968).

[21] A. Schick, Systems politics and systems budgeting, Public Admin. Rev. 29, No.2 (1969).

[22] H.I. Ansoff, Management on the threshold of the post industrial era, forthcoming.

* For summary and conclusions see abstract.

[23] H.I. Ansoff, R. Decierck and R.L. Hayes, From strategic planning to strategic management, forthcoming.

[24] H.I. Ansoff, The firm of the future, Harv. Business Rev. (Sept.–Oct. 1965).

[25] R.H. Jones, GE's new strategy for faster growth, Business Week (July 1972) 52.

[26] W. Reitman, Heuristic decision procedures, open constraints and the structure ill-defined problems, in: Human judgement and optimality, eds. M. Shelly and G. Bragan (Wiley, New York, 1964).

[27] Michael Morton, S. Scott, Management decision systems (Harvard Press, Boston, 1971).

M. Ross, ed., OR '72. North-Holland Publishing Company (1973)

13

ROLE DES MODELES DANS LES PROCESSUS DE DECISION GLOBAUX: PORTE-PAROLE 1

Role of models in corporate decision making: discussant 1

JEAN CHARLES HOLL

Groupe METRA-Sema, Paris, France

L'ensemble des problèmes évoqués par les docteurs Ansoff et Hayes à propos du rôle des modèles dans le processus global de prise de décision répond tellement à mes préoccupations du moment que je dois bien avouer, qu'à titre personnel je regrette seulement de n'avoir pas eu plus de temps à consacrer à son analyse. Durant ces quelques minutes de présentation, je voudrais me placer strictement du point de vue de l'acceptabilité des modèles par les *hauts dirigeants* des entreprises.

Cette étude refleté très clairement le malaise dont les anciens de notre profession souffrent et précise le but vers lequel nous devrions tendre. J'en recommende la lecture attentive a tous ceux qui ont une foi suffisante en notre métier pour qu'une vérité finalement assez désagréable à accepter ne les entraîne pas à changer de profession. Je dois dire en fait qu'il n'est pratiquement aucun point de l'étude des docteurs Ansoff et Hayes sur lequel je ne sois pas d'accord. Dans ces conditions si, comme nous disons en France, "de la discussion jaillit la lumière", il y a aura peut-être de ma part discussion, il ne saurait en aucun cas y avoir contestation mais seulement projection d'un nouvel éclairage de ces problèmes à partir d'expériences vécues dans ce pays prétendument cartésien qu'est la France.

Ce qui me paraît le plus frappant est le conflit qui existe à l'intérieur d'un même individu, entre "l'esprit d'étude scientifique" et "l'esprit de décision et d'action". Presque tous ceux qui ont été à l'origine des hommes d'étude et sont devenues, au prix de quelques années de travail, des hommes de décision, ont profondément souffert de ce conflit qui leur a parfois donné le sentiment que leur précédente activité, celle d'étude, était d'une incroyable pauvreté face à la complexité de leur nouvelle activité, celle de décision. Et comme cela est très bien expliqué dans le premier schéma du texte, une bonne part de ce sentiment provient de l'incapacité des modèlisateurs à traiter l'ensemble du processus de décision, notamment les phases 7 et 8. Il est parfaitement exact que trente années d'effort des chercheurs opérationnels ont eu très d'impact sur l'image du management scientifique et sur son développement; je crois qu'il faut avoir aujourd'hui la franchise de le reconnaître et d'en analyser les causes en bons analystes que nous sommes, le courage d'y trouver des remèdes et la ténacité nécessaire pour les mettre en oeuvre dans un esprit de décision et d'action, ce qui peut impliquer un certain changement dans nos sociétés nationales et la Fédération qui nos réunit.

Je n'ai pas la prétention, dans une aussi courte discussion, de régler tous ces problèmes. Je voudrais seulement m'efforcer de préciser ce que je crois être quelques causes intermédiaires plus accessibles aux réformes et indiquer des voies pour ces réformes. Le divorce y est fort bien expliqué en termes de "qualité" et d'"applicabilité" des modèles, en termes de problèmes "partiels" ou "globaux", en termes pourrait-on dire de raisonnement "logique" et "analogique", enfin en termes de "confiance" et de "defiance". A ce haut niveau d'abstraction, les remèdes sont difficiles à imaginer. Essayons donc de trouver des causes intermédiaires.

J'en vois essentiellement quatre:

(1) Comme tous les metiers nouveaux celui de la recherche opérationnelle s'est initialement développé sur la base de nouvelles *techniques* mais nous n'avons pas su passer de cette phase d'artisanat technique à une phase de comportement industriel et ceci sur deux plans:

Nous avons dépensé beaucoup d'énergie à créer ce qui nous appelions de nouveaux modèles et fort peu à améliorer l'acceptabilité des anciens (un observateur encore plus sévère pourrait dire que nous n'avons d'ailleurs développé que quatre modèles: la programmation linéaire, la programmation dynamique, la programmation en nombres entiers et la programmation combinatoire).

Nous avons fondé nos actions de promotion (livres, revues, congrès...) sur ces techniques et non pas sur leur utilisation; comme il est dit dans le rapport, nous avons cherché des problèmes justiciable de nos solutions et non pas des solutions à des problèmes.

(2) Nous avons travaillé avec une majorité de gens *ignorant le fonctionnement d'une entreprise* soit parce que trop jeunes pour le connaître, soit parce que trop vieux dans notre métier pour ne pas le ramener à un ensemble d'équations.

(3) Nous avons subi l'effet de masque de l'*informatique,* qui en raison de son chrome, de son nickel, de son prix, se montre alors que nous ne nous montrons pas. Le paradoxe réside ici dans le fait que nous n'avons pratiquement pas profité du développement fulgurant... et anarchique... de l'informatique de gestion, alors que nous somme en train de souffrir de la désaffaction temporaire qu'éprouvent les chefs d'entreprises à son égard. Ceci parce que nous n'avons pas su nous en démarquer à temps.

(4) Nous avons laissé se transformer petit à petit notre *image* de la situation initiale A à la situation schématique actuelle B. L'image A était "la recherche opérationnelle est la réflexion scientifique d'un groupe d'hommes de compétences diverses face à un problème complexe". L'image B est devenue "la recherche opérationnelle est l'application de techniques mathématiques à la résolution d'un problème".

Je ne puis bien entendu dans ce cadre donner les moyens de réformer cette situation volontairement dramatisée; je n'en aurais d'ailleurs aucunement la compétence; il est tout de même possible d'indiquer quelques axes dans lesquels ils devraient se situer:

(1) Sans diminuer la qualité de technique de nos publications, y mettre l'accent bien plus sur les problèmes et les résultats que sur les méthodes; ne pas omettre cependant de préciser que de bons résultats nécessitent des méthodes qui ne sont pas à la portée de n'importe qui. Demander aux chercheurs opérationnels vétérans de ne plus traiter que des problèmes "globaux". Faire participer les dirigeants à nos associations.

(2) Considérer que l'enseignement du comportement des organisations est une chose aussi importante pour le jeune chercheur opérationnel que celui des techniques mathématiques. Cet enseignement doit être dispensé par des gens qui ont eu des responsabilités de décision pendant quelques années.

(3) Entreprendre une campagne pour nous démarquer de l'informatique de gestion qui demeure un des moyens de choix au service du management scientifique mais qui n'est que l'un d'entre eux.

(4) Revenir à l'état d'esprit initial de la recherche opérationnelle, précisément en travaillant sur des problèmes qui impliquent la présence conjuguée d'hommes de disciplines différentes.

Enfin j'ose à peine formuler ma dernière remarque sous la forme d'une question: que devons nous penser de la marque "recherche opérationnelle"? A la limite, ne faut-il pas réfléchir à son changement puisque la perception qu'en ont les hauts dirigeants est devenue trop étroite?

M. Ross, ed., OR '72. North-Holland Publishing Company (1973)

14

ROLE OF MODELS IN CORPORATE DECISION MAKING: DISCUSSANT 2

Rôle des modèles dans les processus de décision globaux: porte-parole 2

ALEXIS K. STRAUS

Swiss Federal Institute of Technology, Zürich, Switzerland

The authors presented a wide spectrum of ideas, so that my first thought was: how can I possibly bring a new viewpoint into discussion? Therefore I will merely pick out and comment a few details which it seems to me, might be of some importance for our discussion.

The model shown in fig. 1 (p. 136) and entitled "Management cycle" (in the text also referred to as "Sequence of information processing events" and "total decision process [modelling]") is hardly different from many similar models by various authors*. The headings in these models comprise the expressions problem, solving, system, design, process, engineering, phases, decision and so on. In this eleven-step-model (fig. 1) step 7 is described as follows: "*communication and leadership* is concerned with communicating the chosen programmes to the people who will have to carry them out and with creating positive attitudes toward this work". In my opinion "leadership" belongs to a different category affecting the entire system, not only step 7. The complex problems of our age require that a large number of participants in the problem-solving process are in command, not only of the methods and techniques of problem-solving, but also of the methods and techniques of leadership.

---

* In his survey Kline [1] shows eight such models (p.30), Murdick [2] seventeen (although referring to MIS development), and Witte [3] presents an extensive bibliography as well as an attempt at theoretical justification. The most comprehensive bibliography may be found in Johnsen [4].

Often a solution can only be found if both skills are present. But even if step 7 consisted only of communication, this would not be satisfactory. In our experience those people who have to carry out the programme had best be heard when the programme is defined (step 5) or even before, when the objectives are defined. It would seem that "communication" too should not be restricted to one step but function at all steps; it is therefore a category by itself. The "total decision process" management cycle, fig. 1, incidentally only encompasses a part of managerial activities: "Decisions are necessary only from time to time; usually no decision is needed in order to know what is due" [5, p.13].

I believe that planning systems, information systems and control systems can be created not only by omitting certain steps in the eleven-step-model, but also in a different way. We can apply one and the same basic process to solve different problems, for instance to design a control system, to design a planning system, to design an information system. If we look at things this way, we shall be able to apply the basic "total decision process" to a wide range of problems far beyond the scope of a corporation. As to the control system defined by the authors (inputs 9 and 10 are suppressed) I would like to point out that according to control theory steps 9 (trends) and 10 (prospects) may be considered as disturbances and the whole loop as a feedback control system; therefore suppression is not an indispensable condition for a control system.

The authors say that system analysis "is not decision process modelling of eleven steps of fig. 1". The content of system analysis, as the authors see it, is an extensive "system philosophy" offering few and rudimentary, but impressive models. I agree with the first sentence. But here, too, it is possible to see things differently. Suppose "systems engineering" is a generic term: in that case system analysis as well as decision making process are parts of systems engineering. The very advantage of systems engineering is in fact that it offers a philosophy, a way of thinking, especially how to think about problems and their solutions. I do not say that system thinking is the best way of thinking, but I am a pragmatical person concerned with practical work and as such I believe that at present and even more in the future system thinking will enable managers to do better work.

Time is growing short, and I now proceed to the authors' conclusion: "Today's management science is primarily a collection of model libraries, richer in variety of techniques than in variety of distinctive models". A practical person will completely agree with the authors. Not much of what mathematicians developed under the heading of "management science" has so far been put to practical use in management. But we must not forget that the mathematical sciences have received a considerable impetus from considering practical problems and that their application has been profitably used in other fields if not yet in ours. "In case of doubt it is more important to meet urgent practical requirements than to play. Everyday life has priority. Therefore, mathematics have stronger justification in investigating everyday requirements than in play, even though playing may be considered a thoroughly dignified human activity" [6, p.182]. Similarly: "As a mathematician I have a firm conviction that, despite of apparent richness of internally generated research, there is urgent need for infusion of entirely new classes of concepts and structures, and I believe that the management sciences are an important potential source for a wide variety of challenging new mathematical problems" [7, p.B358].

I concur with the authors that problem identification (setting problem agenda) and sometimes also program decision are the key points of a decision process. Thus, we must be able to ask questions in a reasonable way and think in a reasonable way and we need knowledge, knowledge about men's actions, knowledge about knowledge, knowledge about management of knowledge. Therefore, we need science and men of science, and we need concepts, and we need teachers enabling us to find our path in the future and to solve our problems with responsibility and dignity [6, 8–12].

References

[1] B. Kline and W. Lifson, Systems engineering, in: Cost-effectiveness. The Economic evaluation of engineered systems, ed. J.M. English (Wiley, New York, 1968).

[2] R.G. Murdick, MIS development procedures, J. System Mgmt. (Dec. 1970) 22.

[3] E. Witte, Phasen-Theorem und die Organisation komplexer Entscheidungsverlaufe, Z. Betriebswirtschaft (Okt. 1968) 628.

[4] E. Johnsen, Studies in multiobjective decision models (Student-literatur, Lundt, 1968).

[5] H. Lübbe, Theorie und Entscheidung, Studien zum Primat der praktischen Vernunft (Rombach, Freiburg, 1971).

[6] H. Seiffert, Marxismus und bürgerliche Wissenschaft (Beck, München, 1971).

[7] R.M. Thrall, On mathematicians and management science, Mgmt. Sci. 15, No.8 (1968) B357.

[8] C.W. Churchman, The design of inquiring systems (Basic Books, New York, 1972).

[9] H. Cleveland, The future executive (Harper and Row, New York, 1972).

[10] A. Rapoport, Operational philosophy – Integrating knowledge and action (Harper and Bros, New York, german edition: Darmstadt, 1970).

[11] H. Seiffert, Einführung in die Wissenschaftstheorie 1, (Beck, München, 1st ed. 1969, 5th ed. 1972).

[12] H. Seiffert, Einführung in die Wissenschaftstheorie 2 (Beck, München, 1st ed. 1970, 3rd ed. 1971).

M. Ross, ed., OR '72. North-Holland Publishing Company (1973)

15

INFORMATION SYSTEMS FOR DECISION AND CONTROL

Systèmes d'information pour les décisions et le contrôle

H. WEDEKIND

Darmstadt Technical University, Darmstadt, West Germany

Abstract. Research in the field of information systems in the last decade has put emphasis on either the conceptional classification of divers conceivable decision and control systems or has concentrated on the question of how to implement a particular system in a particular environment. One aspect in the classification approach is the degree of computer orientation from a conventional manual system up to a total business system (TBS), in which both decisions and controls are automated and are embedded in a cybernetic feedback cycle. The particular system approach, very often entitled the "how-did-it-approach", did not try to find any generalization at all. Both approaches were rather disappointing; the one, because of wishful or too ambitious thinking without the restrictions of the implementation phase (which is indeed futurology), and the other, because of its case study output. Influenced by the operating systems people, who are building systems which are likewise complicated, one started in the last few years to think about methods of how to design an information system. The development methodology stressed today is called the "life cycle approach" and tries to describe in a systematic way the mapping of the "computer environment". The life cycles are: fact analysis, finding the objectives of the new system, designing the new system (i.e., finding in a hierarchical way the systems specification), implementation of the new system, and last but not least, the operating and maintenance. We are going to describe in more detail the phases of the life cycle approach, in particular we are stressing the role of operations research in the designing phase. OR can be sought of as a field supplying the systems designer with algorithms or supporting him by finding optimal trade-offs in his specifications.

1. Introduction

A new research — development of information systems established in the last three years — has already reached such a level of sophistication in the

United States and Europe that a full graduate study curricula has been developed and introduced into several universities [1]. In the very beginning of this new discipline, publications on computer-oriented information systems emphasised either the conceptional classification of divers conceivable decision and control systems or else the question of how to implement a particular system in a particular environment. The classification approach was characterized by the varying degrees of computer orientation which ranged from a conventional manual system up to a total business system (TBS) in which both decisions and controls are fully automated and are embedded in a cybernetic feedback cycle. The other, or "practical" approach, very often called the "how-I-did-it approach", did not try to generalize. Both approaches have proved rather disappointing; the first, because wishful or too ambitious thinking about possible systems caused the design and implementation phases to be overlooked, and the other, because of its case study output. These approaches can be contrasted with another – the systems development approach – which we will describe briefly here.

In this development approach the stages are called the system life cycles and the methodology the life-cycle methodology. The basic life cycles are: system analysis, system design, system implementation and system operation. The paper first outlines the basic concepts and methodology of the development approach*. Next it concentrates upon some typical design problems for which OR techniques are undoubtedly applicable, since OR algorithms are the cornerstones of an automatic or half-automatic design process.

It is curious that no design process in engineering, architecture or other fields is so rudimentary (i.e., entirely manual) as in information systems design in which the outcome is an automatic product. The rapid progress in hardware and system software (operating system, compilers, interpreters, utilities, etc.) puts great pressure on the development of application software because the number of economically feasible applications has increased dramatically. All these systems can not be developed manually. Information systems should be regarded as very complex application systems in which the computer is the core element and not a paper-producing machine. According to a governmental report [6], Germany needs roughly 100 000 people up to 1978 in the area of application of system development. This number is far outside of any realistic range. The situation is similar in the United States and other countries. Teichroew and his group, working at the University of

----

* Since it is not intended to analyze this approach in great detail in this paper the reader is referred to [2–5].

Michigan on a general design language [7], state that the development of a design language and design algorithms should be supported as a scientific program.

2. The methodology of information system development

The system terminology has become a "meta-language" useful to describe different types of abstract, concrete or social phenomena. Very often, however, the system language is abused in order to explain thoughts which are only "meta-clear" to their author. In order to establish a common terminological basis, Ackoff [8] in his "system of systems concepts" outlines the syntax and semantics of this interdisciplinary language. A system is a set of at least two elements, which are related to each other. A system can be divided into subsystems or elements, called "components" or modules if we take the point of view of correctness, exchangeability (implying systems reliability) and division of labour. The dialectic counterpart of a system, a system component or a system element, is its environment. The state of a system or the state of the environment is the set of relevant properties. The meaning of "relevant" depends upon the pragmatic view of the particular application. In developing a system, the relevant properties are called "specifications", which are either functional or performance specification (function per time). Specifications are not given a priori; they are the result of a decision.

From a methodological point of view, there are two basic development approaches depending upon the decision sequence in time [9]. The first, or "outside-in", approach starts with the environment of systems to be developed and tries to find specifications by successively developing decisions. Looking at the development process as an hierarchy, one can say, that specifications at a higher level are restrictions on decisions concerning specifications at a lower level. The problem of what the system should do is solved prior to the question of how to meet the specification. The disadvantage with the approach is that the specifications may be too ambitious and cannot be realized. Following the second and opposite "inside-out" approach, one tries to estimate the specifications of the environment upon which it was decided that the system can be built. The danger here is that the system or system component developed may prove useless.

In developing information systems, the outside-in approach is chosen mainly because the task is to map the manual organization of a business onto a computer. The standard application software, supplied by most manufacturers, relies on products developed by the opposite inside-out approach.

Inside-out products must be highly parameterized so that they can be tailored and built into a specific environment. In developing a system, one must keep in mind that the early decisions about specifications are highly irreversible, i.e., they are strategic. The later decisions are easy to alter and are tactical. The basic rule of system development is to keep the degree of irreversibility as small as possible, since a change of specifications is the greatest danger. The dilemma of systems development is that highly irreversible decisions result in fairly general specifications which are expensive. The art of system development is to find the appropriate trade-offs (compromises).

In the development of information systems, the following phases (life cycles) are of vital interest:

(a) System analysis of the existing system.

(b) Feasibility study.

(c) Logical design.

(d) Physical design or implementation.

(e) System operation.

The above sequence corresponds with the outside-in approach.

3. System analysis

Building an information system consists of four separate stages: definition, investigation, description and fact analysis.

3.1. System definition

System definition which deals with the problem of finding a subset which is appropriate for computerization, starts out from the need for a new system. One has to be careful not to define too big a system which under present technological and manpower restrictions can never be analysed, redesigned and implemented on a computer. The euphoria of management information systems (MIS) followed this total system approach and failed to come down to earth. It is therefore better to define small systems and to keep them open-ended.

3.2. System investigation

System investigation, which deals with the problem of getting a true picture of an existing and bounded system, uses the techniques of interview-

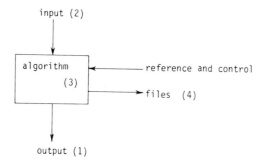

Fig. 1. Information flow.

ing, questionnaires, observations and estimations. In particular, the analyst has to investigate four basic elements of a general information flow (fig. 1). System analysis and system development is product-oriented (output-oriented). Therefore the investigation starts with the output (1) and attempts to find out what input (2), algorithms (3) and reference and control files (4) are required in a subsystem. The output is used as input for other subsystems. Algorithms comprise mathematical procedures, legal regulation, organizational procedures, etc.

3.3. System description

The description of an information system needs special languages or tools. Besides the natural language and mathematical representation diagrams (system diagram, flow charts, media diagrams, etc.), forms (record structure forms, decision tables, etc.) were introduced to describe systems in a succinct way. Andersen et al. [10] give an excellent introduction to system description and to the recorded form, the system documentation. Documentation is not only required for interpersonal communication; in the design phase it can also be regarded as a design tool [2, p.23]. Two important characteristics of a description must be considered: first, the level of detail, and second, the description of pure states, pure function and state/functions. In particular, Walsh [11] shows how to provide several levels of detail to address different professional groups.

3.4. Fact analysis

Fact analysis tries to identify those features among the many found in a system investigation which are relevant to the development of new systems.

4. Feasibility study

This phase answers the basic question of whether the system is feasible from economical, technical and operational points of view. The feasibility study comprises the setting of system objectives, the preliminary design and the justification of the new system.

5. Logical design

In the last three years, all publications on development of information systems stress the necessity to distinguish sharply between logical and physical design. Logical design is concerned with the production of specifications and the interrelationships between them without taking the physical system (the hardware) into consideration.

Logical design implies, for example, the structuring of records without specifying the track format on a disk or the blocking factor on a tape. The development of generalized data base management systems [12] (GDBM) relieved designers from getting too involved in the physical world of a computer. The GDBM-called DBTG language [13] (data base task group, a subgroup of the Codasyl Committee) is a newly designed system to manage all types of data structure without any knowledge of the physical storage structure. The GDBM can be regarded as the basic tool for the development of information systems in the future.

Besides the organization of system output (distribution of information) and system input (data collection, data transformation), the logical design of information systems is concerned with the design of (a) algorithms and (b) files.

5.1. The design of algorithms

Algorithms which produce a proposal for a decision are generally more complicated than pure control algorithms. Whereas in the classical business environment, the algorithms are very simple and the files are rather complicated, an information system for decision and control requires both complicated algorithms and complicated file structures. The logical design of an algorithm refers to such questions as convergence, finiteness, definition of an iteration cycle, selection rules, etc. The physical design solves problems of data storage, partitioning because core storages are too small, computing time, etc. Integer programming is a good example of excellent logical design with disappointing physical consequences. The dichotomy of logical and physical design goes through the whole design process of information systems. A brilliant "theory" (brilliant in an esthetical sense) and a good physical design have very often no "common divisor".

5.2. File design

Although file design is not an area with which operations researchers are generally familiar it became apparent in the last few years that OR can be used to support the logical and physical design of file organization if developed for use as a design tool. Today, rough guesses, simple computations and sometimes simulations are used to find an appropriate file organization. These methods however, are usually unsatisfactory. It is beyond the scope of this paper to state specific file design problems for information systems or to present solutions. [14–17] in the bibliography deal with some general and specific problems of file design.

The logical design of file organization is the problem of finding the best trade-offs between data density (used space), retrieval speed and maintenance. The retrieval speed is subdivided into retrieval by key (e.g., personal number) and attribute (e.g., name, town, street). The capability (insertion or deletion of a record) and the speed of changing the contents of a record in the batch or transaction mode are important evaluation criteria [19].

In fig. 2 the qualitative properties of five well-known types of file organizations are shown. In particular, chained files and complex-structured files (trees and networks) are used in large data bases. These file organizations however, can be combined. One segment of a file can be accessed by the random technique whereas another segment is searched via tables of an inverted file. The general file design problem can be stated as follows:

Given the access and maintenance statistics of a file (if unknown, take these magnitudes as parameters). Given further the storage space to be covered by that file (parameter). Try to find a file organization or a combination of file organizations in data bases such that the speed of retrieval and maintenance is minimal. This problem has not yet been solved, but it must be solved in an heuristic or exact way because system designers need this help. In

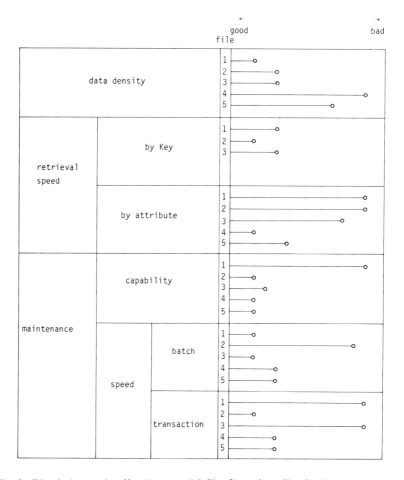

Fig. 2. File design trade-offs. 1) sequential file, 2) random file, 3) chained file, 4) inverted file and 5) complex-structured file (trees and networks).

fact, it is a combinatorial extremum problem; the finding of a solution should be automated to obtain a design tool which is urgently needed.

6. Physical design

The determination of the physical design of a system is called implementation. A logical design is composed of a large volume of logical diagrams, information flow diagrams and layouts of logical files. The problem of physical design is how to get this volume into a machine. Physical design has to do with the selection of programming languages (system software), the selection of machines (hardware), the programming of algorithms, the creations of files, component and systems tests, and last but not least, the implementation of software or hardware devices for data protection and data security. OR techniques (integer programming) were proposed but never used to support the selection procedure of computer hardware [20]. Queueing theory and simulation, however, have been used intensively to find balanced configurations of the physical input-output process [25–27]. The input-output devices (disks, tapes, terminals) are attached to a channel (service station). Under some not very restrictive assumptions concerning the I/O traffic, one can solve the problems of what and how many devices can be attached without loss of efficiency. Gaver [28] even tries to put the whole physical system of a computer into a queueing model. Although the model is relatively simple, the results can be used for long range planning purposes [29].

7. System operation

System operations has to do with various topics such as performance measurement and performance accounting, load planning of machines, regulation of computer usage (priority), keeping logs, system maintenance and the management of system libraries.

8. Education

Supported by the American National Science Foundation, a Curriculum Committee on Computer Education for Management (chairman Dr. Teichroew, University of Michigan) of the Association for Computing Machinery (ACM) has prepared a position paper [1] presenting conclusions concerning requirements for education relevant to information systems in organizations. The report presents a graduate level curriculum for those who will develop complex information systems. Today, the body of knowledge of information systems development is offered in diverse fields. The curriculum, which will be outlined briefly, is an attempt to combine this knowledge and adds new definition and perspective to these activities. The course material in this report may also be integrated into existing programs of industrial engineering, operations research, computer science and business administration.

As a model for a curriculum of information system design, fourteen basic courses are specified in the report. These fall into four groups:

Administrative information systems:
(A1) introduction to systems,
(A2) management decision systems,
(A3) information management for decision systems.

Basic concepts for system development:
(B1) computers and computer programming,
(B2) operations analysis (operations research),
(B3) human and organizational behaviour,
(B4) social implications of information technology.

Computer technology:
(C1) information structures,
(C2) computer systems,
(C3) file and communication systems,
(C4) program design.

Development of information systems:
(D1) information system analysis,
(D2) information system design,
(D3) system development projects.

Group A has as its purpose the understanding of the management process from a system perspective. Course A1 concentrates upon the system concept, in particular, with respect to accounting systems. Course A2 deals with the functions of the most common systems for supporting managements decisions in the areas of marketing, production, finance and procurement. Course A3 concentrates upon the analysis of information requirements.

Group B provides prerequisites in programming, algorithms and social implications.

Group C provides a basic understanding of technology and methods to build complex information systems. Course C1 introduce logical relationships and design principles. Course C2 is hardware and software oriented. Course C3 deals with the physical design of information systems. Course C4 considers large programs with real-time requirements with respect to programming style, maintenance, documentation and interfacing with other programs.

The D courses provide a synthesis of the material presented in groups A, B and C. All life cycles of a development project are worked through with emphasis on case studies.

References

[1] Professional education in information systems development, to be published in Conf. Proc. of the ACM (1972).
[2] R.J. Benjamin, Control of the information systems development cycle (Wiley–Interscience, New York, 1971).
[3] J.K. Lyon, An introduction to data base design (Wiley–Interscience, New York, 1971).
[4] M.L. Rubin, Handbook of data processing management, Vol.1–6 (Auerbach Publ., Princeton, 1970/71).
[5] H. Wedekind, Entwicklung von Anwendungssystemen – Systemanalyse, Systementwurf, Systemimplementierung (Carl Verlag, Munchen) to be published.
[6] Zweites Datenverarbeitungsprogramm der Bundesrepublik Deutschland (Universitatsdruckerei, Bonn, 1971).
[7] D. Teichroew and H. Sayani, Automation of system building, Datamation 17, No.16 (1971).
[8] R.L. Ackoff, Towards a system of systems concepts, Mgmt. Sci. 17 No.11 (1971) 661.
[9] P. Naur and B. Randell, Software engineering, report on Conf. sponsored by the Nato Science Committee, Garmisch (1968), distributed by the Nato Science Committee, Brussels.
[10] C. Andersen, M. Arentzen and A. Petersen, Systems description (Akademisk Forlag, Copenhagen, 1971).
[11] D. Walsh, A guide to software documentation (McGraw–Hill, New York, 1969).
[12] Feature analysis of generalized data base management systems, Codasyl Tech. Rep. (May 1971), distributed by IAG, Amsterdam.
[13] Data base task group, Codasyl Tech. Rep. (April 1971), distributed by IAG, Amsterdam.
[14] A.G. Merten, Optimum assignment of data to sequential storage devices, Univ. of Michigan, Ann Arbor ISDOS Working Paper 50 (Aug. 1971).
[15] D.E. Knuth, Optimum binary search trees, Stanford Univ. Tech. Rep. CS 149 (Jan. 1971).
[16] H. Wedekind, Die Konstruktion eines optimalen Zugriffsbaumes fur Datenorganisationen innerhalb einer Datenbank, Elektron. Datenverarbeitung 11, Heft 12 (1969) 555.
[17] A.G. Merten, Some quantitative techniques for file organization, Univ. of Wisconsin, Computing Center, Tech. Rep. (June 1970).
[18] C.V. Ramamoorthy and P.R. Blevins, Arranging frequency dependent data on sequential memories, in: Proc. of the Spring Joint Computer Conf. (AFIPS Press, Montvale, 1971) p.545.
[19] P. Geodfry, Advanced file organization, IAG Seminar, distributed by IAG, Amsterdam.
[20] W.F. Sharpe, The economics of computers (Columbia Univ. Press, New York, 1969).
[21] File organization, selected papers from File 68, an IAG Conf., distributed by IAG, Amsterdam.
[22] D. Lefkovitz, File structures for on-line systems (Wiley, New York, 1967).

[23] M.S. Morton, Management decision systems (Harvard Univ. Press, 1971).

[24] L.I. Kraus, Computer-based management information systems, Am. Mgmt. Assoc. (1970).

[25] G.H. MacEwen, Performance of moveable-head disk storage devices, presented on NATO-APOR Conf. Munich (August 1971).

[26] P.H. Seaman, R.A. Lind and R.A. Wilson, An analysis of auxiliary storage activity, IBM Systems J. 3, No.5 (1966) 158.

[27] H. Wedekind, The application of queueing theory to determine I/O-configurations, presented on NATO-APOR Conf., Munich (August 1971).

[28] D.P. Gaver, Probabilistic models for multi-programming computer systems, J. ACM 13, No.14 (1967) 423.

[29] F. Hanssmann, Long range planning of minimum cost systems based on the Gaver model, presented on NATO-APOR Conf., Munich (August 1971).

[30] J.F. Nunamaker, A methodology for the design and optimization of information Joint Computer Conf., AFIPS Press, Montvale (1971) p.283.

M. Ross, ed., OR '72. North-Holland Publishing Company (1973)

INFORMATION SYSTEMS FOR DECISION AND CONTROL: DISCUSSANT 1

Systèmes d'information pour les décisions et le contrôle: porte-parole 1

B.M. BROUGH

B.E.A., Ruislip, Middlesex, England

In a general descriptive review of the concepts and methodology pertaining to what he defines as the "systems development approach" the author draws attention to the rudimentary character of the system design process and identifies certain design problems to which the techniques of OR clearly have application. He rightly claims that OR needs to be developed so that it can be used as a more effective design tool.

However, although the paper touches on, and contrasts, the distinction between two basic development approaches — referred to as the outside-in (topdown) approach and the inside-out (bottom-up) approach — and draws attention to the dangers inherent in following either, it is disappointing not to find this question explored in greater depth.

Within the business context, there is growing evidence that absence of an explicit system design strategy may well be the root cause of the lack of success that has so far surrounded many attempts to develop what the paper refers to as the total business system (TBS). But this point is not dealt with, and a significant weak point in the argument lies in the suggestion that the outside-in approach is chosen "mainly because the task is to map the manual organisation of a business onto a computer". This may be frequently seen as the goal of such an approach, but need this be so?

An alternative might well be to avoid deliberately taking a polarised view of the two basic development approaches discussed. But this only becomes possible by adopting a somewhat different view of the outside-in approach. If, in the formulation of TBS strategy, instead of seeking merely to map existing systems onto the computer an attempt is made to develop, as a planning goal, the shape of the TBS that it appears practical to achieve in the longer term with due regard for the potential and foreseeable development of decision models, and a compatible management structure capable of interacting with such models, then development becomes less hidebound by current systems and management decision practices.

In this way the inherent danger in the outside-in approach can be avoided. Moreover, if concurrent with the formulation of a long-range strategic TBS plan on this basis, development work then proceeds at the tactical level based on inside-out approaches, but subject to constraints and goals implicit in the long range strategy, many of the dangers inherent in the latter approach, as discussed in the paper, can also be prevented.

The author claims it is better "to define small systems and keep them open-ended". But in the absence of an overall strategy the purposes for which they are being left open-ended remains unclear, with the attendant risk that development will proceed along many diverse, misguided and uncoordinated paths.

In other words, the two fundamental system development approaches discussed in the paper should not be seen as representing a dichotomy of choice. It would appear reasonable to propose that both can exist concurrently: with long range TBS strategy being guided by outside-in thinking, and tactical development, within the framework of this strategy, being based mainly on the more traditional inside-out approach. But the total system plan needs to remain adaptive. Experience gained at the tactical level must be continually applied to update and enhance the strategic plan in the light of results achieved from systems already implemented, and as OR studies lead to increased understanding of the overall goals of the business and related managerial decision processes.

Ultimately, as development progresses, it is to be expected that detailed planning at the tactical level will converge towards meeting the goals implicit in the longer range strategic plans. As yet, however, it would appear that many organisations still have a very long way to go before attaining this level of development. A further major problem is, that at the present time, there are few heuristics available to guide outside-in thinking towards the development of an explicit TBS long-range strategy. But these may be sought in the growing body of knowledge concerned with management cybernetics. It is the application of this knowledge to the formulation of long-range strategic concepts for the development of information systems for decision and control that constitutes the 'art' of TBS design. This area of thinking is clearly one to which OR thinkers have the potential to make a strong, and possibly their major, contribution.

M. Ross, ed., OR '72. North-Holland Publishing Company (1973)

INFORMATION SYSTEMS FOR DECISION AND CONTROL: DISCUSSANT 2

Systèmes d'information pour les décisions et le contrôle: porte-parole 2

J.F. DONOVAN

Allied Irish Banks, Dublin, Ireland

In considering this subject and in particular the field of information systems in an OR conference, one would superficially think about the use of models and simulation within a data processing environment to help decision-making. However, I believe that there are many problems in information systems which could be of great interest to OR workers and where it certainly would be very gratifying to data processing practitioners who are involved in the design and implementation of information systems, if their OR colleagues were to come up with even partial solutions.

One of the first areas where the systems people run into difficulty is in the economic justification of information systems, particularly of the more sophisticated variety. The field of what Professor Adrian McDonagh [1] calls "information economics" is one which I would like to see more work done by OR workers. McDonagh has done a lot of valuable work in this field. He has pointed out that there are five important areas to be considered when one is examining the economics of information. These five areas are:

(1) *Surveillance* which refers to all those activities by which a better perspective on an Organisation and its environment is obtained. It includes coverage of both external and internal situations. It includes immediate and long-range circumstances. In effect it can cover every aspect of an organisation but practically an organised surveillance effort must be very selective. This surveillance surely must ring a bell with some of the earlier research work in OR in the military field.

(2) *Criteria or measures of performance.* There is a great need for an evaluation of performance of different information systems both in terms of the economics and efficiency to attain the objectives of the information system.

(3) *Classification.* We all know that information systems depend on classification and yet we really have very little knowledge about how to structure good classifications. Information systems are file-oriented and classification systems are the foundations of the structure of these files.

(4) *Documentation.* This is an important area in the development of information systems but may not necessarily have a close affiliation to OR.

(5) *Boundaries.* The question of the integration of subsystems and how they can be put together and the depth of a particular system scope with the practical economic and personnel constraints under which an integrated system has to be designed certainly calls for an OR approach. The optimum system is not an easy one to design and even to be sure that one has reached an optimum would be of great value to the systems designer.

Information systems are the foundation of the decision-making process and there is a connection between decision-making and profit. There is also a connection between decision-making and time, and between decision-making and accuracy of information. The relationship of timeliness and the effects of delays in information systems on profit, I have always believed, are areas which would be well worthwhile investigating.

When one considers decision-making, particularly for top management, one finds as one goes up the hierarchy of an organisation, a greater emphasis on qualitative rather than quantitative information, a greater emphasis on external rather than internal information, and a greater emphasis on long-term rather than short-term implications. The balancing of these elements in an information systems is certainly something to which OR workers could make a contribution.

There is a fundamental link between information systems and the objectives of an organisation. Information systems are created to support decisions which are made to attain objectives and these decisions are carried out by people in an organisation. Conventionally, people often consider information flows within an existing organisation. Perhaps the system should be turned around and information flows should be examined in the light of decisions and objectives and only then should an organisation be created which in fact would be logically made a consequence of information systems rather than the converse.

In designing information systems, the systems analysts will have to resolve the whole question of off-line versus on-line versus real-time information systems. This may very well be an economic problem but it will also probably have serious implications flowing from the nature of the particular decision-making and operational cycles of the organisation. In the case of these different types of systems, the whole question of discipline of response from the decision makers arises. The man/machine interface, in areas like cockpits of aircrafts, machine tools and other areas of a non-management nature now enters the Board room and senior management offices. In fact, one might consider that some analogue devices will have to be married to digital devices for information systems in this field.

In the area of the response, we should also mention the training of top management to handle information systems. Generally, people worry about the training of systems designers in information systems and Professor Wedekind largely confined himself, both in his references and in his last section on education to the workers in the design of information systems. I believe that there is a very big need also for the training of top management in the handling of information systems.

When one considers decisions, one is emphasising particularly a particular output and one is exploring and weighting alternatives. However, the question arises as to who is to find the alternatives and whether in fact modern computers and management sciences can create systems which will explore and define and suggest alternatives automatically. This is a field of wide connotation for OR workers.

In any information system there are a number of major areas or elements. One can list: (a) data capture, (b) data processing, (c) data analysis and interpretation, (d) the decision-making itself.

The structuring of these elements covering both hardware and software and the human element is a real OR problem.

Returning to the question of surveillance, the whole question of the evaluation of opportunities, the searching out of opportunities and the evaluation of risks in the environment are fields which should be incorporated into any integral information system for decision making. I mentioned earlier the fundamental relationship between information systems and organisation and the evaluation of the efficiency of information systems which in turn give rise to the evaluation of the competency of organisations which are of course only there to carry out decisions. A common problem for systems designers in information systems is the establishment of priorities and criteria in a particular firm.

When one considers either the structured or the unstructured decisions in an organisation, one immediately finds oneself in the realms of probability. Somebody has said that the major contribution of management sciences to decision making is to lower the degree of risk or to measure the probabilities.

Information systems, of course, particularly with the high-power computing available today, can readily incorporate probabilistic approaches and analysis of variance in the building up of models for the decision maker.

I mentioned earlier that information systems are largely file oriented and Wedekind has touched on the importance of file structure. I believe that the application of mathematical logic to this whole field would be a very fruitful one and could legitimitely be incorporated into an OR approach.

Professor Amstutz [2] has identified five dimensions along which the evolution of a wide variety of management information systems (MIS) may be traced. He has suggested that these dimensions may be used to evaluate the particular systems and to isolate similarities and differences among alternative systems or stages of system development. The treatment of these five dimensions can in itself be a rather fruitful OR problem. The first dimension he has advised is that of *information recency* which refers to the time lapse between the occurrence of an event and the inclusion of data describing that event in the system. The second dimension is that of *information aggregation* which describes the detail with which information is maintained in system data files. The third dimension is the *degree of analytical sophistication* referring to the sophistication of models or structure encompassed by the system. The fourth dimension of evaluation system, *authority delegated to the system*, is closely associated with analytical sophistication. Management is more willing to delegate authority to sophisticated systems and conversely as management places greater demands on information system, a greater level of analytical sophistication is required. The final dimension is that of *management access* or manager/system interaction. This covers the whole question of response which I mentioned above.

Various criteria are often applied in the design of MIS. It is rarely mentioned that a MIS should provide the information required for the development of advanced scientific management techniques, such as OR. All OR practitioners have been faced with the difficulty of data collection and I believe that the time has come when in fact serious consideration should be given to the design of the information systems which throw up some of this data.

The most fundamental question that one has to ask oneself is whether MIS is adequate. Certainly if decisions are not affected by it, then it is questionable whether it should exist at all. Someone once said that there are companies already dead but that they don't know this because of an inadequate information system!

References

[1] A.M. McDonagh, Information economic and management-systems.
[2] A.E. Amstutz, European Business (July 1968).

M. Ross, ed., OR '72. North-Holland Publishing Company (1973)

GENERAL SYSTEMS RESEARCH

Recherche des systèmes généraux

GEORGE J. KLIR

School of Advanced Technology, State University of New York,
Binghamton, New York, U.S.A.

Abstract. General systems research is a collection of concepts, views, principles, tools, problems, methods, and techniques associated with general properties of systems, i.e., properties which are meaningful for all systems independent of the traditional classification of science, engineering, the arts, and humanities. Isomorphism, homomorphism and other relations are used to identify similarities among systems belonging to various disciplines. This leads to a nontraditional classification of systems. Although each class contains systems from different disciplines, all the systems in the class share certain general properties. When abstracting these properties, we obtain a general system which may serve as a representant of the class. This leads to investigation and, ultimately, to the development of a methodology of general systems.

This paper, prepared for IFORS with the compliments of the Society for General Systems Research, outlines the state of the art and current trends in the area identified as general systems research.

1. Introduction

Although the concept of a system may have different meanings under different circumstances and for different people, it ordinarily stands for "a set or arrangement of things so related or connected as to form a unity or organic whole" (Webster's New World Dictionary). Diverse kinds of things and their interrelations represent different systems.

In sciences (natural, behavioral, social) the concept of system is understood as an abstraction which must be used when nature is examined from the viewpoint of the pertinent scientific discipline. Although we always confine ourselves to only some part of nature, which is the object of our interest, our facilities do not usually permit us to study it in all its complexity. We therefore observe, or measure, appearances of a limited number of certain attributes concerning the chosen object; in other words, we observe or measure values of a limited number of selected variables. Clearly, these observations, or measurements, are made on a certain resolution level and with the objective of finding a simple expression of time-invariant relations (deterministic or stochastic) between instantaneous and/or past and/or future values of the variables involved. Sometimes we also attempt to find the manner in which these relations are composed by simpler relations.

In engineering the system has the same traits as in the sciences; as a rule, however, the problems solved in it are different. The relation between its variables is usually prescribed and we are to design it in such a manner that implementing it with the aid of available technical resources satisfies best certain objective criteria (system synthesis); or, conversely a distinct realization is given and we are to find the relation between some of its variables (system analysis).

In abstract disciplines, systems are not assigned to objects. They are defined by an enumeration of certain variables, their admissible values, and their algebraic, topological, grammatical, and other properties.

Basic system traits can frequently be identified in various arts (music, theater, ballet, poetry). System problems in this area may include the determination of time-invariant relations, decomposition, synthesis, analysis.

Although the notion of "system" is an old one, the concept of general systems is a relatively new concept which has only come into general use in the last two decades. It is based on the realisation that there exist certain system properties which do not depend on the specific nature of individual systems as far as traditional classification of human activities is concerned. Some of these properties were first understood as various kinds of simple system similarities (geometric, kinematic, thermodynamic). Two systems were considered similar if variables of one system were of the same physical nature as those assigned to them in the second system and if values of the assigned variables were proportional at corresponding times.

Later, the meaning of similarity was extended to include systems whose variables are of different physical natures. This kind of similarity, now usually referred to as the analogy between systems, is based on a similarity in the algebraic or differential equations describing the systems involved.

The above mentioned similarities, which are special cases of isomorphic relations, represent initial steps in the development of the concept of general systems. The relation of similarity, in the sense described above, is reflective, symmetric, and transitive. As such, it is an ordinary equivalence relation which partitions systems from different disciplines into equivalence classes. Each equivalence class, which may contain systems from different disciplines, can be represented by a single system – representative of the class. Results obtained by investigating those properties of the representative which are preserved by an isomorphic relation can be transferred, using this relation, to each system in the class.

When mathematical isomorphism is extended to any pair of relations, whether expressible by equations or not, then the concept of general systems acquires its proper meaning. It is a contentless (mathematical) representative (model) of a particular equivalence class, obtained when an isomorphic relation (which is always an equivalence relation) is applied to certain systemic traits.

Thus, mathematical isomorphism is crucial to any form of general systems theory. A study of various aspects of isomorphism, its modifications, and its generalized form – homomorphism, within individual conceptual frameworks – is very important for developing areas of general systems methodology with clearly specified applications. Let us note that the homomorphic relation between systems classifies but does not partition them. Nevertheless, some problems concerning all systems in a class can be solved in terms of its representative – a homomorphic model.

2. Systems approach

Several aspects can be identified in the area of human activities referred to as general systems research. They may roughly be classified into four classes: systems approach, various general systems theories (and their methodologies), a meta-theory of general systems, and general systems education.

The systems approach contrasts with the classical (Newtonian) approach to science. The latter regards an object of scientific investigation as a collection of isolated parts or at most pair-wise interactions. It tries to derive various properties of the whole object directly from the properties of its parts without considering possible interactions between the parts at all or, at most, to derive them by superposition of pairwise interactions. The systems approach, on the contrary, is based on the assumption that properties of the whole object depend not only on the properties of its parts but also on all possible interactions between them.

While the classical approach provides fairly good results in mechanics, it leads to a rather poor understanding of biological, psychological, or social phenomena. Therefore, biology, psychology, and sociology were among the areas within which the systems approach arose; major credits for promoting it belong to Ludwig von Bertalanffy, a biologist.

Although, the systems approach in its pure form (incorporating all interactions between the parts) was well motivated, it appeared to be an utopia. A practical obstruction in applying the pure systems approach is firmly rooted in a limited power of our computing facilities, a theoretical obstruction is represented by the so-called Bremermann (or quantal) limit.

By simple physical considerations based on quantum theory, Bremerman had made the following conjecture [1] : "No data processing system, whether artifical or living, can process more than 2×10^{47} bits per second per gram of its mass". Then he calculated the total number of bits processed by a hypothetical computer the size of the earth within a time period equal to the estimated age of the Earth. Since the mass and the age of the Earth are estimated to be less than 6×10^{27} grams and 10^{10} years respectively, and each year contains approximately $\pi \times 10^7$ seconds, this imaginary computer cannot process more than 10^{93} bits. It is not difficult to find problems, often associated with only medium-size systems, which fall far beyond this limit.

Hence, the pure systems approach is highly desirable but too frequently leads to problems that are practically unsolvable. Some of them cannot be solved due to the limited power of existing computers but most of them can never be solved. In such cases, simplification is necessary. This means that certain simplifying assumptions must be made on the basis of which some of the interactions are neglected.

The systems approach proper is thus characterized by a deep involvement in the study of simplifying assumptions to find ways of yielding a minimal simplification. The word "minimal" means here that the simplification enables us to solve the problem under consideration and preserves essential properties of the original system as much as possible. This leads to the investigation of appropriate measures of "amount" or "importance" of interactions between the system elements. One such concept is W. Ross Ashby's concept of least safe capacity [2].

Hence, an important trend in general systems research consists in developing methods that enable us to construct conceptual systems where interactions between the elements are sufficiently, but not completely, incorporated. The pure systems approach transmutes into something which might be called "theory of simplification" or, as suggested by Gerald M. Weinberg [2] "science of simplification". Some aspects of this new problem area appear to be treated in the recently evolved constraints theory [3].

It seems appropriate to close this discussion concerning the development of the systems approach by quoting Weinberg [2] :

"Newton was a genius, but not because of the superior computational power of his brain. Newton's genius was on the contrary, his ability to simplify, idealize, and streamline the world so that it became, in some measure, tractable to the brains of perfectly ordinary men. By studying the methods of simplification which have succeeded and failed in the past, the general systems theorist hopes to make the progress of human knowledge a little less dependent on genius".

3. General systems theories

Though the whole area of general systems research is often referred to as the general systems theory, it is not a theory in the formal sense (an axiomatic theory) but rather a collection of concepts, views, principles, tools, problems, methods, and techniques associated with general systems. However, it embodies some formal theories of general systems.

In the first of these, the Mesarovic theory*, a general system S is defined as the relation:

$$S \subset \underset{i \in I}{\mathbf{X}} V_i , \tag{1}$$

where $\mathbf{X}$ denotes a cartesian product and I is an index set. More mathematical structure is added when systems with more specific properties are studied. For instance, sets V_i can be partitioned into input sets

$$X = \underset{i \in I_x}{\mathbf{X}} V_i ,$$

and output sets

$$Y = \underset{i \in I_y}{\mathbf{X}} V_i .$$

The system S is then a relation

$$S \subset X \times Y . \tag{2}$$

---

* This was initiated by Eckman and Mesarovic at the beginning of the 1960's [4] and further developed mainly at the Systems Research Center of Case Western Reserve University in Cleveland, Ohio [2,5].

Further specialization may consist in the assumption that X and Y are time functions, that time is represented by a set of integers (discrete time), etc.

Some specific aspects are closely associated with the development of the Mesarovic theory:

(1) Goal-seeking (teleological, decision-making) specification of systems, in which the binary relation (2) is described implicity in terms of a goal-seeking process.

(2) A strong involvement in the elaboration of the theory of general hierarchical systems, where the goal-seeking description of behavior plays an important role [6].

(3) Applications of the theory to metamathematical problems associated with consistency and completeness of axiomatic theories [7].

Another general systems theory, formulated by A. Wayne Wymore in 1967 [8], was developed to subsume both the theory of discrete automata and continuous systems defined by differential equations. Wymore's definition of system is based essentially on a state-transition structure. As such, it incorporates various models of finite-state discrete systems [9] but extends them to continuous functions requiring neither a finite number of states nor a finite number of stimuli. The theory is applicable, therefore, to hybrid systems, which contain both continuous and discrete variables, as well as systems defined on infinite sets. For instance, various Turing machines, whose tapes are potentially infinite in both directions, can easily be described in terms of the Wymore theory. As a consequence, various formal languages (not necessarily finite-state) can be formalized within the Wymore theory.

Wymore formalizes the notion of a coupling of systems which extends the theory to collections of coupled systems and makes the problems of system analysis and synthesis meaningful. He also uses the concept of system homomorphism (or isomorphism as a special case) to formalize the principle of modelling and simulation. He requires the model to exhibit the same input— output performance as the original (model of behavior).

Wymore, like Mesarovic, has intentionally developed his conceptual framework independently of any specific form of mathematical representation. This has allowed him enough freedom to choose a suitable representation for a given purpose. Applications* have been oriented mainly to problems of systems engineering in the broadest sense, including problems associated with health care systems, ecological systems, political systems, and the like.

In my own approach [10], I had followed an inductive path in contrast to

---

* Most of the work on the Wymore theory has been done at the Department of Systems Engineering of the University of Arizona in Tucson, Arizona.

the deductive approach used by Mesarovic and Wymore. Rather than defining the concept of a system axiomatically, as Mesarovic and Wymore do, I identify system traits before I define a system as such. The identification is based on intuitive recognition of systems and system-type problems in various disciplines (natural and social sciences, engineering, mathematics, the arts). Those system traits are compiled which are independent of a specific nature of the variables involved (behavior, states, transitions, elements, couplings, etc.). The compiled traits are then classified and formalized. Any definition of the system is required to satisfy the following conditions:

(1) It is based only on constant traits.

(2) It is based on characteristic traits that are supposed to be completely known.

(3) It is based on those traits which make it possible to determine uniquely for each of the other traits whether or not it is consistent with the given traits.

In addition to these conditions, it is required that any basic definition of the system does not contain redundant traits, i.e., those which are not necessary to satisfy requirement 3. Applying all these requirements, five basic definitions of systems are arrived at [10]. Each of them can be supplemented by additional traits, or several of them can be used together to define a system.

A spectrum of system definitions is thus used in my theory, each of which is associated with a particular class of system-type problems. Adopting the conceptual framework, Robert A. Orchard suggested in [2] a generalization within which it is possible to view a sequence of systems as a system of its own. His definition consists of a set of time values, a collection of acceptable system definitions, and a system procedure which prescribes a passage from one system to another in time.

The Orchard definition allows any changes in the system under consideration but does not allow us to change the procedure which effects these changes. However, it can be extended as follows: Instead of a single system procedure, the system may be subject to several system procedures. It may pass from one procedure to another but at any time only one of them is effective. The passage from one procedure to another is then prescribed by a meta-procedure.

We can proceed still further: The system may be subject to several meta-procedures which are made effective by a meta-meta-procedure, the system may be subject to several meta-meta-procedures, etc. This generates hierarchical structures of system procedures which make it easier to solve problems associated with some phenomena such as growth, evolution, self-reproduction, self-organization, adaptation, learning.

4. Meta-theoretical aspects

The fact that the general systems theory is not unique is the reason for a development of a general systems meta-theory. A remarkable study of the role of this meta-theory in general systems research was made by Lars Lofgren and the following is a quote from his presentation in [2]:

"We want to interpret the concept of general systems theory not necessarily as a formal theory, but rather as a common scientific language, that is, as a meta-language in which we can discuss the effects of various logical bases for effective explanations of certain types of systems phenomena. ...There are many ways of formalizing theories, depending on how the logical basis is chosen. However, I believe that agreement on a suitable logical basis constitutes far less of a problem for a group of scientists than to interact without formalizing their ideas. ... As soon as a scientist believes that he has produced a theory for some phenomenon, he should try to formalize the theory so as to make it effectively communicable. ... Everything that can be effectively explained can be formalized".

Questions concerning the explicatory and predictive power of a general systems theory, its communicability, its syntactic information, and the problem of reducing one theory to another are among those to which the general systems meta-theory is addressed.

So far, various general systems theories have been evolving spontaneously and individually, without any significant coordination. It seems that a stage of evolution has been reached where some sort of integration might be beneficial. Clearly, this integration can be accomplished only within the general systems meta-theory.

The first step in the integration of general systems theories was made by Sirajul Islam [11]. He compared the Mesarovic theory with the Wymore theory in an attempt to unify them. Although a complete unification of the two theories has not been achieved, Islam managed to identify an isomorphic relation between them which is valid under certain minor assumptions.

An important task of the general systems meta-theory is to study the role of topological structures in general systems theories. This study was started by Joseph V. Cornacchio [2]. He demonstrates the need for topological structures in general systems theories and shows that a natural topological structure for the Wymore theory is not the classical topological space but the generalized closure space suggested by Preston Hammer [12].

As pointed out before, there is a general trend to formalize general systems theory so as to make it communicable. It turns out, however, that the process of formalization often narrows the original semantic meaning of the concepts involved. This "poverty of fully formalized concepts" is a serious disadvantage of the formalization in its present form despite its many advantages. New developments in mathematics can help significantly in this respect. Involved are both a modification of existing mathematical concepts (e.g., the extended topological space suggested by Hammer [2, 12]) and the creation of new mathematical concepts (e.g., the Zadeh idea of fuzzy sets [13–15]).

5. Education

People involved directly in general systems research are usually referred to as generalists, while those working in a classical discipline are called specialists. However, if one works solely on general systems research, he then becomes a general systems specialist. He specializes in systems generalizations. Let us call him a specialized generalist.

In recent years, an increasing amount of cooperation has been demanded of general systems theory from such areas as biology, psychology, health care, economics, management, sociology, and political science. On this account, a danger arises: The specialized generalist may try to solve any problem presented to him by the specialist. It is very possible that he may find a solution which is correct from the system point of view but does not solve the problem proper.

My assertion is that the fixed idea of a powerful system theorist, who can solve almost all problems for almost all disciplines, should be recognized as a myth and treated accordingly. A system theorist specializes in a study of general properties of systems, and a few hours, days, or even weeks of concentrating on another discipline can give him only a very naive understanding of its peculiarities, needs, and problems. He cannot spend several years of study of each discipline where his advice is sought. If he claims that he is able to solve problems in various disciplines because of his knowledge of general principles of systems, then he is either naive or dishonest.

A specialized generalist cannot master all the disciplines in which his cooperation might be sought. On the other hand, a specialist in, say, health care can easily grasp basic concepts and principles of general systems in a relatively short time. He might be called a generalized specialist or, following Boulding, "the specialist with a universal mind" [16].

It is my belief that the generalized specialist is the person who will be increasingly in demand. He can be characterized as follows: He is essentially specialized in a discipline; at the same time, he is familiar, to a reasonable depth, with general systems foundations. In addition, he is aware of the capabilities and limitations of contemporary computers. Even though he is not expected to solve complex system-type problems in his discipline, he is able to communicate them properly to system theorists and interpret correctly the results obtained from the latter.

Hence, the role of general systems education consists not only in advancing general systems research but also in making it applicable in the areas where the real system-type problems arise. Three aspects of general systems education should be stressed:

(1) A need for training a sufficient number of system specialists to extend and accelerate basic research in the methodology of general systems. The isolated courses in general systems theory which have been offered so far are no longer sufficient. They should be extended into organized curricula, based on a systemic conceptual framework, including courses on sophisticated mathematical tools, computer programming, principles of modelling, simulation techniques, operations research, principles of measurements, automata theory, theory of languages, control theory, information theory, and other pertinent aspects.

(2) A need to familiarize specialists in various disciplines with fundamental concepts and simple principles of general systems, to make them able to communicate with systems specialists and with people from other disciplines. Scientific and engineering disciplines, as well as humanities and the arts, should be included.

(3) A need for restructuring education in special disciplines to identify more clearly system properties. This involves, for example, modification of text materials in individual disciplines to make them more communicable to other disciplines. It is appropriate to quote Kenneth Boulding in this context [16]:

"Unless the output of most specialists becomes the input of others, knowledge breaks up into a mere aggregation of related entities and ceases to be a single body".

6. Trends in general systems research

Let us summarize now what seems likely to be the most important trends in general systems research in the 1970's:

(1) A development of the systems approach into a theory of simplification as described above.

(2) A unification of contemporary general systems theories.
This involves: (a) clarification of terminology and notation, (b) identification

of minimal assumptions under which different theories are isomorphic or homomorphic, (c) integration of existing general systems theories.

(3) A development of general systems theories (or a unified theory). The most important aspects are: (a) an elaboration of a rigorous classification of systems and associated problems, (b) a development of an organized general systems methodology (in particular, a development of the methodology of general stochastic and fuzzy systems), (c) an investigation of the use of computers for solving problems of large-scale systems, (d) a design of interactive computer networks through which a large portion of the general systems methodology will be available to specialists in various disciplines.

(4) Further study of various meta-theoretical aspects of various general systems theories, including a possible rise of new mathematical concepts.

(5) Universal changes in education. As discussed above, this involves: (a) a development of general systems curricula to educate systems specialists, (b) a preparation of texts and courses providing basic concepts and principles of general systems for students majoring in various other areas, (c) a change of educational patterns in special disciplines to take advantage of general systems properties which are shared by all of them.

A description in depth of contemporary trends in general systems research is the subject of [2].

References

[1] H.J. Bremerman, Optimization through evolution and recombination, in: Self-organizing systems, eds. M.C. Yovits et al. (Spartan Books, Washington, 1962) p.93.

[2] G.J. Klir, Trends in general systems theory (Wiley, New York, 1972).

[3] G.J. Friedman and C.T. Leondes, Constraints theory, IEEE Trans. Systems Sci. and Cybern. SSC-5 (1969) 48, 132, 191.

[4] D.P. Eckman and M.D. Mesarovic, On some basic concepts of general systems theory, in: Proc. Third Intern. Conf. on Cybernetics, Namur (1961) p.104.

[5] T.G. Windeknecht, General dynamical processes (Academic Press, New York, 1971).

[6] M.D. Mesarovic et al., Theory of hierarchical, multi-level systems (Academic Press, New York, 1970).

[7] M.D. Mesarovic, On some metamathematical results as properties of general systems, Math. Systems Theory 2 (1968) 357.

[8] A.W. Wymore, A mathematical theory of systems engineering (John Wiley, New York, 1967).

[9] G.J. Klir and M.A. Marin, A multimodel and computer oriented methodology for synthesis of sequential discrete systems, IEEE Trans. Systems Sci. and Cybern. SSC-6 (1970).

[10] G.J. Klir, An approach to general systems theory (Van Nostrand–Reinhold, New York, 1969).

[11] S. Islam, Toward integration of two system theories, by Mesarovic and Wymore, Int. J. General Systems 1, No.1 (1973).

[12] P.C. Hammer, Advances in mathematical systems theory (Pennsylvania State Univ. Press, University Park, 1969).

[13] L.A. Zadeh, Fuzzy sets, Inform. and Control 8(1965) 338.

[14] L.A. Zadeh, Fuzzy sets and systems, in: System theory, ed., J. Fox (Polytechnic Press, New York, 1965), p.29.

[15] J.A. Goguen, The logic of inexact concepts, Synthese 19 (1968–69) 325.

[16] K.E. Boulding, The specialist with a universal mind, Mgmt. Sci. 14, No.12 (1968).

GENERAL SYSTEMS RESEARCH: DISCUSSANT 1

Recherche des systèmes généraux: porte-parole 1

HASSO VON FALKENHAUSEN

McKinsey and Company, Düsseldorf, West Germany

From my experience with papers and presentations on general systems theory, this topic can be dealt with in an esoteric or enigmatic way such that the general practitioner is utterly lost. I should like to extend my appreciation and respect to the author of this paper for a clear and easy to grasp definition of the means and ends in general systems research. As a user of systems whose primary interest is cost-effectiveness when developing or operating systems, I will group my comments under two headings: the expectations of a user for further results of systems research and for future developments in educating systems specialists. In both cases, a system can be a hardware or software product. For example, it can be the set of material-handling equipment and its manual and EDP-operating processes; it can be the entire logistic system for supplying automobile spare parts from factories to distributors and dealers; and it can be an LP-package to be used in an optimization model.

1. Expectations from systems research

The author groups his discussion of systems research under three headings, and I would like to follow this structure in my comments.

The author's concern about an orderly process for simplification in a *systems approach* is shared by the user who feels that in all the writing on systems approach very little is being said about the pitfalls in simplification. Further efforts in general systems research should therefore focus on developing procedures for testing the validity of a system that is to represent reality *in statu nascendi*. This test is necessary to evaluate the sensitivity of a system to changes in input data (to make a "what if" approach economically feasible) and to test the instability of a system in order to define the bad properties in advance. This set of procedures could, for example, be

(a) a checklist to be rigidly followed for evaluating a systems design when the first draft of a structure has been completed,

(b) a method for defining operating characteristics, like those for a quality control plan.

In *systems theory* the user would highly welcome a better definition of terms for describing a system and its major components. A definition, e.g., should deal with the assumptions underlying the development of the system, the definition of output variables, the definition of input variables, and, finally, the definition of transfer functions that describe the process between input and output. The plagued user is worried by a great deal of sad experiences with the dismal state of systems descriptions that have resulted in many man-months lost due to omissions or misplaced statements in systems manuals. The consumer's concern about "clauses in small print" in contracts is equally shared by those who operate large and complex systems and are left in the dark about some crucial properties of their black boxes.

In *meta-theoretical aspects* the user is looking for a big leap forward comparable to progress made 15 years ago by algorithmic languages in computing that suddenly allowed for a simple and orderly handling of sub-systems in a larger context. Systems command languages like Simscript or Dynamo have made systems users lazy and unconcerned about details, and this state of mind provides for a significant increase in effectiveness compared to those "happy" times when a simulation project meant in the first place writing a simulator program in machine code.

As a systems user, I feel strongly that I have the right to these expectations. I do not accept the piece of advice offered in resignation by a disgruntled user: "Don't try to understand the system, simply get used to it". Operating a badly designed system with incorrect behavior that is insufficiently described and extremely cumbersome to handle is an inhumane burden that should not be accepted by anyone.

2. Expectation from systems education

The author pleads for an education of systems researchers that is based on in-depth training in one discipline such that the student has been exposed in a field well known to him to the thorny problem of simplifying a complex relationship and validating in test runs the results of his design. The author quotes from Gerald M. Weinberg*:

"…. By studying the methods of simplification which have succeeded and failed in the past general systems theorist helps us to make the progress of human knowledge a little less depended on genius."

While I do agree that a Newtonian genius is not what we need in systems design, I would like to make a strong plea for a different kind of genius. If one looks at well-designed systems that work to the full satisfaction of all users you will usually find as a designer a man, or a group of men, who over and above being well educated and intelligent had a great deal of insight, perspective, and judgment. In my experience, these characteristics usually grow with experience, but they grow faster and easier on an education that covers the real world as well as its simplified description in abstract terms such that improvements can be made, rather than on an education that puts its emphasis on detailed knowledge of methods and procedures that can be used exclusively in the abstract space.

Insight, perspective, and judgment built on an education that is oriented toward one aspect of reality will, eventually, offer the opportunity for systems designers to move into managerial positions, just like their peers trained and experienced in one of the classical functions like sales, production, or finance. Unless we keep career objectives in mind when designing curricula for systems research, we will have difficulties in attracting outstanding men to this subject that, under the perspective of insight into corporate interrelationships, should offer exceptional chances for promotion.

The Greek word συστημα means, as quoted by the author "a set or arrangement of things so related or connected as to form a unity or organic whole". In the classic Greek literature, this word has taken on different meanings. Plato has used it for describing the structure of a phalanx that is being prepared for an attack. In later times, the term was used in the sense of putting together several verses into a larger literary opus. In systems design, we expect besides the ability to work with complex interrelationships a sense of application (for building the phalanx) and a sense of proportion (for forming the poem). For we want to be certain that our future systems designer can fight his battle or sing his song without tripping over trivia.

---

* Main paper, page 193.

SIMULATION AND VALIDATION

Simulation et validation

THOMAS H. NAYLOR

Duke University, North Carolina, U.S.A.

Abstract. This paper reviews the state of the art of simulation methodology with special emphasis placed on the problem of validation. Definition of the problem, formulation of a mathematical model, formulation of a computer program, validation, experimental design and data analysis for computer simulation experiments are treated in this paper. A number of methodological problems are defined and where solutions exist, they are described. The problem of validation is treated from three different perspectives: philosophical, methodological, and practical.

1. Computer simulation defined

We shall define simulation as a numerical technique for conducting experiments with certain types of mathematical models which describe the behavior of a complex system on a digital computer over extended periods of time. The starting point of any computer simulation experiment is a model of the system to be simulated. Although computer simulation has been applied to many different types of models, in this paper we shall concentrate primarily on models of business and economic systems. We shall also assume that a model has already been formulated and its parameters have been specified. The principal difference between a simulation experiment and a "real-world" experiment is that, with simulation, the experiment is conducted with a model of the real system rather than with the actual system itself.

2. Methodology

We now turn to a brief summary of the methodology of computer simulation. Experiments with models of economic systems usually involve six steps*:
(1) formulation of the problem,
(2) formulation of a mathematical model,
(3) formulation of a computer program,
(4) validation,
(5) experimental design,
(6) output analysis.
In this paper we shall concentrate on the last three steps.

3. Validation

Validating simulation models is indeed difficult because it involves a host of practical, theoretical, statistical and even philosophical complexities. It is part of a more general problem in validation of any hypothesis. The basic questions are: what does it mean to validate an hypothesis? and what criteria should be used? The criteria depend entirely upon the analyst's objective, be it forecasting, system design, optimization, general exploration, or merely a training exercise. In view of the complexity of most computer models of business and economic systems, a multi-stage validation procedure seems most appropriate.

The first stage, the formulation of a set of postulates, requires a diligent search for what Kant has called "synthetic a priori" using all possible information at our disposal. The set of postulates is formed from the researcher's "general knowledge" of the system or his knowledge of "similar" systems that have already been successfully simulated. The researcher must select, on essentially a priori grounds, a limited number of all possible postulates for further detailed study, thereby rejecting an infinity of postulates on the same grounds. This selection includes the specification of components, the selection of variables as well as the formulation of functional relationships. This a priori approach means that we recognize these basic postulates as tentative hypotheses about the behavior of a system.

The second stage requires the analyst to "verify" the postulates subject to the limitations of existing tests. Although we cannot solve the philosophical

* A complete description of each of the six steps is contained in [1].

problem of what it means to verify a postulate, we can apply the "best" available statistical tests to them.

But in economics we often find that many of our postulates are either impossible to falsify by empirical evidence or extremely difficult to subject to empirical testing. We have the choice of either abandoning them entirely, arguing that unverifiable postulates are scientifically meaningless, or we may retain them as "tentative". If we reject them, we must continue searching for other and verifiable postulates. If we retain them, we may argue that there is no reason to assume that they are invalid just because they cannot be tested.

The third stage consists of testing the model's ability to predict. The degree to which data generated by simulation conform to observed data, can be tested either by historical verification (retrospective predictions) or by forecasting (prospective predictions).

Descriptive analysis seeks to produce a model that would predict the behavior of the system while prescriptive analysis involves predicting behavior under different combinations of controllable conditions from which the most desirable set of conditions will be chosen. In descriptive analysis, the actual historical record can be used as a check on the accuracy of the predictions, and hence on the extent to which the model fulfilled its purpose. But prescriptive analysis involves choosing the one historical path along which the system will be directed. Therefore, only the historical record of the path actually traveled will be generated, and the historical records of alternative paths corresponding to alternative policies will not be available for comparison. Although, in this instance, the historical record cannot be used as a direct check on whether the model did actually point out the best policy to follow, the actual outcome of the policy chosen can be compared with the outcome predicted by the simulation model as an indirect test of the model. In either case, the predictions of the model are directly related to the purpose for which the model was formulated, whereas the assumptions that make up the model are only indirectly related to its purpose through their influence on the predictions. Hence the final decision concerning the validity of the model must be based on its predictions.

Thus far, we have concerned ourselves only with philosophical considerations. What practical considerations do social scientists face in verifying computer models? Some criteria must be devised to indicate when the time paths generated by a computer simulation model agree sufficiently with the observed or historical time paths. That agreement cannot be attributed merely to chance. Specific measures and techniques must be considered for testing the model's goodness-of-fit, i.e., the degree of conformity of simulated time-series to observed data.

As we have previously indicated, these measures and techniques are entirely dependent on the experimental objectives. At the outset we must indicate whether we are primarily interested in observing the average behavior of the system, the variance of the system, the statistical distribution of some particular random variable, or some other descriptive measure of the performance of the system.

Some potentially useful *measures* are: number of turning points, timing of turning points, direction of turning points, amplitude of the fluctuations for corresponding time segments, average amplitude over the whole series, simultaneity of turning points for different variables, average values of variables, exact matching of values of variables, probability distribution, variance, skewness, kurtosis.

Some of the more important statistical *techniques** available are listed below together with a number of references which describe their use as goodness-of-fit tests with simulation models in complete detail: analysis of variance [1], chi-square test [1], factor analysis [1], nonparametric tests [1], regression analysis [1], spectral analysis [2], Theil's inequality coefficient [3], Theil's information inaccuracy test [4].

4. Experimental design

In the next two sections I wish to show the relationship between existing experimental design and data analysis techniques and the design of computer simulation experiments with models of economic systems†. Now I shall describe and suggest techniques for four problems that arise in the design of simulation experiments. These problems concern (1) stochastic convergence, (2) size, (3) motive, and (4) multiple response.

4.1. The problem of stochastic convergence

Most simulation experiments are intended to yield information about population quantities or averages. As estimates of population averages, the sample averages we compute from several runs on a computer will be subject to

---

* Although a number of statistical techniques exist, for some unknown reason economists have, more often than not, restricted themselves to purely graphical (as opposed to statistical) techniques.

† The reader may wish to consult [1] for an in-depth treatment of the problem of experimental design with simulation experiments with models of economic systems.

random fluctuation and will not be exactly equal to the population averages. The convergence of sample averages for increasing sample size is called stochastic convergence.

The problem with stochastic convergence is that it is slow. If the standard deviation, σ for a single observation, measures the amount of random fluctuation inherent in a chance quantity, then for n observations its value is $\sigma/\sqrt{n}$. Thus, in order to halve the random error, one must quadruple the sample size n; to decrease the random error by a factor of ten, one must increase the sample size by a factor of one hundred. It can easily happen that a reasonably small random error requires an unreasonably large sample size.

Clearly other methods are required if we wish to reduce random error. In real world experiments these usually involve including factors such as blocks or concomitant variables that are not of basic interest to the experimenter. If some of these factors can be controlled or observed, then their effects will no longer contribute to the random error, and the standard deviation will be reduced.

In a computer simulation experiment with a given model, the inclusion of more factors is not possible as it requires a change in the model. Once the model has been specified, all the uncontrolled factors have been irretrievably absorbed in the probabilistic specification for the exogenous inputs. There are, however, error reduction techniques that are suitable for computer simulation experiments. The underlying principle of these Monte Carlo techniques is to use knowledge about the structure of the model, the properties of the probability distributions of the exogenous inputs, and the properties of the observed variates actually used for inputs to increase the precision (i.e., reduce random error) in the measurement of averages for the response variables.

Moy [1] describes four Monte Carlo techniques in detail: (1) regression sampling, (2) antithetic-variate sampling, (3) stratified sampling, and (4) importance sampling. He applies each of these techniques to an example model and compares the simulation results.

4.2. The problem of size

What we have called the problem of size could easily be called "the problem of too many factors". In a factorial design for several factors the number of cells required is the product of the number of levels for each of the factors in the experiment. Thus, in a four-factor experiment with a model of the firm, if we have six different employment policies, five alternative marketing plans, five possible inventory policies, and ten different equipment replacement policies, then a total of $6 \times 5 \times 5 \times 10 = 1500$ cells (or factor combinations) would be required for a full factorial design. If we had a ten factor experiment and if we used only two levels for each of these factors, the full factorial experiment would require $2^{10} = 1024$ cells. It is evident that the full design can require an unmanageably large number of cells if more than a few factors are to be investigated.

If we require a complete investigation of the factors in the experiment (including main effects and interactions of all orders), then there is no solution to the problem of size. If, however, we are willing to settle for a less than complete investigation (perhaps including main effects and two-factor interactions), then there are designs that will accomplish our purpose and that require fewer cells than the full factorial. These fractional factorial designs include Latin square and Greco—Latin square designs.

Thus far the problem of size reduction has been discussed in terms of an analysis of variance, which is appropriate when the factors are qualitative. However, if the response Y is functionally related to the qualitative factors, $X_1, X_2 ... X_k$, then regression analysis may be more appropriate. The functional relationship, $Y = f(X_1, ..., X_k)$, called the response surface, can be fitted to observed data using least squares regression analysis.

Where regression analysis is used, factorial design may not be optimal. Several authors, primarily George Box, have developed "response surface designs" which have an important advantage over comparable factorial designs in reducing the required size of the experiment without causing a corresponding reduction in the amount of information obtained.

4.3. The problem of motive

The experimenter should specify his objectives as precisely as possible since the design that will best satisfy his objectives depends on whether he wishes (1) to find the combination of factor levels at which the response variable is maximized (or minimized) in order to optimize some process, or (2) to make a rather general investigation of the underlying mechanisms governing the process under study. This distinction is less important when the factors are qualitative rather than quantitative. Unless certain interactions can be assumed to be zero, the only way to find the optimum response is to measure the response at all combinations of factor levels (that is, the full factorial design). Even if interactions are assumed negligible in an experiment with qualitative factors, the design is likely to be the same whether the aim is to optimize or to explore. In an experiment with quantitative factors the picture is quite different. Hence, the continuity of the response surface can usually be used to guide us quickly and efficiently to the optimum. In this case two sampling methods in general use are systematic sampling and random sampling: (1) the uniform-grid or factorial method, (2) the single-factor method, (3) the method of marginal analysis, and (4) the method of steepest ascent.

Since general explorations are usually a less precisely specified goal than optimization, it is difficult to identify a "best" experimental design. However, we can state a guiding principle: when the aim of an experiment is to further general knowledge and understanding, it is important to give careful and precise consideration to the existing state of knowledge and to the questions and uncertainties on which we desire the experimental data to shed light.

4.4. The multiple response problem

This problem arises when we wish to observe many different response variables in a given experiment – a common occurrence in simulation experiments with economic systems. For example, salary, security, status, power, prestige, social service, and professional excellence, to mention only a few, might all be treated as response variables in a simulation experiment with a model of an organization.

Often, it is possible to bypass the multiple response problem by treating an experiment with many responses as many experiments, each with a single response. Or several responses could be combined (for example, by addition) and treated as a single response. However, this is not always possible; often multiple responses are inherent to the situation under study. Unfortunately, for these cases design techniques are virtually nonexistent.

Any attempt to solve the multiple response program is likely to require the use of utility theory. Gary Fromm [5] has taken an initial step in this direction by using utility theory to evaluate the results of policy simulation experiments with the Brookings model. His specific problem was how to choose among alternative economic policies that affect a large number of different response variables in many different ways. He treated utility as a response variable and developed a discounted utility function over time that depends on the values of the endogenous variables of the model, as well as on the mean, variance, skewness, and kurtosis of these variables.

5. Output analysis

The great bulk of experimental design techniques described in the literature use the analysis of variance as their method of data analysis. Accordingly, we shall investigate several special cases of this technique, including the F-test, multiple comparisons, multiple rankings, spectral analysis and sequential sampling as applied to the analysis of output data generated by simulation experiments with models of social systems.

5.1. F-test

Suppose that we are interested in testing the null hypothesis that the expected payoffs associated with each of five production strategies are equal; a straightforward procedure would be the F-test. If the null hypothesis is accepted, then one tentatively concludes that the sample differences between strategies are attributable to random fluctuations rather than to actual differences in population values (expected payoffs). On the other hand, if the null hypothesis is rejected, then further analysis, such as multiple comparisons and multiple rankings, is recommended. The F-test rests on three important assumptions: (1) normality, (2) equality of variance, and (3) statistical independence. The author has published [1] a number of applications of this use of the F-test.

5.2. Multiple comparisons

Typically, management scientists are interested not only in whether alternatives differ but in how they differ. Here multiple comparison and multiple ranking procedures are often the relevant tools. In contrast with the analysis of variance, these methods emphasize the use of confidence intervals rather than the testing of hypotheses. For example, if one is interested in comparing the means of different populations, then a number of $(100 - \alpha)$ percent confidence intervals for the differences between population means may be constructed. The two books by Naylor [5,1] contain several applications.

5.3. Multiple rankings

Frequently, the objective of computer simulation experiments with models of social and administrative systems is to find the "best", "second best", "third best", and so forth. Although multiple comparison methods are often used, multiple ranking methods represent a more direct approach. A good estimate of the rank of a set of alternatives is simply the ranking of the sample means associated with the given alternatives. Because of random error, however, sample rankings may yield incorrect results. Basically, multiple ranking procedures attempt to answer this question: with what probability can we say that a ranking of sample means represents the true ranking of the population means?

A number of multiple ranking procedures are described in [6] and a number of applications in [1].

5.3. Spectral analysis

Spectral analysis, frequently employed in the physical sciences and more recently applied by economists to analyze the behavior of economic time-series, has relevance for our study for at least four reasons.

First, output generated by computer simulation experiments is usually highly autocorrelated – for example, births in a period t are likely to be highly correlated with births in period $t-k$. Autocorrelation in sample data will lead to underestimates of sampling variances (which are unduly large) and inefficient predictions if classical statistical techniques are used. Several methods are available for treating this problem, apart from the trivial case of ignoring it.

(1) Divide the sample record length into intervals that are no longer than the intervals of major autocorrelation and work with the observations on these supposedly independent intervals [7]. This method suffers from the fact that "the choices of sample record length and sampling interval seems to have neither enough prior nor posterior justification in most cases to make this choice much more than arbitrary" [7].

(2) Replicate the simulation experiment and computer sample means and variances across the ensemble rather than over time. This method may lead to excessive computer running time and fail to yield the type of information desired about a particular time series.

(3) Use a technique such as spectral analysis, which is based on a model in which the probabilities of component outcomes in a time series depend on previous outcomes in the series. In this way the problems associated with method (1) can successfully be avoided without replicating the experiment.

Second, "When one studies a stochastic process, he is interested in the average level of activity, deviations from this level, and how long these deviations last, once they occur" [7]. Spectral analysis provides this kind of information.

Third, with spectral analysis, it is relatively easy to construct confidence bands and to test hypotheses for comparing two or more alternative simulation runs. Frequently, it is impossible to detect differences in time-series generated by simulation experiments when one restricts himself to simple

graphical analysis. Spectral analysis provides a means of objectively comparing time-series generated with a computer model.

Fourth, spectral analysis can also be used as a technique for validating a
model of a social system. By comparing the estimated spectra of simulated
output data and corresponding real-world data, one can infer how well the
model resembles the system it was designed to emulate [7].

Fishman and Kiviat [7] have written a path-breaking article on the use of
spectral analysis in analyzing data generated by computer simulation models.
Naylor et al. [2] have applied spectral analysis to the analysis of simulation
experiments with econometric models. Spectral analysis has also been used to
compare output generated by computer simulation experiments on a model
of the textile industry with corresponding real-world data as a technique of
verification [1].

5.4. Sequential sampling

Output generated by computer simulation experiments (observations) is
costly. This cost may be greatly reduced if at each stage of the simulation the
analyst balances the cost of additional observations (generated by the computer) against the expected gain in information. The objective of sequential
sampling is to minimize the number of observations (sample size) for obtaining the information that is required from the experiment. Sample size, n, is
considered a random variable dependent on the outcome of the first $n-1$
observations and so is not fixed in advance. In this way the objective is to
minimize cost by generating only enough observations to achieve the required
results with predetermined accuracy.

For example, a sequential test on a computer model of a firm could be
designed to determine if the profits obtained by using a certain investment
policy in combination with various production policies differed significantly.
The sequential method has a procedure for deciding at the ith observation
whether to accept a given hypothesis, reject the hypothesis, or continue
sampling by taking the $(i+1)$th observation. Such a procedure must specify the
ith observation, a division of the i-dimensional space of all possible observations into three mutually exclusive and exhaustive sets: an area of preference
A_i for accepting the hypothesis, an area of preference B_i for rejecting it, and
an area of indifference C_i where no statement can be made about the hypothesis and further observations are necessary. The fundamental problem in the
theory of sequential sampling is that of a proper choice of the sets A_i, B_i and
C_i. (See chapter 8 in [1] for an application.)

6. The interface between simulation experiments and real-world experiments

Recently the staff members of the "social system simulation program" at Duke University have embarked on a major research project to explore the interface between computer simulation experiments and real-world experiments. The objectives of this project are (1) to develop a methodology for designing policy experiments with real-world economic systems utilizing preliminary screening experiments which take the form of computer simulations with models of the actual economic systems; (2) to investigate the feasibility of "evolutionary operations procedures" for designing economic policy experiments with real-world economic systems; (3) to consider a number of experimental design and data analysis problems associated with the development of such a methodology.

Richard Day [8] has proposed an interesting application of a relatively new technique called "evolutionary operations procedures" (EVOP) to both real-world experiments and computer simulation experiments with economic systems. EVOP is an experimental design technique developed by George Box and others for the control of chemical production processes. Typically, processes of this type are characterized by the fact that they are so complicated that the production functions of the firm are unknown and classical optimization techniques are analytically intractable. "Box's procedure involves the managers in a sequential game played with their own plants as the environments in which they experiment with controls to allow local estimation of the plant payoff function, and on the basis of which sub-optimization incremental changes and controls can be exercised" [8].

Day has proposed a three-stage procedure for applying EVOP to a national economy – national evolutionary operations procedure (NAEVOP): (1) an initial set of simulation experiments are used to update and evaluate the current planning model; (2) a second round of experiments is conducted to form a broadly representative opinion survey about preferences of possible policy, economic-evolution combinations; and (3) control modifications are attempted in a direction representing the current conception by the policymakers of the public interest. Day envisages for NAEVOP "a real-time, four-way communication network between government planners, political representatives, other economic block representatives (labor unions, industrial executives) and private citizens" [8].

The social system simulation program at Duke University is developing a two-stage methodology for designing experiments with real-world economic systems which involves the use of computer simulation as a type of screening procedure. Basically we hope to develop a generalized methodology which integrates the six-step methodology developed by Naylor for simulation experiments into a framework suitable for real-world experiments. Such a methodology will probably include the following steps:

(1) Formulation of the problem.

(2) Formulation of the overall experimental design.

(3) Formulation of a mathematical model.

(4) Formulation of a computer program.

(5) Validation of the model.

(6) Formulation of the experimental design for the simulation experiment.

(7) Execution of the simulation experiment.

(8) Analysis of the data generated by the simulation experiment.

(9) Execution of the real-world experiment.

(10) Analysis of the data generated by the real-world experiment.

Of course, it will usually be necessary to repeat one or more of the aforementioned steps in order to achieve satisfactory results.

References

[1] T.H. Naylor, Computer simulation experiments with models of economic systems (Wiley, New York, 1971).

[2] T.H. Naylor, K. Wertz and T. Wonnacott, Spectral analysis of data generated by simulation experiments with econometric models, Econometrica 37 (April, 1969).

[3] T.H. Naylor and J.M. Finger, Verification of computer simulation models, Mgmt. Sci. 14 (Oct. 1967).

[4] H. Theil, Economics and information theory (North-Holland, Amsterdam, 1967).

[5] T.H. Naylor, The design of computer simulation experiments (Duke Univ. Press, Durham, 1969).

[6] J. Kleijnen, T.H. Naylor and T. Seaks, The use of multiple ranking procedures to analyze simulations of management systems, Mgmt. Sci. 19 (Feb. 1972).

[7] G.S. Fishman and P.J. Kiviat, The analysis of simulation-generated time series, Mgmt. Sci. 13 (March 1967).

[8] R.H. Day, Comments on the two above papers, in: Frontiers of quantitative economics, ed. M.C. Intrilligator (North-Holland, Amsterdam, 1971).

[9] A.V. Gafarian and C.J. Ancker, Mean value estimation from digital computer simulation, Opns. Res. 14, No.1 (1966).

[10] M.J. Gilman, A brief survey of stopping rules in Monte Carlo simulations, Digest Second Conf. on Applications of Simulation (Dec. 1968).

[11] J. Kleijnen, The statistical aspects of simulation, unpublished paper, Tilburg School of Economics and Business Administration, Tilburg (Feb. 1972).

[12] T.H. Naylor, Experimental economics revisited, J. Polit. Econ. 80 (March–April 1972).

[13] T.H. Naylor and J.M. Vernon, Microeconomics and decision models of the firm (Harcourt, Brace and Jovanivich, New York, 1969).

[14] H. Reichenbach, The rise of scientific philosophy (Univ. of California Press, Berkeley 1951).

M. Ross, ed., OR '72. North-Holland Publishing Company (1973)

21

SIMULATION AND VALIDATION: DISCUSSANT 1

Simulation et validation: porte-parole 1

P. JACQUET

Air France, Paris, France

You were careful in your paper to define your terms clearly, so as to avoid frequent sources of misinterpretation. You point out that your comments apply mainly to simulations of economic systems, implying that they might not be valid for other systems. As you did not specify what you mean by economic system, I feel that a reminder of its chief features will serve for a better comprehension of the extent of your considerations.

Models of any system, whether economic or not, are composed of input data, output data, and a set of rules that specify their relationship. Models of an economic system have the following specific features:

(1) Input and output data are generally abstract macroeconomic variables defined as an aggregate of elementary variables for which a unit of measure has been defined. These elementary variables are always concrete physical data: (a) work supplied by a human being, (b) material used for performing a task. These elementary variables are numerous and varied in nature. Their very definition is sometimes difficult and unstable over time. It is essential to aggregate them (if one wishes to understand economic phenomena) but it must not be forgotten that the basis for aggregation is arbitrary.

(2) The set of rules, likewise purely abstract, that link the outputs and inputs of the model is deemed to represent schematically a complex set of real mechanisms in which human behaviour intervenes permanently. This behaviour is itself not stable in time, as even ethics changes in the course of time.

(3) Lastly, past observations of both input as well as output variables, are generally few. So comments must always be limited over the period of time during which the variables remain stable in definition.

I agree that, from the formal point of view, validating a simulation, raises several philosophic problems as to the selection of criteria, which themselves depend on the aim pursued. As a practitioner, I consider that the immediate aim must, above all, be to place an instrument at the disposal of decision centers capable of helping them to understand everyday reality better and avoid their taking decisions that might have unfortunate future consequences. Hence, from this point of view, a simulation model becomes mainly an instrument capable of monitoring in advance the consequences of all human action.

From my past experience model validity tests boil down to checking, if as the input variables are given the values observed, that the output variables also take as values those that have been observed, or at least similar values. If the deviation between calculated values and observed values is too great, I feel it is always possible – given the characteristics of the economic system which I precisely recalled – to build up a model step by step by multiplying the variables and modifying its logic until finally it gives an excellent representation of the past. This is all the easier as past observations are few in number. I shall even say that, at the very limit, the model might be indeterminate.

I am afraid that, in these conditions, even if the validity test is positive, this cannot be an adequate guarantee of the model's validity in the future.

Finally, testing a model's validity *a posteriori,* i.e., by comparing the scheduled results with those effectively achieved, already supposes that the values taken by the input variables are the same in the model and in reality. This is practically never the case, particularly when some of the input variables are random: the probability that the *scheduled* values of input variables are effectively those that will be *achieved* is at zero limit when the variables are continuous. One could of course check that, with the values achieved from input variables, the values of the output variables are the same with the model and with reality. But this is no test of the merits of the decision which has been taken on the basis of another system of values.

To sum up, I feel that despite the many tests than can be carried out, decisions taken on the basis of results supplied by a model may be entirely false in certain cases if man does not intervene himself to check the results themselves from his own experience. But then again, this is unfortunately not a guarantee. However, is it not in the very nature of things that every decision is attended by a risk that cannot be eluded.

M. Ross, ed., OR'72. North-Holland Publishing Company (1973)

22

SIMULATION AND VALIDATION: DISCUSSANT 2

Simulation et validation: porte-parole 2

ROY H.W. JOHNSTON

Trinity College, Dublin, Ireland

I welcome Dr. Naylor's paper; it puts the philosophy of simulation before us in a comprehensive yet concise manner. In my comment I make, and attempt to defend, three assertions.

(1) The ratio of simulation to analysis in a model can have any value between zero and one; it is not a binary variable.

(2) An experimental structure, which is a model of a real system, ought to be designed so as to produce a big signal, well above the noise level, if insights are to be gained.

(3) There is a need for some objective common measure in multiple-response situations; subjective measures, such as utility, are of doubtful value.

Dr. Naylor gives the impression that he regards simulation and analysis as two quite separate camps. I suggest that it is possible to build hybrid models, containing elements described analytically, interacting in response to signals one or more of which are simulated.

If I may take an example from my own experience, in the early days of real-time airline reservations systems, (1963–64), little or nothing was understood about the statistics of the response of random access computer systems to an environment which manifested itself as a stochastic demand for service of randomly varying type. Serious errors were made in the design of real-time systems as a result. Simulation experiments were done subsequently to try and discover the nature of the design faults, and valuable experience was gained.

Round about this time I was working for an airline and I produced an "analytical simulation" of a real-time system, in which I used the results of queue-theory to predict waiting-times consequent on the demand for services for the central processor, for the channel serving the files and for the files themselves. The demand for services for each of these elements was calculated from a knowledge of the number and type of "messages" which were "in the system". "Messages" were specified by patterns of demand for service by the central processor and files. The "next message" was chosen by the one "Monte Carlo" procedure in the model. This "analytical simulation" gave results in broad agreement with the traditional simulation developed by the manufacturers; it predicted the same bottleneck, namely, the file-access channel. Multiple channels were subsequently introduced. The manufacturers' simulation took some man-years to develop, and hours to run. The analytical simulation took some man-months, and minutes. (This work is on record in the 1965 AGIFORS proceedings at Chicago.) I was convinced by this experience of the wisdom of practicing the maximum economy in the use of random variables.

I turn now to my second point: the need to design the experiment so as to produce a big signal. Nature has provided an abundance of noises with which the signals describing the states of our systems are masked. The philosophy of experimentation which I imbibed when working as a physicist consisted in constructing an experimental model of the system which reduced to the minimum the extraneous noise and focussed on those signals which were considered to be the key to the essential dynamics. I get the impression that the type of simulation philosophy expounded by Dr. Naylor is at variance with this: he feels it necessary to make the noise-level of the model system comparable to that in the real system, so that he is in the happy position of being able to use all the tricks in the statistician's bag to pick the signal out. When I was working in physics, the lore used to be that if a man had to resort to sophisticated statistical techniques, his experiment was suspect. This may be seen by some as an extreme view, but it is useful to bear it in mind when setting the experiment up.

Fortunately, in business systems nature has provided a filter with which the experimenter can pick out the relatively small number of significant variables from the mass of background. This filter is the judgement and experience of the manager: those who have not developed a feel for the significant variables from the experience of working the system are unlikely to have survived. Thus the "problem of many factors", while theoretically present, can in practice often be avoided.

It therefore becomes possible to make meaningful simulations of complex systems which give large and clear signals if we allow ourselves to use judgement and experience in the suppression of irrelevant noise. I, personally, prefer this road to that mapped out by Dr. Naylor. If this restricts the class of problem open to me, I accept this restriction. I have no doubt that there are many who would reject it. I suggest that the ultimate arbiter is the client, who will pay for that which gives him most insight per dollar.

Finally, I feel I must contribute to the discussion on multiple responses and Dr. Naylor's proposed approach via utilities. I would like to see someone working on an alternative approach in which the sole measure is the survival probability of the system as a viable organism. There are insights to be gained from current work on ageing in biology; this depends on information-theoretic concepts such as garbling of coded data, entropy levels, etc.

I suggest that an approach to the problem of viability of an economic organism can be made via a thermodynamic model, with temperature and entropy defined in information-theoretic terms. One can envisage an economic organism (a firm) ingesting nutrient from a disordered environment, ordering the ingested raw material into finished products, which are placed with precision in a disordered market. Each step involves entropy reduction, which costs money. It is useful to reflect that the product of entropy and temperature has the dimensions of energy, which is the same thing as money. Each step in the process has an entropy change associated with it; this entropy change occurs at a "temperature", which may be conceived as a measure of management ability. A "hot" management can reduce entropy rapidly.

An economic organism is viable if its revenue from sales exceeds its total costs; the cost function includes "volume × unit cost" terms and "temperature × entropy" terms. This approach, therefore, contains the embryo of a theory of management costs or "overheads", as the core of its approach to the question of viability of the economic organism. I commend this approach to the theoreticians. It is, as I said, related to a body of theory which is developing in biology with sound roots in physics, thermodynamics and information theory. It represents a radically different approach to that of utility theory, although both relate to measures of value. It substitutes for a multiplicity of subjective sub-goals a single over-riding goal, survival; this goal is of very deep significance and has deep roots in biological and sociological evolution.

Finally, may I take a plea that the theoreticians should pay more attention to the challenges thrown by by the practice of OR. The theory–practice ratio in OR is out of proportion to that which obtains in other branches of applied science. Because theoreticians are solving problems posed by each other and neglecting the experimenters' world, important areas such as that outlined by

Dr. Naylor are neglected. Consequently their development is stultified and pushed into repetitious applications of statistical filtering of dirty signals, which we have all seen before. We need more insights into the inside of the black box, illuminated by good theory. We need more analysis in our simulations. We need to design our experiments so as to keep the noise level down, and finally we need to develop an integrated theoretical approach to the measurement of system viability which could possibly be based on thermodynamic concepts.

M. Ross, ed., OR'72. North-Holland Publishing Company (1973)

Paul Naor Memorial Session

STOCHASTIC PROCESSES

Processus stochastiques

F.G. FOSTER

Department of Statistics, Trinity College, Dublin, Ireland

Abstract. The theory of stochastic processes is applied in OR to provide insights to problems in management control of complex systems. For this purpose, many special stochastic models have been developed in the OR literature and their properties explored.

In this paper, a survey is presented of some of the more fundamental models drawn chiefly from the areas of storage and queueing. Their control aspects and their operating characteristics are discussed and it is demonstrated how a simple calculus of expectations can be applied in a unified manner to derive basic formulae both exact and approximate.

Some of the most recently developed models have arisen in connection with the efficient use of computer systems in which the hardware is time-shared by a number of users communicating concurrently through on-line remote terminals. A general model of basic interest is the so-called "processor-sharing" model. This model which has some surprising features, is singled out for more detailed discussion, and its operating characteristics are derived.

The paper concludes with some general observations on stochastic modelling in OR.

I met Paul Naor at the first IFORS Conference, in Oxford in 1957. On one afternoon we went for a walk around the town and I was pleased to be able to show him the colleges, familiar to me since I had previously studied there. We talked about our mutual interests and it was for me a memorable experience. At subsequent meetings, he recalled the sight-seeing tour of the Colleges which he found fascinating and I remember not the details of the conversation but an attitude to research which impressed me at a time when I was still in the process of formulating my own approach.

At that Conference, Paul read a paper on the subject of machine interference on which he had recently obtained some basic results. The problem of machine interference applies in many situations but is usually stated in terms of a group of machines that break down from time to time. A number of repair men are available to service the machines, but if more machines are broken down at any time than there are repair men available, the machines have to wait for service, so that in addition to the normal loss due to time spent in servicing machines there is the interference loss due to the fact that sometimes servicing is thus delayed. A model of machine interference is a stochastic process in which attention is fixed on the fluctuating number through time of broken down machines and of busy repairmen as the operating characteristics in economic considerations of the system. It is frequently necessary only to consider expected values.

This eminently practical branch of stochastic processes, like indeed the general theory of stochastic processes, ante-dates the time when operations researchers self-consciously regarded themselves as such. The first treatment of machine interference seems to be due to Khintchine [1]. Other early workers in this field were Palm [2] and Ashcroft [3]. The model of machine interference is often referred to as Palm's model. Paul Naor's contribution [4, 5] was to show how numerical results can conveniently be obtained from tables of the Poisson distribution. This solution has been extensively tabulated by Peck and Hazelwood [6].

1. Random modification of a distribution

Before embarking on the main theme of my talk, there is one point in particular in Paul Naor's Conference paper on which I should like to make a remark because I shall want to refer to it again later. In his paper he gave a name for the first time, I believe, to a concept which has been referred to quite often since. The concept is that of the "random modification" of a probability distribution function. The idea is this: Suppose an inspector makes checks at random times on a machine that has a running time which is distributed with a density $f(t)$ possessing a mean β and a variance σ^2. Then after such a random check, given that it occurs during a running time, what is the expected residual running time of the machine? It is not in fact $\frac{1}{2}\beta$. The density of the residual running time, x, can on reflection be seen to be

$$g(x) = \frac{1}{\beta} \int_x^\infty f(t)\, dt \ .$$

This is because the probability that the inspector's check falls in a running time interval of length t is proportional both to t and to the frequency $f(t)$. It is then easily calculated that the mean value is

$$E(x) = \tfrac{1}{2}\beta(1 + \sigma^2/\beta^2) \ . \tag{1}$$

Thus the expected residual time is seen to depend significantly on the coefficient of variation, σ/β, of $f(t)$. (It could easily exceed the mean running time β.) This paradoxical result, which belongs to renewal theory and is much used in queueing theory, originated with Khintchine [7].

This machine interference model, which I have been speaking about although not originally recognised to be so, is in fact abstractly identical with the telephone traffic model in which "machines" become subscribers and "repairmen" become channels (see, for example, [8–10]). The original work on the telephone traffic model was of course done by Erlang (see [11, 12]).

2. A basic relation

Now it is not my intention to survey the field of stochastic processes, which would be quite impossible in a single paper, or indeed by one person. The field is vast and extends far beyond the boundaries of OR into many branches of science. Any general survey would be so general as to be devoid of content and boring. There are stochastic process models in astronomy, medicine, sociology, physics, genetics, biology. The theory is used in communication and control problems and in problems of smoothing and prediction in time-series. Some of the earliest studies were concerned with population growth and decay and date back to the 19th century to the work of Francis Galton and to the English clergyman, the Rev. Watson [13], on the phenomenon of the extinction of family surnames.

Rather I want to continue to consider some of the more basic types of model in the management science area and to discuss one or two very general ideas common to them all that happen to interest me. I do not propose to enter into any technicalities, and if I can demonstrate the self-evident nature of the ideas I am referring to, then the demonstration will be worthwhile.

Many of the practical results depend on a very few basic propositions in the theory of probability. One of the most useful of these relates to expected value. It is not obvious, for example, that if we are interested in the sum of two random quantities, then, even though the value of one of them affects the distribution of possible values of the other, nevertheless the expected value of the sum is equal to the sum of their separate expected values.

I will take as an appropriate starting point a remark made by Paul Naor [4]. In considering a machine-repair system with M machines and r repairmen such that the average running time of a machine is α and the average repair time is β, he defines a as the average number of machines working and b as the average number being serviced (which is the same thing as the average number of repairmen working) and notes that

$$b/a = \beta/\alpha .$$ (2)

"Obviously these two ratios must be equal", he observed. But why are they equal? This is one of those obvious propositions the obviousness of which has to be demonstrated, and once demonstrated only then becomes obvious. We can observe that over a time T the amount of production obtained from the machines is aT while the amount of servicing required is bT. Thus the left-hand side represents the amount of servicing expended per unit of production obtained. Now $1/\alpha$ represents the number of stops per unit of productive time, so that β/α is again the servicing required per unit of production. Defining β/α as the *servicing factor*, we can rewrite the relation as:

servicing rate = production rate × servicing factor .   (3)

Let us now turn to another branch of stochastic processes, inventory models. Here the basic operating characteristics of interest are sales rate, λ, average stock level, S, and turnover, τ, measured as the average time a unit is held in stock. We again have an obvious relation:

average stock/sales rate = turnover .   (4)

Is there any connection with the machine interference relation? Before discussing this, let us look at a third branch of stochastic processes, queueing models. Consider any general queueing system into which units arrive at a given rate and are served by a number of servers according to some queue discipline before quitting the system. The basic parameters are the arrival rate, λ, the expected time, D, a unit spends in the system (delay time) and the expected number of units in the system, N. Again we can write down an "obvious" relation:

expected number in system = arrival rate × delay time .

Why is this obvious? One way of seeing it, is to look at the system from an economic point of view. In a unit of time the total expected amount of delay to units is N. On the other hand, the expected number of arrivals is λ each of which carries an expected delay D. Thus λD is the total amount of delay generated per unit time. On which basis one pays for delay, is a matter of book-keeping convenience.

This last relation will be recognised as Little's relation. It was first discussed by Morse [14] and has been proved three times over in papers in the Operations Research Journal [15–17]. The first proof occupied seven pages of the journal, the second took up eight pages, and the third, although more "heuristic", took two pages. Another formal proof would be necessary only if it was short. For that reason, I cannot resist giving such a one. Let $D(t)$ be the cumulative distribution function of the delay time in equilibrium. The mean is

$$D = \int_0^\infty [1 - D(t)]\, dt .$$

Now consider the contribution to the number of units present now in the system (in equilibrium) made by arrivals at time points in the past. At a time t ago there was an arrival with probability λdt and this unit is still present with probability $1 - D(t)$. The expectation is $\lambda[1 - D(t)]\, dt$. Integrating over all t, we get the expected number present now,

$$N = \int_0^\infty \lambda[1 - D(t)]\, dt = \lambda D . \tag{5}$$

None of these proofs, however, is completely general. Because it seems that arrivals can be batched, for example, or dependent in any old way, so long as there exists an overall expected rate of arrival. Another way of looking at the relation is to write it as:

$$\lambda = N \times (1/D) .$$

Now $1/D$ is the expected departure rate of each unit present. Therefore, N/D is the overall departure rate. Thus the relation says that the input rate equals the output rate. It is difficult to envisage any stochastic process in equilibrium of the type we are considering for which such a throughput is not defined as the common value of an input and output rate, given that the rates are carefully and properly worked out.

The point I now want to bring out, of course, is that, besides the queueing relation, the inventory and the machine interference relations are all simply Little's relation in different guises. Let us take the inventory relation. Since we must assume that all units sold came into stock and only units in stock are sold, the sales rate equals the input rate of units into stock. Now, as in the queueing example, S/τ measures the rate of output of units. (τ is the expected length of time a unit remains in stock.) Thus,

input $= \lambda = S/\tau =$ output .

This is our relation (4).

Now take the machine interference relation. Since a is the expected number of machines running at any time and $1/\alpha$ is the rate of stoppage of any one machine, a/α represents the overall rate at which machines stop. Likewise b/β represents the overall rate at which machines get repaired. Thus again we equate an input and an output rate:

input $= a/\alpha = b/\beta =$ output .

This gives our relation (2).

3. Inventory models

Having now fairly exhaustively explored this basic relation and accepting, if we may, its obviousness we should consider its value. For this purpose, let us take a few examples. Consider first an inventory model in which when stock falls to a given level, R, it is reordered in a fixed quantity, q, that then arrives into stock after a lead-time, t. Suppose that demand is at the rate λ, so that the expected demand in the lead-time is λt. If all demand is eventually met, then λ is also the throughput: this is the backlogged case. Then, the amount of demand, L, that is not met from stock in the lead-time can be calculated from the distribution of demand in the lead-time. Thus the expected stock-level just before the replenishment arrives is $s = R - (\lambda t - L)$. If the unsatisfied demand is immediately met on arrival of the new stock, the level just after replenishment is $R - \lambda t + q$, the amount by which stock is actually increased being $q - L$. Taking an unweighted average of these two levels would now give a good approximation to the average stock level, N. However, for illustration we can apply Little's relation in the form

$$N = \lambda D , \tag{6}$$

where D is the average turnover of a unit of stock. Now to calculate D, we observe that for each replenishment, q, the time in stock is zero for the L units that cancel the backlog and for the remaining $q - L$ units it comprises first the time to clear the s units already in stock, which is s/λ together with the time i/λ if the unit in question is the ith unit in the batch of $q - L$ units. Now since this unit is equally likely to be the 1st, 2nd, ... $(q-L)$th unit, the expected turnover is

$$\frac{q-L}{q} \left[\frac{s}{\lambda} + \frac{1}{q-L} \left(\frac{1}{\lambda} + \frac{2}{\lambda} + ... + \frac{q-L}{\lambda} \right) \right],$$

and this equals

$$\frac{q-L}{q} \left[\frac{s}{\lambda} + \frac{q-L+1}{2\lambda} \right].$$

Therefore the average stock level in the backlogged case is

$$N = \frac{q-L}{q} \left[s + \tfrac{1}{2}(q-L+1) \right]. \tag{7}$$

In the present context, it is of interest to observe that the distinction between this case and the lost sales case is that in the latter λ is not identical with the throughput, since only demands that can be met from stock are met. Thus the average levels just before and just after replenishment are $s = R - \lambda t + L$ and $s + q$. The expected turnover is then

$$\frac{s}{\lambda} + \frac{q+1}{2\lambda}.$$

Now we have to calculate the throughput rate. For this purpose we find the interval between replenishment points. Just after a replenishment the excess of stock over the reorder level, R, is $s + q - R = q + L - \lambda t$. The time until this is reduced to zero is $(q+L-\lambda t)/\lambda$. Therefore, the length of the interval between replenishments is

$$t + \frac{q+L-\lambda t}{\lambda} = \frac{q+L}{\lambda}.$$

Therefore, the throughput rate is $\lambda q/q + L$. It follows that the average stock level in the case of lost sales is

$$N = \frac{q}{q+L} \left[s + \frac{q+1}{2} \right], \tag{8}$$

which is the same as (7) with the recorder quantity increased to $q + L$.

4. Queues

Although there may be some novelty in the method, these results are not new: my purpose is merely to illustrate the generality of an approach. This approach is more interesting when we turn to queueing models. Let us consider first the simple system in which units arrive at an average rate λ, are served one at a time on a first-come-first-served basis and successive service times are independently distributed with a mean β and variance σ^2. Look at the unit, if any, being served at the head of the queue. We can calculate the expected number being served (which is 0 or 1). For since the throughput rate is λ, units arrive into the service position at the rate λ and stay there for an expected time β. Therefore, by Little, the expected number is $\lambda\beta$, which is the quantity usually called the traffic intensity, ρ. If $\{p_j\}, j = 0, 1, ...,$ is the equilibrium probability distribution of the number in the system, then the expected number being served is $1 - p_0$, so that we have $p_0 = 1 - \rho$.

In a similar way we can calculate the expected number, N, in the whole system. For this purpose, however, it is necessary to restrict the arrival process to being Poisson. The significance of this assumption, as has been pointed out by many authors, is that the queue then looks the same to an arriving customer as to an observer at a random instant. An explicit proof was recently given by Strauch [18]. Now, we have our relation (6), and D is the delay time of an arrival. However, the arrival finds the same expected number N ahead of him, of which an expected number, ρ, is being served. The residual service of any unit being served is the mean, v, of the random modification given by (1). Therefore, the expected delay is

$$D = (N - \rho)\beta + \rho v + \beta .$$

Substituting in the relation (6), we obtain

$$N = \rho + \frac{\rho}{1-\rho} \lambda v = \rho + \frac{\rho^2}{1-\rho} \tfrac{1}{2}(1 + \sigma^2/\beta^2) . \tag{9}$$

In particular, if service times are exponentially distributed (so that $\sigma^2 = \beta^2$), then $N = \rho/(1-\rho)$. In this case, however, it is no more difficult to write down the complete distribution using the same approach. Define

$$P_j = \sum_{i=j}^{\infty} p_i \; .$$

Let us number the positions in the queue as in the diagram

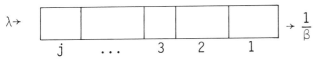

position 1 being the service position. Call the jth position S_j. The probability that S_j is occupied is P_j. Now an arriving unit will eventually pass through S_j if and only if S_{j-1} is occupied on its arrival. Therefore, the throughput rate for S_j is λP_{j-1}. A unit remains in S_j for an expected time β. (This is true whether or not it enters S_j directly or from S_{j+1} because the mean of the random modification of an exponential service time is unchanged.) Therefore, since the expected number of units in S_j is P_j,

$$P_j = \lambda P_{j-1} \beta = \rho P_{j-1} \; ,$$

from which it follows that

$$p_j = (1-\rho)\rho^j \; . \tag{10}$$

This is the basic result in queueing theory.

It is instructive to observe what happens to this argument when we no longer assume that arrivals are Poisson (but keeping exponential service times). Since the queue no longer looks the same to an arrival as to an observer at a random time-point, the throughput for S_j is no longer λP_{j-1}. It is λP_{j-1}^A, where P_j^A is the upper tail of the distribution, $\{p_j^A\}$, for the number in system facing an arrival. Thus, again by Little's relation (6),

$$P_j = \rho P_{j-1}^A \; .$$

This only gives a useful relation between the equilibrium distribution, $\{p_j\}$, and the distribution at arrival time-points. However, the latter distribution can still be obtained by a simple argument due to Winsten [19]. Suppose the system facing an arrival, is currently in state j, the probability for which is p_j^A. It must have been in state $j-1$ at some arrival time-point in the past.

Suppose it was at $j-1$ *for the last time* n inter-arrival times ago and let γ_n be the probability of going from $j-1$ to j in n steps without ever dropping to $j-1$ again. Then, summing over all n, we have

$$p_j^A = p_{j-1}^A(\gamma_1 + \gamma_2 + ...) = p_{j-1}^A \gamma ,$$

say, and clearly γ is independent of j. It follows that

$$P_j^A = \gamma^j , \qquad j = 0, 1, ... ,$$

so that

$$P_j = \rho\gamma^{j-1} , \qquad j = 1, 2, ... ,$$

and

$$p_j = \rho(1-\gamma)\gamma^{j-1} , \qquad j = 1, 2, ... \tag{11}$$

with

$$p_0 = 1 - \rho .$$

The parameter γ depends on λ and β and the shape of the inter-arrival time distribution.

5. Machine interference

I want to return now to the machine interference problem. Consider the model in the diagram

Brokendown machines line up in the lower numbered positions, and the machine in position 1 is being repaired at a rate $j\mu$ when there are j broken-down machines, $j \leqslant r$, and at the rate $r\mu$ when $j > r$. When repair times are exponential with mean $\beta = 1/\mu$, and provided we need not distinguish between machines, this is equivalent to allowing machines to be simultaneously repaired up to a maximum of r under repair. When there are i machines running, breakdowns occur at the rate $i\lambda$.

As previously, let $S_j = 1$ when the jth position is occupied by a broken-down machine, and let $P(S_j = 1) = P_j$ at a random time. We want to find the distribution $\{p_j\}$ of the number of brokendown machines, where

$$p_j = P_j - P_{j+1} , \quad j = 0, 1, ..., m \quad (P_{m+1} = 0) .$$

Suppose first $j \geq r$. Then whenever $S_j = 1$, there must be at least r broken-down machines. The output rate from S_j is therefore $r\mu P_j$. Now consider the input rate to S_j. All input to $S_i, i \geq j$, is eventually also input to S_j. Therefore the input rate to S_j is

$$\lambda [p_{m-1} + 2p_{m-2} + ... + (m-j+1)p_{j-1}] .$$

Therefore we have for $j \geq r$,

$$\rho [p_{m-1} + 2p_{m-2} + ... + (m-j+1)p_{j-1}] = rP_j ,$$

so that by increasing j by 1 and subtracting, we get

$$\rho(m-j)p_j = rp_{j+1} , \qquad j = r-1, r, ..., m-1 . \tag{12}$$

Suppose secondly that $j \leq r$. The output rate from S_j is now

$$\mu [jp_j + (j+1)p_{j+1} + ... + rp_r + rp_{r+1} + ... + rp_m] .$$

The input rate is as before. Therefore for $j \leq r$,

$$\rho [p_{m-1} + 2p_{m-2} + ... + (m-j+1)p_{j-1}] = jp_j + ... + r(p_r + p_{r+1} + ... + p_m) .$$

Again, by increasing j by 1 and subtracting, we get

$$\rho(m-j)p_j = (j+1)p_{j+1} , \qquad j = 0, 1, ..., r-1 . \tag{13}$$

These, together with the previous set (12), are the basic recursion formulae originally obtained by Palm [2], from which the distribution, (p_j), is, in turn, easily obtained.

It is worth noting that the method does not need the assumption of exponential machine running times, provided only that the repair times remain exponential.

6. Processor-sharing model

The method I have been exhibiting for the analysis of stochastic models has not in this lecture as yet produced anything other than classical formulae. Perhaps therefore I should end with an application where it does.

I want finally to take a look at a stochastic model that arises in computer technology. In a time-shared computer system, a number of jobs may share the processor under round-robin scheduling, each job in turn getting a slice of processor time, or quantum, before going back to the end of the queue. If we allow the quantum to be infinitely small, we get an idealized model of the situation in which all jobs present are processed simultaneously, the rate of processing being inversely proportional to the number of jobs present. This is the processor-shared model. An operating characteristic of central interest in such a system is the expected response time of a job, i.e., the time it takes to process it.

We suppose that jobs arrive into the system in a Poisson stream with rate λ and that their lengths are distributed with distribution function $H(t)$. That is, a random job alone in the processor will take a time t to be processed that is distributed as $H(t)$.

Let us follow the progress of a job that arrives, the "tagged job". Conditional upon this job having length t and meeting n jobs in the system on arrival, define $R_n(t)$ to be the expected response time. Then the expected response time conditional only on t is

$$R(t) = E_n\{R_n(t)\} ,$$

and the unconditional expected response time is

$$R = \int_0^\infty R(t)\, dH(t) .$$

Define the random variable $v(x)$ to be the number in the system (excluding the tagged unit) at the instant when the tagged unit has received the amount x of its service. Then for any x,

$$E\{v(x)\} = N ,$$

the expected number in the system at a random time point. The actual response time conditional on t is the random variable

$$\int_0^t \{1 + v(x)\} \, dx \,.$$

Therefore,

$$R(t) = E \int_0^t \{1 + v(x)\} \, dx = \int_0^t E\{1 + v(x)\} \, dx = \int_0^t (1 + N) \, dx = t(1 + N) \,.$$

It follows that the unconditional response time is

$$R = \int_0^\infty t(1 + N) \, dH(t) = \frac{1}{\mu}(1 + N) \,.$$

Now, by Little,

$$N = \lambda R = \rho(1 + N) \,.$$

Therefore,

$$N = \frac{\rho}{1 - \rho} \,,$$

so that

$$R(t) = \frac{t}{1 - \rho} \tag{14}$$

and

$$R = \frac{1}{\mu(1 - \rho)} \,. \tag{15}$$

The surprising feature of this last result is that it is identical with the expected response time in a first-come-first-served system *with exponential service times*. The conditional expected response time is, however, different in the latter system; it is

$$D(t) = N \frac{1}{\mu} + t = \frac{\rho}{1 - \rho} \frac{1}{\mu} + t \,.$$

If this is written in the form,

$$D(t) = \frac{t}{1-\rho} + \frac{\rho}{1-\rho} \left(\frac{1}{\mu} - t \right) , \tag{16}$$

it shows that for $t < 1/\mu$, $R(t) < D(t)$, while for $t > 1/\mu$, $R(t) > D(t)$. Thus the processor-shared system improves response time for shorter than average jobs.

We can go further and examine the expected response time, $R_n(t)$, conditional on both n and t.

The key to the solution is the recognition that the expected response time, $R_n(t)$ is unchanged if we think of the original $n+1$ units as being processed one at a time, units arriving during each of these processing times forming first generations of descendants and being subsequently processed, units arriving during each of their processing times forming second generations of descendants, and so on.

The tagged unit is allocated a processing time t and each of the n units present is allocated an amount t, or its unexpired load, whichever is the lesser. If a unit has an allocation up to x, a unit of its first generation that arrives when it has received y will be allocated up to $x - y$.

Define $u(x)$ to be the total expected load due to an arriving unit that is allocated up to x togetl er with the load due to all its descendants. Then $u(x)$ is given by the relation

$$u(x) = \int_0^x \{1 - H(y)\} \, dy + \lambda \int_0^x \{1 - H(y)\} \, u(x - y) \, dy .$$

The first term gives the expected load of the arriving unit. In the second term, $1 - H(y)$ is the probability that the original unit has a processing time of at least y, λdy is the probability of an arrival in the instant dy and $u(x - y)$ is the total expected service load of this unit and all its descendants.

Let us now make the assumption of exponential service loads,

$$H(y) = 1 - \exp(-\mu y) .$$

Substituting for $H(y)$ above, we obtain

$$u(x) = \int_0^x \exp(-\mu y) \, dy + \lambda \int_0^x \exp(-\mu y) \, u(x - y) \, dy ,$$

the solution of which can be found to be

$$u(x) = \frac{1}{\mu - \lambda} \{1 - \exp(-\overline{\mu - \lambda}x)\} .$$

Now the expected load due to the tagged unit and its descendants is

$$t + \lambda \int_0^t u(t-x)\, dx ,$$

and the expected load due to any one of the n originally present units is $u(t)$. *This is because the unexpired service load of any unit originally present has the same exponential distribution as any new arrival.*

Therefore we now have

$$R_n(t) = t + \lambda \int_0^t u(t-x)\, dx + nu(t) .$$

Substituting for $u(t)$ we obtain

$$R_n(t) = \frac{t}{1-\rho} + \left(n - \frac{\rho}{1-\rho}\right) \frac{1}{\mu - \lambda} \{1 - \exp(-\overline{\mu - \lambda}t)\} . \tag{17}$$

If we give n its expected value of $\rho/1-\rho$, we get back to our previous results (14). This last result (17) has been obtained by Coffman et al. [20] by a quite different method. The result (14) for general service load distribution has been obtained by Sakata et al. [21, 22] using a rather complicated argument based on taking the limit of the result for round-robin scheduling. An important unsolved problem is the generalization of (17) to the case where the service loads are not assumed to be exponentially distributed.

7. Concluding remarks

I will conclude with some general remarks on stochastic modelling. The primary purpose is to gain insight into phenomena: it is not the proving of theorems that is important but the finding out about what is really going on. In a sense it is only after some result has become intuitively obvious that it becomes worthwhile proving it rigorously.

This is of course true of all modelling, whether stochastic or deterministic. What is special about stochastic models is the random component which cannot be dropped without robbing the problem of its significance. It is particularly important as a first step to isolate this essential component and then to strip the problem of all other inessential stochastic elements. To find out what is the essence of a problem, it does not matter that the model is not a realistic one. Looking back on the developments in stochastic processes over the last 20 years, I would say that it is in the simplification of the stochastic concepts that the significant advances have resided. Through the wider assimilation of these ideas the range of their applicability to the real world has been correspondingly widened.

References

[1] A.Y. Khintchine, Über die mittlere Dauer des Stillstandes von Maschinen, Mat. Sbornik 40 (1933) 119.

[2] C. Palm, The distribution of repairmen in servicing automatic machines, Industri-tidn. Norden 75 (1947) 75, 90, 119.

[3] H. Ashcroft, The productivity of several machines under the care of one operator, J. Roy. Statist. Soc. B12 (1950) 145.

[4] P. Naor, On machine interference, J. Roy. Statist. Soc. B18 (1956) 280.

[5] P. Naor, Some problems of machine interference, in: Proc. First IFORS Conf., Oxford (1957) p. 147.

[6] L.G. Peck and R.N. Hazelwood, Finite queueing tables (Wiley, New York, 1958).

[7] A.Y. Khintchine, Mathematisches über die Erwartung von einen öffentlichen Schalter, Mat. Sbornik 39 (1932) 73.

[8] R. Syski, Congestion theory in telephone systems (Oliver and Boyd, Edinburgh, 1960).

[9] F.G. Foster, A unified theory for stock, storage and queue control, Opnl. Res. Q. 10 (1959) 121.

[10] F.G. Foster and I. Elce, A simulation program for machine maintenance, telephone traffic and stock models, Opnl. Res. Q. 14 (1963) 333.

[11] E. Brockmeyer, H.L. Halstrøm and A. Jensen, The life and works of A.K. Erlang, Acad. of Technical Sciences, Copenhagen (1948).

[12] T.C. Fry, Probability and its engineering uses (Van Nostrand, Princeton, 1928).

[13] H.W. Watson and F. Galton, On the probability of the extinction of families, J. Anthropol. Inst. 4 (1874) 138.

[14] P.M. Morse, Queues, inventories and maintenance (Wiley, New York, 1958).

[15] J.D.C. Little, A proof of the queueing formula $L = \lambda W$, Opns. Res. 9 (1961) 383.

[16] W.S. Jewell, A simple proof of $L = \lambda W$, Opns. Res. 15 (1967) 1109.

[17] S. Eilon, A simpler proof of $L = \lambda W$, Opns. Res. 16 (1968) 915.

[18] R.E. Strauch, When a queue looks the same to an arriving customer as to an observer, Mgmt. Sci. 17 (1970) 140.

[19] C.B. Winsten, Geometric distributions in the theory of queues, J. Roy. Statist. Soc. B21 (1959) 1.

[20] E.G. Coffman, R.R. Muntz and H. Trotter, Waiting time distributions for processor-sharing systems, J. ACM 17 (1970) 123.

[21] M. Sakata, S. Noguchi and J. Oizumi, Analysis of a processor-shared queueing model for time-sharing systems, in: Proc. 2nd Hawaii Intern. Conf. on Systems Sciences (1969) p. 625.

[22] M. Sakata, S. Noguchi and J. Oizumi, An analysis of the $M/G/l$ queue under round robin scheduling, Opns. Res. 18 (1970) 371.

24

STOCHASTIC PROCESSES: DISCUSSANT 1

Processus stochastiques: porte-parole 1

ALEC M. LEE

Rolls-Royce (1971) Ltd., Derby, England

Professor Foster has done us a service by reminding us first of the formal unity of many stochastic processes, and second by demonstrating that non-trivial, useful results can be obtained by relatively simple mathematical means.

In opening my discussion of Prof. Foster's admirable paper I have the virtues of simplicity very much in mind. I shall first state an empirical law which I shall call the Iron Law of Mathematical Models. This Law says that the more a mathematical model captures reality, the less likely it is to be capable of practical application.

The familiar mathematical models of stochastic processes, of which Palm's machine-interference models and Erlang's telephone traffic models are excellent examples, are undeniably simplistic. That is, they make assumptions that are strong, simplifying views of reality. Yet these models are capable of practical application. For example, operational researchers did, and many industrial engineers still do, use the results derived from simple machine-interference models in everyday affairs. There are two reasons why such models are usable. First, their parameters are few and well-defined, the data needed to estimate them are simply obtained and simple statistical reduction of these data yield the parameter estimates. Second, calculation of outputs from the models is simple and inexpensive.

Now, the more one looks at stochastic processes in the real world, the more complex many of them are seen to be, and it is understandable that operational researchers should try to construct mathematical models which reflect more of this complexity.

The Iron Law ensures that the majority of such efforts must fail. The Law is manifested in three causes of failure, one or more of which may be operative:

1. The more realistic mathematical model cannot be manipulated to yield solutions in analytic terms.
2. The data requirements are excessive and their preliminary statistical reduction is complicated, as it is not only necessary to estimate independent parameters but to determine the shape of, and estimate the constants in, functional relationships between the parameters.
3. The amount of calculation required to obtain numerical results is very large and expensive.

Operational researchers who want their models to capture reality have therefore largely abandoned mathematical models and turned to simulation models. Simulation is certainly a means of avoiding the first cause of failure. But it does not, in itself, eliminate the problems of data collection and data reduction nor guarantee a reduction in the amount and cost of calculation.

In my opinion the pursuit of more realistic models of stochastic processes and hence the recourse to simulation is sometimes an irrelevant extravagance. Approximate solutions, sufficient for all practical purposes can frequently be obtained by the imaginative use of simpler models. But if one agrees that greater realism is a prerequisite for acceptable solutions, then the triumph of simulation is an inexorable consequence of the Iron Law.

It now seems apparent that in the practice of operational research the only mathematical models of stochastic processes to be much used are old-style, simplistic models. They are primarily used first to obtain solutions to problems which do not merit the time and expense of simulation. They are used second to compute initial conditions of simulation runs. They are used third to provide a rough check on the validity of the outputs from simulation runs. They are used finally when the data requirements of more complex mathematical or simulation models cannot be met.

The Iron Law is not the only reason for this state of affairs. Another is that operational research into stochastic problems such as machine-interference, inventory control and queueing predominantly is informed by the attitudes of the planner. The end product is a planning statistic such as the repairman/machine ratio, or the number of berths to be provided in a new harbour. To put it another way it is often more concerned with the initialisation of systems than with their on-going operation. There is time for elaboration and for simulation.

Simulation is, however, of little direct use in the control of an on-going, man-made system with stochastic elements. There is not time to discuss such control problems here in any depth, but I should like to give an example. One of the problems of airline operation is to assign and re-assign aircraft to flights so as to maintain an acceptable schedule performance in spite of such random events as technical failures, or of delays caused by traffic congestion, or by bad weather, or of many other circumstances. These assignment decisions are taken by human operations controllers who have access to information on the present and short-term future state of the system. These controllers commonly reach their decisions by applying rather simple, often inconsistent, empirical rules. The performance of such a control system could be improved if either the optimal response to an event could be computed quickly or, less ambitious, each controller could be provided with a rapid but accurate assessment of the consequences of any decision he might think of taking. In physical terms this means providing each controller with access to an on-line computer.

Whilst the optimal response to an event might be provided by a computer with acceptable speed and at bearable expense on the basis of a mathematical model, it is in general unlikely that it could be so provided by means of stochastic simulation. To provide, on the basis of stochastic simulation, a rapid assessment of the consequences of a response generated by an experienced controller would be almost as difficult. Man/machine control of stochastic systems is a field in which mathematical models have, at least potentially, the advantage over simulation.

Advances in the general theory of stochastic processes, and in the development of mathematical models of specific stochastic processes, are likely to be of interest in the practice of operational research insofar as they relate to problems of control.

For other problems, particularly planning problems, where realism seems necessary, simulation techniques will tend to be employed wherever possible. The practical interest of more elaborate but non-computable, mathematical models of machine-interference, inventory and queueing is slight, and possibly decreasing. Does anyone disagree?

M. Ross, ed., OR '72. North-Holland Publishing Company (1973)

25

STOCHASTIC PROCESSES: DISCUSSANT 2

Processus stochastiques: porte-parole 2

Optimal dimension of a system with great variability in manhours input

ERNESTO RUIZ PALÁ and CARLOS AVILA BELOSO

Hispano Olivetti S.A., Barcelona, Spain

Certain situations arise in the running of some departments of production, administrative or services firms which, as a result of their psychological effect on the persons working in these departments, have an unfavourable influence on the true output of these departments. Men are not machines capable of working at a constant or predetermined rate and speed. Nevertheless, the purpose of our study *is not* the determination of the environmental conditions influencing the good or ill will that the worker puts into the performance of his job. Our aim is quite different; it refers to those conditions which provoke a logical reaction in man, totally unconnected with ethics.

Any manual or intellectual worker engaged in tasks received at irregular intervals who believes that once the current job is finished it is quite likely that he will remain inactive for some time before being asked to do another job, will react logically by lowering his rate. This is because he will prefer to be constantly occupied than pass through the disagreeable situation of periodic inactivity, even though there is no question of financial loss. On the other hand, an excess of work on hands can cause him a crisis of discouragement when he realises that in spite of his best intentions, he cannot meet the demand.

Both cases perplex the worker. This perplexity has direct repercussions on his attitude to persons directing the organisation.

It is no easy task to find an optimum solution, by intuition or otherwise, when the jobs to be done are of irregular duration and also arrive at very irregular intervals. Thus, in practice compromise, rather than optimum solutions, are employed. Where these irregularities exist, the output of the persons or departments affected is usually quite low, although for short periods, intensive activity occurs.

It is of interest, therefore, to find a *quantitative* solution providing us with sufficient elements of judgement which will enable us to exert a favourable influence on the determining causes of the system. In this way we can approach the optimum system by means of such hypotheses as our observations of real life behaviour prove valid.

Some features of the problem, associated with Queueing Theory, make an analytical solution hard to come by:

1. The duration of the service times is modified according to the momentary state of the system by the "rate equation". This rate equation, which we shall give later on, is derived from observing that, in practice and *within certain limits*, the rate of the individual or group depends on the number of jobs awaiting attention.

2. Exponential distributions, which make the study of waiting line problems easy, more often than not do not occur in real life. Rather we have bell type distributions with a modal value situated to the left of the average value. Sometimes these distributions may resemble the hypoexponential distributions, but in this case with rather high t values.

This similarity could help in the difficult task of finding an analytical solution. However, any simplification implying a disarrangement of the true distribution should only be made with great care.

Useful results depend precisely on a strict adjustment of both the rate equation and the distributions of the arrival intervals, together with the service times to the true behaviour of the system.

For these reasons we have decided to carry out a simulation study with the aid of an IBM 1620 computer. We produced some graphs based on the numerical example studied which may help point the way to a future analytical solution.

In presenting our study, we shall adopt the terminology developed by Jay W. Forrester:

(a) The system is Grade One since it concerns the activity of one sole homogeneous group.

It is single loop.

It has negative feedback with a trend towards a state of balance.

(b) The system level, depending on the time factor, is defined by the number of outstanding jobs.

(c)The rate depends on the level, through the rate equation (independent of time).

(d)The rate's effect on the level includes the time factor.

Study of the case

For us the problems arose while we were making observations in departments concerned with Materials Reception, Engineering, and Administration, but, no doubt, they exist in many branches of Production, Administration and Services.

We shall study first the "rate equation", then the problem of the "waiting line or queue" and then move on to how the system works.

The "rate equation" is exponential of the type

$$x = 1 + \frac{b}{a^{Kn}} \qquad \begin{cases} n = 0 \\ x = 1 + b \end{cases} \qquad \begin{cases} n = \infty \\ x = 1 \end{cases} \ ,$$

where x corresponds to the rate, n corresponds to the number of jobs pending, and K is a parameter with a value of $K \geqslant 1$.

We have observed that the slowest rate occurs where the worker realises that since there is no other job waiting he runs the risk of being inactive as soon as he finishes the job on hand. For this reason, there can be quite a big difference in working rate depending on whether there is another job waiting or not. If two jobs are waiting, the rate may be modified further, although psychologically the risk of being inactive has diminished. Nevertheless, this influence on the rate is notably lower than in the previous case. Following the same reasoning, the practical result is that with short queues of 3 to 4 jobs, the maximum rate is reached.

With reference to the parameter K, it turns out to be an inverse function of the service time.

$$K = f(T_s^{-1})$$

The study of this function would require a statistical application to several particular cases. In all probability some other environmental parameter also enters into it.

The problem of the waiting line is the one corresponding to "single or multiple service station with single queue". Nevertheless, our case also allows for the possibility that certain units entering the system have priority over the remainder. This priority is not pre-emptive; that is, when a non-priority job is being done, any priority job arriving must wait until the non-priority one has been served.

Using the standard symbols of queueing theory, we have:

T_a	= average time interval between two consecutive arrivals
T_s	= average service time
$\lambda = 1/T_a$	= average arrival frequency
$\mu = 1/T_s$	= average service frequency
$\rho = \lambda/\mu$	= coefficient of utilisation of the system
W	= average time unit remains in system
P_0	= fraction of time system is inactive
$P_1 P_2 \dots P_n$	= fraction of time in which there are 1, 2, ..., n priority units in the system
$P'_1 P'_2 \dots P'_{n'}$	= fraction of time in which there are 1, 2, ..., n non-priority units in the system
n	= number of units in system (priority)
n'	= number of units in system (non-priority).

The structure of the system in our case corresponds to a centre where jobs arrive according to an exponential curve and are completed in time periods which collectively form a normal distribution. Since the study is quite general, any other hypothesis could be proposed.

Two levels of urgency are used to classify jobs as they arrive, but this priority is only known to the manager at the centre who distributes the work and not to the people doing the work. The latter only know the total number of jobs outstanding.

Table 1

Valves of parameters fed into computer[*]

	A	B	C	D	E	F
T_1	0.5	0.5	0.5	0.5	0.5	0.5
σ_1	0.05	0.05	0.05	0.05	0.05	0.05
T_2	(0.5)	(0.5)	0.06	0.06	0.06	0.06
σ_2	(0.05)	(0.05)	0.006	0.006	0.006	0.006
λ_1	(0.5)	(0.5)	1.00	1.00	1.00	1.00
λ_2	(0.5)	(0.5)	1.66	3.33	5.00	6.67
$\gamma(1)$	1.00	2.00	2.00	2.00	2.00	2.00
$\gamma(2)$	1.00	1.37	1.37	1.37	1.37	1.37
$\gamma(3)$	1.00	1.14	1.14	1.14	1.14	1.14
$\gamma(4)$	1.00	1.055	1.055	1.055	1.055	1.055
$\gamma(\geqslant 5)$	1.00	1.00	1.00	1.00	1.00	1.00
ρ_t	0.5	0.5	0.6	0.7	0.8	0.9

[*] Independent variable: λ_i = arrival frequency for non-priority units.

The frequency of arrival and service of the non-priority units may be different from the priority ones.

We have considered the following hypotheses:

A. A single type of job. Constant, optimum rate.

B. A single type of job. Variable rate.

C, D, E and F. Two types of job, priority and non-priority. Case A and B jobs retain their priority, but an ever increasing number of non-priority jobs are introduced into the system.

The values of the parameters for these hypotheses are given in table 1. The values for Hypotheses A and B given in brackets are fictitious but included with a view to being able to employ the same programme in the computer for all six hypotheses.

$K = 1$ and the values of the following table have been considered in the "rate equation".

$n = 1, 2, 3, \geqq 4.$

These values have been fed into the computer and two graphs have been drawn. The horizontal axes of both graphs give the values of $\rho = \lambda/\mu$ (coefficient of use of the system) and the corresponding system efficiency values: e.

With reference to the vertical axes, fig. 1 gives the values of P_0 (fraction of inactivity), P (fraction of time occupied in priority units) and P' (fraction of time occupied in non-priority units).

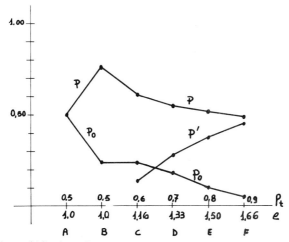

Fig. 1. Working and idle time of system.

Horizontal axis: (above) coefficient of utilization of system (ρ_f); (below) system efficiency (e).

Vertical axis: fraction of time in %.

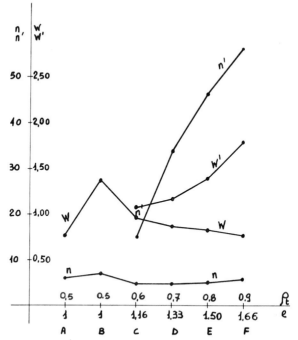

Fig. 2. Total mean waiting-time (W, W') and mean number (n, n').
Horizontal axis: (above) coefficient of utilisation of the system (ρ_t); (below) system efficiency (e).
Vertical axis: (right) total mean waiting-time; (left) mean number of units.

Fig. 2 gives the values of:

W = waiting time of priority unit in the system

W' = waiting time of non-priority unit in the system

n = average number of priority units in the system

n' = average number of non-priority units in the system .

   In fig. 1, we observe that when we pass from constant rate (A) to variable rate (B), the inactivity ratio P_0 drops sharply, since the time spent inactive is reduced as a consequence of working more slowly. From case C onwards, when non-priority units are introduced into the system s, P_0 continues to drop. The fraction of time spent on priority units P drops, although the efficiency increases. The time spent on non-priority units increases, as does the efficiency.

   The practical results may be seen better in fig. 2. Here we see that if in the theoretical case (A), the average time W taken to clear out a job was

$W = 0.75$, it runs out to $W = 1.4$ under the hypothesis of variable rate. When non-priority jobs are introduced into the system, this time W drops sharply and then continues to drop slowly to approach its original theoretical value. The number n of priority units in the system remains practically constant. The number n' of non-priority units increases since this is precisely the independent variable of the system.

Also W' (time necessary to clear out a non-priority job) increases, although relatively less than n' because of the increase in rate.

Observing fig. 2, we deduct that the optimum situation, in our case, corresponds to (C) where:

1. The waiting time W is only slightly higher than the theoretical value.
2. The efficiency of the system has gone up by 16% and at the same time $n' = 15$ non-priority jobs have been done (at zero cost).
3. The number of non-priority jobs awaiting attention is relatively low. This point is of interest with a view to achieving a psychological balance.

M. Ross, ed., OR '72. North-Holland Publishing Company (1973)

BEHAVIORAL SCIENCE MODELS

Modèles de science du comportement

JOHN STRINGER

Institute for Operational Research, London, England

Abstract. The paper considers why, although OR and behavioural science have much to offer each other realisation of this potential has been sparse. Some modest examples of such collaboration in the author's experience are examined in terms of the relative OR and behavioural science components in: (1) understanding and facilitating OR as a social process (relations between researcher and client; effectiveness of problem-solving groups), (2) understanding the nature of objectives in a situation involving an organisation and its personnel, (3) understanding the kinds of skills needed for planning in a multi-agency situation, and (4) understanding mutual learning relationships to be incorporated in a decision model.

It is suggested, in the light of these experiences that OR and behavioural science require the stimulus of working together on decision problems of a significance and urgency which transcend disciplinary and professional trivia. Some social problems are considered from this point of view. They are seen to violate the assumptions implicit in much OR theory and practice; for example that there is a relevant, identifiable, single, decisionmaker; or again, that conflicts may be resolved by reference to a sufficiently high authority.

1. Introduction

As this is billed as a "State of the art" paper, it is only fair to start by admitting that it will be no such thing. Contact with social scientists heightens one's awareness of the interaction between personal biases and objectivity and the theme of the paper is certainly grounded in the former, as follows.

First the relevance of OR to the problems that matter for people is not immediately obvious; it may even be detrimental to their interests. Second, there is an unfortunate tendency to force OR into the mould of a "discipline in its own right". Since a discipline has to have its distinctive content, what is essentially a body of method gets treated as a body of knowledge about the real world. These and other influences result in stultifying pressures to restrict OR to problems "with some OR in them". Third, OR often starts when there is a decision impending, thereby avoiding the equally serious questions of how a decision came to be needed, and how it is "made" (as distinct from "taken").

These observations are concerned with social factors in the various senses that an OR study is itself a social process; that the need for it arises in a social or political context; and that the variables in our models represent, however abstractly, real factors in the lives of real people. In each of these respects, therefore, a merging of the insights and methods of the social and behavioural sciences with those more commonly associated with OR seems highly desirable, to say the least.

A little progress is being made in this direction. A cautious flirtation took place at the 1964 International Conference on OR and the Social Sciences [1]. After referring to the lack of mutual contact, the editor's preface continues:

"..... (there have) been one or two objections that the whole concept of separation is a chimaera, and, for example, that social scientists have co-operated with other disciplines within operational research teams. That this has sometimes happened one would not deny, but, as we shall stress later, it is not sufficiently widespread to have led to a single paper for this conference."

The caution has persisted. Thus [2] :

"The difficulty seems to lie in the fact that social and psychological concepts are rarely rigorously enough defined to be included in the modelling of the operational researcher .,... We ..... have to make the further step ..... before social scientists drop the notion that there is a domain of qualities into which the OR man cannot safely be allowed."

As Emery implies, given the need and the opportunity for a merging of insights into a more socially relevant OR (or a more operational social science – whichever term is palatable) it can only finally come about as a result of a painful process of mutual adjustment in the course of working together.

During the period spanned by these two quotations an Institute for Operational Research (IOR) grew up within the Tavistock Institute of Human Relations (TIHR) in England and since it is in the experience of working together that progress of future significance will come, it may be useful to try to draw conclusions from some modest examples in this setting.

2. Facilitating operational research as a social process

The importance of the relationships between researcher and client, and within the research team, is well illustrated by an old example – old enough for time to have softened the strong emotions generated at the time.

The building communications project ended prematurely in 1964. A few years earlier the national organisations representing builders, architects, etc., having identified communications as a root cause of the industry's difficulties, commissioned a pilot study [3] which aroused strong enthusiasm for research on communications. (Vagueness here as to what the communications problem was, accurately reflects the uncritical nature of this enthusiasm.)

Money was raised, a research committee formed and a mixed OR/behavioural science team commissioned to undertake "the research". A series of case studies was undertaken; the most significant outcome of which, from the scientific point of view, was the contribution to the understanding of the design process [4].

However, the "practical" people, contractors, plumbers and so on, began to fidget. They could see nothing in the design process of interest to them. When we turned attention to the co-ordination of operations on site, the architects began to lose interest.

Typically the first site co-ordination meeting would start with hearty expressions of willingness to collaborate. At later meetings, when delays and mistakes were apparent, behaviour would become defensive. Each would wait for another to fail, hoping that his own shortcomings would thereby be covered up. Tension would mount until somebody cracked.

Faced with its own conflicts of interest, the research committee behaved in the same way, typical of the industry. The research team were accused of "not delivering the goods", by which each of the accusers meant something different. In fact, we were trying to make the committee face the question "What do we mean by improvement in communications?" for it seemed that there were vested interests in the state of near chaos and that what would be an improvement for one would seem a disadvantage to another. The argument which polarised between the "research" and "industry" members of the committee over the definition of improvement, might equally well have polarised between architects and builders, or between behavioural scientists and operational researchers. Clearly some of these strains had to come out into the open before further progress could be made. That the split occurred the way it did, was accidental.

Then the money ran out. The research committee had been too pre-occupied to raise further funds. So what might have been a constructive emergence of conflict, became the excuse for the premature end of the project. The interim reports [5] were well received by the trade press, but it is doubtful whether they made much impression on the industry.

What can we learn?

(1) The pilot study was a reasonable diagnosis of the industry's problems but the resulting enthusiasm for research was misleading. Expectations were unrealistically high but the tough task of defining aims should have been undertaken.

(2) The research committee should have included representatives of the purchasers of buildings, their users and the community at large. Had such interests been present, they might have transcended the parochial objectives of the industry members, and provided a focus for resolving conflicts of values.

(3) We should have checked our implicit assumption that the industry accepted the need for a change from "crisis management" to a more sophisticated style.

(4) Any major project needs to have a showdown about values and criteria. In the process the divergent views of client and research team as to the nature of the expected outcome can (hopefully) be resolved. We should have had this showdown whilst there were still time and money left to work on with a realistic understanding of what could be achieved.

No doubt any researcher working on public or on multi-organisational problems could give equally telling examples (e.g. [6]). Anecdotal evidence, however, does not take us far enough. Recognising the need for analytical rigour in considering client/researcher interactions, Shipp [7] has described a "communication model of an OR project" intended as a conceptual framework for distilling experience. His model runs on the following lines.

The project is a co-operative venture between a client, who has direct experience of the problem and of the environment in which any solution must work, and an OR scientist, who has analytical skills. The *aim* is to mobilise the knowledge and intellectual resources of both so as to arrive at a solution. The *means* is a willingness by both to make this contribution, which requires them to maintain effective communication. The *difficulty* lies in the communication process.

The OR scientist has two frequently incompatible aims. As well as meeting professional standards which may be unfamiliar to the client, he must also establish his credibility or "right to be heard" in terms the client accepts.

The client knows that the purpose of the study is to change his day-to-day working life. He wants to have an adequate say in these changes and is concerned about being left with an unrealistically demanding task. He holds his personal view of the study within a wider framework of social or political factors in his own environment. He may find it embarrassing to make the criteria or constraints he uses explicit to a virtual stranger, or indeed impossible to do so because he does not apply them consciously. Even if he did spell out these constraints, it may not be possible to include them in a quantitative analysis.

Unless the scientist appreciates the "hidden" factors which affect the client's attitudes and behaviour, he will not be able to maintain a co-operative relationship and open communication and will tend to regard the client as an impersonal source of information. The text books and published case studies normally reinforce this view.

In the problem definition phase the bulk of the overt flow of information is from the client and his organisation to the scientist. However, there is also an informal undercurrent in which the client seeks information from the scientist in order to assess his capabilities (hence the frequent questions about past studies). Without any very clear idea of what OR is or what OR scientists do, managers must do the best they can in judging capabilities; the initial assessment (which may change later) may therefore be influenced by appearance, dress, accent, etc., as much as by more relevant abilities.

The OR scientist, meanwhile, overtly explores the context of the problem to establish its scope. At the undercurrent level he is trying to find out whether the client is presenting a symptom of a more basic problem; but if he asks his questions ineptly, he lays himself open to a charge of arrogance.

The end of the first phase can be defined as the reaching of mutual agreement on realistic expectations for a problem to be tackled. Difficulties are likely to arise unless the agreement also specifies the "other decision-makers" (e.g., trades unions, staff of other departments, users, etc.) whose implicit sanction is necessary if successful implementation is to be achieved, and about the extent to which they must be kept abreast of the study.

Proceeding in this way through the "solution" and "implementation" phases Shipp builds up a framework in which the patterns of communication, both explicit and implicit, can be systematically analysed and related to defined stages of agreement (or collusion) between the parties. He then extends the model to more complex client/researcher situations. There may, for example, be a state of "client confusion" with financial and technical responsibility for the project resting in different parts of the client organisation, and with the subject of the project lying within the area of responsibility of a third party. The constraints imposed by these relationships on the progress and possible outcomes of the project can be severe. For example, those parts of the client system with responsibility for the technical aspects of the project may, in an understandable attempt to protect their own position, insist that all communication between the external OR team and the third party for whom the work is really being done, should be routed through themselves. If the research team cannot maintain the appropriate relationship with the third party concerned – the "real" client – they will be restricted in the nature and quality of the information they can get about informal, but nevertheless real, values and constraints in the situation.

It would be equally possible to analyse project team organisation in communication terms.

To sum up, the view of OR as a process of social interaction is worthy of systematic development. The value of a sound conceptual model of these interactions is greatest where the "client" is itself a complex system and where the research team incorporates several disciplines.

3. Organisations and their personnel

Difficulties over client confusion are especially likely in projects dealing with manpower planning or personnel policy. The values of those concerned in the situation are to some extent in conflict, to some extent in agreement and furthermore the mutual perceptions of them may well be incorrect. Culturally determined attitudes to work do not necessarily follow economic models, for example. The implicit value assumptions of the researchers may also obtrude. An important test for the potentialities of OR/behavioural science collaboration lies, therefore, at the interface between the macroscopic approaches of manpower planning on the one hand, and the particular requirements of personnel management as applied to individuals, on the other. Little work has been done by the "statistical" manpower planners in terms of indicating how precisely their results are to be implemented. In the same way, behavioural scientists have tended to neglect the aggregated effects of their policies for the organisation as a whole. The "middle ground" of career planning has therefore been chosen by IOR as one of its programme foci.

One concern has been with the effects, both on individuals and on their organisation, of changes in recruitment, posting and promotion policy. Taking a particular example, there is a contrast between "specialist" and "generalist" policies. Under a specialist policy people achieve a fair degree of experience of a particular kind or in a particular part of the organisation and then continue to apply this experience and thus develop specialised expertise. On the other hand, a generalist policy aims to transfer people between the various parts of the organisation sufficiently frequently for them to obtain a wide range of experience so that they could fill any of a wide range of jobs at least adequately.

These extremes of policy differ in terms of career prospects, of the build-up of experience, of availability of suitable candidates for new positions and of the trade-offs between current performance and future capabilities.

The considerable body of behavioural science knowledge about job evaluation and personnel appraisal provides some useful indicators at the micro level. However, the outcomes of alternative policies are manifest only in the context of the larger system. This work has therefore developed gaming and simulation models of the recruitment, posting and promotion process [8] in parallel with attempts to quantify concepts as "experience" on which the models depend. For example, it has to be ascertained whether people do learn more rapidly in their first years in a new post, whether personal abilities and motivations greatly affect the learning rates or whether these factors are themselves influenced by career development practice within the organisation. In pursuing such questions and considering their relationship to a system model, disciplinary boundaries are starting to lose their former relevance.

The same may be said of another example described by Drake et al. [9]. Their work in an organisation faced with problems of management succession included a systematic collection of data on the preferences of individuals, their managers, and the personnel function, with regard to promotion or transfer, and the use of these data in an information system based on an assignment model.

Drake et al. conclude:

"It may be argued that the practical difficulties inherent in asking people to state their own preferences for jobs in an organisation are such as to make it an unattractive course of action. The experience of this research, however, is that given the opportunity to express their work interests people respond in a way which has provided a workable basis for the organisation to arrive at decisions about its allocation of people to jobs.

... other applications of the assignment model ... differ ... in that they involve greater numbers of people and jobs and there did not appear to be a particular need to negotiate moves either with individuals concerned or their managers. Furthermore, in the present application the model has been used to develop a number of 'good' solutions rather than to find a single optimum in relation to a set of arbitrarily defined weights. In this way the management concerned can take other criteria into account in choosing between good solutions. Among these criteria have been the fit in terms of personalities of assigning particular individuals to groups.

... The research also suggests that career planning should be regarded as an iterative process involving systematic feedback between the planners and the planned and that some effort is necessary to create the conditions in which this can take place."

These examples are on a relatively small scale, what is significant in them is the extent to which the OR scientists have been able to relinquish the "analyst" role for that of the "change agent" whilst the behavioural scientists have been able to accept the OR model as a guiding framework for their activities.

4. The art of forming networks

An earlier paper [10] discussed some of the problems of conducting OR in multi-organisational systems. Recent work on this theme by a team of operational researchers and political scientists [11] has highlighted the importance of "reticulist" (i.e., network-forming) skills. From close observation of a town expansion scheme, they argue that planning involves a continuous (but not necessarily convergent) process of adjustment and that skilful management of networks of inter-agency relationships is an integral part of this process. The skills of network management require ability to combine appreciation of problem structure and of "opportunity space", with an appreciation of political structure, and must be regarded as a scarce resource to be deployed selectively. Organisations can act only as a constraining or enabling influence, hopefully by providing appropriate supports to individuals who have reticulist skills or are capable of acquiring them.

This model helps in diagnosing difficulties in the public planning process and hence can assist in developing appropriate forms of OR. For example, innovations in methods for exploring alternatives which Friend et al. have proposed, can help to enhance the scope for timely adjustment between agencies. Research skills and network managing skills are complementary and are in practice subject to similar constraints; for instance, accounting conventions do not normally reveal the benefits of spending additional effort in order to reach better decisions. The processes of inter-agency adjustment are also constrained if one agency possesses a preponderance of either of these skills, for this tends to bring out obstructive attitudes in the others. Again the deployment of network managing skills or of research skills requires access to exploratory processes which may be politically sensitive and this access can sometimes only be bought by accepting constraints on the use of sensitive information.

This highly summarised account of some constraints in the processes of public planning and the skills required to overcome them, add further point to the view of OR as a social process rather than as a technical one.

5. Discussion

In none of the examples illustrated was it possible even to contemplate the assumptions implicit in a great deal of OR theory; for example, that there is a relevant, identifiable, single, decision-maker; or that conflicts can be resolved if only they are referred to a sufficiently high authority. Nevertheless progress was made.

The natural style of behavioural science is to work with existing organisations, helping the people in them to see and to acquire insights into their own problems, so facilitating a process of self-help. Whilst this is to some extent true of OR also, the use of system models does seem to provide the integrative focus for the practical use of concepts and data from the social sciences, and their extension to more complex situations than those from which they derived originally.

The collaboration should be especially valuable, therefore, in enabling the two kinds of skill to deal with those problems — many of a social nature — which existing organisations and institutions do not adequately cover. Such problems include:

Social deprivations such as poverty, mental ill-health, educational failure, delinquency, joblessness, in which transmission from parents to children seems to be a factor along with environmental influences and the deliberate interventions resulting from social policies. It is one thing to measure, say, the correlation between broken homes and child delinquency, and another to indicate how something can be done about it.

Planning public services. Rising expectations and rising sensitivities are giving rise to increasing demands for "participation" in all forms of public planning, but how can these pressures be reconciled with the increasing technical complexity of the services themselves? Can alienation between planners and planned-for be reduced, e.g., by extension of the processes of eliciting preferences used by Drake et al. cited above?

Work and the use of resources. The need of the individual to work continuously in order to survive is no longer self-evident. In many societies, cultural expectations and psychological needs derived from the historic nature of work may now be in conflict with such factors as the consumption of natural resources. Such problems are not to be solved at the physical or economic level alone. Is it possible to design a new order of things which simultaneously satisfies the physical, behavioural and political constraints?

Compared with those on which working relations between OR and behavioural science have already been established, these are problems of a different order. The outcomes are more difficult to identify, the research design hard to imagine, the client system not apparent. But, surely this does not mean that there is no alternative but to fall back on doom-mongering [12] or on scholarly comment as the only contribution we can make? What is necessary for *operational* research on such questions? It seems worth exploring whether for the higher order problems, the appropriate researcher/client relationship would be a reinforcement by OR and behavioural and social science skills of whatever reticulist roles are evolving in relation to these problems.

This, in turn, requires a more stable base for the growth of the interdisciplinary research capability and the evolution and maintenance of its system of values than the usual "jobs for clients" or "in house" arrangements can provide. The problem of intra-team communication is not just the obvious one which requires each member to learn something of the language of the others; the differences are more deeply rooted in underlying value systems. This is especially a difficulty when the values of the client system cannot be made sufficiently explicit to have an overriding influence. Since the ultimate client is often the community at large, the difficulty of disparate values amongst the research team can easily obtrude, with detrimental effect.

Perhaps the only answer is to be aware of the problem and in the long run, by team self-education, to develop professional standards about how to apply and use values which purport to represent those of the community at large whether or not these coincide with those of the researcher. It may have to be someone's role to be continuously insistent upon revealing the value systems from which research team members operate. For example, the economist who slips from "economic man would be expected to behave as follows ..." into saying "everyone should behave as follows ..." would not be allowed to go unchallenged.

Which argument leads to the conclusion that to realise the potentialities of OR with behavioural science is a long-term matter, requiring the continuous support of an institutional setting dedicated to the challenge of important social problems. Recent indications are that in several countries, steps are being taken to establish institutions of this sort.

References

[1] J. Lawrence, Operational research and the social sciences (Tavistock Publ. London, 1966).

[2] F.E. Emery, Organisational behaviour: an introduction, in: Approaches to the study of organisational behaviour, ed. G. Heald (Tavistock Publ. London, 1971).

[3] G. Higgin and W.N. Jessop, Communications in the building industry (Tavistock Publ., London, 1965).

[4] J. Luckman, An approach to the management of design, Opnl. Res. Q. 18, No. 4 (1967).

[5] C. Crichton, Interdependence and uncertainty: a study of the building industry (Tavistock Publ. London, 1966).

[6] I.A. Lowry, Reforming rent controls in New York City: the role of research in policymaking, Policy Sci. 3 (1972) 47.

[7] P.J. Shipp, A study of client relations, Inst. Opnl. Res. internal paper (1972).

[8] P.J. Farmer, A simulation study of career planning policies, paper presented to Third Joint Conf.: Industrial relations and manpower organisation; Inst. Opnl. Res., internal paper, No.638 (1971).

[9] R.I. Drake, J.R. Morgan, J. de B. Pollard and P. Quinn, A career planning system integrating an assignment model with subjective information and individual aspiration, NATO Conf. Cambridge (1971).

[10] J. Stringer, Operational research for multi-organisations, Opnl. Res. Q. 18, No.2 (1967).

[11] J.K. Friend, C.J.L. Yewlett and J.M. Power, Beyond local government reform: some prospects for evolution in public policy networks, Inst. Opnl. Res., internal paper (1971).

[12] D. Meadows et al., The limits to growth: a report for the Club of Rome's project on the predicament of mankind (Universe Books, New York, 1971).

M. Ross, ed., OR '72. North-Holland Publishing Company (1973)

27

BEHAVIORAL SCIENCE MODELS: DISCUSSANT 1

Modèles de science du comportement: porte-parole 1

ERIK JOHNSEN

School of Economics and Business Administration, Copenhagen, Denmark

As I agree with John Stringer's conclusions my comment will be indirect, outlining our own frame of reference for merging OR and the behavioral sciences.

In traditional OR we work with following equation

$$V(x) = f(x,y).$$

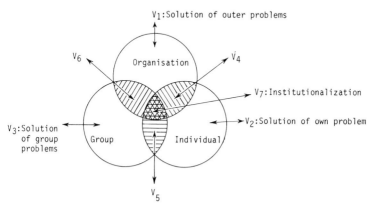

Fig. 1. The actual problem complex, $V_1(x)$, $V_2(x)$, $V_3(x)$, $V_4(x)$, $V_5(x)$, $V_6(x)$, $V_7(x) = f(x,y)$.

Table 1

Means	Relation	Objective
value theory	rational man	maximum utility
economics	economical man	maximum profit
psychology	psycholical man	dynamic satisfaction (search–learn)
sociology	group man	efficiency and social satisfaction
organization	organizational man	satisfaction via job
political science	politician	power
systems theory	systems man	control of complex environment
societal science	societal man	development of society

In the actual problem complex we are always faced with human problems in terms of organizational-, group- and individual problems as well.

This is sketched in fig. 1. The solution of "the outer problem" is only one side of the complex. We must solve the "inner problem" of the group/organization as well. And we must solve (or help to solve) individual problems connected with it.

When turning to the actual problem-solving activity we can draw on knowledge from the behavioral disciplines sketched in table 1.

It is our experience that the problem-solving process in itself should be

Table 2
Problem solving

Process	Discipline (language)		
	Decision theory	Systems theory	Behavioural theory
analysis	make a satisfactory decision	design a function-able system	prescribe behavior in specified situations
interaction	decision maker *and* consultant together produce a decision rule	change a function-ing system	change a social process by own or consultant help
search–learning	search for a decision rule and improve the search procedure	make interaction between system and environment for mutual effect	change adequate means and ends

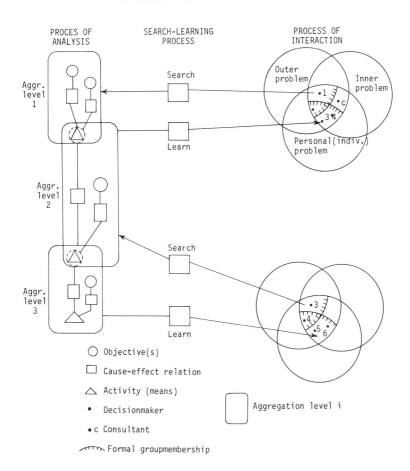

Fig. 2. Problem solving.

organized as a search-learning process in which overlapping groups and a consultant participate. Together they produce information in terms of partial decision models linked together in a total systems model (fig. 2). I could give many examples from our practice that this strategy works for the practitioner as well as for the researcher.

This experience again gives information on a systematization of problem-solving strategies and problem-solving languages (disciplines). This is given as table 2 and should be self explanatory.

Again this means that OR and behavioral sciences is so deeply inter-woven that they simply are parts of each other. Because as an OR-man you are working with all combinations in table 2, depending on your problem.

M. Ross, ed., OR '72. North-Holland Publishing Company (1973)

28

BEHAVIORAL SCIENCE MODELS: DISCUSSANT 2

Modèles de science du comportement: porte-parole 2

A. YOUNG

The New University of Ulster, Coleraine, Northern Ireland

Mr. Stringer has pointed out that a test of the potentialities of OR/behavioral science collaboration lies at the interface between the macroscopic approaches of manpower planning on the one hand and particular requirements of personnel management as applied to individuals on the other. Further he has commented that needs and attitudes of personnel are changing. I wish to enlarge on these points in relation to manpower models designed to be of predictive use in planning, particularly in hierarchically structured management systems.

The literature of industrial sociology and psychology is very largely American with some Western European contributions. Almost all that I know (which may of course reflect my ignorance) is describable as being in the Western, Anglo-Saxon, Puritan tradition in which work is an end in itself or a moral imperative. Recently I have been encountering situations where this is manifestly not the case and in some societies (Ireland for example) work is a means to an end. I suspect this is increasingly the case in many societies. Young entrants to firms seem decreasingly to regard their first job as their career job and it is a matter of direct statistical observation that labour wastage patterns are changing. If we are to recognise such changes in order to make predictive models, mathematically trained modellers like myself must gain the cooperation of behavioral scientists to formulate models of group behaviour. That the problems are formidable can be illustrated by simple case histories.

When a British insurance firm dispersed its central records office just after the war it decided on the basis of the known labour wastage of the educated and skilled female punched card machine operators that it could run down the central staff by natural wastage, stopping recruitment but not declaring redundancies. Wastage stopped entirely and after about six months the firm restarted recruitment against the danger of wastage, when it restarted, being catastrophic. Why did these women stay longer than they had done previously? In a factory making radio and electronic equipment, the advent of cheap foreign parts simultaneously with a change in British budgetary policy led to a run-down. This firm also decided to rely on natural wastage to run down the labour force. Semi-skilled men responded by staying longer, as was the case for the skilled women in the insurance company mentioned above, but the unskilled women assembly workers responded in exactly the opposite manner. The personnel manager told me that some of these women actually stated that it was not fair of them to take the firm's wages without doing proper amounts of work in return. Why these different reactions? Given an anticipated change in staffing requirements, can behavioral science give us some indication in advance what the staff response will be?

As another example firm S hardly recruited at all during the slump of the 1930's and the war years. In 1952, fewer than 5% of its managerial grades of staff had less than 5 years' service and well over 70% had 20 or more years' service. Its recruitment literature emphasised good working conditions, excellent welfare and pension provisions and security. After the war, the firm expanded rapidly. As recruitment proceeded and elderly staff retired the service-distribution of staff changed radically. By 1959, about 42% of the staff had less than 5 years' service and well over 70% had 20 or more years' dropped to under 35%. By 1966 the proportions were about 48% and 12%. In the early 1960's therefore staff with very short lengths of service were being promoted into the upper-middle ranges of management and by 1966 they were reaching top-management grades in contradistinction to the situation in the early 1950's when people with long service were in quite junior positions*.

What was very evident, even to a mathematician, was the changing attitude of staff. Recruits in the 50's could see that they would achieve rapid promotion. Ten years later recruits of similar abilities could see their near-contemporaries already occupying more senior positions and relatively few of the senior posts were occupied by people of long service – hence promotion blockages lay ahead. It is not within my competence to analyse the sociolo-

* This is illustrated in fig. 5 on page 93 of [1]

gical attitudes of staff, but the statistical analysis did show changes in leaving rates related to changing promotion prospects. How does one disentangle the sociological causes and effects? Certainly the firm did change its recruitment style and stopped emphasising job-security, pension rights, etc. Can behavioral science tell us what the group-dynamics are likely to be? Can it separate out causes and effects internal to the firm from the changes in the social climate generally outside the firm? Can it provide clues which we can build into our models so that they become more precise planning tools?

More recently I have become engaged in comparative analyses of the management staffs of a number of British and Irish companies, chosen from different industries and operating in a variety of locations in the United Kingdom. The analyses are already highlighting areas where we seem to be in need of support from behavioral scientists, and producing problem situations which I suggest the sociologists might usefully explore. Comparing two companies, one a large marketing organization, the other in the engineering industry but both operating in the same regions, nation-wide, we find that leaving rates of executives in four of the British regions are roughly in the proportions:

Midlands   1.0
Northern   1.4
Scotland   3.7
Southern   2.4

in both firms. It may be widely believed that executives pine for the South, or at least London, and it may be that jobs are still relatively plentiful in the London area, so job-changing in the South is easy enough to achieve. But in the other three regions leaving rates are almost inversely proportional to the regional rates of unemployment. Moreover, both these firms say that among their "shop-floor" work forces labour turnover is greatest where the local unemployment is heaviest. Is there a group-dynamic which can be specified closely enough for OR modelling to become effective?

Finally, I would like to mention an encouraging result being investigated by one of my research students, P. Vassiliou. My linear Markov model of hierarchical management systems works well up to a point, as does Bartholomew's replacement model. Indeed in conditions of steady expansion or of constant size, the two models are virtually equivalent at least in mathematical terms. Both models fail when conditions change rapidly. I have mentioned the link between promotion prospects and wastage. This suggests we need non-linear feed-back models. Now firms are collections of a biological species (man) and we might look for models from ecological population-dynamics. Happily for mankind, though perhaps unhappily for mathematicians, man is distinguished from most biological species by his ability to think and take anticipatory action. Thus we have to build into our feed-back model terms which express human reactions to the developing situation. This we may attempt to do by black-box techniques, hoping that we can prescribe inputs and mechanisms which give us outputs which fit observations.

Mr. Vassiliou suggests that the firm has some sort of "desired" hierarchy, overtly-stated or otherwise. Those at all levels concerned with making immediate decisions about recruiting and promoting staff, however, have a "perceived" hierarchy based on the aggregate of their individual but intimate knowledge of the parts of the structure with which they are concerned. A principle of inertia operates (a system continues in its state of rest or of uniform motion unless acted upon by external forces) and the firm in actuality operates towards an "inherent" hierarchy which may change with time but which is the result of the interaction between the desired and perceived hierarchies and the forces working on the system. The inherent hierarchy can (hopefully) be deduced by statistical analysis of movements within the staff over a period of years assuming particular mechanisms within the black-box. Tentative results for firm S indicate that this kind of analysis can yield better predictions than the linear models do. It is my hope that behavioral science will become involved in the analysis of the group sociology at work so that we can gainfully use their insights to improve our black-boxes.

Reference

[1] D.J. Bartholemew and B.R. Morris, Aspects of manpower planning, (EUP, London, 1971).

PART V

NATIONAL CONTRIBUTIONS

Contributions Nationales

Contributions from societies in

Belgium	Brazil	Canada
Denmark	France	Greece
Germany	India	Ireland
Israel	Italy	Japan
Netherlands	Norway	Spain
Sweden	Switzerland	United Kingdom

Contents

Applications to News Media

Education and Research

Railways and Airlines

Coal and Power

Health

Other Applications

Mathematical and Computer Techniques

M. Ross, ed., OR '72. North-Holland Publishing Company (1973)

29

CONSTRUCTING AN ADAPTIVE STRATEGY
FOR A NATIONAL NEWSPAPER

Construction d'une stratégie adaptive
pour un journal national

DAVID B. HURST

Thomson Organisation Ltd., London, England

Abstract. The methods actually used in a long-range planning exercise for a national newspaper are described. The process of constructing the plan consisted of three main phases: (1) selection of preferred future state (target horizon scenario) for the newspaper (it was found that best values of the various alternative horizon scenarios that were considered could be obtained by optimising the output variables of a simple model), (2) selection of a fail/safe implementation programme, (3) establishment of a monitoring and control system whereby the target horizon scenario and implementation programme can be modified in light of further information.

The paper considers phase 1 in some detail, and briefly describes the procedure adopted for phases 2 and 3. Particular attention is given to the nature of management involvement in the project.

1. Introduction

Constructing a strategy for a product has certain parallels with the scientific process. A structure of hypotheses is built up to describe a particular system or organism and how it behaves in its environment. If it seems possible to predict measurable results, experiments are designed and carried out, and the hypotheses are added to, discarded or modified according to the results. In business, hypotheses are built up about the way a particular product interacts with its environment, i.e., how customers, suppliers, competitors, etc., are effected by changes in an attribute of the product like quality, price, availability, etc., and these hypotheses are tested by experience. Hypothesis structures can often be developed which repeatedly produce adequate predictions and these tend to be elevated to the status of law. When eventually new data or new unanticipated influences arise which repeatedly upset the predictions, a crisis occurs where the laws become inappropriate to the real situation. The extent or intensity of the crisis depends upon the degree of change required of the system in order for it to be adapted successfully and the strength of belief in the original hypothesis structure.

The way an organisation resolves a crisis is very similar to the way an individual tends to act after the death of a close relative. Fink et al. [1] distinguish four phases:

(1) *shock* where decision making becomes paralysed,

(2) *defensive retreat* where the organisation reverts to old patterns of behaviour and management reacts expediently to day-to-day affairs only,

(3) *acknowledgement* where it becomes recognised that change is necessary and management begins to explore new methods and opportunities,

(4) *adaptation and change* where a new successful mode of operation is evolved and adopted.

The time that an organisation takes to go through these four stages depends on the severity of the crisis, and the longer it takes before the crisis is resolved, the more costly it is likely to prove. The length of this "grief cycle" is further extended if the defensive retreat phase is reinforced by comparatively good results or if the hunting behaviour exhibited in the acknowledgement phase cannot be resolved.

This may occur respectively, where a crisis occurs at the trough of an economic cycle or where the product under consideration is no longer commercially viable.

In order to avoid the ill-effects of the "grief cycle" it is not necessary to avoid organisational crises as such. It is sufficient to be able to foresee the crisis in due time in order to be able to switch straight to the adaption and change phase without any of the intermediate steps. To do this, a strategy must be devised which can be quickly modified if necessary in light of current data and findings about the product.

2. Background to the problem

Newspapers being a communicating medium are a peculiar product in that they sell the two direct markets simultaneously. Sales are made to the receivers of the information provided by the medium (the circulation market) and also to other transmitters of information who wish to share the medium with the publishers (the advertisement market). Major "grief cycles" can be identified for the National Newspaper Industry in the UK during the last 100 years which can be related to structural changes in these two markets.

The current crisis in the British National Newspaper Industry can be identified with the end of the circulation boom during the Second World War and the decline in National Press Advertising as a proportion of Gross Domestic Product which began about 1960, when Commercial Television began to take an increasing share of the total advertising budgets. Four national newspapers in fact closed down or merged in 1960/61. Crisis indeed.

Meanwhile the general policy of the National Newspapers remained one of circulation and advertisement volume maximisation rather than optimisation. The labour force had become static in size, even declining and consequently was showing an older and older age-profile. However, wage rates continued to rise as fast as they had in the boom years of the 1950s and redundancy and recruitment especially in the production area were regulated by Trade Union control.

The situation was one where the "defensive retreat" phase of the grief cycle was reinforced each time by comparatively good results. The levelling off of advertisement expenditure was obscured by a four to five year advertising cycle where annual growth rates in real money terms varied by 10–15%. The dramatic fall off in advertising revenue in constant money terms experienced by the National Newspapers in 1961/2 and 1966/7 were counteracted by the upswings in the advertising cycles of 1963/4 and 1968/9 which had the effect of reinforcing the traditional attitudes and strategies. By the downturn of 1970/1, however, it seemed that, with one exception, even the most profitable papers were only likely to make a marginal profit.

It was at this point that a special unit was set up to consider the problem.

3. Method of approach

The terms of reference of our study were: "to define a strategy which would increase cash flow in the short term as a basis for further increasing profit in the long term".

As a working definition, we saw a strategy as comprising three distinct elements:

(1) to define a preferred possible future state for the newspaper (target horizon scenario) satisfying the objectives thereof and constraints thereon whether explicit or implicit,

(2) to establish broad decision rules towards achieving such a state,

(3) to delineate a suitable monitoring and strategy adaption system.

We approached the problem initially by:

(1) collecting ideas and opinions from key individuals within the company,

(2) evolving a series of models to describe the operation of the newspaper and assembling the relevant quantitative data,

(3) deriving a "surprise-free extrapolation" of revenues and costs from historical data. This "surprise-free extrapolation" was derived independently from the model that generated the horizon scenario and was based on projections of consumer expenditure and aggregate economic data. It will not be described in detail in this paper.

4. Collection of ideas from key individuals

Construction of suitable hypothesis structures demands creative thought. In principle, the more creative ideas that are available, the wider the range of hypothesis structures that it should be possible to construct.

We therefore placed great importance in collecting value judgements and ideas about the newspapers from as many individuals as possible. These were collected in three stages:

4.1. Initial questionnaire

An initial questionnaire was constructed and 31 individuals were interviewed, 21 within the company and 10 outside the company connected with ancillary industries such as advertising, distribution and retailing.

As a result of these interviews, several hundred ideas were received relating to all aspects of the newspaper and its competitors. A preliminary model was developed to describe qualitatively the impact of these ideas on revenue and costs (fig. 1). A classification system based on the various elements within this model was used to analyse the ideas put forward.

This model that we used was exclusively concerned with the effects of the variables within management control; the effects of exogenous variables such as government actions, economic cycles and competitors's activity are not shown directly, but affect each one of the model elements.

It will be noted that various positive and negative feedback loops can be identified within the model, for example if the cover price is raised, the number of buyers (circulation) is reduced, readership falls, less advertisements are placed in the paper, the value of the paper drops and circulation reduces even further.

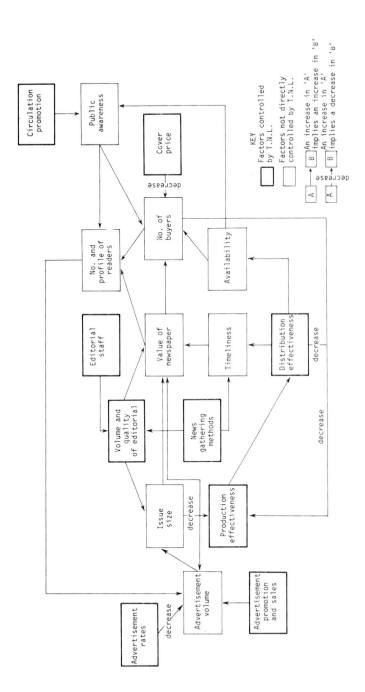

Fig. 1. Qualitative model.

4.2. Strategy questionnaire

11 individuals within the company, mostly directors or their senior sub-ordinates were selected to devise "intuitive" strategies of their own with a common format derived from the qualitative model in fig. 1.

The primary purpose of this stage was to identify alternative horizon scenarios on which to base the final choice, to clarify further the inter-relationships that needed to be built into the model and to give top management the chance to contribute to the strategy. The secondary and probably more important purpose was to identify which key individuals would be likely to support our final recommendations and which would be likely to oppose them. Our selling effort could then be pitched accordingly.

11 complete strategies were received altogether, including the pilot strategy devised by the leader of the planning unit to test the strategy question-naire form.

For preliminary analysis, the strategies were classified by the implied values of four major variables. These variables were advertisement rate (A), cover price (P), pagination, or pages per issue (S), and circulation (C). An advertisement rate higher than the projected 1975 level is denoted by A_1 and a lower rate by A_0. Similar notation is used for the other variables. An analysis of the strategies that we received is shown in table 1.

The fact that there was no concensus as to what the best strategy for the newspaper should be, is consistent with what one might expect from an organisation in the acknowledgement phase of the grief cycle. As a rough guideline, however, opinion appeared to be polarised between a $S_0C_0A_1P_1$ and a $S_1C_1A_0P_1$ type strategy.

The internal logic of each contributed strategy and the ideas inherent in them were analysed qualitatively using the model in fig. 1. The various ideas

Table 1
Number of strategies received by category

	S_0C_0	S_0C_1	S_1C_0	S_1C_1	Totals
A_0P_0	–	–	–	1	1
A_0P_1	–	–	2	3	5
A_1P_0	–	–	–	–	0
A_1P_1	4	–	–	1	5
Totals	4	0	2	5	11

that merited further consideration were then graded as follows:

(1) strategic ideas, ideas concerning the extent of variation of the various elements in the model in fig. 1;

(2) tactical ideas, ideas concerned with the actual implementation of changing the values of the strategic variables which would involve significant expenditure (be it to introduce them or to reverse their effects);

(3) peripheral ideas, ideas concerned with implementation which would not involve significant expenditure either upon introduction or cessation.

It was decided that in our final report it would be necessary to deal with the interactions of the strategic variables and ideas in detail and to quantify the effects of the major tactical ideas. A list of suitable peripheral ideas could be appended without comment.

4.3. Feedback

As the final step, copies of all the received and synthetic strategies were re-circulated to each individual for comments and criticisms. The purpose of this stage was:

(1) to clarify the logic of the newspaper model and to identify any objectives and constraints that has not yet been expressed,

(2) to identify strategies, tactics and peripheral ideas that were impracticable owing to internal inconsistencies or resource constraints,

(3) to identify the likely reactions of each individual to various different strategy proposals as an aid to our selling effort for final recommendations.

We were thus able to isolate five tactical ideas and forty peripheral ideas which were suitable for including in our final report.

5. The optimisation model

Fig. 2 shows the qualitative model in fig. 1 in a form suitable for quantification. Circulation revenue is a function of advertisement volume and advertisement rate. Variable costs are a function of editorial promotion, pagination, circulation, etc. A large proportion of the costs varies with the total number of pages printed per issue, i.e., is a function of the product of circulation and pagination.

Rather than treat the model in the most general way possible, we hope to clarify the exposition by taking only one category of advertising and one category of editorial and describe the model in its simplest form.

There are in fact various different categories of advertising, each with their

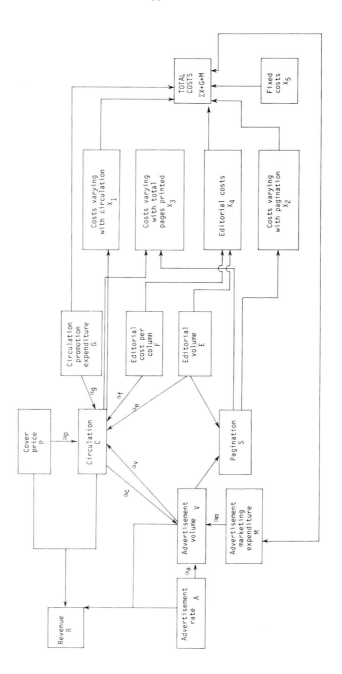

Fig. 2. Model for quantification.

own rate structure and response to variations in rates, circulation and marketing effort. Similarly different categories of editorial have different effects on circulation. It is left to the reader to elaborate as he chooses.

This model can be used in two ways: with and without inbuilt time lags.

5.1. Model with time lags

Changes in most of the controllable variables are by their nature discrete, especially changes in cover price or advertisement rate. Time series analysis indicates that it takes between three and six months for circulation to settle down after an increase in cover price. Readership data is published every six months based on an average for the previous year. It may take 18 months or more, therefore, for an advertiser to be fully aware of the effects of a cover price increase and adjust his advertising appropriation accordingly.

The time lagged model was used to devise the implementation plan.

5.2. Model without time lags

For the purpose of constructing a strategy, it is not necessary to introduce time lag effects into the model, since we are primarily interested in the nature of alternative possible states of equilibrium rather than in how we can arrive at them. Let $S(i, j)$ be the ith possible state of the newspaper at a time j.

Given the current state of the newspaper $S(0, 0)$ we can project a no-change state $S(1, 0)$ where the changes in the controllable variables in the recent past have worked through the various time lags to a situation where each variable in the model is in a state of equilibrium.

By changing the values of the controllable variables, we can then transform $S(1,0)$ to derive an alternative equilibrium state $S(r,0)$ and possible even an optimal profit situation $S^*(r,0)$. It will not, however, be possible to move from the state $S(0,0)$ to the state $S(r,0)$ immediately. Not only will the time lags apply, but it will probably only be feasible to achieve the new equilibrium situation in a series of stages.

Meanwhile, after a time, t, the effects of inflation and economic cycles will have distorted the original equilibrium position to a state $S(1,t)$.

The essence of our approach was accordingly to devise a "surprise-free" projection of a possible state $S(1,t)$ and to transform this by use of the model to a "target horizon scenario" $S^*(r,t)$. This would indicate the direction we should at present be going in changing prices, rates, editorial expenditure, etc., and the rate of change needed to achieve the new situation within a given time. To make the strategy effective and to avoid "grief cycle" effects, it would also be necessary to institute some system of updating the value of $S^*(r,t)$, so that the direction could be changed in light of changes of the values of the various variables, interrelationships and constraints inherent in the model.

6. Quantification

The measurements used for the various variables under consideration are shown in fig. 2. They are essentially crude, since the impact of items such as editorial quality or circulation is dependent on factors such as flair, appeal and fashion, which are extremely difficult to quantify. The assumption has to be made that the editor would use any extra cost per column available to him to improve quality proportionately.

Similar assumptions have to be made in respect of the other controllable variables. Annual, or in some cases six-monthly, averages were taken for each variable to eliminate seasonal effects and to enable variables, such as cover price and pagination, which are essentially discrete, to be treated as continuous.

The constraints that were built into the model were basically derived from our original tactical constraint that cash flow should be increased in the short term. This meant that it was out of the question to aim for a target horizon scenario which demanded early investment in new assets or facilities that would be likely to exceed the amount of extra profits that could be generated during the first few years of the plan. The capacity of the presses was therefore restricted to its present level and it was considered unlikely that the distribution network could be reasonably extended in its present form. Maximum limits for circulation and pagination could therefore be established.

To evaluate the interrelationships between the variables it was necessary to select suitable forms for the equations describing the interrelationships.

Such equations will be of the form:

$$V = \phi_1(A,C,M),$$

where V = advertisement volume, A = advertisement rate, C = circulation, M = marketing expenditure; α_a, α_c, α_m are constants related to the above 3 variables, ϕ_1 is a functional operator.

A similar function will apply for circulation:

$$C = \phi_2(P,E,F,G,V).$$

Since there was no a priori reason to select a particular function ϕ, we decided to test the simplest model available, namely

$$V = \alpha_a\, A + \alpha_c\, C + \alpha_m M + \text{constant}.$$

In terms of proportional changes, this can be expressed as

$$v = \alpha_a a + \alpha_c c + \alpha_m m,$$

which represents a chord of the response surface for small incremental values of a, c and m even if the function ϕ is in fact non-linear.

Unfortunately values of α_a, α_c, α_m, etc., could not satisfactorily be derived directly from a series of multiple regression equations. This was because:

(1) it was not considered that more than ten year's back data would be relevant to the current situation,

(2) the model ignores the effects of competitive activity, inflation or economic activity.

Two newspapers were considered to be competitors for circulation and six for advertising. Assuming all the data to be available in the first place, a complete analysis would entail at least 17 independent variables for circulation and 20 for advertisement volume.

We therefore confined ourselves, as far as competitive activity was concerned, to identifying where competitive action significantly affected our market shares in volume terms.

For cases where data concerning the competitors were unavailable or where there were significant effects, the assumption was made that circulation and advertisement volume would respond to changes in the relevant variables in the same way as they had in the past. That is that if the effects of our activity and that of the competitors were interdependent, then the competitors' activity would be such that the historical relationship between each of our controllable variables and their dependents would remain valid.

It was found that the variables within our control could be divided into those with short-term effects and those with long-term effects. Cover price, advertisement rates and circulation promotion expenditure tended to have a short-term effect and, circulation, advertisement marketing and editorial expenditure longer-term effects. The effects of the short-term variables could be identified from seasonally adjusted and smoothed time series of circulation and advertisement volume. The longer-term effects could then be derived by a series of multiple regressions using historical data, adjusted (a) for the short-term variable changes and (b) for inflation and economic cycles on the same basis as those used for the static projection $S(1,t)$.

Since it was expected that we might be able to achieve a new target equilibrium state for the newspaper in four years time, e, c, m, etc., were taken as four year changes in the adjusted value of E,C,M, etc. Reasonably satisfactory correlations were obtained.

7. Optimisation

Given the constraints on C and S and the relationships shown in fig. 2, it should be possible to construct some optimal values for the controllable variables in the model to optimise an objective profit function.

$$Y = R - \Sigma X,$$

where Y = profit, R = revenue, ΣX = costs.

The result of this optimisation will be to produce a profit Y_0^* corresponding to the target horizon scenario, T_0^*. T_0^* will not necessarily correspond to the true optimal state S_0^* unless the behavioural relationships are in fact linear.

Now the current situation S_0 can be transformed in a series of steps, S_1, S_2......S_n towards the target horizon scenario T_0^* such that the controllable elements of S_r lie within the range of the controllable elements of S_{r-1} and T_{r-1}. At any stage S_r, the linear relationships can be re-evaluated and a new target horizon scenario T_r^* can be derived. If at any point s, the increments required to transform S_s to T_s^* are all small, then the linear approximations to the behavioural formulae will apply such that $T_s^* = S_s^*$. Thus if $(T_r^*-S_r)$ is a convergent series, for all elements of T_r^* and S_r, then $T_r^* \to S_r^*$, and thus a method of deriving an optimal situation can be established, even if the behavioural relationships are non-linear. That the series $(T_r^*-S_r)$ is convergent, is stated without proof, but if it in practice is not convergent, then it will indicate that this method of using the model should be abandoned and replaced by a new hypothesis structure.

Upon examining the absolute values of the interrelationships it was found that the values of $|\alpha_m|$, $|\alpha_v|$, $|\alpha_f|$ and $|\alpha_g|$ were significantly smaller than $|\alpha_p|$, $|\alpha_a|$, $|\alpha_c|$ and $|\alpha_e|$. The model equations could therefore be simplified:

$$c = \alpha_e e + \alpha_p p, \quad v = \alpha_c c + \alpha_a a, \quad s = (1-q)e + qv, \quad x_4 = e.$$

$$Y = \text{profit} = CP(1+c)(1+p) + AV(1+a)(1+v) - X_1(1+c)$$

$$- X_2(1+s) - X_3(1+c)(1+s) - X_4(1+e) - (X_5 + G + M).$$

This is shown in fig. 3.

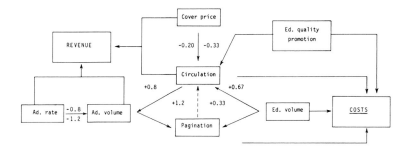

Fig. 3. Simplified model.

Expressed in terms of s, c and a only:

$$e = \phi_1(a, c, s), \quad p = \phi_2(a, c, s), \quad v = \phi_3(a, c),$$

where ϕ are linear functions. Hence

$$\frac{\partial Y}{\partial c} = \phi_4(a, c, s), \quad \frac{\partial Y}{\partial a} = \phi_5(a, c), \quad \frac{\partial Y}{\partial s} = \phi_6(c).$$

Equating the partial differentials to zero, we can solve for a, c and s and derive values for e, p and v, to obtain an optimal value for Y.

The formulae that we actually used were somewhat more complicated than the above, since we considered more than one category of advertisement and several additional cost structures were incorporated into the model. However, the method described above is in principle no different from the one we adopted. Equations using these "optimising" formulae, were made, using a range of values for α_c, α_e, α_p and α_a to allow for the uncertainty inherent in our quantification of these interrelationships. The extreme values of these ranges are shown in the diagram of the simplified model in fig. 3.

To revert to the situational notation used earlier, we thus found ourselves with a range of target horizon scenarios $S^*(r,t)$, with corresponding profits Y^*. The expected value of Y^*, $E(Y^*)$ corresponding to $E(S^*)$ was found to be about £2 m. above the profit arising from $S(1,t)$, the surprise-free extrapolation of $S(0,0)$.

The range of values of Y^* was quite large with an upper limit of £5.2 m. improvement and a lower limit of £0.1 m. Throughout most of the range, $S^*(r,t)$ was found to be constrained by the upper limits established for circulation and pagination.

Although the values of $S^*(r,t)$ corresponding to the lower values of Y^* were fairly close to $S(1,t)$, $E(S^*)$ implied large changes in some of the controllable variables. In broad terms, it was evident that the future of the newspaper depended upon product improvement, with a long term emphasis upon editorial volume of the same quality, impact and appeal as that already in the newspaper, backed up by circulation promotion and advertisement marketing to offset the effects of time-lags and seasonal variations. It was reckoned that increases in editorial were likely to have a decreasing marginal effect and that at some point in the future other variables would have to be introduced into the model as their effects became more important.

7.1. Implementation and control

Having developed a target horizon scenario, $E(S^*)$ it was now necessary to develop:

(1) an implementation plan delineating a possible path towards the target horizon scenario within the time t,

(2) a control system for comparing expected outcomes with actual and revising the target horizon scenario accordingly,

(3) a sales approach for convincing top management to adopt the strategy in principle.

Our main concerns in developing the implementation plan were:

(1) to introduce as little change as possible into the system at any stage in order: (a) to enable any changes that produced adverse effects to be reversed as cheaply as possible (the "fail-safe" facility), and (b) not to exceed the consumer's maximum price thresholds at any time in cases of increase in cover price or advertisement rates,

(2) to allow sufficient time between changes for their effects to be assessed so that the target horizon scenario could be updated,

(3) to enable the target horizon scenario situation to be reached as soon as possible while at no point reducing profit below that anticipated in any year in the "surprise free" extrapolation.

As things turned out, owing to the expected upturn in the British economy in 1972, it was possible to devise an implementation plan which did not diverge significantly from current policy until 1973.

The control system consisted of three elements, a short term forecasting system, a monitoring system and a simplified strategy updating system. The short term forecasting system was based on the model incorporating time lags, outlined briefly above, and the monitoring system required values of circulation and advertisement volume to be assessed at specific intervals after each step change had been made. If either were found to be significantly different from the predicted variables, this would be taken as a signal that the target horizon scenario should be updated.

The simplified strategy updating system was to evaluate the target horizon scenario based on the current situation of the newspaper, $S(0,0)$ rather than the surprise free extrapolation $S(1,t)$. We tested this method on our original data, and found that $S^*(r, 0)$ indicated a similar policy direction to $S^*(r, t)$. We therefore recommended this method should be installed, with the proviso that if $S(0,0)$ and $S^*(r,0)$ began to converge that the method should be reassessed.

To enable a new target horizon scenario to be evaluated quickly, a simple computer program has been written which can be used in the interrogative mode on a terminal.

In selling top management the concept of our recommended strategy, it was apparent that we would have a problem. Only one of the submitted strategies corresponded to ours in the binary classification system, and only three advocated the same logic for achieving the target horizon scenario. It was therefore to be expected that our recommendations would be likely to take a considerable time to be accepted. Luckily our strategy does not demand any substantial change from existing policy until 1973. Meanwhile, at least two vital components of our final target horizon scenario have become generally accepted.

Acknowledgements

My thanks are due to the other members of the Strategic Services Unit, P. Rivers, G. Randall and B. Elliott, and to the various TNL directors and executives who helped us in the formulation of the strategy.

Reference

[1] S.L. Fink, J. Beak and K. Taddeo, Organisational crisis and change, J. Appl. Behavioural Sci. 7, No.1 (1971).

M. Ross, ed., OR '72. North-Holland Publishing Company (1973)

30

LA METHODE ELECTRE II
Une application au média-planning

The Electre II method, an application to media planning

B. ROY

Université de Paris et METRA, Paris, France

et

P. BERTIER

E.S.S.E.C. et METRA, Paris, France

Résumé. Pour choisir dans un ensemble fini d'objets, en tenant compte de plusieurs critères difficilement réductibles à un seul, il faut faire appel à des approches nouvelles, la théorie de l'utilité se heurtant à deux obstacles: une connaissance imparfaite des préférences du décideur et une information imprécise pour caractériser chaque objet. De même que Electre I, Electre II est fondée sur des relations de surclassement, définies à partir des notions de concordance et de discordance entre critères; ces relations caractérisent le risque que l'on prend en déclarant qu'un objet surclasse un autre. Electre II donne deux préordres "extrêmes" et un préordre "médian" sur les objets.

Outil de portée générale, il a été mis au point à propos du problème de la sélection des titres où passer les annonces d'une campagne de publicité, pour lequel il fallait faire intervenir non seulement le prix de l'espace mais aussi des caractéristiques qualitatives telles que le contexte rédactionnel, l'image, la qualité de reproduction du titre.

L'objet de la communication est, en prenant appui sur un exemple numérique, d'expliquer cette méthode qui est largement utilisée dans le groupe Paris-Match.

1. Introduction

Dans cette communication, le problème général sous-jacent, mais non étudié en tant que tel, est celui du choix "multicritère": étant donné un ensemble fini X d'objets, comment guider le choix en prenant appui simultanément sur plusieurs critères — disons n — non aisément réductibles à un seul. Ces critères peuvent prendre des formes diverses: présence de caractéristiques, appréciation d'un facteur non quantifié, degré d'accomplissement d'un objectif, valeur résultant d'un calcul économique, etc. Nous désignerons par E_i l'ensemble fini complètement ordonné (échelle) des appréciations possibles pour le critère i. Pour un objet $x \in X$, l'appréciation portée sera notée $\gamma_i(x) \in E_i$.

Confrontée à une telle hétérogénéité, la voie qui consiste à expliciter une fonction d'utilité maniable et réaliste s'avère souvent impraticable. Soulignons-en les trois principaux obstacles:

(1) d'abord, une connaissance imparfaite des préférences du décideur, principalement pour ce qui relève de la manière dont peut s'opérer la compensation entre un gain sur un critère et des pertes sur plusieurs autres, en tenant compte de leurs amplitudes et des divers niveaux auxquels ces gains et pertes se situent;

(2) ensuite, une information imprécise pour caractériser chaque objet selon chaque critère (jugements subjectifs, évaluations grossières, calculs approximatifs, ...);

(3) enfin, beaucoup des méthodes fondées sur la détermination d'une fonction d'utilité exigent l'hypothèse de l'indépendance des contributions de chaque critère à l'utilité globale. Cette hypothèse est souvent peu conforme à la réalité.

Ce sont ces trois obstacles qui justifient pour une très large part l'intérêt et l'essor [1–3] des approches purement multicritères, telle celle présentée ici.

La méthode Electre I [4, 5] permet de sélectionner un sous-ensemble de X renfermant les objets les plus intéressants et les moins comparables. Utilisée depuis plusieurs années, elle a montré que souvent il était préférable pour le décideur de disposer, non d'une simple dichotomie séparant les bons des moins bons, mais d'un véritable classement des objets. La méthode Electre II est le fruit de cette constatation. Des motivations de même nature et des développements semblables à Electre I se retrouvent d'ailleurs dans [6, 7].

2. La méthode Electre II

2.1. Notion de surclassement

La méthode Electre II est fondée sur le concept primaire de relation de "surclassement" (introduite par l'un des auteurs dans [4]): il faut entendre par là une relation binaire définie sur X telle que l'affirmation: "x surclasse y" ($x, y \in X$) traduise une préférence de x relativement à y, suffisamment bien assise (en dépit des deux obstacles (1) et (2) signalés en introduction) pour que l'on soit en droit d'accepter le "risque" de la considérer comme acquise.

Il ne découle nullement de cette définition qu'une relation binaire de surclassement S soit transitive. En effet, si l'on peut prendre le risque d'accepter xSy et ySz, il n'en résulte pas nécessairement que l'on puisse prendre le risque d'accepter xSz: x et z peuvent être incomparables selon S ou, on peut même avoir zSx (ce qui crée un circuit). Lorsque deux objets x et x' apparaissent comme indifférents, il est naturel d'adopter xSx' et $x'Sx$. Même lorsque S n'est pas transitive, il sera légitime de considérer comme indifférents deux objets x et x' appartenant à un même circuit dans S. Pour plus de précisions sur le concept de relation de surclassement, voir [8].

Dans Electre II, comme dans Electre I, le surclassement se définit à partir d'une notion de concordance et d'une notion de discordance entre les critères (mais de nombreuses améliorations ont été apportées par rapport à Electre I): pour tout couple (x, y) d'objets de X, on accepte le risque de décider "x surclasse y" si un test de concordance et un test de non-discordance sont satisfaits.

2.1.1. Test de concordance

On demande au décideur de définir, en tenant compte d'une éventuelle redondance des critères, pour chaque critère i un indice d'importance p_i (notion apparentée à celle de poids mais qui ne donnera lieu à aucune multiplication par $\gamma_i(a)$). Pour chaque couple (x, y) on définit la trichotomie de l'ensemble I des critères en posant:

$$I^+(x, y) = \{i/\gamma_i(x) > \gamma_i(y)\} ,$$

$$I^=(x, y) = \{i/\gamma_i(x) = \gamma_i(y)\} ,$$

$$I^-(x, y) = \{i/\gamma_i(x) < \gamma_i(y)\} .$$

(On a fait l'hypothèse non restrictive des préférences croissant dans le même sens que les γ_i) et on introduit *

$$P^+(x, y) = \sum_{i \in I^+(x,y)} p_i , \qquad P^=(x, y) = \sum_{i \in I^=(x,y)} p_i ,$$

$$P^-(x, y) = \sum_{i \in I^-(x,y)} p_i , \qquad P = P^+ + P^= + P^- .$$

Soit c un seuil de concordance défini par le décideur. Le test de concordance

---

* Σ pouvant être remplacé par un opérateur autre que l'addition.

est accepté si

$$\frac{P^+(x,y) + P^=(x,y)}{P} \geqslant c \quad \text{et si} \quad \frac{P^+(x,y)}{P^-(x,y)} \geqslant 1 ,$$

c'est-à-dire si l'importance relative dans l'ensemble des n critères du "super-critère" constitué de la réunion des critères pour lesquels x est meilleur que y est "suffisamment forte".

2.1.2. Test de non-discordance

Pour chaque critère i, le décideur définit un ensemble de discordance D_i. Soit E_i l'ensemble des modalités notées e_i que peut prendre le critère i.

$$D_i \subset E_i \times E_i , \quad e_i \in E_i, \ e_i' \in E_i , \ e_i < e_i' .$$

On dira que le couple de modalités (e_i, e_i') est discordant si on ne peut en aucun cas accepter le risque de décider qu'un objet x présentant la modalité e_i selon γ_i surclasse un objet y présentant e_i'. On posera alors $(e_i, e_i') \in D_i$. Le test de non-discordance x surclasse y est satisfait si il n'existe pas d'indice i tel que:

$$(\gamma_i(x). \gamma_i(y)) \in D_i .$$

L'originalité d'Electre II provient de l'usage qui est fait ensuite de ce concept de surclassement pour établir un préordre complet sur l'ensemble des objets. Signalons tout d'abord deux aspects importants de cette procédure de classement:

(1) Elle repose non point sur une mais sur deux relations de surclassement correspondant à des niveaux de risque différents: S_F traduisant un surclassement fort et S_f un surclassement faible (moins solidement assis). S_F et S_f sont définies respectivement par des seuils de concordance c_F et c_f et des ensembles de discordance D_i et D_i^* tels que $c_F \geqslant c_f$ et $\forall i\, D_i^* \subset D_i$.

(2) Elle fournit non point un mais trois préordres solutions: deux notés v' et v'' apparaissent comme "extrêmes", le troisième $\bar{v}$ occupe une position "médiane".

2.2. Construction des préordres

Pour définir le préordre v' supposons que le surclassement fort S_F ne crée pas de circuit (lorsqu'il en est autrement, on substitue à X l'ensemble des classes d'indifférence). Introduisons l'ensemble:

$$C = \{x \,|\, x \in X, \, \nexists \, y \in X \text{ tel que } yS_F x\} \,,$$

constitué des objets qu'aucun autre ne surclasse fortement. L'absence de circuit implique $C \neq \emptyset$.

Le surclassement faible S_f peut créer des circuits dans C: notons B l'ensemble des classes d'indifférence qui en résultent dans C. Soit alors A le sous-ensemble des objets figurant dans les classes de B non faiblement surclassées dans B. A constitue par définition la première classe du préordre v'. La seconde est définie de la même manière sur $X - A$ et ainsi de suite.

Le préordre v'' est défini de façon identique à ceci près que l'on procède en sens inverse: on cerne tout d'abord la dernière classe, puis l'avant-dernière, etc. Pour cela on raisone sur le sous-ensemble des objets qui n'en surclassent fortement aucun, puis l'on isole parmi eux ceux qui n'en surclassent faiblement aucun.

L'utilisateur est invité à comparer ces deux préordres. Si les divergences de classement de certains objets dépassent la marge d'indétermination qu'il peut tolérer, il faut, s'il veut les réduire, affiner ses évaluations et/ou reconsidérer les paramètres qui, au-travers des conditions de concordance et de discordance, caractérisent les risques acceptés.

S'il aboutit à des divergences tolérables, il peut adopter un préordre situé "entre" v' et v'' tel le préordre médian $\bar{v}$ proposé dans Electre II (pour plus de précisions, voir [9]).

2.3. Considérations théoriques et pratiques

Les trois préordres complets ainsi élaborés apparaissent comme compatibles avec le surclassement fort en ce sens que:

$$xS_F y \Rightarrow \text{classe de } x \text{ antérieure à classe de } y \,,$$

le surclassement faible n'étant utilisé que localement (afin de ne pas prendre trop de risques) pour départager des objets incomparables selon S_F.

v' comme v'' et $\bar{v}$ peuvent être altérés par adjonction d'un nouvel objet. Cette instabilité est au premier abord choquante; elle est d'ailleurs contraire aux axiomes classiques de la théorie de la décision. Pourtant, elle s'explique fort bien et parait même inévitable, lorsque le caractère qualitatif de certaines des échelles, ou l'hétérogénéité des unités relatives aux autres, ne permet pas de prendre le risque que représente l'acceptation de l'une au moins des deux propositions:

$$xSy, ySx \qquad \forall x, y \in X$$

du moins en ne considérant que les seules évaluations des deux objets x et y. On est alors bien forcé d'admettre que la comparaison de deux objets x et y à un même troisième z peut apporter une information déterminante dans la décision finale de l'ordre relatif de x et y.

Electre II est un outil d'aide à la décision susceptible d'applications fort variées en raison de la généralité du problème qu'il cherche à résoudre et de la simplicité des procédures qu'il met en oeuvre. Ces applications possibles concernent, entre autres, les problèmes de: choix de projets de développement régional ou urbain, sélection de projets de recherche ou de développement d'une organisation, élaboration de plan d'équipement ou d'investissement lourd, recrutement de personnel, configurations d'ordinateur, marketing et publicité, ...

3. Le problème de la sélection des supports de presse

C'est à propos d'un problème de média-planning que la méthode Electre II a pris sa forme définitive et qu'un programme a été écrit. Avant d'exposer un exemple, nous allons décrire rapidement les méthodes actuelles et leurs limites, exposer quels sont les critères pertinents pour le problème du choix de la liste des magazines dans lesquels seront insérées les annonces d'une campagne de publicité.

3.1. Les méthodes actuelles

Les méthodes actuelles [10] reposent sur les données recueillies par le Centre d'Etude des Supports de Publicité dans son enquête sur la lecture des magazines nationaux. La séquence est à peu près la suivante [11, 12]:

(1) A partir de poids donnés aux modalités des caractéristiques socio-économiques des lecteurs, on détermine une population "utile" pour le publicitaire, les poids traduisant les objectifs de la campagne publicitaire.

(2) On calcule pour chaque magazine son audience (nombre de lecteurs) utile et le coût aux mille lecteurs utiles. Ce coût permet de mettre un ordre sur les titres.

(3) On introduit alors une "courbe de réponse" qui synthétise par un coefficient compris entre 0 et 1 l'intérêt de toucher quelqu'un x fois.

(4) L'ordre précédent permet d'élaborer des combinaisons de plusieurs titres appelées "plans de campagne"; et l'on calcule l'efficacité d'un plan à l'aide de la courbe de réponse.

Des algorithmes permettent de trouver les plans les plus efficaces pour un coût donné. Cette démarche fait donc appel à des méthodes d'optimisation.

3.2. Principales limites

(Voir [13].) Dans l'enquête du Centre d'Etude des Supports de Publicité, les erreurs d'échantillonnage sont importantes, l'estimation des audiences est imprécise, le coût aux mille lecteurs utiles est mal connu et l'extrapolation des résultats enregistrés dans l'enquête à l'ensemble de la population française est malaisée [14].

Des difficultés importantes apparaissent lorsqu'il s'agit de saisir le phéno-mène "lecture": on s'aperçoit que le libellé des questions joue un rôle déter-minant sur les réponses, qu'il s'agisse de saisir des habitudes ou des comporte-ments. Et le phénomène n'est actuellement qu'assez grossièrement approché par cette enquête.

La limite fondamentale des méthodes actuelles tient cependant à une autre raison. Les deux éléments pris en compte – coût aux mille lecteurs utiles et courbe de réponse – apparaissent comme gravement insuffisants pour saisir le phénomène de l'efficacité d'un plan dans toutes ses dimensions. Par ailleurs, ils font intervenir des chiffres dont la précision n'est en aucun cas garante de l'exactitude.

3.3. Critères à prendre en compte

Les critères ou points de vue selon lesquels on peut vouloir analyser les conséquences d'un plan de campagne sont divers et nombreux. R. Abgueguen en analyse 22 dans [14] et M. Marc en introduit encore quelques uns dans [15] et [16]. Cette revue assez complète ne doit pas dispenser, dans chaque cas particulier, de chercher si une dimensions importante n'a pas été oubliée. Dans tous les cas, il faut retenir au plus une dizaine de critères, relativement indépendants, c'est-à-dire tels qu'ils saisissent des conséquences distinctes non liées par leur définition même. Voici une description sommaire des six critères qui ont été retenus dans l'exemple traité ci-après:

(1) *Le coût aux mille lecteurs utiles, exprimé en francs*. Et le sens de la préférence est bien sûr celui des coûts décroissants.

(2) *Le contexte rédactionnel*. Si l'on pense qu'il est souhaitable d'harmo-niser au mieux le contenu du magazine et le contenu des annonces publici-taires, que le premier crée une ambiance propre à la réception du second, on comprend pourquoi pourront être mieux cotés (de 0 à 10, par exemple, dans le sens des préférences croissantes) les magazines pour lesquels les deux con-tenus coïncident.

(3) *La puissance*. Ce critère est lié d'abord à l'audience du support (plus elle est grande, plus la chance est grande d'obtenir de nombreuses occasions de voir) et à la fiabilité de l'information (d'autant plus grande que l'audience est grande). La note la plus forte est donné au support le plus puissant.

(4) *Le degré d'affinité du support avec la cible*. Il s'agit ici de saisir le pourcentage de la cible utile inclus dans l'audience. En effet, il ne faut pas que les lecteurs "utiles" soient marginaux dans le support: le support doit être bien centré sur la cible. La note la plus élevée (9) correspond au pourcentage le plus élevé dans la liste de supports retenue au départ.

(5) *La régularité de lecture*. On peut définir ce critère comme le pourcentage de lecteurs réguliers dans l'audience (avec la note 8 pour le plus élevé, et ceci à partir des données du Centre d'Etude des Supports de Publicité comme pour les critères 1, 3 et 4) lorsque l'objectif de la campagne est de présenter par des annonces différentes une gamme de produits et qu'il faut toucher chaque lecteur utile un minimum de fois.

(6) *Le prestige du support*. Les journaux, comme les produits, ont une image et il est important, lorsqu'il s'agit de promouvoir des produits considérés comme prestigieux, de mieux noter (de 1 à 10 dans le sens des préférences croissantes) les journaux les plus prestigieux.

4. Un exemple d'application d'Electre II

Déjà M. Marc avait essayé d'introduire Electre dans le problème de la selection de titres pour lequel il avait obtenu des résultats intéressants [16] et dans un problème plus large, celui du choix entre les grands médias: cinéma, radio, presse, TV, ... [15]. En 1971, R. Abgueguen a repris le problème dans le cadre du Groupe Paris-Match; il nous a demandé de mettre au point la méthode décrite précédemment; il l'a appliquée sur l'exemple qui va être analysé ci-après et que l'on trouvera aussi dans [14].

Il s'agit de choisir des titres de magazines pour une campagne de publicité dont l'objectif est de présenter une gamme de produits assez luxueux destinés essentiellement aux femmes habitant des villes de plus de 10 000 habitants, âgées de 20 à 40 ans et faisant partie des catégories aisées de la population. La séquence de travail a été la suivante: choix des critères à retenir (cf. 3.3), constitution de la liste des magazines à étudier, évaluation des critères pour chaque magazine, choix des poids et des seuils, passage d'Electre II, analyse et discussion des résultats.

Tableau 1
Données numériques

Supports	Critères					
	Contexte	Coût aux 1000 (en Fr.)	Régula-rité	Puissance	Affinité	Prestige
Poids cas no. 1	6	4	2	3	3	2
Poids cas no. 2	7	5	4	3	4	2
l'Express (Ex)	4	114	6	3	9	7
Jours de France (JF)	10	58	5	6	7	9
Modes de Paris (MP)	7	48	7	5	5	5
Mlle Age Tendre (MAT)	6	77	6	3	5	3
Elle (E)	10	51	4	5	8	9
Femmes d'Auj. (FA)	7	62	6	5	6	5
Intimité (I)	5	74	8	2	5	3
Nous Deux (ND)	5	125	7	2	5	3
Modes & Travaux (MT)	6	55	6	9	5	4
Echo de la Mode (EM)	6	86	6	3	5	4
Marie-Claire (MC)	10	59	4	6	8	9
Marie-France (MF)	9	59	4	5	7	7
Femme Pratique (FP)	7	51	4	4	7	6
Jardin des Modes (JM)	10	65	4	2	8	10

Tableau 2
Ensembles de discordance

	Contexte	Coût aux 1000	Régularité	Puissance	Affinité	Prestige
D_i^*	(1.10)(2.10) (3.10)(4.10) (1.9)(2.9) (1.8)	30 %	(1.9)(2.9) (3.9)(4.9) (1.8)(2.8) (3.8)(1.7)	(1.9)(2.9) (3.9)(1.8) (2.8)(1.7) (2.7)	(1.10)(2.10) (3.10)(4.10) (5.10)(1.9) (2.9)(3.9) (4.9)(1.8) (2.8)(3.8) (1.7)(2.7) (1.6)	(1.10)(2.10) (3.10)(4.10) (1.9)(2.9) (3.9)(1.8) (2.8)(1.7)
$D_i - D_i^*$	(5.10)(3.9) (4.9)(2.8) (3.8)(1.7)	20 %	(5.9)(4.8) (2.7)	(4.9)(3.8) (1.6)	(6.10)(5.9) (4.8)(3.7) (2.6)	(5.10)(4.9) (3.8)(2.7) (1.6)

4.1. Evaluation des magazines

Une liste de 14 magazines a été retenue, comprenant ceux qui paraissaient les plus adaptés à la campagne; certains, peu adaptés, ont été conservés aux fins d'expérimentation. On trouvera dans les tableaux 1 et 2 toutes les données utilisées. Il a été admis que, lorsque l'indice de concordance était supérieur à 3/4, il fallait un écart de 30 % sur le coût aux 1000 pour refuser le surclassement fort; lorsque cet indice était compris entre 2/3 et 3/4, un écart de 20 % suffisait pour le refus. Deux jeux de poids ont été pris en compte pour étudier la sensibilité des résultats.

4.2. Analyse et discussion des résultats

On trouvera dans le tableau 3 les ordres v', v'' et $\bar{v}$ pour les deux distributions de poids envisagées (cas no. 1 et 2). Ces résultats appellent les remarques suivantes:

(1) Les ordres v' et v'' sont assez voisins l'un de l'autre dans les deux cas. Il est donc raisonnable de postuler l'existence d'un ordre latent et l'ordre médian $\bar{v}$ a une signification.

(2) Dans le cas no 1, seul le magazine Jardin des Modes change de rang (4e pour v' et 8e pour v''), car ce magazine, relativement mal noté sur les critères coût aux 1000 et puissance, n'a que peu de relations de surclassement fort avec les autres. Dans le cas no. 2, Modes de Paris passe du 4e au 6e rang, parce qu'il n'est pas surclassé fortement.

Tableau 3
Résultats

Ordres		Classes 1	2	3	4	5	6	7	8	9	10	11	12	13	14
Cas no. 1	v'	E	JF	MC	JM	MF	MP	FP	FA	MT	MAT	EM	I	Ex	ND
	v''	E	JF	MC	MF	MP	FP	FA	MT JM		MAT	EM	I	Ex	ND
	$\bar{v}$	E	JF	MC	MF	MP	JM	FP	FA	MT	MAT	FM	I	Ex	ND
Cas no. 2	v'	E	JF	MC	MP JM		MF	FP	FA	MT	MAT	EM	I	Ex ND	
	v''	E	JF	MC	JM	MF	MP	FP	FA	MT	MAT	EM	I	ND Ex	
	$\bar{v}$	E	JF	MC	JM	MP	MF	FP	FA	MT	MAT	EM	I	Ex	ND

(3) Le coût aux 1000 est minimum pour Modes de Paris, qui n'arrive qu'au 5e rang dans les 2 cas étudiés.

(4) La différence entre les cas no. 1 et 2 est minime; par exemple on observe sur $\bar{\nu}$ un seul changement, permutation de Marie-France et de Jardin des Modes, qui s'explique par la baisse relative du poids du critère puissance (entrainant la progression de Jardin des Modes).

(5) Les ordres trouvés sont assez conformes à ceux que l'on attendait intuitivement. Cependant, si l'intuition est solide pour les 2 ou 3 premiers éléments de l'ordre, l'utilité d'Electre II apparait pour le choix des 3 ou 4 suivants.

4.3. Conclusion

La revue des critères à prendre en compte dans une campagne de publicité (3.3) montre la difficulté d'intégrer, d'agréger ces critères, plus ou moins qualitatifs, dans un modèle synthétique. Il fallait donc chercher une méthode, pas trop ambitieuse et présentant les qualités suivantes:

(1) Simple à comprendre et à mettre en oeuvre. Viser une méthode complexe aurait requis des données difficiles à rassembler et à traiter, aurait entrainé des coûts importants de mise au point et d'exploitation, aurait été comprise de quelques spécialistes seulement et finalement n'aurait pas été utilisée par des publicitaires.

(2) Ne faisant pas dire aux données plus qu'elles ne peuvent, qu'il s'agisse d'informations qualitatives ou d'informations quantitatives ne pouvant être qu'imprécises.

(3) Souple pour permettre d'étudier la sensibilité des résultats. Il faut en effet permettre aux décideurs de mesurer facilement l'incidence d'un changement dans les données.

Electre II, qui répond à ces trois désirs, est utilisée en time-sharing environ une fois par jour dans une séquence de calcul permettant de générer et d'évaluer des plans de campagne; un passage portant sur 50 titres avec 10 jeux de poids coûte environ 100 F.

D'autres applications sont en cours (cf. 2.3).

Enfin, Electre II utilisée comme outil d'exploration (jeux de poids) est une méthode qui, relevant des méthodes d'agrégation d'ordres, est proche de méthodes d'analyse et de structuration de données.

Bibliographie

[1] J. Antoine et B. Roy, Les techniques préparatoires de la décision, intérêt et limites, Rev. PROJET 33 (mars 1969).

[2] P. Bertier et J. de Montgolfier, Comment choisir en tenant compte de points de vue non commensurables? Analyse et Prévision 11 (1971).

[3] B. Roy, Décisions avec critères multiples: problèmes et méthodes, Rev. METRA 11, No. 1 (1972).

[4] R. Benayoun, B. Roy et B. Sussmann, Electre: une méthode pour guider le choix en présence de points de vue multiples, N.T. No. 49, D.S., Groupe METRA (juin 1966).

[5] B. Roy, Classement et choix en présence de critères multiples, Rev. Informatique et Recherche Opérationnelle, 2e année, No. 8 (1968) 57.

[6] Electre Air France: une méthode de classement d'objets en fonction de leurs qualités selon divers points de vue, Air France, Dir. Informatique (1968).

[7] Ventura, Concours d'urbanisme d'Evry; méthode d'analyse multicritère, C.G.E. Note No. 50 (sept. 1971).

[8] R. Roy, How outranking relation helps multiple criteria decision making. Commun. to the Univ. of South Carolina, Seminar (Oct. 1972).

[9] B. Roy et P. Bertier, La méthode Electre II (une méthode de classement en présence de critères multiples) N.T. No. 142, D.S., Groupe METRA (avril 1971).

[10] D.H. Gensch, Computer models in advertising media selection. J. Marketing Res. (Nov. 1968).

[11] La recherche opérationnelle appliquée à l'élaboration des plans médias, IREP, Paris (1966) p. 354.

[12] M. Irrmann, L'utilisation des modèles pour la mise au point du plan média, Intern. Marketing (juillet–août 1970).

[13] A.D. Shocker, Limitations of incremental search in media selection. J. Marketing Res. (Feb. 1970).

[14] R. Abgueguen, La sélection des supports de presse (Robert Laffon, Paris, 1971).

[15] P. Bertier et M. Marc, Choix des médias, Rev. METRA 7, No. 1 (1968).

[16] P. Buffet, J.P. Gremy, M. Marc et B. Sussmann, Peut-on choisir en tenant compte de critères multiples? une méthode (Electre) et trois applications, Rev. METRA 6, No. 2 (1967).

[17] J.L. Grolleau et J. Tergny, Manuel de référence du programme Electre II (méthode de classement Electre II en présence de critères multiples) D.T. No. 24, D.S., Groupe METRA (déc. 1971).

[18] J. de Montgolfier et J. Tergny, Les décisions partiellement rationalisables (avenir incertain et critères multiples) Rev. METRA 10, No. 2 (1971).

M. Ross, ed., OR '72. North-Holland Publishing Company (1973)

31

INDUSTRIAL DYNAMICS MODEL
OF A JAPANESE UNIVERSITY

Modèle industriel dynamique d'une université Japonnaise

TOSHIRO SHIMADA

Meiji University, Tokyo, Japan

Abstract. This report represents an application of Industrial Dynamics [1] to a Japanese university. We divide the whole university system into ten sectors corresponding to the seven faculties, the Junior College, University Finance, and Annuity. Each of the four leading faculties is subdivided into a day and a night school sector. Further, each faculty contains subsectors for education research and faculty finance. Variables and functional relationships in the Law Faculty Sector and University Finance Sector are explained.

Three simulation results are shown: first, the basic run, second, a case in which governmental aid is assumed, and third, given a constant value for average hours worked in the day school.

1. Introduction

1.1. A Japanese university

My second [2] case study using the industrial dynamics model was applied to a Japanese private university, partly because data could be easily gathered but also because the university problem is now a matter of primary concern in Japan. The university selected is 90 years old and typical of universities in Tokyo. Recorded data was supplied by the university authorities and from other sources. This was supplemented by other data, such as working conditions, obtained through inquiries from instructors and administrators of the university.

1.2. The objectives

The objectives of this ID research project were as follows:
(1) To develop a simulation model for the operation of a university faculty that could be applied to the complex of faculties forming the university.
(2) To investigate system structures in the areas of instruction, research and other activities by using simulation.
(3) To make a comparative study of alternative policies: e.g., changes in teaching time, the number of freshmen, the number of teaching staff members, tuition, governmental aid and so on.

2. General description of the model

2.1. Introduction

The university system is divided into 10 sectors; the seven faculties of **Law** (4), Commerce (C), Politics (P), Literature (L), Management (M), Engineering (E), and Agriculture (A), the Junior College (J), University Finance, and Annuity *. Characters in parentheses identify the faculties.

Law, Commerce, Politics, and Literature faculties are subdivided into day and night schools, represented as 1 and 2, respectively. In this paper we will be concerned with two sectors only – the Law Faculty (and here only the instruction-research subsector) and University Finance. Other faculty sectors will follow easily by analogy.

2.2. Instruction-research subsector in the Law Faculty Day School

2.2.1. Staff working hours
The average working time per individual teacher (TWT41), assumed to be a table function of the average age of teaching staff members (Y), is divided into 5 categories: actual instruction (ATH4), preparation for instruction (PHE4), outside activities (OWH41), miscellaneous (MH41) and research (RH41). Actual instruction (ATH4), which includes lectures, seminars, practicals, experiments, etc. was given as an average in the base model. On the basis of inquiries among staff members preparation time (PHE4) was assumed to be a table function of (ATH4) above. Outside activities (OWH41) are self explanatory while miscellaneous (MH41), which represents hours spent by

* The explanation of annuity is not given in this paper.

teaching staff members at faculty and committee meetings, student guidance and so on, was given a constant value (different from those of other faculties). Research (RH41) was given the residual value after all other activities had been deducted, i.e.,

$$RH41 = TWT41 - ATH4 - PHE4 - OWH41 - MH41 . \tag{1}$$

2.2.2. Students

The total number of students (men) (TS41) is the sum of the members of freshmen, sophomores, juniors and seniors, i.e.,

$$TS41 = S141 + S241 + S341 + S441 . \tag{2}$$

Values for S241, S341, S441 may be easily obtained from S141 [the number of freshmen (men/year)] given the student equation. (Student variables of this type are called a rate [3].)

$$S141.KL = CS141 . \tag{3, R}$$

CS141 is assumed constant at first.

2.2.3. Number of staff

The desired number of full-time teaching staff (DT41) can be derived from the total number of students (TS41). The process is as follows: Data supplied by the university enabled me to estimate average hours of instruction per student (ASH41). Total student hours of instruction (TSH41) is therefore:

$$TSH41 = (TS41)(ASH41) . \tag{4}$$

From university data I was able to assume in the basic model that 60 students was the desired level of enrollment (DSE41) in classes in which enrollment was limited. Therefore the required teaching hours of all staff members (REH41) is:

$$REH41 = TSH41/DSE41 . \tag{5a}$$

These must be shared by all staff members. Now if we have the desired teacher hour per head (DTH41) — set at 8 hours per week in the basic model — we obtain the desired number of teaching staff members (DT41):

$$DT41 = REH41/DTH41 . \tag{5b}$$

Now from this desired value (DT41) the calculated number of full-time teaching staff (NT41) at any time is determined as follows starting from an initial value of 44 (i.e. NT41 = 44):

$$NT41.K = NT41.J + (DT)(HT41.JK - RT41.JK) . \tag{6, L}$$

(This is a *level* equation [3]) where HT41: newly hired teaching staff members (men/year), RT41: retiring teaching staff members (men/year), DT: delta time, the time interval between situations of the equations (year).

To calculate eq. (6) we need to know the numbers retiring each year:

$$RT41.KL = (CRT41)(NT41.K) . \tag{7, R}$$

Here, the ratio of retiring staff members to the total number of teaching staff members is assumed to have a constant value in line with experience over a ten year period.

Eq. (6) also requires the number of new staff and, here, the desired level (DT41) enters the picture:

$$HT41.KL = RT41.JK + (1/DFHT4.K)(DT41.K - NT41.K) , \tag{8, R}$$

where DFHT4 (years) is the delay factor in hiring teaching staff members due to FC, the financial constraint on the cash balance, viz.:

$$DFHT4 = DHT4/FC , \tag{9}$$

where DHT4 is the delay itself in hiring staff.

Eq. (8, R) says that the number of newly hired staff members equals the number of retiring staff members during the previous interval plus the difference between the number of desired staff members (DT41) and the actual number of teaching staff members (NT41) divided by the delay (DFHT4). FC, the cause of this delay, will be discussed later in (34).

Next we calculate education time (ET41), the total classroom hours taught by full-time staff members, as the product of full-time staff members and the average number of daytime hours per full-time staff member (ADH41):

$$ET41 = (NT41)(ADH41) . \tag{10}$$

ADH41 is assumed to be a decreasing table function of the number of full-time staff members (NT41).

Now we can calculate the number of outside teachers (OT41) from the difference between total required teaching hours (REH41) and the actual hours taught by full-time staff (ET41);

$$OT41 = \frac{COT4}{AOT41} (REH41 - ET41) . \tag{11}$$

COT4 represents a delay; AOT41, the average hours taught by outside teachers, is initially given a constant value.

2.2.4. Quality considerations

If we define the hours of preparation multiplier (PHM4) as

$$PHM4 = PHE4/ATH4 , \tag{12}$$

and the education time multiplier (ETM41) as:

$$ETM41 = REH41/ET41 , \tag{13}$$

then we can define educational quality (EQ41) as

$$EQ41 = PHM4/ETM41 . \tag{14}$$

Similarly if the (unitless) research hours multiplier (RHM41) is defined as

$$RHM41 = RH41/TWT41 , \tag{15}$$

teachers' quality (TQ41) may be defined as

$$TQ41 = (PHM4)(RHM41) . \tag{16}$$

Student quality (SQ41) is a function of teachers' quality, educational quality and the original quality of students, which is represented by the ratio (EXR41) * of examinees (EXM41) to freshmen (S141).

---

* See also eq. (22).

$$SQ41 = (CSQ41)(EXR41)(EQ41)(TQ41) , \qquad (17)$$

$$EXR41 = EXM41/S141 , \qquad (18)$$

where CSQ41 is a proportionality constant chosen so that the initial value of SQ41 may approximate the actual initial value.

The quality of facilities in the faculty is measured by the (unitless) room space multiplier (RSM5), which is the ratio of the room space per student on the campus to the average room space per student in all private universities in Japan.

The quality of students, teachers, and university facilities will determine the (unitless) reputation of the faculty (RU41) by means of a reputation factor (RUF41). The latter is defined as:

$$RUF41 = (CRU41)(TQ41)(SQ41)(RSM5) , \qquad (19)$$

where CRU41 is a proportionality constant chosen so that the initial value of RUF41 may approximate the actual initial value.

RUF41 only becomes the reputation of the faculty after a certain time lag. The process may be represented by the next smoothing function:

$$RU41.K = RU41.J + (DT/DRU)(RUF41.J - RU41.J) , \qquad (20, L)$$

$$RU41 = (CRU41)(RUF41) , \qquad (21, N)$$

where DRU, delay in reputation of the university, is assumed to be 4 years in the basic model.

Now the reputation of the faculty may be an important factor which influences the examinees of the faculty (EXM41). Therefore we can write the next rate equation:

$$EXM41.KL = (CEX41)(EXMM.K)(RU41.K)/(EXR41.K) , \qquad (22, R)$$

where CEX41 is a proportionality constant chosen so that the initial value of EXM41 may approximate the actual initial value and the unitless examinee multiplier (EXMM) is an index number representing the change in the number of examinees in the whole country.

Next, we determine the number of administrators starting from an initial value

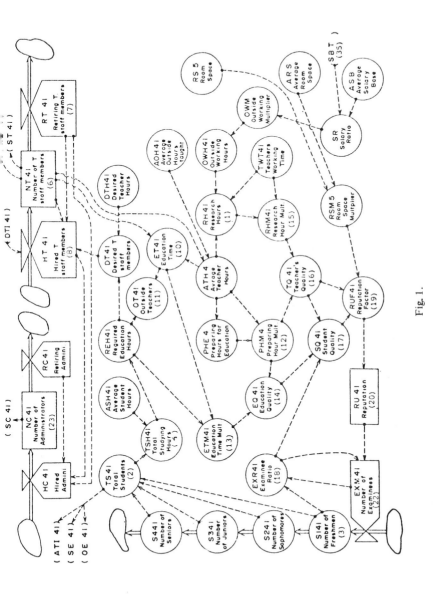

Fig. 1.

$$NC41.K = NC41.J + (DT)(HC41.JK - RC41.JK) ,\qquad (23, L)$$

$$NC41 = 67 . \qquad (24, N)$$

This level equation is quite similar to eq. (6) and may be interpreted accordingly (see also fig. 1).

This description of instruction-research sector is shown as a flow diagram in fig. 1. Numerals below each variable correspond to the equation number.

2.3. University Finance sector

A deficit, where expenditure exceeds income is represented by DTI with the appropriate code numbers following, e.g. DTI41 is the deficit in the Law Faculty. The total university deficit is an aggregate of all deficits:

$$DTI = DTI41 + DTI42 + DTIC1 + DTIC2 + DTIG1 + DTIG2 + DTIL1$$

$$+ DTIL2 + DTIM1 + DTIE1 + DTIA1 + DTIJ1 + DTIA0 . \qquad (25)$$

$-DTI$ means the excess of total income, which is added to the cash balance of the university (CBU) which is set initially at zero.

$$CBU.K = CBU.J + (DT)(-DTI.J + 0) , \qquad (26, L)$$

$$CBU = 0 . \qquad (27, N)$$

Now, we will estimate the expected value (in 1000 yen) of CBU, i.e. ECBU at the end of each fiscal year.

$$ECBU = CBU + CBUC , \qquad (28)$$

$$CBUC.K = CBU.K - PCBU.JK , \qquad (29)$$

$$PCBU.KL = CBU.K , \qquad (30, R)$$

where CBUC is the change in CBU and PCBU its level in the previous year.

In this model we assume that tuition is to be raised if ECBU is negative, and the process of changing tuition is as follows:

$$\text{ATFU61.KL} = (\text{TRF6})(\text{TF161.K}) \quad \text{if ECBU.K} \leqslant 0,$$

$$= 0 \quad\quad\quad\quad\quad\quad \text{if ECBU.K} > 0,$$

(31,R)

where ATFU61 is the amount of tuition raise (1000 yen/year), and TRF6, the rate of tuition raise, assumed to be 0.5 in the basic model.

Once ATFU61 is determined the tuition level follows, starting from an initial tuition (TF161) of 36 000 yen for a freshman:

$$\text{TF161.K} = \text{TF161.J} + (\text{DT})(\text{ATFU61.JK} + 0),$$ (32, L)

$$\text{TF161} = 36 \quad (1000 \text{ yen}).$$ (33, N)

Next year TF161, TF261 and TF361 will become TF261, TF361 and TF461, respectively. These processes can be treated easily by DYNAMO.

Now we can return to the financial constraint, FC.

$$\text{FC} = \text{a table function of CBUM},$$ (34)

where CBUM [the CBU multiplier (unitless)] is obtained by dividing the cash balance of the university (CBU) by 100 million yen, i.e., CBUM = CBU/100 000. As seen from eqs. (8) and (9) this financial constraint influences policy in hiring staff members.

Now we will treat the salary base of teaching staff members (SBT), for which we use the average salary base of instructural public personnel (ASB) which is derived from a time series. Now the change in the salary base of teaching staff members (SBCT/1000 yen/man/month/year) is assumed to rise from an initial level of 50 in proportion to the rate of change in the average salary base of instructural public personnel (ASBC/1/year), viz:

$$\text{SBT.K} = \text{SBT.J} + (\text{DT})(\text{SBCT.JK} + 0),$$ (35, L)

$$\text{SBT} = 50,$$ (36, N)

$$\text{SBCT.KL} = (\text{KT.K})(\text{ASBC.K})(\text{SBT.K}),$$ (37, R)

$$\text{ASBC.K} = \frac{\text{ASB.K} - \text{ASB.J}}{\text{ASB.J}},$$ (38)

where KT is a unitless proportionality constant.

3. Simulation results

Specifications for the simulation are as follows:

(1) The simulation was run for the 32 years from 1961 to 1993.

(2) The main inputs were the number of freshmen and the average salary base for the instructural public personnel.

(3) The time interval between computations (DT) was one year.

(4) The time intervals between printing and plotting the results of the model were one year in the basic model.

3.1. Comparison of simulation results with historical data

For the period between 1961 and 1970, the following variables in our simulation fit the historical data well: the tuition of Day School freshmen, those of Night School and of the Engineering Faculty, the salary bases of the teaching and administrative staffs of the university, the total numbers of the teaching and the administrative staffs, and the total expenses by the university. The fit was less satisfactory for the numbers of the examinees, of the teaching staff, and of part-time lectures from the outside, in each faculty. We tested student quality, which is an ambiguous, difficult variable, against the average points at the university's uniform examinations given to the juniors but the fit is not yet satisfactory.

On the whole this model merits consideration as a basic simulation model for the university concerned.

Now let us look at three different simulations which we carried out.

3.2. First run

Governmental aid (GF) may be given in accordance with the salaries of full-time teaching staff members (ST) and at a rate (GFC):

$$GF41 = (GFC41)(ST41).$$

In the first run GFC41 was set at 0, and ADH41 made a decreasing function of the number of teaching staff members; in other words, no governmental aid, and the average hours worked per head in day schools assumed to decrease as the number of teaching staff members increased. This run was remarkable in that the tuition did not exceed the salary base of teaching staff members. In this model tuition was assumed to rise at a certain rate whenever the expected cash balance of the university became negative, but for all that, the tuition did not go up too high, though it could be changed in accordance with the change in the salary base of teaching staff members.

This run shows, therefore, that a tuition raise which would enable the university management to keep the salary base at a corresponding level to that of the instructural public personnel, is highly feasible in so far as the university enjoys a high reputation.

The total amount of part-time lecturers' salaries, in spite of their being a sizable proportion of the total were, surprisingly, much smaller than that of full-time staff members. This is true of most private universities in Japan and tends to lower the quality of the education provided while making management easier.

The number of the teaching staff were assumed to increase at the expense of part-time lecturers from outside. Even so the university can keep the quality of its education at a high level while staying sound financially.

(This model did not contain building expenses, which are treated in the second model.)

3.3. Second run

In this run GFC41 was assumed to be a table function of time, as follows: 0.1 for 3 years from 1970, 0.2 for the next 3 years, and 0.3 after 1976, and to be at the same rate for all faculties other than Law Faculty.

The tuition curve was different from that of the first run, indicating the extent to which a change in the rate of governmental aid influences the change in tuition.

3.4. Third run

In the first run ADH41 was assumed a decreasing function, but actually hours worked per teacher could be left unchanged. In this run, however, ADH41 was given a constant value of 9.5 hours, i.e., the same value as at present.

In these results the number of examinees was smaller than in the first run. This may be because the heavy teaching load meant less hours spent in preparation and research, so that the quality, first, of teachers and then, of students went down, with a consequent fall in the reputation of the university. This induced a decrease in the number of examinees.

4. Conclusion

These results confirm our belief that an industrial dynamics model will be of considerable use to us in making a comparative study of teaching and administrative policies.

Acknowledgement

This work has been done under the grant from the scientific research fund of the Ministry of Education and the grant from the Institute of Sciences and Technology of Meiji University.

References

[1] J.W. Forrester, Industrial dynamics (M.I.T. Press, Cambridge, 1961).
[2] T. Shimada, Industrial dynamics model of weekly stock prices, a case study, Bull. Arts and Science, Meiji Univ., No. 42 (1968).
[3] A.L. Pugh, DYNAMO user's manual, 2nd ed. (M.I.T. Press, Cambridge, 1963).
[4] T. Shimada, Industrial dynamics model of a private university, part 1: Systems analysis of a private university (in Japanese) Mem. Inst. Sci. Technol. Meiji Univ. 9 (1970).

M. Ross, ed., OR'72. North-Holland Publishing Company (1973)

32

A DYNAMIC PROGRAMMING APPROACH
TO ESTABLISHING TEACHING POSTS
IN A CENTRALIZED EDUCATIONAL SYSTEM

*Méthode de programmation dynamique en vue de
l'établissement de postes de personnel enseignant
dans un système d'éducation centralisé*

D.P. PSOINOS

Supreme Hellenic Armed Forces Command, Athens, Greece

and

D.A. XIROKOSTAS

Public Power Corporation, Athens, Greece

Abstract. An educational system is a purposive one. It has goals and objectives which it strives to achieve within financial constraints. Apparently, OR can influence positively the effectiveness of such a system. In this paper, apart from discussing several problems of a centralised educational system susceptible to optimisation, a dynamic programming approach to establishing teaching posts in schools is developed, according to certain criteria of system's effectiveness. Such criteria are minimum overtime, fair distribution of working load among teaching personnel, etc. Results of a case study concerning the Greek educational system are discussed.

1. Introduction

The demand for education in all countries of the world has reached tremendous proportions. However, educational systems can only provide services to meet this demand within limits imposed by financial and other type constraints. Although this problem is different from those in industry, OR can contribute towards its solution, thus improving the effectiveness of such systems.

An examination of the literature on management and planning of educational systems [1–3] leads us to the conclusion that, although considerable work has been done on the development of mathematical models for planning purposes *, very little has been done on tactical problems facing a manager optimizing the operations of the educational system.

In many cases the result is an inability to implement the increasingly detailed plans prepared by these sophisticated techniques. Often planning then gives the impression of being isolated from the realities of the policy and decision making processes which it is supposed to serve.

In this paper, apart from discussing a few problems of a centralized educational system which are susceptible to optimization, certain criteria of systems effectiveness are used to develop an approach to establishing teaching posts in schools. These criteria include minimum overtime, fair distribution of working load among teaching personnel, etc.

2. Certain educational problems susceptible to optimization

Certain problems in the management of educational systems, are susceptible to optimization. These are very briefly discussed below:

(a) *Transfer of teachers*, in a centralized educational system in which teaching personnel constitute a hierarchy, are controlled using different criteria. Examples of such criteria are: uniform level of staffing the schools, satisfaction of the maximum number of applications for transfer under some specified constraints, teachers maximum service time in the same post, and minimization of the total time posts are vacant.

(b) *Establishing teaching posts in higher education* on the basis of the teaching and research load of a chair or a department.

(c) *Systematic analysis of the decision making mechanism in an educational system.* From our own experience this would be beneficial since it seems that decision making is not consistent with the organizational structure of an educational system. Furthermore, the mechanism appears to be less diversified than in many other organized systems. Possible measures of performance might combine many different factors, such as the duration of the decision, the number of people affected by it, etc.

---

* These concern: students flow, forecasting manpower needs and supply, forecasting enrolments at different levels of education, forecasting demand and supply of teachers, etc.

3. Establishing teaching posts in schools

3.1. Problem formulation

Let us assume that we have $i = 1, 2, ..., n$ schools and a number N of available teachers to cover A_i teaching hours at each school. The objective is to establish posts so as to optimise a performance criterion subject to the teaching hours at each school being covered.

The choice of the performance criterion involves two considerations: the economy, which results from the minimization of the total overtime of the system, and the effectiveness of teaching, that may be assumed to increase as the teaching load among teachers becomes more equal. Therefore, more than one criteria may be defined, each of them serving one of the above considerations or a combination of them.

Each one is considered below.

3.2. Minimum total overtime

If x_i is the number of established teaching posts at school i then the function,

$$U_i(x_i) = A_i - hx_i \tag{1}$$

gives the overtime at this school, provided that $U_i(x_i) > 0$, where h is the standard weekly teaching hours per teacher. The problem then is to determine the values of x_i which satisfy the criterion,

$$U = \min \sum_{i=1}^{n} U_i(x_i) . \tag{2}$$

This may be solved as follows: Teachers are placed sequentialy one at a time at every school in which the conditions,

$$U_i(x_i) \geqslant h , \quad x_i > 0 \tag{3}$$

are satisfied. Then two cases will be faced:

(a) the total number of teachers is placed so that the required optimal solution is obtained *.

* In this case more than one optimal solution satisfying the criterion (2) exists, but the one found in the way outlined above has the advantage that it gives a more uniform distribution of teaching hours per teacher than any solution.

(b) At the end of the above procedure some teachers still remain to be placed. These remaining teachers are placed one at each school according to the amount of hours left, starting from the largest and proceeding towards the smallest. Thus the required optimal solution is obtained.

3.3. Minimum total overtime with upper limit on the allowed overtime per teacher

Obviously the above optimal solution may result to any amount of over-time per teacher, depending on the total number of available teachers, N, and the total of teaching hours at each school. Since in some cases the teaching load may be excessive an upper limit of overtime per teacher should be imposed. This may be a percentage of h, i.e. bh, where $b < 1$.

$$V_i(x_i) = \frac{A_i - hx_i}{x_i} = \frac{U_i(x_i)}{x_i} \tag{4}$$

gives the overtime per teacher in terms of the teaching posts x_i for every school i, provided again that $U_i(x_i) > 0$.

The constraint to be satisfied for every school is:

$$V_i(x_i) < bh , \quad x_i > 0 . \tag{5}$$

The objective now is to determine the values of x_i which satisfy the criterion (2) under the new constraints (5).

The procedure used in section (3.2) will give a solution provided N is large enough to cover the requirements under the constraints (5). Otherwise b should be increased.

3.4. Maximum effectiveness of teaching

We assumed that teaching effectiveness increases as the teaching load among teachers becomes more even. Granted this premise the objective now is to minimise overtime per teacher averaged over the whole educational system, $(V_i \max)$, which we have selected as a surrogate measure of evenness in the teaching load. The solution was found by an iterative procedure which uses the computation procedure of the previous section (3.3) starting from large values of the limit bh, for which a feasible solution exists, and proceeding towards smaller values until the last value for which a feasible solution exists is reached. This solution then is the one which, given the stated assumptions, achieves the most uniform distribution of the teaching load among teachers and therefore the maximum effectiveness of teaching. Total overtime increases as the limit *bh* decreases until at the solution it takes its maximum value, i.e., the maximum among the minima.

3.5. Minimum total sum of overtime and idle time per teacher in the whole educational system

A criterion that combines, in an indirect manner, both economy and teaching effectiveness, is the sum over the whole educational system of overtime and idle time per teacher (i.e., the difference between a teacher's actual and the standard weekly teaching hours, *h*). Overtime per teacher relates to teaching effectiveness, and idle time to the economy of the system.

In mathematical terms this criterion is expressed as follows:

$$V = \min \sum_{i=1}^{n} |V_i(x_i)| = \min \sum_{i=1}^{n} \frac{|A_i - hx_i|}{x_i} \ . \tag{6}$$

A realistic solution requires an upper limit on the overtime per teacher, i.e., constraint (5). Moreover, only the first negative value of $V_i(x_i)$ for the idle time per teacher need be considered because it is meaningless to allocate more teachers to a school than those required to cover its teaching hours fully.

Therefore, the problem in this case is stated as follows: Determine the values of x_i that satisfy the criterion (6) under the above mentioned restrictions.

This problem may be solved by dynamic programming [4] since the functions $V_i(x_i)$ are non-linear (fig. 1) and furthermore separable. For this purpose each school is considered as one stage of a multistage process. Thus, by applying the principle of optimality, the following functional relationship is derived:

$$f_n(N) = \min_{x_n} [|V_n(x_n)| + f_{n-1}(N - x_n)] \ , \tag{7}$$

where $f_n(N)$ is the minimum total sum of overtime and idle time per teacher for *n* schools with *N* teachers available, i.e. *V*. For $n = 1$ (i.e., one school) evidently

$$f_1(N) = V_1(x_1) = V_1(N) \ . \tag{8}$$

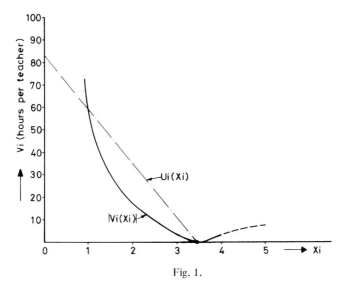

Fig. 1.

From that function we may determine $f_2(N)$, etc. up to $f_n(N)$. Then from the values of these functions the optimal solution is determined by the known steps in dynamic programming.

As it is known, the presence of constraints results in a reduction of the computational effort in dynamic programming solutions. The present problem is no exception. The constraints mentioned above restrict the range of values of the functions $f_1(N)$, $f_2(N)$, ..., $f_i(N)$, ..., $f_n(N)$, which are required to be computed, as follows:
For $f_1(N)$

$$x_1^\ell \leqslant N \leqslant x_1^u , \tag{9}$$

where x_1^ℓ is the value of x_1 for which $V_1(x_1)$ first takes a value smaller than bh, x_1^u is the value of x_1 for which $V_1(x_1)$ becomes negative for the first time.
For $f_2(N)$

$$x_2^\ell + N_1^\ell \leqslant N \leqslant x_2^u + N_1^u ,$$

where x_2^ℓ and x_2^u as above for x_2 and $V_2(x_2)$, and N_1^ℓ is the value of N that corresponds to the first value of $f_1(N)$ that was computed, N_1^u is the value of N that corresponds to the last value of $f_1(N)$ that was computed.

Hence, in general, for $f_i(N)$

$$x_i^\ell + N_{i-1}^\ell \leqslant N \leqslant x_i^u + N_{i-1}^u .\tag{10}$$

The reduction of the computation due to the above constraints is so drastic, that the problem is tractable on a digital computer, even for very large educational systems.

A variant of the criterion (6) is to consider the squares of the overtime and idle time instead of their absolute values, i.e.,

$$V' = \min \sum_{i=1}^{n} [V_i(x_i)]^2 = \min \sum_{i=1}^{n} \frac{(A_i - hx_i)^2}{x_i^2} .\tag{11}$$

This criterion, in fact, is expected to give a more uniform distribution of the teaching load among teachers than the criterion (6), since the larger deviations are weighted heavier than the smaller and therefore are precluded from the optimal solution.

The problem is again solved by dynamic programming.

3.6. Minimum total teaching cost of the educational system

If it was possible to assign to the effectiveness of teaching a numerical value in the form of an increasing cost $C(V_i)$ of overtime per teacher V_i, as for example shown in fig. 2, then an economic criterion could be formulated that combines both economy and teaching effectiveness as follows:

The cost of the school i due to overtime and teaching effectiveness is given by:

$$K_i(x_i) = U_i(x_i)C_0 + V_i(x_i)C[V_i(x_i)] ,\tag{12}$$

where C_0 is the cost of one hour of overtime. The problem then is to determine the values of x_i that satisfy the criterion

$$K = \min \sum_{i=1}^{n} K_i(x_i) ,\tag{13}$$

under the constraints (5).

This problem can be solved by dynamic programming, in a similar manner to (3.5).

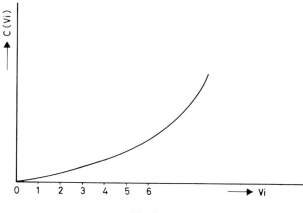

Fig. 2.

4. Results of a case study

The above theory was applied to the Greek educational system in the region that comprises Athens and its suburbs. This region has 102 high schools and about 900 teachers available to teach ancient and modern Greek. The weekly total hours required in all schools, A, was 23 122 and the standard weekly teaching hours per teacher, h, was 24.

The criteria described in sections 3.2, 3.4 and 3.5, referred to here as criterion 1, 2 and 3, respectively, were programmed on a digital computer and the results obtained are summarized in table 1.

As expected criterion 1 gives the minimum total overtime but a less uniform distribution of working load among teachers, as derived from both the values of $(V_i \max)$ and (V).

Table 1

Criterion	Total overtime U	Maximum value of overtime per teacher in the region $V_i \max$	Total sum of overtime and idle time per teacher V
1	1522	15.0	$210 + 0$ [a] $= 210.0$
2	1658	3.3	$163.6 + 35.4$ [a] $= 199.0$
3	1627	7.9	$155.5 + 25.9$ [a] $= 181.4$

[a] Sum of idle time per teacher over the whole region.

On the other hand, criterion 2 gives the largest total overtime but the fairest distribution of teaching load among teachers, since the value of $(V_i\max)$ is the smallest and that of (V) fairly small. Although criterion 3 gives the smallest value of (V), it cannot be said that it provides a fair distribution of the teaching load, since the value of $(V_i\max)$ is relatively high. It was felt, therefore, that it should be replaced by the variant criterion (V'), eq. (11), which is expected to give more consistent results with regard to both (V') and $(V_i\max)$.

The existing allocation of teaching posts was found to come very near to minimizing total overtime, a situation which, as was pointed out above, gives the worst distribution of teaching load. Therefore, there is a scope in applying the criterion 2 $[\min(V_i\max)]$ or the variant of the criterion 3 (V') or the minimum total teaching cost of the educational system [eq. (13)], which is the best criterion whenever it can be evaluated.

The above results refer to a case where there is a shortage of teachers in the system. If teachers are not scarce there is no problem since solutions by all criteria are almost identical. However, in most educational systems today significant shortages of teaching personnel occur (in some cases up to 30%) [5, 6].

References

[1] Directory of current educational models in OECD member countries, OECD, Paris (1969).
[2] Mathematical models in educational planning, OECD, Paris (1969).
[3] R.M. Durstine and R.G. David, Educational planning in developing countries; a possible role for operations research, Opns. Res. 17 (1969) 5.
[4] R.E. Bellman and S.E. Dreyfus, Applied dynamic programming (Princeton Univ. Press, Princeton, 1962).
[5] Study on the supply and demand for teachers in primary and secondary education, OECD, Paris (1969).
[6] Training, recruitment and utilisation of teachers in primary and secondary education, OECD, Paris (1971).

M. Ross, ed., OR'72. North-Holland Publishing Company (1973)

33

BICRITERION FUNCTIONS
IN ANNUAL ACTIVITY PLANNING

Fonctions bicritères dans la planification d'activités annuelles

H. PASTERNAK

Agricultural Engineering Institute, Beit-Dagan, Israel

and

URY PASSY

Technion, Israel Institute of Technology, Haifa, Israel

Abstract. A method for finding optimum planning using bicriterion functions is developed. The problem arose at the Beit-Dagan Agricultural Engineering Institute. The necessary theory is developed and illustrated with an example consisting of nineteen projects. It was proved and illustrated that the solution can be found after generating only part of the efficient points. The saving in computations increases significantly with the size of the problem.

1. Introduction

In recent years much effort has been devoted to the theory of multicriteria programs [1]. These represent reality more closely than the single criterion program.

The present problem, which has two criteria, originated at the Beit-Dagan Agricultural Engineering Institute, Israel. The institute has several research units engaged in government-sponsored agricultural projects and employs seventy researchers and other personnel. Its annual budget is approximately IL 2 million.

There are three main departments:

(1) Harvest Mechanization, mainly concerned with developing harvesting machinery;

(2) Packing and Handling, dealing with the mechanization of the sorting and packing processes and the development of control equipment for the cold storage of fruits and vegetables;

(3) Production and Marketing, whose main concern is the economic evaluation of manual work methods and management systems.

Some seventy projects are proposed each year, but only about half of these can be accepted. Since a partially completed project has no practical value each project can either be accepted or rejected completely. It can be assumed that the value of a particular project as well as the relevant inputs are independent of all other projects, thus, linear criterion functions and constraints can be used.

Economic value, $\quad f(x) = \sum_{j=1}^{n} c_j x_j$, $\hfill$ (1a)

personal satisfaction, $\quad g(x) = \sum_{i=1}^{n} d_j x_j$, $\hfill$ (1b)

manpower and budget requirements define the constraint set S,

$$\sum_{j=1}^{n} a_{ij} x_j \leqslant b_i , \qquad i = 1, 2, ..., m , \hfill (2a)$$

$$x_j \in [0, 1] . \hfill (2b)$$

This problem will be referred to as I.P.

The successful solution of such a problem requires the full cooperation of the management and of the staff, and it was therefore decided first to study 19 projects as an example (table 1). The work was divided into two phases: Phase one consisted of the estimation of the various parameters through discussions with the staff and the management. In the second phase a computer code for sorting efficient points was developed. The optimal solution was located in the final step. The various constraints and the coefficients of the two criteria are given in table 2.

2. Selecting projects for the institute

The Agricultural Institute initiates and receives projects in agricultural engineering. The selection is based on two criteria:

(1) economic value: the expected increase in farm income due to application of the research results,

(2) personal satisfaction: the subjective satisfaction of the research worker engaged in the project.

Table 1
Projects in the Institute Problem

No.	Project
1	Evaluation of citrus hand grading methods
2	Sorting and grading of roses
3	Improved management technique for cooperative settlements
4	The computer as a management tool in flower export
5	Optimal policy for producing and marketing frozen chickens
6	Mechanized tomato harvest for canneries
7	Mechanized pepper harvest for processing
8	Mechanized onion-bulblets harvesting
9	Development of a peanut salvager
10	Development of a pecan-nut salvager
11	Experimentation in mechanical grapefruit harvesting
12	A system for waxing melon
13	Controlled conditions for prying onion-bulblets
14	A citrus fruit wrapping machine
15	The influence of citrus packing on fruit physiology
16	Precooling of citrus fruit
17	Banana handling and packing
18	Tomato handling
19	Machine for sorting carrots by length

The economic value is the net present value of the expected returns due to the implementation of the results of a given research project. The net returns equal the difference between the returns due to the use of the newly developed technique and those from the best available alternative. Several factors were considered when evaluating the net returns:

(1) the expected increase in income over and above that obtained from ordinary technological improvements,

(2) expenses due to equipment amortization and interest payments,

(3) the extent of the utilization of the technique developed, which depends on the size of the farms and on the rate of expansion of the relevant produce,

(4) obsolescence of a technique. This may be due to several causes. Obviously, if a particular cultivation is abandoned, the project ceases to yield returns. In addition it may become obsolete if the technique becomes commercially available from other sources or is superceded by more advanced ones.

All these factors are quantified and summarized in table 3.

Table 2

The tableau for the Institute Problem. Researchers value is obtained from table 3 after multiplying by 10 the total scientific value of each project (done for scaling reasons). The economic values were obtained from table 3 in the following fashion: The annual net income figures were multiplied by the probability of success, to derive the expected annual net income. This in turn was discounted over the period of technical amortization using a 10% discount rate

Project no.	Econ. value (10^4 IL)	Res. value (unit)	Budget (10^3 IL)	Mechanization of the crop and its harvesting res. (month)	Mechanization of the crop and its harvesting techn. (month)	Packing and handling of products res. (month)	Packing and handling of products techn. (month)	Production engineering and marketing res. (month)	Production engineering techn. (month)	Marketing techn. (month)
1	205	400	90					12	12	12
2	90	300	40					18	6	6
3	49	300	50					48	6	18
4	106	450	150					12	–	–
5	34	500	20					12	6	18
6	211	600	300	42	36					
7	154	920	80	80	40					
8	116	430	40	24	12					
9	228	650	90	12	12					
10	48	750	77	12	10					
11	49	500	300	30	18					
12	160	510	12			6	6			
13	29	300	50			12	24			
14	157	1050	180			36	36			
15	111	800	70			24	24			
16	2870	1350	200			42	54			
17	306	480	25			30	6			
18	91	700	25			12	9			
19	13	750	70			12	6			
b			1200	34	80	78	72	42	36	18

It was assumed that published papers, accumulation of knowledge, and increased local prestige, may serve as indicators for the degree of satisfaction. After discussions with the staff it was possible to introduce a scale so that the relative contribution of the various factors to the personal satisfaction could be expressed quantitatively. A paper in an international journal was worth up to 40 units, while a paper published in a local journal or a patent contributed not more than ten units. Accumulation of knowledge is affected through various channels: reading technical literature, learning new technical methods, and testing techniques and acquiring information by data collection. The relative contribution of the various factors were six, seven and six units, respectively. Local prestige contributes up to twenty units. The contributions of each research project to the personal satisfaction are listed in table 3.

3. Method of solution

It was assumed that the utility function is a monotonic-increasing one in both criteria, e.g., economic value and personal satisfaction. Thus, the solution can be found among the efficient points of f and g [eqs. (1)].

It was also assumed that the utility function $\phi(f, g)$ can be extended over the convex hull of S [eqs. (2)], and its extension, $\Phi(f, g)$, will be strictly quasiconcave. Obviously,

$$\Phi[f(\pmb{x}), g(\pmb{x})] = \phi[f(\pmb{x}), g(\pmb{x})] \qquad \forall \pmb{x} \in S .$$

However, the most serious assumptions were the following:

(1) The existence of a utility function, $\phi(.,.)$ (Von Neumann–Morgenstern axioms [2]).

(2) If Ω is the set of efficient points, then the management can directly compare any two elements of Ω. Either one is preferred to the other, or the two are equally desirable (or undesirable).

(3) The preference relation is transitive.

With these assumptions the solution to the IP can be found, once a code for generating efficient points and a search scheme have been developed.

Efficient points of two functions f and g can be found by the following two parametric programs, respectively called A_α and B_θ.

(1) A_α parametric program:

$$\max \alpha f(\pmb{x}) + (1-\alpha) g(\pmb{x}) ,$$

subject to the constraints eqs. (2).

Table 3
The data for the tableau given in table 2

Project no.	Physical units	Volume (10³ unit) current	planned	new b)	Price /unit (IL)	Income /unit (IL)	Net income /year (10³ IL)	Techn. amort. (year)	Prob. of success (%)
1	ton	1265	1603	600	580	1.4	840	7	50
2	dunam a)	0.6	0.8	0.8	–	288	230	6	90
3	–	–	–	–	–	–	90	10	90
4	–	–	–	–	–	–	350	5	80
5	–	–	–	–	–	–	150	5	60
6	ton	32	180	120	120	14.3	1710	5	90
7	ton	–	12	12	300	30	360	8	80
8	ton	1	3	1.85	1100	–	242	8	90
9	dunam	50	50	20	900	23.7	474	8	90
10	ton	0.5	2.2	1.4	5750	90	126	8	90
11	ton	–	50	50	–	3.4	170	5	50
12	ton	3.5	5	2.4	1250	350	840	4	90
13	ton	1	1	0.8	1100	66	53	10	90
14	ton	–	–	180	580	5.5	990	4	50
15	ton	–	–	385	–	29.3	11280	3	20
16	ton	–	–	441	580	40	17300	8	70
17	ton	15	15	13.5	52.8	41	554	10	90
18	dunam	0.15	1.5	1	–	165	400	5	90
19	ton	5	5	2.5	262	2	5	7	90

a) One dunam is equal to ¼ of an acre.
b) Volume processed with the newly developed techniques.

Table 3 (continued)

| Project no. | Development costs | | | | Scientific value | | |
	costs excl. labor (10^3 IL)	res. services (month)	techn. services (month)	publications	accumulation of knowledge	local prestige	total scientific value
1	90	12	24	20	10	10	40
2	40	18	12	10	10	20	40
3	50	48	24	10	10	10	30
4	200	12	–	10	15	20	45
5	20	12	24	20	15	15	50
6	185	44	36	30	10	20	60
7	60	96	36	60	12	20	92
8	40	21	12	15	15	13	43
9	90	12	12	30	15	20	65
10	77	12	12	40	15	20	75
11	175	30	15	25	10	15	50
12	12	6	6	25	10	16	51
13	50	12	24	10	10	10	30
14	130	36	36	80	15	10	105
15	100	60	60	50	15	15	80
16	200	60	108	90	15	20	135
17	6	28	7	20	8	20	48
18	25	6	8	40	15	15	70
19	70	8	8	50	15	10	75

(2) B_θ parametric program:

$$\max f(\boldsymbol{x}) \, ,$$

subject to the constraints defined by eqs. (2) and by

$$g(\boldsymbol{x}) \geqslant \theta \, .$$

The constraint set for problem A_α is denoted by S, that of B_θ by S_θ. Clearly $S_\theta \subseteq S$. Program B_θ will generate all the efficient points of f and g if θ varies over the range $[\theta_1, \theta_2]$ defined by:

$$\theta_1 = \{ g(\boldsymbol{x}) / f(\boldsymbol{x}) = \max_{\boldsymbol{y} \in S} f(\boldsymbol{y}) \} \, ,$$

$$\theta_2 = \max_{\boldsymbol{x} \in S} g(\boldsymbol{x}) \, .$$

The proof of the above assertion is published elsewhere [3]. The parametric program A_α generates only those points which are both vertices and efficient relative to the convex hull of the set of all efficient points. In the example considered, only six points out of a total of thirteen were generated by the A_α program (see fig. 1). As can be seen from the example, much computational effort could have been saved, if the solution to IP had been generated by the A_α program.

Unfortunately, that program does not always generate a solution. However, there is a certain relationship between the best solution found among the set of efficient points generated by A_α and the solution to IP. That relationship is described in the following section. The set of points $\boldsymbol{y}_i \in S$, $i = 1, ..., P < \infty$ associated with the efficient points generated by A_α, i.e., $f(\boldsymbol{y}_i), g(\boldsymbol{y}_i)$ is efficient, will be designated by Y. The set Y is finite since $Y \subseteq S$ and S is finite. It is possible to define an order on the set Y, viz. $\boldsymbol{y}_i > \boldsymbol{y}_j$, if $f(\boldsymbol{y}_i) > f(\boldsymbol{y}_j)$.

Let us now define the following auxiliary program, called $(AP)_\alpha$:

$$\max_{\boldsymbol{x} \in X} \alpha f(\boldsymbol{x}) + (1 - \alpha) g(\boldsymbol{x}) \, .$$

The set X is defined by the constraints

$$\boldsymbol{x} = \sum_{i=1}^{P} u_i \boldsymbol{y}_i \, , \qquad \boldsymbol{y}_i \in Y \, , \qquad \sum_{i=1}^{P} u_i = 1 \, , \qquad u_i \geqslant 0 \, .$$

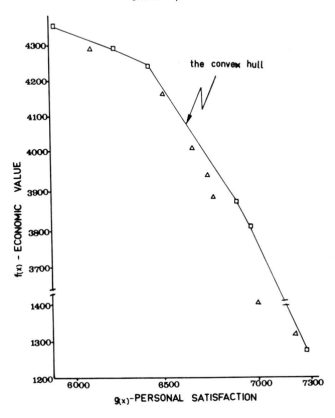

□ efficient points generated by A α

△ efficient points not generated by Aα

Fig. 1. The convex hull of all efficient points $f(x)$, $g(x)$. As can be seen only those points generated by the A_α programs are vertices of the convex hull.

The set of optimal solutions of $(AP)_\alpha$ for a fixed value of α is designated by $Y(\alpha)$. Define

$$H(\alpha) = \max_{x \in Y(\alpha)} \Phi[f(x), g(x)] , \tag{3}$$

$$H(\alpha^*) = \max_{\alpha \in [0,1]} H(\alpha) .$$

It has been shown [4] that

$$\max_{x \in X} \Phi\left[f(x), g(x)\right] = H(\alpha^*) .$$

Finding α^* is a one-dimensional search. The effectiveness of any search depends primarily on how readily $H(\alpha)$ can be computed. In the next paragraph, therefore, the method of computing $H(\alpha)$ is explained.

The unit interval can be divided into P subintervals according to the following rule:

$$I_{i-1} = [\alpha_i, \alpha_{i-1}] = \{\alpha/\alpha f(\mathbf{y}_i) + (1-\alpha) g(\mathbf{y}_i) = \max_{x \in X} \alpha f(\mathbf{x}) + (1-\alpha) g(\mathbf{x})\} ,$$

where $i = 1, ..., P-1$, $\alpha_0 = 1$ and $\alpha_i < \alpha_{i-1}$.

$$I_{P-1} = [\alpha_P, \alpha_{P-1}] = \{\alpha/\alpha f(\mathbf{y}_P) + (1-\alpha)g(\mathbf{y}_P) = \max_{x \in X} \alpha f(\mathbf{x}) + (1-\alpha)g(\mathbf{x})\} .$$

The parameter α_P equals unity.

It is now possible to define an optimal solution function of $(AP)_\alpha$, namely $\mathbf{y}(\alpha) = \mathbf{y}_i$ if $\alpha \in I_i$. The function $\mathbf{y}(\alpha)$ is an n valued function on $[0, 1]$ which is piecewise constant.

Theorem: (For the proof see [4]). Let $\mathbf{y}(\alpha)$ be given. For each point of discontinuity α', $\underline{\mathbf{y}}(\alpha')$ and $\overline{\mathbf{y}}(\alpha')$ are defined as the left-hand and right-hand limits, respectively, of $\mathbf{y}(\alpha)$ at α'. Then at every point of continuity in $[0, 1]$:

$$H(\alpha') = \Phi\{f[\mathbf{y}(\alpha')], g[\mathbf{y}(\alpha')]\} , \tag{4a}$$

at every point of discontinuity in $[0, 1]$:

$$H(\alpha') = \max_{0 \leqslant \lambda \leqslant 1} \phi\{\lambda f[\underline{\mathbf{y}}(\alpha')] + (1-\lambda) f[\overline{\mathbf{y}}(\alpha')], \lambda g[\underline{\mathbf{y}}(\alpha') + (1-\lambda)g[\overline{\mathbf{y}}(\alpha')]\}. \tag{4b}$$

If at α^* $\mathbf{y}(\alpha^*)$ is continuous and $\alpha^* \in I_i$, then $H(\alpha^*) = \Phi[f(\mathbf{y}_i), g(\mathbf{y}_i)]$. Since $S \subseteq X$ and Φ agrees with ϕ on S, $\mathbf{y}_i$ is the solution to IP. However, if at $\alpha^* \in I_i$ $\mathbf{y}(\alpha^*)$ is not continuous, then it may happen that $H(\alpha^*) = \Phi[f(\mathbf{y}), g(\mathbf{y})]$ for some $\mathbf{y} = \lambda \mathbf{y}_i + (1-\lambda)\mathbf{y}_{i-1}$ which satisfies eq. (4b). In this case the solution of IP is not necessarily a member of Y.

Suppose that $\mathbf{y}(\alpha)$ is discontinuous at α^*, and let $\mathbf{y}_r$ and $\mathbf{y}_{r+1}$, respectively, be the right- and left-hand side limits of $\mathbf{y}(\alpha)$ at α^*. According to Geofferion [4] $H(\alpha^*) = \Phi[f(\mathbf{y}^*), g(\mathbf{y}^*)]$ for some $\mathbf{y}^* \in X$ located on the line segment

$[\mathbf{y}_r, \mathbf{y}_{r+1}]$, i.e., $\mathbf{y}^* = \lambda \mathbf{y}_r + (1-\lambda)\mathbf{y}_{r+1}$.

The following lemma relates $\mathbf{y}_r$, $\mathbf{y}_{r+1}$, $\mathbf{y}^*$ to $\mathbf{x}^*$ ($\mathbf{x}^*$ is the solution to IP).

Lemma. Let $\mathbf{x}^*$ be the solution of IP and $\mathbf{y}^*$, $\mathbf{y}_r$ and $\mathbf{y}_{r+1}$ be as defined above then

$$f(\mathbf{y}_r) \geqslant f(\mathbf{x}^*) \geqslant f(\mathbf{y}_{r+1}) , \qquad f(\mathbf{y}_r) \geqslant f(\mathbf{y}^*) \geqslant f(\mathbf{y}_{r+1}) ,$$

$$g(\mathbf{y}_r) \leqslant g(\mathbf{x}^*) \leqslant g(\mathbf{y}_{r+1}) , \qquad g(\mathbf{y}_r) \leqslant g(\mathbf{y}^*) \leqslant g(\mathbf{y}_{r+1}) .$$

It follows, therefore, that IP can be solved in two steps:

(1) Performing a search for $\mathbf{y}_r$ and $\mathbf{y}_{r+1}$ by repeatedly solving A_α. (It should be noted that $H(c)$ is quasiconcave [4].)

(2) Generating all efficient points in the interval $[g(\mathbf{y}_r), g(\mathbf{y}_{r+1})]$ by repeated application of B_θ.

The algorithm for solving the A_α or B_θ programs will now be described.

4. The algorithm for generating efficient points

The algorithm for locating an efficient point associated with a fixed value of α or θ is a variant of Balas' implicit enumeration method [5]. It belongs to the branch-and-bound category. The Boolean program solved at each step, i.e., fixed α and θ, is

$$\max \sum_{j=1}^{n} c_j(\alpha) x_j , \tag{5}$$

subject to the following conditions:

$$\sum_{j=1}^{n} a_{ij} x_j \leqslant b_i , \qquad i = 1, ..., m , \tag{6a}$$

$$\sum_{j=1}^{n} d_j x_j \geqslant \theta , \tag{6b}$$

$$x_j \in [0, 1] . \tag{6c}$$

It is understood [see eqs. (1)] that

$$c_j(\alpha) = \alpha c_j + (1-\alpha)d_j , \qquad j = 1, ..., n ,$$

$$d_j = d_j \qquad [\text{eq.} (6\text{b})] \, , \qquad j = 1, ..., n \, .$$

If the problem is an A_α problem, then $\theta = -\infty$, i.e., only eqs. (6a, c) define the constraint set. If the problem is B_θ, then α is made equal to unity, i.e., $c_j(\alpha) = c_j$. A solution to A_α or B_θ is any n-dimensional vector $\boldsymbol{x}$ that satisfies eq. (6c). A feasible solution is one that satisfies all the associated constraints eqs. (6a, c) [or eqs. (6a, b, c)]. The solution to IP is feasible for the B_θ problem and optimal for some $B_{\theta'}$, but only feasible for the A_α problem (sometimes even optimal for some $A_{\alpha'}$).

However, too many feasible solutions may exist. The implicit enumeration technique is, therefore, a method for systematically examining only some of the feasible solutions in a way which ensures that all solutions have been implicitly examined.

There are two main differences between this method and the one developed by Balas:

(1) Balas' method is a maximization technique, in which the coefficients, c_j, of the objective function are fixed and non-negative. (If $c_j < 0$, it is possible to define a new variable $y_j = 1 - x_j$ and to eliminate x_j from the problem.) Thus, it is possible to renumber the components of $\boldsymbol{x}$. If efficient points are to be generated, it is no longer possible to keep $c_j(\alpha)$ constant and non-negative. Therefore, there is no way to renumber the components of $\boldsymbol{x}$. Balas' method will systematically assign values of 0 or 1 to some components of $\boldsymbol{x}$. A set of assignments

$$\Psi_s = \{x_{j_1}^{(s)} = \delta_{j_1}^{(s)}, ..., x_{j_q}^{(s)} = \delta_{j_q}^{(s)}\} \, ,$$

where $\delta_j^{(s)}$ $(j = j_1, ..., j_q)$ is either 0 or 1, and $1 \leqslant q \leqslant n$ will be called a pseudo-solution. If the components of $\boldsymbol{x}$ are renumbered, then $j_1 = 1$, $j_l = l$ and $j_q = q$. Hence a set of assignments Ψ_s is a sequence of zeros and units with q elements. If $c_j(\alpha)$ is not positive, Ψ_s can no longer be represented by a sequence of zeros and units. In that case, Ψ_s is represented by a sequence of n (not q) numbers which can be 0, 1 or 2.

If the jth term of the sequence equals 0 or 1, then $x_j^{(s)} = 0$ (or $x_j^{(s)} = 1$). The number 2 symbolizes a free variable, i.e., that no value has yet been assigned to $x_j^{(s)}$. For example, if $\boldsymbol{x} \in B^{(5)}$, an assignment Ψ could be $\{20112\}$, which is equivalent to the following statements: $x_2 = 0, x_3 = 1, x_4 = 1; x_1$ and x_5 are free.

(2) In the Balas method the number of arcs emanating from each node varies from n to zero. In the method here described only two arcs leave each node and· thus, it is suggested, the number of trial points generated and

checked during the process will be reduced significantly. The complete details of the algorithm can be found in [6].

5. The search method

The search is divided into two steps:
(1) Locating y_r and y_{r+1} (see lemma in section 3).
(2) Generating all efficient points by the B_θ when θ varies over the interval $[g(y_r), g(y_{r+1})]$.

It was shown previously (lemma) that the solution to IP, x^*, satisfies the relation $f(y_r) \geqslant f(x^*) \geqslant f(y_{r+1})$. The optimal parameter α^* is located in the interval $I_r \cup I_{r+1}$, where $y_r = y(\alpha)$ $\forall$ $\alpha \in I_r$ and $y_{r+1} = y(\alpha)$ $\forall$ $\alpha \in I_{r+1}$. Finding y_r and y_{r+1} is, therefore, equivalent to locating an interval I that satisfies the following relations:

$$I \subseteq I_r \cup I_{r+1} , \tag{7a}$$

$$I \cap I_r \neq \emptyset \quad \text{and} \quad y(\alpha) = y_r \quad \forall \ \alpha \in I \cap I_r , \tag{7b}$$

$$I \cap I_{r+1} \neq \emptyset \quad \text{and} \quad y(\alpha) = y_{r+1} \quad \forall \ \alpha \in I \cap I_{r+1} . \tag{7c}$$

An interval I that satisfies (7a, b, c) could be found by a sequential search for the maximum of $H(\alpha)$ [eq. (3)]. The function $H(\alpha)$ is piecewise constant and quasiconcave (see fig. 2). An outcome of two different trials made at α_1 and α_2 ($\alpha_1 < \alpha_2$) may be:
(1) $H(\alpha_1) > H(\alpha_2)$, in this case $\alpha^* \in [0, \alpha_2]$ and $I \subseteq [0, \alpha_2]$;
(2) $H(\alpha_1) < H(\alpha_2)$, in this case $\alpha^* \in [\alpha_1, 1]$ and $I \subseteq [\alpha_1, 1]$;
(3) $H(\alpha_1) = H(\alpha_2)$ and $y(\alpha_1) \neq y(\alpha_2)$, in this case $\alpha^* \in [\alpha_1, \alpha_2]$ and $I \subseteq [\alpha_1, \alpha_2]$;
(4) $H(\alpha_1) = H(\alpha_2)$ and $y(\alpha_1) = y(\alpha_2)$, in this case $\alpha^* \notin [\alpha_1, \alpha_2]$.
The search starts according to the golden section rule [7] as long as the outcome is not of type (4), i.e., $y(\alpha) = y(\beta)$, $\alpha \neq \beta$. The algorithm is given below:

Step -1): Let $a_0 = 0$, $b_0 = 1$ and $k = 0$.
Step 0): Solve A_{α^*}, where $\alpha^* = 0.618 (b_k - a_k)$.
Step k): 1) Let α_k satisfies $b_k - \alpha^* = \alpha_k - a_k$. Solve A_{α_k}.
 2) $k = k + 1$.
 3) If $H(\alpha_{k-1}) > H(\alpha^*)$ and $\alpha^* < \alpha_{k-1}$ ($\alpha^* > \alpha_{k-1}$) then $a_k = \alpha^*$, $b_k = b_{k-1}$ and $\alpha^* = \alpha_{k-1}$ (respect. $a_k = a_{k-1}$, $b_k = \alpha^*$ and $\alpha^* = \alpha_{k-1}$). If $b_k - a_k > \epsilon$ go to 1) else go to 14).

4) If $H(\alpha_{k-1}) < H(\alpha^*)$ and $\alpha^* < \alpha_{k-1}$ ($\alpha^* > \alpha_{k-1}$) then $a_k = a_{k-1}$, $b_k = \alpha_{k-1}$ (respect. $a_k = \alpha_{k-1}$, $b_k = b_{k-1}$). If $b_k - a_k > \epsilon$ then go to 1) else go to 14).

5) If $H(\alpha_{k-1}) = H(\alpha^*)$ and $y(\alpha_{k-1}) \neq y(\alpha^*)$ and $\alpha_{k-1} < \alpha^*$ ($\alpha_{k-1} > \alpha^*$) then $a_k = \alpha_{k-1}$, $b_k = \alpha^*$ (respect. $a_k = \alpha^*$, $b_k = \alpha_{k-1}$). If $b_k - a_k > \epsilon$ then go to 0), else go to 14).

The following part of the algorithm deals with the search scheme following an outcome of type (4).

6) If $H(\alpha_{k-1}) = H(\alpha^*)$ and $y(\alpha_{k-1}) = y(\alpha^*)$ then, if $\alpha_{k-1} < \alpha^*$, $a_{k,1} = a_{k-1}$, $b_{k,1} = \alpha_{k-1}$, $a_{k,2} = \alpha^*$, $b_{k,2} = b_{k-1}$ Respect. if $\alpha_{k-1} > \alpha^*$ then $a_{k,1} = a_{k-1}$, $b_{k,1} = \alpha^*$, $a_{k,2} = \alpha_{k-1}$, $b_{k,2} = b_{k-1}$).

7a) Let $\alpha_{k,1} = \frac{1}{2}(b_{k,1} + a_{k,1})$; solve $A_{\alpha_{k,1}}$.

8) $k = k + 1$.

9a) If $H(\alpha_{k-1,1}) > H(b_{k-1,1})$ then $a_k = \alpha_{k-1,1}$, $b_k = b_{k-1,1}$, $\alpha^* = \alpha_{k-1,1}$ go to 1).

10a) If $H(\alpha_{k-1,1}) = H(b_{k-1,1})$ and $y(\alpha_{k-1,1}) \neq y(b_{k-1,1})$ then $a_k = \alpha_{k-1,1}$, $b_k = b_{k-1,1}$ go to 0).

11a) If $H(\alpha_{k-1,1}) = H(b_{k-1,1})$ and $y(\alpha_{k-1,1}) = y(b_{k-1,1})$ then $b_{k,1} = \alpha_{k-1,1}$, $a_{k,1} = a_{k-1,1}$ go to 7b).

12a) $a_{k,1} = \alpha_{k-1,1}$, $b_{k,1} = b_{k-1,1}$.

7b) Let $\alpha_{k-1,2} = \frac{1}{2}(b_{k-1,2} + a_{k-1,2})$; solve $A_{\alpha_{k-1,2}}$.

9b) If $H(\alpha_{k-1,2}) > H(a_{k-1,2})$ then $a_k = a_{k-1,2}$, $b_k = b_{k-1,2}$, $\alpha^* = \alpha_{k-1,2}$ go to 1).

10b) If $H(\alpha_{k-1,2}) = H(a_{k-1,2})$ and $y(\alpha_{k-1,2}) \neq y(a_{k-1,2})$ then $a_k = a_{k-1,2}$, $b_k = \alpha_{k-1,2}$ go to 0).

11b) If $H(\alpha_{k-1,2}) = H(a_{k-1,2})$ and $y(\alpha_{k-1,2}) = y(a_{k-2,2})$ then $a_{k,2} = \alpha_{k-1,2}$, $b_{k,2} = b_{k-1,2}$ go to 13).

12b) $a_{k,2} = a_{k-1,2}$, $b_{k,2} = \alpha_{k-1,2}$.

13) If $(b_{k,2} - a_{k,2}) + (b_{k,1} - a_{k,1}) > \epsilon$ then go to 7a) else $b_k = b_{k,2}$, $a_k = a_{k,1}$.

14) Generate all efficient points in the interval $[g\{y(a_k)\}, g\{y(b_k)\}]$ by the B_θ parametric program.

The search scheme for the example is shown in fig. 2. The left part of fig. 2 represents the first part of the search step -1) to step 13). In this part, the parametric program solved was the A_α program. It was solved for six different values of the parameter α. The right side of the graph represents step 14) of the algorithm. In this step four additional efficient points have been generated together with the optimal solution $x^{(5)}$. All the efficient points for the example solved are listed in table 4.

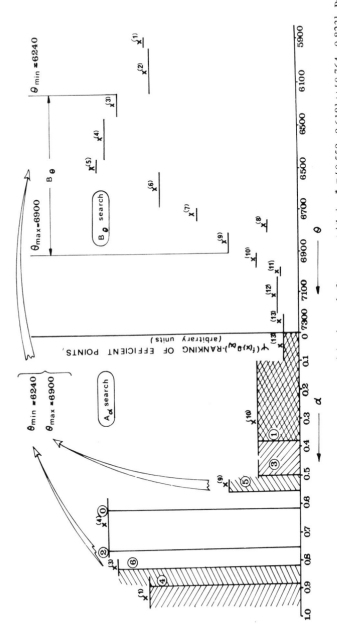

Fig. 2. The search for the optimal solution. The remaining interval after seven trials is $\alpha^* \in [0.559, 0.618] \cup [0.764, 0.823]$. By applying the B program all efficient points y satisfying $x^{(3)} > y > x^{(9)}$ were generated together with the optimal solution $x^{(5)}$.

Table 4

List of all efficient points for the example solved. As can be seen, only six points out of thirteen are generated by A_α. The range of a given solution is given by the interval $[\alpha_L, \alpha_U]$

	1	2	3	4	5	6	7	8	9	10	11	12	13
Econ. value (10^4 IL)	4340	4284	4283	4227	4160	4012	3945	3877	3865	3798	1388	1332	1265
Res. value (unit)	5920	6120	6240	6440	6510	6660	6730	6780	6900	6970	7010	7210	7280
$\alpha_U(X)$	1.000		0.849	0.781					0.560	0.511			0.109
$\alpha_L(X)$	0.849		0.781	0.560					0.511	0.109			0.000

Project no.

	1	2	3	4	5	6	7	8	9	10	11	12	13
1	1	1	1	1	1	1	1	1	1	1	1	1	1
2	1		1								1		
3													
4	1	1	1	1	1	1	1	1	1	1	1	1	1
5		1		1	1	1	1	1	1	1	1	1	1
6	1	1											
7			1	1	1	1	1	1	1	1	1	1	1
8	1	1	1	1	1	1	1	1	1	1	1	1	1
9	1	1	1	1	1	1	1	1	1	1	1	1	1
10	1	1	1	1	1	1	1	1	1	1	1	1	1
11											1	1	1
12	1	1	1	1	1	1	1	1				1	1
13										1			
14											1	1	1
15											1	1	1
16	1	1	1	1	1	1	1	1	1	1			
17	1	1	1	1	1		1						
18						1		1	1	1			
19									1	1	1	1	1

References

[1] B. Roy, Problems and methods with multiple objective functions, Math. Programming 1 (1971) 239.

[2] P.G. Fishburn, Decision and value theory (Wiley, New York).

[3] H. Pasternak and U. Passy, Annual activity planning with bicriterion functions, Mimeograph Ser. No. 110, Fac. Ind. and Mgmt., Eng., Technion, Israel (1972).

[4] A. Geoffrion, Solving bicriterion mathematical programs, Opns. Res. 15 (1967) 39.

[5] E. Balas, Discrete programming by the filter method, Opns. Res. 15 (1967) 915.

[6] H. Pasternak and U. Passy, Bicriterion mathematical programs with Boolean variables, submitted to Math. Programming.

[7] D.J. Wilde, Optimum seeking methods (Prentice–Hall, Englewood Cliffs, 1964).

[8] H. Pasternak and U. Passy, Finding global optimum of bicriterion mathematical programs, Opns. Res., Statist. and Econ., Mimeograph Ser. No. 91, Fac. Ind. and Mgmt, Eng., Technion, Israel (1972).

OPTIMAL TRAIN SCHEDULING
ON A SINGLE TRACK RAILWAY

Circulation optimale de trains
sur un chemin de fer à voie unique

BERNARDO SZPIGEL

Companhia Vale do Rio Doce, Vitoria, E.S., Brasil

Abstract. This paper concerns a single track railroad in eastern Brazil. The basic problem was: Given the routes and departure times of the trains on a single track railway, what are the best crossing and overtaking locations? A detailed description of this problem suggested that it had a structure analogous to the general job-shop scheduling problem developed by Greenberg. A more general formulation is given to the constraints and a more meaningful objective function is adopted. A technique is introduced that significantly reduces the number of nodes created by the branch-and-bound algorithm. Some results of computational experiments are presented at the end.

1. Introduction

This paper concerns a single track railroad in eastern Brazil – Companhia Vale do Rio Doce – where iron ore transportation plays the major role and passenger and freight trains are of lesser significance.

By definition a single track railroad has only one track which is used for circulation in both directions. In our example only at the stations is there additional track, parallel to the main line where trains can cross or overtake. Track between two consecutive stations will be called a *track section*.

During their travels, trains may have to stop for clearance of sections ahead. Such a situation is depicted in fig. 1, by means of a type of graph in common use by railroads to represent train movements. The vertical axis represents the relative positions of the stations and the horizontal the time.

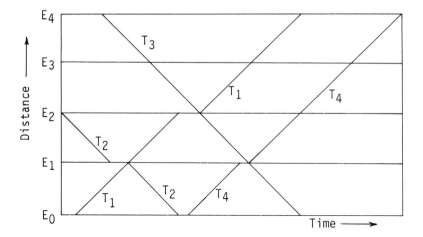

Fig. 1. Graph of train movements.

Fig. 1 displays the movement of four trains in four single track sections. As an example, train T_1, which is running from E_0 towards E_4, had to stop at station E_2 while waiting for train T_3.

Given that two trains must cross, a decision must be made as to where (which station) this is to occur. In general, this decision involves a choice among alternatives that affect differently the movement of other trains.

The selection of crossing points is made as an operational routine in two different operational functions. The first is the *time-table* preparation, which sets a pattern to be followed in the movement of trains. The second function is *train dispatching*, which is required when disturbances of the planned time-table occur.

Train scheduling decisions may have different economic effects. Sequences that reduce travel times may decrease investments in cars and engines as well as crew and fuel costs. Regularity and transportation velocity, which also depend on the schedule, are important factors to the satisfaction of customers needs and thus are related to railroad income.

In any railroad the importance of train scheduling problems increases with the number of trains per day. Decisions can be efficiently made by trained man-power until a certain degree of complexity is reached. From this point on, better means of finding good solutions are required.

2. Model

Train scheduling can be regarded as analogous to the problem of scheduling jobs (train travels) on a set of machines (track sections).

While most reported applications in job-shop scheduling have been based on heuristic approaches several authors [1–4] have formulated mathematical programming models for the "minimize the latest job completion time" form of this problem. In addition Manne [3] minimizes the average flow (travel) time and Greenberg [4] total machine idle time.

The model described here builds on Greenberg's formulation but includes more general constraints and an objective function which fits better the economic characteristics of the scheduling situation treated in this paper.

2.1. Constraints

Let n be the number of trains to be scheduled on m track sections. The ordered set of track sections that must be travelled by a train to complete a trip will be named a *route*. The route of train i will be represented by a vector with m_i components, where m_i is the number of track sections in this route. Component $r(i,k)$ of this vector is the kth track section to be travelled through by train i.

Let $t_{ir(i,k)}$ be the entrance time of train i into section $r(i,k)$ and let $a_{ir(i,k)}$ be the minimum time interval between the entrances of train i in track sections $r(i,k)$ and $r(i,k+1)$, then

$$t_{ir(i,k)} + a_{ir(i,k)} \leqslant t_{ir(i,k+1)} , \qquad k = 1, 2, ..., m_i-1 , \qquad (1)$$

$$t_{ir(i,k)} \geqslant 0 \quad \text{for all } i \text{ and } k , \qquad (2)$$

Constraints (1) express the sequence in which track sections must be travelled. Note that a route must be composed of adjacent sections. These sections, however, may be arranged in any form of network.

Constants $a_{ir(i,k)}$ may have different interpretations. The usual one is $a_{ir(i,k)} = d_{ir(i,k)}$, where $d_{ir(i,k)}$ is the time needed by train i to cover section $r(i,k)$. A more general interpretation is $a_{ir(i,k)} = d_{ir(i,k)} + s_{ir(i,k)}$, where $s_{ir(i,k)}$ is a non-negative constant. This is the general case in which a time interval is required between the releasing of a section and the seizing of the following one. Examples of this case are: (1) scheduled stops of passenger trains for embarkation and disembarkation and (2) train lengths considerably shorter than station yards and thus requiring a travel time to reach the following track section.

Departure times are constrained by

$$t_{ir(i,1)} \geqslant t_{i0} \quad \text{for all } i , \tag{3}$$

where t_{i0} is the time when train i is ready.

The ordering of trains i and j in section p are specified by

$$(t_{ip} + b_{ijp} \leqslant t_{jp}) \quad \text{or} \quad (t_{jp} + b_{jip} \leqslant t_{ip}) , \tag{4}$$

the "or" being exclusive.

For convenience of the discussion in section 3 we shall renumber the constraints contained in (4) as

$$t_{ip} + b_{ijp} \leqslant t_{jp} , \tag{4a}$$

$$t_{jp} + b_{jip} \leqslant t_{ip} . \tag{4b}$$

Constraints (4) must be specified in every track section p for any pair of trains that travel through this section.

Constants b_{ijp} also may have different meanings. If a train is not allowed to seize a section while it is occupied by another train this can be expressed by setting $b_{ijp} = d_{ip}$. This is clearly the case for any pair of trains running in opposite directions. For trains running in the same direction it is possible, in some railroads, to have them simultaneously in the same track section, provided they do not get closer than a predetermined safety distance. In these cases b_{ijp} may be less than d_{ip} and its value is defined by the minimum time interval allowed between the passages of trains i and j through any point of section p.

In some railroads, track sections cannot be seized immediately after being released by a train. Examples: (1) Traffic control procedures may be significantly time consuming. (2) Trains at a standstill waiting to seize a section may have to spend time in acceleration. In these cases, constant b_{ijp} can be given a third interpretation: $b_{ijp} = d_{ip} + u_p$, where u_p is the additional time required to clear section p after the passage of a train.

Constraints (4) can be alternatively formulated using 0–1 variables [4]. The present formulation is more convenient for the branch-and-bound algorithm described in section 3.

In this model it is assumed that the station yards can accomodate any number of trains that are likely to be there simultaneously. The importance of this assumption must be analysed for each railroad. In many real cases the constraints on the maximum number of trains in a station are seldom active.

2.2. Objective function

There is no standard objective function for train scheduling problems. The specific conditions of each railroad determine the criteria to be used. The objective proposed below is to minimize the weighted average of train travel times. Let F_i be the travel time of train i, i.e., the time interval between its ready time (t_{i0}) and its arrival at the destination, then the objective function can be expressed as

$$z' = \sum_i c_i F_i = \sum_i c_i [t_{ir(i,m_i)} + a_{ir(i,m_i)} - t_{i0}] , \tag{5}$$

or equivalently as

$$z = \sum_i c_i t_{ir(i,m_i)} , \tag{6}$$

since t_{i0} and $a_{ir(i,m_i)}$ are constants. Coefficients c_i express the general situation in which trains differ in economic importance or priorities.

Objective function (6) may be applied to some scheduling situations. In particular it is a good objective function when a considerable number of trains travel between the terminals with no scheduled intermediate stops (e.g., ore trains continuously travelling between loading and unloading terminals). It can also represent situations in which, for a relatively small number of trains, previously assigned arrival and departure times at intermediate stations should be obeyed as closely as possible (e.g., passenger trains). This can be achieved by setting high values to the correspondent c_i together with an adequate definition of constants $a_{ir(i,k)}$.

The model proposed in this section is to minimize (6) subject to (1)–(4). This will be named problem P.

3. Solution method

Problem P can be solved by a branch-and-bound algorithm as presented in [4]. In this section a brief description of this solution method is followed by a presentation of some modifications which improve on Greenberg's original algorithm.

The problem associated with the starting node is problem P without constraints (4). Call it problem P'. It is a linear programming problem and can be solved as such. If the solution of P' satisfies P the latter is solved. Otherwise we start the first branching operation by selecting two trains i and

j, in a section p and then creating two new problems: one is P' together with the additional constraint (4a); the other is P' with constraint (4b). These two problems, which correspond to two new nodes in the branch-and-bound tree, are also linear programming problems. We now select one of the newly created nodes for another branching operation.

For notational convenience we shall write $(i, j; p)$ when referring to trains i and j in section p. The solution method proceeds through a sequence of node selecting and branching. At any point, branching from a selected node creates two problems, each of which will result from the inclusion of one of the constraints (4a) or (4b) in the problem associated with the node currently being branched. These constraints must be associated with an $(i, j; p)$ which has not been fixed for the current branching node. The expression "fixed $(i, j; p)$" will mean that the relative order of trains i and j in section p is fixed.

The solution of the linear programs associated with the nodes provide the lower bounds which are used to guide the selection of nodes for branching and to identify optimal solutions.

3.1. Branching rules

For each iteration the branching rules must specify: (1) which node is to be branched and (2) which $(i, j; p)$ is to be fixed.

3.1.1. Node selection

A node which has not been branched will be named an *open node*. An *active node* will be any candidate for branching. An active node (1) must be an open node, (2) cannot correspond to a feasible solution to problem P and (3) cannot have a value greater or equal to the best known feasible solution. The solution method begins with an active node – the starting one – and finishes when there is none. At each iteration the branching node is selected from among the active nodes.

The following rules are compared in our study:

(a) *Select the least value active node* – the rule used by Greenberg [4].

(b) *Select the latest active node created.* In this rule, described by Little [5], open nodes (active or not) are arranged in a list in accordance with its creation time. The node to be selected is the last active one in this list.

(c) *Select the latest node created if it is active. Otherwise, select the least value active node.* This rule may be regarded as a mixture of rules (a) and (b).

Branching rules can be compared in terms of (1) number of nodes created; (2) computer storage requirements; (3) computer time required to obtain the first (good) feasible solution, and (4) computer time required to obtain an optimal solution.

While rule (a) is best, given criterion (1), it is by far the worst, given criteria (2) and (3), which are more important for practical applications. Rules (b) and (c) produce good feasible (and very often optimal) solutions using considerably less time than rule (a). However, they require additional time to ensure optimality.

3.1.2. Selection of (i,j;p) to be fixed

This section describes a technique that significantly reduces the number of nodes explicitly enumerated by the solution method as compared to Greenberg's algorithm.

After defining a node to be branched, we must select two trains i and j on a track section p, to fix their relative order in that section. A simple rule is:

(a) *Select any (i,j;p) which has not been fixed in the node being branched.* This rule leads us to one of these two conditions: (1) Neither constraint (4a) nor constraint (4b) is satisfied; or (2) only one of them is satisfied (and the other is not). There is no other possibility. In the first condition we shall say that trains i and j are in *conflict* on section p. A feasible solution to problem P cannot have any conflict. When, for a particular $(i,j;p)$, condition (1) occurs, the inclusion of one of the constraints (4a) or (4b) will eliminate the conflict for this $(i,j;p)$. Where condition (2) occurs, the additional constraint will be redundant for one of the two new problems.

The disadvantage of fixing an $(i,j;p)$ under condition (2) becomes clear when we are branching from a node without conflicts (i.e., the node solution is feasible for problem P). This can happen (and it generally does) before fixing all possible $(i,j;p)$. In this case it is pointless to continue fixing $(i,j;p)$ because we already have a feasible solution.

The above discussion suggests the following rule:

(b) *select an (i,j;p) such that trains i and j are in conflict in section p.* This rule requires that we undertake some additional computational work in order to find conflicts. This must be traded off against the additional number of nodes required when using rule (a). As an example, the 3 job-2 machine problem solved by Greenberg after creating 19 nodes under rule (a) can be solved searching only 7 nodes using rule (b). This saving increases with problem size.

3.2. Node evaluation

The problems associated with all nodes are linear programming problems. Two ideas for reducing the computational burden of obtaining their solutions were employed in the computer codes developed to test the model. Problem

P', associated to the starting node, can be easily solved:

$$t_{ir(i,1)} = t_{i0} \quad \text{for all } i,$$

$$t_{ir(i,k+1)} = t_{i0} + \sum_{l=1}^{k} a_{ir(i,l)}, \quad k = 1, 2, ..., m_i-1,$$

$$z = \sum_i c_i [t_{i0} + \sum_{l=1}^{m_i} a_{ir(i,l)}].$$

For any other node we can use the dual simplex algorithm, more specifically in Beale's column tableau form [6]. When a new node is created, its related problem results from the inclusion of an additional constraint to a problem (associated to the current branching node) for which a solution is already known. By applying the dual simplex algorithm we can obtain the new optimal solution with few (very often only one) iterations.

4. Computational experiments

The solution method was coded in Fortran and processed in an IBM/360 model 40 computer with 64K of core memory. Three versions were developed, each using one of the branching rules for node selection mentioned in section 3. Version 1, based on rule (a) was considered too inefficient for application purposes and was abandoned before the end of the experiments.

Table 1 illustrates computer codes performance for some test problems. In all problems the railroad is composed of five track sections linking two terminals. All trains travel at the same speed and each one spends the same amount of time in any of the five track sections. In each problem, half of the trains run in each direction.

The maximum size of the problems that we were able to solve was not satisfactory. Fields for future developments could be both suboptimization procedures and ways of increasing maximum allowed problem size. The approach presented in this paper can be further explored in these developments. The interruption of the algorithm after obtaining a good feasible solution is an obvious suboptimization scheme. Furthermore, partitioning a problem into smaller subproblems, as described in [7], can be a useful device to increase problem size.

Table 1
Computational results

Prob-lem	Track sections × trains	Branching rule [a]	Time (nodes created) [b]				Feasible solution/ optimal solution [c]		
			T1	T2	T3	T4	1	2	3
1	5 × 4	b	0.5 (8)	* 0.6 (10)	0.8 (14)	—	1.018	1.0	—
		c	0.5 (8)	0.8 (14)	* 0.9 (16)	—	1.018	1.009	1.0
2	5 × 6	b	1.3 (14)	* 1.9 (22)	3.0 (34)	—	1.018	1.0	—
		c	1.3 (14)	* 2.6 (30)	3.2 (36)	—	1.018	1.0	—
3	5 × 8	b	1.9 (18)	* 4.8 (46)	9.6 (92)	—	1.009	1.0	—
		c	1.9 (18)	* 4.4 (42)	9.6 (92)	—	1.009	1.0	—
4	5 × 10	b	3.2 (24)	4.5 (34)	*21.7(160)	39.3 (298)	1.018	1.014	1.0
		c	3.0 (24)	5.4 (44)	* 6.9 (56)	29.8 (244)	1.018	1.011	1.0

a) The branching rules are those for node selection in section 3.

b) $T1$ is the time at which the first feasible solution was obtained; $T2$, $T3$ and $T4$ are the times at which either a better feasible solution was obtained, or the program stopped after having ensured optimality (in this case the correspondent Ti is the last time value recorded for the problem). The time at which the optimal solution was achieved is marked with "*". Times are measured in minutes and are approximate. The values in parentheses are the number of nodes created up to that moment. Example: In problem 1 with rule b, the first feasible solution was obtained after 0.5 minutes, the second one (which is already optimal) after 0.6 minutes but the program stopped after 0.8 minutes.

c) These columns contain the ratios of the value of a feasible solution to that of the correspondent optimal solution for the problem. The order is the same as that in which the feasible solutions were obtained.

References

[1] E. Balas, Discrete programming by the filter method, Opns. Res. 15 (1967) 915.
[2] J.M. Charlton and C.C. Death, A generalized machine scheduling algorithm, Opnl. Res. Q. 21 (1970) 127.
[3] R.W. Conway, W.L. Maxwell and L.W. Miller, Theory of scheduling (Addison–Wesley, Reading, 1967); see especially Manne, and Brooks and White.
[4] H.H. Greenberg, A branch bound solution to the general scheduling problem, Opns. Res. 16 (1968) 353.
[5] J.D.C. Little, K.G. Murty, D.W. Sweeney and C. Karel, An algorithm for the travelling salesman problem, Opns. Res. 11 (1963) 972.
[6] T.C. Hu, Integer programming and network flows (Addison–Wesley, Reading, 1969).
[7] B. Szpigel, Train scheduling, unpublished M. Sc. Thesis, Pontificia Universidade Catolica of Rio de Janeiro, Brazil (1972).

35

A METHOD OF PLANNING YARD PASS TRAINS ON A GENERAL NETWORK

Méthode de planification des trains "yard pass" *
sur un réseau général

SHIGEMICHI SUZUKI
Railway Technical Research Institute, Japanese National Railways,
Kokubunji-shi, Tokyo, Japan

Abstract. One of the most important problems in train formation planning in railway freight transportation is to determine, considering freight traffic flow and other operation characteristics, the sections on which direct service of yard pass trains is provided so as to minimize the total transit time of freight cars or the total cost of transportation. First, the problem in a general yard network is explained and then formulated as a discrete programming problem. Since it is practically impossible to obtain an optimal solution of the problem, an approximate numerical method is developed. It is able to treat the problem for a general network containing up to fifty yards within reasonable computing time. Newly developed graph-theoretic analytical tools are useful in formulating the problem and devising an algorithm for solving it. Although the analysis is carried out primarily for determining a nearly optimal pattern of yard pass trains in a railway freight transportation, it can be applied to other types of planning of transportation where grouping or batching of freights or passengers are essential.

1. Introduction

In railway transportation trains move freight cars from one station to another. Only exceptionally is the demand for transportation between a pair of stations large enough to warrant running a train between them every day. Therefore, it is a common practice to transport freight cars by relaying them in a series of trains. One method of doing so, which we will call the basic scheme, is to construct a number of marshalling yards in the railway network

* Yard pass: trains qui passent les dépôts.

and to operate two types of trains between adjacent yards: local trains, or pick up and delivery trains, which stop at intermediate stations, and inter-yard trains which do not stop.

Transportation of freight should be planned so as to minimize the total transit time or the total cost of transportation (in this paper the total transit time is chosen as an objective function). From this point of view, if there exist a sufficiently large number of freight cars at a certain yard A for another yard B and beyond, it may be profitable to establish a train from A to B, in addition to the basic scheme. A train of this type, called a yard pass train or a maintracker, saves standing time of freight cars at intermediate yards. However, freight cars on yard pass trains must wait at a departing yard until a sufficient number of other cars are ready to travel in the same direction or until a train is scheduled to leave. This idle time is called an accumulation delay. Therefore, our problem is to determine sections on which direct service of yard pass trains is provided together with the flows on the train network so as to minimize the total transit time of freight cars. We call this train formation planning.

The problem is an old one but needs a new outlook. In 1959 Odaira took up the problem [1] and formulated it as a discrete programming problem for a linear yard network. He also presented a branch and bound type method for obtaining an optimal solution. Kanamatsu [2] devised also for a linear network a method of successively improving a solution. His method relies on heuristic rules and the algorithm is not specified in its details. He extended the method to a tree type network. Methods for a linear or tree type network have also been studied by Kutukova [3, 4], Borovoy [5], Trubin [6] and Berngard [7]. Some successes are reported for these methods, even though the details of the methods have not been known to the present author. All suffer from inherent limitations when it comes to handling large problems, especially those of a general yard network. After completing this work, a paper by A. Truskolaski [8] was called to the author's attention. It is presumably the only method that can deal with a general network. It has some features in common with this paper, although it seems an experimental study applicable to a network of small size.

The purpose of this study is twofold. One is to develop a systematic method for handling the problems of a general network. The other is to devise a practical algorithm which gives within a reasonable length of computing time a train formation plan for a real network containing from fifty to a few hundred marshalling yards.

2. Definitions and basic concepts

The traffic volume from yard i to j is denoted by w_{ij}. The transportation route from i_1 to i_m, $R_{i_1 i_m}$, is defined to be a sequence of yards through which freight cars from i_1 to i_m are transported. The transportation routes are assumed to be given for the present problem. When the route from k to l contains s and t as intermediate yards, we shall assume that the transportation route from s to t, R_{st}, is the part of the route R_{kl} which begins with s and ends in t. Now let $R_{ij} = (i, r_{ij}, \ldots, j)$. The $n \times n$ matrix $R = (r_{ij})$ is said to be the transportation route table. The transportation route graph $G(j)$ to destination j is the graph consisting of the $(n-1)$ directed arcs $\{(i, r_{ij})\}_{i \neq j}$ with j fixed. It indicates the transportation route from each i to j.

Suppose that a certain number of yard pass trains are set up in a yard network. If a yard pass train is set up from k to l along the transportation route to j, then some freight cars with destination j may be transported by the yard pass train. In this case add an arc from k to l to $G(j)$. The graph which is obtained after all such arcs associated with yard pass trains are added to $G(j)$ is called the train transportation route graph to destination j and is denoted by $GT(j)$. There are several routes in $GT(j)$, in general, from yard i to j. An optimal route is defined to be the longest route. The length of arcs will be defined shortly. The graph which consists of all the arcs in the optimal routes in $GT(j)$ is called the optimal car route graph to destination j and is denoted by $CR(j)$.

If the transportation route from a yard k different from i to j passes through yard i, k is said to be subordinate to i in $G(j)$. The set of yards which are subordinate to i in $G(j)$ is called the set of background yards of i with respect to $G(j)$ and is denoted by $B_i(j)$. The set of yards which appear in R_{ij} and do not contain i is called the set of foreground yards of i with respect to $G(j)$ and is denoted by $F_i(j)$.

The through traffic volume from k to l, W_{kl}, is defined as

$$W_{kl} = \sum_{R_{kl} \subset R_{st}} w_{st}. \tag{1}$$

Each term of the right hand side of (1) is called a component of W_{kl}.

The transit time of a freight car consists of actual running time, operation time and accumulation delay at stations and marshalling yards. Actual running time and accumulation delay at departing and arriving stations and yards can be considered to be independent of a train formation plan. Hence our objective is to minimize the sum of the total operation time and the total accumulation delay at intermediate marshalling yards.

Let τ_i be the time required for yard operations per freight car at yard i. The total operation time saved per freight car carried by a train from k to l is denoted by τ_{kl}. Associate τ_{kl} to the arc from k to l in GT (j) as its length.

If the average number of freight cars to be carried by a train from yard k to l is q_{kl} and the rate of accumulation of freight cars is uniform, then the accumulation delay per day, T_a, due to the trains from k to l can be expressed as $T_a = 12\ q_{kl}$. In practice, however, fluctuations occur in the rate of accumulation. By taking these into account, we express the accumulation delay as

$$T_a = a_{kl} + b_{kl}\ q_{kl},\tag{2}$$

where a_{kl} and b_{kl} are constants to be estimated.

Let X_{kl} be the number of freight cars to be carried by yard pass trains from k to l. The change of the total transit time of the freight cars due to the yard pass trains from k to l, ΔT_{kl}, is

$$\Delta T_{kl} = (a_{kl} + b_{kl}\ q_{kl})\ \delta\ (X_{kl}) - \tau_{kl} X_{kl} = s_{kl}\ \delta\ (X_{kl}) - \tau_{kl}\ X_{kl},\tag{3}$$

where $\delta\ (x)$ is a function which takes the value 0 or 1 depending on whether its argument is zero or not. $\delta\ (x) = 1$ indicates that yard pass trains are set up between two yards and $\delta\ (x) = 0$ otherwise. Our problem is to find a train formation plan which minimizes the sum of ΔT_{kl}.

3. Formulation of the problem

In order to obtain a train formation plan, it is necessary to know not only the sections, (k, l)'s, on which yard pass trains or inter-yard trains are established but also the number of freight cars with final destination j to be carried by trains from k to l for each eligible combination of k, l and j. "Eligible" in this case means that the route R_{kj} contains the route R_{kl} as a sub-route. Let $x_{kl}^{(j)}$ be the said number of freight cars, then they are the variables which completely determine a plan. Now we are in the position to formulate the problem.

Consider the transportation route graph G (j) with destination j. Take yard i different from j in G (j). Then the equation of conservation of freight cars flow should hold at yard i, namely

$$\sum_{l \in F_i(j)} x_{il}^{(j)} - \sum_{k \in B_i(j)} x_{ki}^{(j)} = w_{ij} \qquad (i \neq j). \tag{4}$$

The equation for $i = j$ can be derived by summing up all the constraints for $i \neq j$. Obvious non-negativity constraints should also be imposed,

$$x_{kl}^{(j)} \geq 0 \quad \text{for every eligible combination of } k, l \text{ and } j. \tag{5}$$

A solution $x_{kl}^{(j)}$ satisfying (4) and (5) is feasible because the solution yields a plan which realizes transportation of w_{ij} freight cars from i to j following the prescribed transportation route for every pair of i and j.

Next we will consider the objective function. By measuring the change of standing time ΔT of freight cars in the intermediate marshalling yards due to yard pass trains and taking the situation in the basic scheme as a reference point, the following relation can be obtained from (3),

$$\Delta T = \sum_{k,l} \Delta T_{kl} = \sum_{k,l} \{ s_{kl} \, \delta \, (X_{kl}) - \tau_{kl} X_{kl} \}, \tag{6}$$

where the summation should be taken over all the possible yard pass trains. In order to obtain a more explicit expression for ΔT, we will express the through traffic volume W_{kl} in terms of its components,

$$W_{kl} = \sum_{p=1}^{N_{kl}} w_{\alpha_p(k,l), \beta_p(k,l)} \, , \tag{7}$$

where N_{kl} is the number of components of W_{kl}. We will omit k and l in α_p and β_p except in the case where explicit representation is necessary. Then

$$X_{kl} = \sum_{p=1}^{N_{kl}} x_{kl}^{(\beta_p)} \, . \tag{8}$$

Hence

$$\Delta T = \sum_{k,l} \left\{ s_{kl} \, \delta \left(\sum_{p=1}^{N_{kl}} x_{kl}^{(\beta_p)} \right) - \tau_{kl} \left(\sum_{p=1}^{N_{kl}} x_{kl}^{(\beta_p)} \right) \right\}. \tag{9}$$

Therefore the problem is to minimize ΔT in (9) subject to (4) and (5). This is a discrete programming problem since $\delta \, (x)$ is a step function.

Taking the number of yards as a parameter table 1 gives an idea about the scale of the problem for different numbers of variables and the constraints. Although the formulation presented above gives a precise statement of the problem, attempting to solve it by any of existing methods for discrete programming is not realistic. This fact motivated the development of the approximate method to be described in the next section.

Table 1
Scale of the problem for a linear network (one way only)

No. of yards n	No. of constraints $n(n-1)/2$	No. of variables $(n+1)n(n-1)/6$
10	45	165
50	1 225	20 825
100	4 950	166 650

4. Approximate method of solution using through traffic volume

The algorithm consists of two alternately executed stages. In one of these stages yard pass trains are successively introduced to reduce standing time of freight cars at intermediate yards and a pattern of such trains determined. In the other stage the optimal car routes to yard j with respect to the present pattern of yard pass trains are computed for each j and the flow of freight cars is allocated along these optimal car routes. Now we return to the first stage and continue to set up favorable trains. The process is iterated until further reduction of standing time cannot be expected. A general flow chart of the algorithm is shown in fig. 1.

A few comments will be added to clarify the meaning of the flow chart. After the initialization favorable yard pass trains are set up one by one until min ΔT_{ij} becomes non-negative. The modification of the OD table and the through traffic volume table in step 3 is carried out according to the following rules,

$$w'_{\alpha_p,\beta_p} = 0, \quad w'_{\alpha_p,k} = w_{\alpha_p,k} + w_{\alpha_p,\beta_p}, \quad w'_{l,\beta_p} = w_{l,\beta_p} + w_{\alpha_p,\beta_p},$$

$$w'_{ij} = w_{ij} \text{ for other } w_{ij}, \qquad p = 1, 2, \ldots, N_{kl}, \tag{10}$$

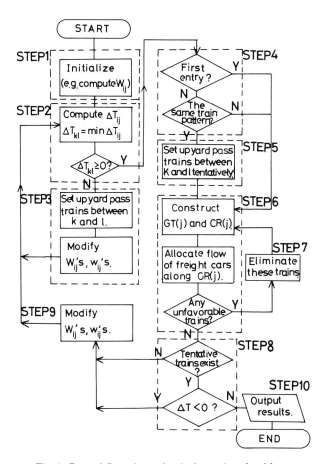

Fig. 1. General flow chart of train formation algorithm.

$$W'_{st} = W_{st} - \sum_{\substack{R_{st} \subset R_{\alpha_p,\beta_p} \\ R_{st} \neq \emptyset}} w_{\alpha_p,\beta_p}, \qquad (11)$$

where primes denote quantities after modifications. A yard pass train is set up on a tentative basis in step 6 even if $\Delta T_{kl} > 0$. If the actual merit of the train is proved in step 8, then the establishment will become final. Trains are deemed unfavorable in step 6 if the number of freight cars on them is less than a predetermined value or ΔT_{jj} becomes positive.

The algorithm was programmed in Fortran and was tested on FACOM 230/60 and CDC 3600. Among the problems handled there was one with thirty six yards through which about 20 000 freight cars are transported daily. In this problem yard pass trains were set up on 163 sections and then 22 trains removed in the optimization stage. The results show a considerable reduction of standing time of freight cars compared to the one in practice. The computation time was ten to twenty minutes.

5. Concluding remarks

A method for a freight train formation planning in a general yard network is presented. A graph-theoretic approach turns out to be useful in both formulating and solving the problem. Although the method is primarily intended for planning yard pass trains, it can be applied to other types of planning of transportation where grouping or batching of freight or passengers is essential.

Some extensions of the present method are now under development. One of them is train formation planning which includes through trains from a set of stations to another without any yard operations.

Acknowledgement

The author wishes to thank Mrs. A. Fujieda for her painstaking programming work.

References

[1] H. Odaira, On a grouping policy of freights cars (in Japanese), Pre-report 58–225, Railway Tech. Res. Inst. (1958).
[2] M. Kanamatsu, Computational method of a grouping policy of freight cars (in Japanese), Keiei-Kagaku 4, No. 2 (1960) 113.
[3] G.A. Kutukova, Numerical evaluation of a train formation plan by digital computer (in Russian), Report of the All-Union Sci. Res. Inst. of Railroad Transportation, U.S.S.R., No. 1 (1968) 60.
[4] G.A. Kutukova. An algorithm for computing a plan of single-group trains (in Russian), Railroad Transportation No. 8 (1968) 41.

[5] N.E. Borovoy, Simultaneous computation of a plan for through and inter-yard trains by digital computer (in Russian), Report of the All-Union Sci. Res. Inst. of Railroad Transportation, U.S.S.R., No 8 (1968) 54.

[6] V.A. Trubin, On determination of an optimal plan for single-group trains (in Russian), Report of the All-Union Sci. Res. Inst. of Railroad Transportation, U.S.S.R., No. 7 (1969) 57.

[7] K.A. Berngard, A computational method for distribution of sorting operations and for expansion of stations (in Russian), Report of the All-Union Sci. Res. Inst. of Railroad Transportation, U.S.S.R., No. 4 (1970) 1.

[8] A. Truskolaski, Application of digital computers to the optimization of freight train formation plans, Bulletin of I.R.C.A.: Cybernetics and Electronics on the Railway 5, No. 5 (1968) 311.

[9] S. Suzuki, Determination of grouping policy for freight cars by through traffic volumes (in Japanese), Report No. 672, Railway Tech. Res. Inst. (1969).

M. Ross, ed., OR'72. North-Holland Publishing Company (1973)

36

THE IMPLEMENTATION OF OR MODELS
IN PLANNING PROCEDURES

L'application de modèles de la recherche opérationnelle
dans les processus de planification

NORMAN TOBIN and TERRY BUTFIELD

British European Airways, London, England

Abstract. Over the past two years BEA's operational research branch has been developing and implementing a set of interrelated planning models on an inhouse time-sharing
system on a DECsystem-10 computer. In the course of these developments many lessons
have been learned about the evolution and maintenance of models and their integration
into the planning process.

The models constructed during this period cover a wide range of tactical and strategic
planning areas, but they all have one feature in common. Each one has become firmly
embedded in the planning procedures, seen by the planners themselves as an essential
part of their equipment. The paper discusses what are believed to be the main reasons for
this high degree of implementation, using various models to illustrate particular points. It
is not possible to describe all the models in one short paper, but a diagram is appended
showing the full range of models in order to indicate the broad base of experience from
which the lessons have been drawn.

1. Introduction

In this paper, an attempt is made to distil from a much longer paper [1]
those points that would seem to be of most interest and value to operational
research workers in general rather than the solely airline audience for which
the earlier paper was written. At the same time, the ideas have been updated
to some extent in the light of further experience. These ideas, which form the
distinctive approach of the BEA group as a whole, have evolved in the course
of developing a wide range of tactical and strategic aids to planning.

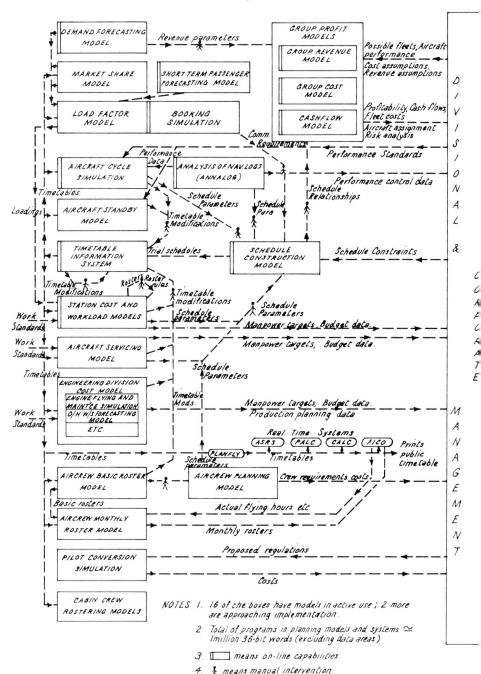

Fig. 1. BEA computerised models for planning. Simplified diagram: i.e., some boxes repre
large suites of related models or system programs.

During the last two years, the OR group in BEA has had considerable success in implementing OR models into the planning procedures of the airline. There are many factors contributing to this success, some of which would appear to be specific to the airline industry, to BEA, to the OR branch or to the computer facilities available for this work in BEA. However, we suspect that many of the lessons we have learned have much wider relevance. About 40 inter-related models or sub-models and extensive supporting systems have already been constructed.

In this short paper, little will be said about the models themselves, as the purpose is rather to discuss the reasons why they are all in active use. However, fig. 1 gives some indication of their range and scope.

2. Models in planning

2.1. OR in airline planning

In any industry one can never properly plan the different parts of the enterprise completely in isolation. At the very least there is likely to be competition for financial resources, interaction between what can be produced and what can be sold, and relations between the make-up of the order book and the balance of productive resources. The airline industry is one where planning of the various parts is inter-related in a much more detailed and complex way, for the interactions are primarily in the construction of the timetable, which is itself a voluminous and detailed plan. The sales, operational and engineering functions, all interact through the timetable during planning, and it is through the timetable that the airline's planning interacts with that of the customer. Thus, the timetable is both the instrument and the expression of a large amount of the planning and is essentially the product of complex interactive decision-making. Operational Research should be concerned with the central processes of planning, with the interaction of different parts of the enterprise, with balance and consistency in planning, and therefore with the timetable.

In an airline there are two special features that lead OR into a particular overall approach. The first is that most of the important decisions are repetitious or cyclic, giving rise to the seasonal operational plan and its implications throughout the airline. The trail of decisions leading to a particular schedule stretches over several years, but every year each stage of the decision-making must be repeated for the appropriate years ahead. Thus OR must put its first priority on developing improved methods or systems for repetitious decision making rather than helping in one-off decisions. This is not to say that one-off decisions should be shunned completely, but many decisions that seem to be of this type can anyway be better seen as special cases of repetitive decision processes.

The second feature is that these decisions are basically concerned with or expressed through a timetable (or the route/frequency plans leading up to it). The distinctive approach of OR is to build models, and in this case they must handle very large amounts of data, to show the broad effects of detailed interactions of numerous variables that cannot sensibly be regarded as random. There is also an obvious need for speed in these processes, as one ideally needs to repeat the calculations a number of times with varying assumptions, to test the cost or other implications of alternative policy decisions. Speed will also allow one to obtain answers much sooner, or alternatively to wait until more reliable data is available before beginning the calculations.

In short, the OR man in airline planning is obliged to build computer models of repetitious decision problems. He can only begin to make his real regular contribution to planning when the proposed timetables (and/or route frequencies) are, as a matter of normal routine, on computer files.

2.2. The purpose of models in planning

On a more basic level, it is necessary to consider what is the nature of the contribution the models can make to planning. Obviously they cannot actually plan. It has already been noted that planning is highly interactive in an airline and one part cannot be planned rationally in isolation. Thus the computer cannot actually do the planning unless it does all the planning, which is manifestly not possible. It can, however, carry out various procedures and calculations accordingly to predetermined logic, on the basis of specified or implied policies and assumptions and show the best answer to a problem within these limitations. But these will always be at best an approximation to the real situation and if management is unhappy with the answer it must always be possible to re-examine the assumptions or policies or logic, or in some situations simply to override the computer.

3. The BEA approach

3.1. Computing facilities available for planning in BEA

Three years ago it was realised in BEA that the difficulties inherent in trying to develop models for planning on computers that were primarily devoted to other purposes, real-time and batch, were making it impossible to realise the very great benefits to be obtained in this field. The decision was made to acquire a separate computer installation dedicated to planning purposes and a DECsystem-10 computer was installed in 1970. The installation now includes 96K of core store, 4 disc drive units, 2 magnetic tape drives, a line printer and a card reader. At night it operates in a batch mode on production, but during day time it operates in timesharing mode with 14 teleprinters and 2 display units on-line, most of which are devoted to model development while the remainder are being used by planners with on-line models.

Some of the advantages of an in-house timesharing facility are obvious, even if it were treated simply as a very-fast-access batch system for program development, but the impact on model development and use has been much more profound and impressive. New software and programming methods taking full advantage of the interactive possibilities of timesharing facilities have brought tremendous acceleration in program development. This in turn has reinforced and stimulated new approaches to model development that are faster, more flexible and more responsive to the user's needs. These advances have brought new power and scope to the planner, who has changed his own approach to his task. The programmer, the model builder and finally the planner not only work faster, but find themselves using new thought processes to achieve new and better results.

The following subsections are each primarily devoted to one feature in the BEA approach. This is to some extent artificial, as the various ideas interact and reinforce one another and it will sometimes be convenient to refer to the same model by way of example in different sections, but it helps to underline the principal points.

3.2. Evolution from simple models

Lengthy discussion in early OR literature on the dangers of sub-optimisation has led to a quest for completeness that has been neither completely necessary nor always beneficial. In the realities of an airline with its high interactivity even at the tactical level, the search for a solution to the "whole problem" is seen more easily than elsewhere as a wild goose-chase. But even here, incompleteness is seen as needing excuses and there is often an urge to include as much as possible as soon as possible in a model, subject to time constraints and technical difficulties. In our view this is a fundamental error in approaching any repetitive planning problems and leads directly to many of the most frustrating difficulties of implementation.

It is almost always best to begin by constructing the simplest model that will actually be useful for planning. It is then possible, through experimental use of the simple model, to get the users really involved with OR in constructive thinking about where to proceed and how far. The limitations and potential of the first simple model become common ground for a dialogue between the planner, whose understanding of his problems may go far beyond the limitations implied by his current procedure, and the OR man, who is better equipped to formulate these problems in terms of the capabilities of computerised models.

The point is not merely that the first simple model gets the dialogue started; it provides a much freer, more stimulating basis for development than a first complex model, with less inhibitions from commitment to ideas and justification of resources spent.

The aircraft cycle simulation is a good example of this precept. The first BEA model concerned with punctuality was a relatively complex simulation of the movement of all the BEA fleet around the network. It was built in 1962 and had some limited success in application, but it had serious defects. It was inflexible, took a long time to set up for a run, and quickly became out of date owing to the immense amount of primary data to be updated. It was also thought to be lacking in realism, and this, with its inflexibility, were seen at the time as its main disadvantages, so work was begun on a more realistic and flexible model. After some time, it was realised that the answer was not to go to the more complex, but to the more simple. A new simulation was quickly developed, concerned with one important factor contributing to punctuality or unpunctuality. This was the stability of an aircraft cycle, i.e., the likely punctuality that would obtain if an aircraft tried to operate its cycle of flights for a typical day under reasonably normal conditions. This model was rapidly put into use by the schedulers. The simplicity of the model allowed a precise and useful meaning to be attached to the results, and the schedulers and OR soon realised that the way ahead did not lie in increased complexity. The requirement was rather for a much faster service (much faster than overnight) and an on-line version was developed.

3.3. Involvement with users

This example also shows the advantage of getting the user departments actively interested from an early stage in thinking about the purpose and nature of the model. If this is not done it is very hard to build something that will be firmly implemented as part of the ongoing planning system. Much has been written about the importance of involving the users during various stages of development, but all too often the involvement achieved is ineffectual, however keen and interested the users may be. The reason is not hard to find. If a planning model is to be really effective, it will not merely make planning easier or quicker but change its very nature. Careful prior discussions about the desirable features of a complex model are likely to produce a tool that is more relevant to the problems as they were seen by OR and the planners at the beginning of the study than to the new realities of a new planning environment. If on the other hand a simple model is implemented first, a more meaningful dialogue is established, and new tools and methods are evolved in parallel in the light of common experience.

3.4. Integration of the model into the planning processes

It is our belief that a planning model has not been implemented in a real sense unless it is an integral part of the planning system, seen by the planners themselves as an important part of their equipment. This implies understanding not only the logic of the decisions and the abstract information flow, but also how the information provided by the model will actually fit into the modes of thought of the planners as they are doing their job. This is only possible by watching the planners in action and it is much easier if they can be seen attempting to use a simple model to the best advantage. Their contributions are much more meaningful under these conditions and give much better insight into their needs than relatively abstract prior discussions.

In BEA, many of the models have reached a very high degree of integration into the planning processes. The process of timetable development is now seen as a series of interactions between schedulers and a succession of models and systems, some in an interactive on-line mode. It would perhaps still be possible to produce timetables by the old methods, but no-one would any longer be satisfied with the results. In the corporate planning field, the processes of aircraft fleet planning again involve an extensive series of exploratory interactions between the planners and a series of OR models that were developed in the simplest usable forms and extended as a cooperative effort in the light of problems in actual use. At a more tactical level, the station workload and cost model (actually an extensive suite of submodels) is increasingly seen as an essential tool in planning the manpower required to cope with operational plans.

3.5. Validation and maintenance of the logic

In classical OR studies there is often a ceremony called "validation of the model". A test procedure is agreed with the potential user, a time is agreed and the test is staged. If the test is successful and the political quicksands are not too dangerous, the model is implemented. Often this is the last that is heard of the model. If on the other hand the model is evolved through a process of experience in use, there is no occasion for this touching and hazardous ceremony. The model is tested progressively and repeatedly in the course of development and its (one hopes increasing) efficacy is assessed and re-assessed through the results obtained in practice.

When the model appears to have reached its final form, this merely means that the process of development has slowed down. The model is now suited to the current needs of planning, but the world will change and the tools of the planners must be re-fashioned. OR must accept a continuing responsibility for maintaining the logic of the models in accordance with the changing needs of the planners and the changing realities of the environment. If this is not done, they have built a tool not for the workshop but for the museum. In BEA this responsibility is taken very seriously. It represents a lasting diversion of OR effort from potential new developments, but the alternative of allowing active models to fall out of use is a far greater waste of effort. When certain sections of ground handling staff at Heathrow airport were re-organised, the OR team working on the station workload and cost model dropped all new developments and concentrated on re-programming several submodels affected. This has maintained not only the model, but the credibility of OR methods and of the new approaches to planning.

3.6. Updating and modification of data

The maintenance discussed above is concerned with the logic of the models, but most of them need inputs of data relating to past experience and current practical constraints, and this must also be maintained. In many cases the volume of data is very large, and then it is essential to find some automatic means of updating. Otherwise the model is unlikely to be a feasible tool for the ongoing process of planning. While OR, in cooperation with the schedulers, were developing successive improved versions of the aircraft cycle simulation, OR, together with operations division, were tackling the problem of automatic updating of the data base. This was achieved through a new system for analysis of navigation logs.

In the more unstructured areas of planning (normally those involving assumptions about the environment, such as marketing and corporate planning), other problems of updating arise. A basic requirement is to be able to explore easily and quickly the implications of varied sets of assumptions about relationships or the future values of external variables, or internal ones that are difficult to control. It is a common feature of our models in the area of corporate planning (for evolving aircraft fleet procurement and allocation policies and for financial planning), that such assumptions can readily be changed by the planner sitting at a teleprinter and using a simple but powerful command language to amend the relevant files. The "standard" set of assumptions can thus be modified temporarily for such purposes as sensitivity or risk analysis, or more permanently as the "standard" view of the future environment changes.

3.7. Linking the planning and control functions

A planning tool may be very useful on its own, but its value will be very greatly enhanced if it can be linked closely to the control function. This has not by any means been achieved with all of BEA's planning models, but progress is being made and in some cases the link is very strong. The system for analysis of navigation logs, which supports the aircraft cycle simulation, also provides monthly control information to a high level body overseeing the planning and control of punctuality. The importance of this is not only in common use of the same data in both planning and control, but also in the adoption of a common philisophy in assessing the performance and capabilities of the operating functions.

4. Conclusion

Several points have been made: that a first simple solution should be actively sought rather than accepted reluctantly; that the intended users must be closely involved in the development; that real implementation is only achieved when the planners themselves see the model as an essential tool; that OR must accept a continuing commitment to maintenance of the logic of the planning models; that updating and manipulation of data must be simple, quick and flexible and often automatic; that planning models are better if they are linked with control; that all these features are interactive and mutually supporting. Many of these propositions seem dangerously close to platitudes, but the danger is in seeing them as platitudes, as evident truths whose influence will somehow inform our projects without our conscious effort. In BEA they are at the forefront of our minds at all stages of a project. The results give strong support to the great importance we attach to them.

Reference

[1] N.R. Tobin and T.E. Butfield, OR models and their implementation in the airline's planning cycle, 10th AGIFORS Proc. (Oct. 1970).

M. Ross, ed., OR'72. North-Holland Publishing Company (1973)

37

SIMULATION OF A COMPUTER-CONTROLLED
CONVEYANCE SYSTEM FOR AIR PASSENGERS' LUGGAGE

*Simulation d'un système de bandes transporteuses
contrôlées par ordinateur destinées au
transport des bagages de voyageurs en avion*

ROLF HEINE

Frankfurt/Main Airport Co., West Germany

Abstract. In the new terminal at Frankfurt/Main airport a luggage conveyance and distribution system has been installed. It is proposed to transport the luggage of about 30 million passengers per year. The system consists, of about 240 check-in counters for boarding passengers' luggage, about 30 check-in-points for transfer-luggage, about 30 km of conveyor sections, a store for the early-arrival luggage and empty pallets (capacity about 6 000 storage positions), several hundred distributing and adjoining switches, lifts, stackers and destackers and of about 40 points to discharge the pallets. Furthermore there are reading and counting stations, switchboards and three process control computers to lead the pallets to their destination.

The simulation model describes in detail all the various elements, the transportation of each pallet and the development and servicing of queues. The local and global strategies determining the flow of the pallets are considered. The influences coming from the environment — such as irregularities of the timetable, the disposition of aircraft parking positions and of pallet dischargement points are realized by a pre-simulation. Furthermore the behavior of the passengers, the development of queues at the check-in-counters and the flow of transfer-passengers are exactly simulated. The results of the simulation give the basis for continuing planning and show the premises and conditions which have to be fulfilled in order to guarantee the accurate performance of the entire system.

During the last few years air traffic had an unprecedented boom, making aircraft a mass traffic media. In the process Frankfurt has become a turntable in air traffic. Currently more than 60 carriers in airline service and an additional 160 in charter traffic make approx. 5 000 direct connections with 190 cities in 90 countries each week. By 1975 a passenger yield of 18 million is expected and 30 million by 1980. The foreign share of this is about 65%, the share of transfer passengers about 40%. The amount of luggage to be dealt with corresponds to the number of passengers. The high transfer share brings with it special sorting problems. In addition, the timetable has a special structure characterized by four peak periods of 1.5–2 hours duration during each of which approximately 60 flights have to be handled.

At Frankfurt Airport the need to cope with these high demands was anticipated early enough. In the new Air Terminal, which was opened in March 1972, a luggage conveyer system has been installed at a cost of approximately DM 110 million. With this conveyer system the entire luggage of boarding and transfer passengers can be transported fully automatically and directly from the luggage check-in points to any delivery place at the aircraft parking positions at the building or to a central clearing place for aircraft which are not close to the building. The volume involved can reach a maximum of ≈13 000 pieces of luggage per peak hour.

More than 10 000 containers serve to receive the air passengers' luggage. Each has a different binary coding which makes it possible to identify any individual piece of luggage being transported from the 240 counters or 30 transfer luggage stations to their destination points. These loaded pallets are transported just like the empty pallets, through the same system consisting of more than 30 km of conveyer sections – belt conveyers and express wheeled tracks – 380 junctions, lifts and accumulating and waiting routes with a maximum speed of 2.5 m/sec.

Destination control is carried out with the aid of three process control computers AEG-60-50 and a central distributor consisting of three parallel rings, 650 reading points for identifying the pallets as well as 450 counting points. Attached to the distributor is an early-luggage store with a total capacity of ≈6 000 units and with 15 revolving tracks which is designed both to accumulate the luggage whose destination is not yet known, and to store unnecessary empty pallets in stacks of four. Process control computers supervise the reserves and supply of empty pallets to the decentral stores located in front of the check-in points where luggage from either transfer or new passengers is checked in. Stackers pile empty pallets into stacks of four at ≈40 luggage delivery positions, considerably reducing the space requirement and the transportation time for empty containers. The corresponding de-stackers are found at the check-in places which are supplied as necessary. This luggage conveyer system is thus a closed circuit, the check-in positions are sinks of empty pallets and sources of loaded pallets, the delivery places are sinks of loaded pallets and sources of empty pallets.

The central airport computer provides the link with the environment by providing the process control computer with the basic information, e.g., time-table and control information such as begin of conveyance, end of convey-ance, destination, counter groups, etc. Messages about interruptions and breakdowns of the system, critical loads etc. are transmitted back to the central computer.

Without simulation the reaction of this complex system could only be found out very inexactly, if at all, especially since floating loads are frequent. Simulation shows the critical points of the system and how to avoid environ-mental influences, bottlenecks in the system, disturbances due to breakdowns of system parts, etc., which can impede the faultless functioning of the system and lead to a disruption of air traffic.

The simulation model distinguishes between the environment, the system and the interactions between system and environment. The environment comprises the timetable, the actual arrival and departure times of the aircraft, the behaviour of the boarding passengers and of the transfer-pas-sengers, the aircraft parking positions and the assigned luggage delivery positions as well as the luggage check-in places for transfer-passengers, the handling capacities at the delivery and check-in places, the number of luggage-units per passenger or the number of passengers per flight.

The simulation is carried out in two stages. In the first the actions of the central airport computer are simulated. Based on the schedule, the actual arrival and departure times for each flight are derived using random number generators and distribution curves for the irregularities in minimum ground times pertaining to national, Berlin, European and transcontinental or charter flights. At the same time the most suitable aircraft parking position for each flight is calculated from the aircraft type, the number of passengers, the ground time and the flight classification. In addition, an appropriate luggage delivery place and the necessary conveyance time are estimated. The average number of passengers and the average number of luggage units for transfer passengers are also calculated from an extensive set of statistics.

The second step, the simulation of the actual system, either uses all this data as input or derives the necessary control information from it. Other data required for the second stage include the assignment of the individual luggage check-in counters to the various airline companies, selection list of possible luggage check-in positions for transfer-passengers' luggage for each aircraft parking position, as well as the various service rates at the luggage check-in or delivery positions.

The queues occurring at the counters are now simulated. The transport of the containers in the system itself is described in great detail, as queues at any junction can decisively impede the behaviour of the entire system.

The topology of the system can be described in a directed graph. The nodes of this graph can be interpreted as switching elements – junctions or other connections of various conveyance elements – which determine each time if and in what direction a pallet should be conveyed further. These switching elements implicitly contain that part of the luggage computer strategy which determines destination control, whereby the possible destinations are carried in code in each of these elements (≈ 1400). There are in all more than 100 different types of these switching elements.

The simulation on the computer is now carried out by establishing the changes in the system from one cycle time to the next. The transport must hereby be arranged at locally constant speed. For this the individual conveyer belts are divided up into the respective number of possible places for the containers. The cycle time is the time which is necessary to convey a container on the fastest belt from one place to the next and corresponds to ≈ 1 sec real time.

The transport of the containers is presented by pushing the imaginary end of each conveyer element against the direction of conveyance until the original end of the preceeding element is reached. Then the container code numbers are first transferred. If, however, the imaginary end of a belt has reached a storage place which contains a pallet, the transition to a following conveyer element is fixed over the assigned switching element.

At junctions one container can enter at the same time on each approach route. Then one of them is stopped on a preceding waiting route until there is a possibility of being conveyed further. The control of junctions is made using both local criteria for the switching elements as well as global criteria. For this we must determine the requirements of, e.g., empty containers at the various check-in places or the number of pallets at the waiting routes preceding the delivery positions.

Redundant empty containers are sent to the early-luggage store and can be recalled from there when additional requirements occur. The same is true of the loaded containers whose destination is not yet known or which cannot be delivered. The loaded containers must await delivery until after a certain number of simulation time units it is decided whether they can now be conveyed. In that case delivery starts.

The check-in counters and the check-in position for transfer-passengers' luggage as well as the delivery positions are handled separately. In each case after 60 cycle times the number of the passengers just arrived and their luggage units are determined for each flight with the aid of the appropriate distribution function and are sent to the shortest queue at the counters opened for them. If the length of the queue is greater than a prescribed threshold value the next counter of the airline is opened. This determines the respective counter requirement.

While the counters are constructed as double counters – i.e. the handling of the passengers is made at two different desks, the luggage, however, is transported on a common belt – no constant service rate can be assumed. Such an exact representation is necessary in order to simulate the individual queues at the check-in counters and a realistic transport of the luggage.

The check-in places for the transfer-passengers' luggage operates in principle just like the counters. The difference is that two units are not combined into one functional unit. In addition here a suitable check-in point must be planned in advance for each flight and at a time when it cannot be known if this service position will be free.

The luggage delivery positions do not operate at a constant clearing speed either. Dependent on the waiting routes preceding them and on the number of persons working there, the removal speed fluctuates and can lead to back pressures in the system.

Through detailed simulation with the help of the computer extremely accurate predictions about the behaviour of the system under the most varied conditions can be made. For example, the state of parts of the system, or also of the entire system, can be made available at any time for individual examination. The waiting times of luggage units on the various track sections as well as the loading of the store and main transport routes enable exact conclusions to be drawn about critical spots or bottle-necks in the system. In addition personnel disposition plans at the counters, check-in points for transfer-passengers' luggage and at the delivery positions can be obtained.

The course of individual cases can be followed by means of their characteristic values: flight number, counter where the piece of luggage was checked in, time of entry into the system, time of waiting in a queue, period of stay in early luggage store, time of removal from the system. The number of units which did not leave the system punctually is established for each flight.

A first simulation run for a period of 16 hours with the timetable of 1971 showed that, although short-term congestions may occur in peak periods, and although the early luggage store is at times very full, the maximum transport times of the individual luggage pieces exceeded the estimated average transport period only occasionally. Generally the times were considerably shorter.

As already described, the simulation model was compiled in two stages. The first part was carried out by our data processing department (operations research), the second by the company AEG–Telefunken commissioned by, and in cooperation with Frankfurt Airport.

Fortran IV was chosen as the programming language. The run for the presimulation was done on a Siemens 4004/45 with 256 KB. The run of the main simulation was carried out on a Telefunken computer TR 440 with 256 K words. The latter lasted approx. 5.5 hours for 16 hours real time.

The preparatory work took about a year, since the collecting and editing of the data necessary for the simulation required a greater effort than the programming itself.

Irregularities in the timetable were discovered by comparing the scheduled with the actual times for a period of ten weeks and then evaluated accordingly. In all, about 12 000 flights were covered.

Transfer-passengers' streams were represented by collecting over a period of 2.5 months about 11 000 passenger-transfer messages from the most important airlines of Frankfurt, Deutsche Lufthansa and its handling partners, and Scandinavian Airlines, BEA, PANAM, Air Canada and Swissair. About 80% of all transfer passengers could be assigned on this basis. To determine service times at counters, transfer-passengers' luggage check-in positions and luggage delivery positions, we had to use either estimated or experienced figures. We were able to use the records of the Deutsche Lufthansa and our own data bank to establish the passenger arrival rates and the number of luggage units per passenger.

The considerable outlay we made for our simulation was necessary because no luggage conveyer system of this size had ever been installed before, so we could not fall back on the experiences of other large airports or other service works.

M. Ross, ed., OR '72. North-Holland Publishing Company (1973)

38

SIMPREP,
A COMPUTER MODEL FOR COAL PREPARATION

Un modèle d'ordinateur pour la préparation du charbon

K. GREGORY and C. RUSSELL

National Coal Board, Harrow, England

Abstract. In medium and long term planning, engineers and managers concerned with coal preparation are obliged to undertake lengthy and at times approximate calculations to determine quality, price and other characteristics of future saleable products. Factors influencing these calculations include alternative types of processing equipment, market trends and changes in raw material.

The paper describes the development, validation and some applications of a simple, flexible planning tool − a computer model for coal preparation (SIMPREP) − carried out by the Operational Research Executive and Computer Services of the National Coal Board in cooperation with management staff. Whilst maintaining a facility to process crude information, SIMPREP allows engineers for the first time to deal scientifically and exhaustively with the detailed coal analyses now commonly available. Because of the underlying simplicity of the system, this can be done without the aid of OR specialists.

1. Introduction

A modern coal preparation plant may cost up to £1.5m to build and process 1m tons/year of raw coal to give proceeds of £5m per annum. The National Coal Board has 240 of these plants, although not all of them are so large or so modern. To help with the problems of planning the design and longer term operation of these plants a computer model, SIMPREP, has been built. The model was developed by the operational research executive in conjunction with computer services and Coal Preparation Branches of the National Coal Board. This paper describes the development of SIMPREP together with its validation and some applications.

Section 2 of the paper gives some background of the work; section 3 describes the model; section 4 the validation; section 5 its uses with two applications; and section 6 discusses some of the technicalities of the computer system which have been built around the basic model.

2. Background of the work

2.1. Coal preparation

A coal preparation plant prepares coal straight from the mine (known as run-of-mine coal) into marketable grades. A single plant may contain as many as 50 different items of equipment each with a separate job to do. These pieces of equipment are connected in some order (by conveyor belt or pipes) so that the coal may be washed (extraneous dirt removed), dried, crushed, screened and blended. The different grades of coal produced vary in size consist and quality and are suitable for different markets.

2.2. The role of a coal preparation engineer and the problems of planning

An area coal preparation engineer is responsible for the operation and planning of possibly 20 coal preparation plants. A breakdown at one of these plants can cost £3000 per hour in lost production, hence his time is predominantly spent on operational problems. The planning problems facing the engineer can be broadly summarised by the four questions:

(1) What is the best design for a new or extended plant?

(2) What is the effect of changes in run-of-mine coal on products, proceeds and plant capacities?

(3) What is the effect of market changes on saleable products?

(4) How can proceeds be maximised?

The data available in a major planning exercise will include a full scientific analysis of the coal being mined so that its behaviour in a coal preparation plant may be forecast. This is normally represented by matrices of "washability" data which could be as large as 16 X 10 X 3 and there could be several of these matrices representing different seams of coal. It is clearly impossible for any man, let alone a busy one, to make full use of this data and to do a rigorous planning exercise, considering all possible combinations of equipment within a plant.

It was against this background, therefore, that the Operational Research Executive of the National Coal Board were asked to develop a computer model to help with planning problems.

2.3. The choice of technique

Earlier work by ORE in coal preparation had made use of linear programming and dynamic programming techniques. However, it proved difficult to build a generalised model which could be easily formulated to represent any coal preparation plant using either of these techniques. Essentially the techniques were orientated towards coal flows rather than items of plant equipment. Hence it was very difficult to consider alterations in plant layout.

To overcome this problem, and bearing in mind that many of the engineers' problems are unconnected with optimisation, it was decided to build a deterministic model based on broad mathematical descriptions of the actions of plant items on the coal. This approach had the added advantage of being readily understood by management.

3. The computer program (SIMPREP)

A coal preparation plant can be considered as consisting of different pieces of equipment connected by conveyor belts, along which coal flows. SIMPREP has been built up in the same way. The main types of equipment are represented by sub-models in the program. Individual pieces of equipment are connected by "coal flows": matrices of washability data. A sub-model representing, say, a screen, processes a "coal flow" (matrix of data) and produces

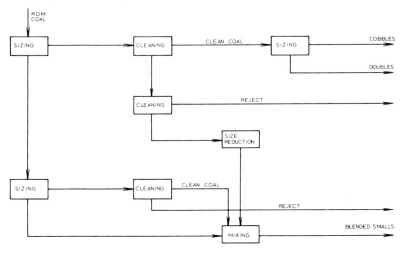

Fig. 1. Flow diagram of a simple coal preparation plant.

two new matrices representing the oversize coal and undersize coal, respectively. These new coal flows are further processed by other sub-models until eventually one or more flows are produced which represent the saleable products.

3.1. Plant layout

Fig. 1 shows the flow diagram for a simple coal preparation plant. The arrows represent coal flows and the boxes represent sub-models. The run-of-mine (ROM) coal is firstly sorted into two size ranges by a screen (represented by the sizing sub-model).

(1) The oversize coal is then cleaned in two stages, the clean coal again being screened to produce two grades of coal, cobbles and doubles for the domestic market. The middlings (inferior quality coal), is crushed (size reduction) and added to the blended smalls (a power station fuel).

Table 1
A typical coal flow. Tons flowing per unit time = 300

| Size (mm) | Overall | | | |
	wt %	ash %	sulphur %	moisture %
150 × 50	6.1	42.1	0.85	2.0
50 × 12.5	30.9	37.0	1.51	2.5
12.5 × 6.4	14.4	37.8	1.18	4.2
6.4 × 0.5	35.6	43.4	1.13	6.1
0.5 × 0	13.0	50.7	1.02	8.3
	100.0			

| Size (mm) | Floats at SG 1.4 | | | Floats at SG 1.8 | | |
	wt %	ash %	sulphur %	wt %	ash %	sulphur %
150 × 50	2.9	3.2	1.10	3.1	6.5	1.30
50 × 12.5	15.6	3.0	1.24	18.2	6.8	1.45
12.5 × 6.4	7.5	2.9	1.33	8.5	6.2	1.50
6.4 × 0.5	16.7	3.3	1.31	21.1	6.1	1.48
0.5 × 0	6.0	4.0	1.21	6.9	7.4	1.27
	48.7			57.8		

(2) The undersize coal from the primary screen is again screened, with the very small coal (which is more difficult and expensive to clean) being added to the blended smalls. The oversize from this screen is cleaned, with the clean coal being added to the blended smalls.

3.2. A coal flow matrix

Any coal flow can be described numerically by a matrix of numbers, each number corresponding to a measurable physical property of the coal. An example of such a matrix is shown in table 1.

Each row of the matrix refers to a particular size range given in the first column. Referring to the second row (for the size range 50 mm $\times$ 12.5 mm) it can be seen that 30.9% of the coal flow lies in that size range and that the range has ash, sulphur and moisture contents of 37.0%, 1.51%, 2.5%, respectively. If all of the size range is placed in a liquid of specific gravity (SG) 1.4, then the amount that floats is 15.6% of the coal flow and this floating part has an ash level of 3.0%. Notice that the floats at 1.8 has a higher ash level, namely 6.8%.

For a full analysis of a coal flow as many as ten specific gravities and sixteen size ranges may be quoted.

3.3. Example of a sub-model

A sub-model operation is probably best explained by taking an example of sizing. Consider a screen taken at 12.5 mm (0.5 inch) and with an efficiency

Table 2
Oversize from screen. Tons flowing per unit time = 129.9

Size (mm)	Overall wt %	ash %	sul- phur %	mois- ture %	Floats at SG 1.4 wt %	ash %	sul- phur %	Floats at SG 1.8 wt %	ash %	sul- phur %
150 × 50	14.1				6.7			7.2		
50 × 12.5	71.5				36.0			42.0		
12.5 × 6.4	5.4	as table 1			2.8	as table 1		3.2	as table 1	
6.4 × 0.5	6.6				3.1			3.9		
0.5 × 0	2.4				1.1			1.3		
	100.0				49.7			57.6		

Coal and power

Table 3
Undersize from screen. Tons flowing per unit time = 170.1

Size (mm)	Overall wt %	ash %	sul-phur %	mois-ture %	Floats at SG 1.4 wt %	ash %	sul-phur %	Floats at SG 1.8 wt %	ash %	sul-phur %
150 × 50	0				0			0		
50 × 12.5	0				0			0		
12.5 × 6.4	21.3	as table 1			11.1	as table 1		12.6	as table 1	
6.4 × 0.5	57.6				27.0			34.2		
0.5 × 0	21.1				9.7			11.2		
	100.0				47.8			58.0		

of 90% (i.e. 90% of 0.5″ coal goes to the undersize, and 10% to the oversize). Allowance is made for the fact that most of the misplaced coal is only just less than 0.5″. The sizing sub-model acts on the matrix shown in table 1 and produces two new matrices table 2 (oversize) and table 3 (undersize). The new weight %'s are expressed as percentages of the coal present in their respective coal flows. The ash, sulphur and moisture contents remain unchanged since only the quantity and not the quality of a coal in a size range is altered.

These 2 new coal flows could then be further processed by, say, the cleaning sub-model (oversize and by sizing again (undersize)) and further coal flows produced.

3.4. The sub-models available

In addition to sizing, there are eight other sub-models available. Six represent processes: cleaning 1 ("partition curve" approach), cleaning 2 ("ad hoc" approach), slurry treatment (for fine coal), mixing, splitting and size reduction. The other two represent pricing and the degradation of coal at any point in the plant. The "partition curve" approach to cleaning was developed after extensive data collection and curve fitting by the Mining Research and Development Establishment. A partition curve relates the probability of coal of a certain size and specific gravity "floating" in the separator with a certain reference specific gravity. Use of these curves requires extensive washability information on the original input to the preparation plant, but in the absence of such information there is an alternative, simple model — "ad hoc".

3.5. Data requirements

Each sub-model is written in a general manner, e.g., the sizing sub-model can represent any type of screen. To represent an individual screen, the screen size and its efficiency need to be stated. For cleaning (partition curve) the main data requirements are the nominal specific gravity and the type of washbox.

Similarly, for each sub-model, a few numbers transform from the general to the particular.

3.6. Data output

A coal flow matrix may be printed out at any point in the program. The most important coal flows are those which represent saleable products. In addition to tonnages, size consist, and ash, sulphur and moisture contents (both for each size range and overall), the price/ton and proceeds may be given for each product.

4. Model validation

4.1. Data

In order to test the validity of the model a full scale scientific test was carried out at one coal preparation plant. The particular model of the plant was more complex than the one shown in fig. 1 and contained 18 sub-models. The test was carried out over a period of one shift when 1500 tons of coal were being washed. 830 samples, weighing in total 14 tons, were taken at 17 points. The samples were analysed to give extended washability data for the run-of-mine coal at a point below ground, for the input to the washing unit and for the products of the plant (including the discard). More limited analyses were carried out for the other sampling points within the plant.

4.2. Method of approach

The method of approach was to feed the run-of-mine washability data into the model together with first estimates of process parameters. Part of the other data was compared with predictions of the model and adjustments were made to the process parameters until a reasonable fit was obtained. A sensitivity analysis revealed that in some cases estimates of these parameters were adequate and gave results within sampling errors. In other cases accurate fits to the data were required. The next step was to compare predicted data at all points in the plant with the scientific data.

4.3. Goodness to fit

The model predicted the correct tonnages, ash and moisture for each plant product and for the discard to within 5% in some cases, 1% in others (sulphur was not an important variable at this mine). The fit to the data was considered good.

5. Possible uses for SIMPREP and an application

SIMPREP may be used to determine:

(1) What plant parameters are required to maximise proceeds?

(2) Can the existing plant meet different marketing constraints? If not, what alternations are required?

(3) Can the existing plant cope with a change in the raw coal input? How does this affect products and proceeds?

(4) When new plant is being considered: What are the effects of serving different markets? What is the best plant configuration? What plant capacities are required? What is the difference in products and proceeds if the washing is done by Baum boxes or dense medium cyclone? How susceptible would the plant be to a changing feed?

5.1. A planning application

A proposal to build a new coal preparation plant for the production of a 1.25″ × 0 coking coal involved the evaluation of five alternative design schemes under a strict constraint on the ash content of the product. Other constraints included the desirability, but not the necessity, to supply a well-established domestic market. The schemes were based on combinations of the following choices open to the planners:

(1) Type of washing equipment.

(2) Special treatment of very fine coal or not.

(3) Separate washing of large and small coal or size reduction of large coal.

(4) Domestic market to be supplied or given up.

Within each of these basic choices there were several subordinate questions on plant settings. Without the aid of SIMPREP the task of accurately calculating proceeds from these alternatives would have been impossible. Twenty runs were required taking up approximately thirty minutes in execution time (using an IBM 360/65).

Each scheme considered had a different capital investment associated with it and with accurate proceeds available it was possible for management to conduct a discounted cash flow exercise for the most likely schemes.

6. The systematised version of SIMPREP

SIMPREP is intended to be used for line management who are not necessarily familiar with OR or computer techniques. As a result any package built

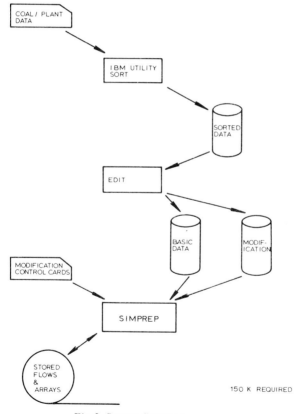

Fig. 2. System flowchart.

round the basic program would have to ensure that minor errors in input data be easily tracked down and that input should be kept to a minimum by having the facility to store information on coal flows and flow diagrams. This facility of storage means that "later-date" inputs consist of two or three punch cards.

There are four main programs in the system: SORT, EDIT, UPDATE and SIMPREP. There are two permanent files held on magnetic tape or disc: the MASTER file and SOLUTION file. The MASTER file stores all the input data for the original job and the SOLUTION file stores all the flows and related data which are calculated from the original input. The EDIT program checks the output from the SORT, and rejects invalid cards. Assuming an earlier MASTER file is already in existence the UPDATE program creates a new MASTER file from the earlier one and the cards that have been accepted by the EDIT. The EDIT allows a transfer of information from one project to another. Thus a simple instruction will allow the engineer to discover the effect of washing coal from a particular colliery at several preparation plants in the area.

The system flow chart is shown in fig. 2.

7. Conclusion

Apart from mathematical and programming technicalities associated with the operation of particular items of equipment, SIMPREP is an unsophisticated deterministic model. The great strength of the model lies in its simplicity: it uses calculations which management readily understand; it produces results which are immediately testable by common sense and experience; it can be used by managers themselves.

The area of uncertainty in coal preparation, as illustrated by the list of possible uses for the model, has been considerably reduced and it is confidently expected that SIMPREP will become a standard tool in planning exercises.

Acknowledgements

The authors would like to acknowledge the assistance given during the development of SIMPREP by NCB Computer Services, Headquarters Coal Preparation Department, Area Coal Preparation and Scientific Departments and the Mining Research and Development Establishment. We would also like to thank the other members of the Operational Research Executive who contributed to the success of the project, in particular D.A.V. Edmonds and G.A. Parkin for their assistance and advice throughout the development of the model, and in the preparation of this paper.

Any view expressed are those of the authors and are not necessarily those of the National Coal Board.

DETERMINING THE COAL WAGON REQUIREMENTS IN THE RHENISH LIGNITE MINES

Calcul du nombre nécessaire de wagonnets de charbon dans les mines de lignite Rhenanes

H. MÜLLER-OEHRING

Rheinische Braunkohlenwerke, Cologne, Germany

Abstract. Raw lignite is transported by means of belt conveyors and railways from the open cast sites to the power stations and briquetting plants. Within the next few years the power stations will be enlarged and the excavator's capacities increased. The only change in the transportation facilities involves the possible acquisition of additional wagons costing 100 000 DM each. It is essential to determine how many will be required up to 1976 subject to these conditions: (1) One fixed excavator's capacity shall be fully used. This excavator is dredging coal and overburden in changing proportions. Thus the quantity of coal delivered by it varies. (2) Supplies to coal consumers, must be guaranteed even in cases of breakdown.

Linear programming was used to determine the optimum distribution of coal for each of the various operating conditions, taking into account changing proportions between coal and overburden at that mentioned excavator for every single year. The duration of operations proved to be Erlang distributions. Their parameters differ depending on whether it is a case of loading, unloading, waiting before signals or travel. In the latter case average speed increases with distance. Previous data were used to calculate the present reliability of supply and then to form the basis on which operating conditions could be simulated for several years into the future. Several different simulations were performed with varying assumptions about the coal–overburden ratio and the waiting times per train. Out of all requirements calculated those were selected which required the fewest wagons having regard to all the technical restrictions. The method used required that 26 fewer wagons (13%) be bought than was suggested by the conventional mode of analysis thus affecting a saving of 2.6 million DM.

This paper is a new assessment of an earlier investigation [1] into opencast lignite mining in the Rhineland. The earlier study sought to minimize total costs of exploitation, transport and tipping associated with the various types of overburden and lignite. It was formulated as an nth dimension transport problem with additional restrictions and solved by means of the "Simplex-algorithm". The new assessment seeks, instead, to determine the necessary number of coal wagons for two opencast sites. It consists of a one-dimensional transport problem with additional restrictions solved by linear programming and connected to a simulation section.

The abundance of lignite in the German Federal Republic provides ample means of heating at low prices. In 1970, it provided 17% of the total production of primary energy and had a share of 27% of the production of electric power at all thermal power stations in the Federal Republic. The favourable heating costs gave power stations using lignite an average of 7000 h/a running time, compared to an average of 4900 h/a for all thermal power stations. 75% of the lignite output went to produce electric power; the balance to briquette factories. The Rhineland accounted for 86% of the lignite output and 89% of the briquette production. Here an installed capacity of 7 700 MW provides more than 87% of the total capacity of all lignite power stations in the Federal Republic. This figure will reach 11 500 MW by 1975.

Lignite mining in the Rhineland is located west of Cologne in a triangle whose sides are about 40 km long with four of the five opencast mines between the cities of Brühl and Grevenbroich and one north of Eschweiler. Their combined output, in the region of 90–100 million tons annually supplies power stations and briquette factories in the immediate vicinity. Thus, the distances over which low-grade raw lignite has to be transported are comparatively short.

Coal is, however, only a part of the total output. The overburden lying above the coal has to removed and tipped. This is because up to the present, no technique has been developed which would make it more economical to extract raw lignite from underground mines.

Opencast extraction of overburden and coal is carried out on several levels, one above the other. The bucket-wheel excavators used can each handle up to 100 000 m^3 a day. Thus, in less than five minutes one of them can excavate the volume of a family-home. Machines of corresponding capacity (stackers) are used for tipping of the overburden. The vertical distance between two levels which can be up to 40 m, is determined by the geological conditions and the operating height of the excavators. The height of a tip is given by the machine construction, the combination of soils transported and the level of the rebuilt earth surface.

Train and conveyor belt systems are used from the excavators to the coal consumers and to the stackers. These two different means of transportation are used partly in tandem and partly in conjunction. The rail wagons used – mostly standard gauge with up to 10 times the capacity of normal freight wagons – travel on a network more than 400 km long. The conveyor systems have a belt width of up to 2 m and operate at a speed of over 20 km/h. Their total length is more than 100 km.

One of these train or conveyor routes starts from each excavator. It joins other routes coming from other excavators at the next signal-box area or belt junction point. The routes branch off again and join other routes, until one route finally reaches each receiver. Thus, the transport connections between sender and receiver form a network in which there is a choice of various routes for the transportation from a particular excavator to a particular receiver. Sections of these routes are used in common. Fig. 1 provides a highly simplified illustration. A load to be carried from sender A to receiver A' can either follow sections 1, 2 and 3, or sections 1, 4, 7, 5 and 3. Similarly two routes go from B to B', from A to B' and from B to A'. Sections 2, 4, 5 and 7 can be used for transports from each sender to each receiver. Sections 1, 3, 6 and 8, on the other hand, are allocated to particular senders or receivers.

About 30 km of railway connects all opencast mines, power stations, and briquette factories in the main mining area. In this way, each excavator is connected to each power station and briquette factory. This layout guarantees maximum security of supply.

Our task was to determine how many coal wagons would be needed in the two northern opencast sites in the years up to the year 1976. This is no

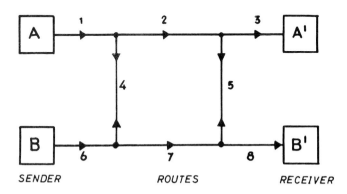

Fig. 1. Scheme of possible transports in network-like structure of connections.

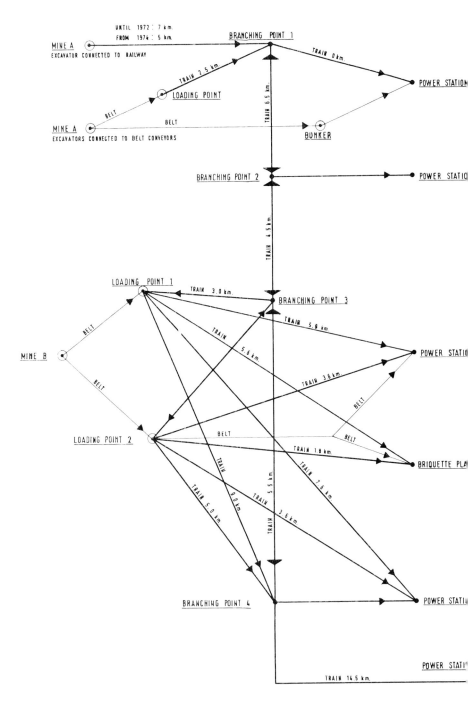

Fig. 2.

optimization project in its narrowest sense, but rather one which required that the situations in the years up to 1976 be simulated.

Coal wagons will be needed to transport the raw lignite from the excavators at the opencast sites, or from the loading installations to the bunkers of the coal consumers, i.e., the power stations and briquette factories, as long as conveyor belts are not used for that work. In fig. 2, you can see the available connections between the two opencast sites and coal consumers I to VI*. The coal consumers are provided with raw coal bunkers to bridge them over Sundays and holidays. These bunkers must be replenished on resumption of the coal supply. In general, we can assume that the requirements of the relevant bunker characterize the requirements of a consumer. However, the bunker of power station I, which is supplied by a conveyor belt system, can only supply one part of the power station with coal and therefore must be given special consideration. Another special case is the trainloading excavator at site A which extracts both overburden and coal in the proportions found on the site. For operational reasons this excavator should be employed to its fullest capacity.

The changing operating conditions at the opencast sites and at the coal consumers mean that the circuit times of the trains have random rather than fixed values. Thus there are no fixed timetables so that internal transport is irregular. However, all available techniques are used for security and speed of the train journeys, track diagram switching, road gates, locomotive radio-contact.

Table 1 gives the daily capacity and requirements of the coal consumers from 1970 onward. Power stations II and III will be extended during this period. Capacity at site A will be increased parallel to this. The train loading excavator at this site is shown with four different capacities in each year. They represent different assumptions about the proportion of coal in the total volume excavated, and are based on alternative forecasts of the changing conditions which may occur as the mining progresses.

Unfortunately, no operation runs exactly according to plan. Transport capacity must be sufficient to cope with the inevitable disruptions. Special

---

* The actual conditions have been simplified as much as this project would allow. The conveyor belt installations, for example, have been summarized. Railway triangles and circuits have not been illustrated, but their distances have been kept. At the junctions shown, branch-offs or rejoining points of transportation routes are given. The opencast and transport installations whose capacity must be taken into account in the calculation are marked with circles. The arrows show the possible transport directions on individual route sections.

Table 1
Typical illustration of annual coal-capacities in the mines and coal requirements
in 10^3 t/d [a]

	1970	1971	1972
Excavator connected to railway, mine A	15/30/45/60	15/30/45/60	15/30/45/6(
Loading point, mine A	60	60	60
Excavators connected to belts, mine A	150	150	150
Belts K 11/12, mine A	60	60	60
Bunker 2, power station I	60	60	60
Loading points 1 + 3, mine B	200	200	200
Loading point 2, mine B	100	100	100
Power station I	80	80	80
Power station II	0	0	27
Power station III	36	47	47
Briquette plant IV	20	20	20
Power station V	30	30	30
Power station VI	33	29	21

[a] The table gives the years 1970 to 1972. Similar estimates are available from 1972 onwar

attention must be given to those which, by their nature and length, could cause bottlenecks and breakdowns in total Federal power supplies. A survey revealed eight situations to be critical. Among these were the failure of the belt from site A to the bunker of power station I, the blocking of the track section between junction 2 and 3, and the disruption of loading point 2 at site B.

A conventional type analysis compared these eight disruptive situations with the normal situation and found that wagon requirements were greatest when loading point 2 at site B was out of order. Conventional procedures for the calculation of the wagon requirements, based on the average circuit times of the trains and on the daily coal requirements of consumers (drawn from the annual planning), showed that 200 coal wagons would be needed in 1973 and 1974 and that 213 wagons would be needed in 1976, compared with 172 wagons at present on the sites. 28 wagons, therefore, must be bought by 1973 at a cost of 2.8 million DM. The size of the costs involved justified the somewhat more difficult simulation analysis being undertaken. This will now be described.

Linear programming was used to minimize the ton-kilometers involved. Due to the four different assumptions about the proportion of coal excavated, set out in table 2, the relatively small matrix of 31 columns and 22 lines

Table 2

Optimal coal distribution in normal case with full employment of train loading excavator at mine A in 10^3 t/d [a]

Overburden:coal ratio	1970				1971				1972			
	3:1	1:1	1:3	coal only	3:1	1:1	1:3	coal only	3:1	1:1	1:3	coal only
Train loading excavator mine A to power station I	15	30	45	60	15	30	45	60	15	30	45	60
Loading point mine A to power station I	5	–	–	–	5	–	–	–	5	–	–	–
Belts mine A to power station I	(60)	(50)	(35)	(20)	(60)	(50)	(35)	(20)	(60)	(50)	(35)	(20)
Train loading excavator mine A to power station II	–	–	–	–	–	–	–	–	–	–	–	–
Loading point 1 mine B to power station II	–	–	–	–	–	–	–	–	27	27	27	27
Loading point 2 mine B to power station III	(36)	(36)	(36)	(36)	(47)	(47)	(47)	(47)	(47)	(47)	(47)	(47)
Loading point 2 mine B to briquette plant IV	(20)	(20)	(20)	(20)	(20)	(20)	(20)	(20)	(20)	(20)	(20)	(20)
Loading point 1 mine B to briquette plant IV	–	–	–	–	–	–	–	–	–	–	–	–
Loading point 2 mine B to power station V	30	30	30	30	30	30	30	30	30	30	30	30
Loading point 1 mine B to power station V	–	–	–	–	–	–	–	–	–	–	–	–
Loading point 2 mine B to power station VI	14	14	14	14	3	3	3	3	3	3	3	3
Loading point 1 mine B to power station VI	19	19	19	19	26	26	26	26	18	18	18	18

[a] Illustration for years 1970 to 1972.

had to be worked out four times for each of the seven years, or 28 times altogether. This gave the optimal method of transport for one of the nine given cases (i.e. normal or disruptive). The transition from one case to the next was made by setting capacity allotted to one installation at zero for all years, and by entering the values given in table 2 for the aggregate which has previously zero. The normal case was calculated for each year under two conditions: (1) the train loading excavator at site A must be used to capacity, (2) the utilisation (if any) of this excavator must not exceed its capacity. In the eight critical situations full use of any piece of equipment was deemed subsidiary to the task of supplying all consumers adequately, so that the train loading excavator need not be fully employed.

Again, as was the case with the conventional calculation, simulation showed that the failure of loading point 2 at site B was the disruption which required the greatest number of wagons. Here, the range in wagon requirements (rather than the total figure) was calculated using the total number of ton-kilometers shown to be necessary.

The remaining simulation analysis could now be limited to three cases:

(1) normal case with full employment of the train loading excavator at site A,

(2) normal case without full employment of that one excavator, and

(3) failure of loading point 2 at site B.

The following data were available and could be used without conversion:

(1) engineers' data on the average times for loading, tipping, waiting and travelling per train circuit from each loading point to each tipping point,

(2) the corresponding minimum values of these times,

(3) the transported quantities from each loading point to each tipping point, and

(4) the capacity per coal train as ascertained from past data.

The number of circuiting trains (Z), to which reserves are to be added, is calculated using the formula

$$Z = \sum_i \frac{U_i L_i}{t_i I}.$$

If subscript i represents route i then for that route: U_i is the circuit time in minutes, L_i the daily tonnage of coal to be transported, t_i the total time (in minutes) available each day to transport the quantity of coal L_i,* and I the train capacity in tons.

---

* t_i is the total time (for several circuits) available for the transport of coal via route i. In general it amounts to 24 hours per day. In case of the train loading excavator there are

Probability distributions for loading, tipping, waiting and travelling times were constructed using the average and minimum times, from which one could read the probability that the actual time would be less than a particular time. A 90% guarantee of supply, considered adequate for consumers, was taken as a basis on which to determine circuit times and from these, the number of wagons required. The result was unsatisfactory. Wagon requirements were 30 to 40% higher than in the results of the conventional calculation. Instead of an expenditure of 2.8 million DM, the figure was now 3.5 million DM.

The mistake was soon found. The average times given by the engineers already contained safety margins, whose extent could no longer be determined. Accordingly direct measurements had to be resorted to. For nearly two weeks a total of 47 train circuits at both opencast sites was registered in detail. The data were evaluated separately by site. The statistical time distributions obtained made it reasonable to assume that the ideal distributions were "Erlang distributions", as is frequently the case with time distributions of real events, and especially irregular internal transport.

The time distribution for loading a train has the same parameters for both opencast sites, in spite of independent and separate recordings and evaluations. The average values almost coincide with the figures given by the engineers. The Erlang distribution in fig. 3 is a total frequency curve, which is easier to construct and interpret than the simple frequency curve.

The Erlang distribution of tipping times (fig. 4) differed from one site to the other due to a difference in the tipping mechanism. The average value of the time distribution was about 30% lower than that originally given by the engineers.

The distribution of the waiting times (fig. 5) deviated most from the engineers' figures with measured averages about 300% above the estimated values. Thus, depending on distance, waiting times were from 30 to 60% of the total train circuit time. For this reason it was advisable to vary the waiting times in the remaining calculations, using first the full, then 3/4, then a half and finally 1/4 of the measured waiting times. These last times, which correspond to the engineers' figures, may be considered practicable for a well-developed circuit organization.

special conditions. If there is a proportion of one part overburden to one part coal the excavator needs the half time of the day for excavating the overburden. So the loading and transport of the coal from this excavator to the receivers has to be done within the other half of the day, i.e. within 12 hours.

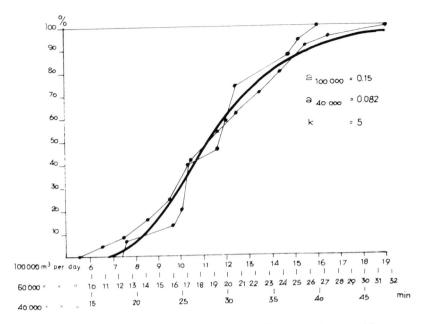

Fig. 3. Safety margin for loading quicker than shown, in mines A and B.

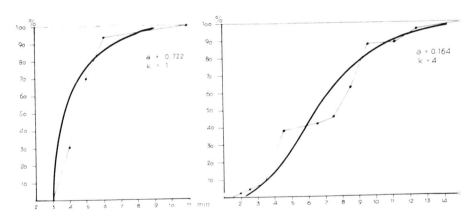

Fig. 4. Safety margin for tipping quicker than shown, mine A (left), mine B (right).

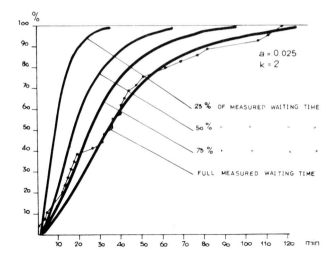

Fig. 5. Safety margin for waiting less than shown (stationary railroad).

An intermediate calculation was necessary, to determine the time distribution of pure journey-times. The calculation had to ascertain the rate at which the average speed of the trains increases, as the distance between loading point and tipping point increases. A straight regression was made, from which a straight line could be drawn to relate time to minimum distance and from that, the random time distribution.

By combining the four time-distributions and the straight regression line we have the distributions for the total duration of individual train circuits between the various end points of the routes. Now if we know the required safety margin (level of probability) train requirements can be calculated using the formula already given. The safety margin to be used was the one which existed in the past. Again, data was collected and a past safety-margin of 82.5% established. The train circuit times which could be achieved with this margin of safety were entered in the formula (see table 3). The quantities to be entered in the formula are the optimal quantities of the relevant year over route i for each of the three cases, i.e., normal operation with and without full employment of the train loading excavator, and the special situation at site B. These were each estimated for the four different capacities of the excavator. Furthermore, the number of trains was determined for the whole measured waiting time, for 3/4 of this waiting time, for the half and for 1/4 of the measured waiting time. In this way, a total of up to 48 different requirement figures were produced for each year corresponding to the 48 sim-

Table 3
Distances and circuit times with 82.5% safety and varied waiting times

		Circuit distance (km)	Circuit time with 82.5% safety in min	
			with full measured waiting times	with 25% of measured waiting times
Train loading excavator mine A to power station I	till 1972	14.0	175.0	87.0
	1973	14.0	165.5	77.5
	from 1974	10.0	159.1	71.1
Train loading excavator mine A to power station II	till 1972	31.0	202.6	114.6
	1973	31.0	193.1	105.1
	from 1974	27.0	183.6	95.6
Loading point mine A to power station I	till 1972	5.0	118.1	70.1
	from 1973	5.0	108.6	60.6
Loading point mine A to power station II	till 1972	22.0	154.6	106.6
	from 1973	22.0	136.1	88.1
Loading points 2 and 3 mine B to	power station II	19.0	131.3	83.3
	power station III	7.2	112.2	64.2
	briquette plant IV	3.6	106.3	58.3
	power station V	7.2	112.2	64.2
	power station VI	44.0	171.8	123.8
Loading point 1 mine B to	power station II	19.0	131.3	83.3
	power station III	11.8	119.6	71.6
	briquette plant IV	11.2	118.6	70.6
	power station V	15.2	125.1	77.1
	power station VI	48.0	178.3	130.3

Table 4
Number of coal wagons required in mines A and B 1971–1976

		1971	1972	1973	1974	1975	1976
Full waiting time	normal case 1 a)	252	278	343	330	330	369
	normal case 2 b)	174	200	187	161	174	200
	critical case c)	239	265	291	278	291	317
75% of measured waiting time	normal case 1	226	252	304	278	278	317
	normal case 2	148	174	161	148	161	187
	critical case	213	226	252	252	252	278
50% of measured waiting time	normal case 1	187	213	252	226	226	252
	normal case 2	135	148	135	122	135	161
	critical case	187	200	200	200	213	239
25% of measured waiting time	normal case 1	148	161	200	187	187	213
	normal case 2	109	122	122	109	122	135
	critical case	148	161	174	174	174	200

a) Full employment of train loading excavator in mine A.
b) Without full employment of train loading excavator in mine A.
c) Failure of loading point 2 at mine B.

ulations. From these requirement figures up to 12 were selected by choosing from each set of four assumptions about the ratio of coal to overburden the one which required the most wagons (table 4). Practicable requirements can now be estimated from these twelve using certain criteria:

We must take into account that at the time of calculation, 172 wagons were available. Since no new wagons could be obtained by 1971, in that year we must dispense with requiring the full employment of the train loading excavator and with requiring certainty of coal supply should loading point 2 at site B fail. Under these circumstances 174 wagons suffice, so that two more wagons would have to be obtained. By 1972 delays occurring during the train circuits should have been reduced by 25%. In that year the 174 coal wagons already available are ample under the same conditions. Indeed, should the conditions of 1972 persist, this number of wagons would be sufficient up until 1975. In fact, it even offers the necessary assurance of supply in the special situation of the failure at site B. When the emergency occurs, it is merely necessary to reduce the waiting times per train circuit to the time given by the engineers. Full employment of the train loading excavator cannot, however, be achieved entirely with 174 wagons. The simulation shows that not until 1976 it is necessary either to obtain additional wagons, or to reduce the waiting times further. Additional wagons will then guarantee supply even in an emergency. If we consider, however, that a new planning environment will come to be by 1976, it will be wiser to carry out a new simulation calculation well before 1976.

Finally, let me summarize the way in which the result deviates from the conventional calculation: According to the original calculation 200 coal wagons were needed for 1973 and 1974. Of these, an additional 28 had to be obtained at a cost of 2.8 million DM. The simulation calculation showed that one can get by with 174 coal wagons, i.e. an additional 2 wagons costing 200 000 DM. In this way, investments of 2.6 million DM can be deferred until 1975 and only 7% of the originally calculated investment is made. On the other hand, dispensing with 26 coal wagons clearly requires a reduction of waiting times during break-down situations.

Reference

[1] Entwicklung eines L.P. Modells zur Behandlung von Forderaufgaben im Braunkohle Bergbau, reviewed in: Intern. Abstracts Opns. Res. (1970) 131.

M. Ross, ed., OR'72. North-Holland Publishing Company (1973)

40

OPERATIONAL GAMING IN THE PLANNING OF THE GEOLOGICALLY TROUBLED COLLIERY

Jeu opérationnel dans la planification de la houillère sujet à des complications géologiques

D.M. HAWES*

R.J. Travers Morgan and Partners, Milsons Pt. N.S.W., Australia

Abstract. Uncertainty about the location of hazards in the coal measures worked by a colliery can cause producing coalfaces to be halted unexpectedly, resulting in serious financial losses. To reduce this risk of losing output, management may either buy information through exploratory tunnelling, provide insurance in the form of spare face capacity, or accept production variability and maintain supplies from surface stocks. Each of these policies is expensive and the traditional planning procedures, which are more concerned with individual faces than with the colliery as a whole, have proved to be unsuitable for developing a robust and economic mining strategy.

This paper describes an improved means of colliery planning, based on an operational gaming approach, which was developed to overcome the problem of imperfect geological knowledge. Alternative mining strategies are prepared by the colliery management and these are evaluated by simulating their operation (by hand) against patterns of geological hazards, produced on the basis of information gained in surrounding workings. The manager acts as decision-maker in this process, the nature of "future" geology being unknown to him until hazards are encountered by faces or tunnels. Deficiencies in a strategy can thus be identified and the strategy modified and retested. The related problem of monitoring colliery performance for control purposes is also discussed.

The issues are illustrated by means of a case study.

1. Introduction

This paper describes the application of operational gaming to the design and evaluation of mining strategies for the geologically troubled colliery. The

* Formerly: National Coal Board, Harrow, England

problems of developing a suitable scheme are complex, involving the deployment of resources between productive and tunnelling functions and the selection of an evolutionary pattern in order to secure the balanced physical growth of the colliery through time. The application is novel, both for the structure of the problem and for the fact that operational gaming is integrated into a routine planning procedure.

A coal seam may be thought of as a two dimensional plane containing hazards which act as barriers to producing faces. Although the overall pattern and intensity of disturbances can be anticipated from information gained in previous workings, the location of hazards within an area will not be known until mining operations there are well-advanced. The unforeseen discovery of an impediment by a face can result in expensive production losses and also will usually necessitate the redeployment of resources, rescheduling of activities and modification to the intended layout of workings. To avoid or reduce such losses, management may choose a strategy which incorporates exploratory and/or insurance components in order to ensure the availability of sufficient productive capacity at all times. Thus the manager must decide the broad deployment of resources between the different seams available and for each seam, the allocation of men and machines between the driving of tunnels which provide insurance or advance information, and face operations which provide the coal. He must decide which areas of the seam should be worked, the sequence and method of working, and thus where and when roads should be driven. Frequently the choice will be constrained by such factors as manpower availability, previous actions and technical factors such as depth of the seam. Alternatively, production losses could be accepted if proved cheaper, supplies being drawn from surface stocks. The costs of these policies and the sums to be won or lost dictate that full use be made of the available geological, mining and financial data in evolving and evaluating suitable alternatives if a robust yet economic scheme is to emerge.

The remainder of the paper is divided into four sections, viz.:

(1) Description of the colliery and its geological environment.

(2) Statement of the problem and its characteristics.

(3) Description of the gaming approach.

(4) Monitoring of colliery operations.

A brief case study is given at the end of the paper to illustrate the type of issue involved and to demonstrate the application of the gaming approach and the nature of the "answers" produced.

2. The colliery and its geological environment

The modern coalface is highly mechanised, normally costing about £250 000 to equip with roof-supports, cutting machine and conveyors. In essence, it is a line some two hundred yards long which sweeps through the seam, the overlying strata being allowed to collapse once the equipment has passed. The ends of the face are linked to the arterial roads housing the trunk services (transport, ventilation, power, etc.) by two gateroads which flank the panel being extracted and provide access for men and materials and transport for the coal. The main features of the (advancing longwall) face are illustrated in fig. 1. Typically, a colliery might have only three or four working faces and produce a million tons of coal per year, so earning £6 million in revenue. As the major part of costs is fixed, the profitability of the colliery is extremely sensitive to the extended loss of production from a face.

Ideally, the seams to be worked would be level, unbroken and consistent in height and composition. In practice, fluctuations in thickness and constitution occurred during deposition, subsequent stresses in the strata have displaced, tilted and otherwise distorted the seam, whilst volcanic activity has substituted hard rock for coal in some areas. Such impediments certainly

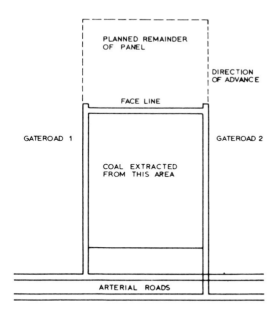

Fig. 1. Essential features of a coalface.

affect the positioning of workings (for an example, see the case study) and unless adequate precautions are taken, can cause unexpected losses of production. It is certain that geological troubles cost the N.C.B. many million pounds per annum in lost revenue.

To reduce the impact of geology on production, the manager may:

(1) develop additional faces so as to provide spare capacity,

(2) attempt to explore and map the seam by driving exploratory tunnels in advance of production operations.

In both cases, roadways costing up to £100 per yard are driven earlier than would otherwise be necessary (representing several £ 00 000's invested), and to provide spare capacity also implies under-utilisation of costly capital equipment. Exploration may also require the driving of additional roadways.

Exploration by the advanced drivage of arterial roads assists in the improved siting of faces whilst pre-drivage of gateroads makes it possible to identify when faces will be stopped, so enabling replacement capacity to be scheduled. By driving additional arterial roads, a fuller picture of the seam is obtained (at a correspondingly greater cost) although this serves to constrain future production operations, roads acting as barriers to faces.

Clearly, the amount of information gathered by a tunnel may depend on the direction of drivage (the aim is to find rather than avoid hazards), although the choice is often restricted by technical factors such as the inclination of the seam. The value of the information gained depends on its timing; if a road is not sufficiently far advanced, information will arrive too late to be of use.

3. The problem

The cost of mining coal is inevitably increased by the presence of hazards in the seam. If their position is known in advance, this increase can be held to a minimum. If, however, there is uncertainty about the location of impediments, it is necessary to pay a premium for insurance or exploration in order to maintain supplies. The problem facing management is thus to minimise this premium, the price of uncertainty, by choosing the policy best suited to the colliery and its environment. The strategy chosen must take account of historical actions and of any constraints on resources and their deployment. Possible strategies must also be viewed in the broader context of area and national programmes for production, stocking and marketing.

The problem is characterised by the following features:

(1) There is partial knowledge about the likely intensity and pattern of hazards in an area, but not of their location.

(2) Collieries are complex, growing in space through time and producing both coal and information.

(3) The ability to maintain output depends upon the balance between productive and tunnelling activities and their relative positions in space and time.

(4) The decision processes are complex and involve the consideration of many factors of varying importance together with inferential procedures incorporating the latest geological information.

(5) The impact of today's decision may be felt within a few weeks (production decisions) or not for several years (development decisions).

Fortunately, this situation differs from many other search problems in so much as nature "played her hand" long ago and cannot respond to the exploratory activity undertaken, thus making it possible to chart the "future".

On tackling the problem, the first difficulty lies in making use of the available geological knowledge. This information takes the form of (imperfect and incomplete) data gathered from roads and faces already driven in the vicinity. To draw inferences about the pattern and intensity of disturbances in the new area, there must exist some means of analysing this information. Hazards take the form of both lines and areas and for fault lines alone, it is necessary to consider length, direction, throw, curvature and spacing. It is thus difficult to prepare a numerical description of such a pattern to take full account of the factors affecting mining operations, although basic summary statistics have been devised.

The second difficulty lies in assessing the impact of geology on the colliery. When one face is stopped, the ability to maintain production depends upon the position and manning-up of other faces and developments at that point in time. The full impact of such interference can only be measured if the long run implications of the short-term expedient are examined. For example, the loss of a face has frequently resulted in a subsequent reduction of effort on long-term arterial development work (to provide extra production shifts), the impact of this change of balance not being reflected in output for a year or more. Thus in the evaluation of a strategy, it is necessary to examine the working of the colliery as a whole over an extended period rather than consider its individual faces in isolation.

Several possible means of tackling the problem have been considered. Only an operational gaming approach, however, can make full use of all available geological information and permit realistic modelling of the operation of the colliery. Other approaches considered, including decision trees and computer simulation, were unsuitable for modelling the complex decisions and inferential process involved, whilst the nature of the information involved clearly eliminated analytical methods.

4. An operational gaming approach

The planning approach adopted is essentially a simulation against nature in which the colliery manager or planner acts as decision maker and interpreter of strategy. Nature is represented by a set of conjectural maps of geological hazards, prepared by the colliery geologist so as to reflect the likely range of possible structures for the area. These must be consistent with the intensity and pattern of disturbances as observed in previous workings in the vicinity (numerical descriptors and visual pattern recognition), and must agree with the actual positions of those impediments found by roads and faces bordering the area.

The process is broadly as follows. The manager first states the initial strategy to be evaluated, specifying resources and their deployment, performance levels and a skeletal layout design. The working of this scheme is then simulated by hand, on paper against one from the set of conjectural geologies. The position of hazards is not made known to the manager until they are found by faces or roads, whereupon he must decide the future of the affected unit, and if necessary, redeploy resources and modify the layout. The information so gained is available for this and subsequent decisions as it would be in the real-life situation. The set-up and mechanics of this procedure are described in outline below.

One of the geologies is placed on a glass-topped tracing table (illuminated from below) and a print showing the present position of bordering workings is correctly positioned above it. A blank sheet of tracing material is placed on top of these and all three sheets are firmly secured together. The geology is then only visible with the table-light turned on. Apart from the planner or manager, a second person is required to act as assessor to ensure that the rules are obeyed and to record the progress of the roads and faces.

The main steps are then:

(1) With the light off, the manager details on the tracing sheet all development and production work expected to be completed in the next period (generally of three or six months).

(2) With the light on and the manager absent, projected workings are examined by the assessor to see if they have encountered any hazards. If necessary, the manager must amend the plan, a further examination being carried out to check that no other troubles have been found. Once finalised,

all work completed is firmly drawn in and the monthly advance of faces is recorded. All hazards encountered are shown on the tracing (at the points where they have been found), this information then being available for subsequent use.

(3) Steps (1) and (2) are repeated until the required number of years has been simulated.

The choice of a time-based rather than event-based procedure was dictated by the difficulties of finding the first event, the frequency of events (finding hazards) and by comparison, the relative ease of modifying workings on a time-based model.

When completed, monthly outputs are calculated by the conversion of the advances of roads and faces into tons. Thus a picture is obtained of the likely level and variation of output over the period covered by the game. The process is repeated for different geologies and other strategies as is appropriate.

A series of runs for a strategy will indicate its robustness and will serve to identify its weaknesses, so permitting improvements to be made. Alternative strategies can then be costed, and whilst the approach does not necessarily find an optimal strategy, it does permit decisions to be made on the basis of a considerable amount of synthetic operating experience. Suitable alternatives can then be considered in relation to broader objectives as expressed in area of national plans.

For the colliery manager, the approach provides a plan to which he can now work: a broad layout for workings, resource requirements and their deployment, rates of drivage, etc., are all specified. Additionally, the importance of specific roadway developments or other activities to the overall growth of the colliery can be highlighted; these can then be assigned a priority status. As with other gaming exercises, this approach also has an educational or learning value. The manager can condense many years operating experience into a few hours, making it possible to link decision and effect and permitting alternative courses to be explored.

This approach was developed and refined in a series of practical applications at geologically troubled collieries, each with slightly different problems and circumstances. It is now part of the routine planning procedure for several major collieries and continuing effort is being devoted to extending the implementation so far achieved.

5. Monitoring colliery operations

As workings progress into the new area, the data so generated must be used to check both the validity of the assumptions about geology and the performances on which the strategy is founded, and to track implementation of the scheme. A suitable monitoring system must be capable of:

(1) monitoring the operation of the colliery as a whole rather than closely specified sub-tasks,

(2) transforming the physical positions of workings and their progress into a statement about the balance between production and tunnelling operations and future ability to produce,

(3) being operated and comprehended by existing staff.

The approach adopted makes use of information collected in the gaming studies to provide a means of relating tunnelling work (measured in yards) to ability to sustain output (measured in tons).

Arterial roads and gateroads can be viewed as producing the colliery's work-in-hand: accessed blocks of reserves and developed faces. As with any other industry, the flow of these intermediate products must be capable of supporting the long-run rate of output whilst stocks must be sufficient to cover short-term fluctuations in their flow (caused both by geology and performance variability). A strategy may thus be restated in terms of a broad layout and the necessary stocks and flows of arterial and gateroad development.

By reference to the gaming studies, the long-run average contribution of

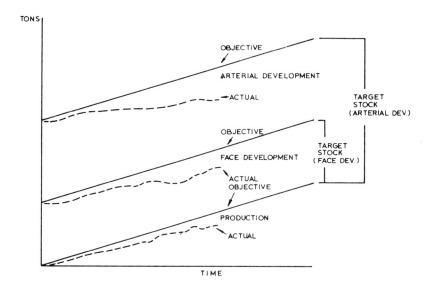

Fig. 2. Monitoring chart.

both types of road (their tonnage equivalents) can be calculated in terms of expected output per yard driven. These will depend primarily on geology and the type of layout. The requirements for stocks will have been explicitly estimated (in terms of how far roads should be in advance of production operations) and may be converted into tonnage terms by use of the equivalents above. It is now possible to relate actual and objective stocks and flows of both types of drivage and production on the same axes. Fig. 2 shows how this information may be displayed (in this example, productive and tunnelling activities are initially in balance, objectives lines therefore are parallel).

In this stage of the process, the system is maintained by converting monthly progress on drivages to tons assuming the veracity of the tonnage equivalents. Less frequently (or as events dictate) the assumed and observed geological situations must be compared and if necessary, the impact of changes on the strategy evaluated, tonnage equivalents recalculated and the monitoring records revised.

Research in this field is still continuing, with alternative methods of presenting and revising the information currently being tested.

6. A case study

The type of considerations involved in the planning of a geologically troubled colliery and the contribution to be made by the gaming approach are best illustrated by an actual study.

The colliery in question produced approximately 500 000 tons in 1967/68, making a small profit (before interest). Since then, the performance deteriorated rapidly to a situation where in 1969/70, approximately 375 000 tons were produced at a loss exceeding £500 000 (before interest). Examination of past records suggested that inadequate development, resulting in insufficient face capacity, was largely responsible.

The colliery works two seams of different qualities and thicknesses. It is more costly to produce from the thinner of the two seams (as there is less coal per yard advance) but marketing needs dictate continued production from both. The reserves to be worked in both seams are several miles out from the shore, beneath the sea, although some areas have been over- or underworked in other seams.

Extensive workings closer to the shore in several seams in this and other (now exhausted) collieries provide a good picture of the frequency and pattern of hazards (almost exclusively faults) in the vicinity. Additionally, the position of major faults already found can be reasonably projected as these tend to run in straight lines in this region.

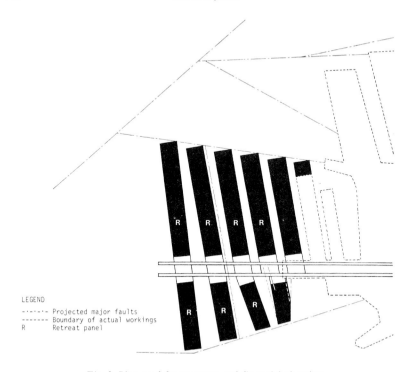

Fig. 3. Plan used for resource and financial planning.

The nature of the traditional planning process and the application of the gaming method can now be shown by reference to only one seam, although in practice the colliery was treated as a whole since information found in one seam could be projected to the other and there was some scope for adjusting the resource balance.

The layout of future workings (black) proposed by the management is shown in fig. 3. It is based on projection of previously found major faults. Four arterial roads are to be driven to the West to open up new areas of reserves, faces being worked to either side of these. Because of uncertainty about the location of faults, gateroads were to be pre-driven for all panels with an R in it. (It would be impossible to do this for the first faces to be developed because of a lack of men, machines and time.) The aim is to have two faces producing at all times, one on three shifts, the other on two. As the single face in the other seam was also to be treble-shifted, a face lost would result in two idle shifts. Resource and performance requirements were calculated on the basis of the layout shown in fig. 3 with a "blanket" relaxation applied to allow for possible geological interference.

On testing this scheme against three conjectural geologies it was apparent that the proposed development capacity was nowhere near adequate to support the objective output. Because of faults slowing drivages, gateroads could not be pre-driven and the arterial roads were insufficiently far advanced to be of much assistance in positioning faces to avoid faults.

Because of the location of the colliery, the management felt that development capacity could not be increased by recruiting additional teams. The alternative was thus to increase the performance of the existing teams by investing in high-speed tunnelling machines.

Fig. 4 shows one of the simulations carried out to test the modified scheme. It is immediately obvious that:

(1) faces were frequently shorter than planned and often had to be angled to avoid faults,

(2) advance to the West has to be far more rapid than planned whilst the percentage of the reserves actually extracted was lower,

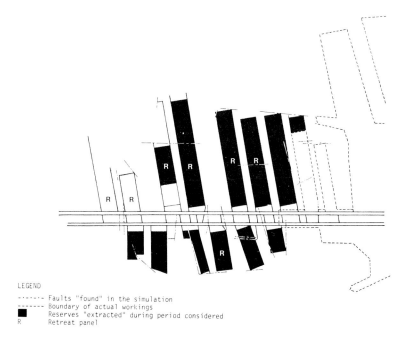

LEGEND
------- Faults "found" in the simulation
------- Boundary of actual workings
■   Reserves "extracted" during period considered
R   Retreat panel

Fig. 4. Result of one simulation using a modified strategy.

(3) it was still impossible to pre-drive all gateroads as originally intended. On the basis of this study, it was possible to set target drivage rates to allow for the necessary build-up of development stocks, and also to highlight the financial advantages of concentrating production to a single seam. The crucial importance, in the early years at least, of the projected positions of certain of the previously found fault lines was also indicated. Because of time constraints, other layouts could not be considered initially, but it was proposed that alternatives be considered when the position of one particular projected fault was proven.

Acknowledgements

A simulation approach was first suggested by A.M. Clarke, Deputy Chief Geologist to the N.C.B. Contributions to the development of a useable and acceptable technique have since been made by staff of the Operational Research Executive, the Geological Branch and the Mining Department.

Thanks are due to several people in the Executive, notably G.H. Mitchell and D.J. White, for reading and commenting upon the draft, and to the N.C.B. for permission to deliver the paper. The views expressed and any errors remaining are of course entirely personal.

M. Ross, ed., OR '72. North-Holland Publishing Company (1973)

41

AN ALGORITHM FOR OPTIMAL RELOADING OF PRESSURIZED WATER REACTORS

Un algorithme pour le rechargement optimal des réacteurs nucléaires du type PWR

J.P. BRANS, M. LECLERCQ

University of Brussels, Brussels, Belgium

and

P. HANSEN

Institut d'Economie Scientifique et de Gestion, Lille, France

Abstract. The problem of reloading a PWR considered in this paper is the following: given two sets of fresh and exposed assemblies, of known reactivity, determine the location pattern of these assemblies which maximizes the reactivity of the core under a constraint on the power-distribution form factor. After linearization, this problem may be reduced to a sequence of assignment problems with a side condition. These problems are solved by an implicit enumeration routine. The algorithm can also be used as a simulation tool for the comparison of reloading modes.

1. Introduction

Power reactors of the PWR type are nuclear reactors fueled with enriched uranium, moderated and cooled by pressurized light water. The uranium is contained in fuel elements regularly disposed in the reactor core. As the reactor operates the fissile material in some of the fuel elements is depleted in such way as to require their replacement by fresh ones. If $Q(t)$ denotes the number of neutrons emitted by the fission process at a given time and able to induce successive fissions and $I(t)$ denotes the number of neutrons at the next generation, the ratio

$$\rho(t) = \frac{I(t) - Q(t)}{I(t)}, \tag{1}$$

called the *reactor reactivity* allows us to distinguish three cases

(1) $\rho(t) < 0$: The chain reaction cannot sustain itself and dies out quickly; the reactor is subcritical.

(2) $\rho(t) = 0$: The chain reaction is self sustaining at a certain level of power but cannot develop further; the reactor is critical.

(3) $\rho(t) > 0$; the number of neutrons is increasing at each neutron generation and the chain reaction diverges; the reactor is over-critical.

Theoretically, with a fresh core, the reactor will be over-critical. In practice, to compensate for this overcriticality a neutronic poison, usually soluble boron is introduced in the reactor core to keep it at the critical level. As the fissible material content of the fuel elements decreases while the parasitic neutron absorption in the fission products grows the concentration of the boron solution is reduced consequently. When no boron remains the reactor must be reloaded unless the reactivity becomes negative.

The time interval between two reloadings is called the *reactor cycle*. Its length depends on the initial boron concentration and hence on the initial reactivity: the higher the initial reactivity is, the longer will the cycle be.

Let us consider a sequence of cycles $k = 1, 2, ..., K$. Let X_{k-1} denote the state of the fuel at the end of the $(k-1)$th cycle, D_k the vector of the decisions which must be taken during the kth cycle and $p_k = f(X_{k-1}, D_k)$ the corresponding energy production cost. In order to minimize the total energy production cost during these cycles, it is necessary to determine the optimal decisions of the following sequential decision process:

$$\min\left[\sum_{k=1}^{K} p_k = \sum_{k=1}^{K} f(X_{k-1}, D_k) \right] , \tag{2}$$

under the constraints:

$$F \leqslant F_0 , \tag{3}$$

$$E \leqslant E_0 , \tag{4}$$

where (3) is a constraint on the core power-distribution form factor which cannot allow for a peak higher than F_0 and (4) is a constraint on the peak exposure of the discharged fuel.

Following Melice [1], we consider that each vector D_k ($k = 1, 2, ..., K$) contains *exterior decisions* and *interior decisions*. The exterior decisions concern the number and enrichment of the fresh fuel assemblies to be loaded into the core. The interior decisions concern the initial boron concentration and also the reloading pattern, i.e., the way the assemblies of different burn-up states (exposures) are disposed in the core.

Hence the sequential decision process (2)–(4) encompasses both an *interior problem* and an *exterior problem*. In principle these problems are linked together. However, following the reference cited above, we shall admit that it is possible to solve first the interior problem and then the exterior problem (separability assumption). We propose hereunder a new method to solve the interior problem and then give some indications as to the way to solve the exterior problem. The interior problem may be formulated as follows:

"Dispose in the reactor's core N assemblies of different but given burn-up states in order to maximize the reactivity while satisfying the constraint concerning the form factor".

We shall use an iterative method. Let us consider the reactivity and the form factor as functions of the exposures E_i (i = 1, 2, ..., N) of the fuel assemblies, i.e., of the cumulated specific energies released by the fuel assemblies. At each iteration we shall proceed by linearization, limiting the expressions to the first order terms of Taylor's expansion. Hence we assume any increase of a function f depending on the exposure $E = (E_1, E_2, ..., E_N)$ may be written

$$\Delta f = \langle \frac{\mathrm{d}f}{\mathrm{d}E}, \Delta E \rangle = \sum_{i=1}^{N} \left(\frac{\partial f}{\partial E_i} \right)_i \Delta E_i . \tag{5}$$

The quantities $(\partial f/\partial E_i)_i$ (i = 1, 2, ..., N) will be called *statistical weights*; they are defined for each place where an assembly is located. Codes which allow us to compute the reactivity ρ and the form factor F are available. One of these, due to Melice [2], gives also the values of the statistical weights $(W_\rho)_i = (\partial \rho/\partial E_i)_i$ and $(W_F)_i = (\partial F/\partial E_i)_i$ of the reactivity and the form factor, respectively.

This method called *linearization–iteration* was introduced by Kromov et al. [3] and used by several authors. Their aim was to determine the optimal reactivity profiles assuming these profiles to be continuous. The determination of the reloading pattern was then empirically determined by using these continuous profiles. Contrary to that procedure we propose a combinatorial method which proceeds from feasible pattern to feasible pattern until the optimal one is reached.

2. Canonical form of the interior problem

Let us assume, when reloading a reactor, that a core pattern of irradiated and fresh fuel assemblies is known which satisfies the form factor constraint. The reactivity of the core is not, in general, maximum for this pattern; therefore, an improved pattern must be found. Let us introduce boolean variables x_{ij} defined for $i, j = 1, 2, ..., N$ and such that x_{ij} is equal to 1 if the ith fuel assembly is assigned to the jth location and x_{ij} is equal to 0 if not. In other words, x_{ij} is equal to 1 if the ith fuel assembly is put in the place previously occupied by the jth fuel assembly and x_{ij} is equal to 0 if not.

Hence, an iteration of the interior problem may be written as

$$\max \sum_{i=1}^{N} \sum_{j=1}^{N} (E_i - E_j)(W_\rho)_i x_{ij} \, , \tag{6}$$

under the following constraints

$$F + \sum_{i=1}^{N} \sum_{j=1}^{N} (E_i - E_j)(W_F)_i x_{ij} \leqslant F_0 \, , \tag{7}$$

$$x_{ij} | E_i - E_j | \leqslant \alpha \, , \tag{8}$$

$$\sum_{i=1}^{N} x_{ij} = 1 \, , \tag{9}$$

$$\sum_{j=1}^{N} x_{ij} = 1 \, , \tag{10}$$

$$x_{ij} \in \{0, 1\} \, , \tag{11}$$

where α is a given constant.

The objective function (6) requires that we seek the feasible assignment of fuel assemblies to locations (or, equivalently, the feasible permutation of fuel assemblies) which gives the highest possible increase in reactivity. Constraint (7) is on the form factor. Constraint (8) limits the variation of exposures in order to keep the linearization approximation valid. Thus, this last constraint also limits the increase in the reactivity; therefore, an iterative method must be used. Constraints (9) and (10) express that one and only one assembly must be assigned to each location and conversely.

Let successively

$$(E_i - E_j)(W_\rho)_i = \tilde{c}_{ij} , \tag{12}$$

$$(E_i - E_j)(W_F)_i = \tilde{d}_{ij} , \tag{13}$$

$$c_{ij} = \max_{i,j} \tilde{c}_{ij} - \tilde{c}_{ij} , \tag{14}$$

$$d_{ij} = \tilde{d}_{ij} - \min_{i,j} \tilde{d}_{ij} , \tag{15}$$

$$F_1 = F_0 - F + N (\min_{i,j} \tilde{d}_{ij}) . \tag{16}$$

Furthermore, put c_{ij} equal to a large positive value M for each couple (i,j) for which constraint (8) is not verified when $x_{ij} = 1$; the interior problem may then be written in the following *canonical form*:

$$\min \sum_{i=1}^{N} \sum_{j=1}^{N} c_{ij} x_{ij} , \tag{17}$$

under the following constraints

$$\sum_{i=1}^{N} \sum_{j=1}^{N} d_{ij} x_{ij} \leqslant F_1 , \tag{18}$$

$$\sum_{i=1}^{N} x_{ij} = 1 , \tag{19}$$

$$\sum_{j=1}^{N} x_{ij} = 1 , \tag{20}$$

$$x_{ij} \in \{0, 1\} , \tag{21}$$

where the coefficients c_{ij} and d_{ij} are non-negative for all i and j.

This problem is an assignment problem with an additional constraint. The resolution of the canonical problem (17)–(21) gives a new feasible pattern. For this pattern the reactivity, the form factor and the statistical weights are computed. A new problem of the form (6)–(11) is written, transformed and solved as indicated previously. This iterative procedure is continued until a stable pattern is obtained.

Remark: If symmetry axes are given (which in practice is nearly always the case) it is only necessary to consider one quarter of the core. This does not change anything of the form of the equations written above.

3. Algorithm for the canonical problem

3.1. Bounds

We propose hereunder an implicit enumeration algorithm to solve the canonical problem. Let us first introduce some definitions:

A *particular assignment* is a couple (i, j) of indices, where i is the index of a fuel assembly and j the index of a location. A particular assignment will be said to be *included* (or *excluded*) if and only if the corresponding variable x_{ij} is equal to 1 (or 0). A particular assignment, which is not included or excluded, will be said to be *free*; the value of the corresponding variable x_{ij} will be noted φ.

A *partial assignment* Y is an ordered set of N^2 particular assignments which may contain free particular assignments. To each partial assignment corresponds a φ-boolean vector (cf. Kuntzmann [4]) with N^2 components.

A *complete assignment* X is an ordered set of N^2 particular assignments which contains no free particular assignment. A boolean vector with N^2 components corresponds to each complete assignment.

According to these definitions a complete assignment is a particular case of a partial assignment. Complete assignments may be obtained by including, or excluding, the free particular assignments of a given partial assignment, i.e., by giving a boolean value to every variable $x_{ij} = \varphi$. The complete assignments thus obtained will be called *completions* of the given partial assignment.

A complete assignment will be said to be *feasible* if it satisfies the constraints (18)–(20). The problem is thus to determine a feasible complete assignment which minimizes the objective function (17). At a current iteration of the algorithm, some particular assignments will be included, some will be excluded and some will be free. The situation is, therefore, characterized by a partial assignment Y. The tests of the algorithm will make use of lower bounds of the values taken by the objective function and by the left-hand side of the constraint (18) on the set of completions of this partial assignment. These bounds will be called respectively "of type C" and "of type D".

3.1.1. Bounds of "type C"

(a) Let $V_1(Y)$ denote the sum of the coefficients c_{ij} corresponding to the included assignments:

$$V_1(Y) = \sum_{(i,j)|x_{ij}=1} c_{ij} \ . \tag{22}$$

(b) Let $c_i'(Y)$ denote the smallest coefficient of the ith line of the matrix $\mathbf{C} = (c_{ij})$ corresponding to a free particular assignment:

$$c_i'(Y) = \min_{j|x_{ij}=\varphi} c_{ij} \ . \tag{23}$$

If there is no index j such that $x_{ij} = \varphi$, let $c_i'(Y) = 0$.
For all i and j let

$$c_{ij}' = c_{ij} - c_i(Y) \ , \tag{24}$$

and let $c_j''(Y)$ denote the smallest element of the jth column of the matrix $\mathbf{C}' = (c_{ij}')$ which corresponds to a free particular assignment:

$$c_j''(Y) = \min_{i|x_{ij}=\varphi} c_{ij}' \ . \tag{25}$$

If there is no index i such that $x_{ij} = \varphi$, let $c_j''(Y) = 0$.
Further, let

$$V_2(Y) = \sum_i c_i'(Y) + \sum_i c_j''(Y) \ . \tag{26}$$

Clearly, the matrix

$$\bar{\mathbf{C}}(Y) = (\bar{c}_{ij}(Y) = c_{ij} - c_i'(Y) - c_j''(Y)) \ , \tag{27}$$

which will be called the current *reduced matrix* of $\mathbf{C}$, contains at least one zero in each line and in each column, in which one $x_{ij} = \varphi$ at least remains.

(c) With every coefficient $\bar{c}_{mn}(Y)$ of $\bar{\mathbf{C}}(Y)$ equal to 0 and such that no coefficient of the same line or of the same column corresponds to an included particular assignment, i.e.

$$\forall \bar{c}_{mn}(Y) = 0 | \nexists x_{mj} = 1 \ , \qquad \nexists x_{in} = 1 \ , \tag{28}$$

the second minimum $\theta_{mn}(Y)$ of the nth column of $\bar{\mathbf{C}}(Y)$, where only the coefficients corresponding to free particular assignments are considered:

$$\theta_{mn}(Y) = \min_{i \mid x_{ij} = \varphi,\, i \neq m} \overline{c}_{in}(Y) . \tag{29}$$

If there is only one coefficient corresponding to a free particular assignment in the column n of $\overline{\mathbf{C}}(Y)$, $\theta_{mn}(Y)$ is fixed at an arbitrary large value M.

Let $p(i)$ denote the number of coefficients $\theta_{ij}(Y)$ corresponding to the ith line of $\overline{\mathbf{C}}(Y)$. Clearly, if Y has at least one feasible completion, $p(i) = 0$ if $\exists x_{ik} = 1$ and $p(i) \geqslant 1$ if $\nexists x_{ik} = 1$. Let the $\theta_{ij}(Y)$'s corresponding to each line such that $p(i) > 1$ be ranked in the order of decreasing values:

$$\theta_{ik_1(i)}(Y) \geqslant \theta_{ik_2(i)}(Y) \geqslant \ldots \geqslant \theta_{ik_{p(i)}(i)}(Y) \geqslant 0 . \tag{30}$$

Further, let $V_3(Y)$ denote the sum, for all indices i such that $p(i) > 1$, of the sums of the second to last $\theta_{ij}(Y)$'s:

$$V_3(Y) = \sum_{i \mid p(i) > 1} \; \sum_{j = k_2(i),\, k_3(i),\, \ldots,\, k_{p(i)}(i)} \theta_{ij}(Y) . \tag{31}$$

Theorem: $V(Y) = V_1(Y) + V_2(Y) + V_3(Y)$ is a lower bound of the values taken by the objective function (17) on the set of completions of the current partial assignment Y.

Proof. If the assignment Y is complete, it is obvious that $V_1(Y)$ is equal to the value of the objective function and that $V_2(Y) = V_3(Y) = 0$; thus the theorem holds. If the assignment is partial let us first note that the bounds $V_1(Y)$ and $V_2(Y)$ are those proposed by Little et al. for the travelling salesman problem in a well-known paper [5]; these bounds are valid for the assignment problem too.

Clearly, $\theta_{mn}(Y)$ is an increase to be given to $V_1(Y) + V_2(Y)$ if the particular assignment (m, n) is excluded. If all $p(i) \leqslant 1$, i.e., if there is at most one coefficient $\theta_{ij}(Y) > 0$ for each index i, $V_3(Y) = 0$. If there is an index m such that $p(m) > 1$, at least $p(m) - 1$ free particular assignments corresponding to coefficients equal to 0 in the mth line of $\overline{\mathbf{C}}(Y)$ must be excluded in every completion of the current partial assignment. The increases corresponding to these exclusions may be given to $V_1(Y) + V_2(Y)$ and, clearly

$$S(m) = \sum_{j = k_2(m),\, k_3(m),\, \ldots,\, k_{p(m)}(m)} \theta_{mj}(Y) \tag{32}$$

is a lower bound of the sum of these increases.

Furthermore, a similar reasoning may be applied to all lines i such that

$p(i) > 1$ and the lower bounds $S(i)$ may be added because if two coefficients $\theta_{il}(Y)$ and $\theta_{kl}(Y)$ correspond to coefficients in the same column of $\bar{c}(Y)$ they are obviously both equal to 0.

3.1.2. Bounds of "type D"

The left-hand side of (18) has the same form as the objective function. It is therefore possible to compute a lower bound $W(Y)$ of the values taken by the left-hand side of (18) on the set of completions of Y in a similar way as above. Let

$$W(Y) = W_1(Y) + W_2(Y) + W_3(Y) \tag{33}$$

denote this bound, where $W_1(Y)$, $W_2(Y)$ and $W_3(Y)$ are defined as $V_1(Y)$, $V_2(Y)$ and $V_3(Y)$ the d_{ij}'s replacing the c_{ij}'s. The quantities corresponding to $\theta_{ij}(Y)$ and to $p(i)$ will be noted by $\tau_{ij}(Y)$ and $q(i)$.

3.2. Algorithm

The algorithm uses *direct* and *conditional tests*. Direct tests are sufficient conditions for the set of completions of the current partial assignment to contain no better complete assignment than the one already obtained or no feasible complete assignment. Conditional tests are sufficient conditions for certain free particular assignments to be included or excluded in all optimal completions of the current partial assignment.

3.2.1. Initialisation

Set all components x_{ij} of Y equal to φ. Give to $V(Y_{opt})$, the value of the best solution Y_{opt} yet obtained, or ceiling the value of the initial feasible complete assignment.

3.2.2. Direct optimality test

Compute $V_1(Y)$ and $V_2(Y)$. Compute the $\theta_{ij}(Y)$'s and rank them in the order of decreasing values line by line. Compute $V_3(Y)$ and $V(Y)$.
If $V(Y) \geqslant V(Y_{opt})$ go to 3.2.7 (regression step).
If $V(Y) < V(Y_{opt})$ go to the next test.

3.2.3. Conditional optimality tests

The following tests are to be applied for all indices i such that $p(i) \geqslant 1$; if $p(i) = 1$, consider $\theta_{ik_2(i)}(Y)$ to be equal to 0.

(a) If

$$V(Y) + [\theta_{ik_1(1)}(Y) - \theta_{ik_2(i)}(Y)] \geqslant V(Y_{opt}) \, ,$$

fix $x_{ik_1(i)}$ at 1. Then fix all $x_{ij}, j \neq k_1(i)$ and all $x_{lk_1(i)}, l \neq i$ which were equal to φ at 0.

(b) If

$$V(Y) + [\theta_{ik_1(i)}(Y) - \theta_{ik_\lambda(i)}(Y)] \geqslant V(Y_{opt}) \, ,$$

fix $x_{ik_\lambda(i)}, x_{ik_{\lambda+1}(i)}, ..., x_{ik_{p(i)}(i)}$ at 0.
This test is to be applied for $\lambda = 3, 4, ..., p(i)$.

(c) If $p(i) > 1$ and

$$V(Y) + \theta_{ik_1(i)}(Y) \geqslant V(Y_{opt}) \text{ for } j \neq k_1(i), k_2(i), ..., k_{p(i)}(i) \, ,$$

fix all x_{ij} which were equal to φ at 0.

When tests (a) to (c) have been applied to all indices i such that $p(i) \geqslant 1$, go back to test 3.2.2. if one variable at least has been fixed at 1 or 0 by these tests. Otherwise go to the next test.

3.2.4. Direct feasibility tests

(a) If there is an index i such that all x_{ij} are fixed at 0, go to 3.2.7.

(b) If there is an index j such that all x_{ij} are fixed at 0, go to 3.2.7.

(c) Compute $W_1(Y)$ and $W_2(Y)$. Compute the $\tau_{ij}(y)$'s and rank them in order of decreasing values line by line. Compute $W_3(Y)$ and $W(Y)$.

If $W(Y) > F_1$ go to 3.2.7.

If $W(Y) \leqslant F_1$ go to the next test.

3.2.5. Conditional feasibility tests

The following tests are to be applied for all indices i such that $q(i) \geqslant 1$; if $q(i) = 1$, consider $\tau_{ik_2(i)}(Y)$ to be equal to 0.

(a) If

$$W(Y) + [\tau_{ik_1(i)}(Y) - \tau_{ik_2(i)}(Y)] > F_1 \, ,$$

fix $x_{ik_1(i)}$ at 1. Then fix all $x_{ij}, j \neq k_1(i)$ and all $x_{ik_1(i)}, l \neq i$ which were equal to φ at 0.

(b) If

$$W(Y) + [\tau_{ik_1(i)}(Y) - \tau_{ik_\lambda(i)}(Y)] > F_1 ,$$

fix $x_{ik_\lambda(i)}, x_{ik_{\lambda+1}(i)}, ..., x_{ik_{q(i)}(i)}$ at 0.
This test is to be applied for $\lambda = 3, 4, ..., q(i)$.

(c) If

$$W(Y) + \tau_{ik_1(i)}(Y) > F_1 \quad \text{for } j \neq k_1(i), k_2(i), ..., k_{q(i)}(i) ,$$

fix all x_{ij} which were equal to φ at 0.

When tests (a) to (c) have been applied for all indices i such that $q(i) \geq 1$, go back to test 3.2.2. if one variable at least has been fixed at 1 or 0 by these tests. Otherwise, if one variable at least remains equal to φ go to the choice step; if no variable x_{ij} remains equal to φ an improved complete assignment Y has been found. Update Y_{opt} and $V(Y_{opt})$ and go to 3.2.7.

3.2.6. Choice step

Choose the particular assignment $[m, k_1(m)]$ such that

$$\theta_{mk_1(m)}(Y) - \theta_{mk_2(m)}(Y) = \max_i \; [\theta_{ik_1(i)}(Y) - \theta_{ik_2(i)}(Y)] ,$$

where $\theta_{ik_2(i)}(Y)$ is considered as equal to 0 if $p(i) = 1$ and give the value 1 to $x_{mk_1(m)}$. Then return to test 3.2.2.

3.2.7. Regression step

Consider the last variable x_{kl} chosen in the choice step and fixed at 1. If such a variable remains, liberate (i.e., give the value φ) all the variables fixed by the conditional tests after this variable was chosen, fix x_{kl} at 0 and return to test 3.2.2. If no such variable remains the resolution is finished. Y_{opt} is the optimal assignment and $V(Y_{opt})$ its value.

4. Management of a reactor

Clearly, the algorithm given in the previous section allows us to solve the interior problem. It can also be used to analyse the exterior problem.

First, the usual reloading modes, such as third by third, quarter by quarter, salt and pepper, etc., can be compared. It is indeed easy to take into account the restrictions on location of fuel assemblies, which characterize these reloading modes, by modifying the value of some c_{ij}'s.

The sensitivity of the value of the solution when specific constraints are imposed or omitted can also be studied. New reloading modes could perhaps be suggested by the results of this comparison and sensitivity analysis.

Further results may be obtained provided a simulation program is available which gives the state X_k of the fuel at the end of the k cycle when X_{k-1} and D_k are known. Then exterior decisions may be compared cycle by cycle during the transient phase until stationary is reached.

Acknowledgements

The authors thank M. Melice for suggesting the problem studied in this paper and for several fruitful discussions. They are also grateful to M. Decressin for helping in the final paper presentation.

References

[1] M. Melice, Nucl. Sci. Eng. 37 (1969) 451.
[2] M. Melice, Code A. Conf. 49-E. 287.
[3] B. Kromov, A. kusmin and A. Kachutin, At. Energ. (USSR) 27 (1969) 186.
[4] J. Kuntzmann, Algèbre de Boole (Dunod, Paris, 1965).
[5] J.D.C. Little, E.G. Purty, D.W. Sweeney and C. Karel, Opns. Res. 11 (1963) 972.

M. Ross, ed., OR '72. North-Holland Publishing Company (1973)

42

APPLICATION DE LA RECHERCHE OPERATIONNELLE A UN PROBLEME DE SANTE PUBLIQUE: L'ORGANISATION DES SECOURS D'URGENCE

Application of OR to a problem of public health: the organisation of the emergency services

F. FAGNANI

INSERM, Paris, France

Résumé. Le problème de l'organisation d'un dispositif cohérent de secours et soins mobiles d'urgence débouche sur un certain nombre de questions relatives à la part qu'il faut accorder aux différents éléments qui constituent ce dispositif, pour aboutir à l'élaboration d'un système efficace. En d'autres termes, supposant connue la demande de soins d'urgence au niveau d'un secteur géographique donné, il s'agit de définir le type d'utilisation qui doit être fait des ressources disponibles et des moyens techniques actuels afin d'améliorer le plus possible le système existant: (1) amélioration de l'alerte, par une réduction des délais (augmentation du nombre de postes téléphoniques le long des routes pour les accidents de la circulation, par exemple); (2) amélioration de l'intervention sur les lieux: diminution des délais et amélioration de la qualité des soins dispensés, par exemple; (3) amélioration de la qualité des soins des hopitaux d'acceuil (développement de la pratique de la réanimation, permanence des services d'acceuil, etc.). Les réponses qu'on pouvait fournir jusqu'à présent à ce type de problème se dégageaient de l'expérience nécessairement fragmentaire des responsables de ces activités, chirurgiens, réanimateurs notamment.

L'étude développée par l'INSERM a pour but de fournir des éléments d'appréciation précis et quantitatifs aux responsables des décisions. Après une observation du système dans un département (Côte d'Or) sur l'ensemble des accidents de la circulation et les autres urgences mettant en jeu le dispositif de secours, un modèle est construit qui permet de simuler l'ensemble des évènements qui surviennent dès le début de l'urgence jusqu'à l'accueil à l'hopital. Ce modèle permet de porter des appréciations sur les différents types d'investissements possibles et constitue une base utile pour un développement coordonné des services dans le domaine exploré.

1. Une information statistique insuffisante, des choix politiques hasardeux

La nécessité d'organiser rationnellement le dispositif mobile de secours et de soins d'urgence a été ressentie depuis plusieurs années en France, au niveau de différents responsables politiques et médicaux. Cette prise de conscience, liée à la croissance dramatique des accidents de la circulation s'est traduite par un ensemble de mesures réglementaires et d'équipements. Toutefois la connaissance de la nature et de l'ampleur des besoins et de la façon dont ils sont satisfaits au niveau d'un secteur géographique donné est trop réduite pour permettre une estimation de l'efficacité réelle des diverses mesures d'intervention possibles. Cette connaissance est déjà relativement réduite en ce qui concerne les accidents de la circulation; elle devient presque inexistance pour les accidents domestiques; elle est dispersée et disparate pour les accidents du travail. Quant aux problèmes de soins d'urgence relatifs aux maladies évoluant en phase aiguë, leur connaissance souffre des mêmes lacunes que celle de la morbidité générale de la population dont ils constituent un aspect particulier.

Du point de vue des moyens d'intervention également, l'information se réduit dans les meilleurs cas à une liste d'équipements: ambulances, lits, personnels, etc. Mais on ignore comment ces moyens sont utilisés, pour quel type de pathologie et avec quel succès. Ainsi l'effort en matière d'équipement n'a pas été accompagné par la mise en place d'un outil d'observation permettant le contrôle du secteur en question. Un tel outil est en fait difficile à définir car cela nécessite au préalable une analyse approfondie du système d'intervention dans son ensemble. C'est dans le double but de préciser les lignes directrices d'une action collective pertinente et de déterminer les concepts fondamentaux d'une politique de l'information en matière de soins et secours d'urgence que l'Institut National de la Santé et de la Recherche Médicale (INSERM) a entrepris l'étude qui est exposée ici [1, 2].

2. Des besoins considérables

Il nous suffira de rappeler qu'en 1970, pour ce qui concerne les seuls accidents de la circulation, les statistiques pour la France furent les suivantes (tableau 1).

Si la croissance actuellement observée pour les accidents de la circulation se poursuit dans l'avenir, on a calculé que plus de la moitié des Français nés au cours des dernières années seront victimes au cours de leur vie d'un accident (blessé ou tué).

De façon plus générale, les morts violentes constituent la première cause

Tableau 1

	Nombres absolus	Pourcentage annuel d'accroissement
Accidents	236 000	3,6
Blessés	319 544	3,5
Tués	15 113	2,6

de décès chez les jeunes (pour les hommes de 15 à 34 ans elles représentent les deux tiers des décès totaux).

Un certain nombre d'innovations en matière de techniques médicales permettent à présent de maintenir en vie des blessés et des malades évoluant en phase aiguë. Les techniques de réanimation cardiaque et respiratoire donnent lieu à des interventions efficaces dans des cas qui auraient été jugés désespérés il y a seulement quelques décades. Toutefois les problèmes qui sont posés par la diffusion de ces innovations en vue de répondre efficacement aux besoins dépassent les limites du "système de santé" dans ses structures actuelles. En effet, un ensemble de tâches de nature non médicale doivent être accomplies préalablement ou parallèlement aux soins. Il faut alerter un service spécialisé, transporter la victime en un lieu approprié, avertir les personnels nécessaires, prendre éventuellement des mesures de sauvegarde ou de sécurité pour d'autres usagers, etc. Or ces tâches mettent en jeu le système social presque dans son ensemble: on peut, par exemple, concevoir une éducation générale de la population en matière de secourisme (il en est ainsi au Danemark); il est nécessaire d'informer le plus largement le public de l'attitude qu'il convient d'adopter face à un certain nombre de détresses. Il faut enfin préciser les rôles respectifs des divers institutions ou groupes qui entrent pour une part dans le processus des secours: Sapeurs–Pompiers, ambulances privées, Gendarmeries et Polices Urbaines, Hopitaux, medecins de ville, etc.

3. Délimitation du problème

Il s'agit de définir et de comparer les différents moyens propres à réduire les conséquences des détresses de toute nature survenues à la suite d'accidents ou de maladies évoluant en phase aiguë. Toutefois, l'étude laisse de côté les points suivants:

(1) Les moyens de prévention suceptibles de modifier et de réduire la demande actuelle. On fait donc l'hypothèse que l'efficacité de la prévention

est réduite au point de n'influencer que faiblement la structure et l'importance des besoins actuels. Si une telle supposition peut être considérée comme justifiée en matière d'accidents de toute nature, elle demanderait à être précisée pour les maladies. Il est probable en effet que nombre d'entre elles pourraient être évitées par des mesures préventives adéquates mais dont les effets seraient de toute façon à long terme.

(2) Les moyens permettant de faire apparaître une demande potentielle actuellement méconnue. Cet aspect du problème touche également aux urgences médico-chirurgicales de nature diverse qui, faute d'une information adéquate du public ne donnent pas lieu à une demande de soins d'urgence.

(3) Certains aspects spécialisés de l'urgence: urgences néonatales (réanimation du nouveau-né après l'accouchement), urgences psychiatriques et cardiovasculaires (exemples de domaine où les mesures de prévention devraient être prises en compte ainsi que les moyens de faire apparaître la demande potentielle).

(4) Les soins d'urgence fournis par le canal de la médecine de ville sauf si ceux-ci aboutissent à une demande de transport ou de soins spécialisés.

(5) Les problèmes consécutifs à la prise en charge dans un établissement spécialisé. On se limite donc à la période qui s'écoule entre l'évènement qui déclenche le processus de l'urgence et l'arrivée du patient en un lieu médical adéquat pour recevoir les soins les meilleurs que son état requiert.

(6) Les problèmes relatifs aux moyens à mettre en oeuvre lors d'évènements catastrophiques faisant d'un coup de nombreuses victimes. Des dispositions particulières sont en effet à prévoir pour ce type d'évènement dont la fréquence est destinée à croître dans les années à venir. En France, il s'agit d'un ensemble de règles regroupés sous le qualificatif de "Plan ORSEC". Cet aspect a également été volontairement écarté de l'étude.

Remarque: Il faut insister sur le fait que le problème qui est traité ici, n'est pas de définir une organisation idéale destinée à être construite "ex nihilo". En fait, tout un ensemble de moyens et de règles existent dont le but est de répondre à des besoins relativement mal définis. Il s'agit d'établir plutôt les lignes directrices des changements à promouvoir compte tenu des objectifs, des contraintes et des possibilités de collaboration des divers acteurs d'un système fortement décentralisé. Aucune autorité établie n'est en mesure d'imposer à l'ensemble des acteurs en question, les formes d'une organisation que le calcul aura révélé être la plus efficace. Les conclusions de l'étude ne doivent donc pas être recherchées sous l'aspect d'une "solution optimale" plus ou moins illusoire. Il s'agit plutôt d'approfondir et de préciser des objectifs techniques plus fins que ceux qui existaient implicitement auparavant. C'est aux acteurs concernés de faire valoir ensuite les critères qui les concerneront et de promouvoir les changements dans la mesure de leur pouvoir et de leur possibilité d'action.

4. Analyse qualitative du problème

L'interaction entre deux variables fondamentales (les délais et les niveaux de soins disponibles) constitue la base du problème tel qu'il a été délimité. Il importe en effet de réduire au maximum les délais tant que le niveau de soins le meilleur (relativement à l'état du patient) n'est pas disponible. A partir de l'instant où celui-ci intervient, la prise en compte des délais perd tout intérêt; la notion même d'urgence disparait. Le problème est donc pour l'essentiel de trouver la stratégie la meilleure au niveau de la combinaison de ces deux variables, dans une situation où les deux acteurs principaux du drame qui se joue (la victime et le personnel opérant les secours) convergent l'un vers l'autre à partir de positions initiales aléatoires. L'analyse des délais est relativement simple. On peut les décomposer en trois catégories suivant la figure 1.

L'analyse de la qualité et de la nature des soins disponibles est par contre plus complexe. Peut-on se contenter de la référence au niveau de qualification du personnel qui les dispense? Enfin les soins dépendent largement de l'état du patient qui est censé les recevoir. Comment appréhender un tel besoin dans la diversité apparemment infinie des situations pathologiques consécutives aux accidents et aux maladies. En fait, la pratique de la médecine de réanimation réduit cette diversité en un nombre limité de catégories. Le dénominateur commun à ces situations de détresse est en effet l'existence d'un certain nombre de déficits de fonctions vitales essentielles: respiration, circulation, conscience, mutuellement dépendantes, qu'il s'agit de compenser dans des délais précis pour éviter le décès ou des séquelles irréversibles. On sera donc amené à définir les états transitoires des patients par référence à de tels déficits et à leurs combinaisons, appréciés à partir de signes fonctionnels simples.

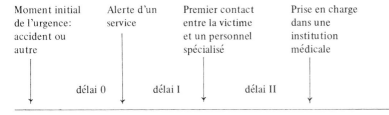

Fig. 1.

Le passage d'un état transitoire à un autre est directement influencé à la fois par ce qui s'est passé auparavant et par les soins actuellement fournis.

Deux niveaux de soins ont été finalement retenus en plus du niveau 0 correspondant à une absence totale de soins (évolution naturelle), soins de secourisme et soins de réanimation, résumant dans chaque cas l'ensemble des gestes qui peuvent être accomplis par un secouriste et un médecin réanimateur disposant du matériel et de l'équipement qu'on peut placer dans une ambulance. A côté de cette définition évolutive de l'état des blessés et malades, on peut enfin caractériser celui-ci par la donnée du diagnostic de la pathologie ayant entraîné l'urgence. Selon les cas, il s'agira d'une pathologie précise ou d'un ensemble plus ou moins homogène de conséquences d'un traumatisme: hémorragie, polytraumatisme, fractures, etc. Là encore un problème de regroupement se pose, face à la diversité des cas qu'on peut entrevoir. Mais le mode de regroupement sera à présent lié, non pas à une pratique médicale mais à un même mode d'évolution physioloque au cours du temps; pour des diagnostics très différents, des déficits de même nature peuvent s'installer conduisant à une dégradation comparable des fonctions vitales.

On voit, en conclusion qu'un travail important de conceptualisation a été nécessaire, dans le cadre de la présente étude pour aborder le problème traité. Les concepts qu'il a fallu élaborer, en collaboration avec les médecins réanimateurs n'étaient pas directement imposés ni par la pratique clinique ni par la réflexion épidémiologique. Ce travail a finalement était le plus délicat parmi les tâches accomplies; il a été mené en parallèle à l'exploitation de l'enquête entreprise en Côte d'Or et doit de toute façon être considéré comme inachevé.

5. Enquète sur le terrain

La démarche suivie a consisté dans un premier temps à rassembler les données nécessaires à l'analyse de la situation actuelle. Celle-ci a été étudiée au niveau d'un secteur géographique constituant une unité administrative (département de la Côte d'Or), choisie en raison de sa diversité et de son caractère représentatif d'une situation française typique: vaste zône rurale traversée par des voies à grande circulation, métropole régionale dotée d'un centre hospitalier important, petites agglomérations périphériques disposant de moyens médicaux réduits, ... Une enquête réalisée de mai à juillet 1968 a permis d'observer l'ensemble du système au cours de la période étudiée, grâce à la participation de la totalité des services publics concernés. La demande actuelle de secours d'urgence a été analysée selon son origine, la structure des diagnostics, le degré de gravité des états observés à l'arrivée des secours et à l'entrée à l'hopital. Les differents facteurs susceptibles d'influencer cette demande ont été appréhendés (localisation, heures de la journée, etc.). Enfin du point de vue de l'offre, on a tenté dans la mesure du possible d'apprécier les différents délais déjà définis et la nature des soins fournis lors des phases successives du sauvetage.

6. Construction d'un modèle

Comme dans la plupart des applications de la recherche opérationnelle en santé publique, la difficulté essentielle est de simuler le processus d'évolution d'une pathologie au niveau d'une population avec assez de réalisme d'une part, tout en conservant un degré de simplicité permettant le calcul, d'autre part. Différentes stratégies d'intervention se marquent par des modifications sur les paramètres de ce processus, aboutissant à des trajectoires différentes que l'on pourra tenter d'apprécier au moyen de critères économiques, épidémiologiques ou démographiques. Le problème se présente dans le cas présent dans des termes identiques bien qu'il ne s'agisse pas de pathologie précise.

On a supposé ici qu'il était à la fois possible et justifié de définir une probabilité de passage d'un état de dégradation des fonctions vitales à un autre au cours d'une unité de temps à définir; qu'une telle probabilité ne dépendait enfin que d'un nombre limité de facteurs: le type de diagnostic, l'unité de temps choisie, le niveau de soins disponible au cours de la période de temps en question et, la nature et la durée des états antérieurs; enfin que les médecins réanimateurs avaient une idée assez précise de l'évolution probable de patients ainsi définis, pour que cette connaissance, bien que faisant partie d'une "expérience" apparemment incommunicable puisse être traduite en termes quantitatifs. Ainsi, les variables qui ont été retenues et qu'on vient de citer rapidement, ont été prises en compte sous leur forme la plus simple compatible avec les exigences de précision du médecin pour pouvoir apprécier les modes d'évolution.

Les diagnostics ont été rangés en trois grandes catégories selon la valeur de l'unité de temps avec laquelle il s'est révélé nécessaire d'étudier l'évolution des états:

(1) Avec comme unité de temps 3 minutes, on a placé les diagnostics comportant des risques de déficit respiratoire.

(2) Avec comme unité de temps 15 minutes, ceux qui peuvent entraînner des déficits circulatoires.

(3) Il a été regroupé dans une dernière catégorie, les diagnostic où les fonctions vitales ne sont pas touchées et qui constituent donc en quelque sorte de

"fausses urgences". Pour une fracture simple, par exemple les délais d'arrivée des secours important peu d'un point de vue médical strict et sans dépasser pour autant certaines bornes!

Dans le première catégorie (3 minutes), on trouve dix types de diagnostics qui ont fait l'objet du modèle qu'on vient d'esquisser: (1) électrocution, (2) noyade, (3) intoxications par gaz et vapeurs, (4) intoxications par barbituriques (médicaments), (5) affections de l'appareil respiratoire avec défaillances respiratoires, affections et syndromes neurologiques avec défaillance respiratoire et de la conscience, (6) affections cérébro-vasculaires, (7) traumatismes craniens et traumatismes associés, (8) polytraumatismes, (9) fracture du crâne, du crâne et de la face, (10) pendaison.

Dans la seconde catégorie, on a regroupé les diagnostics en quatre sous-groupes (unité de temps: 15 minutes): (1) brûlures, plaies avec déficit circulatoire, fractures ouvertes avec hémorragies externes, fracture de cuisse, hémorragies extériorisées, urgences obstétricales, syndrome abdominal aigu, (2) oedème aigu du poumon, insuffisances cardiaques décompensées, autres affections cardio-vasculaires décompensées, (3) infarctus du myocarde sans arrêt cardiaque, (4) traumatismes thoraciques, fractures pluri-costales, traumatismes de l'abdomen et du bassin.

Pour chacun de ces groupes de diagnostics, les probabilités de passage d'un état transitoire à un autre dans l'unité de temps correspondante ont été estimées. La matrice obtenue pour les polytraumatismes est reproduite en tableau 2. Onze états transitoires apparaissent dans la seconde colonne du tableau. Pour certains d'entre eux, la notion de la durée pendant laquelle ces états se sont manifestés a été introduite en plus de la définition médicale de ceux-ci. Il s'agit seulement d'un artifice simple pour obtenir un modèle markovien dans une situation où la réalité ne l'est manifestement pas. Pour chacun de ces états, trois ensembles de probabilité figurent dans le tableau, selon trois lignes horizontales. Du haut vers le bas, on trouve successivement les évolutions sans soins, avec secourisme et avec soins de réanimation. Dans la première colonne, on a noté la distribution des états initiaux estimée également à partir de jugements d'experts. Il faut remarquer ici que les valeurs finalement retenues ont fait l'objet de vérifications de cohérence avec les résultats obtenus dans l'enquête et avec des informations publiées par ailleurs dans la littérature spécialisée. Cependant, ces vérifications sont restées qualitatives et relativement sommaires faute d'une observation statistique assez important et assez précise.

Le modèle permet ensuite toutes les manipulations nécessaires à la comparaison d'efficacité (mesurée par un critère de mortalité à l'entrée à l'hopital) de différentes modifications du système de secours par rapport à la situation

Tableau 2
Example d'une matrice de transition: les polytraumatismes (unité de temps: 3 min)

Etats initiaux	Etats aux temps T		1	2	3	4	5	6	7	8	9	10	11
0,01	Sans déficit	1	1										
0,05	Intervalle libre	2		0,90 0,90 0,90	0,10 0,10				0,10				
0,25	Coma + trouble respiratoire	3			0,50			0,50					
	Encombrement respiratoire	4								0,99	0,01		
0,25	Coma + encombrement respiratoire < 3'	5			0,80		1	0,90					0,05
	Tension basse ou pincée ou collapsus	6			0,05 0,05				1				
0,39	Coma sans trouble respiratoire	7	0,60 0,60 0,60		0,20 0,05				0,20 0,35 0,40				
	Coma + encombrement respiratoire de 3 à 6'	8			0,80				1	0,99 0,19	0,01 0,01		
	Coma + arrêt respiratoire	9							0,50			0,50	
0,05	Coma + arrêt respiratoire + arrêt cardiaque	10										1 1 0,50	1 1
	Décès	11											1 1

Tableau 3
Efficacité des différentes actions

Objectifs	Milieu urbain (toutes urgences, Dijon)		Milieu rural (accidents circulation, hors Dijon)	
	Moyens	Efficacité (nombre de morts évités pour 1970) (intervention ou réanimation)	Moyens	Efficacité (nombre de morts évités pour 1970)
Réduction délai d'alerte.	• Unification du numéro d'appel. • Information du public. • Information du personnel médical et paramédical.	Diminution moyenne du délai d'intervention (*) : — de 5 mn : 17 morts évités, — de 10 mn : 27 morts évités.	• Téléphone avec ligne directe le long des routes. • Information du public. Unification du numéro d'appel.	Diminution du délai d'intervention (*) moyen : — de 5 mn : 16 morts évités. — de 10 mn : 33 morts évités. — de 15 mn : 58 morts évités.
Réduction délai d'arrivée d'une ambulance.	• Choix des lieux de stationnement des ambulances. • Amélioration des transmissions de l'alerte.		• Détermination des secteurs d'intervention.	— 26 morts évités.
Pratique des soins sur place avant l'arrivée d'une ambulance.	• Enseignement et recyclage sur la réanimation pour le personnel médical. • Enseignement du secourisme.	Non envisagée en milieu urbain.	• Enseignement généralisé du secourisme dans le public. • Enseignement et recyclage sur la réanimation pour le personnel médical local.	Si la réanimation peut être pratiquée sur place par le personnel médical : 90 morts évités.
Amélioration de la qualité des soins pendant le transport.	• Réanimation assurée sur ambulance du C.H.R.	32 morts évités.	• Secteur d'intervention des ambulances du C.H.R.	Secteur d'intervention optimal en réanimation à partir du C.H.R. : délai d'intervention (*) ≤ 1 heure 7 morts évités.
	• Interdiction du transport des blessés en voiture particulière. • Réglementation des transports primaires en ambulance privée (secouriste obligatoire).	4 morts évités.	• Interdiction du transport des blessés en voiture particulière. • Réglementation des transports primaires en ambulance privée (secouriste obligatoire).	9 morts évités.
alternative — Réduction délai de transport.	• Permanence du service de garde.	Non envisagée si on pratique la réanimation.	• Hélicoptère ou autre moyen.	Non envisagée si on pratique la réanimation sur place.
Réduction des coûts.	Problèmes de coordination et d'organisation d'un système intégré d'alerte, de secours et de soins.			

(*) Délai d'intervention = délai d'alerte + délai d'arrivée d'une ambulance sur les lieux.

actuelle. A la combinaison des diagnostics correspond la structure de le demande actuelle. A la combinaison de délais et de niveau de soins qu'on utilise pour le calcul, correspond une forme particulière de l'offre de secours et de soins d'urgence. On a représenté dans un tableau les résultats du calcul effectué pour différentes modifications du système actuel, regroupées selon les objectifs généraux qui sont notés dans la première colonne (tableau 3). Il s'agit là de nombre de décès évités pour l'ensemble du département de la Côte d'Or sur l'année 1970 consécutifs à la mise en oeuvre des différents moyens d'intervention qui sont envisagés.

7. Critères de choix utilisés

On a tenu à conserver une pluralité de critères exprimant chacun une certaine "dimension" du choix collectif en question. On a affaire en effet à des actions alternatives très hétérogènes quant à leur importance politique et budgétaire, à leur étalement dans le temps, à leur degré d'indépendance mutuelle, à l'incertitude relative qui pèse sur leur possibilité réelle de réalisation. A côté des critères pouvant être considérés comme des "résultats" directs de l'étude provenant de l'utilisation du modèle et des analyses budgétaires, on a donc placé des commentaires destinés à nuancer et à enrichir les résultats quantitatifs précédents. C'est l'ensemble de ces informations qui doit, finalement être pris en compte par les utilisateurs. La nécessaire synthèse qu'implique un choix, impose alors d'opérer une pondération entre les différents aspects évoqués. Le mode actuel de la prise de décision en matière sociale est tel qu'il parait parfaitement illusoire d'apporter une sophistication excessive dans les études qui ont pour fonction d'améliorer ce processus. La fonction pédagogique et explicative semble actuellement plus importante que les résultats eux-mêmes.

Un tableau résume, dans cet esprit les principaux résultats de l'étude relatifs à cinq programmes (tableau 4). La première ligne de ce tableau, notée Service d'Aide Médicale Urgente (SAMU) concerne la création d'un service hospitalier spécialisé dans l'accueil et le transport des urgences; ce service comprend dans le cas présent une unité de soins intensifs de 8 lits ainsi qu'un ensemble de services techniques pouvant fonctionner sans interruption.

Tableau 4
Coûts-efficacité de cinq programmes

Actions	Coût sur 5 ans (1) (en millions de francs)	Coût actualisé sur 5 ans (2) (en millions de francs)	Nombre de morts évités sur 5 ans	Ratio : coût actualisé Nombre de mort évités (sur 5 ans)
S.A.M.U.	6,630 7,07 (*)	5,02 5,36 (*)	195	25 800 27 500 (*)
Secourisme généralisé.	0,51	0,386	78	4 950
Réanimation par corps médical local.	4,040	2,77	270	10 250
Téléphones le long des routes.	0,5	0,379	80	4 750
Réglementation des transports en ambulances privées, voitures particulières.	0,007	0,007	52	135

(1) A francs constants.
(2) Taux d'actualisation (10 %) ne tenant pas compte de l'évolution des prix relatifs.
(*) *Avertissement :* les actions ayant été étudiées séparément, l'efficacité globale n'est pas ég<
compte des liaisons existant entre les actions.
(*) **Estimations** obtenues à partir des données réelles d'amortissement.

8. Conclusion

Indépendamment des résultats directement utilisables qu'elle a fournis, l'étude a eu pour fonction de démontrer les possibilités offertes par l'analyse de système et l'utilisation des modèles en matière de santé publique. Dans ce secteur les méthodes quantitatives sont encore essentiellement descriptives ou utilisées dans le cadre d'expérimentations statistiques contrôlées; celles-ci se révèlent incapables de fournir l'information pertinente pour les principaux choix techniques et politiques. L'approche de la recherche opérationnelle

Tableau 4

Problèmes associés	Hypothèses et commentaires	Liaisons entre les actions
— problèmes généraux de l'anesthésiologie en milieu hospitalier public. — pénurie actuelle d'anesthésistes-réanimateurs. — organisation de l'urgence en milieu hospitalier.	Le SAMU est un investissement complexe dont l'objectif est beaucoup plus large que ce qui concerne le relevage des blessés ou malades.	Action indépendante.
— participation et motivation du public par rapport au secourisme. — motivation des praticiens pour assurer cet enseignement.	Secourisme pratiqué par 10 % de la population active ; hypothèse : dans ces conditions, il y a au moins un secouriste parmi les témoins d'un accident.	Particulièrement lié à la création des SAMU et au recyclage des médecins praticiens.
— préparation des médecins praticiens à assumer de nouvelles responsabilités, ... — problèmes d'organisation du dispositif d'alerte.	Réanimation disponible en milieu rural dans les conditions de délais actuellement observées.	Actions liées à la création des SAMU.
— étude de répartition optimale des bornes téléphoniques et des moyens de financement.	Installation de 20 bornes d'appel placées de façon optimale. Réduction du délai moyen d'alerte de 5 minutes.	Action indépendante. Possibilités de financement autres que budgétaires.
— problèmes de réglementation et de contrôle.	Possibilité de secourisme assurée pour tous transports en urgence.	Action dépendante d'une organisation cohérente et efficace du système de secours d'urgence.

la somme des efficacités de chacune des actions ; les coûts doivent être interprétés en tenant

peut jouer un rôle important dans ce secteur dont le développement est considérable mais qui continue encore souvent à fonctionner selon un mode artisanal. Mais la crédibilité de cette approche est liée semble-t-il à l'effort de synthèse qui pourra être opéré avec les acquis de l'épidémiologie et des sciences sociales.

Bibliographie

[1] D. Minvielle et F. Fagnani, Etude du système mobile de secours et soins d'urgence, Bull. INSERM 26, No. 2 (1971).

[2] F. Fagnani, Application de la recherche opérationnelle à l'organisation des secours d'urgence, Cahier Sociol. Demographie Med. 11, No. 4 (1971).

M. Ross, ed., OR '72. North-Holland Publishing Company (1973)

43

IMPROVING THE PERFORMANCE OF A LOCAL AUTHORITY AMBULANCE SERVICE

Amélioration de l'efficacité du service d'ambulance des autorités locales

J. CANTWELL, B. LENEHAN and J. O'FARRELL

Department of Finance, Dublin, Ireland

Abstract. The operation of a local authority ambulance service in a sparsely populated area in the west of Ireland was examined, with a view to improving its performance, particularly in relation to emergency calls. In addition, it was important to ensure that the non-emergency aspects of the service were not neglected.

The characteristics of the area and the demand pattern for service were analysed in detail. The performance of the service was measured by the percentage of emergency cases reached within certain specific time-periods from the moment the call was received. A general model was developed which enabled the number and deployment of ambulances for any given level of service to be determined. The model is easily adaptable to each of the other local authority areas in the country.

In its main recommendations, the study proposed changes in the number and distribution of the ambulances and in the staffing arrangements. A modified form of the proposed scheme was implemented in a portion of the area for a trial period, and the results obtained are compared with the performance as forecast by the model.

1. Introduction

This paper is based on a study carried out by the Irish Government OR Unit on behalf of a Consultative Council set up by the Minister for Health to examine the ambulance service. The service caters for both emergency and non-emergency requirements but the prime concern of the Minister was to remove any inadequacies in the performance of the service in dealing with emergency calls.

There are many factors which influence the effective operation of an ambulance service, ranging from the availability of efficient means of communication between the public and the ambulance control centres to the type of vehicle used. The main concern is to get the patient to hospital as quickly as possible, but the time required to transport a patient to hospital is governed principally by the distance to the hospital, a factor over which there is no control since the locations of the hospitals are fixed. The time required to summon an ambulance to the scene depends on how long it takes to contact the service plus the time which elapses before the ambulance reaches the patient. This latter aspect of the problem, the time required for an ambulance to reach a patient from the moment a call is received (the response time), is governed essentially by the number of ambulances available to service a given area and the way in which they are deployed throughout the area. It is this aspect of the problem which is discussed in this paper, although other factors including the organisation, staffing and control of the service were examined during the course of the study [1]. The response time to emergency calls is particularly important, but an adequate level of service must be provided for all calls including non-emergency calls. Non-emergency calls involve the transportation of both stretcher and ambulant patients to and from hospitals and out-patient clinics.

The area administered by the Western Health Board was selected for a pilot study. This area, which is composed of Counties Galway, Mayo and Roscommon, covers 5442 square miles and has a widely scattered population of 320 000. When the study was carried out there were 19 ambulances in the area allocated among 9 depots (fig. 2). Each depot had its own radio transmitter and controlled its own ambulances, each of which was equipped with suitable receiving/transmitting apparatus. Each depot however was virtually autonomous; it serviced the calls it received itself and calls were rarely transferred to other depots.

2. Data analysis

An analysis of a sample of data for two months of 1969 selected at random, revealed that approximately 1600 emergency and 4700 non-emergency calls were made in the area during the year. The number of calls per day averaged 17 and was uniformly distributed throughout the week. The number of calls per hour was also constant and had a Poisson distribution with a day-time average of 1.14 calls per hour and a night-time average of 0.3 calls per hour. Emergency calls averaged 0.2 calls per hour during the day-

Table 1
Present approximate performance of the ambulance service in the WHB area

	Time (min)				
	15	30	45	60	90
Percentage of emergency cases reached within the specified time	41	60	78	90	99.9

time and 0.16 calls per hour during the night, while non-emergency calls averaged 0.9 calls per hour during the day-time and 0.14 calls per hour at night.

The number of calls per 1000 inhabitants varied from county to county and from district to district within each county. No reason for this variability could be found and regression analysis failed to establish any significant relationship between the number of calls and such factors as distance from hospital or ambulance depot, population density, age profile or wealth of the community.

It was agreed with the Ambulance Consultative Council that the performance of the ambulance service would be measured by the speed of its response to emergency calls. When this measure was applied to the existing system the result shown in table 1 was obtained. These figures are an approximation as the records did not contain sufficient data for an accurate calculation to be made.

3. Method of approach

At first glance the problem might appear to be a straightforward queueing situation, but it can be shown that even with relatively few ambulances and an unlikely long response time the probability of a queue forming is negligible.

Assume, for example, an average service time* of 120 minutes exponentially distributed and 5 ambulances serving the area. Then for day-time

---

* Service time is the time which elapses from the moment the ambulance leaves its base until it returns to its base. Response time, which is the time taken to reach a patient, is less than half the service time. The average response time in the WHB area is (service time/2 − 5 minutes).

operation, when the distribution of the time of arrival of calls is exponential with a mean of 52.5 minutes, the probability of six or more customers in the system, i.e., the probability of a queue forming is 0.034. If the number of ambulances is increased to six then the probability of a queue forming is reduced to 0.003. As the number of ambulances is increased and the response time improved the probability of a queue forming is reduced.

In addition, it was evident from the records that emergency calls never had to queue for service. An ambulance was always available yet the service provided was not considered adequate. It was unlikely, therefore, that an improvement in service would introduce a queueing factor into the waiting time. These considerations suggested that the response time is influenced more by the distances the ambulances have to travel to reach the patient than by the actual demand for service. The problem thus involved the determination of both the number of ambulances required and where they should be stationed so that the response time would be within acceptable limits.

An analytic solution is possible [1] but the method is cumbersome and was discarded in favour of a heuristic approach using a simulation model. A model was developed which simulated the existing system in the WHB area. The model is general and can be used to simulate an ambulance service for any given area.

4. The model

The area was divided into 42 districts of approximately equal size. Each district is described in the model by the Cartesian coordinates of its demographic centre of gravity. A similar method is used to describe the location of both hospitals and ambulances.

Distances between points are calculated as the sum of the absolute differences of the coordinates. Similarly, an ambulance having covered, say, one third of the distance between two points is taken to have travelled one third the x distance and one third the y distance. A check on the accuracy of this method of calculating distances gave a correlation coefficient of 0.98 when compared with the actual road distance.

Considerable difficulty was experienced in devising a method to calculate the response time. The records gave only the overall service time, i.e., the time from departure to return, no record was kept of the time to reach a patient. Furthermore, the distribution of service times did not follow any recognised pattern.

To overcome this difficulty service time was considered to consist of two elements, a minimum time determined by the distance the ambulance had to travel and a random component. The travelling time to each call was cal-culated on the basis of an average speed of 30 mph. When this component was subtracted from the recorded service time for each call the residual time was found to have a gamma distribution ($r = 2$) of mean 22 minutes. This component of the response time was considered to consist of the time spent at the scene of the accident or at the patient's home, plus an element which, since it was assumed that all calls came from the demographic centre of gravity of the district, could be attributed to the distance to the patient from this point. Observations revealed that the time spent at the scene of an accident or at the patient's home was exponentially distributed with a mean of 10 minutes. The remaining component then, which had an exponential distribution of mean 12 minutes, was a function of the distance to the patient from the demographic centre of gravity of the district.

Thus it was assumed that the time taken to reach a patient was composed of the time to travel to the centre of the district plus a random component sampled from an exponential distribution of mean 6 minutes.

Calls are divided into two categories, emergency having priority 1 and non-emergency having priority 2. A priority 1 call can pre-empt a priority 2 call provided the priority 2 patient has not been picked up. All calls are dealt with immediately they arrive and each call is serviced by the nearest available ambulance. When an ambulance becomes free, if there are no priority 1 calls in the queue, the position of other ambulances travelling on priority 1 calls is checked. If this free ambulance is nearer the emergency it takes over. During the driver's meal times ambulances are considered to be available for emer-gency calls but not for non-emergency calls.

The arrival of a call generates another call of the same type at a time sampled from the appropriate distribution. Each call is assigned to a district. This is done by a random process having regard to the frequency of calls from each district. A destination for the patient is assigned by a random process which chooses in proportion to the hospitals used by the district.

Calls are held in a circular queue, and attended to on a first come first served basis according to priority. The method used is a modified form of that used by Tocher [2].

5. Experimental results

Experiments were performed using different numbers of ambulances. Each experiment simulated a year's operation of the service. The input for each

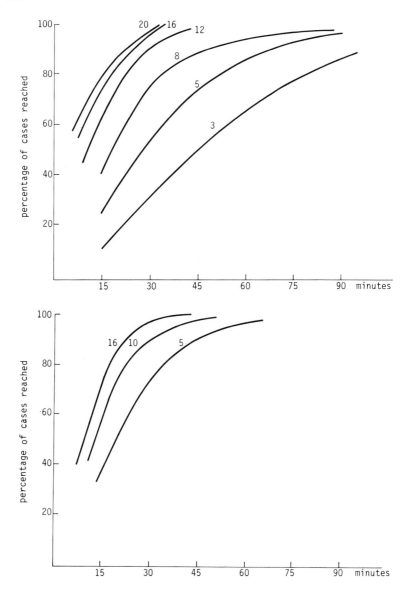

Fig. 1. Percentage of emergency cases reached within various time periods for different numbers of ambulances. Upper: day-time; lower: night-time.

experiment consisted of specifying the number of ambulances to be allocated to the area and where they should be stationed. The output gave details of response time, the average time to reach both emergency and non-emergency patients, the longest time an emergency and a non-emergency patient had to wait for an ambulance after it was called, the number of times patients had to queue for service and the length of time each patient spent in the queue. In addition, information was provided on ambulance utilisation and the number of times ambulances were diverted from non-emergency calls to service emergency calls.

The ambulances were located where it appeared they would be most effective. When the resultant output was obtained, the least utilised ambulances were moved towards the busier ones and the experiment repeated. This process was continued until improvements in performance were negligible. This procedure was not as time consuming as it might appear since many locations were obvious e.g. the large towns. Furthermore, the options were reduced by the desirability of leaving at least one ambulance at each existing depot. Different experiments were performed for day-time and night-time operation because of the different levels of demand.

The results of some of the experiments are shown in fig. 1.

It is interesting to compare the response time to emergency calls for day-time and night-time operation. Five or six ambulances on duty during the night would be capable of providing an appreciably better service than a similar number during the day. However, the difference in performance becomes less pronounced as the number of ambulances increases. There are two main reasons for this: (1) If a small number of ambulances was on duty during the day, queues of emergency cases would form; this would not happen during the night due to the low demand for service. (2) The number of ambulances required for a high level of service is determined more by the distance the ambulances have to travel than by the level of demand.

6. Interpretation of results

The Ambulance Consultative Council indicated that it would be satisfied to be able to guarantee a response time of 30 minutes to 95% of all emergency cases. Reference to the results of the experiments reveals that for day-time operation 14 ambulances suitably dispersed would be able to reach 96% of emergency cases within 30 minutes. When the coordinates of each of the 14 ambulance bases were marked on a map it was found that some adjustments to their locations had to be made to cater for the heavily

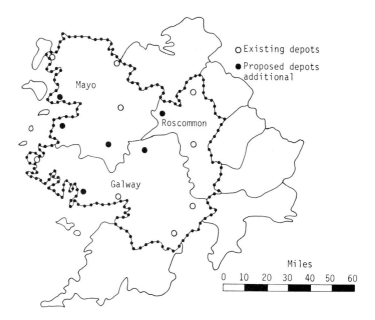

Fig. 2. Location of existing and proposed new depots.

Table 2
Expected performance of the 16 ambulances

	Time (min)		
	15	30	45
Percentage of emergency cases reached within the specified time	76	98	100

	Waiting-time (min)	
	average	maximum
Emergency	13	45
Non-emergency	16.5	60

indented coastline of counties Galway and Mayo. Other minor adjustments were made so that all ambulances would be stationed in towns or large villages. As a result of these adjustments two further ambulances were allocated to the area so that the actual performance of the 16 ambulances would at least equal the theoretical performance of the 14 ambulances as predicted by the model. The expected performance of these 16 ambulances is given in table 2. The location of existing and proposed new depots are shown in fig. 2.

Fifteen ambulances would be required at night to guarantee the same level of services as that being provided during the day. However, the utilisation of these ambulances would be so low that a fleet of that size on duty during the night could hardly be justified. It may be more realistic to reduce the number of ambulances on duty during the night to five or six. If such a decision was taken by the WHB it would at least be taken with full knowledge of its effect of the level of service.

7. Sensitivity analysis

The scheme for day time operation was subjected to a sensitivity analysis. The demand was increased in steps to four times the 1969 demand and the experiment repeated in each case. The results are shown in table 3. The deterioration in service with increasing demand is remarkably small. Again this supports the theory that due to the large area and relatively sparse population the number of ambulances required is influenced more by the size of the area than by the demand for service.

Table 3
Sensitivity analysis performed on the scheme requiring 16 ambulances

Demand	Percentage of emergency cases reached within (min)				Average waiting-time (min)
	15	30	45	60	
(1969)	76	98	100		13.0
(1969) × 1.5	71	96	99	100	14.1
(1969) × 2	69	94	99	100	14.6
(1969) × 3	63	92	99	100	16.3
(1969) × 4	60	90	98	99	17.3

8. Trial run

With the cooperation of the Local Authority in Co Mayo a scheme based on the study was operated for a trial period of 5 weeks. The purpose of the trial was to (a) check the validity of the model and (b) discover what difficulties might arise in implementing the proposal in the whole WHB area. Table 4 shows the level of service as predicted by the model and that actually obtained during the trial period.

Two reasons are suggested which may explain the discrepancy between the predicted and the actual performance:

(1) Some of the ambulances were staffed by two men but others had to get a nurse from the local hospital to accompany the driver before setting out on an emergency call. This created a tendency on the part of the controller to use the ambulances staffed by two men as often as possible to obviate the necessity of looking for a nurse.

(2) The discrepancy in the short haul cases might be due to attributing too slow a speed to the ambulances and too little time to the search process. These compensating errors would not be noticed on long journeys.

Table 4
Actual compared to predicted performance for the trial run

	Percentage of emergency cases reached within (min)				Maximum waiting-time (min)
	15	30	45	60	
Forecast	51	83	90	98	90
Actual	44	79	87	97	86

9. Conclusions

The recommendations made as a result of the study were accepted in principle by the Ambulance Consultative Council and arrangements are under way for their implementation in the Western Health Board area. The solution obtained appears reasonable, that is, that the ambulances should be dispersed more widely throughout the area; they should, in effect, be located as near as possible to the source of the demand for the service. This principle could be equally applicable to other areas of health service organisation, although the tendency now appears to be to centralise services in order to achieve economies of scale. This tendency may have the effect of depriving the people of these services or, at least, making them more difficult to obtain. This is something which needs to be examined, can we achieve the advantages of economy of scale while at the same time not take the services away from the people they are supposed to serve?

References

[1] The local authority ambulance service, report presented to the Ambulance Consultative Council (May 1971).
[2] K.D. Tocher, The art of simulation (English Univ. Press, 1963).

44

A GENERALIZED COST-EFFECTIVENESS MODEL FOR HEALTH PLANNING *

*Modèle d'efficacité du coût generalisé
de la planification de la santé*

GEORGE W. TORRANCE

McMaster University, Hamilton, Canada

Abstract. The cost-effectiveness approach to health planning is generalized by combining it with a new morbidity-mortality health index. The index for a particular health state is the utility of that state as perceived by society. The index-day can then be viewed as a disease- and program-independent measure of health, and the model structured to maximize these units, thus maximizing health utility, for the given set of constraints.

Two techniques are investigated for measuring the required utilities: a time trade-off technique developed specifically for this research and a von Neumann-Morgenstern standard gamble approach. Equations are developed for use in calculating the effectiveness of any particular health care program. Two computational algorithms are presented for analyzing a set of potential health care programs to select the optimal subset: a cost-effectiveness ranking algorithm developed for this project and a standard zero–one integer programming algorithm. The model is tested and demonstrated by applying it to three different programs in the health service system: tuberculosis screening, prevention of hemolytic disease, and kidney dialysis and transplantation.

1. Introduction

Cost-benefit and cost-effectiveness analysis, the traditional analytical tools for program planning and evaluation in the public sector, have serious shortcomings when applied to health care programs. Cost-benefit analysis measures the economic, but not necessarily the health, consequences of a

* Supported in part by the Ontario Department of Health, Research Grant PR 118; and McMaster University Summer Research Support Program.

program [1–3]. Cost-effectiveness analysis measures the health benefits in program-specific units, thus precluding inter-program comparisons [4–6].

Dissatisfaction with these two traditional approaches led to the development of an alternative model [7,8] that attempts to combine the advantages of the other two. Basically, the new model is an extension or generalization of the cost-effectiveness approach achieved by combining it with a new morbidity-mortality health index. This paper presents a brief summary of the proposed model.

2. Health index

Many researchers have discussed the need for a combined morbidity-mortality health index and several approaches have been proposed [9–12]. None was considered satisfactory for the needs of this model, and a new approach founded on utility theory was developed.

Health is considered a three-dimensional phenomenon consisting of physical, emotional and social components. Each dimension has a large range of possible states, varying from perfect health to total absence of function. The health of an individual at any one time (a health state) can be considered as a point in three-dimensional space, with the axes representing physical function (x_1), emotional function (x_2) and social function (x_3). Most points in this three-dimensional space are feasible – people may at times be functioning quite poorly on one of the three scales and yet quite well on the other two.

In this research, the index value for a particular health state is the *utility of that state as perceived by society*. In this way, the model attempts to allocate resources in the health service system in a manner which will maximize the total health utility achieved by society. If h represents the index value, h is a function of the health state; i.e., $h = f(x_1, x_2, x_3)$. However, rather than attempting to define this function explicitly, the index value for any health state of interest is measured directly, by defining the health state precisely and then employing a utility measurement technique on an appropriate sample of subjects from the population of interest. The utility of a particular health state will differ for each individual in the sample, and indeed, it will vary over time for any one individual. The general index, however, is an aggregate utility for the population of interest, and thus, exhibits greater stability.

The health index is measured on a linear interval scale, standardized at a value of one for the healthy state $(h_1 = 1)$ and zero for the dead state $(h_n = 0)$. The index value for a state is measured in such a way that it represents the average utility of the state over a specified time period (t), independent of prognosis and financial considerations.

Two measurement techniques are available: the classical von Neumann-Morgenstern standard gamble approach and a new time trade-off technique, developed specifically for this research. In both cases, the first step is the determination of the time period of interest (t) for each state; if several states have identical time periods, they can be grouped together for convenience. The procedure for measuring a group of states begins by asking the subject to preference rank the states, assuming the same time period t for each state and assuming identical prognoses. Let $i = 2, 3, ..., n-1$ represent the preference rankings for a particular respondent ($i = 1$ and $i = n$ are reserved for the reference states, healthy and dead, respectively). The utilities for this respondent are then measured using either the von Neumann-Morgenstern standard gamble approach or the time trade-off technique as described below.

2.1. Von Neumann-Morgenstern standard gamble

Fig. 1 shows the measurement of state $n-1$, the morbidity state least preferred in the ranking. The subject is asked to choose between two alternatives: alternative 1 (the certainty alternative) – healthy for time t, state $n-1$ for time t, followed by death; alternative 2 (the gamble alternative) – healthy for time t, followed by a hypothetical drug which has a probability p of keeping him healthy (completely asymptomatic) for time t followed by death, and a probability $1-p$ of causing immediate death. The probability p is varied to locate the point at which the respondent is indifferent between these two alternatives. At this indifference point, the required utility is calcu-

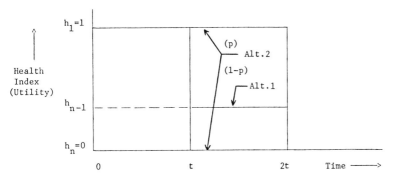

Fig. 1. Standard gamble for state $n-1$.

lated as follows:

Utility of alternative 1 = utility of alternative 2

$$h_1 t + h_{n-1} t = h_1 t + h_1 tp + h_n t(1-p) \,.$$

Using $h_1 = 1$ and $h_n = 0$ (by definition), this simplifies to:

$$h_{n-1} = p \,.$$

The apparently superfluous requirement that in each alternative the respondent begins by being healthy for time t is in fact necessary to ensure that at all times, the respondent is dealing with his future death and never his immediate death. This precaution not only improves the reliability of the resultant utilities, but is consistent with their eventual use — in planning decisions concerning future health programs where the trade-offs to be evaluated will all be in the future.

The utility of any general state i, other than $n-1$, could be measured in the same way; however, a modified procedure is recommended in which the reference states are 1 and $i+1$ rather than 1 and n, and the common future prognosis is state 1 rather than state n. These modifications have the advantage of avoiding continual reference to state n (dead), and more importantly, of avoiding extremely small indifference probabilities which are difficult for the subject to estimate.

2.2. Time trade-off method

An alternative technique for measuring the required utilities was developed as part of this research. Fig. 2 shows the application of this method to state $n-1$. Here the respondent is asked to choose between two certainty alternatives: alternative 1 — state $n-1$ for time t followed by death; alternative 2 — healthy for time $x < t$, followed by death. The respondent's indifference point is located by varying the time x. The average utility for state $n-1$ over time period t, h_{n-1}, is determined by equating the utilities of the two alternatives:

Utility of alternative 1 = utility of alternative 2

$$h_{n-1} t = h_1 x + h_n(t - x) \,,$$

$$h_{n-1} = x/t \,.$$

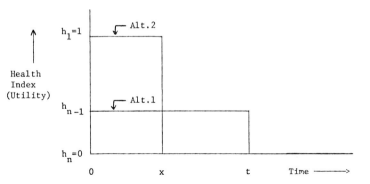

Fig. 2. Time trade-off for state $n-1$.

For any general state i, other than $n-1$, the alternatives become: alternative 1 — state i for time t followed by healthy, and alternative 2 — state $i+1$ for time $x < t$ followed by healthy. Again x is varied to determine the indifference point, at which the required utility is

$$h_i = 1 - \frac{x}{t}(1 - h_{i+1}) \ .$$

3. Effectiveness and cost measures

When health index values have been determined for all relevant health states, it is a relatively straightforward calculation to determine the effectiveness (E) of a program, measured in health-days (index-days). From an analysis of the program, determine $d_{jk}(y)$, the number of man days changed from health state j to health state k during the year y as a result of the program. Since the matrix of state changes is skew-symmetric $[d_{jk}(y) = -d_{kj}(y)]$ let $D_{jk}(y) = \max [0, d_{jk}(y)]$. Next, define $E(y)$ as the health effectiveness of the program in year y, measured in health days and representing the change in health utility in year y caused by the program. It can be found from:

$$E(y) = \sum_{j=1}^{n} \sum_{k=1}^{n} D_{jk}(y)(h_k - h_j) \ ,$$

where h_j and h_k are the utilities of states j and k, respectively. Let E be the change in health utility (health effectiveness) for all years affected by the program, with future changes discounted to their equivalent present value at an annual rate r.

$$E = \sum_{y=1}^{\infty} (1+r)^{-y} E(y) .$$

Substitution for $E(y)$ yields the following formula for the program health effectiveness

$$E = \sum_{y=1}^{\infty} (1+r)^{-y} \sum_{j=1}^{n} \sum_{k=1}^{n} D_{jk}(y)(h_k - h_j) . \tag{1}$$

The cost of the program has four components: $C_1(y)$ is the direct cost of the program in year y, $C_2(y)$ is the indirect cost of the program in year y (earnings lost due to program participation), $C_3(y)$ is the reduction in the direct costs of health care in year y as a result of the program, and $C_4(y)$ is the reduction in the indirect costs of disease, disability and death in year y as a result of the program (the indirect costs are measured in terms of lost earnings).

C_1 and C_2 represent resources consumed by the program; C_3 and C_4 represent resources released or created by the program; thus, the net cost of the program to society in year y is:

$$C(y) = C_1(y) + C_2(y) - C_3(y) - C_4(y) ,$$

and the total net cost of the program over all years, with future costs discounted at an annual interest rate i, is:

$$C = \sum_{y=1}^{\infty} (1+i)^{-y} C(y) . \tag{2}$$

In practice, the summation over y in eqs. (1) and (2) can be truncated at a value sufficiently large that, because of the discounting factor, little error is introduced.

4. Optimization

The criterion for optimization of the model is to maximize the total effectiveness for the given constraints, thus maximizing the increase in health utility for society. Two algorithms are available: a cost-effectiveness ranking algorithm or a mathematical programming algorithm.

The cost-effectiveness ranking algorithm, listed below, can be used on problems with mutually-exclusive programs and a single constraint on total cost. Let e_i and c_i represent the effectiveness and cost of the ith program respectively.

(1) For each set of mutually exclusive programs, determine the best initial program and add it to the list of candidate programs.
(a) If a set has any $c_i < 0$, the best initial program is the point with the minimum c_i. In case of a tie, select the point with the maximum e_i.
(b) If a set has no $c_i < 0$, the best initial program is the point with the maximum $\Delta E/\Delta C$. (For the initial list $\Delta E/\Delta C = e_i/c_i$.) In case of a tie, select the point with the minimum ΔC.

(2) Select the best program from the list of candidate programs using the same criteria as step 1 above, and enter it into the solution.

(3) Replace this program in the list of candidate programs by the next best program from the same mutually exclusive set. If program r is currently in solution, the replacement for it is that program i which maximizes $\Delta E/\Delta C$, $\Delta E > 0$, where $\Delta E = e_i - e_r$ and $\Delta C = c_i - c_r$. In case of a tie, select the increment with the minimum ΔC.

(4) Repeat steps 2 and 3 until programs for consideration are exhausted.

(5) The sequence with which programs enter the solution gives their cost-effectiveness priority ranking.

This algorithm has been programmed and implemented on a time-shared computer system. (The program listing is available in the original research [7].) The basic output of the algorithm is a list of programs ranked in their cost-effectiveness priority sequence with cumulative and marginal costs and effectivenesses.

An alternative approach to this optimization problem is to use a standard 0–1 integer programming formulation. Here the basic model, equivalent to the problem solved by the cost-effectiveness ranking algorithm, is formulated as follows:

$$\text{Maximize} \sum_{i=1}^{n} e_i x_i , \qquad \text{subject to} \sum_{i=1}^{n} c_i x_i \leqslant C ,$$

$$x_i = 0, 1; \quad i = 1, 2, ..., n, \quad \sum_{i \in I_j} x_i \leqslant 1, \quad j = 1, 2, ..., p , \tag{3}$$

where $x_i = 1$ implies the ith program is in the solution (accepted), $x_i = 0$ implies the ith program is not in the solution (rejected), e_i is the effectiveness of the ith program, c_i is the cost of the ith program, C is the total budget available, and I_j is the jth set of mutually exclusive programs.

The major advantage of this formulation is its great flexibility in handling additional constraints. For example, suppose that it is desired to individually constrain the amount of physician time, the amount of nurse time, and the number of hospital bed-days to no more than the total amounts available; P, F, and B, respectively. Let p_i, F_i and b_i be the amounts of each of these resources used by the ith program. Then, the following three additional constraints should be included:

$$\sum_{i=1}^{n} p_i x_i \leqslant P , \qquad \sum_{i=1}^{n} f_i x_i \leqslant F , \qquad \sum_{i=1}^{n} b_i x_i \leqslant B .$$

Note that this formulation allows the analyst, through parametric analysis, to investigate the marginal value of additional units of each type of resource. That is, it can answer the question: How much additional health would be created by adding an additional unit of physician time, of nursing time, or of hospital beds?

Readers familiar with mathematical programming will appreciate that further constraints can readily be added to handle any number of more complicated variations of this basic problem. However, unless additional constraints are required, it has been found [7] that the basic problem as formulated in (3) is best solved by the vastly more efficient cost-effectiveness ranking algorithm.

5. Application

The model was tested and demonstrated through application to three different health-care programs: tuberculosis screening, prevention of hemolytic disease of the newborn, and kidney dialysis and transplantation. The three basic programs were partitioned into sub-programs and expanded into program variations, making a total of 669 different programs for evaluation.

Utility values were required for five health states in addition to the healthy and dead states. As a pilot project, the utilities were measured on a small convenience sample of eleven physicians; a sample size that was too small to provide precise results, but was sufficient to demonstrate the feasibility and the reliability of the proposed measurements techniques. Further research to measure utility values on a larger random sample of the general public would be valuable as an additional test of these techniques.

Available data on program outcomes and costs and the health state utility data discussed above were used in eqs. (1) and (2) to calculate the effectiveness and the cost of each of the 669 programs. Both optimization algorithms were implemented, with the cost-effectiveness ranking algorithm proving immensely more efficient. In fact, the 0–1 integer programming formulation was so inefficient that the problem had to be reduced significantly before it could even be run. Otherwise, no particular difficulties were encountered in the application.

6. Discussion

The generalized cost-effectiveness model described in this paper takes a society-wide view of costs; however, it is sufficiently flexible that other cost definitions could be readily substituted if desired. Benefits (i.e., health days) are assumed to be additive. This is a consequence of the linearity of the health index scale and the fact that every person is given the same weight in the model. The contribution of one health day to the indicated program effectiveness is the same regardless of the person experiencing that day of health. If desired, the model could be easily modified to handle other weighting assumptions.

The health index described in this model is currently somewhat cumbersome in that specific utilities must be measured for each application of the model. Further research to develop a general health utility scale to circumvent this requirement would be useful. Furthermore, the index described here, in addition to its application in the model, could prove independently useful for measuring, comparing and monitoring community and national health levels.

The model appears to be applicable to a wide variety of health programs, perhaps all. In this research it was applied to three different programs and no particular difficulties were encountered. The requirement for accurate data about the effect of a given program on patient outcomes can presumably be met by appropriate health care experimentation; otherwise, currently available data may constitute a practical limitation. While the scope of applicability requires verification by further research, it appears that, given adequate data, the model could be used to optimize the total health service system, allocating health resources to programs and activities so as to maximize the overall utility achieved.

References

[1] H.E. Klarman, The economics of health (Columbia Univ. Press, New York, 1965).

[2] A.R. Prest and R. Turvey, Cost-benefit analysis: a survey, Econ. J. 75 (1965) 683.

[3] D.P. Rice, Estimating the cost of illness, Health Econ. Ser., No. 6 (U.S. Govt. Printing Office, Washington, 1966).

[4] H.E. Klarman, J. Francis and G.O. Rosenthal, Cost effectiveness analysis applied to the treatment of chronic renal disease, Med. Care 6, No. 1 (1968) 48.

[5] L. Lipworth, Cost effectiveness of a preventive program in renal disease, Milbank Mem. Fund Quart. (1969) 70.

[6] K.M. McCaffree, The economic basis for the development of community mental health programs, Med. Care 6, No. 4 (1968) 286.

[7] G.W. Torrance, A generalized cost-effectiveness model for the evaluation of health programs, working paper, Res. Ser. No. 101, Fac. of Business, McMaster Univ., Hamilton (1970).

[8] G.W. Torrance, W.H. Thomas and D.L. Sackett, A utility maximization model for the evaluation of health care programs, Health Serv. Res. 7, No. 2 (1972) 118.

[9] C.L. Chiang, An index of health: mathematical models, Ser. 2, No. 5 (Public Health Serv., Washington, 1965).

[10] S. Fanshel and J.W. Bush, A health status index and its application to health-services outcomes, Opns. Res. 18, No. 6 (1970) 1021.

[11] A.I. Kisch et al., A new proxy measure for health status, Health serv. res. 4, No. 3 (1969) 223.

[12] D.F. Sullivan, Conceptual problems in developing an index of health, Vital and Health Statistics, Ser. 2, No. 17; Public Health Serv. Publ. No. 1000 (1966).

M. Ross, ed., OR '72. North-Holland Publishing Company (1973)

45

OR ASPECTS OF A MANAGEMENT INFORMATION SYSTEM*

Aspects de la recherche opérationnelle d'un système informatique de gestion

C.G. DE LEEUW

N.V. Philips' Gloeilampenfabrieken, Eindhoven, The Netherlands

Abstract. The control of materials flow increasingly calls for computer based information systems, (MIS) which are either systems for registration and retrieval or systems with built-in decision rules. Strong doubts exist about the applicability of the second category since the "classical" OR approach aims mainly at the study of the individual components or at relatively small systems.

To meet the needs of management and dispel any doubts about the difficulties of OR, a Philips research team has designed and analysed an integral information system for the control of the materials flow from the purchasing and production stages through to sales. This system is called "initiating production by sales orders" (IPSO). The design is based on a combination of well-known OR systems, while the control of integration and coordination is mainly product-oriented rather than department-oriented. To avoid the pitfalls of classical OR the methods of analysis were based on the assumption that simplified approximations to solutions of many aspects of complex stochastic control systems are more useful than the exact solution of one aspect of a small problem. IPSO has been evaluated for a specific situation containing about 6000 products.

1. Introduction

The increasing complexity of business activities and the necessity to react quickly and economically to changes in the environment (e.g. the market)

---

* This paper presents some results of a study performed by a research team of the N.V. Philips' Gloeilampenfabrieken in the Netherlands, see also [1].

brings with it a growing need for computer-based information systems to assist in management decision-making. These systems, usually called management information systems (MIS), can be divided into two main categories: first, systems for information storage and retrieval only – management will make decisions based on information provided by these systems – and second, systems with built-in decision rules, i.e. information control systems. These latter perform in addition the routine part of decision procedures so that their output can be used either as "decision" or – if additional information is available – as guidance for management decisions. Since these systems contain formalised decision rules, OR might be expected to play an important role in their design and analysis. However, the failure of classical OR to do so adequately has raised strong doubts about their practical value.

In this paper we will compare the classical OR approach with a more pragmatic one, which seems to be more successful in dealing with complex situations. We will illustrate this "system engineering approach", using results obtained by a research team at the Philips company in the Netherlands. A brief outline of this research will be given in section 2.

2. The project

In 1967 the research group of the ISA department* was asked to design and analyse an information control system for the control of the flow of materials from the purchasing and production stages through to sales. Moreover they were to investigate whether it could be implemented as a computer system which would offer economic advantages as compared with current methods for control. The name of the project IPSO (Initiating Production by Sales Orders) emphasizes the objective of designing an integral control system.

An environment was chosen for investigation, for which the flow of materials has the following characteristics:

(1) All products are manufactured in one factory.

(2) The production process is a "flow shop".

(3) The products are so-called catalogued products.

(4) All products and parts should as a rule be deliverable from stock.

The factory concerned produces about 500 types of finished fluorescent light units from about 4000 different kinds of components and raw materials.

The chosen flow of materials is outlined in fig. 1.

* ISA stands for information systems and automation.

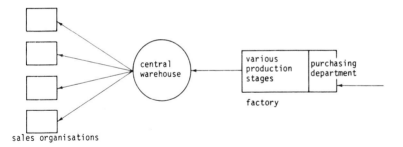

Fig. 1

A vast amount of data necessary for analysis and evaluation had to be collected from this environment. Moreover, a number of managers and staff personnel were involved in the design of the system, and an experimental field for implementation was obtained. The design, analysis and evaluation of the system took roughly 17 man-years to complete including 14 man-years expended by the research group. At present experiments are being carried out to prepare the way for full-scale implementation.

3. The design

3.1. The classical approach

The classical approach to the design of a control system mainly consists of the following:

(1) formulation of the problem,

(2) determination of the restrictions,

(3) construction of an objective function,

(4) construction of an algorithm to determine the optimal control (e.g. dynamic programming).

The main disadvantage of this approach is, that it can only be applied successfully to problems with a relatively simple structure, e.g., stock control of a single product, the s,S inventory policy and the linear decision rule for production smoothing.

The structures of information control systems are, however, far more complex. As an example, the materials flow in the IPSO project forms a network of about 5000 stocks with many complex interdependencies which are, inter alia, caused by restricted production capacity. Such a network can, of course, be scaled down considerably without losing its essential characteristics, but even so the structure will remain too complex for classical OR. Therefore another approach to design the control system had to be found.

3.2. The system engineering approach

This approach starts from the idea that control does not necessarily have to be optimal (in some restricted sense) but should rather be an improvement over the current situation. Furthermore, the following points are of importance:

(1) The principles of the control system must be understood by the manager.

(2) The design must permit the system to be analysed in order to determine the values of the control parameters and the economic evaluation of the system.

(3) The system should be as uniform as possible in order to keep down the costs of implementation and the running costs of the computer system.

Usually ideas about improvements exist in a more or less intuitive way; the project name (initiating production by sales orders) is a good example of this. However, for specific situations these ideas should be verified and preferably more ideas found.

One possible approach uses historical data to analyse the current control policies to find those aspects having adverse effects and seeks to avoid such effects as much as possible in designing a new control system. It also seeks to benefit as much as possible from the optimal results of the classical approach by basing the decision rules on these results and by adapting and extending them in such a way that they become applicable to complex situations with interdependent components.

3.3. Some IPSO examples

First, some examples will be given of adverse effects which were found by analysing the current control methods with the aid of mainly aggregated data for a period of up to ten years. These effects were mainly brought to light by the realization that warehouse and factory stocks as well as production and work force fluctuate considerably more than market demand. The examples are:

(1) the effect of department-oriented planning: Each department in the materials flow tries to optimize its own results. This leads to suboptima which can deviate considerably from the overall optimum.

(2) the batch effect: By ordering in batches the fluctuations in demand at

the warehouse and at the factory caused by the stochastic fluctuations in market demand are amplified. This leads to either high safety stocks or low performance (service level).

(3) the acceleration, or Forrester, effect: Changes in standard stock levels, brought about by changes in demand, cause magnified fluctuations in inventory of semi-finished products and materials as well as in production.

(4) the "growth psychosis" effect: Random fluctuations in demand are interpreted as trends, which are extrapolated for planning purposes.

The IPSO control system was designed with a view to avoiding these effects. The decision rules are mainly adaptations and extensions of well-known rules from the classical approach and consists of three parts:

(1) a forecasting procedure for market demand (to avoid the growth psychosis effect),

(2) a short term control system (to avoid the batch effect),

(3) a medium term control system for production smoothing (to avoid the acceleration effect and the effect of department-oriented control).

To illustrate the design the short term control system will now be discussed briefly.

3.4. The short term control

Short term control uses the u,s,S system, which combines the s,S ordering system and a runout list, and consists of two steps.

First, net requirements are planned as follows: Market demand forecasts, the present stock levels and a s,S ordering system are used to calculate the replenishment batches expected to be needed in the near future by the sales organizations. Each batch is assigned a priority index, u, which measures the interval from the present moment to the time when the replenishment is expected to be really required. This information is automatically passed on to the next level within the information system where it is combined with present stock levels to calculate future replenishment batches of that level together with their priority indices. And so on up to and including the purchasing department. The net requirements planning is illustrated in fig. 2.

In the second, or scheduling step, purchase orders, a production schedule and a transport schedule are made following the sequence of priority indices. All batches with a priority index smaller than a preset value (u_{max}) are considered in this step. This allows batches to be processed before they are actually needed (production in advance). The production and transport schedule also take account of the actual stock levels of necessary parts and available capacity.

IPSO

SHORT TERM CONTROL

NET REQUIREMENT PLANNING

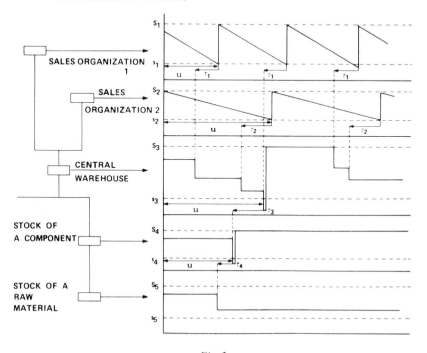

Fig. 2.

Roughly speaking the scheduling procedure can be considered as a queueing policy with dynamic priorities. Suppose the manufacture of products $i_1, i_2, \ldots$ on production unit M, requires parts $j_1, j_2, \ldots$ (see fig. 3). The first batch of i_1 is denoted by $Q_{i1,1}$, the second by $Q_{i1,2}$ and so on. Batches of $i_1, i_2, \ldots$ are standing in the queue for M in the order of their priority indices. Before the batches are actually scheduled, the sequence can change because

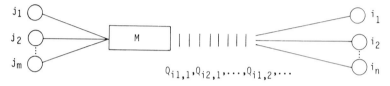

Fig. 3.

of the dynamic priorities. Moreover, a small amount of overcapacity of M will set bounds on the growth of the queue, while the use of u_{max} on the other hand will set bounds to production in advance, or, in other words, to the growth of stocks of the products $i_1, i_2,...$ The control procedure will be carried out at frequent intervals to ensure that decisions concerning purchase orders, the production schedule and the transport schedule will be based on the most recent and most accurate information. In the IPSO project a frequency of once or twice a week is optimal.

4. The analysis

As stated above, analysis of the control system is essential for both the economical evaluation and the determination of the values of the control parameters (e.g. the s and S levels and u_{max}). Again – as in the case of design – the classical approach and a system engineering approach can be distinguished.

4.1. The classical approach

While in principle the analysis will be carried out in a mathematically exact way, the classical analysis only takes account of those aspects which can be analysed as a whole, i.e., in one model. This implies that either only relatively simple systems can be analysed or – in the case of more complex systems – not all effects can be taken into account. In the latter case the different components are usually analysed separately, ignoring the interdependencies. Furthermore, unrealistic assumptions are sometimes made to make problems amenable to analysis in the classical sense.

As the most important effects, such as coordination, are usually the most difficult to analyse, analytical models of complex control systems, if at all possible, only resemble reality in a defective way. As a consequence they cannot provide those numerical values of control parameters necessary to obtain some important benefits of the control system, e.g., the effects of coordination. It is thus very doubtful whether economic advantages can be achieved at all.

4.2. The system engineering approach

This approach requires that all important effects be taken into account. However, since the available mathematical tools are insufficient for an exact analysis of complex systems, some additional methods are needed, viz:

(1) the use of approximations and upper limits (especially for evaluation),

(2) separate models to analyse only those effects, which are independent or of which the dependencies do not considerably affect the final results,

(3) hypotheses about effects which cannot be handled in another way.

These methods may, however, yield final results which are far from correct. Thus, the classical approach produces exact solutions from defective models, while the systems engineering approach obtains defective solutions from realistic models. However, in the latter case, the correctness of the solutions can be estimated with the aid of a simulation model. The analytical model must continue to be improved until the correctness of the solutions are within preset boundaries, obtained from a sensitivity analysis of the cost model.

4.3. Some IPSO examples

In illustrating the system engineering approach by some examples from the IPSO analysis, no derivations of formulae will be given, but one of the central formulae will be discussed and some interdependencies will be shown.

The classical approach to optimisation of inventory control usually considers stock-out costs. As it was not possible to estimate these costs, it was decided to take the service level of the finished products at the sales organisations as independent variables which can be set by management. The service levels of all other products (such as parts and raw materials), however, result from the optimisation procedure.

It is now necessary to relate the service level to the s-level based on the probability distribution of the safety stock *,v. The distribution of v is approximated by a function, whose standard deviation σ_v in particular, plays an important role in the analysis. The formula derived for σ_v has the following form:

$$\sigma_v = [\bar{\tau}\sigma_e^2 + \bar{d}^2\sigma_\tau^2 + \sigma_y^2(1) + \sigma_y^2(T)]^{1/2} \tag{1}$$

with: τ = the expected throughput time; σ_e^2 = the variance of the error in the demand forecast per time unit; $\bar{d}$ = average demand per time unit; σ_τ^2 = variance of the throughput time τ; $\sigma_y^2(T)$ = variance of the size of the drop in the stock below the s-level during a time T; T = period of control.

---

* This is defined as the algebraic stock level just before a batch arrives. The algebraic stock level is the physical stock level less backlog. The algebraic stock can be negative.

The first two terms are a variant of the well-known formula for the standard deviation of stochastic demand during a stochastic lead time. The third term gives the influence caused by depletion of the stock occurring in fluctuating batches, the last term reflects the fact that control is not continuous but performed at periodic intervals of length T.

4.4. Interdependencies

Consider a product i_1, manufactured on a production unit M, on which the products $i_2, i_3, \ldots$ are also manufactured. In addition, i_1 has as parts the products $j_1, j_2, \ldots$ while i_1 itself is one of the parts for the products $k_1, k_2, \ldots$ (see fig. 4).

(1) An increase in the average batch size of the products $k_1, k_2, \ldots$ affects σ_y^2 of product i_1 which appears in formula (1). This means that σ_v of i_1 will be increased.

(2) An increase in the average batch size of the products $i_2, i_3, \ldots$ affects the waiting time for the production unit M and, consequently, the throughput time τ for i_1. Again σ_v of i_1 will increase because of an increase in $\bar{\tau}$ and σ_τ.

(3) An increase in the average batch size of the products $j_1, j_2, \ldots$ will reduce the probability of stock-out of these products. This will reduce the waiting time for parts of i_1 and, consequently, the throughput time. In this case the σ_v of i_1 will decrease.

Mathematical formulae are derived for these interdependencies and embodied in a coherent analytical model together with many others. In an optimisation procedure they are weighed against each other.

4.5. A hypothesis about "coordination"

The first term of formula (1) is of special interest. The first step of the u,s,S system can be interpreted as follows: Demand for all other products is

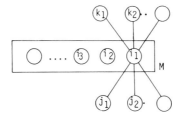

Fig. 4.

derived from the forecast of demand for finished products, but is dependent on the state of the system.

As the analysis of such a state-dependent forecast gave rise to severe problems, a hypothesis was stated, i.e., that the variance of the forecast errors can be determined directly from the forecast errors of a higher level, without taking into account the fact that demand is batched. In this way the determination of the variance of the forecast errors can be reduced to the determination of this quantity for finished products.

The underlying argument is that the amplifying effect on the uncertainty due to batching is avoided by the first step of the u,s,S system, which provides a forecast of the batch sizes and their due times (priority indices). This is one of the benefits of the system. Non-integral control (e.g., in the s,S policy) must consider the amplifying effect of batching, which will considerably enlarge the first term of formula (1). The consequence is that the u,s,S system reduces inventory costs considerably as compared with non-integral control, while having the same performance. Simulation has shown the hypothesis to be a reasonable approximation.

5. Concluding remark

In this paper we have tried to show that the system engineering approach can be successfully applied to the design and analysis of information control systems. The methods, however, can be improved so that they may be applied more broadly. Unfortunately, OR literature rarely deals with these methods and the question arises whether any systematic research on this subject is being done at all. Clearly it would be worth while to do so and we hope that this paper will stimulate work in that direction.

Reference

[1] H. Grünwald, Entwurf und Analyse eines Management Informationssystems für die Steuerung einen grossen industriellen Organisation, in: Planungsforschung–Forschungsplanung (Springer, Wien, 1972).

OPERATIONS RESEARCH IN THE
SWISS TELECOMMUNICATION SERVICES

Recherche opérationnelle dans les
services de télécommunications Suisses

JÜRG WETTSTEIN

PTT, Bern, Switzerland

Abstract. The telecommunication services form part of the Swiss PTT, a public corporation. Foremost in their business policy comes the principle of public utility, under which meeting requirements in an optimum way must take precedence over maximum results. Operations research can be successfully used in numerous fields of telecommunication. In this paper the three models "optimum organization of Regional Telecommunication Directorates", "warehousing and optimum purchasing policy", "maintenance and replacement of telephone exchanges" are treated in greater detail. Making use of these models, very substantial savings have been achieved through OR work.

1. Objectives and tasks of the Swiss telecommunication services

The telecommunication services form part of the Swiss PTT, which is a public enterprise. Public service is foremost in their business policy so that meeting requirements in an optimum way must take precedence over maximum results. The enterprise aims at covering its costs. Net profits, where they occur, are small and go to the public exchequer. Principles of managerial economics are strictly observed since subsidies are ultimately chargeable to the public funds and diminish the overall results of the national economy.

A staff of 13 000 in the telecommunication services build, operate and maintain the Swiss telephone, telegraph and telex systems as well as the radio and television networks. Radio and television programmes are the responsibility of the Swiss Radio Corporation, from whose studios they are broadcast.

At present there are 961 telephone exchanges, 14 510 000 km of telephone lines and 481 radio and television transmitters and transposers. More than 2 000 000 subscribers average 1 000 telephone calls each annually. 1.8 million people in Switzerland possess a radio receiving licence, 1.3 million a television licence. Capital invested averages 425 000 francs per employee.

In 1970 total revenue from these services was 1 492 million francs. While some services yielded a net profit of up to 13%, others showed deficits. In general, net profits of the telecommunication services make up the deficit of the postal services. In 1971 the PTT showed an overall deficit for the first time in many years.

2. The planning principles of the telecommunication services

The telecommunication services have set up a 10-year plan for the years 1966–1975. Studies of population and telephone density enable the yearly expansion of the operating plant to be forecast, and from this credit and staff requirements and the future relation of operating revenue to expenditure for the various services can be projected. Currently an average of 85 000 new subscribers are connected yearly. The 10-year plan hopes to do better and eliminate the backlog of unfulfilled demand for telephones which has accumulated as a result of restrictions during the last few years. This will require a joint effort by the PTT and industry, and will only succeed if the PTT obtains the necessary funds and sufficient staff.

Under these circumstances it is certainly good policy to seek accurate planning data for the telecommunication services and to examine to what extent the methods of OR can be used to advantage.

Inland and international calls as well as subscribers' main stations and telephones were correlated with both the nominal and the real gross national product, overall construction activity, the total number of housing units, the newly built homes and buildings. The correlation coefficients of the 25 correlations ranged from 0.965 to 0.997. The correlation coefficient for the linear function, real gross national product (base 1958) and subscribers' main telephone stations, was 0.9957. From accurate estimates undertaken by federal commissions and universities it appears that the development of the real gross national product will be linear in the years ahead. Thus, it can be inferred that the growth of the Swiss telecommunication services over the next few years will be linear and continuous, too, unless an unexpected economic crisis arises. This assumption forms an important overall condition for the mathematical solution of the problem discussed below.

3. Optimum organization of the Regional Telecommunication Directorates

3.1. Formulation of the problem

17 Regional Telecommunication Directorates (RTD) are responsible for running the telecommunication services. Working closely with the General Directorate they plan telephone exchanges, amplifier installations, extensions to trunk, junction and local cable systems, VHF transmitters and television transposer stations. Their responsibilities also cover personnel and financial requirements. To fulfill its many assignments each RTD is subdivided into six departments. Given the great number of such Regional Directorates, the complexity of their tasks and the large work force of over 13 000 employees the first task we set ourselves was to determine z, the optimum number of RTD – and thereby reduce costs to a minimum.

3.2. Model for the optimal organization of the RTD's

Linear regressions relating the number, y, of employees in a department to the number, x, of subscribers' main stations, took the values given in table 1.

Table 1

Department	Coefficient of x	Constant	r
Administration	0.000485	14.16	0.95
Operating	0.00451	−40.61	0.97
Building	0.000592	74.70	0.93
Materials & Transport	0.000218	15.59	0.95
Telegraph	0.000118	−47.23	0.90

From cost accounting data it was possible to develop the relationship between travel costs, K_r, and personnel costs for senior positions, K_p, respectively on the one hand and the number of RTD's on the other up to a limit of 52 possible RTD's (i.e. $z \leqslant 52$), viz:

$$K_r = 6\,351\,250 - 33\,430\,z\,, \qquad 1 \leqslant z \leqslant 52, \qquad (1)$$

$$K_p = 522\,763 + 232\,556\,z\,, \qquad 18 \leqslant z \leqslant 52. \qquad (2)$$

Experience has shown that today's complement of senior staff cannot be reduced if a first class service is to be maintained so eq. (2) is only valid for between 18 to 52 RTD's. Below that number senior personnel costs are constant.

These equations show that if there were only a few RTD's, considerably higher travel costs would result than in the case of an organization with many Directorates, as on a national level the same amount of supervisory work would have to be done. However, an increase in RTD's would also entail an increase in personnel costs for senior positions which would offset the savings in travel expenses.

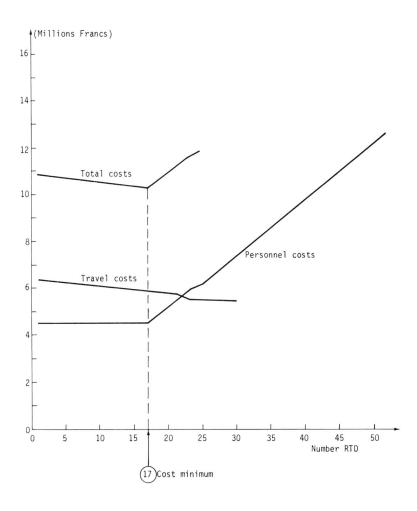

Fig. 1. Costs = f (number of RTD).

3.3. Derivation of a solution from the model

As the total number of staff has been found to be a linear function of the number of subscribers' main stations, the minimum travel and personnel cost for senior positions is very easy to determine. Fig. 1 shows clearly that the cost minimum lies at 17 RTD's as at present.

3.4. Discussion of the solution

If the number of Regional Directorates is to change at all, it can only be to increase, especially as the number of subscribers' main stations will continue to grow in the years ahead. An increase implies subdividing the largest Directorates, where the large number of telephone subscribers might make it too difficult for the supervisors to oversee the proportionally large staff required. This condition only applies in one Directorate today. However, political interests are also apt to come into play, and politics evades OR methods.

Thus the present organizations of the Regional Telecommunication Directorates can be said to be satisfactory.

4. Storage and optimum purchasing policy

The telecommunication services place orders of more than 800 million francs value with about 1 500 companies each year. These orders are allocated to the greatest possible number of firms all over the country, due regard being paid to their being competitive. Some firms abroad are also considered. Purchase is generally made by restricted competition, several contractors being invited to bid.

To ensure that RTD's can obtain their requirements readily stocks, worth almost 100 million francs, are kept at the central and regional warehouses. Therefore it is of advantage to determine the optimal purchasing policy.

The mathematical model, used in the analysis, consists of the following variables: contract frequency, administrative cost of the conclusion of a contract, initiating and handling a delivery, frequency of deliveries, value of yearly requirements, interest rate, rate of storage cost, rate of transport cost and overhead cost per storage item. The solution suggests that contracts should be concluded as infrequently as possible and run for as long as possible, within the limits imposed by the uncertainty in the development of prices and demand. Such contracts, extending over long periods, in addition benefit from quantity discounts.

In the light of these considerations it was decided to fix a five-year period as the upper limit for the duration of contracts, although a 10-year plan is in operation in the PTT. The reason for this time-limit is that manufacturing machines and tools in the telephone section of the PTT services are completely amortized within five years as a rule. Moreover, the technical development within this period can be more easily reviewed. Price adjustments can usually be made every year, so that only the administrative costs of initiating and handling a delivery from storage still accrue.

The application stage also required a model for determining the general rise of the prices. Essentially this model used the Federal Industry and Labour Office indices for salaries and wholesale prices as well as the coefficients for the fixed, the salary-dependent, and the material-dependent cost portions of the individual product or of a product group.

By his two model procurement method, we achieved good distribution of orders among suppliers, streamlining of the manufacturing programme, standardization and efficient purchasing. Above all, underutilisation of development capacity could be avoided. As a result the suppliers of the PTT can achieve productivity gains which generally exceed the Swiss average. The Swiss PTT, on the other hand, benefit from quantity discounts which are often considerable.

5. Maintenance and replacement of telephone exchanges

Efficient maintenance of the operating plant is achieved by abandoning the previous method of systematic preventive maintenance at fixed intervals in favour of selective preventive maintenance, under which maintenance work is only performed after a specific need has been established. Experience has shown that this new method results in substantial staff savings for the same standard of service.

The maintenance work of all telephone exchanges, which handle approximately 2 million subscribers, can be split up as follows: 28% preventive mechanical maintenance work, 36% preventive electrical maintenance work, 11% equipment cleaning work, and 25% clearing of faults. In the exchange service 10.5 employees are needed to handle each 10 000 subscribers' main stations (inclusive of trunk calls).

Telephone exchanges can be considered entities of decreasing efficiency. Therefore we examined the possibility of cost reductions by replacing these exchanges. Modifying a replacement model by Churchman we found we ought to keep the plant in operation as long as possible. In support of this

conclusion it was observed that today, Swiss telephone exchanges are replaced after 20 years service as a rule, while in the United States they do
service for 40 years. In replacement the decisive factor is the life span of the
different switching components, rather than maintenance cost. The electric
relays, which possess the shortest life, can cope with 10^9 switchings without
substantial impairment of their efficiency. Heavily loaded circuits such as the
registers, must handle about 3.5×10^6 switchings a year. This results in a life
of 28 years for the critical circuits. If these critical elements were to be
replaced after this period, it would be possible even in Switzerland to keep
the telephone exchanges in operation for 40 years.

6. Future operations research studies in the telecommunication services

Given our successful application of OR to date it is planned to make
available additional models for decision making, planning, organization and
control and, moreover, to unite them into one "telecommunication model".
We will have to investigate whether such a model would be suitable for
so-called business games, for training of executive officers in the telecommunication services. Provided that the model in such a business game is sufficiently realistic, optimal business strategies can be realized, which can be very
useful for management in the decision making process.

M. Ross, ed., OR '72. North-Holland Publishing Company (1973)

47

A WORKING PLAN FOR PROGRAMMING AND SUSTAINING THE GROWTH OF SMALL SCALE INDUSTRIES AROUND CALCUTTA, INDIA

Plan pour le programmation et le développement de petites industries autour de Calcutta

B.P. BANERJEE

Vice-President of IFORS

Abstract. Recent surveys indicate that the power-operated small scale industries in the Calcutta Metropolian District, now suffering from severe under-utilisation of capacity, can become as viable and productive as their counterpart in the large scale sector given proper support. This observation gains further relevance when considered in the context of India's planning philosophy according to which full and effective utilisation of the abundant human resources is a focal point of socio-economic policies.

This paper identifies raw materials procurement, sales and supply of working capital as the major areas of weakness for the small scale units. It thereafter suggests a working plan for programming and sustaining the growth of small scale industries in the region — using minimisation of factor inputs for a requisite or pre-specified growth in employment as the criterion. The plan is designed to be operational, quantifying the requisite factor inputs and developing the required organisational set-up. Possible uncertainties in input-output relationship are noted.

1. Background of the study

For quite some time now the State of West Bengal has played a rather interesting and important role in Indian political and intellectual life. Starting from an early position of preeminence and leadership, the state has suffered a decline since World War II and the distinct signs of stagnation in industrial growth have inevitably led to political turmoil. The period 1966–72 witnessed the installation of a left wing government in the state. This should be seen in the context of a centrist and neutralist Federal Government on the one hand and on the other the first outburst from a rising and violent ultra-leftist movement (called Naxalism after a remote village) which is largely concentrated among and capturing the imagination of the educated youth.

In consequence, the last five years have been a period of trial for this state: galloping unemployment, a slowdown in industrial growth, increased violence and complete collapse of the social and educational system. Calcutta, at the hub of the states' industrial and cultural life, has been showing all signs of bursting at the seams.

The birth of Bangladesh, bordering on West Bengal in India, followed by the victory of Prime Minister Indira Gandhi's party in the recent assembly election, has brought about change in the situation. Violence is on the wane, and there is an all-round sense of urgency that the respite obtained must be used to put things right.

The extent of enemployment invariably gets a preeminent position in the list of wrongs, being variously estimated at between 2.84 and 4.8 million in a total population of 55 million, or between 15.5 and 26.2% of the workforce. Between 1966 and 1969, it increased by about 44% and, by all evidence, is growing at the rate of 15% annually.

Table 1

New jobs created in Calcutta offices (1969–70) by qualification types

Qualification	Number of jobs	Average number of applicants per job filled
graduate plus (technical)	4302	38
school plus (technical)	800	42
other graduates	1280	170
management qualification	5900	17
clerical	2200	560
typists, etc.	1500	20
non-qualified	500	5 [a]
total	16482	

a) The low ratio is due to non-open connection-based hiring.

A second aspect is the preponderance of the educated amongst the unemployed. A survey result is typical and revealing (table 1). It is no wonder, therefore, that unemployment has been identified as the most pressing problem for West Bengal. Indeed this has been recognised for quite some time and various suggestions have been put forward for ameloration of the situation. This paper reports on one such set of suggestions arising out of a series of studies. These studies were, however, somewhat limited in scope in that they were confined to the small scale industries sector in the Calcutta Metropolian area.

2. Early phase

It is well known that the Government of India has made the encouragement of small scale industries a cornerstone of its economic policy. The basis for this policy is not purely economic, a whole complex of political, ideological and other arguments are put forward in favour of this policy. A survey carried out in the Calcutta Metropolian area shows that given proper support, small scale industries employing less than 25 people (or, more specifically, employing between 11 and 24 persons) with power-operated equipment, can be rendered as viable and productive (both in terms of labour productivity and wages) as their larger counterparts (see table 2).

The same survey also reveals that these small units have a very considerable under-utilisation of capacity (table 3). This would seem to indicate that considerable potential exists for creation of additional employment without significant additions to capital assets through better utilisation of capacity already installed.

An unique concentration of innumerable power-operated small scale units in the Calcutta Metropolian region also had a significant impact on the economy and employment situation of the region. (It may be mentioned that this sector currently has a total employment of 308 194, fixed assets of Rs. 979.4 millions, working capital of Rs. 1014.0 millions and gross output of

Table 2
Estimated gross value added and wages per employee

N (number of people employed)	Gross value added (Rs 100/−)	Wages (Rs 100/−)
$N \geqslant 100$	49	14
$50 \leqslant N < 100$	38	11
$25 \leqslant N < 50$	40	11
$1 \leqslant N < 25$	32	10
$11 \leqslant N < 25$ [a]	47	11.4
Combined	41	12

a) With power-operated equipment.

Table 3
Estimated rate of utilisation of capacity of small scale units in the
Calcutta Metropolitan District

Industry group	Percentage utilisation
engineering and metal	24.6
chemical	24.3
wood	25.0
food, drink, etc.	23.8
textile	28.4
glass and ceramic	26.5
leather and rubber	22.9
paper and printing	25.7
miscellaneous	23.2
Combined	25.6

Rs. 1476.2 millions.) Thus it is a justifiable candidate for detailed study in the context of the problem briefly outlined above.

As already indicated, at present Indian policy aims at helping the small units. It takes operational form in several possible ways, e.g., by reserving for them the production of certain commodities and by the provision of subsidies, exemption from duties, loans on easy terms, machinery on hire-purchase, factory space in the Industrial Estates, etc. None of these instruments gives any incentives aimed at the best utilisation of capital resources. As a consequence policy has hardly been effective in sustaining this sector.

The relative inadequacy of units of the small scale sector is most conspicuously when it comes to the organisation facilities for:

(1) procuring raw materials and other inputs,

(2) prompt disposal of finished goods,

(3) obtaining necessary working capital and finances, and

(4) obtaining modern managerial expertise on problems of planning, pricing, industrial relations, etc.

There is, therefore, justification for providing centralised or planned assistance, in respect of these items.

The nucleus of an organisation for such centralised guidance already seems to exist in the Government-run Small Industries Services Institute, and, given a proper programme, it is conceivable that the necessary organisation for its implementation can be built up under the aegis of this institute.

Such a programme should have five distinct phases:

(1) Determination, in quantitative terms, of the specific input over time of

the factors (labour, raw materials, capital stock), as also the other supports and assistance necessary to ensure and sustain any desired rate and direction of growth.

(2) Matching these requirements with the corresponding availability and drawing up a concrete programme.

(3) Determination, in quantitative terms, of the outputs which were not readily marketable and would require specialised marketing efforts and creating a suitable central marketing organisation for the purpose.

(4) Determination of the centralised management services necessary to render the units continuously viable.

(5) Framing the organisational set-up necessary to sustain such a programme and its implementation.

3. The methodology

The inputs of an unit or industry in the small scale industries sector consists of (a) capital stock, (b) labour, broadly classified into skilled, semi skilled and unskilled, and (c) raw materials coming partly from other units or industries in the small scale sector and the balance, which we will term *imports*, from outside the sector, either indigenously or from foreign sources. The responsibility for arranging and managing the imports would rest with the centralised agency.

Outputs from the sector would either be: (a) consumed as raw material either by the unit or industry itself or some other unit or industry within the sector, (b) used to create new capacity for the same industry or another within the sector, (c) sold, or made available for selling outside the sector; i.e. *exports*. Here again the proposed centralised agency would act as the sole selling agent.

The objective was to create additional employment and the vehicle of analysis was a dynamic linear programming model due to Garvin and others and the planning horizon chosen was five years. Thus, in specific terms, the objective in the model was to minimize the total centralised input of materials and finances, subject to conservation and other constraints. For this purpose the following industrial groupings were assumed: engineering and metal, chemicals, wood, textiles, paper and printing, leather and rubber, glass and ceramics, miscellaneous.

The model was run several times to determine the capital outlay, raw materials requirements and inventory build up at the Central Agency for the specific growth rates, and these were simultaneously matched with availability and the proposed organisational and managerial capability of the Central Agency until a balanced result was obtained.

It was found that this sector could sustain a growth rate of employment of 15% (uncompounded). The corresponding resource requirements would be: Rs 101.5 millions in fixed assets, Rs 112.5 millions in working capital; also Rs 164.1 millions in raw materials "bank", Rs 197.0 millions in finished goods "export" inventory. Responsibility for procuring an average of Rs 980 million worth of raw materials and selling an average of Rs 790 millions worth of finished goods per year would rest with the Central Agency. This growth rate of 15% compares with an average growth rate of 1.2% per year in the total industrial sector of West Bengal during the period 1961–1970.

4. Future work

The study reported above aroused the interest of State planners. The extremely high level of unemployment, overall deficiency in food and other agricultural output in the State and the advent of high yielding varieties of seeds have, however, shifted the focus of attention of the State planning authorities to the rural sector.

Thus, today the gross cultivated area in the state is 18.4 million acres and the average number of crops per acre is 1.35. This provides full employment to 5.2 million persons. It is estimated that introduction of double cropping in this total area would generate new employment opportunity for 2.8 million people. Use of high yielding varieties of seeds, and modern agricultural techniques would simultaneously increase the yield by more than 100%, thereby deficiency in food supply in the state.

The advent of high yielding varieties, however, necessitates a large number of industrial inputs into agriculture, in terms of capital equipment, consumables and maintenance facilities. Proximity and other necessities lead to the concept of a large number of rural service centres. This, together with the under-utilisation of capacity of the existing units of small scale sector, encourages an extension of the planning approach briefly described in the paper to bring about a comprehensive and integrated agro-industrial development model.

References

[1] Survey of manufacturing industry—1962; Calcutta Metropolitan District, Vols. 1–3, Calcutta Metropolitan Planning Organ., Govt. of West Bengal (1967).

[2] Survey of small engineering units in Howrah, Reserve Bank of India (1964).

[3] B.P. Banerjee and A.N. Bose, Productivity of small scale industries: a survey, Calcutta Productivity Council Newsletter (1965).

[4] B.P. Banerjee and A.N. Bose, Impact of under-utilisation of capacity, Calcutta Productivity Council Newsletter (1966).

[5] A.N. Bose, Implication of capacity utilisation; a study of the Calcutta Metropolitan District (Das Gupta & Co., Calcutta, 1966).

[6] B.P. Banerjee, Impact of under-utilisation of capacity on export costs, in: Cost reduction for exports (Indian Inst. Foreign Trade, New Delhi, 1967).

[7] W.W. Garvin, Introduction to linear programming (McGraw—Hill, New York, 1960).

[8] B.P. Banerjee and P.K. Ghosh, A working plan for programming and sustaining the growth of small scale industries around Calcutta, India (interim report) CORSI Bull. Calcutta Branch of Opnl. Res. Soc. of India (1968, 1969).

[9] Report of the Survey Committee on the Engineering Industry in West Bengal (1951—1968).

[10] West Bengal; an analytical study, Bengal Chamber of Commerce and Industry (1971).

[11] B.P. Banerjee, West Bengal's role in the industrial development in India, in: Focus on West Bengal; problems and prospects (Oxford Book & Stationery Co., Calcutta, 1972).

[12] A memorandum on a perspective plan for Calcutta Metropolitan district and West Bengal 1971–1989, Calcutta Metropolitan Planning Organ., Govt. of West Bengal (1971).

M. Ross, ed., OR '72. North-Holland Publishing Company (1973)

48

BUDGET SIMULATION: A TOOL FOR ADAPTIVE PLANNING

Simulation de budget: un instrument pour la planification adaptive

PER STRANGERT

Research Institute of National Defence, Stockholm, Sweden

Abstract. A budget simulation model was developed for long-range planning of a complex resource system. By making the description of the state in the model sufficiently comprehensive, it was possible to depict the inert properties of the system when attempting alterations of its composition. Some applications are presented including planning of adaptations, analysis of the cost of postponement of choice, and related topics important when evaluating different policy alternatives.

1. Introduction

It is safe to say that uncertainty is always present in planning problems. However, instead of describing it by probability distributions of some variables one must often represent it by a broad spectrum of qualitatively different outcomes. For simple decision problems it may be possible to sketch a decision tree, but in large, complex systems one has to deal with system inertia as a macro effect due to numerous conspiring factors.

As I see it, it is possible to study large systems by simulation using simple concepts from decision theory if one proceeds carefully in designing the model. It may be necessary to refrain from the push-the-button solutions of optimizing models, but instead the analyst may gain a fingertip feeling of important dynamical interactions within the system.

To support this suggestion, I will describe a rather comprehensive investigation undertaken for the Swedish Army. First, however, I should like to make the following comments. When discussing planning in this context, the primary interest concerns the plans themselves, not the process that creates them in some organizational environment. Courses of action and forecasts of uncertain variables are considered only as representative samples out of the very large set of possible ones. An *adaptive plan* is a decision tree conditional to the gradual resolution of uncertainty in time, i.e., a strategy in the sense of game theory.

2. The Swedish Army cost model

2.1. The model

A cost model was developed for the Swedish Army using fictitious data which were, however, quite consistent with the facts. The model might be characterized as a deterministic simulation, using forecasts and tentative plans as input data. The analyst looks for successive approximations converging, in some sense, toward an acceptable plan. The model structure is in part conventional, but in some respects includes features that make the model more useful in adaptive planning.

The register areas of the computer program contain the Army's current personnel and material supplies. The possible register contents define a set of states. The simulation is time-controlled. Some updating of the states is performed autonomously by the program. Other changes are controlled by external decisions, arranged in sequences forming a "plan".

The following examples show that the state registers must be carefully defined in order to make the model respond to decisions in a dynamically correct way. (1) The personnel register must contain the numbers of men in different age groups. By an adequate updating routine, the development will be correctly described. (2) The formal decisions on the procurement of equipment mean that a number of inputs (such as payment, delivery, generation of operating costs, and scrapping) are transformed into commitments. During the simulation, the decision is simulated by storing the component inputs in a buffer register which is scanned once every period for transactions to be performed.

The outputs from the runs, on the one hand, provide feedback information for the iterative runs; on the other, and this is our primary interest, they give the year-by-year costs and a feasible development of force structure.

2.2. Using the model in methodological investigations

When studying methodology, I chose to study the relationship between the initial power and the endurance of a force structure. On the one hand the relative importance of these effects is influenced by future doctrines, treaties, and technological development. The uncertainty of these factors is to some extent resoluble. On the other hand, endurance is achieved by personnel-intense structures, and initial power by material-intense ones. Therefore, changing the structure in this respect will be a slow and inert process.

For the purpose of illustration in this context, a two-dimensional scale of merit has been constructed, measuring endurance (e_1) and initial power (e_2). It seems to be valid, but must be regarded as only provisional.

2.3. Finding the feasible objectives

First, given an initial state, the set of feasible objectives was investigated by several simulation runs. A possibility frontier of feasible, non-dominated objectives could be estimated and, furthermore, proved useful as a basis for the approximate prediction of further points (see fig. 1). Here and in the following the frontier consists of effect combinations attained in the fifteenth year. Also, unless otherwise stated, the budget level remained constant and equal in all runs.

Because some long-run effect maximization was attempted, every plan is represented by a trajectory up to a point on the frontier. The trial-and-error process sought acceptable sample plans which did not show excessive dips from the frontier during the planning period. The development of this process made considerable progress in the course of the study. This is an interesting by-product, especially as line people themselves can participate in the work.

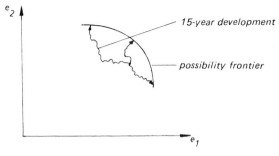

Fig. 1.

2.4. Formulating a general condition on the description of the state

If the model is to be valid, the description of the state by registers, on the one hand, must correspond with the nature of the decisions in an input sequence and the program routines processing them, on the other. If the simulation model is to be useful for adaptive planning, the inputs, apart from those reflecting external influence, should correspond to what is perceived by the planner as real decisions, leading to commitments. This imposes a condition on the state description which is fulfilled in the Army model, e.g., by introducing the age grouping and the decision buffer register.

3. The study of adaptations

3.1. The development of options when an effect-maximizing policy is followed

If one follows a plan making successive decisions, the system gradually becomes specialized in the corresponding direction. But international politics may change in an unforeseen way, so that the premises of the defence policy of a small country must be revised. Therefore, an important question is: if the goal should change, would it then be possible to make a satisfactory adaptation, i.e., to switch over to another plan leading to another objective? In general, this is a problem posed by the inertia of the system.

There are several factors that cause inertia in the Army. R&D projects require some minimum time. Because of limited training capacity, it will be impossible to set up new kinds of force units in a short time. Moreover, given funds are limited, equipment can only be acquired at a limited rate. Therefore, it will in general be difficult to change the direction of the development of the Army as fast as may be desired, and the evaluation of a plan should also consider the possibility of adapting the plan of development if changes in goals or external factors occur. The greater the probability for such changes, the more desirable will adaptability be. In the new Swedish defence planning system the short-term effect, on one hand, is explicitly balanced against the long-term effect and the adaptability resulting at the end of the medium-term plan, on the other. So, methods for studying adaptations are important.

After some deliberation I chose a plan leading to a point on the possibility frontier and conducted a five years simulation of the plan. The final state of the system was taken as the initial state for several runs in which efforts were made to change the effect combination in various directions. The strategies in

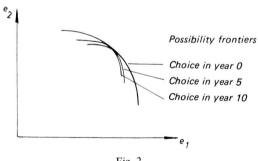

Fig. 2.

the various cases contained such measures as speeding up the acquisition of equipment or training of new categories of recruits. Using the same representation as before the results are shown in fig.2. Also the frontier corresponding to an adaptation in the tenth year has been plotted.

It will, of course, always be possible to reach the goal initially chosen. For other e_1/e_2 proportions, some effect must be given up. The inertia of the system is correctly represented thanks to the fact that the inputs of the model correspond exactly to real decisions such as may be used to change the development pattern of the Army.

3.2. Increasing the adaptability

We shall now use the same method as in the previous section to evaluate another medium-term planning policy. Instead of aiming at maximal long-

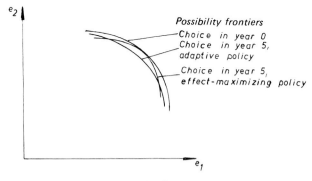

Fig. 3.

term effect, we shall try to maintain options and postpone decisions about the goal to be reached.

The adaptability may be increased by such measures as initiating parallel R&D activities and buying non-specialized equipment. Personnel may be trained for many types of force units. Because all resources are not directed to one single goal, some effect will then be sacrificed.

The investigation was conducted as before. By trial and error, a five-year plan was constructed which contained such measures as mentioned above and which could be continued in the fifteen-year perspective, as is shown in fig.3.

It is no longer possible to reach a point on the outer frontier, because this presupposes an effect-maximizing policy to be followed during the whole planning period. Instead, some options are retained longer than before.

By this method, one can construct any feasible medium-term plan and study the development of the options. Of course the nature of the uncertainty of future preferences is a decisive factor that determines how long-term effect should be traded off for adaptability. In any case, the meaning of the concept "optimal plan" seems somewhat obscure when one faces this balancing problem. Effect maximization may be incompatible with freedom of choice.

Using the same experimental design I have found that to maintain to-day's options five years longer than in the reference case would require a model Army budget about 10–15% higher than would otherwise be necessary.

3.3. Adaptations in the case of uncertain parameters

Uncertainty applies not only to goals, but also to many technical and economical factors. But as it is gradually resoluble, adaptations may be a countermeasure to be considered explicitly.

When the Army cost model was used, investigations of the impact of future changes in price relations were especially urgent. The interest focussed on the relative price indices of manpower and equipment. If the goal is to maximize the effect, the optimal allocation of resources between these categories depends on these indices. To test this I constructed two models in which I sought to maximize $e_1 + e_2$ in the long run under the alternative assumptions that the trend favoured a rise in the price of manpower relative to equipment or that the reverse held.

First, it was assumed that information about the target development would be available in the very near future. In this case, two effect-maximizing plans could be constructed (fig.4). In the simulation runs, one alternative of the price development and the corresponding decisions were used conjointly as inputs to give the combined effect.

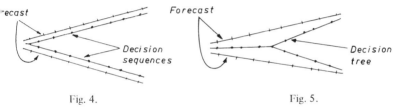

Fig. 4.   Fig. 5.

Then it was assumed that information would not be available until the
'th year. Therefore a decision tree had to be constructed (see fig.5) with a
're-year common branch containing measures to maintain the necessary op-
ons. When designing this conditional plan some guidance was provided by
rlier results on goal uncertainty. However, space does not permit me to give
ore details here. In any case there was, as expected, a certain loss of effect
the second case as compared with the first one, which was due to the
formation delay assumed.

Concluding remarks

Both theory and the applied work described underline the importance in
ort and medium-term planning of paying attention to the state changes of a
stem rather than simply calculating the immediate effects upon flow varia-
es, such as cost and effect (revenue, benefit). Simulation models which
tisfy the conditions mentioned in this paper provide one method of com-
ring alternative states resulting from different medium-term plans. The eval-
ation then can also take in long-term consequences and the freedom of
oice.

My work has also given me a very thorough grasp of system behaviour in a
namic sense. As the model was operated by successive trial-and-error runs,
e analyst gradually got an increased, intuitive feeling of what decision
ains would lead to the desired results. Also, the method has been easy to
plain, and the results could be communicated to line people in a way that
emed uncomplicated as well as persuasive. The response suggests that both
e contents and the process of planning have improved.

SIMULATION LANGUAGES: FROM BATCH
TO CONVERSATIONAL MODE

Simulation discrète: en s'approchant de l'interactivité

ADRIANO ALLOISIO

ENEL, Centro Ricerca di Automatica, Milan, Italy

BRUNO MARTINOLI

OR Department, Italsider, Genoa, Italy

MATILDA DE MATTIA

OLIVETTI S.p.A., Ivrea, Italy

and

OLGA VARALLI

A.R.S. S.p.A., Milan, Italy

Abstract. The effectiveness of the simulation approach depends on structure and power of the available simulation languages, and on the interaction level they allow between analyst and model. The interaction takes place in many phases of the work; for each of them, the languages have been provided with special facilities (modularity, data structures handling, graphics, tracing).

In this paper, a definition of conversational simulation is given, and a survey is made to explore at what extent conversationality, in the limits allowed by the language facilities, can contribute to improve the yield of simulation in these phases.

Some conclusions are: (1) The conversational interactions have to be inserted in the simulation logic as normal events, scheduled by the operator and controlled by the simulation time-advance device; (2) Interactive simulation seems to be useful to get insight into the model. Practical experiments are in progress in this field; (3) Interaction effectiveness depends chiefly on the availability of an 'ad hoc' software interface to avoid logical conflicts in the model; (4) A low-level conversationality, especially useful in the debugging phase, can be obtained at a low cost, starting from the available simulation languages.

1. Introduction

Simulation, as we well know, is a deductive device, but when considered as a "last resort" technique it brings the operations researcher to engage in a kind of empirical behaviour. Thus, simulation assumes some of the characteristics of an experiment. Simulation languages have been also devised to cater for the particular need of a strong interaction between analyst and model, which materializes in the flexibility of defining or changing the model itself, in the facilities provided to measure and identify the behaviour of the system or to control its "side conditions". Moreover, each simulation model runs through some simulation device (SD, from now on), such as the computer program, which generally follows a rather intricate pattern far removed from the original model logic (for instance, the time advance and events scheduling device, data structures and lists handling, sophisticated storage allocation, etc.). Thus we need further devices to facilitate the communication with the analyst (several types of statements for events scheduling and lists scanning, facilities for the creation and destruction of sets of data, routines for debugging and tracing). The effectiveness of simulation and ease of usage depend rather heavily on the means at hand to deal with the above mentioned types of interaction. In fact, we usually measure and compare the power of simulation languages by means of these parameters.

Now, the progressive diffusion of time-sharing systems puts at the disposal of many users the possibility of effective interaction taking place during the simulated time, thus bringing up the problem of the advantages to be obtained by digital conversational simulation. In this particular field the experiences achieved seem to be limited to a few research centers or confined to certain specific classes of problems. On the other hand the effectiveness of this approach can be evaluated only after an intensive exploitation by several researchers who choose to modify their work-methods of simulating. However such exploitation could require the rather costly implementation of an ad hoc language. Do we really need a new language to obtain interactive simulation? Are general and powerful interaction facilities really useful in the every-day simulation? In dealing with these problems, we first try to focus this paper on the theoretical limits of any discrete conversational simulation, and second, suggest a very simple methodology by which to bring a typical general purposes simulation language to a conversational level at a very low cost, although with some slight restrictions.

2. Conversational simulation: an approach

We shall develop our analysis by considering interactive simulation as a natural extension and improvement on batch simulation. We are not going to deal with the cases in which the simulation is intended as an educational, or training, or real-time process control support. The terminology we shall use is derived from Simscript, one of the more widely known simulation languages; in its "world-view" the dynamic system to be simulated is resolved into individual entities whose status is expressed by the values of a record of attributes. Simulation develops through instantaneous events, that is, through changes in the status of entities, occurring at discrete points of the simulated time. These events are defined by algorithms (operating on some status variables such as attributes, or on the future events list, or on the composition of some sets of entities, etc.) and are executed in time order.

Interaction can take place when the simulation run is suspended by a request for data sent from the computer to an input device, such as a teletype. As soon as the operator will have entered the requested data on the console, the simulation can restart, for instance, from the last system status which had been reached. Therefore, we find an immediate answer to a question we must put: when can we interact?

Owing to the very structure of the discrete simulation, every interaction can take place only at discrete points of the simulated time, corresponding to scheduled events. In fact the modelled system "exists" only in these instances, so that the interaction itself must be considered as any event which can be scheduled in the future events list in one of the following ways: (1) in the stream of exogenous events, before the simulation run, for some predetermined moments, (2) when other events occur, (3) by the last interaction event, as one of the actions at the operator's disposal.

Another important question arises in connection to the actions possible when interacting. They could run as follows: (1) scheduling of the next interaction, (2) analysis of the SD status, (3) changes in the SD status and in the SD structure, (4) control of the simulation flow.

2.1. Scheduling of the next interaction

The operator can enter on the console the time he wants to assume the control of the simulation. He can also choose the conditions which must be satisfied in order to set-up the new interaction. To do this, he has to introduce into the SD a new type of event, or insert these conditions into an already existing event.

2.2. Analysis of the SD status

Devices for the analysis of the SD status can be found in every simulation language (debugging, tracing, dump routines). Using these facilities in a conversational way allows us to know the status of only those SD elements we are interested in, and only when we want to, thus eliminating a great amount of information which might have proved useless or misleading. Such an analysis, based on a question-answer system, turns out to be much more effective than a sequence of tests planned in advance. Thus we can check whether the SD works correctly, and are able to detect unexpected patterns in the behaviour of the model. The efficiency of this type of interaction depends particularly, of course, on the availability of a sharp and immediate visualization of the SD messages we get through the software and hardware equipment.

2.3. Changes in the SD status and structure

By "changes in the SD status", we mean a set of actions on the SD, starting from the actual status and leading to a new one; these actions may consist of the modification of the values of the entities attributes, the creation of entities with specific characteristics, or their destruction, the alteration of the future events list, or the changes in the sets composition, etc. These types of actions require special attention: in fact, the SD devices are heavily interdependent and in order to make just one change we must coordinate several points of the SD, along a given line known only to those thoroughly acquainted with the simulation program; otherwise we risk creating an "unfeasible" SD status, with catastrophic consequences. Thus the operations leading to changes in status should have automatic safeguards built in, whose nature and implementation may be different according to the specific model. Now let us consider the changes in the SD structure. They could be: (1) the insertion of a new class of events, or entities, or sets, (2) the insertion or deletion of already defined events, or entities, or sets, (3) the insertion or deletion of statements in the events algorithms.

Generally the SD logic is rather involved, so that the first type of changes is not straightforward and easy to introduce quickly. In fact we consider it useless to attempt major changes in the model within the short time allowed by an interaction in a simulation run. On the other hand minor changes are often useful, but – if extemporaneous – they need an ad hoc interpretative language to avoid recompilations, or in any case costly software devices designed for this purpose. The logical difficulties in changing status mentioned above are even more relevant to a change in the model. We wish to point out that in the simulation runs with which we were concerned the most significant changes made through interaction had been planned in advance in the SD setting-up phase, making the problem of status and structure changes trivial. Provided the SD has been equipped so to allow the operator to choose one from among a number of predetermined alternatives (by setting some logical switches activating or disactivating some parts of the program), we can achieve some minor changes at a very low cost whenever we have at our disposal a general compilative simulation language.

2.4. Control of the simulation flow

Supposing we have a file on which to record the most significant statuses run by the SD, and can restart from any of them, we can get a "tree-like" system evolution, in which the nodes mark the actions of the operator and the branches correspond to the segments of the simulation run made under different hypotheses. In this way the operator can go back on his decisions and choose, among several alternatives of model changes, the one that turned out to be the best.

3. Using Simscript as a conversational language: some technical details

Our experiences have been with the Simscript 1 language as implemented in the Honeywell 6000 series (in this section we will take for granted that the fundamentals of this language are known). The Simscript compiler and library we used do not run under the control of the time-sharing system. The operating system at our disposal * permits each compiled program to have direct access to a specified input/output file which may correspond, for instance, to a teletype, so that the time-sharing operating system module is not used. In this way we can run programs requiring a large core storage, although maintaining the same immediateness in the response time, and can utilize Simscript with all its original facilities.

The most natural way to implement an interaction is to consider it as an endogenous event (which we called DIALOGUE). This event starts by calling the operator, the conversation goes on, and ends up with a new scheduling of DIALOGUE itself for a future time, by activating the well-known CREATE

---

* We used a computer GE 635, under the control of the operating system GECOS III, and a DATANET 30 unit for the control of remote-batch and time-sharing terminals.

and CAUSE statements, already embedded for this purpose in the program. Furthermore, any of the other events can, depending on the operator preferences, originate a DIALOGUE on their own by setting the proper switches during the period of interaction. The DIALOGUE event routine assists the operator with several types of actions. A status analysis can be easily made by calling the various dump functions offered by Simscript, and by activating preprogrammed reports. We can also create or destroy temporary entities of a predefined type. By keeping track of the addresses the computer gives them, we can retrieve them at any moment we like and modify their attributes. To do so it is not necessary to mention the name of the required attributes, it is enough to know the locations the programmer gave them in their entity records.

Other possible operations are the filing, or the removal, of entities into, or from, sets, and the scheduling of any endogenous event. In all these cases (with the exception of the modification of temporary attributes) any change to be made by interaction requires us to have programmed in advance some statements explicitly referring to the names of the system variables, the entities, the sets and the event notices used in the specific program, so that a DIALOGUE routine must be written each time we have a new model. However, such a routine could be automatically generated by a Fortran precompiler program, which takes its input exclusively from the information contained in the Simscript Definition Form, and gives as its output a Simscript subprogram devised to interpret the operator instructions. Considering the conversational features needed in a simulation program, such an implementation, even if of general application, may often be a luxury.

We wish to underline at this point that it is not sufficient to create, for instance, a new entity in order to carry out an effective change in the model or in the status; in fact we must file this entity in a convenient set, or schedule an event for it, etc., so that from now on the SD will handle it automatically. Unfortunately, these coordinating actions cannot be easily generalized. Referring to the interactive simulation control flow, we find in the Simscript language appropriate statements, such as RECORD MEMORY and RESTORE STATUS, which conveniently combined with the facilities for changing the model, allow the operator great flexibility of action.

4. Two typical applications

We now intend to outline briefly two models, one simulating a job shop, the other simulating a city traffic network, for which we implemented some conversational features.

With minor changes, the job shop model is the same as that suggested by Ferguson and Jones [4] for a manager-computer interaction test. The most significant decisions available to the operator during the simulated time are:

(1) accepting or rejecting the orders on arrival at the shop, or putting them in storage for processing later,

(2) turning a machine on or off, in order to balance fixed costs against setup costs,

(3) choosing from among the several rules at hand, for each machine one specific priority rule to apply to the orders waiting in queue,

(4) altering the operations sequence that the order has to follow on the machines, in order to plan an equivalent routing,

(5) going back to some previously recorded system statuses, in order to carry out a new set of decisions.

Depending on the particular aim of the simulation, the operator can enter his decisions on the console, after examining reports at the desired level of detail, on the status of queues, orders, machines, on the due dates which are most critical. Interactions can be scheduled according to one's wish, or can be automatically activated by the arrival of an order at the shop, or by the completion of the order processing by a machine. The model has been written in a simulation language (Simscript) and, therefore, its implementation — including conversational facilities — requested only one man-month of work. The straightforward logic of the model did not provide the possibility that the particular advantages deriving from the interactive features could stand out during the debugging phase. However, even in such a simple case we were faced with some instances of erroneous actions by the operator, against which the SD had not yet been protected. Also we never felt the need to introduce important and not forecast changes in the model structure during the simulated time.

The second model simulates the flow of cars in a city network completely controlled by traffic-lights. In a particular phase of our work, we aimed to define the motion law by which each car follows the one in front. We used a discrete form of a continuous simulation scheme, in which events are equally spaced at sufficiently short time intervals. It is possible to modify the parameters of the motion laws at any time we decide to do so; it is also possible to impose a particular behaviour on a car, for instance, a sudden stop or an acceleration, just as if the operator were the driver of that car, in order to examine the consequences on the motion of the cars behind it. The operator has other possibilities of interaction, such as switching manually the intersection-lights, or introducing at the sources of the flow a stream of cars interspersed as he wants. Graphic reports varying over time are displayed on a video unit giving thus a very immediate system representation.

The structure of this model, which has been programmed in Fortran, is quite different from the one we referred to all through this work, since it is somewhat similar to the structure of continuous simulation models. We want to emphasize here that in this type of scheme conversationality can be introduced in a more flexible way than in the discrete scheme, and seems to be more effective. In fact the simulated system "exists" in the SD so that the operator can follow its evolution in a closer way. On the other hand our traffic model required some elaborate core allocation and sets handling devices, so that even in this case other sophisticated actions had to be programmed accurately in advance.

5. Some conclusions

Generally speaking there does not seem to be any compatibility between a strict methodology – from the statistical point of view – in the simulation and the insertion of an active interaction by the operator into some samples, necessarily limited in number. Apart from obtaining some valid results in a statistical sense, interaction can be effective in getting an insight into the SD and into the model. But what kind of an insight do we get? The debugging phase is the one to benefit most from interactions; on the other hand in the operational phase the analyst can create the best experimental conditions as the situation evolves; interaction turns out also quite useful in the optimizing phase, if any, if the model is sufficiently deterministic, by switching from one pre-embedded alternative to another; we can also "simulate" through the operator behaviour certain parts of the model which are going to contain some decision rules not yet defined or implemented. In this connection let us not forget that sometimes we meet certain simulation problems for which it becomes convenient to give up modelling human behaviour and its individual decisions. If we wish to emphasize the latter we can enlarge the model and the SD to include through interaction the man itself.

In our analysis we noticed that there are many promising possibilities of interaction. The batch simulation languages we have at our disposal nowadays, seem to provide such flexibility, provided we build the SD to keep track of what we have in mind to do during the interaction. We found out that it is very hard to conceive and to implement more general, powerful and "spontaneous" actions on the system during the simulated time, while they can be made without any trouble before rerunning. Our experiences made us realize that no particular effort is necessary to bring up the simulation models to a useful conversational level, in the sense we outlined beforehand. We met with some difficulties in exploiting the conversational features immediately and completely, but as the interactive simulation became a habit, these difficulties kept decreasing more and more. However, at the present time, it is rather difficult to determine when this additional dimension, which conversationality seems to offer to simulation, really improves the quality of the results or only becomes a "side-advantage" to the operations researcher. Even as such, it can be validly justified on its own merits.

References

[1] J.G. Laski, Using simulation for on-line decision-making, in: Digital simulation in operational research, ed. S.H. Hollingdale (English Univ. Press, Londen, 1965).
[2] H.M. Markowitz and R.C. Steorts, Modify and restart routines for Simscript games and simulation experiments, Rand Corp. Mem. RM-4242-PR (1965).
[3] M. Greenberg and M. Jones, On line, incremental simulation, in: Simulation programming languages, ed. J.N. Buxton (North-Holland, Amsterdam, 1968).
[4] R.L. Ferguson and C.H. Jones, A computer aided decision system, Mgmt. Sci. Appl. Ser. 15, No. 10 (1969).

M. Ross, ed., OR '72. North-Holland Publishing Company (1973)

50

SOME CHARACTERISTICS OF PROJECT DURATION
FOR A CLASS OF STOCHASTIC ACTIVITY NETWORKS

Caractéristiques de la durée d'un projet
pour une classe de réseaux d'activité stochastique

M. KRISHNAMOORTHY
India Institute of Management, Calcutta, India

and

J. SUDARSANA RAO
Coca-Cola, O.R. Group, Essen, W. Germany

Abstract. A general formula for any GERT network configuration of "exclusive–or" type giving the expected project duration and its variance is derived in section 1 of this paper with the help of signal flow graph method and Mason's rule. Two special cases of this formula are of interest here. In case one the activities are all deterministic. In case two they are probabilistic (discrete or continuous) with the restriction that the expected value is equal to the variance. The difference between the project variance for these two cases has been shown to be equal to the expected value of project duration. For any network containing a mixture of these two extreme cases, the difference in variance at the project level will be less than its expected value. This measure, therefore, provides boundary conditions for project variances. Similar quantitative measures between the variances can be readily obtained from the general formula for any explicit relationship between standard deviation and expected value at the activity level. The utility of the general formula, thus, lies in providing a basis for a detailed sensitivity analysis of GERT networks. Section 2 of this paper uses a conditional probability approach to obtain these measures under certain restrictive assumptions. Section 3 provides an equivalence between the two for a trivial case under the assumption of geometric cycling.

1. Signal flow graph approach

Consider an "exclusive–or" "event-on-node" GERT network [1–10] having feedback loops of activities. The network is described by events $i = 1, 2, \ldots$ $\ldots, N$ and activities $(i, j) \in A$ having probabilistic durations t_{ij} with expected values μ_{ij} and standard deviations σ_{ij}^2.

Let the network have paths $k = 1, 2, ..., K$, each path having A_k activities in sequence. Let h be a set of activities forming a loop ($h = 1, 2, ..., H$). For the rth order of combination of non-touching loops for the path k let l_{rk} represent the set of r numbers of elementary loops h and let there be L_{rk} such combinations for the rth order ($r = 1, 2, ..., R_k$). At the graph level let l_{rg}, L_{rg} and R_g represent the corresponding limits.

The graph transmittance w_g is built up from activity transmittance w_{ij} in the following manner.

$$w_g = \frac{\sum_{k=1}^{K} w_k \left[1 + \sum_{r=1}^{R_k} (-1)^r \left(\sum_{l_{rg} \in L_{rg}} w_{l_{rk}} \right) \right]}{1 + \sum_{r=1}^{R_g} (-1)^r \left(\sum_{l_{rk} \in L_{rk}} w_{l_{rg}} \right)} = \frac{u}{v}, \tag{1}$$

where

$$w_k = \prod_{(i,j) \in A_k} w_{ij} \, ,$$

$$w_{l_{ry}} = \prod_{h \in l_{ry}} \left(\prod_{(i,j) \in h} w_{ij} \right) = \prod_{h \in l_{ry}} w_h \, , \qquad y = g, k \, , \tag{2}$$

$$w_{ij} = p_{ij} M_{ij} = p_{ij} E \left[\exp (s t_{ij}) \right] \, ,$$

given that p_{ij} is the probability of realisation of activity (i, j) and M_{ij} is the moment generating function of its activity duration t_{ij}.

The expected value μ_g and variance σ_g^2 at the project level are calculated by using the formulae (3) and (4) derived from the first principles, differentiating the numerator u and the denomenator v of (1) and putting $s = 0$ as required.

$$\mu_g = \left(\frac{u_0'}{u_0} \right) - \left(\frac{v_0'}{v_0} \right) \, , \tag{3}$$

$$\sigma_g^2 = \left(\frac{u_0''}{u_0} \right) - \left(\frac{v_0''}{v_0} \right) - \left(\frac{u_0'}{u_0} \right)^2 + \left(\frac{v_0'}{v_0} \right)^2 \, . \tag{4}$$

1.1. Calculation of the expected project duration

Let A_x represent any one of the sets of activities in series as in A_k or in a loop as in h. Then

$$w_x = \prod_{(i,j)\in A_x} w_{ij} = \prod_{(i,j)\in A_x} p_{ij} \prod_{(i,j)\in A_x} M_{ij} = P_x \prod_{(i,j)\in A_x} M_{ij}, \quad (5)$$

$$w'_x = P_x \sum_{y\in A_x} \prod_{(i,j)\in[A_x-y]} M_{ij}M'_y. \quad (6)$$

Hence

$$w'_{x0} = P_x \sum_{y\in A_x} E(t_y) = P_x\mu_x, \quad (7)$$

using (7) to calculate u_0, v_0, u'_0 and v'_0 as in (3)

$$\mu_g = \frac{\sum_{k=1}^{K} P_k \left(\mu_k + \sum_{r=1}^{R_k} (-1)^r \sum_{l_{rk}\in L_{rk}} P_{l_{rk}}(\mu_{l_{rk}} + \mu_k) \right)}{\sum_{k=1}^{K} P_k \left(1 + \sum_{r=1}^{R_k} (-1)^r \sum_{l_{rk}\in L_{rk}} P_{l_{rk}} \right)}$$

$$- \frac{\sum_{r=1}^{R_g} (-1)^r \sum_{l_{rg}\in L_{rg}} P_{l_{rg}}\mu_{l_{rg}}}{1 + \sum_{r=1}^{R_g} (-1)^r \sum_{l_{rg}\in L_{rg}} P_{l_{rg}}}, \quad (8)$$

where

$$P_{l_{ry}} = \prod_{h\in l_{ry}} P_h = \prod_{h\in l_{ry}} \prod_{(i,j)\in h} p_{ij}, \qquad y = k, g, \quad (9)$$

and

$$\mu_{l_{ry}} = \sum_{h\in l_{ry}} \mu_h = \sum_{h\in l_{ry}} \sum_{(i,j)\in h} \mu_{ij}, \qquad y = k, g. \quad (10)$$

Since μ_g does not contain any $\sigma_{ij}, (i,j)\in A$,

$$\mu_g = \mu_{gI} = \mu_{gII} = \mu_{gIII} \, , \tag{11}$$

representing three different types of networks, having activities A_I, A_{II} and A_{III}, respectively, where A_I contains only deterministic activities (A_1), A_{II} contains only probabilistic activities (A_2) and A_{III} has both deterministic (A_1) and probabilistic (A_2) activities.

$$A_I \ = A \,|(A_1 = A, A_2 = \emptyset; \sigma_{ij}\,|(i,j) \in A_1 = 0) \, ,$$

$$A_{II} = A \,|(A_1 = \emptyset, A_2 = A\,; \sigma_{ij}\,|(i,j) \in A_2 > 0) \, , \tag{12}$$

$$A_{III} = A \,|(A_1 \neq \emptyset, A_2 \neq \emptyset, A_1 \cup A_2 = A) \, .$$

1.2. Calculation of the variance of project duration

Differentiating w'_x once again, from (6) we get

$$w''_x = P_x \sum_{y \in A_x} \left[\prod_{(i,j) \in [A_x - y]} (M_{ij} M''_{ij}) \right.$$

$$+ \sum_{z \in [A_x - y]} \left. \left(\prod_{(i,j) \in [A_x - y - z]} (M_{ij} M'_z M'_y) \right) \right] , \tag{13}$$

$$w''_{x0} = P_x \sum_{y \in A_x} \left[E(t_y^2) + \prod_{z \in [A_x - y]} E(t_y) E(t_z) \right] . \tag{14}$$

Using the relationship for any activity y,

$$E(t_y^2) = \mu_y^2 + \sigma_y^2 \, , \tag{15}$$

we get

$$\dot{w}''_{x0} = P_x(\mu_x^2 + \sigma_x^2) \, , \tag{16}$$

and

$$u''_0 = \sum_{k=1}^{K} P_k \ (\mu_k^2 + \sigma_k^2) + \sum_{r=1}^{R_k} (-1)^r \sum_{l_{rk} \in L_{rk}} P_{l_{rk}} [(\mu_k + \mu_{l_{rk}})^2 + \sigma_k^2 + \sigma_{l_{rk}}^2] ,$$

$$\tag{17}$$

$$v_0'' = \sum_{r=1}^{R_g} (-1)^r \left(\sum_{l_{rg} \in L_{rg}} P_{l_{rg}} (\mu_{l_{rg}}^2 + \sigma_{l_{rg}}^2) \right) . \tag{18}$$

From (3), (7) and (8), it can be shown that

$$u_0 = \sum_{k=1}^{K} P_k \left[1 + \sum_{r=1}^{R_k} (-1)^r \left(\sum_{l_{rk} \in L_{rk}} P_{l_{rk}} \right) \right] , \tag{19}$$

$$v_0 = 1 + \sum_{r=1}^{R_g} (-1)^r \left(\sum_{l_{rg} \in L_{rg}} P_{l_{rg}} \right) , \tag{20}$$

$$u_0' = \sum_{k=1}^{K} P_k \left[\mu_k + \sum_{r=1}^{R_k} (-1)^r \left(\sum_{l_{rk} \in L_{rk}} P_{l_{rk}} (\mu_{l_{rk}} + \mu_k) \right) \right] , \tag{21}$$

$$v_0' = \sum_{r=1}^{R_g} (-1)^r \left(\sum_{l_{rg} \in L_{rg}} P_{l_{rg}} \mu_{l_{rg}} \right) . \tag{22}$$

Using (17) to (22) and the relationship (4), the value of σ_g^2 can be shown as a function of expected values, variances and probability of occurrence of various paths and combinations of non-touching loops.

$$\sigma_g^2 = f(P_x, \mu_x, \sigma_x^2 ; x = k, l_{rk}, l_{rg}) . \tag{23}$$

Since σ_x^2 occurs only in u_0'' and v_0'' as in (17) and (18), the difference between the project duration variance σ_{gII}^2 for the completely probabilistic case $(A = A_{II})$ and that of the deterministic case σ_{gI}^2 can be shown as in (24).

$$\sigma_{gII}^2 - \sigma_{gI}^2 = \frac{\sum_{k=1}^{K} P_k \left[\sigma_k^2 + \sum_{r=1}^{R_k} (-1)^r \left(\sum_{l_{rk} \in L_{rk}} P_{l_{rk}} (\sigma_k^2 + \sigma_{l_{rk}}^2) \right) \right]}{\sum_{k=1}^{K} P_k \left[1 + \sum_{r=1}^{R_k} (-1)^r \left(\sum_{l_{rk} \in L_{rk}} P_{l_{rk}} \right) \right]}$$
$$- \frac{\sum_{r=1}^{R_g} (-1)^r \left(\sum_{l_{rg} \in L_{rg}} P_{l_{rg}} \sigma_{l_{rg}}^2 \right)}{1 + \sum_{r=1}^{R_g} (-1)^r \left(\sum_{l_{rg} \in L_{rg}} P_{l_{rg}} \right)} . \tag{24}$$

By virtue of (24), the project duration variance σ_{gIII}^2 for the mixed case $A = A_{III}$, $(A_1 \neq \emptyset, A_2 \neq \emptyset, A_1 \cup A_2 = A)$ will lie between σ_{gII}^2 and σ_{gI}^2

$$\sigma_{gII}^2 > \sigma_{gIII}^2 > \sigma_{gI}^2 \ . \tag{25}$$

Situation 1: Comparing (8) and (24) it is seen that

$$\left[\sigma_{gII}^2 - \sigma_{gI}^2 \left| \begin{array}{l} \sigma_{ij}^2 = \mu_{ij} \ , \ (i,j) \in A_{II} \\ \sigma_{ij}^2 = 0 \ , \quad (i,j) \in A_I \end{array} \right. \right] = \mu_g \ . \tag{26}$$

The deviation of particular solutions from the generalised model (26) given above in discrete and continuous cases satisfying the properties mentioned may be verified by inspection of the respective m.g.f. of Poisson, $\exp[\mu(e^s - 1)]$, gamma, $(1 - s)^{-\mu}$, and normal $\exp[\mu s(1 + \frac{1}{2}s)]$, which take into account the relationship $\mu = \sigma^2$.

Situation 2: Since eq. (24) is not in any way dependent upon an imposed relationship such as $\sigma_{ij}^2 = \mu_{ij}$ or $\sigma_{ij} = \mu_{ij}$, it is valid in all cases. However, the compact form of (26) is unique for the assumption $\sigma_{ij}^2 = \mu_{ij}$.

2. Conditional probability approach

Let every loop h $(h = 1, 2, ..., H)$ of a network having a single path containing A_k activities be traversed B_h times before the project attains completion. It is assumed that t_{ij}^b, $(i, j) \in h$, $h = 1, 2, ..., B_h$ are independent sets of independent random variables for fixed B_h as i, j and h are varied and they are identically distributed. The B_h themselves are independent non-negative integral random variables.

The total project duration T_g is then given by

$$T_g = T_k + \sum_{h \in H} \sum_{b=1}^{B_h} T_h^b \ , \tag{27}$$

where

$$T_k = \sum_{(i,j) \in A_k} t_{ij} \ , \qquad T_h^b = \sum_{(i,j) \in h} t_{ij}^b \ . \tag{28}$$

Let the expectation and variance of T_k and T_h be μ_k, σ_k^2, μ_h and σ_h^2, respectively. Then

$$E(T_g|B_h, h \in H) = \mu_k + \sum_{h \in H} B_h \mu_h \,, \tag{29}$$

and

$$V(T_g|B_h, h \in H) = \sigma_k^2 + \sum_{h \in H} B_h \sigma_h^2 \,. \tag{30}$$

Hence

$$\mu_g = E(T_g) = \mu_k + \sum_{h \in H} \mu_h E(B_h) = \mu_{gI} = \mu_{gII} = \mu_{gIII} \,, \tag{31}$$

and

$$\sigma_g^2 = V(T_g) = E[V(T_g|B_h, h \in H)] + V[E(T_g|B_h, h \in H)] \tag{32}$$

$$= \sigma_k^2 + \sum_{h \in H} \sigma_h^2 E(B_h) + \sum_{h \in H} \mu_h^2 V(B_h) \,. \tag{33}$$

By putting $\sigma_h^2 = \sigma_k^2 = 0$ in (33), we get

$$\sigma_{gI}^2 = \sum_{h \in H} \mu_h^2 V(B_h) \,, \tag{34}$$

and

$$\sigma_{gII}^2 - \sigma_{gI}^2 = \sigma_k^2 + \sum_{h \in H} \sigma_h^2 E(B_h) \,. \tag{35}$$

Comparing (35) and (31) for the case $\sigma_{ij}^2 = \mu_{ij}$

$$\left[\sigma_{gII}^2 - \sigma_{gI}^2 \left| \begin{array}{l} \sigma_{ij}^2 = \mu_{ij}, (i,j) \in A_{II} \\ \sigma_{ij}^2 = 0 \,, (i,j) \in A_{I} \end{array} \right. \right] = \mu_g \,, \tag{36}$$

as before in (26) indicating the equivalence of these two approaches under restrictive assumptions.

3. Solution of $E(B_h)$ and $V(B_h)$

Even though the rules given in section 2 of this paper are free from the geometric nature of feed back loops which is assumed before, it has the drawback of missing the interdependence of cycling that may exist in the network. Hence the equivalence shown here is only upto the first two moments and it may breakdown in terms of equivalence of m.g.f. except in the case of a single path containing non-touching loops under the assumption of geometric cycling.

Consider a network with only one path (i.e., $k = 1$) and where the loops h ($h = 1, 2, ..., H$) do not have any common node among them. This implies that $R_g = H$ and the denomenator in (1) can be rewritten as $\Pi_{h \in H}(1 - P_h M_h)$. Since there is only a single path, there will be no non-touching loops with respect to the path and the numerator in (1) is simply (w_k). Hence

$$w_g = \frac{P_k M_k}{\displaystyle\prod_{h \in H}(1 - P_h M_h)} = \frac{u}{v}. \tag{37}$$

For the simplified network described here, it can be shown that

$$u_0 = v_0 = P_k = \prod_{h \in H}(1 - P_h), \tag{38}$$

and

$$v'_0 = -P_k \sum_{h \in H}\left(\frac{P_h}{1 - P_h}\right)\mu_h. \tag{39}$$

Hence

$$\mu_g = \mu_k + \sum_{h \in H}\left(\frac{P_h}{1 - P_h}\right)\mu_h. \tag{40}$$

Comparing (40) with (31), we get

$$E(B_h) = \left(\frac{P_h}{1 - P_h}\right), \qquad h \in H, \tag{41}$$

which conforms to the expected value of a geometric distribution.

The value of v'_0 in (39) is obtained from

$$v' = -\sum_{h \in H}\left(\prod_{y \in [H-h]}(1 - P_y M_y)P_h M'_h\right). \tag{42}$$

Accordingly,

$$v'' = - \sum_{h\in H} \left[\prod_{y\in[H-h]} (1 - P_y M_y) P_h M_h'' \right.$$

$$\left. - \sum_{z\in[H-h]} P_z M_z' P_h M_h' \left(\prod_{y\in[H-h-z]} (1 - P_y M_y) \right) \right]. \tag{43}$$

Therefore, using (38) and (43)

$$\left(\frac{v_0''}{v_0} \right) = - \sum_{h\in H} \left[\left(\frac{P_h}{1-P_h} \right) (\mu_h^2 + \sigma_h^2) - \sum_{z\in[H-h]} \mu_z \mu_h \left(\frac{P_h}{1-P_h} \right) \left(\frac{P_z}{1-P_z} \right) \right]. \tag{44}$$

Hence

$$\sigma_g^2 = \sigma_k^2 + \sum_{h\in H} \mu_h^2 \left(\frac{P_h}{[1-P_h]^2} \right) + \sigma_h^2 \left(\frac{P_h}{1-P_h} \right). \tag{45}$$

From (40), (41) and (45) it is obvious that

$$V(B_h) = \frac{P_h}{(1-P_h)^2} = E(B_h)(1+E(B_h)), \qquad h \in H, \tag{46}$$

which also conforms to the variance of a geometric distribution. Furthermore,

$$\left\{ \sigma_{gII}^2 - \sigma_{gI}^2 \left| \begin{array}{l} \sigma_{ij}^2 = \mu_{ij}, \ (i,j) \in A_{II} \\ \sigma_{ij}^2 = 0, \ (i,j) \in A_I \end{array} \right. \right\} = \mu_g. \tag{47}$$

References

[1] H. Eisner, A generalised network approach to the planning and scheduling of a research project, Opns. Res. 10 (1962) 115.
[2] S.E. Elmaghraby, An algebra for the analysis of generalised activity networks, Mgmt. Sci. 10 (1964) 494.
[3] S.E. Elmaghraby, On generalized activity networks, J. Ind. Eng. 17 (1966) 621.
[4] A.A.B. Pritsker, GERT: graphical evaluation and review technique, RAND Memo RM – 4973, NASA.
[5] A.A.B. Pritsker and W.W. Happ, GERT: graphical evaluation and review technique, Part I: Fundamentals, J. Ind. Eng. 17 (1966) 267.
[6] A.A.B. Pritsker and G.E. Whitehouse, GERT: graphical evaluation and review technique, Part II: Probabilistic and industrial engineering applications, J. Ind. Eng. 17 (1966) 293.

[7] G. Whitehouse, Model systems on paper with flowgraph analysis, Ind. Eng. (June 1969) 30.

[8] A.A.B. Pritsker, The status of GERT, in: Project planning by network analysis, Proc. Second Intern. Congr., Amsterdam (Oct. 1969) ed. H.J.M. Lombaers (North-Holland, Amsterdam, 1969).

[9] F.S. Settles, GERT network models of production economies, Ph.D. Dissertation, Arizona State Univ. (1969); presented at the AIIE Nat. Conf., Houston (May 1969).

[10] M. Krishnamoorthy and J. Sudarsana Rao, Some properties of stochastic feed back activity networks, presented at the Fourth Ann. Conv. of the Opnl. Res. Soc. of India (March 1972).

M. Ross, ed., OR '72. North-Holland Publishing Company (1973)

51

PROCESSUS DE DECISION DECOMPOSABLES

Decomposition processes

RAMON COMPANYS-PASCUAL
l'Université Polytechnique de Barcelona, Barcelona, Spain

Résumé. Dans plusieurs cas la traduction fidèle de la déscription verbale d'un processus évolutif à un modèle mathématique conduit à des processus Markoviens de décision dans lesquels on peut séparer l'évolution naturelle du système de l'évolution induite par les décisions. Ce fait est courant dans les problèmes de rénouvellement et de stocks.

Il est intéressant de profiter de la structure du modèle pour son traitement numérique dans les applications. La communication débute par un exposé théorique décrivant des algorithmes de résolution et les critères qui permettent d'assurer son applicabilité, en raison de la convergence du processus subjacent.

On présente plusieurs cas d'applications. Les uns issus des problèmes réels (barrage "El Pastoral"), d'autres de la litérature existante ou bien dérivés des problèmes généraux. Dans tous les cas la modelisation a été aisée et les algorithmes ont donné satisfaction, même dans des conditions défavorables.

Le schema présenté paraît très adapté aux problèmes de rénouvellement dont un aperçu de deux cas est donné, et aux problèmes de stocks qui font l'objet de la présentation d'un cas-exemple.

Les idées développées dans le présent texte sont le resultat des travaux de plusieurs personnes, réalisés pendant les dix dernières années. La première partie présente une famille de modèles et un algorithme de résolution, la dernière décrit plusieurs essais, avec une base réelle ou académique. Les processus décomposables trouvent son intérêt dans le fait qu'ils traduisent exactement l'exposition verbale de plusieurs processus courants, tels que ceux qui se présentent dans les stocks ou les procedures de rénouvellement d'équipement. L'algorithme proposé découle aussi directement du modèle et présente de belles performances dans les applications numériques.

1. Introduction

Beaucoup de phénomènes auxquels s'intéresse la RO peuvent être décrits au moyen d'un système qui subit une évolution dans le temps, en changeant d'état. On dit que le système passe d'un état à un autre, ou que le système se trouve dans un état donné. Nous assumerons:

(a) Le processus est discret dans le temps, c'est à dire, nous nous intéressons à l'état du système en instants discrets, également séparés, que nous écrivons: 0, 1, 2, ..., t, ... Entre deux de ces points temporels s'écoule une période, et pendant la période le système subit l'évolution d'un état a un autre (qui peut être le même initial).

(b) Les états forment un ensemble denombrable et fini. Nous écrivons les états 1, 2, ..., i, ..., n.

(c) A l'évolution du système est associée une fonction économique. La valeur de cette fonction au cours de plusieurs périodes s'obtient par agrégation (normalement addition) des valeurs associées à chaque évolution d'une seule période.

(d) En plus l'évolution élémentaire dans chaque période est fonction de l'état initial et de la valeur que prend une variable d'action liée à la période. Le nombre de valeurs que peut prendre cette variable est fini, $u = 1, 2, 3, ...$ ..., k, ..., m_i.

(e) Le processus est Markovien dans le sens où toute l'information pertinente pour décrire l'évolution future du système se trouve dans l'état présent et dans les valeurs successives des variables d'action. L'évolution passée n'apporte pas de renseignements supplémentaires.

Nous avons défini ainsi des processus Markoviens de décision étudiés par plusieurs auteurs. Il y a une caractéristique en plus présenté souvent dans des problèmes réels. Dedans de chaque période l'évolution est décomposée en deux parties: une partie qu'on appelera *évolution propre ou naturelle du système* (phase H) et une autre *évolution induite par la décision* (phase D). Un processus de ce type est dit décomposable, et en suivant l'ordre de phases dans la période on peut distinguer les processus H–D et les processus D–H (ou bien *processus de correction* et *processus de prévision*). Evidemment il pourrait avoir plus de deux phases dans une période, mais nous n'allons pas suivre cette voie.

Dans les processus H–D, le système passe d'un état i à un état intermédiare j (quelques fois sans signification réelle) en forme spontanée, indépendante de l'action du décideur. La décision de celui-ci fait passer le système de j à un état k, de la même nature qui i. Tant à la transition de la phase H comme à celle de la phase D sont associées des valeurs économiques élémentaires $S_{ij}(t)$

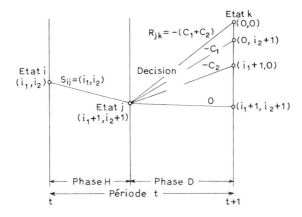

Fig. 1.

et $R_{jk}(t)$. Il pourrait exister des valeurs économiques attachées aux états eux-mêmes, mais le développement resterait sensiblement le même et nous allons continuer dans le sens précédent.

Bien que la première phase soit designée H (lettre initiale du mot "hasard"), la transition de i à j peut être déterministe. En fait le cas indiqué dans la fig. 1 correspond à un schéma de ce type basé sur le problème bien connu suivant:

"Un système se compose de deux machines principales. Son rendement est fonction des âges de machines. Si ces âges sont i_1 et i_2 le rendement ou bénifice pendant l'unité de temps est $\phi(i_1, i_2)$ où ϕ est une fonction décroissante de ses variables. Les machines peuvent être renouvellées. C'est-a-dire, changées par d'autres d'âge 0 à un prix indépendant de l'âge de la machine changée, et égal à C_1 pour la première maxime et C_2 pour la deuxième. Quelle est la meilleure politique de substitution des machines?"

En ne tenant pas compte, pour l'instant, de la question posée nous voyons que la schema de la fig. 1 corréspond au problème. L'état i est le couple (i_1, i_2) formé par les âges des machines. L'évolution naturelle porte l'état du système à $(i_1 + 1, i_2 + 1)$ avec une valeur $\phi(i_1, i_2)$. Il y a quatre actions possibles a entreprendre:

changer les deux machines, coût $(C_1 + C_2)$,

changer la 1ère machine seulement, coût C_1,

changer la 2ème machine seulement, coût C_2,

ne changer pas aucune machine, coût 0.

Nous étudierons, néanmoins, le cas plus général, et plus stable, dans lequel la transition de i à j n'est pas déterminée à l'avance; à partir de i on peut atteindre plusieurs états j et il existe une loi de probabilité de passage, $H_{ij}(t)$. Les valeurs de $H_{ij}(t)$, pour des i et j concrètes forment une matrice stochastique $\mathbf{H}(t)$.

Dans le cas des décisions nous pourrons aussi former une matrice stochastique $\mathbf{D}(t)$, avec des éléments $D_{jk}(t)$, si nous pensions utiliser des stratégies mixtes. Dans des cas plus complexes (jeu submergé dans un processus Markovien) les stratégies mixtes pourront nous intéresser, mais ici nous allons nous limiter à des stratégies pures, de la forme $k = k(j, t)$. Une suite finie ou non de stratégies sera appelée *politique*. Nous allons étudier les stratégies et politiques que dans un certain sens soient optimales.

Tout ce qui vient d'être dit pour les processus H–D pourrait être répété pour les D–H, sauf l'inversion des phases. En fait les deux types de processus sont identiques, mais certains problèmes se posent tout naturellement dans l'une des formes de préférence à l'autre.

Bien que les modèles décrits soient directement utilisables (les arbres de décision sont des processus D–H finis) nous allons nous fixer sur les processus homogènes dans le temps, c'est-à-dire, tels que S_{ij}, R_{jk} et $\mathbf{H}$ sont indépendants de t.

Dans cette dernière optique soient $v_i(N, P_n)$ l'espérance mathématique de la valeur économique à obtenir en N periodes consécutives quand initialement le système se trouve a l'état i et la politique qu'on va utiliser est P_n, et soit $v_i^*(N)$ la même valeur quand la politique est optimale, P_n^*. Soit aussi $k_n^* = k^*(j, n)$ le premier élément de la politique P_n^*. Nous pouvons écrire:

$$a_j^*(N) = S_{jk_n^*} + v_{k_n^*}(N) = \underset{k}{\text{OPT}} \ [S_{jk} + v_{k*}(N)] \ , \quad j = 1, 2, ..., m \ , \tag{1}$$

$$v_i^*(N+1) = q_i + \sum_j H_{ij} a_j^*(N) \ , \quad i = 1, 2, ..., n \ , \tag{2}$$

ayant fait

$$q_i = \sum_j H_{ij} R_{ij} \ . \tag{3}$$

Si on utilise l'écriture matricielle, avec des vecteurs a^*, v^* et q, et des matrices $\mathbf{H}$ et $\mathbf{S}$, nous aurons

$$a^*(N) \quad = \mathbf{S} \otimes v^*(N) \ , \tag{4}$$

$$v^*(N+1) = q + \mathbf{H} \cdot a^*(N) \ , \tag{5}$$

où l'opération matricielle de (4), le "optproduit", traduit l'opération indiquée en (1), ce qui est numériquement valable.

Pour mémoire il est convenable de dire que dans certains cas il est nécessaire d'introduire le facteur d'actualisation $\beta(0 < \beta < 1)$, qui d'ailleurs assure la stabilité de la politique à long terme. Dans ce cas (5) sera substituée par

$$v^*(N+1) = q + \beta\, \mathbf{H} \cdot a^*(N) \ . \tag{6}$$

2. Détermination de la politique optimale

Dans les problèmes avec la structure précédente nous nous intéressons souvent à la politique optimale à long terme, ce qui veut dire les stratégies optimales correspondant à des valeurs de N non fixées mais élévées. Heureusement dans la plupart de cas, quand N croît, la politique optimale subit une stabilisation, soit en forme périodique (de période au dessus de 1), surtout et presque obligatoirement si la phase H est deterministe, soit non périodique ou de période 1, c'est-à-dire avec k_N^* indépendant de N, k^*, pour N superieur à une certaine valeur finie, et quelques fois très réduite. Dans ce dernier cas, l'unique vraiment utile, on peut montrer que:

$$v^*(N) \rightarrow N g X_1 + w \ , \tag{7}$$

où la flèche veut dire équivalence dans la limite, X_1 et w sont des vecteurs, X_1 à toutes ses composantes égales à 1, et N et g sont des scalaires. La valeur g est la valeur économique moyenne à long terme par période (c'est-à-dire le bénéfice ou le coût moyen par période).

Pour trouver la politique optimale à long terme il est possible d'utiliser plusieurs méthodes. Il existe l'itération dans l'espace des politiques, proposé par Howard, procédé bien connu ce qui permet de ne pas le décrire. Il y a aussi l'alternative d'employer le jeu d'éqs. (4) et (5), en partant d'une $v^*(0)$ convenable, attendant la stabilisation pour des valeurs de N suffisamment importantes. Il existe ici une complication due à la difficulté de comparaison des succesifs vecteurs $v^*(N)$ entre eux.

Une remarque très simple permet d'apporter une amélioration sensible. En tenant compte de la nature de la matrice $\mathbf{H}$, dont la somme des lignes est égale à 1, nous voyons que si on ajoute ou on retranche la même quantité, x, à toutes les composantes de $v^*(N)$, la stratégie optimale k_N^* reste sans changement, et les vecteurs $a^*(N)$ et $v^*(N+1)$ subissent la même transformation, c'est-à-dire, toutes les composantes sont augmentées ou diminuées par x.

Soit alors le procédé suivant de "normalisation" des vecteurs $\boldsymbol{v}^*(N)$: On retranche de chaque composante une d'elles, par exemple la dernière

$$\bar{v}_i^*(N) = v_i^*(N) - v_n^*(N) , \qquad i = 1, 2, 3, ..., n . \tag{8}$$

Le vecteur $\bar{\boldsymbol{v}}^*(N)$ a systématiquement sa dernière composante nulle. La politique optimale, et donc la politique optimale à long terme, n'est pas changée, et le problème a perdu une unité de sa dimension, ce qui est un beau résultat déjà. Le nouveau jeu d'équations sera maintenant

$$\boldsymbol{a}^*(N) \quad = \mathsf{S} \otimes v^*(N) , \tag{9}$$

$$v^*(N+1) = q + \mathsf{H} \cdot \boldsymbol{a}^*(N) , \tag{10}$$

$$\bar{v}^*(N+1) = \mathsf{R} \cdot v^*(N+1) , \tag{11}$$

$$g_{N+1} \quad = v_n^*(N+1) , \tag{12}$$

où R est la matrice qui fait la transformation (8). Il est très facile à montrer que dans l'hypothèse de convergence contenue dans (7) nous aurons:

$$g_N \rightarrow g , \tag{13}$$

$$v^*(N) \rightarrow \mathsf{R} \cdot \boldsymbol{w} . \tag{14}$$

3. Critère de convergence

Pour etre assurés de la convergence des équations de recurrence (9) à (12) il nous faudrait un critère simple. Il est facile a démontrer que un critère valable est:

$$\sum_j H_{kj} H_{lj} \neq 0 , \qquad \text{a tout couple } (k,l) . \tag{15}$$

Si la matrice H a une colonne d'éléments non nuls, par exemple, le critère est satisfait et il y a convergence. Beaucoup de cas sont tels que la condition de la colonne non nulle est implicite dans son structure même. Evidemment le critère est une condition suffisante; mais pas nécessaire. Le critère met en jeu seulement la matrice H. La partie décisionelle du processus n'intervient pas, et évidemment peut jouer son rôle dans les cas où H n'assure la convergence, a travers la matrice S. L'analyse de cette possibilité reste ouverte. La convergence, dans les cas ou elle existe, est normalement exponentielle, ce qui permet l'usage de plusieurs artifices pour son accélération.

Les problèmes dont la nature se prête a sa modelisation en processus décomposable, sont facilement formulés au moyen de (4) et (5), et la variable auxiliaire $a^*(N)$ trouve tout son intérêt dans la résolution numérique à travers des expressions (9) à (12). Une autre formulation exige habituellement plus de calculs.

4. Cas d'application

4.1. Détermination de la courbe de sécurité d'un barrage

Il s'agit de la première partie d'une étude plus approfondie sur la gestion du barrage "El Pastoral". La courbe de securité, de risque α, donne le niveau auquel il faut conserver celui du barrage dans la mesure du possible, pour être assuré de pouvoir fournir en aval une certaine quantité d'eau par unité de temps avec probabilité $1 - \alpha$. Les données du problème étaient:

N, niveau maximum: en prenant le système Sau et Susqueda groupé 385 Mm^3;

M, écoulement maximum par les tourbines – le goulot d'étranglement était $50m^3/seg$;

C, quantité d'eau à fournir en aval: $12m^3/seg$;

A, apportation maximale; on disposait d'une statistique des apportations du fleuve Ter sur 36 années.

Le niveau recherché de securité qu'on garantie étant G, le problème se présente avec la structure de la fig. 2. La politique est imposée par la définition même de courbe de securité. Soit j l'était ou niveau au debut de la phase D. Alors:

si $N + M \geqslant j \geqslant G + M$ tourbiner M et passer à l'état $k = j - M$,
$\quad G + M \geqslant j \geqslant G + C \qquad j - G \qquad\qquad k = G,$
$\quad G + C \geqslant j \geqslant C \qquad\quad C \qquad\qquad\quad k = j - C ,$
$\quad\quad C \geqslant j \geqslant 0 \qquad\qquad j \qquad\qquad\quad k = 0.$

Dans le dernier cas il y a défaillance, puisqu'on ne fournit pas la quantité C. Pour en tenir compte, on introduit une pénalisation de $+1$ chaque fois où la transition se fait de $j < C$ à $k = 0$. La phase H comporte le passage de i à $j = i + a$ en vertu de l'apportation a. La probabilité de passage a été déduite de la sta-

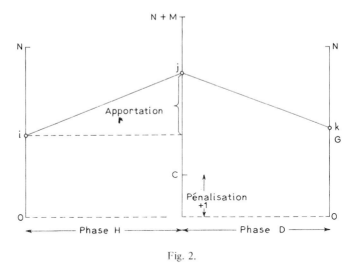

Fig. 2.

tistique sur 20 ans, à travers l'ajustement d'une loi normale-logarithmique, à paramètres différents pour les différents mois. L'ajustement était très satisfaisant, comme plusieurs tests statistiques ont montré, mais il existait une forte corrélation entre deux mois succesifs.

Pour la détermination de G on a tenu compte de l'observation suivante. Avec la valeur juste de G la politique choisie sera telle que la valeur économique moyenne par période sera α. On peut utiliser donc α pour la "normalisation" du vecteur $v(N)$

$$\bar{v}_i(N) = v_i(N) - \alpha, \tag{16}$$

et l'indice i de la composante nulle de $\bar{v}(N)$ correspondra au niveau G.

Nous pouvons commencer l'itération avec une valeur de G quelconque (pas trop mauvaise si possible) et la changer à chaque itération par le niveau l correspondant à la composante nulle de $v(N)$. Dans l'application concrete on a choisi comme période le mois. Puisque il y a douze mois différents quand au comportement du fleuve, il y a aussi douze valeurs différentes. L'itération comporte douze périodes distinctes à l'intérieur d'une macro-période annuelle.

La convergence a été très satisfaisante mais le résultat obtenu confronté aux statistiques n'était pas valide, dû à la forte corrélation des mois. On a compliqué la phase H en tenant compte de la corrélation entre deux mois successifs, ce qui correspondait à une chaîne de Markov de 2ème ordre et à une forte augmentation du nombre d'états. La convergence néanmoins a été

atteinte, dans des conditions de temps convenables. Le résultat, là-aussi, présenté des traits mauvais, dû à la corrélation, et ayant testé la méthode, le
problème a été abordé d'un façon différente bien que très rapprochée.

On a utilisé un calculateur GE 415 programme en Fortran.

4.2. Problèmes de renouvellement

Nous avons fait plusieurs tests pour connaître la portée des idées théori-
ques précédentes. Nous avons repris le problème de l'automobile de Howard
qui s'exprime de la façon suivante: Nous voulons savoir quand il faut changer
l'automobile et quelle doit être l'age de la nouvelle voiture achetée. L'age de
la voiture est exprimée en trimestres, ce qui nous donne un indice i, exprimant l'état, compris entre 0 et 40. La limite de dix années est prise entre
d'autres choses, pour limiter les calculs. Les données sont

P_i, probabilité de passage de l'age i à l'age $i + 1$ en un période ou trimestre.
$1 - P_i$ exprime la probabilité d'une avarie importante qu'oblige au changement de voiture. Dans les conditions énoncées $P_{40} = 0$.

T_i, valeur a la vente d'une voiture d'age i;
C_i, prix d'achat d'une voiture d'age i $(C_i > T_i)$;
E_i, coût moyen d'entretien de la voiture pendant le trimestre i.

Dans la fig. 3 on peut trouver la structure du problème en processus H–D,
nous croyons qu'elle enlève la necessité d'une déscription plus complète.

La politique optimale trouvée coincidait avec celle donnée par Howard:

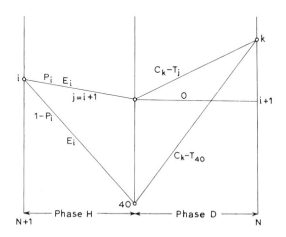

Fig. 3.

maintenir la voiture entre l'age de 6 mois et 6 ans et demi, hors cette bande, l'échanger pour une voiture d'age 3 ans.

Nous avons utilisé un calculateur IBM 360/30 à 32K. L'algortihme a été programmé en Fortran, et en plus de la procédure d'itération on y a introduit une procédure d'accélération. Le nombre d'itérations, pour arriver a une différence entre vecteurs $\bar{v}^*$ succesifs de 10^{-4} a été 185, et le temps total ordinateur de six minutes.

Nous avons abordé aussi les cas de deux pièces en série et en parallèle, étudiant spécialement le problème du "bladder" cité par Bellman et Dreyfus et des variantes du problème aléatoire analogue au réprésenté dans la fig. 1. Nous avons utilisé ici le langage PL/I et un ordinateur plus puissant l'IBM 360/40 à 128K.

4.3. Gestion de stocks

Une classe de problèmes qui se prête facilement à notre formulation est l'étude de modèles de stocks à approvisionnement périodique et délai d'approvisionnement pratiquement constant. Dans ce cas il est plus pratique utiliser les processus D–H, mais il est aussi possible d'employer le même schema général que précédemment. La fig. 4 montre un cas où le délai d'approvisionnement est égal à la période.

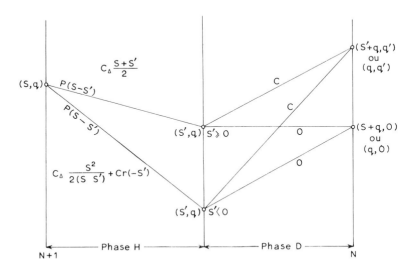

Fig. 4.

Nous avons traité plusieurs cas, avec différentes variantes, dans un IBM 360/30 à 32K, programmé en PL/I. Les temps et les résultats ont été satisfaisants.

Notes

(1) L'idée des processus décomposables a été conçue au cours d'un travail de récherche sur la substitution d'équipement, en traduisant exactement l'exposition verbale du problème. Elle a fait l'objet de deux Notes de Travail à diffusion restreinte [1, 2], et par la suite à la publication [3]. Plusieurs auteurs ont recueilli l'idée: Kaufmann (qui était à la base de la récherche initiale) Fauré, Muller, Chacon, etc. [4, 5]. Les processus décomposables ne sont différents en leur essence de ceux étudiés par Howard [6].

Le problème du système avec deux machines, décrit au moyen de la fig. 1 se trouve en [7] et il a été traité au moyen des processus en [8].

(2) La détermination de la politique optimale à long terme se trouve en plusieurs textes cités dans la note 1, par exemple [3, 6].

(3) Le critère de convergence et l'étude d'accelerateurs a fait l'objet d'une thèse par Ramos [9].

(4) Les exemples d'application ont des sources diverses. Le cas du barrage "El Pastoral" est développé en [10] et en plusieurs documents à diffusion restreinte. L'exemple de la voiture se trouve en [6] et aussi en [12] et il est plus développé en [9, 11]. L'exemple du "bladder" vient de [12] et il est développée en plusieurs variantes en [9, 11], avec résultats qui ne concordent exactement avec [12]. Les exemples de stocks se trouvent aussi en [9, 11].

Bibliographie

[1] R. Companys, Gestion d'un ensemble composé de plusieurs sous-ensembles ou pièces, Note de Travail (1961).
[2] R. Companys, Décisions séquentielles en processus en chaîne de Karkov, Note de Travail (1961).
[3] R. Companys, Procesos de decisión en la gestión de equipos industriales complejos, Cuadernos de Estadistica Aplicada e Investigación Operativa 2, fasc. 3 (1962).
[4] A. Kaufmann et R. Cruon, La programmation dynamique (Dunod, Paris, 1965).
[5] R. Bellman, The theory of dynamic programming (Princeton Univ. Press, Princeton, 1957).
[6] R. Howard, Dynamic programming and Markov processes (MIT Press, Cambridge, 1960).
[7] D.J. White, Dynamic programming (Oliver and Boyd, Edinbury, 1969).

[8] R. Companys, Programmación dinámica, 2a Version (CPDA, 1972).

[9] E. Ramos, Procesos azar, Decision convergencia y aplicaciones, Tesis de Doctor Ingeniero, Universidad Politecnica de Barcelona (1972).

[10] R. Companys et R. Puigjaner, Calcul de la courbe de securité d'un barrage simulé par un processus hasard-décision, présentée à Conf. Intern. sur la R.O. et l'Energie Electrique, Athenes (1968).

[11] R. Companys et E. Ramos, Diversas aplicationes de los procesos azar-decision, Cuadernos de estadistica applicada e Investigación Operativa Vol VII, fasc. 2, 1970.

[12] R. Bellman et S. Dreyfuss, Applied dynamic programming (Princeton Univ. Press, Princeton, 1962).

M. Ross, ed., OR '72. North-Holland Publishing Company (1973)

52

RANKING OF INTERDEPENDENT INVESTMENT PROJECTS

*Rangement des projets d'investissement interdépendants
asujettis à des contraintes budgetaires*

INGE THYGESEN

IMSOR, Technical University of Denmark, Lyngby, Denmark

Abstract. A set of projects is proposed to expand the capacity of a system of inter-related activities meeting a growing demand. Resources are scarce, but the final budget allocations are not necessarily known a priori. It shows how the optimal ranking, which exists among independent projects, can be generalized to a set of efficient rankings of interdependent projects. The optimal plan corresponding to any series of annual budget allocations may then be found by timing the projects within each efficient ranking using the simple first-year-benefit criterion and choosing the best of the resulting plans.

Thus, a two-phased planning procedure is suggested in which only the second phase, the timing routine, has to be repeated in the case of budget revisions. The determination of efficient rankings in the first phase takes advantage of certain regularities often found in the development of the relative effectiveness of alternative states of an expanding system.

1. Introduction

The problem considered in this paper is well-known to most heads of divisions managing an expanding system of interrelated activities. They are faced with a list of projects they want to carry out in order to increase the capacity of the system or to make it work more effectively. They know capital resources are scarce, and so they want to be able to communicate with top management to claim their share of the available funds. Finally, they look for advice on how to choose the best programme of investments possible within the budget constraints given or foreseen.

The method described below is developed to meet these needs. For expositional reasons only a very simple case is treated in detail (sections 2–4). However, possible generalizations are listed afterwards (section 5). Some empirical results and comparisons with other methods are found in the conclusion (section 6).

2. Formulating the problem

Initially a *set of investment projects* enumerated by index $j = 1, 2, ..., n$ has been formulated. It is assumed that all projects may be combined freely (see, however, section 5) and thus, there exist 2^n alternative *states of the system*. These are to be specified by a n-dimensional binary vector $x = \{x_1, ..., x_j, ..., x_n\}$, where x_j is equal to one if project j has been carried out and zero otherwise.

The *effectiveness* of the system in a given year is assumed to depend only on the state of the system in that year, as defined by the initial state and the projects implemented in previous years regardless of age. Let $b_t(x)$ denote an evaluation (in monetary terms) of the differential net benefit obtainable in year t by operating the system in state x instead of continuing in the initial $X_0 = \{0, ..., 0\}$. The *capital costs* of switching from one state to another is assumed to be equal to the sum of the capital costs of each project involved. C_j denotes the capital costs of implementing project j, evaluated at the time of completion, i.e., at the end of the last year before the project changes the state of the system. For simplicity all capital costs are assumed to be constant (cf. section 5).

The problem is to find the best *programme*

$$X = X_1, ..., X_t, ... ,$$

where

$$X_t = \{X_{t1}, ..., X_{tj}, ..., X_{tn}\}$$

indicates the states of the system for each $t = 1, 2, ... $.

The *optimality criterion* used is maximization of the net present value $V(X)$ of the programme measured by the (net) benefits generated by operating the system in the states defined by the programme instead of continuing in the initial state, minus the capital costs involved in expanding the system. The direct capital costs are modified by the shadow value of capital reflecting the *annual budget allocations* imposed upon the system by higher levels of the organization.

Let r denote the *rate of discount* expressing time preference and let λ be the *shadow value of capital* evaluated in the year in which it is spent using the discounted value of marginal opportunity costs. It is assumed that the scarcity of capital is constant and, therefore, that λ is independent of t. This assumption turns out to be unnecessarily restrictive (see section 5), but it simplifies the mathematical expressions considerably.

The objective function becomes

$$\max_{X} V(X) = \max_{\{X_t\}} \sum_{t=0}^{\infty} \left[b_t(X_t) - (1+\lambda) \sum_{j=1}^{n} C_j(X_{t+1j} - X_{tj}) \right] (1+r)^{-t} . \tag{1}$$

Making use of the initial condition that $X_{0j} = 0$ for all j and remembering that $b_0(X_0) = 0$, (1) can be reformulated as follows:

$$\max_{X} V(X) = \max_{\{X_t\}} \sum_{t=1}^{\infty} \left[b_t(X_t) - (1+\lambda) r \sum_{j=1}^{n} C_j X_{tj} \right] (1+r)^{-t} , \tag{2}$$

which, supplemented by the physical constraints,

$$X_{tj} = 0 \text{ or } 1 , \tag{3}$$
$$t = 1, 2, \ldots \quad \text{and} \quad j = 1, 2, \ldots, n ,$$
$$X_{t+1j} - X_{tj} \geqslant 0 , \tag{4}$$

constitutes the model. It is important to note that each term of the summation (2) refers to the state of the system in one year only. However, the whole programme is connected through the constraints (4), which express the irreversibility of changes in the system.

Expression (2) shows that the value of a programme can be found as the sum of the discounted values of the surpluses generated in every year of the programme. The *surplus* in year t is equal to the operating benefit $b_t(X_t)$ minus the interest charge and the opportunity cost of the capital $\Sigma_j C_j X_{tj}$ so far invested. Had it not been for the constraints (4), the optimal programme could evidently be found by choosing for each year the state promising the largest surplus (as just defined) in that year.

3. Solution in the special case of independence

To prepare the ground for the method proper, let us assume that the projects are independent, i.e., not only the capital costs, but also the benefits of the projects are additive. Let b_{jt} denote the potential benefit in year t from having implemented project j. It is a sufficient condition for the solution given below that b_{tj} is non-decreasing over time corresponding to a growing demand for the goods or services produced by the system.

The model becomes

$$\max_{X} V(X) = \max_{\{X_t\}} \sum_t \left[\sum_j b_{tj} X_{tj} - (1+\lambda) r \sum_j C_j X_{tj} \right] (1+r)^{-t}$$

$$= \max_{\{X_t\}} \sum_j \sum_t [b_{tj} - (1+\lambda) r C_j](1+r)^{-t} X_{tj} , \tag{5}$$

under the same constraints (3) and (4) as above. In this case the solution is immediate, as the model may be decomposed into submodels involving only one project each.

3.1. λ given: the pure timing problem

Evidently, each project should be put into operation the first year it promises a positive contribution to (5) in the form of a surplus: For each j:

$$\text{FYB}_{tj} = b_{tj} - (1+\lambda) r C_j \quad \begin{cases} \leqslant 0: X_{tj} = 0 , \\[2mm] > 0: X_{tj} = 1 . \end{cases} \tag{6}$$

As the left-hand side of the inequality is non-decreasing over time, constraints (4) are fulfilled. (6) is the well-known first-year-benefit *criterion for timing* presented, e.g., by Marglin [1].

3.2. λ unknown: the pure ranking problem

In a multi-level planning process the budget allocations and the implied shadow values are unknowns to be found. Heads of divisions may contribute significantly by ranking their projects and indicate the consequences of marginal changes in their budgets.

In the present case there exists an *optimal ranking* * of projects to be put into operation in year t given by the following priority index: For year t:

$$FYRR_{tj} = b_{tj}/C_j. \qquad (7)$$

to be interpreted as the First-Year-Rate of Return. The project topping the index has the best chances of fulfilling the implementation requirement in (6) for any fixed value of λ and should thus be given top priority. A similar reasoning holds for the remaining projects.

Programming is carried out sequentially (starting with $t = 1$) by computing the priority index (7) for all projects not yet selected for implementation and including as many of these projects as possible within the suggested annual budget. The index for the marginal project implicitly determines the marginal opportunity costs [the cut-off point being $(1+\lambda)r$]. Note that future budgets need not be known and that the optimal ranking may change over time.

4. Solution in the case of interdependence

Under certain assumptions (to be specified below) the optimal programme may be found by a generalization of the techniques described in the preceding section. The planning procedure suggested below has two phases, i.e., ranking and timing of projects, of which the former is independent of the shadow value of capital (λ) and only the latter has to be repeated in the case of budget revisions.

4.1. Phase 1: determination of efficient rankings

A ranking of projects may be transformed into a ranking of states defined by adding to the initial state projects one by one in the order prescribed by the ranking. There exists $n!$ such rankings of states. The goal is to determine a much smaller set of rankings, which includes all rankings involved in optimal programmes corresponding to any budget allocations, i.e., rankings implied by the solution to the model (2)–(4) for any value of λ.

This is obtained by utilizing the relative cost-effectiveness of alternative states of the system in a single year as an indicator of the sequence, in which the states should be attained. Evidently, such conclusions have as a prerequi-

---

* It is assumed that the budgeting procedure is flexible enough to make up for the discontinuities intrinsic to project implementation.

site a certain regularity in the development of the relative effectiveness of alternative states. This is a typical feature in expanding systems.

The relative cost-effectiveness of alternative states in a single year (t) may be illustrated by an *efficiency-diagram* (fig. 1) showing the benefit $b_t(x)$ accruing from each state x as a function of the total capital cost $C(x) = \Sigma_j C_j x_j$ required to attain this state.

Disregarding for a moment the physical constraints (4), the optimality criterion (2) shows that an arbitrary state x is preferable to all more expensive states which imply an additional benefit smaller than or equal to the interest charge of the additional costs. This criterion for dominance among states is independent of λ and shown graphically as the shaded area in fig. 1.

If one had a free choice of state for that year, one would evidently choose one of the *efficient states* (indicated by an $\times$ in fig. 2) depending on the budget available. However, the state of the system in the previous year $(t-1)$ as well as the states of the system in the following years $(t+1, t+2, ...)$ may indicate the choice of an inefficient state in this year (t). Nevertheless, the set of efficient states proves to be a useful starting point.

Dominance and efficiency may be generalized to apply to the rankings of states. One ranking dominates another, if any state in the second ranking is dominated by at least one state in the first ranking. Thus, there exists a set of *efficient rankings* (see the example shown in fig. 3). Any efficient state belongs to at least one efficient ranking. A systematic and simple way of determining the total set of efficient rankings for a given year has been developed by the author [2], tested and programmed by Mørdrup [3] and Holm [4] (see also section 6 below).

The crucial question is, how these sets of efficient rankings (one set per year) develop over time. Let successive sets of rankings be called non-decreasing, if all efficient rankings in one year are included in the set of efficient rankings in later years with the understanding that an early ranking may have been extended by more states which only become efficient in later years.

If the set of efficient rankings for successive years are non-decreasing, there exists a *limiting set of efficient rankings*, which include the optimal rankings for all values of λ. This is the set we were looking for. However, to be useful the limiting set of efficient rankings should be a small set and should show up within a reasonable planning horizon. Experience gained from the systems so far analyzed has been very promising in this respect.

However, the assumption of non-decreasing sets of efficient rankings is much more restrictive. A *sufficient condition* is that the annual increases in benefits obtained from a state belonging to an efficient ranking is non-decreasing with the ranking of the state. Thus not only must the benefit of a given

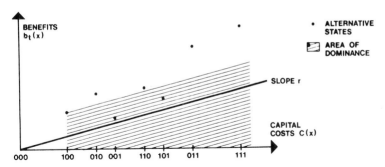

Fig. 1. Efficiency diagram for year *t*. Dominance and efficiency among states.

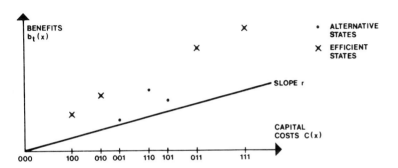

Fig. 2. Efficiency diagram for year *t*. Set of efficient states.

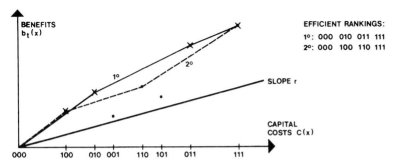

Fig. 3. Efficiency diagram for year *t*. Set of efficient rankings.

state be increasing over time, but it must also be increasingly profitable with larger expansions. Fortunately, these conditions are often met in practice.

4.2. Phase 2: timing of efficient rankings and choice of optimal programme

It is now a simple matter to prepare the optimal programme corresponding to a suggested shadow value of capital (λ) and thus the suggested budget allocations.

First, each of the efficient rankings in the limiting set must be transformed to an efficient programme. This is done by timing each change of state, i.e., each project in the ranking, in the prescribed order by the first-year-benefit criterion (6), where b_{tj} should be interpreted as the additional benefit obtainable from the considered change of state.

Finally, the *optimal programme* is found by maximizing the net present value $V(X)$ of the few efficient programmes using (2). To avoid terminal problems it is often advantageous to use as the planning horizon the first year, in which all efficient programmes coincide by specifying the largest efficient state (i.e., normally $\boldsymbol{x} = \{1, ..., 1\}$). If this occurs too far in the future, relative terminal values of the efficient programmes have to be introduced in (2).

Frequently, one finds that the ranking involved in the optimal programmes is very insensitive to changes in λ. Sometimes there exists only one optimal ranking for all realistic values of λ. This ranking may then be treated as described in the last paragraph of section 3. Otherwise optimal programming for the first year is only possible in light of all future budget allocations.

5. Possible generalizations

The model discussed so far was deliberately simplified by making several assumptions, some of which are unnecessarily restrictive.

First of all, it turns out that the limiting set of efficient rankings is the same if (a) the scarcity of capital is non-increasing over time even if (b) the capital expenditures in carrying out projects are spread over several years. Furthermore, the method is easily generalized to cover the case in which the capital costs of all projects increase at the same rate over time.

Finally, it is quite possible to include mutual exclusiveness and contingency relationships between projects (see e.g. Weingartner [5]). However, such relationships usually imply that more projects have to be considered, and that the limiting set of efficient rankings grows substantially.

6. Conclusions

The method was developed for planning investments in road networks, where it has proved very useful. However, only fairly small problems have been tried. First, Mørdrup [3] tried an interurban network involving 128 alternative states. He found 10 efficient rankings of which one turned out to be optimal for all realistic values of λ ($0 \leqslant \lambda \leqslant 3$).

Later, Holm [4] worked on an urban network (114 home nodes, 375 other nodes and 1102 branches) for which 30 projects were proposed. He managed to group the projects into fairly independent subsets thereby reducing the 2^{30} alternative states of the system to combinations of only 124 substates. Computer times (IBM 360/75) were for ranking: 1,3 sec, and for timing and choice: 1 sec per value of λ or a total of 1 min for the full procedure allocating given budgets.

There seems to be a close correlation between the number of efficient states and the number of efficient rankings. Computer time grows only linearly with these numbers and is likely to be quite insignificant compared to the cost of estimating the effectiveness of alternative states (3 min per state in the above example).

Other efforts have been made to solve the problems involved in non-linear interdependence between projects, notably Bergendahl [6, 7]. However, within its range of applicability, the method suggested in this paper appears to be superior in two important respects. First, it has the advantage of implying a very significant cut in data requirements (often found prohibitively expensive to fulfil in larger systems) as the benefits $(b_t(x))$ need only be computed for selected values of t and x. Finally, a major new feature is, that the procedure assures the decision-maker of a high degree of preparedness in case of budget revisions and thereby of an ideal position for negotiating his claims with top management.

References

[1] S.A. Marglin, Approaches to dynamic investment planning (North-Holland, Amsterdam, 1963).
[2] I. Thygesen, Investment planning; improved decision-making through operational research (in Danish) (Polyteknisk Forlag, 1971).
[3] I. Thygesen and E. Mørdrup, Planning road investments (in Danish) IMSOR, Techn. Univ. Denmark (1969).
[4] J. Holm, Planning the extension of networks (in Danish) IMSOR, Techn. Univ. Denmark (1971).

[5] H.M. Weingartner, Mathematical programming and the analysis of capital budgeting problems (Prentice–Hall, Englewood Cliffs, 1963).
[6] G. Bergendahl, A combined linear and dynamic programming model for interdependent road investment planning, Transp. Res. (July 1969) 211.
[7] G. Bergendahl, Models for investments in a road network (Bonniers, Stockholm, 1969).

M. Ross, ed., OR '72. North-Holland Publishing Company (1973)

53

WAREHOUSE LOCATION AND ALLOCATION PROBLEMS SOLVED BY MATHEMATICAL PROGRAMMING METHODS

Situation d'entrepôts et problèmes de repartition resolus par des méthodes de programmation mathématique

SVEND A. KRAEMER

Oslo School of Business Administration, Oslo, Norway

Abstract. The problem of determining the optimal location of a given number of warehouses with respect to the demand and location of another set of fixed facilities (demand centers or customers) is considered. The optimality criterion is that of minimizing the weighted sum of total transportation costs. Mathematical programming formulations of different location–allocation problems are given. A dual formulation of the facility problem is presented, which eliminates the nondifferentiability problem of algorithms used to solve the primal problem. Some numerical examples illustrate the efficiency of an algorithm developed to solve the dual problem.

1. Introduction

Location–allocation problems may involve the location of warehouses with respect to customers and factories, hospitals and other types of community services in cities and rural districts, the design of gas and oil pipeline networks, and computer terminal networks, to name only a small number.

An industry-wide survey [1] indicated that physical distribution costs account for between 10 and 30 percent of net sales income. Thus, the control of these costs should be considered a very important management task.

In this paper we will be concerned with the problem of locating a specified number of warehouses in a distribution system. This is a subproblem of the more general one of determining the number and location of regional warehouses in a factory customer distribution system. Quantitative formulations of this general problem have been presented in the literature [2] as a matter of modelling two conflicting cost functions – one representing the cost of building and operating the warehouses which increases with the number of warehouses, and the other representing transportation costs which supposedly decreases as the number of warehouses increases.

However, given N, the number of warehouses, their optimal location must be determined if the transportation cost function is to be determined. We consider two different approaches and conclude that both approaches complement each other in finding the best solutions to real life problems. We will, furthermore, look into the computational aspects of the dual form of one of these solution approaches.

In the following section, however, we will consider some managerial aspects of the design of physical distribution systems.

2. The design of physical distribution systems

It may be useful to consider the design of distribution systems in two stages:

(1) long range considerations concerning the location and number of facilities (the strategic planning activities),

(2) shorter range considerations concerning the operation of the located facilities (the tactical planning activities).

The quantitative models presented in section 3 of this paper are concerned with the location problem of the stage 1 planning activities.

2.1. Strategic planning activities

Logical planning does seem to require that strategic planning activities are first put into effect since they will be imposing constraints on the shorter range tactical planning activities. This implies that the design of a physical distribution system for an industrial corporation cannot be considered as an isolated planning activity but rather as part of the top management decision-making activities which also includes product and market development, investment decisions, etc.

A distribution system will always be subject to change due to changes in customer locations, demand variations, etc. A planning horizon of more than 2–4 years then, seems unrealistic. In fact, updating the data base for the strategic planning should be an ongoing administrative process.

2.2. Tactical planning activities

Once a plan for the number and location of a system of warehouses has been established, the actual moving of goods through the system can take place. The several classical OR models available include "the travelling salesman problem" and "the truck dispatching problem" which, however, lack solution techniques. Both models have been formulated as integer programming problems [3, Chapt. 13], but computationally feasible solutions often make it necessary to apply heuristic search techniques.

3. Mathematical location and allocation models

Of the two known approaches to modelling warehouse location problems one assumes no knowledge of potential warehouse locations, whereas the other works with a finite set of possible locations.

3.1. Infinite solution space location model

The mathematical formulation of a model where the locations are identified through a cartesian coordinate system is as follows:

$j = 1, 2, ..., P$: index of P known customer centers,
$i = 1, 2, ..., N$: index of N unknown warehouse locations,
$x_i = (x_{i1}, x_{i2})$: the coordinates of the ith warehouse,
$a_j = (a_{j1}, a_{j2})$: the coordinates of the jth customer center,
$d_t(x_i, a_j) = (|x_{i1} - a_{j1}|^t + |x_{i2} - a_{j2}|^t)^{1/t}$: the mathematical distance between the ith warehouse and the jth customer center. [The parameter t $(1 \leqslant t \leqslant 2)$ is to be estimated for the geographical area in question.]
w_{ij}: weight between the ith warehouse and the jth customer center, representing, for example, the required quantity per unit time from the customer center to be supplied by the warehouse mutiplied by the transportation cost per unit distance.

A cost function to be minimized in x_i can now be formulated:

$$F_1(x) = \sum_{i=1}^{N} \sum_{j=1}^{P} w_{ij} d_t(x_i, a_j). \tag{1}$$

Note that in this model we have not considered possible flows of goods between warehouses. This can be easily included by a second term:

$$F_2(\boldsymbol{x}) = \sum_{1 \leqslant i < k \leqslant N} w2_{ik}\, d_t(\boldsymbol{x}_i, \boldsymbol{x}_k) \,, \tag{2}$$

where $w2_{ik}$ represents the weight between the ith and the kth warehouse. The objective function then consists of the following terms:

$$\min F(\boldsymbol{x}) = \sum_{i=1}^{N} \sum_{j=1}^{P} w_{ij}\, d_t(\boldsymbol{x}_i, \boldsymbol{a}_j) + \sum_{1 \leqslant i < k \leqslant N} w2_{ik}\, d_t(x_i, x_k) \,. \tag{3}$$

Similarly, geographical constraints of a certain form may be included in the location model in order to exclude the location of warehouses in, for example, a lake or other inaccessible area [4].

3.2. Finite solution space model

A great deal of attention has been devoted to the location problem given a number of alternative sites where facilities may be constructed, i.e.:

$$\min \sum_{i=1}^{N} \sum_{j=1}^{P} w_j\, d_{ij} y_i z_{ij} \,, \tag{4}$$

subject to

$$\sum_{i=1}^{N} \sum_{j=1}^{P} z_{ij} w_j y_i = \sum_{j=1}^{P} w_j \,, \tag{5}$$

$$\sum_{j \in I} z_{ij} = 1 \,, \quad i = 1, 2, ..., P \,. \tag{6}$$

N: number of proposed warehouse sites,
P: number of demand areas,
w_j: demand per time period from demand center j,
I: index set given as $\{j \mid \text{if } y_j = 1\}$,
d_{ij}: actual distance from demand center j to the proposed ith warehouse,
$y_i = 1$, if a warehouse is placed at location i,
$\quad = 0$, otherwise,

z_{ij} = 1, if demand center j is to be supplied from the ith warehouse,
= 0, otherwise.

The constraints ensure that all demands are assigned to some warehouse, eq. (5), and that each demand center is assigned to only one warehouse location, eq. (6).

The problem is thus to determine the optimal values of y_i and z_{ij}, which is an integer programming problem. Special solution techniques proposed in the literature include heuristic rules [5] and "branch and bound" [6].

From a practical point of view the question of determining the set of possible warehouse locations does, however, seem rather difficult. But here the two approaches for solving the location problem may very well complement each other. Thus, when the infinite solution space model yields a set of coordinates $\{x_i^*\}$ for the location of the N warehouses, it is rather unlikely that the locations will be very close to community facilities where a warehouse must be located for reasons other than minimization of transportation costs.

But on the other hand the solution $\{x_i^*\}$ should form a very good basis for compiling a set of possible warehouse sites needed for the finite solution space model. Furthermore, since this way of using the solution of the infinite solution space model would tend to simplify the problem, eqs. (4)–(6), with respect to the number of possible warehouse sites, in real life situations both methods may usefully be employed simultaneously.

3.3. Location–allocation problems

In a real life situation the model represented by eq. (3) does possess some quite serious drawbacks. One is the assumption of constant weights between the facilities. It is indeed rather unrealistic to assume that we would know the amount of goods to be shipped from warehouse i to customer center j before the location of the warehouse has been determined. Thus, initially the warehouse locations $\{x_i\}$ as well as the weights $\{w_{ij}\}$ must both be variables. We call the problem of determining both $\{x_i^*\}$ and $\{w_{ij}^*\}$ the location–allocation problem.

A two-stage method for solving the location–allocation problem has been suggested [7] when no constraints on the capacity of the warehouses are present. First, an arbitrary solution for the locations is selected. The two-stage procedure is then as follows:

(1) Each customer center is allocated to its nearest warehouse, thus determining a set of w_{ij}.

(2) The function in eq. (3) is minimized in $\boldsymbol{x}$ for the weights determined in stage 1.

Stage 1 and 2 are repeated until no improvements in the objective function is obtained, thus yielding an optimal set of locations $\{\boldsymbol{x}_i^*\}$ and allocations $\{w_{ij}^*\}$.

3.4. Computational algorithms for the location problem with infinite solution space

The problems in eqs. (1) and (3) are convex programming problems. Computational algorithms described in the literature have all involved calculation of a direction vector based on the gradient vector of partial derivatives $\nabla F(\boldsymbol{x})$. An algorithm of the form

$$\boldsymbol{x}^{k+1} = \boldsymbol{x}^k + h\boldsymbol{s}^k \tag{7}$$

is then applied to find successive location vectors $\{\boldsymbol{x}^k\}$, where

k: iteration number,
h: scalar designating the optimum step-size,
$\boldsymbol{s}^k$: direction vector based on the gradient vector $\nabla F(\boldsymbol{x}^k)$ evaluated at $\boldsymbol{x}^k$.

An optimal solution $\boldsymbol{x}^*$ is then reached when $\nabla F(\boldsymbol{x}) \simeq 0$. However, a rather serious shortcoming of this method is that the gradient vector is undefined when one of the variable facilities is located on top of one of the demand centers. This is easily seen when deriving an element of $\nabla F(\boldsymbol{x})$:

$$\frac{\partial F}{\partial x_{i1}} = \sum_{j=1}^{P} \frac{(x_{i1} - a_{j1})}{d_t(\boldsymbol{x}_i, \boldsymbol{a}_j)} . \tag{8}$$

This defect is actually quite serious, since in practical problems the solutions generated by eq. (7) do tend to approach one or more of the demand centers such that $d_t(\boldsymbol{x}_i, \boldsymbol{a}_j) = 0$. However, a dual form of the location problem, which eliminates the non-differentiability problem, has been formulated based upon a duality theorem for nonlinear programming [8, 9].

In the following section we shall only consider the problem of locating a single warehouse with respect to the demand and location of P fixed demand centers:

$$\min F(\boldsymbol{x}) = \sum_{i=1}^{P} w_i d(\boldsymbol{x}, \boldsymbol{a}_i) \, . \tag{9}$$

The dual form of this problem is the following:

$$\min_{u,v} G = -\sum_{i=1}^{P} a_{i1} u_i + a_{i2} v_i \, , \tag{10}$$

subject to

$$\sum_{i=1}^{P} u_i \geqslant 0 \, , \qquad \sum_{i=1}^{P} v_i \geqslant 0 \, , \tag{11}$$

$$u_i^2 + v_i^2 \leqslant w_i^2 \, , \qquad i = 1, 2, ..., P \, . \tag{12}$$

The (u_i, v_i) is interpreted as a vector pointing from $\boldsymbol{a}_i$ to the facility to be located. Note that the dual problem, eqs. (10)–(12), is only given for straight line distances ($t = 2$). It is, however, easily expressed for $1 < t \leqslant 2$.

The development of this dual form was first given by Bellman [10]. Duality properties of eqs. (10)–(12) are discussed by Kuhn [11] who also points out that the nondifferentiability problem of eq. (9) is nonexistent in eqs. (10)–(12).

From a computational point of view it is interesting to note that the dual problem has a linear objective function in u_i and v_i. Furthermore, the problem is decomposable into a linear master program, eqs. (10)–(11), with P nonlinear subproblems, eq. (12). The decomposition principle developed by Dantzig and Wolfe [12] can then be applied to approach the optimal solution vectors (u_i^*, v_i^*).

A decomposition algorithm similar to algorithms developed for pure linear programs was developed by Love and Kraemer [13] for the more general problem, eq. (3), with N facilities to be located and P fixed customer centers. The formulation also includes variation of the distance function parameter t, for $1 < t \leqslant 2$.

The algorithm was programmed in Algol, and several data sets were used to test its efficiency. The coordinates of the fixed customer centers $\{\boldsymbol{a}_i\}$ and the weighting constants $\{w_{ij}\}$ were generated randomly in all cases.

Tables 1 and 2 show the required number of simplex iterations and computing time in minutes and seconds for locating one and more facilities as the

Table 1
Computing times for locating one facility

Number of fixed locations	Number of simplex iterations		Computing time (min, sec)	
	$t = 1.1$	$t = 2$	$t = 1.1$	$t = 2$
20	37	52	0, 30.6	0, 42.8
25	53	46	1, 2.0	0, 56.1
30	56	80	1, 34.0	1, 14.1

Table 2
Computing times for locating 2, 3 and 4 facilities in relation to 10 facilities

Number of facilities to be located	Number of simplex iterations		Computing time (min, sec)	
	$t = 1.1$	$t = 2$	$t = 1.1$	$t = 2$
2	56	66	0, 57.2	1, 2.4
3	82	148	2, 58.7	5, 35.3
4	142	152	9, 59.7	10, 40.7

Table 3
Effect of adding constraints (when constraints become binding) to a problem with 5 fixed locations, 2 locations to be determined ($t = 2$) [13]

Number of constraints	Number of simplex iterations	Computing time (sec)
0	45	14.5
1	51	15.7
2	61	19.0
3	57	16.1
4	39	10.7
5	32	9.1
6	23	5.9

number of fixed customer centers increases. The results are given for both straight line distances ($t = 2$) and for more rectangular distances ($t = 1.1$). Table 3 shows the effect on computing time and adding constraints to the location problem which require that the locations be determined within a certain geographical area. The reduction in computing time when the constraints become binding at the optimum is in contrast to the nonlinear programming primal method for which computing time is greatly increased by adding constraints [4].

References

[1] R.E. Snyder, Physical distribution costs, Distribution Age (dec. 1963) 35.
[2] C. Revelle, D. Marks and J.C. Liebman, An analysis of private and public sector location models, Mgmt. Sci. 16 (1970) 692.
[3] H. Wagner, Principles of operations research (Prentice–Hall, Englewood Cliffs, 1969).
[4] R.F. Love, Locating facilities in three dimensional space by convex programming, Naval Res. Logistics Q. 16 (1969) 503.
[5] R.E. Shannon and J.P. Ignizio, A heuristic programming algorithm for warehouse location, AIIE Trans. 2 (1970) 334.
[6] M.A. Efroymson and T.L. Ray, A branch and bound algorithm for plant location, Opns. Res. 14 (1966) 361.
[7] S. Eilon and D.P. Dexiel, Siting a distribution centre; an analogue computer application, Mgmt. Sci. 12 (1966) B245.
[8] D. Bhatia, A note on duality theorem for a nonlinear programming problem, Mgmt. Sci. 16 (1970) 604.
[9] S.M. Sinha, A duality theorem for nonlinear programming, Mgmt. Sci. 12 (1966).
[10] R. Bellman, An application of dynamic programming to location–allocation problems, SIAM Rev. 7 (1965) 126.
[11] H.W. Kuhn, On a pair of dual nonlinear problems, Chapt. 3, in: Nonlinear programming, ed. J. Abadie (Wiley, New York, 1967).
[12] G.B. Dantzig and P. Wolfe, A decomposition principle for linear programs, Opns. Res. 8 (1960) 101.
[13] R.F. Love and S.A. Kraemer, A dual decomposition method for minimizing transportation costs in multi-facility location problems, Transp. Sci., submitted.

M. Ross, ed., OR '72. North-Holland Publishing Company

54

SOME DEVELOPMENTS IN 0–1 PROGRAMMING*

Quelques développements dans la programmation 0–1

PETER L. HAMMER

University of Waterloo, Ontario, Canada

Most of the available methods for the solution of mathematical programs in 0–1 variables are based either on implicit enumeration, on the use of cutting planes or on Boolean algebra. It has been observed recently that a combination of these techniques can prove more efficient than any of them taken individually.

1. Linear 0–1 programming

The careful examination of the constraints may allow the detection of useful information, and thus the shortening of the process of exploration. Take, for example, the inequality

$$7x + 4\bar{y} + 6z + 8\bar{u} + 3\bar{v} \leqslant \lambda \ , \tag{1}$$

where λ is to be specified below, and where the bars on certain variables represent negations (e.g., $\bar{y} = 1-y$) and were introduced for the elimination of negative coefficients. It is obvious that for very small and for very large values of λ we can "read" this constraint. If, say, $\lambda \leqslant 5$ then we know that in every 0–1 solution of (1) we shall have $x = z = \bar{u} = 0$. If $\lambda = 100$, we know again that the inequality is superfluous and we can delete it from our constraint set. But if λ takes, for example, the value 10, this does not mean at all that

---

* This paper was originally a discussant paper on mathematical programming.

(1) is "illegible". The inequality

$$7x + 4\bar{y} + 6z + 8\bar{u} + 3\bar{v} \leqslant 10 \tag{2}$$

gives us an immediate conclusion of the following nature: x and $\bar{y}$ cannot simultaneously be equal to 1, hence

$$x\bar{y} = 0 \ . \tag{3}$$

Similarly

$$xz = x\bar{u} = \bar{y}u = z\bar{u} = \bar{u}\bar{v} = 0 \ . \tag{4}$$

But (3) is equivalent to the new inequality

$$x \leqslant y \ , \tag{5}$$

while (4) gives similarly

$$x \leqslant \bar{z}, \ x \leqslant u, \ \bar{y} \leqslant u, \ z \leqslant u, \ \bar{u} \leqslant v. \tag{6}$$

The role of these order relations consists in the fact that combining relations of this type derived *from different constraints* may lead either to the determination of the values of some variables (e.g., $x \leqslant y$ and $x \leqslant \bar{y}$ imply $x = 0$; similarly, $\bar{x} \leqslant y$, $y \leqslant \bar{z}$ and $\bar{x} \leqslant z$ imply $\bar{x} = 0$, i.e., $x = 1$), or to the detection of equalities among variables (e.g., $x \leqslant y$ and $y \leqslant x$ imply $x = y$; similarly, $x \leqslant y$, $y \leqslant \bar{z}$ and $\bar{x} \leqslant z$ imply $x = y = \bar{z}$).

Finally, if these relations do not lead to any of the above conclusions, they can still be very useful as *cuts* in the associated linear program.

A method combining this type of reasoning with implicit enumeration and with cutting procedures is described in [1]. Test problems involving 15 constraints and from 30 to 200 variables have been run on a CDC-6600 computer of the Université de Montréal, with durations from 0.35 to 85.41 sec.

2. Quadratic 0–1 programming

The knowledge of the order relations derived from the constraints can not only produce conclusions similar to those obtained in the linear case, but also help to eliminate nonlinearities. For example, the objective function

$$3xy + 2xu - xz + 4yu \ , \tag{7a}$$

subject to the linear constraint (2) would simplify to

$$3x + 2x + 4 - 4\bar{y} - 4\bar{u} \quad , \tag{7b}$$

because according to (3) and (4) we have $xz = 0$, $xy = x$ (implied by $x \leq y$), $xu = x$ (implied by $x \leq u$) and $yu = (1-\bar{y})(1-\bar{u}) = 1-\bar{y}-\bar{u}+\bar{u}\bar{y} = 1-\bar{y}-\bar{u}$.

A method exploring such techniques is described in [2]. Obviously the idea can easily be extended to the handling of other types of nonlinearities too.

3. Nonlinear unconstrained optimization

Many practical problems of operations research (e.g., location problems) can be formulated as optimization problems involving 0–1 variables, no constraints and a polynomial objective function.

A method has been developed in [3] for the solution of such problems, the key element of which is branching. However, branching is not performed according to single variables, but according to groups of variables appearing in the same term of the polynomial.

Test problems have been run on an IBM 360/50 computer at the Technion, Haifa; execution times varied from 0.48 (10 variables, 5 terms) to 239.03 sec. (30 variables, 50 terms). We plan to improve this method by incorporating into it elements of [1] and [2].

4. Conclusions

Combinations of different types of solution methods for 0–1 programs result in efficient ways of solving them. Thus, while the time spent in analysing the problem is somewhat increased at each step, the number of steps to be considered is reduced. It takes of course, some effort to arrive to a good blend with right proportions. But then, it was not overnight that Irish coffee was invented.

Acknowledgement

This research was partly supported by a grant from the Canada Council, No. S72–0107–S1.

References

[1] P.L. Hammer and S. Nguyen, APOSS A partial order in the solution space of bivalent programs, Univ. Montréal, Centre de Recherches Math., Publ. CRM-163 (1972).
[2] P.L. Hammer and P. Hansen, Quadratic 0–1 programming, Univ. Montréal, Centre de Recherches Math., Publ. CRM-186 (1972).
[3] P.L. Hammer and U. Peled, On the maximization of a pseudo-Boolean function, J. Assoc. Computing Machinery 19 (1972) 265.

M. Ross, ed., OR '72. North-Holland Publishing Company (1973)

55

NONLINEAR PROGRAMMING

Programmation non linéaire

G. ZOUTENDIJK
University of Leyden, Leyden, The Netherlands

The question is sometimes posed whether nonlinear programming is actually being applied in practice given that — with a few exceptions — there are no general production codes available. My reply is intended to supplement that of Professor Abadie * which contains some fine examples of applications. Nonlinear programming has been applied for the last ten years to many refinery scheduling and plant optimisation problems. The methods being used — mostly MAP [1] and separable programming [2] — were rough and limited in scope but they worked, at least for the problems they were designed for. Nonlinear programming has also been applied to design and control engineering problems, to approximation problems under constraints, to economic growth problems, to pollution abatement problems and they will probably be applied to solving some of the survival models the Club of Rome and others are urging us to build. In spite of this it must be admitted that the applicability of nonlinear programming has been limited. There are several reasons for this.

Although the world is basically nonlinear it is also highly non-convex. Just imagine what would happen if the energy minimisation problem would be a convex programming problem; we would not be here to-day. The non-convexity of many problems may result in local optima which might be

---

* This paper was originally a discussant paper on mathematical programming to supplement the presentation by J. Abadie.

unacceptable in some cases. A second reason is that nonlinear is negative by definition. When building a model we need to derive the real relation either from theoretical considerations or in an empirical way. In many cases, however, our theoretical knowledge of the process under study is so limited that the model would not be valid anymore. Next we have the problem of data organisation and model updating which is already tremendous in the linear case and could become too complicated in the nonlinear case. Linearisation of the model, even at the cost of oversimplification, might then be easier. Finally, the computer codes that are commercially available do not have the amount of sophistication a linear programming code has.

It is even subject to doubt whether the best methods have been chosen – unless you define as the best method the one that has been programmed since the other ones are not available anyway. The cost of writing a package of proven nonlinear programming computer codes with all the latest developments included is so enormous that it will probably not be done in the near future unless somebody can be found to pay the bill. I would like to make a few remarks on the methods available at present. We can first distinguish between problems with only linear constraints and problems with nonlinear constraints too. In the latter case penalty function methods have received a lot of attention; in these methods a sequence of linearly constrained problems has to be solved; their applicability is limited to problems not exceeding a certain size. For some of the larger problems direct extensions of methods originally developed for the linearly constrained case, like the generalized reduced gradient method or the modified feasible direction method [3], have been succesfully applied.

The linearly constrained nonlinear programming problem is essentially simpler to solve. Methods can be divided into those which are extensions of the simplex method for linear programming or, as far as their computational aspects are concerned, at least very close to it, like the methods of conjugate feasible directions [4] and those which are extensions of unconstrained methods to problems involving linear constraints. In the latter class we find the variable metric methods [5]. Recently, Dixon [6] has proved a very remarkable property, viz. that many of the methods suggested are basically the same in that they lead to the same directions and therefore to the same sequence of intermediate solutions. As far as the extension to linear constraints is concerned, at the recent Nato Summerschool in Fiqueira da Foz, Portugal, Powell reported that the number of perfect linesearches in the case of a quadratic objective function will never exceed $n + l$, in which n is the number of variables and l the number of times the set of active constraints changes.

For the general nonlinear programming problem some recent research on primal-dual methods might be of potential interest. An auxiliary function $\varphi(x, u)$ is constructed, to be called a generalized Lagrangian function – the u's being dual variables – in such a way that the so-called primal problem $\max_x \min_u \varphi(x, u)$ is equivalent to the original problem, while the dual problem $\min_u \max_x \varphi(x, u)$ will have the same value. An attempt is made to solve the dual problem which is a minimisation problem in u with each function evaluation being a maximisation problem in x [7].

A final remark on the theory of nonlinear programming. Professor Abadie made the remark that there is essentially one theorem, the Kuhn–Tucker theorem, and even that is debatable since this theorem can be easily derived from Farkas' theorem in the theory of linear inequalities. In spite of this many interesting articles and even books (e.g. [8]) have been written on the subject with many different theorems which, although related, lead to a coherent and not always simple theory.

References

[1] R.E. Griffith and R.A. Stewart, A nonlinear programming technique for the optimization of continuous processing systems, Mgmt. Sci. 7 (1961) 379.

[2] C.E. Miller, The simplex method for local separable programming, in: Recent advances in mathematical programming, eds. R.L. Graves and P. Wolfe (McGraw–Hill, New York, 1963) p. 89.

[3] G. Zoutendijk, Nonlinear programming, a numerical survey, ISIAM Control 4 (1966) 194.

[4] G. Zoutendijk, Nonlinear programming, computational methods, in: Nonlinear and integer programming, ed. J. Abadie (North-Holland, Amsterdam, 1970) p. 37.

[5] M.J.D. Powell, Recent advances in unconstrained optimization, Math. Programming 1 (1971) 26.

[6] L.C.W. Dixon, Quasi Newton algorithms generate identical points, short communication, Math. Programming 2 (1972) 383.

[7] J.D. Buys, Dual algorithms in nonlinear programming, doctoral thesis, Leiden (1972).

[8] O.L. Mangasarian, Nonlinear programming (McGraw–Hill, New York, 1969).

PART VI

RECENT DEVELOPMENTS IN THE UNITED STATES

Les développements récents aux Etats Unis

National contributions from ORSA/TIMS reviewing developments in:

THEORY

APPLICATIONS

PROFESSIONAL PRACTICE

M. Ross, ed., OR '72. North-Holland Publishing Company (1973)

56

RECENT U.S. ADVANCES IN OR THEORY

Progrès récents aux Etats Unis dans la théorie RO

BERNARD OSGOOD KOOPMAN

Arthur D. Little Inc., Cambridge, Massachusetts, USA

Abstract. "OR theory" is interpreted, as in the case of "physical theory", to mean the perceived structure of a phenomenon or class of phenomena belonging to the subject under discussion. Advances in OR theory involve becoming aware, through observation and practical requirements, of new structures or of new features of old ones. In the process, reasoning based on abstractions is used, and this (by definition) is mathematical in form, as in the case of theoretical physics; but in neither case is a mathematical advance by itself a theoretical contribution to the respective subjects. On this basis, the advances in OR theory are relatively few, but have been occurring. They may be characterized as falling into the five following (somewhat overlapping) categories: sequential evolution of a system (queues, stochastic and deterministic models); extremal phenomena (optima, Lagrange multipliers, minimax); networks (graphs, allocations, flow charts, schematics of complex operations); search (with and without Bohr-Heisenberg assumptions; false targets, pro- and anti-search); information and decision theory. Examples are given of each category. The period covered is the last half dozen or so years.

1. Introduction

In preparing myself to write this outline, and in passing in review the immense number of theoretical papers contained in American periodicals during the last half dozen or so years, it has become apparent that a clear answer has to be given to the question "What is operation research theory?" We suppose, with Phillip Morse, that we know what an "operation" is and that "operational research" is the scientific study of operations, for the double purpose of understanding them and of improving their performance.

As in medical research, understanding of the phenomena of life and disease is sought, and is applied to preventing or treating sickness. In each case, it is the process of *understanding* that, I submit, identifies the conception of "OR *theory*". The distinction between this and "OR *practice*" is similar to that in the case of medical practice: what the doctor does to treat his patient – in the light of the advances of theoretical understanding.

In the case of OR as in medicine, the identification of the "theoretical" is complicated by the fact that in these subjects so many other branches of science are applied. Thus medicine uses biology, chemistry and physics, while OR uses mathematics, statistics, computers, engineering and many other branches of knowledge. Yet nobody would confuse an advance in chemistry with an advance in medical theory – although the former might lend directly to an increase in medical understanding: then it would be this understanding that would be heralded as the medical advance. Similarly, the discovery of a theorem of mathematics in connection with the study of an operation could not, in itself, be regarded as an advance in OR theory. If, however, such a discovery permits the operation to be *viewed in a new light*, so that its *structure* and *inter-relationships* become clearer, we may regard the mathematical advance as leading to such an advance in OR.

What these considerations lead to is the view that a theoretical advance in OR is the increased understanding of the structure of some type of *operation*, regarded as a particular *phenomenon of nature*.

With this conception in mind, the search for advances in OR theory in the massive OR literature becomes rather like the Curie's search for radium in their tons of pitch-blend. Without in the least disparaging the merit and value of a single publication, we can say that their impact has most often been in rather different directions from the increase in the understanding of operation phenomena. The great bulk have been devoted to practical methods, often with the production of mathematical theorems of great abstract beauty, or with graphical and mechanical methods of essential value in solving problems. A number of other papers, while more general in intent, deal with selling OR services, organizing OR work, and, in certain cases, are addressed to the operations of society, with all the political forces and value judgments that such operations inevitably entail. Again without belittling these immensely important and absorbing matters, we must repeat that they do not in themselves constitute advances in OR theory as we are obliged to view it.

There have, however, been such advances. To give them most clearly in the time allowed, we shall divide the whole subject roughly into five categories. There is a danger here: to paraphrase the first Justice of our Supreme Court (John Marshall: "the power to tax is the power to destroy") we must beware lest the power to pigeon-hole become the power to destroy – a process not un-used by bureaucratic managers of science. Accordingly, we must regard our categories as provisional, roughly defined, and often over-lapping. We characterize them by the following catch-words: *decision theory, search, evolution of systems, networks, extremal properties.* These terms refer to the salient features; but most well developed OR studies comprise more than one of them.

2. Decision theory

We place this first since it evokes the most characteristic feature of OR: the interaction of the sequence of physical events of the operation with the mental processes of those who are directing it. Ideally, the latter are quite logical, operating by the most rational use of the uncertainties and the un-known elements, and constantly re-adjusting action to knowledge as it devel-ops in the course of the unfolding operation. The ancillary sciences are logic (intuitive and symbolic) and probability. Use of the former is often by means of *decision trees*, as well as by the equivalent Boolean manipulations. As for the latter, a very marked return to an older conception of probability is oc-curing: the view of it as a "measure of rational belief" rather than as a fre-quency. Furthermore, the modern methods of *sequential decision theory* are being developed and given ever wider application. Much progress has its basis, in essence, on the following idea: at the nth stage of the operation, a decision has to be made between possible courses of action that will lead to the $(n+1)$st stage; to "optimize" things, the situation at the nth stage must be used, and in particular, conditional probabilities based on knowledge only obtainable when the nth stage has been reached. This has a striking implication: apart from very simple cases, it is not sensible to give exact orders or directions in advance – only principles whereby decisions shall be made: orders must be replaced by "meta-orders" (just as modern mathematical logic recognizes "language" and "meta-language").

Under the above aegis come the developments of various forms of sequen-tial testing, dynamic programming, and differential games, all of which are in a state of rapid development in the United States as elsewhere. In these sub-jects, the actual choice at the nth stage is not the difficult thing, so much as the narrowing down of possibilities at the outset – in the simplest case, so that an idealized machine could be programmed to make the decisions se-quentially.

On the other hand, there are situations in which the decision at the nth stage – with all the knowledge available then – is the most conspicuous difficulty. Two approaches have been made, and while in essence they are very old, they have received new life in recent years. One is the *war game*, now extended to the *diplomatic game*: two sides play a game against each other, as in chess, under rules and limitations of knowledge that are intended to parallel the action under study. The results often throw unexpected light on the processes of decision. Another method resembles more a council of war at a high level of command, an ancient process recently fortified by psychological and statistical techniques: the *Delphi* process, in which knowledge of experts is methodically pooled and interrelated. It has in recent years had a great increase in use, in industry and in organizations exploring policy decisions, such as education, public transportation, public health, etc. The method is being used increasingly in other nations.

No discussion of the theory of decision would be complete that did not raise a fundamental issue on the level of logic: the issue of *indeterminacy*. If a decision is to be based on knowing the outcomes of the different options, it may well happen that the total body of knowledge available at the time of decision, however augmented, does not determine the outcome of any reasonable option: to a question of outcomes, the answer "yes" may be just as consistent with this body of knowledge as the answer "no". This is strict *logical indeterminacy*. More relevant to OR problems is the question of determining, within useful limits of accuracy, the probability of the various possible outcomes ensuing from the different options. In most classical cases, this is possible. But there remain situations, sometimes of the highest importance, in which the probabilities cannot be known to any useful degree of precision: this is *probabilistic indeterminacy*. Sometimes methods of minimizing the numerical information of a distribution will give some guidance; but this requires a rather mathematically simple state of affairs. "Gut feeling" is often invoked; but if this is to be more than guessing under the influence of more or less unconscious prejudices, it must have some communicability or reproducibility. I submit that what sometimes occurs – and this represents no mean order of creativity – may be an instance of that trans-logical process of the mind (known in *Gestalt* psychology) of *concept formation*: a configuration, a pattern, is preceived as when a human face is suddenly recognized. This is a case of that third and unsung process of the scientific method, without which the others (experiment and reasoning) would reduce science to a massive catalogue of observations and mathematics to a grandiose tautology.

3. Search

In a military context, this lists among the oldest branches of mathematical OR; but after World War II it rapidly broadened its scope, and is now recognized as playing a role in search for minerals, for markets, customers, and objects sought in commerce; and in medicine and public health, of sources of infection, causes of disease, and is applied in diagnostic procedures. It is almost always complicated by the possibility that when the search turns up an object, it may in fact be spurious: this is the problem of false targets. When action has to be taken as a result of the search, and there may be false targets or false alarms, we are back to a branch of decision theory; but the classical problems of search have enough "local color" of their own to warrant separating their theory from the former.

A particularly interesting issue is raised by certain parts of the theory: does the act of searching merely gain knowledge in a purely passive way, as do the observations of the state of a system in classical physics? Or does the process of searching disturb the situation, either by changing the physical factors or by alerting the enemy? The first case would occur in infra-red photography of a battle-field, the examination of the photographs being made at a distant spot, and nothing changed but the searcher's degree of knowledge. The second case was strikingly illustrated in World War II when the U-boats used search receivers to detect our search radar signals. The search under such conditions may be compared with the observation of the state of an elementary physical system according to quantum theory: an observation of the momentum of a particle disturbs it so that the results of an immediately previous observation of its position are no longer valid. This is known as the "principle of uncertainty" of Heisenberg and Bohr, (a misleading term).

The practical importance of distinguishing between the two search situations set forth in the last paragraph is self-evident. Its theoretical importance is no less: when successive searching operations are contemplated, and when they can gain knowledge in a purely passive way, the probabilities of the various combinations of possible outcomes may be calculated by the direct application of the ordinary laws of probability (including conditional probabilities). When, on the other hand, the act of searching on the first occasion is not a purely passive one, the second search must deal with a modified situation: in the language of probability, it is not the repetition of the first trial, but the performance of a *different kind*, of a nature depending on the outcome of the first. The straightforward application of total and compound probabilities in such a case would be quite wrong, not because the laws are themselves invalid (as had sometimes erroneously been supposed in early writings on quantum physics) but because the logical combinations of disjunction and conjunction cannot be applied to two *incompatible* propositions: the operation defining one rendering impossible that defining the other. We may, with Bohr, illustrate the case by a biological example: a unique rat mutant is to be tested by two toxins; event A is that the first prove lethal, even B that it succumbs to the second; these events being incompatible, their logical sum and product are meaningless. Here, as in the case of quantum physics and search theory, holding to the operational definition of the statements involved (in the sense of P.W. Bridgman) clarifies the whole situation. Long and acrimonious debates have occurred in recent developments of search theory in the U.S. which could have been clarified by the concept of incompatible observations. It is to be hoped that this issue will be recognized in future texts on probability.

A new direction has recently been given to search theory in the U.S. in its application to the arrangement of books in a library, attempting, among other things, to facilitate the process of "browsing". This might be termed "cooperative" search, since, in contrast with the hiding and deceptive devices used by an enemy for whose units we are searching, those responsible for target arrangements wish to have them found.

In mathematical search theory the "probabilistic indeterminacy" discussed earlier shows itself, for example, in selecting a reasonable a priori probability distribution of enemy targets. Sometimes the physical conditions, together with the presumed intentions of the enemy, can be used to formulate an information-minimizing problem, conditioned by the knowledge of certain expected values. Useful results are obtainable in this way (cf. the maximum entropy principle leading to Gibbs' canonical distribution of molecular velocities). Thus under reasonable physical assumptions, when the expected number density of targets in a given area is known, the Poisson distribution having this expected density as a variable coefficient in its parameter, can be derived by the process.

4. Evolution of systems

In a large class of cases it is possible to focus one's mind on a fairly restricted set of interacting things and people, and treat it as an "organism", or, better, a *physical system*; the usual practical questions involve its *evolution* in the course of time. Included in this point of view are *queues*, *duels*, the *Lanchester theory of combat*, and *stochastic processes* in general. They obviously will contain elements belonging to the two former categories; but the point of view of examining their evolution as *physical systems*, emphasizing the mathematical methods and laying much less stress on the human being acting as an individual thinker, warrant giving them a separate place.

There has been a very considerable literature on queues of various types; but there has too often been a methodological "all or nothing" attitude – in this, as well as in so many other parts of OR. According to this, problems have to be solved either in "closed analytic form", or by simulation. Slight extensions have been made to the analytic approach by including infinite processes of very standard types (e.g., classical series and integral transforms). Inasmuch as there are many cases of the greatest practical importance in which the driving elements of the queueing process are strongly time dependent, and are functions that can be observed and tabulated, but cannot be expressed by simple formulas, the analytical method, in the above limited sense, cannot be applied. Workers have been driven to solve such problems by simulation, and while some successes have been obtained in certain simple cases of airport queues by this method, it has no future in making fine distinctions between the improvements of suggested new equipment or operational changes. This is because of the excessively low cost-effectiveness of simulation when reliable results of sufficient accuracy are required.

Fortunately there is a middle ground. Mathematicians have long relegated to the eighteenth century the view that numerical answers can only be obtained by finding closed analytic solutions. Once the problem has been formulated precisely in terms of functional relations, not only can properties of the solution be established (theorems) but the most economical programs of machine computation can be developed. This has recently led to a new method of examining the effects of various improvements on American airport congestion. Its bearing on OR theory is in demonstrating what should always have been known: mathematics *reasons* about *structure*, and is not confined to manipulating formulas.

A somewhat similar change has come over the manner of thinking about certain types of military action, as for example, the duel. Following an apparently irresistible reflex, the usual procedure has been to develop a "computer model", viz., simulation. But it is becoming increasingly apparent that this conceals many assumptions, which, if stated explicitly, might not have been accepted. For one thing, the role of the decision maker is removed. This is appropriate in many studies; but one should be told exactly what conventions have been used in doing this. Secondly, the machine acts as if the system is a Markov process – simply because that is the way machines are made. This may be a useful assumption; but if it is made the machine could be used much more efficiently by multiplying transition matrices than in a Monte Carlo calculation. For these and for many other reasons a swing away from an implicit trust in machine simulation toward methods whose logic is more visible is beginning to take place.

The Lanchester theory of combat has been advancing at a steady although perhaps not a break-neck pace. Larger varieties of interactions are being considered, and results of the movement of forces has been studied quantitatively.

When larger-scale operations are considered, anything like detailed considerations of probability are made impossible by their very complexity. If changes in probability distributions are not studied, but only the evolution of the expected values, serious errors would occur. On the other hand, for purposes of long-range economic planning (e.g., in force level studies) it may be useful to invent a "non-dispersive model", in which the expected value of any (non-linear) functions of a set of variaties is equated to the same function of their individual expected values. While obviously quite wrong as a model of any actual military operation, this may — when used with discretion — provide useful indices for economic policy.

5. Networks

Communication and transportation networks have long been a subject of theoretical OR; they bring in the techniques of topology of graphs. Moreover, in practice, the connectivities can be changed unpredictably; therefore they require methods of probability and stochastic theory. The earliest examples are those of the survival of communication systems under attack: military, civilian sabotage, or natural forces (earthquake, fire and flood). Similarly, for transportation networks.

The networks need not be material; thus, in an assembly line construction, and, more generally, in conducting the steps of a very complicated large-scale process in such a way that the different phases fit together, with such coordination of earlier with later stages that all goes through smoothly to the end, we have in essence an abstract network structure, complete with flow rates. The study of these by methods of *critical paths*, *PERT charts*, and other systematizations is a very active theoretical as well as practical branch of OR in the U.S. as in other countries.

A still more abstract case of graphs and their connectivities, with or without stochastic elements, is in the *allocation problem*. The assignment of missiles to targets, with redundancy to take care of missile outages, and also reassignment possibilities to adjust to destroyed targets has long been a familiar application of OR theory. More recently, problems facing the civil authorities, requiring assignments of police to crime areas and criminal targets are being studied; they have many of the above-mentioned features. There are similar problems in medicine and in disaster areas.

We may conclude the subject of graphs and networks in OR by mentioning the "travelling salesman" problem, which has proved a most provoking stimulant to parts of OR theory, playing a role comparable to the four color map problem in topology or Fermat's last theorem in number theory.

6. Extremal properties

Most of the four categories passed in review above lead to the requirement of "optimizing" some numerical index of effectiveness: OR theory without the concept of extremal properties would be like "The Prince of Denmark" with Hamlet left out.

The subject of extremalizing one quantity under constraints in other related quantities is as old as the calculus of variations; but the striking features that have been exhibited by the OR problems are the new ground and unexpected considerations, both of theory and of method, which they have forced upon our attention. When all the relations and constraints are linear, we have the subject of linear programming: utterly trivial, from the traditional point of view in which variables and functions are thought of as existing in conveniently small numbers; but taxing very high mathematical powers when their numbers run into scores or hundreds, as they do in many industrial problems. When the linearity is an insufficiently accurate representation of the facts, and when some constraints are inequalities rather than equations, as in the elementary theory of optimum distribution of searching effort, we find ourselves in a new field, very incompletely studied in the traditional part of the calculus of variations. Convexity may be a basis of our methods, as in many problems of econometrics; but it may not even be approximately present.

The notion of maximizing several desirable characteristics is an ever-present one; the only difficulty is that in non-trivial cases the process of increasing one good thing to its maximum tends to decrease the others. Three positions may be taken: first, we may insist on not letting all but one of the desirable quantities fall below certain pre-assigned minima; and then maximizing that one. Second, we may adopt the point of view of "trade-off", which usually amounts to maximizing a linear combination of all the quantities. This leads to the modern theoretical developments in Lagrange multipliers, which are having both a theoretical and a practical impact on OR. Finally, after observing that both these methods imply value judgments (by fixing the least acceptable numerical values in the first case, and by selecting the trade-off coefficients in the second), we may separate out and refer back to the "decision maker" that part of the problem that was indeterminate in the absence of the value judgments, and do all that objective quantitative reasoning can do to narrow down his choice. This is not hard to describe in principle: if there are, for example, two desirable quantities, u and v, we consider the set E of points in the plane of these variables corresponding to all possible (reasonable) decisions; it is clear that no interior point is a sensible choice, since by moving to the right, or upwards, or both, we could increase the desirable quantities. Therefore the choices are points on the part of the boundary at which (if E is convex) the tangent (or support) lines have a non-positive slope. If E is not convex, we must refer to the boundary of the minimal convex set containing it. Let the decision-maker narrow his choice to a point by his own value-judgments!

The final subject to be mentioned is the use of minimax, maximin, and game theory in the sense of von Neumann. This subject, which has been a favorite one for military and economic OR workers for over two decades, is continuing, with increasing attention to non-zero sum games.

We conclude by noting that we have not attempted to supply an exhaustive, or even a particularly well-balanced, summary of U.S. advances in OR theory; merely a sampling. Moreover, we have methodically omitted all reference to names of people or organizations who have done the various pieces of theoretical OR work mentioned herein: to have mentioned some (other than the dead) would have been unfair to the far greater number of equally important workers whom limitations of space (and of our knowledge) would have forced us to omit.

NEW APPLICATIONS AND TRENDS IN OR IN THE U.S.

Applications et directions nouvelles dans la RO
aux Etats Unis

ROBERT E. MACHOL

Immediate Past President ORSA, Northwestern University,
Evanston, Illinois, USA

Abstract. The paper examines the meaning of the word "applications" and concludes that, on the one hand, applications is OR; but on the other hand, one man's application is another man's theory. It cites some early papers to indicate that most of the things that one could say today about trends and applications were said many years ago. But it goes on to assert that OR has become more mature; to predict that OR will continue to grow and become more successful; and to indicate some of the lines along which this may take place.

1. Introduction

Six or eight months ago, in response to an appropriate deadline, I submitted the following abstract for this paper.

"Application of OR in the US has been moving away from predominantly military and aerospace areas and into social areas and the application of large-scale models which take into account political as well as physical parameters. For example, there are now a number of large-scale environmental regional models of such problems as water quality control and power-plant siting. It is now the Government agencies and the regulatory bodies who see the need for these models, who are sponsoring them, and who hope to use them in achieving their goals. A number of such examples will be discussed in the paper, including application to urban housing, transportation systems, and distribution of services. In the area of the firm, the classical models of

inventory theory, production control, etc., are being extended to more complete total models which formally include objectives of corporate strategy
and various long-range planning options. System engineering and OR have
tended to merge in some of these newer application areas, a trend which is
partly a result of economic pressures and partly a result of the increasing
sophistication of both the practitioners and the consumers."

In the ensuing months I have been looking at this abstract with increasing
dissatisfaction, and have finally decided it is fraudulent. The reason it is
fraudulent is that it could have been given fifteen years ago at the first IFORS
Conference. In fact it was. I have been rereading the proceedings of that
conference, and every one of these points was made at that time. In fact,
Churchman's paper entitled "A summing-up" [1] makes most of these points
far better than I could make them, and I wish the rules of the game permitted
me to read you his paper instead of mine. Quite apart from the proceedings
of that conference, let me remind you that McKean's book on efficiency in
government through systems analysis [2], which has a preface dated April
1958, is mostly about the application of OR to water resource projects. And
in a book of mine published in 1957 [3], I had made the same point about
system engineering and OR having tended to merge.

There's another reason why I don't want to give the paper described in the
above abstract. It would be easy enough to cite one paper each on plant
siting, transportation, production control, etc., but this would only make
sense if they were in some sense typical; and even then, the only interesting
questions are: what makes them typical? and what are their characteristics?
And still more specifically, how have these characteristics changed? Because I
am certainly unwilling to admit that OR has not changed in the past fifteen
years.

The third reason for not giving that paper is that any attempt to summarize the applications of OR by citing a few examples is certain to be
misleading, if only because of the enormous bulk of applications which are
appearing. At the most recent national meeting of ORSA, for example, there
were almost 700 papers [4]. The majority of these were applications papers.
ORSA has held six such meetings since the last IFORS, as has TIMS; and
there have been numerous meetings of the American Institute of Decision
Sciences, the American Cybernetics Society, the Systems Man and Cybernetics group of the IEEE, the Systems Engineering Group of the AIIE, etc. It
seems probable that the number of OR applications which have been described at professional meetings in the US in this three-year period exceeds
10 000. This is not a surprising number; operational analysts resident in the
United States who are members of ORSA or TIMS or both add up to about

10 000. It would not be surprising if they had averaged more than one application each for the past three years.

Finally, I have decided that the title itself is fraudulent (but to that I plead innocent; the title was given to me). To talk about OR applications is a solecism, a redundancy, like talking about rich millionaires. Seventeen years ago Morse wrote "most of the time of ...conferences on operations research is taken up with attempts to define operations research and to persuade others to try it" [5]. While we do a little more than that today, we are still coming up with definitions of OR; but of all the ones I have seen, I do not recall any that did not include the word "apply" in some form. So I am being asked to speak on applied applications, which is silly.

2. Theory and application

What is an application? Let me tell you an anecdote: Many years ago I had a problem and I asked a friend, a mathematician, to help me with it. He came up to my office and for half an hour I scribbled on the blackboard and told him everything I knew about the problem. He listened carefully and at the end he said "OK, what are the equations?" I said "That's what you're here to help me with", and his response was "Look Bob, I'm an applied mathematician; you write the equations, I'll help you solve them". Now I don't want to get into a semantic discussion, and I recognize that the distinction which this man drew between himself and the chaps who prove existence and uniqueness is a tenable and even a useful one. I am simply making the point that one man's application is another man's theory.

Churchman referred to this point in discussing a paper by Naor (Naor is not here, having died in an airplane accident; we still grieve for him). "The question is", said Churchman "how frequently do the problems he considers actually occur? Perhaps very often, but at the present time no one can tell". If they do occur often, then this is an applications paper; if they don't, then it is theory. Perhaps this distinction won't stand up; it is like the distinction between a trick and a technique: a trick is a technique you haven't seen before, and a technique is a trick which you use frequently.

Some of you may be surprised that I asserted that the majority of papers at the ORSA meeting were applications papers. As I have said, one man's application is another man's theory, but it is clear that there is a very different mix of applications and theory papers at our meetings and in our journal. Despite heroic efforts on the part of our editor, the majority of our published papers continue to be theoretical. This has been the subject of innumerable discussions, of which a charming exemplar is a letter by Woolsey [6] – charming because Woolsey is angry and doesn't care who knows it.

To summarize this lengthy introduction, Koopman has been given the task of talking about "OR theory" and I have been given the task of talking about "OR applications". I think these titles are misleading; Koopman's title should have been "Mathematics useful for OR", and mine should have been "OR". Clearly OR is too big a topic for me to discuss. I shall try, however, to make a few comments, with emphasis on where we stand in applications.

3. Innovation becomes routine

Twenty-one years ago, reviewing the first book on OR, Bronowski wrote [7] "Is there then a future for operations research today, either in industry or in war? I doubt it...What was new and speculative in the battlefield turns out, in the practical affairs of industry, to become only a painstaking combination of cost accounting, job analysis, time and motion study, and the general integration of plant flow...Operations research has done its major work". Six years later, in reviewing the first text on OR, I quoted that remark and added [8] "It is a pleasure to report that Bronowski sounded the knell of OR too early...there is gold lying about to be plucked and the OR teams are plucking it. As Bronowski said 'the field of opportunity will never again be quite so blank, so simple, and so lavish' ". This view, that OR is at a dead end, continues to be expressed, but perhaps this is in the essential nature of OR. To the extent that OR is research, it must continually seek new challenges. Yesterday's problems have already been solved.

Consider, for example, what is perhaps the most famous of all applications papers, Edie on toll booths [9]. Edie's objective was to schedule personnel into the booths, but in order to build his mathematical model he had to investigate the properties of booths, and he discovered incidentally that right-hand booths were much less efficient than left-hand booths. "As a consequence of these findings, the Port Authority is reconstructing all major tolls plazas to provide only left-hand toll booths". That result is now known to everybody – not just operations researchers, but everybody in the toll-booth business. As a result there aren't any right-hand toll booths in the United States, and that particular application is obsolete.

This is not always true. As Wagner says "an application may be standard, yet it need not be routine" [10]. Wagner also speaks of "new applications that are beneficial but no longer technically innovative". Consider the classical inventory problem: the economic lot size formula was invented by purchasing agents a very long time ago for the purpose of buying pencils most efficiently. The first people to realize that this formula was applicable to production control (Whitten and Ackoff independently) obviously made a significant contribution. Subsequently, the theory of inventory control has been greatly expanded and it became a routine "OR application". But in many cases we are approaching the situation where a person can buy a set of software from a computer company (for example IBM Impact), and set up a pretty good inventory control system without knowing anything about OR. That is, to a considerable extent inventory control has gotten out of the OR field and into that of operations. On the other hand, the recent book on inventory control by Reisman et al. [11] indicates that the expertise of an OR man can still be useful in applying classical inventory theory.

The point I want to make here is that the paucity of current applications in such fields is a strength of OR, not a weakness. The old applications should become routinized.

4. The approach to large models

There is another aspect to this inventory control problem. We preach continually the evils of suboptimization, and so many people have tried to extend the successful inventory control model to the model of a firm; as we all know, many such attempts have been catastrophic. In particular, Radnor has studied the birth and growth (and occasional death) of OR groups. He finds [12] a particular growth curve being repeated over and over again: after steady growth, due to a series of successes, the OR group takes on a problem which is too big; it then fails at this big problem, sometimes spectacularly, leading to contraction or even death of the OR group. It is clear that we must continue to build these larger models, though being cautious in their utilization. And it is clear that in the long-term future of OR there will be more successful large models. For example, I happen to agree with Shubik [13] (and Hitch at the conference), that Forrester's models are of dubious utility, but one must certainly applaud their innovative nature.

How then should we assess the status of our applications? It is clear that as we spread from the military to industry in the '50s, we have spread to social and governmental problems in the '60s. And whereas we frequently rushed in where angels feared to tread in the good old days, we are now more mature and better able to understand our own capabilities. I cite the current issue of Operations Research [14] which is devoted largely to urban problems (no such special issue could have been assembled a few years ago). An OR group working with the New York City Fire Department recognized immediately that the twin problems were those of extinguishing fires and preventing fires. They also recognized immediately that the former was easy and the latter hard, but in the long run the latter must be more important. They made their brownie points by making significant and visible progress in aiding with the first. Meanwhile, they are proceeding very slowly in attacking the second.

Another article in the same issue [14], by Szanton, describes an OR group working on the housing problem in a major city. The problem given them was to hasten the completion of new housing developments, but they quickly decided that the real problem was instead to prevent the deterioration and abandonment of older housing (his analogy: "the problem was not to turn the faucet on harder; it was to plug the drain"). They discovered that "the more pervasive problem was that most owners of the controlled housing were not getting enough revenue to maintain their buildings properly", and they "recommended raising ceiling rents". While they were by no means a naive group, the political thicket into which this led them was worse than they had anticipated, and their ultimate success was not great. As Szanton points out, the OR man has long held it self-evident that he must have an unambiguous objective; but to the politician it is equally necessary that his objectives be ambiguous. Thus, for the OR man and the politician to work together effectively on such a problem is going to require some rather special capabilities. But even this is not new. In 1946 Morse and Kimball wrote [15] that "considerable tact must be employed to persuade the administrator" if OR, including its implementation, is to be successful.

5. OR is more mature

And so of course there is nothing new under the sun. And yet, we *have* grown up and become more mature. The question is: can we distill the essence of that maturity in describing applications so that the newcomers can avoid the mistakes of their forebears? and the answer is: I cannot. The wisdom is all there on paper, and has been there for many years (for example, in the papers of the first IFORS Conference), but education is an inefficient process; and I am referring now as much to the school of hard knocks as I am to more formal kinds of education in the university. There are today dozens of groups which I would hopefully turn loose on an urban housing kind of problem (as well as lots of groups for whom I would have more trepidation if they were faced with anything so difficult); but I think there were very few that good ten or fifteen years ago.

The political overtones are by no means the only indication of this maturity. Stark, for example, talks about the classical problem facing a civil engineer; namely, how to build a building. He says that increasingly that same engineer is being asked where to build the building; and perhaps he should insist that in the future he be consulted on the basic question of whether the building should be built at all. This same Stark has written, of all things, a book on OR for civil engineers [16], where linear programming, Markov processes, and all sorts of unexpected things are applied to the building of better buildings.

Another measure of our maturity in applications is our interface with the behavioral sciences. We have always paid lip service to this interface; but we have tended to look down on them because of their lack of good quantitative methodology. As Boodman says, we are concentrating now on trying to "understand the behavior of a manager well enough to make these tools useful to him".

Another trend is away from optimization and toward forecasting and long-range planning, but forecasting and planning of a rather special kind. The earlier and more naive models typically led to recommendations like "make 13 units of product 1 and 27 units of product 2 in order to obtain maximum profit". These are, of course, very useful. But often an executive needs help in making a decision where optimization is not well defined. He would like to know what the effect is likely to be of each of the several possible actions facing him if any one of several possible environments should develop. Increasingly, the OR team is presenting the executive with the output of simulations which will not necessarily optimize anything or even make specific recommendations, but which will aid the executive in making his decision; this is perhaps the ultimate objective of OR.

Of course, this technique has become much more promising because of the tremendous development (in both software and hardware) of simulation capabilities. Other developments, not primarily due to the OR man, have also made his kit of tools more powerful. I cite for example the survey of integer programming algorithms by Geoffrion and Marsten [17]. We have had the Gomory cut for a long time, but real applications were few and far between because the algorithms didn't work in practice. Now they work.

To summarize, let me quote again from Churchman at the first IFORS. He took the famous definition that operations research is what operations researchers do and improved it to "operational research is what our operational research people want or intend to do", and then finally "operational research is what future operational researchers will try to do". And what will they try to do? They will take the kit of tools that we now have, and the better kits of tools that we are going to have, and apply them to ever broader and more important problems. On the fairly easy problems they will work themselves out of jobs by operationalizing the results to the point where they can be utilized by less highly trained operational people. They will build ever larger models, with due humility about interpreting the predictions of those models. And they will work well with behavioral scientists, with politicians, and with managers in order to ensure implementation of their results.

References

[1] C.W. Churchman, in: Proc. First Intern. Conf. on Operational Research, ORSA, Baltimore (1957) p. 514.
[2] R.N. McKean, Efficiency in government through systems analysis (Wiley, New York, 1959).
[3] H.H. Goode and R.E. Machol, System engineering (McGraw–Hill, New York, 1957).
[4] Bulletin of the Operations Research Society of America, Suppl. 1 to Opns. Res. 20 (April, 1972).
[5] P.M. Morse, Physics Today 8, No. 9 (1955) 14.
[6] R.E.D. Woolsey, Opns. Res. 20, No. 3 (1972) 729.
[7] J. Bronowski, Sci. Am. 185 (1951) 75.
[8] R.E. Machol, Mech. Eng. 79, No. 9 (1957) 890.
[9] L.C. Edie, Traffic delays at toll booths, Opns. Res. 2 (1954) 107.
[10] H.M. Wagner, lecture to ORSA Meeting in Dallas (May, 1971), and private correspondence.
[11] A. Reisman, B.V. Dean, M.S. Salvador and M. Oral, Industrial inventory control (Gordon and Breech, New York, 1972).
[12] M. Radnor and R. Neal, The progress of management science activities in large U.S. industrial corporations, to appear in Opns. Res. 21, No. 2 (1973).
[13] M. Shubik, Science, 174 (3 Dec. 1971).
[14] Opns. Res. 20, No. 3 (1972) 463–642.
[15] P.M. Morse and G.E. Kimball, Methods of operations research, OEG Rept. No. 54, Navy Dept., Washington (1946); (Wiley, New York, 1951).
[16] R.M. Stark and R.L. Nicholls, Mathematical foundations for design: civil engineering systems (McGraw–Hill, New York, 1972).
[17] A.M. Geoffrion and R.E. Marsten, Integer programming algorithms: a framework and state-of-art survey, Mgmt. Sci. 18, No. 9 (1972) 465.

M. Ross, ed., OR '72. North-Holland Publishing Company (1973)

THE ORSA GUIDELINE REPORT – ONE YEAR LATER

Le rapport de guidage de l'ORSA – un an après

T.E. CAYWOOD

President of ORSA in 1969, A.T. Kearney, Inc., Chicago, USA

Abstract. Given are a brief discussion of the history and contents of "Guidelines for the practice of operations research", a summary of the published and unpublished reaction flavored by the speaker's personal interpretation of the reactions, a discussion of the position of OR in helping to arrive at decisions on political matters, and suggestions for future acitivies.

1. History and contents of the report

In Spring, 1969, President Nixon presented to the U.S. Congress a program for the development of an anti-ballistic missile defense (ABM). The Department of Defense delineated their plans and justifications for the proposed development. In addition to the government's presented program, operational analyses, both pro and con, were presented by supporters as well as opponents to the program. The subject was quite controversial and the final vote in the U.S. Senate was a tie which was broken by the Vice President of the U.S. in favor of starting the program.

In late November, 1969, ORSA received a request to consider some aspects of professional conduct during this ABM debate. The ORSA Council instructed me as then President of the Society to form an ad hoc committee to look into the specific complaint and "... to develop guidelines for operations researchers and systems analysts in advising sponsors and users of their studies ..." [1, p. 1248].

Our report was published in September, 1971, and was sent to each member of ORSA [1]. In addition to a section on guidelines for professional practice, there was a discussion of the position of the operational analyst in an adversary process. Appendices to the report include an introduction to OR and a presentation as a case study, a portion of the ABM debate with comments from the committee. Our case study concerned testimony given by expert witnesses to a subcommittee of the U.S. Senate as well as letters released by the public press on the matter of U.S. anti-ballistic missile defense.

The specific complaints that prompted our study came from a witness in favor of the proposed development and from a U.S. Senator who has been identified as a Defense Department supporter on this matter. Our investigation found varying degrees of quality of the OR presented, and we commented on many individual items. Unfortunately, most of the deficiencies in research quality seemed to come from the anti-ABM faction. Hence, our analysis and critique of the case study has been identified with the Nixon administration's position.

Before going into the reaction to our report, I'd like to point out that our committee was composed of OR types from a wide variety of backgrounds and each member had been a president of an OR society. The report was a joint effort, and each person approved the final draft. All of us considered the guidelines as only a first step in any future delineation of the position of ethical practice of OR and ORSA's possible future posture in this regard. With respect to the case study considered, although we tended to find more technical deficiencies in the anti-ABM presentations, the majority of our committee members found themselves politically favoring the anti-ABM side which ultimately lost in the U.S. Senate. Perhaps, because of this, we were overly critical of faulty arguments from the anti-ABM faction.

2. Public reaction to report

Since the question of ABM defense is still a lively issue in the U.S., the section of our report on the case study produced comment from many sources. The published reaction started with a statement, included in the report, from certain ORSA Council members. It was taken up by the public press and continued by a large number of *letters to the editor* published in the January–February 1972 issue of Operations Research [2]. An interesting set of comments was recently published in the June 1972 issue of Management Science [3].

The serious criticism of the report seems to center around the fact that the case analysis was sponsored and published by ORSA. I.e.: Was this a legitimate activity for a professional society? It is sad to note that nearly all of this objection comes from sources favoring the anti-ABM position, or friendly to the opponents of the ABM position. One has the feeling that facts and mathematical analysis are irrelevant when reading their comments. Most of this criticism seems to center around the single question: "Why was the report prepared and sponsored by ORSA?" The fact that ORSA was involved seems to them to commit ORSA to a pro-ABM position. Thus, the report, or at least the case study, is considered a political document.

Some objections to our report center around the feeling that we did not go further. Our guidelines have been criticised as being platitudinous and suggestions have been made that even moral guidelines should have been prepared. Our case analysis has been criticised for not having examined the larger problem in which the case was imbedded.

Praise came from those who agreed with our statements and encouraged the continuance of our effort. Sadly again we have praise from those who use our case analysis as a political document justifying their previous positions.

3. Discussion of public reaction

First the "Causa belli". Why was the report written? Our answer is clearly because we, the authors, wished it to be written. I cannot sympathize with any restrictive idea that the report should not have been prepared and published. A relatively large group of persons already find it a credible document which justifies its creation. Our guidelines are elemental and as pontifical as any other first, or basic, statements that can be made with regard to engineering practice. Our report takes a step toward codifying the use of OR as an applied science or engineering discipline. In this sense, we showed extreme concern for the persons who use OR results and the persons subjected to its power. Our principal concern was with the correctness and honesty of the OR developments and presentations. In our opinion OR has the function to inform management regarding the consequences of possible management decisions. Thus, we realized that we were discussing the design of a tool or weapon that could be used for any purpose, good or evil. As a consequence, we have been criticised because we labelled as inferior, or inadequate, certain OR used in a good cause.

In a similar vein, we were criticised because of our incompleteness. Our guidelines were just a beginning, and our critique of the case study did not begin to treat the larger problem in which the discussion was imbedded. We admit to both shortcomings and hope that others will carry on where we left off.

A fair amount of discussion has surrounded the wisdom of publishing the case study along with the guidelines. We felt that the case discussion would add substance to the general guideline presentation. We hoped that the wording of the report and its approval by the Council would not associate ORSA with a pro-ABM position, or an official condemnation of the inferior OR presented by the anti-ABM advocates. However, since ORSA sponsored a committee that prepared a report which in turn ORSA published, ORSA is deemed to have taken a political stand. This chain of logic seems to have been adopted by those who agree with the political stand of the persons whose OR we criticised. I doubt if any ORSA disclaimers would have satisfied them. I also note that some of our critics seem secretly to welcome the persecution of their cause since it gives them an occasion to repeat their arguments.

4. Politics and professional societies

What should be the official position of a technical society with respect to various political issues? Most of us do not wish our professional societies to select a side to champion on a political issue (particularly if we do not agree with the side selected to champion). We will be pressured from time to time, but most technical societies are successful in avoiding political issues. However, I believe that our societies as well as individuals, would like to see various causes represented adequately by OR talent. Since it is generally undesirable to commit a society to a political cause, this means that the commitment should be individual.

I doubt if OR has ever, in the past or today, made a fundamental political contribution to a controversial cause. I don't know of any situation where analytical reasoning had determined a political decision. Politicians seem to be guided more by matters other than scientific truths. However, rather than abandon the political arena, as a start I think we should work from the detail end. In particular, when people present analytical reasoning, their arithmetic should be correct. Next, their logic and algebra should be acceptable. Finally, their analysis should include most of the reasonable alternatives. Now we come to the ethical problem which could be impressed onto an operations researcher. If he is in advocacy position, should he present arguments which can be developed against his position? I think not, I think it is up to the opposition to develop these arguments. The adversary process has been very successful in our civilization, and I doubt if our OR societies wish to rebuild or destroy this process *.

We realize that we placed an extreme amount of faith in the advocacy process in contrast to the sole use of the scientific method. Recently two additional cases were brought to my attention where scientific reasoning and specific testimony was used perhaps incorrectly to sway a political decision. Specifically, scientists were accused of presenting just those findings which support one side of a case. The popular press has stated that "... if a scientist is to be worthy of the name, he must protect the integrity of the scientific method by presenting all his findings, not just those that bolster one side of the case".

This seems to be a naive position which does not recognize the realities of modern life. Our committee report presents more pragmatic guidelines. Thus, for the near future I think our societies should encourage presentations of both sides and make our publications available for serious criticism of OR. Perhaps at some later time when we have developed a large quantity of such criticism we may be able to take additional steps and add to our guidelines.

References

[1] T.E. Caywood, H.M. Berger, J.H. Engel, J.F. Magee, H.J. Miser and R.M. Thrall, Guidelines for the practice of operations research, Opns. Res. 19 (1971) 1123.
[2] Reactions to the guidelines for the practice of operations research, Opns. Res. 20 (1972) 205.
[3] Discussion of the ORSA guidelines, Mgmt. Sci. 18 (1972) B608.

* The following guidelines are taken from the ad hoc committee report indicating how we felt operations researchers should participate in the adversary process:
If an analyst is called upon or volunteers to advocate or support the advocacy of a position, a documented analysis by which he reaches his conclusions should be available for independent and objective appraisal. A write-up of his analysis should be made available in advance, for thorough analysis by the staff of the organization to which he is offering testimony (such analysis by the organization receiving the testimony cannot be accomplished unless it has access to its own staff competent to evaluate the analysis) and by recognized and competent adversaries. Subsequent oral testimony or position papers urging a course of action may be weighed against the analytical background (submitted earlier) from which they sprang.
Responsible decision makers using the adversary process to arrive at a decision should take care to consider technical criticism of operations research as well as rebuttal of this criticism on a technical basis.

PART VII

WORKSHOP SESSIONS

Séances de traveaux pratiques

Chairman: B. BROUGH (United Kingdom)

Reports on:

Education systems, R.L. ACKOFF (USA).

Urban planning, L.C. EDIE, D.C. GAZIS, D.F. BLUMBERG and J.L. SCHLAEFLI (USA).

Guiding technological development, G.W. MORGENTHALER (USA).

Agricultural research, J.B. DENT and R.A. PEARSE (U.K.).

Health and welfare systems, R. ROSSER and V. WATTS (U.K.).

Crime prevention, G. CASSIDY (Canada).

Environmental pollution, D.J. CLOUGH (Canada).

EDUCATIONAL SYSTEMS

Systèmes d'éducation

RUSSELL L. ACKOFF

University of Pennsylvania, Philadelphia, USA

Editorial note: This popular workshop, attended by 70 to 80 persons, did not produce a formal report. Section 2 below reproduces the chairman's statement to the closing session which gives the reasons behind this decision and also provides an insight into some of the topics discussed. At the concluding session the chairman invited a guest participant, Ruth Norden*, to comment on her experience of the workshop. Her account forms section 3 below. Section 1 reproduces the chairman's opening statement of the problem.

1. Statement of the problem

1.1. The critics' case

OR fiddles with schools while education burns.

Education at all levels has been subjected to widespread critical evaluation which has brought most, if not all, of its basic assumptions into question. The indictments levelled at the educational process are too numerous to identify and too basic to describe in detail here. However, a sample of passages from some of its more eminent critics may be sufficient to give you a sense of their intensity and flavor.

In a study of American public schools commissioned by the Carnegie Foundation of New York, Charles E. Silberman [1] wrote:

"It is not possible to spend any prolonged period visiting public school classrooms without being appalled by the mutilation visible everywhere—mutilation of spontaneity, of joy of learning, of pleasure in creating, of sense

---

* Highview School, Hartsdale, New York, U.S.A.

of self... Because adults take the schools so much for granted, they fail to appreciate what grim, joyless places most American schools are, how oppressive and petty are the rules by which they are governed, how intellectually sterile and esthetically barren the atmosphere, what an appalling lack of civility obtains on the part of teachers and principals, what contempt they unconsciously display for children as children (p.10)."

To many observers the primary function of schools is no longer educational. They have become institutional baby-sitters, day-care centers, low-security sleep-out detention homes, and places for those between infancy and adulthood to grow up without bothering their parents or being bothered by them.

James Herndon, in his recent book, *How to survive in your native land* [2], put it even more strongly:

"If their parents do not see that they go to school, the parents may be judged unfit and the kids go to jail... No matter how bad the school, it is better than jail. Everyone knows that, and the schools know it especially (p. 19)."

Of course, not all schools are comparable to jails. But even our most permissive schools are being called into question. Edgar Z. Friedenberg [3], professor of education at Dalhousie University in Halifax, Nova Scotia, observed:

"Even the most enthusiastic supporters of the 'free' or 'experimental' school movement ... are beginning to express severe misgivings about whether young people need schools at all (p. 19). ... schools have a prior commitment ... to segregate their clientele by age and artificial situations rather than help them relate to what is really going on in their community (p. 20)."

One of the principal proponents of elimination of schools is Ivan Illich of the Center for International Documentation in Cuernavaca, Mexico. In his recent book, *Deschooling society* [4], he wrote:

"Many students, especially those who are poor, intuitively know what the schools do for them. They school them to confuse process and substance. Once these become blurred, a new logic is assumed: the more treatment there is, the better are the results; or, escalation leads to success. The pupil is thereby 'schooled' to confuse teaching with learning, grade advancement with education, a diploma with competence, and fluency with the ability to say something new. His imagination is 'schooled' to accept service in place of value...

... the institutionalization of values leads inevitably to physical pollution, social polarization, and psychological impotence: three dimensions in a process of global degradation and modernized misery...

My analysis of the hidden curriculum of school should make it evident that public education would profit from the deschooling of society (pp. 1–2)."

The eminent British psychiatrist, Dr. R.D. Laing, in his book, *The politics of experience* [5], argues that parents and schools unconsciously collude to destroy a child's sense of self. In discussing the work of Jules Henry, the American antrhopologist and sociologist who wrote *Culture against man* [6], Laing observed:

"It is Henry's contention that in practice education has never been an instrument to free the mind and the spirit of man, but to bind them. We think we want creative children, but what do we want them to create?"

Henry had written:

"If all through school the young were provoked to question the Ten Commandments, the sanctity of revealed religion, the foundations of patriotism, the profit motive, the two party system, monogamy, the laws of incest, and so on we would have more creativity than we could handle [6,p.288]."

Laing continued:

"Children do not give up their innate imagination, curiosity, dreaminess easily. You have to love them to get them to do that. Love is the path through permissiveness to discipline, and through discipline, only too often, to betrayal of self.

What schools do is to induce children to want to think the way school wants them to think. "What we see," in the American kindergarten and early schooling process, says Henry, "is the pathetic surrender of babies." You will, later or sooner, in the schools or in the home.

It is the most difficult thing in the world to recognize this in our own culture [5,pp. 71–72]."

Despite the need to face such fundamental questions as these selections raise, OR has been largely occupied with the administrative—not the educational—problems of schools. At a time when the structure and functioning of educational institutions require fundamental redesign, OR is primarily concerned with scheduling classes, students, and faculty; with the running of libraries, cafeterias, school stores, and purchasing departments; with the annual rituals of budgeting and admissions; with administrative information systems, and a number of other problems the solutions to which can have no significant impact on the nature and quality of education.

I hope the workshop will get into the heart of the matter. To this end I propose that it considers five requirements of an effective educational system.

1.2. Five requirements of an effective educational system

1.2.1. Focus on the learning process

Understanding of the failure of formal education must begin with recognition of the fact that it is less efficient than informal education. Evidence of this is plentiful. Children learn their first language at home more easily than they learn a second language at school. Most adults forget much more of what they were taught in schools than of what they learned out of them. The bulk of what adults use in their work and play they learned at work and play. This is even true for teachers. They learn more about what they teach by teaching it than by being taught about it. University professors are not exceptions; they are largely occupied by teaching subjects they were never taught. In more than twenty-five years of university teaching I have never conducted a course on a subject I was taught.

Formal education ignores the effectiveness of learning processes that take place out of school. Most learning takes place without teaching, but schools are founded on teaching, not learning. As Professor Friedenberg put it: "... schools have a prior commitment to teach rather than help people learn..." [3,p. 20]. Teaching—unlike learning—can be industrialized and mechanized; it can be controlled, scheduled, timed, measured, and observed. But teaching is at most an input to the learning process, not an output. Nevertheless, our educational systems operate as though an ounce of teaching is sufficient to produce at least an ounce of learning. Nothing could be further from the truth.

The first requirement of a new educational system, then, is that it be focussed on, and organized about, the learning process, not the teaching process.

1.2.2. Development of desire and ability to learn

Learning outside of school is not organized into subjects, courses, semesters, curricula, or other discrete units. A child's learning of a language, for example, is not separated from its learning of other subjects but is intimately tied to it. Geography and history, economics and mathematics, and philosophy and science may be taught separately, but they are not learned separately.

Subjects and disciplines are categories we create in order to file knowledge. The same material can be filed in many different ways. Filing systems cannot be differentiated by correctness, only by convenience. Although storage of knowledge may require dividing it into categories, using it requires putting its parts back together again. Formal education is preoccupied with taking things apart; most of our lifes out of school are preoccupied with putting them back together again.

What is learned informally is learned without "benefit" of examinations or grades. This, one might argue, is only true for things one wants to learn. But school, one might continue, must teach a child things he needs but does not want to learn. This conception is not only incorrect; it is inhumane. In the New School, the young should be motivated to learn whatever they ought to learn but never forced to learn anything they do not want to. To impose learning is to take the fun out of it and this is much more serious than is the failure to learn any particular subject.

Therefore, the second requirement of the New Education is that it not be organized around rigidly scheduled quantized units of classified subject matter, but around development of a desire to learn and the ability to do so.

1.2.3. Preservation of individuality

Even where numerous entrance requirements are imposed on students, they vary widely in ability, interests, and what they have already learned. Therefore, the same input to different students does not produce the same outputs. Schools based on the industrialized model ignore or minimize the differences between students and thus require them to adapt to the educational production process. The process should be adapted to the students. Individuality should be preserved at all costs. Uniformity and conformity are anathema to creativity and, hence, to progress.

Therefore, the third requirement of the New Education is that it individualizes students and preserves their selves by tailoring itself to students, not tailoring them to it.

1.2.4. Continuing integrated process

Learning is not restricted to a part of one's life. It takes place continuously. In the past, when relatively little was known and it was added to or changed slowly, formal education could be completed in a few years. As knowledge accumulated, more and more formal education was required to absorb it. As the rate of increase of knowledge increased, the problem of keeping up with additions to, and changes of, knowledge also grew. Refresher courses of many types and durations have become commonplace. Continuing education—education after departure from school—is now an integral part of our culture. As it approaches an unbroken continuity it will be apparent that the separation of work, play and education is as undesirable for adults as it is for preschoolers.

The fourth requirement of the New Education is that it be organized as a continuing, if not a continuous, process and that it be integrated with all aspects and stages of life.

1.2.5. Adaptable systems

We do not have answers to basic educational problems. Nor can we find them if by "answer" we mean something that puts a problem to rest once and for all. Social systems exist in continually changing environments. Therefore, what solves an educational problem at any one time and place is not likely to do so at another time or place. Hence we must give up the search for a best educational system, one that operates optimally regardless of time and place, not to mention students.

Therefore, the fifth requirement of the New Education is that it be carried out by a system and subsystems that can learn and adapt effectively. Ideally, such systems should be organized so that each of their participants can experiment with them, and they can experiment on each of their participants.

If consideration of such requirements as I have proposed is not a proper function of OR, then I hope the workshop will behave improperly. It is only by such impropriety that OR can start to unravel some of the social crises that confront us. Society is being degraded more by our failure to face the right problems than by our failure to solve those problems we face.

2. Chairman's statement on the outcome of the workshop

2.1. The reasons for no report

At an early stage the workshop on education concluded that its efforts to learn were being constrained by the need to produce a report that presumably would teach others. Its members unanimously felt the workshop's principal function was to serve its participants and therefore decided to ignore the requirement for a report. Put another way—the group decided that the principal value of a workshop does not lie in output produced for consumption by others, but lies in participating in the workshop process. Thus it rejected a common objective of students, that of teacher-pleasing.

Our workshop recommends that no report of its deliberations be published and it suggests that IFORS conferences as a whole might benefit from the same type of recommendation. Previous proceedings of IFORS conferences have been expensive and time consuming to produce. They do not contribute significantly to an already supersaturated literature. We suffer more from an overabundance of useless literature than we do from a shortage of that which is useful.

The members of the workshop felt its value to them — a value that cannot be shared with non-participants — consisted of three opportunities:

first — the opportunity to become aware of their own educational beliefs, attitudes and assumptions;

secondly — the opportunity to begin to organize these into a conceptual model of the educational process that will increase their abilities to think more fruitfully about education in the future; and

thirdly — the opportunity to become aware of alternative ways of thinking about education and educating.

2.2. The organisation of the workshop

The workshop divided itself into four subgroups — one concerned with learning processes, another with what is now compulsory education, a third with what is now voluntary education, the last with the system as a whole.

These subgroups spent virtually no time in trying to identify deficiencies in current educational systems. They were not concerned about what they did not want, but with what they did want. Therefore, they did not have to walk into the future facing the past. They were occupied with developing concepts, designs and models of the kind of system they wanted to plan towards — not of the kind of system they wanted to plan away from.

Furthermore, they deliberately ignored all practical constraints in order to unleash their imaginations. As a result a number of ideas were generated. No effort was made to extract agreement, or even to identify disagreements — rather the effort was to formulate alternatives to current educational practices and ways of thinking about them that are worthy of study. There was not enough time to put these ideas together into a comprehensive design.

2.3. Some observations and suggestions

Time permits me to identify only a small sample of the observations and suggestions generated — and it does not permit me to describe the rationale behind any of them.

(1) Less affluent parents tend to want their children to be better, and do

better than they. Therefore, they want education for change. Affluent parents tend to want their children to be as good and to do as well as they did. They want education for non-change. In developed countries – and less developed ones that imitate them – the attitudes of the affluent determine the nature of the educational proceeds. A system, which seeks non-change, is more concerned with precluding potential disruptive inquiry than in developing the ability to inquire.

(2) A child and/or his parents should be able to apply for admission to any and every school in a system; selection among applicants should be made at random; each publicly supported school should receive from the government as its only income tuition for each attending student, and the government should provide free transportation to any school in the system. This would create an active educational market place.

(3) Teachers should stop teaching and begin to serve as a resource to be used by students as they see fit to learn, to learn how to learn, and to reinforce the natural, if not innate, desire to learn.

(4) More time in early school should be spent on learning how to convert what is learned out of school into information, knowledge, and understanding – than in obtaining substantive inputs. Currently the child is left on its own to convert raw material into something useful. Put another way the emphasis of school should be on method and process rather than on content.

(5) That for at least some of what is now the pre-school years, parent and child should attend school together.

(6) That school provides a wide variety of subjects and means of access to them – that the student be free to choose from these – and that he has available continuing advice to assist him in these choices. That the mature student and advisor each be aware of the other's state of readiness or capabilities, wants and objectives, and style and personality.

(7) Students should not be assigned and confined to homogeneous age or attainment groups – but should be part of largely self-organising heterogeneous groups in which the opportunity to learn from each other is maximized and the need to learn from a teacher is minimized.

(8) Every so-called teacher at every level of the educational system should be required to be a student at some higher level of the system.

2.4. Now on the university

That universities should have no entrance or exit requirements, and confer no degrees. Students could therefore come and go as they see fit. Students need not be examined on what they have learned unless they want to be.

Examinations and evaluation should be conducted so as to maximize feedback to student. They should be learning, not unlearning, experiences. Records of evaluations should go into a file to which only the student has access. Dissemination of its content within, as well as outside, the university should be completely under his control. Failures, however, should not be recorded. Qualifications of students should be determined by institutions outside the university. Requalification should be frequent to encourage keeping up with developments and to encourage continuing use of the university.

A faculty member should be a student who facilitates the learning of others and who adds to the material worth learning. His selection should be controlled by other faculty members – but his retention should depend on students as well as faculty. Academic freedom should be protected by means other than tenure. Incompetence and unproductivity should not be protected under any guise.

Faculty ranks should be eliminated. Currently the quest for promotion dominates the quest for knowledge.

2.5. On schools generally

Finally, on schools generally – ways of obtaining continuous feedback of information on performance of departed students should be developed. Controlled experiments on educational processes should be continuous. Both feedback and experiments should be incorporated into systematic adaptation and control. OR can make a major contribution to education in this regard. It should be concerned with the design and operation of educational systems that can learn and adapt effectively – not with the effective operation of systems that cannot.

2.6. The guest participants

Our workshop was unique in at least one respect. A number of wives – many teachers or ex-teachers – participated and contributed significantly. We enjoyed and benefitted from their participation and suggest they be encouraged to take part in our meetings in the future whenever they see fit.

We asked one of these wives – Ruth Norden – to comment on her involvement with the workshop.

3. Some invited observations by a guest participant – Ruth Norden

I was thrilled by the invitation your Federation extended to its guests to attend any sessions they wished. As an educator I was naturally curious to observe how operations researchers dealt with the problems of education. I enjoyed the luxury of being a guest, with neither obligation nor commitment. The informality of the workshop and the kind indulgence of its leader and participants made it hard for me to be a passive observer. I appreciated this opportunity and know that many guests were equally grateful.

Hopefully the presence of laymen has also helped to bridge the gap between the theoretical and technical approach of the operations researcher and the real, ongoing responsibilities in the field. I believe this experience has indicated a real need for specialized professional societies to interact, not merely on a coincidental basis, but rather on a deliberate, continuing basis.

Traditionally in education, and I assume in OR, we have attempted to analyze and evaluate those aspects which have been easiest to measure, and refined these while we avoided dealing with the more subjective problems that focus on the true objectives. The emphasis in technological and educational applications research seems to have been more product than process oriented. You hold the means and the expertise to help us deal with complex problems.

My initial concern that an organization, whose reputation is in the field of technology, might focus merely on theoretical measurements and models, was relieved by the emphasis on the human factor in every session I attended from the highlights speakers to the individual workshops and plenary sessions. This awareness, to me, signals great hope for a breakthrough for OR's role in the solution of some of the more universal problems of mankind.

Now for some more specific reactions and suggestions: a workshop format that truly wants to grapple with multi-disciplinary problems might deliberately include: varied *expertise*, not merely of interest amongst its participants; prior preparation to at least insure some common frame of reference [example: for a Learning Process Workshop, OR constituents might investigate research in the field of human learning and innovative teaching programs, while educators might familiarize themselves with models, systems design and decision trees] ; proceedings, at least of significant preplanned contributions should become "preceedings" and be distributed to participants prior to the session.

I know this requires more of a commitment than people are willing to make, but might result in a more fruitful focus on problems which require interactive thinking. Don't get me wrong. I should hate to see excessive structure imposed on the workshop operation. Its greatest value is in the cross-breeding of ideas and in the definition of problems and future needs. But I believe we could address ourselves more productively to this if we are prepared.

It was also my impression that a full-time workshop commitment is frustrating to many members who travel half way round the world to exchange views with fellow professionals and find themselves confined to one group. Perhaps narrowing the wide range of options to several universal needs (as expressed in the highlights session) through strands of workshops which would deal with the "suboptimizing phase" for part of the time, followed by a second strand of workshops that attempt to relate the "sub" to the "grand" problem at several steps along the way, would be worth trying.

In education, the greatest impact has often come from those tangentially related to the field; psychologists, physiologists, behavioral scientists and the medical profession; whereas the implementation process rests with the practitioner or teacher. The two seldom communicate at the most crucial point of interaction of application of theory to practice.

I believe OR could help to offer more systematic means for reaching agreed upon objectives for each learner, institution and society as a whole through diagnosis, prescription, resource allocation (human and other), evaluation, decision making, and feedback to renew and improve the cycle. This is where I see a potential for a society like IFORS to include educators, not only coincidentally, but in the learning process of OR.

The unanimous concern with the human factor, the agreement on educational objectives by widely divergent groups and individuals, the realization of the importance for creating change from within rather than imposing it from above, were a most promising start for a technological OR society. I have hope that operations researchers can and will help us grapple with the complexities of the multitude of unisolatable variables that are part and parcel of every human experiment. We need to develop clearer definitions and guidelines and to implement a multitude of processes by optimizing our utilization of methods, materials, resources to suit the learner. What the best practitioners now do instinctively, OR can help us do deliberately, productively, continuously and more universally.

References to section 1

[1] Ch.E. Silberman, Crisis in the classroom (Random House, New York, 1970).
[2] J. Herndon, How to survive in your native land (Simon & Shuster, New York, 1971).

[3] E.Z. Friedenberg, How to survive in your native land (book review) The New York Times Book Review (April 11, 1971) 19.

[4] I. Illich, Deschooling society (Harrow Books, New York, 1972).

[5] R.D. Laing, The politics of experience (Ballantine Books, New York, 1967).

[6] J. Henry, Culture against man (Vintage Books, New York, 1963).

M. Ross, ed., OR '72. North-Holland Publishing Company (1973)

60

URBAN PLANNING

Planification urbaine

LESLIE C. EDIE

The Port Authority of New York and New Jersey, New York, USA

DENOS C. GAZIS

IBM Watson Research Center, Yorktown Heights, New York, USA

DONALD F. BLUMBERG

Decision Science Corp., Jenkinstown, Pennsylvania, USA

and

JOHN L. SCHLAEFLI

Stanford Research Institute, California, USA

1. Introduction

The nature of urban problems was summarized by Professors Eastman, Johnson and Dortanek of Carnegie-Mellon in the special issue of Management Science devoted to urban problems [1]. They pointed out that,

"Sharp and bitter conflict has become an ingredient of urban life and the public policy affecting that life. This conflict manifests itself in racial rebellions, street demonstrations, increases in violent crime, protest marches, court tests, tax increases, increased drug use, strikes by public employees, new bargaining arrangements, new political coalitions, along with escalating demands for improved housing, employment, education, social and public services by citizens' groups and public officials alike. The precarious financial conditions of cities — many of them almost bankrupt — sustains the boding sense of uncertainty, leaving cities in a more or less perpetual state of foment with policy makers asking: where do we go from here?"

This may apply most aptly to US urban areas. We are possibly ahead of other countries; you might say look at New York City and see the future. How can the methods and techniques of operations research best be used to address these problems. The general goal of the workshop on urban planning was first to identify and assess how OR has helped so far in pointing the way in certain areas, the four named in the program. We selected these four areas not because they are the most critical or important ones but for two other reasons. First, other workshops were devoted to other areas of concern in urban planning like education, crime, welfare and pollution, and we did not want to duplicate or compete with these workshops. Secondly, we picked areas in which we knew some significant OR has been done.

In the first group, Professor Leo Kadanoff, a physicist from Brown University, led the workshop in a consideration of policy models involving land use and urban growth, and gave a state of the art lecture of the analytical work going on in the modeling and computer simulation of the temporal and spatial variation of urban development patterns.

This was followed by a discussion of urban management systems led by Donald F. Blumberg. The workshop problem addressed was that of finding new approaches to the management information and planning systems which are needed to run all of the complex operations of a modern metropolis.

Another group, on urban transportation, was led by John L. Schlaefli of the Stanford Research Institute. An important problem in this area is the decline of mass transportation and the associated traffic congestion and other serious consequences of continued growth of private transportation. The problem of urban goods movement is another which has received far too little attention in urban transportation planning.

The workshop was also concerned with problems of housing and urban services, including computer applications for the analysis of urban housing problems and for the planning and scheduling of essential services, such as police and fire fighting. Dr. Gazis led the discussion of this part of the workshop. The participants were fortunate in considering this area of the urban planning problem by virtue of the fact that a complete report of the work of the New York City Rand Institute was published in Operations Research along with other papers on other aspects of OR in urban services [2].

How well we could do in evaluating the contributions the OR profession has made or could make to these important urban planning areas depended entirely on the talent and experience of the workshop participants. We were fortunate in having members of the planning profession who were not OR analysts but who were well-acquainted with the problems of urban planning. Among the other knowledgeable participants were quite a spectrum of fields and disciplines, including engineering, architecture, management, insurance, law, physics, geography, mathematics, medicine as well as OR scientists and systems analysts.

There were some general questions considered by each group, such as the following: In what organizations and where in those organizations can operations researchers and multiple-discipline teams be placed to be most effective in contributing to urban planning and the implementation of the plans? For which decision makers should the operations researcher work? Should an OR group report to an urban planner, to the mayor or other chief executive, to a city council or legislative body, or whom. One important consideration is just how decisions are made in an urban area, with many over-lapping jurisdictions?

This report covers the three main areas of study addressed in the workshop: "policy models and urban management systems" (combining the first two sections of the workshop), "urban transportation" and "urban services", and these are followed by a summary.

2. Policy models and urban management systems

The increasing complexity of urban and regional growth has led to the growing demand for more powerful systems for urban management. The concept of urban oriented models has been in existence since the development of micro-economic theory and econometrics as part of the general theory of regional economic demand. The basic "gravity" models of the economic literature, which attempted to relate regional and urban growth to transportation, started this area of development. Unfortunately, the gravity model approach proved to be too narrow in scope, and more ambitious and comprehensive structures were found to be needed in order to deal with the issues involved.

The state of the art, thus far, indicates that, to be effective, an urban model designed for use in support of the general urban management process must involve four discrete, yet dynamically related components:

(1) *land use*: the availability of land, its uses, and the physical structures on the land within the community and region,

(2) *economic–social structures*: the characterization of the people living and working in the community and region, and the economic wealth produced,

(3) *transportation*: the movement of goods and people from one area of the community or region to another, and

(4) *utilities and services*: the required supporting services to support a viable existence of the people in the community and region.

These component elements must be both spatially as well as dynamically (i.e., in time) related.

2.1. Urban planning models

Over the last ten years considerable effort has been directed towards the development and application of analytical models and simulation techniques to support urban and metropolitan planning programs and regional design studies. Although progress has been made, such models are not yet fully developed for routine use such as the prediction of the growth and functioning of urban and regional systems. However, they do serve as a supporting framework for the development of advanced systems which can be ultimately used to play a decisive role in urban and metropolitan planning.

Basically, models have been developed for the evaluation of urban, metropolitan and regional systems in terms of the number of substructures. These include:

(1) land use,
(2) transportation,
(3) population,
(4) economic activity, and
(5) utilities and supporting services.

Tables 1 and 2 (based in part on [3]) provide a general overview of urban models * for which published information is available in the United States. A general bibliography describing these models as well as a specific bibliography discussing other related models is also available [4].

2.2. Urban financial policy models

However, the existence of models of elements of, or the complete representation of an urban area, do not, of themselves, provide a solution to the problem of urban management. The urban models provide a "planning framework", a method of examining the future in an orderly way through prediction and extrapolation. They do not, in and of themselves, provide the basic management mechanism for policy and action resolution. It is in this area that a second, in fact, parallel development effort has been underway; focus on urban policy. Most of the quantitative work in this area has been directed toward financial policy because the underlying decision at the local government level, at which urban policy is resolved, is focused on resource allocation and such key question as tax assessment rates, etc.

If the sophistication of urban management systems cannot be realistically simulated by any single "integrated" physical planning model, neither can the

---

* Excluding models primarily oriented to transportation planning.

addition of financial planning considerations make true realism less elusive to modeling. Wood [5] might have intended the following as a caution to those concerned with "total urban systems planning":

"We need a model that encompasses the decision-makers and their activities, but goes further to identify the generators of public matters and the consequences of public actions".

Wood suggested several "identifiable and interlinked components" to be considered in such a model, requiring a reduction in emphasis upon physical development and an expansion of attitudinal surveys drawn from carefully identified "political power centers" to predict acceptability of various program alternatives. Combined attitudinal studies and computer simulations thus together provide one picture to an urban planner of how well policies may succeed, not in physical or financial terms, but in terms of the ultimate evaluators – whether they be "elite" power groups, active minorities, or federal and state bureaucracies playing their part in the resolution of local issues. Consideration of financial planning variables, such as local budgetary and operating expenditure decisions, will most likely be of primary importance to planners.

Laska [6] described how the "planning and program budgeting management information system" in Mineola, Long Island, has enabled a functionally oriented budget to be implemented. The city uses a "cost-effectiveness" analysis of expenditures by program (function) rather than by department organization. Decision makers can thus compare estimated versus actual program expenditures of various departments as one means of obtaining a measure of efficiency (or at least realism) for each department. Such a measure can then be used to choose the most efficient departments to administer subsequent programs and to select the less efficient departments for re-organization. Functional records are maintained to quantify the amount of service performed by each department for the community. Funding may then be allocated according to the type and quantity of service to be performed.

Crecine [7] had developed a computer simulation model of the municipal budgeting process. The computer model designed by Crecine covers the three areas of departmental requests submitted by the respective department heads, the mayor's budget as submitted to the city council for consideration, and the final municipal appropriations as approved by city council.

2.3. Urban data systems

A third area of emphasis in the field of urban management systems has been focused on urban data and information. The USAC program in the

Table 1
Urban and regional planning models

No.	Model name	Author(s)	City	Approx. date
1	Activities allocation model	Scidman	Philadelphia	1964
2	Empiric land use model	Brand, Barber, Jacobs	Boston	1966
3	Land use plan design model	Schlager	S.E. Wisconsin	1965
4	Model of metropolis	Lowry	Pittsburgh	1964
5	Penn-Jersey regional growth model	Herbert	Philadelphia	1964
6	Pgh. urban renewal simulation model	Steger	Pittsburgh	1964
7	Polimetric land use forecasting model	Hill	Boston	1965
8	Probabilistic model for residential growth	Donnelly, Chapin, Weiss	Greensboro	1964
9	Projection of a metropolis – NYC	Berman, Chinitz, Hoover	New York City	1960
10	Retail market potential model	Lakshmanan, Hansen	Baltimore	1964
11	San Francisco C.R.P. model	A.D. Little Inc.	San Francisco	1965
12	Urban Detroit area model	Doxiadis	Detroit area	1967
13	SCANCAP	Blumberg	general	1968
14	PROMUS	Blumberg	Toronto	1970
15	BASS	Graybeal	San Francisco area	1967
16	TOMM	Crecine	general	1968
17	Urban dynamics	Forester	general	1969
18	LAMPS	Decision Sci. Corp.	Nottingham	1972

For bibliography on models see [3, pp. B262–4]

United States, for example, has been emphasizing the development of urban data systems as its basis for improved urban management. The opportunity for expansion and interjection of physical urban planning-oriented models

Table 2
Subjects and methods of the models given in table 1

	Model no.																	
	1	2	3	4	5	6	7	8	9	10	11	12	13	14	15	16	17	18
Subject																		
Land use																		
residential	X		X	X	X	X		X			X		X	X	X	X	X	X
industrial (Mfg.)	X			X		X							X	X	X	X	X	X
commercial	X		X	X		X							X	X	X	X	X	X
govt. or institutions			X															
roads, streets, alleys	X		X															
public open space			X															
Population	X	X	X	X		X	X		X		X	X	X	X	X	X	X	X
Transportation																		
interzonal strips									X		X	X	X	X	X	X	X	X
other transp.																		
Economic activity																		
employment	X												X	X	X	X	X	X
1. retail trade		X		X		X	X		X				X	X	X	X	X	X
2. manufacturing	X	X		X		X	X		X				X	X	X	X	X	X
3. service		X					X		X				X	X	X	X	X	X
trade																		
1. retail								X	X									
2. other						X			X									
personal income	X	X				X	X		X				X	X	X	X	X	X
Method																		
Econometric & stochastic																		
regression	X	X						X				X						
input–output					X				X									
Markov process											X							
Mathematical programming																		
linear programming			X		X													
other analytic forms				X			X		X		X							
Simulation																		
autonomous	X		X		X	X	X				X		X	X	X	X	X	X
with intervention			X	X				X										

and the financial policy planning system has been greatly improved by recent computerization techniques. For example, graphic display devices have
made urban growth models more easily understood and appreciated by plan-

ners outside of the econometric or computer-oriented disciplines. Several data variables could be used in displays of neighborhood allocation patterns and related to social or physical changes.

Kadanoff et al. [8] have reported the development of a computerized urban data system that can be used to evaluate public policy alternatives. Historical data related to real estate transactions, construction and land usage were assembled for the City of Kankakee, Illinois, covering a time frame of over 100 years. These data were then coded for computer input to form a historical data bank of urban development. With application of a computer-controlled graphic display capability to this data bank, urban planners have been able to examine conveniently and in detail the dynamic urban growth pattern of this city of 50 000 people as a function of their own public policies.

Several "decision variables" were recognized as significant public policy factors affecting the patterns of urban growth. By using dynamic sequential CRT map displays representing period-by-period growth patterns changing over selected time frames, planners could observe the addition or removal of various land features in any portion of the city. Using historical land use patterns to "calibrate" predictive mathematical models, measures of reliability could be obtained in addition to predictive information.

In summary, three parallel efforts are underway in the field of urban management systems:

(1) comprehensive urban models for planning,

(2) urban financial policy models, and

(3) urban data systems.

An example of a system which embodies all of the elements is the PROMUS system now being implemented for the City of Toronto and the Province of Ontario, Canada. The system was discussed extensively during the workshop.

2.4. The PROMUS system

The provincial municipal simulation system (PROMUS) is an advanced urban simulation system presently under development [9]. The system (fig. 1) consists of two major subsystems:

(1) *community model subsystem (CMS)*, which describes an existing or new community in terms of size, location, internal diversity, etc., and

(2) *financial policy planning subsystem (FPPS)*, which provides the basis for computing the costs, cash flow, and return on investment of given development and operation programs. Within this system is a specific model used for the financial evaluation of new community or area development programs.

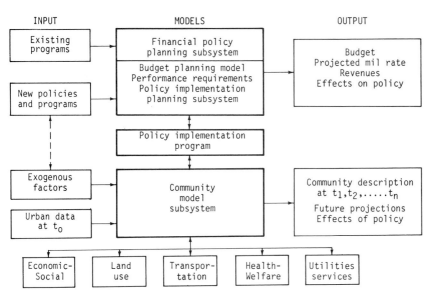

Fig. 1. The PROMUS system.

These two models are connected through a policy implementation program. In essence, the community development plan is first tested in terms of its initial financial viability (i.e., cash flow, basic return on invested capital, etc.). The community structure is then implemented through the community model (through the policy implementation program), and the actual community growth and change is then projected, considering both the internal demographic-economic structure and the exogenous factors which may affect the community. This system, in conjunction with other elements of the financial planning model, will then evaluate and project the effects of the internal development plan of the community on housing mix, community services and government, social factors (which can be quantitatively measured), etc. Thus, the PROMUS system provides the basic capability to evaluate the viability of the community plan, as well as the economic, demographic, social and industrial impact which will result from this plan.

The urban management systems subgroup discussed the state of the art as outlined above and reviewed the design of the PROMUS system during the workshop. In general it was agreed that a variety of models and techniques currently exist which could improve the planning and management of urban areas. The major area of focus should now be placed on application and implementation.

3. Urban transportation

3.1. Introduction

The urban planning workshop set out to identify and assess how OR methods have helped or can help to improve urban planning. A great deal of OR work has already been done on urban transportation problems yet the true contributions of this work and the present state of the art are difficult to determine.

Urban transportation can be thought of as the study, synthesis and control of individual and mass transportation systems in an urban area. Given this definition, it is immediately evident that the field is very broad. Much has been written about urban transportation. Unfortunately, more emphasis has been placed on describing the symptoms and/or prescribing "home remedies" than has been spent on analyzing healthy systems or isolating the causes of the various problems. Perhaps it is of value to consider three commonly mentioned symptoms.

(1) *Congestion*; It does not take OR to demonstrate that most urban areas suffer from vehicular traffic congestion. Large resources have been expended on developing modern streets and highways. Much valuable urban property is being devoted to accommodating vehicular traffic and parking; yet, there is as much congestion as ever.

(2) *Decline of mass transportation*; This symptom seems to go hand in hand with congestion in urban areas. Not only are the cities caught in an ever-expanding spiral of vehicular transportation, but in many areas this is accompanied by a corresponding decline in mass transit. Mass transportation customers are few, costs are inequitably distributed, service is curtailed and customers become fewer.

(3) *Imbalanced travel modes*; This symptom is demonstrated by the fact that on a 400-mile business trip, an executive can spend three hours traveling 60 miles on congested highways and waiting at the airport, but spend only one hour on the inter-city airplane trip.

Admittedly, the above is an extremely simplified presentation of the urban transportation problem. For the purposes intended here, it suffices to say that perhaps the operations researcher has a role to play in defining the urban transportation problem as well as affecting solutions to the many facets of that problem.

3.2. The role of the operations researcher

Some rather extensive work done by the Transportation Science Section of the Operations Research Society of America is relevant to a discussion of the role of OR. In November of 1969, a special meeting of 27 leading transportation scientists and engineers was held in Miami, Florida, to discuss the overall problem in transportation. A number of participants felt that OR work in urban transportation, as reflected in the literature, (1) has not shown the true capabilities of the professionals in the field, (2) has not satisfactorily treated the problems of potential clients, and (3) would improve considerably if there were more interaction of a substantive nature among OR professionals. And while OR professionals have a role in urban transportation, there certainly is much that can be done to improve their effectiveness.

There seems to be little question of potentials of OR in the urban transportation field. The literature exhibits classic papers that range from basic advances in car-following theory through treatments of new exotic urban transportation systems. Yet, there are few papers documenting the solution of a significant urban transportation problem. Each urban area is different, presenting unique problems in private and public transportation. There are no standard solutions but success seems to be imbedded in the ability to put all the pieces together using standard techniques and then following through with the implementation process. Often OR results have not been put into practice to the degree that they should, perhaps due to the diverse nature of the urban problem, the decision structure under which it thrives, and the environment of the practicing OR professional.

Operations researchers themselves are motivated from different points of view, resulting in a significant division of available talents. A large body of talent exists in the college and university community. On the other hand, many of our colleagues work for public agencies directly involved with urban transportation decisions. This latter group is subject to political and administrative constraints that are not easily understood by OR professionals in other environments. A third body of professionals make their living in private enterprise and again, quite different constraints (e.g., profit motive) are in effect. There is significant need to encourage these groups to communicate and come closer together if the contributions of OR to urban planning are to improve.

3.3. Some important topics in urban transportation

A complete evaluation of the state of the art of OR methods in urban transportation was beyond the scope of the urban planning workshop. However, some important topics in urban transportation research were discussed. The topics originated from those suggested as a result of the first ORSA/TSS urban transportation workshop conducted during 1971 [10]. That effort indicated that the following seven areas are extremely important. Improved OR methods are needed for:

(1) predicting demand for new urban transportation systems,

(2) measuring the value of transportation,

(3) developing urban transportation systems configurations,

(4) evaluating the impact of transportation systems within the total urban environment,

(5) evaluating systems for urban goods movement,

(6) analyzing public transportation financing problems, and

(7) evaluating constraints on urban transportation systems.

Of course, there has been substantive work in many of these areas. It is important to point out that previous approaches have been, in most cases, too narrow. A much broader approach (i.e., consideration of economics, land use, community values and community impacts) rather than the narrow approach (i.e., traffic engineering, equipment analysis and subsystem analysis) is required. It also seems that much of the research on urban transportation should be oriented more towards total systems and externalities rather than subsystem or system element problems.

While the OR professional is in a position to attack these problems, it is very clear that in the urban environment he must rely heavily on others in the fields of social science, engineering science, political science, environmental science, economics, and law.

The highlights of the workshop discussion as it related to transportation directly or indirectly are summarized below. These highlights along with the state of the art discussions presented, represent the product of the transportation section of the workshop.

Validation of transportation models. The testing of urban transportation models for their degree of validity is an essential current research need. Little effort has been expended in this area. Even when significant differences between model predictions and actual results are uncovered, simple linear terms are modified or constraints added without serious consideration as to whether the basic form of the model is wrong.

Marginal Impacts. The workshop treated the question of whether changes in urban transportation systems could have major versus marginal effects on the urban area being considered. It seems that often the planner is analyzing the system in the view of dramatic changes when in fact the implementer sees only marginal improvements. Experience to date indicates that the OR professional should look at the problem of analyzing marginal improvements to existing urban transportation systems. An examination of the impact of changing this point of view may be a research topic suitable for presentation and discussion at a future IFORS meeting.

Movement towards people-oriented decisions. Decision makers in the urban environment are beginning to lean strongly toward people-oriented decisions in transportation and urban services. The need for the OR professional to seek help from the social scientists, psychologists, architects, town planners etc. is great. Future attempts of IFORS to promote interaction and communication among these groups is needed.

4. Urban services

There have been numerous applications of OR techniques for the improvement of urban services. From the successes, and failures, of their studies we can draw the following conclusions.

(1) Problems of urban services do involve and must involve a concerned customer who might benefit from the results of OR analysis. Under no circumstances should this work be done in a vacuum, because it often ends up being unrealistic and unused.

(2) Work on urban problems should not be undertaken by dilettantes willing to invest a few afternoons in order to solve the world's problems. The world is just not hungry for OR specialists who can miraculously obtain easy solutions to difficult problems. A great investment of time and effort is needed before an OR analyst can begin to make a real contribution.

(3) The objective function associated with a given service is not generally clear, and is up to the OR analyst to define. Political considerations, often unmentioned but almost always present, tend to make the objective function difficult to define.

(4) Sometimes it is not sufficient to find a solution and give it to the customer. As the New York City Rand Institute people found, it is most often necessary to work with the customer in order to sell the solution to those who control the funds necessary for implementation.

(5) It is wise to question the statement of the problem given by a customer. Sometimes it pays to look for a different approach to a problem, rather than work on marginal improvements of a bad solution.

Among the problems addressed by OR techniques are the following:
fire-fighting,
housing,

ambulance service,
garbage collection,
school bus scheduling,
districting (e.g. for elections), and
police deployment.
In terms of techniques used, these problems may be sub-divided into four categories. The workshop addressed these categories, and the challenges concerning their proper use.

4.1. Vehicle scheduling problems

These include the school bus scheduling and the garbage collection problem. Typically, we are given N locations at which garbage, or students, must be picked up by vehicles starting at one location (garage) and ending at another (school or dump). The pickup must be done as economically as possible, and satisfy some constraints peculiar to the problem. (For example, students must not be kept on a bus for an excessive amount of time.)

The most successful attacks on these problems have been made through applications of extensions of the Clarke and Wright algorithm [11] for scheduling a fleet of delivery vehicles. Typically, the benefit from such solutions is not in obtaining better than the manual schedules, but in lowering the time required in preparing these schedules, through the use of computers, and hence making easy the adaptation of schedules to changing needs.

The challenges in the area are: (1) development of better, cheaper algorithms, (2) better handling of constraints, perhaps through the use of different objective functions, and (3) consideration of systems larger than the vehicle scheduling system, in order to investigate trade-offs obtained by changing some of the ground rules (e.g., changing school starting times in the school bus scheduling problem, to allow better utilization of buses for the transportation of students of elementary, middle and high schools).

4.2. Problems handled by simulation

These include the ambulance service, fire-fighting, and police deployment problems. Typically, a simulation program is prepared which simulates the occurrence of "incidents" over an urban area. The program is (hopefully) validated, and then used to investigate the effect of making changes in the system of providing an urban service. This method was used, for example, to test algorithms for dispatching and redeployment of fire-fighting units in New York City; for deciding on the question of stationing ambulances partly at the hospital and partly at a satellite garage; and for redeploying police forces.

The challenges in this area are: (1) to provide a general enough simulation model for a given service, which can be transferred from one city to another with minimum need for "customizing", and (2) to guarantee that the simulation models can be validated against data that can be collected.

4.3. Facility location problems

The distribution of voting machines over an urban area in order to provide good source to voters is one example of such a problem. Others are the location of a new school, hospital or police station, which, however, are frequently dominated by political considerations rather than merely efficiency considerations.

There is a well developed theory for handling facility location problems in a network so as to minimize the total weighted distance from each mode. Another approach views an urban area as a two-dimensional continuum with non-Euclidean, "Manhattan" distances and yields a methodology for determining boundaries of regions allocated to different facilities which minimize weighted distance of all users of the facilities.

The challenge in this area is to provide a methodology which can consider an objective function other than just the weighted distance, a problem which can now be handled largely by simulation.

4.4. Special advisory computer programs

The decision process, be it at the level of municipal government, other governmental authorities, or entrepreneurs working in an urban environment, can be helped substantially by the availability of advisory computer programs which provide an easy analysis of the effects of alternative courses of action on financial matters. An example is the problem of housing construction by private developers aided by government subsidies. Computer programs are currently available (see for example [12]) which can give the effect of changing costs, policies, and other quantifiable factors on the financial life of a housing project.

The lessons from the use of such programs appear to be the following:

(1) Interactive – Computer programs work best because they provide an analytical tool for a planner or developer without presuming to take over their decision responsibility. Questionable modeling assumptions of human behavior need not be introduced into the computer programs, since the human remains in the decision loop.

(2) It is very helpful to provide a computer program which can be used by persons who are not trained programmers. This can be done by providing a set of command instructions which activate the proper parts of the program, and allow inputting of important parameters in an easy, conversational mode.

(3) Transferability of programs from one location to another, and the creation of data bases of cost data are important considerations in the creation of advisory computer programs.

(4) OR in new town investment — A major discussion of town planning had to do with the problem of investment in services (e.g., fire-fighting, sewers, water treatment, etc.) was held during the workshop. A case study for a small town development in the Netherlands was discussed.* Projections of population trends in terms of changing household make up were analyzed using a linear programming model that related housing starts to demand for services. The objective function involves minimizing the over shoot of required services to minimize the cost of these services over time. This simple model was used to determine the number of housing starts allowed during the first year of development. Needs for sensitivity checks and re-evaluations after the first year were pointed out. Descriptions of these approaches and their effectiveness represents another area in which IFORS can promote information exchange and hopefully improve the state of the art in urban planning techniques.

5. Summary

The urban planning workshop differed from most of the others by having state of the art lectures. Our conclusion was that they are useful for opening a workshop discussion, but in our case more time was needed to develop questions which arose.

For urban policy models a great deal more work needs to be done to make them realistic and useful. New and better models are needed before they can be used.

Planning models currently are available to improve the planning and management of urban areas but they do not give the needed policy kinds of outputs, such as the quality of public health, the levels of crime, pollution, etc. However, when we look at planning models, it seems apparent that experience with those available is needed more than the development of new and better models.

* The discussion was led by Mrs. Diny E. Boas–Vedder, Town Planning Institute, Rotterdam.

In transportation planning, it is apparent that work to date has not yet shown the true potential of OR. For one thing there has been insufficient interaction among OR professionals, and there has continued to be a problem of determining who are the potential clients of operations researchers in urban transportation. In a substantive way, better methods are needed for predicting transportation demands, measuring the values of transportation services, developing system configurations, making impact studies, and dealing with goods movement and the financial problem of mass transit.

In urban problems, OR work must seek to involve a concerned customer in order to be effective. OR studies seeking improvement in urban services should not be undertaken by dilettantes willing to invest a few afternoons in order to solve the world's problems. The world and urban areas are not hungry for OR analysts who can miraculously obtain easy solutions to difficult problems.

References

[1] C. Eastman, N.J. Johnson and K. Dortanek, A new approach to an urban information process, Mgmt. Sci. 16 (1970) 3733.

[2] P.L. Szanton, Systems problems in the city, Opns. Res. 20, No. 3 (1972) 465.

[3] Kilbridge, O'Block and Teplitz, A conceptual framework for urban planning models, Mgmt. Sci. 15, No. 6 (1969).

[4] New communities, Decision Sci. Corp., Jenkintown, Pennsylvania State of the Art Rept. (1971).

[5] H.G. Schaller, Public expenditure decisions in the urban community (1963).

[6] R.M. Laska, Government of the people, for the people, by the computer, Computer Decisions (Jan. 1970).

[7] J.P. Crecine, A computer simulation model of municipal budgeting, Mgmt. Sci. 13, No. 11 (1967).

[8] L.P. Kadanoff, J.R. Voss and W.J. Bouknight, A city grows before your eyes, Computer Decisions (Dec. 1969).

[9] A review of the state of the art in community analysis, simulation and modelling, Decision Sci. Corp. Jenkintown, Pennsylvania.

[10] Urban transportation workshop, conducted by the Transportation Sci. Section of ORSA, Brown Donaldson Center, Maryland (August 1971).

[11] G. Clarke and J.W. Wright, Scheduling vehicles from a central depot to a number of delivery points, Opns. Res. 12 (1964).

[12] A computer model for the financial analysis of urban housing projects, Socio-Econ. Planning Sci. 5 (1971) 125–144.

M. Ross, ed., OR '72. North-Holland Publishing Company (1973)

61

GUIDING TECHNOLOGICAL DEVELOPMENT

Orientation du développement technologique

GEORGE W. MORGENTHALER

Martin Marietta Corp., New York, USA

1. Introduction and workshop objectives

Though a high level of technological development is the salient difference between the "have" and the "have-not" nations, it is apparent that this attainment is far from an unmixed blessing. It has also enabled mankind to wage or threaten wars of unbelievable devastation, to amass economic power that crushes individual and group freedoms, to create social mobility and change at rates disruptive to community values, and to damage or destroy the environment. These effects have been documented in many recent popular conceptualizations of the technocratic society, such as Alvin Toffler's *Future shock* [1] and *The year 2000* by Kahn and Wiener [2]. The basic question concerning technological development has been stated by environmentalist David Brower: "We urge that what man is capable of doing to the earth is not always what he ought to do". We must, it is obvious, learn to understand more completely and to manage better our technological development and its consequences. Our question in workshop III was: what can OR do to help?

Mounting concern for understanding and guiding technological development was evidenced by the participation of some 35 delegates of the IFORS Conference in workshop III. Our aims were to identify and characterize what is currently known about the modern (or institutionalized) R&D technology development process, and to examine how the OR method (with its emphasis on modeling and optimization) could assist in the decision-making that binds together and moves the R&D process.

2. Workshop III objectives

(1) To understand better the technology development process and its effect on participants and society;

(2) To formulate macro- and micro-problems of guiding technology development which must be solved if more effective technology development is to be achieved;

(3) To understand better the technology application and transfer process; and

(4) To identify existing or desired OR models to assist the effective guiding of technological development.

3. The technological development process

Large R&D laboratories have grown up primarily since World War II. In the earlier university tradition, they were often formed around one or more eminent scientists and had rather well understood goals, such as aeronautical development, atomic energy development, or improvement of telephone communications, in which areas specific projects were undertaken. Activities of industrial laboratories were focused quite sharply on creating new products and processes which would increase profits, initially without much concern about the environment or consumerism. By the early 1960's, most large governmental agencies and business firms had formed R&D groups and the United States (which, unavoidably, is the author's primary reference) was soon spending more than $20 billion/year or about 2.5% of GNP on R&D.

Naturally, with this investment, the R&D process and its management became the subjects of intensive study and analysis. The Sloan School of Management Science of the Massachusetts Institute of Technology (MIT) [3]; the Case Western Reserve University [4]; the United States Department of Commerce [5]; private research organizations such as the National Industrial Conference Board [6]; government agencies in the United States such as the Air Force, Army, Navy, and the National Aeronautics and Space Administration [7], the National Science Foundation [8]; and similar agencies in other nations, conducted and documented investigations on what happens in the R&D process and how to manage it.

A great deal has been learned about the R&D process, and two primary lessons are: the necessity for strong focus and establishment of goals, and the necessity for dogged follow-up through the various stages of product or process innovation. The popular image of eccentric researchers in white lab

Table 1
Distribution of cost and time in successful product innovation

Phase	% Cost [5]	Approximate time (years)
Determining the goals for R&D	1 (author estimate)	–
Research, advanced development, basic invention	5–10	2–3
Engineering and design of product	10–20	1–2
Tooling and manufacturing engineering (getting ready for manufacturing)	40–60	1
Manufacturing start-up expenses	5–15	1
Marketing start-up expenses	10–25	1
Total	100	6–8

coats following their fancies and creating new products in an environment free of constraints is a myth. The road to successful innovation is long, costly, demanding, and deliberate and the bulk of the time and money is spent *after* the pure research and conception phase, as is indicated in table 1.

A survey of recent OR literature shows that relatively few attempts have been made to model the kinds of management problems involved in the R&D process. Moreover, these efforts have focused on the selection of specific projects or on the evaluation of markets of proposed innovations, rather than on the more careful selection of the R&D goals or the better management of the later phases of the R&D process where, according to table 1, the larger expenditures occur. In general, management of R&D still proceeds without the use of formal OR tools. (This was borne out in a 1970 survey [9] by the author which also indicated, however, interest in some companies trying to apply such tools.) Some of the reasons for the lack of quantitative models are: little documented data and few case histories exist, one does not know for a long time the results of decisions in the R&D process, and the experience of R&D managers is rather specialized and limited to specific fields and a few laboratories. Transfer and generalization of learning is difficult.

4. Organization of workshop III

To maintain effective workshop communication with 35 participants and still investigate all aspects of the problem, four subgroups were formed, each with a captain and secretary and each devoting attention to a major area:

Subgroup A: Determining the goals for technological development; captain A. Christman (USA), secretary R. Jackson (Denmark).

Subgroup B: Managing the technological development process, given the goals; captain A. Butterworth (USA), secretary J. de Raad (Netherlands).

Subgroup C: The technology transfer and applications process, given the development; captain M. Robbins (USA), secretary P. van Wiechen (Netherlands).

Subgroup D: Human aspects of the technological development process; captain G. Morgenthaler (USA), secretary G. Traversa (Italy).

5. Determining the goals for technological development

As already mentioned, in the early years of most laboratories the goals were understood or relatively easy to identify. In industry the goal was to develop profitable products; in other non-university labs goals were usually mission-oriented, such as defense, space, health, or agricultural improvement. The success in achieving these goals is now legend, but other impacts of these new-found technologies and results (as man continues to press them onward) are proving to be dismayingly detrimental to society. The point is that man needs goals that include imaginative and thorough pre-consideration of the consequences of achievement, and he must develop means – laws, practices, training, education – to preclude certain consequences, to channel others, and in general, to ease the impact of technological changes on society.

Fig. 1 assumes the need to establish goals for technology but raises the question, whose goals? There is indeed a tripolar set of stimuli. First, the needs of increasing population and the business community that serves those needs provide what we may call a market-back goal. Second, the scientist or engineer naturally wants to set the goals for the research and development program. He is motivated by his specific technical interests, dominated by what he believes best in the general development of his technology field. Often he seems to feel that intermediate goals of application are wasteful because further development of theory would be in the better long-term interest of mankind. The third polar view, more and more finding a voice and wanting to be heard in the setting of the goals of science and technology, is that of concerned, or social minded, groups. This view is often negative. You have seen and heard, of course, advocacy that this or that kind of technical development be slowed or stopped completely because of some anticipated consequence to society. The defeat of the US SST program in the Congress is

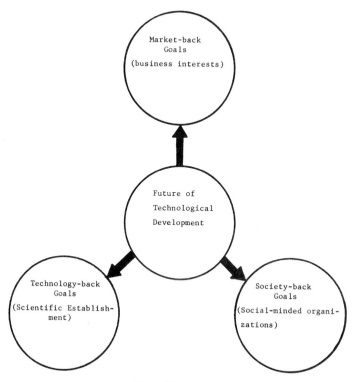

Fig. 1. Whose goals?

probably the most noteworthy example of success in establishing a society-back goal.

Certainly, in the usual situation, no one of these viewpoints or stimuli should prevail. Rather, the question is how to allocate a given amount of resource to the satisfaction of the three kinds of goals for most advantage and least disadvantage in the broadest sense, in a way that will best improve the "quality of life". This problem occupies two recent papers by eminent members of research and development management in the United States. The problem is analyzed, the results are viewed in terms of the impact on the present social and economic establishment in the United States, and a strategy is recommended for the future guidance of technological development in the USA. The first paper is by Herbert Hollomon and A.E. Harger, *The technological dilemma of the United States* [10], and the second is in two parts, also by Herbert Hollomon, called the *Technology in the United*

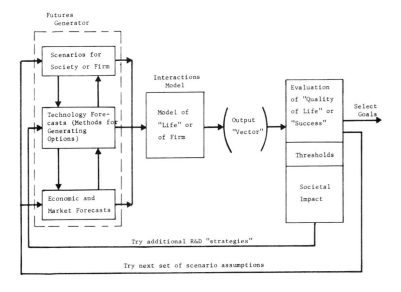

Fig. 2. R&D goal selection methodology.

States: the opinions before us [11]. The US government has also recently convened panels of advisors to consider the problem of better selection of national technology goals [12]. International recognition of this problem has also occurred and resulted in assessments by International Committees [13].

The workshop III group discussed this question and arrived at the schematic goal selection methodology portrayed in fig. 2. Fig. 2 does not itself portray a model, but is a sequence of activities which should lead to better R&D goal selection. The idea in fig. 2 is that the analyst (the R&D manager himself, or an OR analyst working with R&D management) looks at the flow of model activities and attempts to iterate through the flow loop until desired goals are attained. For example, suppose the question involved a major R&D effort to develop a new energy form that, if successful, would supply such needs in a society for the next several decades. On the left of the figure we see a "futures generator". Various scenarios would be developed for the society or agency trying to select the energy goals. They could include, in the case of a nation and a whole economy, for instance, periods of depression or recession, periods of economic abundance, wars, labor strife, etc. Then a technological forecast methodology could be used to assess when, where, and how one could expect the sought for energy technological development to occur. When would the energy approach first reach a pilot plant stage? What would be the cost per unit of power? Finally, economic and market forecasts would be made in each of the scenario situations, and consistent combinations of the three flowboxes on the left would provide alternative futures in which to analyze impacts of this energy technological development.

After the "futures generator" we enter the interaction model. Here a model of the firm (or the nation, or the world) is used to assess the consequences of the proposed technological development. An example of such a model is the "World dynamics model" evolved by the Club of Rome and Professor Forrester of MIT. Forrester's MIT group has been developing other urban models and world models to simulate such interactions.

When the interaction model has processed the inputs, an output would be determined in vector form. A vector output is required because the user (and society) is interested in a *number* of consequences, not a single scalar indicator. In the case of a world or regional model the output vector could include among its components the number of persons, food per person, degree of unemployment, number of housing units, amount of land available for recreation and life support, etc.

Finally, the output is viewed in a "quality of life" evaluation sub-routine or sub-model. Perhaps this is as simple as having persons experienced in the regional economy and having social, medical, artistic, and scientific training judge whether the output was suitable or desirable – a talk-through model, or it could be more formal, with thresholds or minimal values to be surpassed before the output vector is considered adequate. This model could also include specific societal or impact constraints.

In any case, evaluation of "quality of life" would in some sense be accomplished and, if found wanting, or if intuition is strong that other goals or other timetables for the technology would be more beneficial, we iterate by returning to the "futures generator". Certainly, one would return to try alternative scenarios, or different sets of R&D strategies. This analysis, perhaps performed many times, would indicate some output vectors to be more suitable than all others. Obviously, in this case the R&D strategies and goals that lead to these desirable consequences should become the recommended goals for the R&D program.

At this point, the workshop considered whether there indeed existed examples of the various sub-models portrayed in fig. 2. Some such models are listed in table 2.

In the first instance, the fact that meaningful scenarios can be written for society (or for a firm or a principal mission-oriented agency) has been demonstrated through the work of the Rand Corporation, the Hudson Institute, Stanford Research Institute, and other such organizations.

Table 2
Technical interaction models

	Models for studying process improvement	Models for studying product improvement	Models for evaluating "new" products	Models for assessing operations improvement
World, region, or nation level models		input–output economic models [14]		world dynamics [15], urban dynamics [16], world game [17]
Firm or agency level models	capital plant investment models (Allbach)	Weyerhauser model [18]	Weyerhauser model [18]	industrial dynamics [19], simulation

Technology forecasting techniques involve extremely subtle methodologies. Recent articles have identified a variety of such technology forecasting techniques and long range forecasting methodologies. For example, the United States Air Force held a symposium in 1969, followed by publication of *Approaches to long range forecasting* [20]. Other publications, such as the work of Professor Bright [21–23] provide a fairly extensive list of the techniques of technology forecasting including the Delphi method of soliciting informed judgments, trend extrapolation of past parameters giving rise to envelope curves, examining the future to determine needs and assuming that needs will be filled, etc. Another technique has been regression analysis, i.e., fitting of regression surfaces to independent and rather sporadic data in order to develop trend surfaces. Some large corporations, such as TRW [24], have used technology forecasting as an input to their long range planning.

It was remarked by various members of the workshop that other countries have engaged extensively in this type of activity. For example, in the Netherlands the Dutch Central Planning Bureau has developed a model, a 10 year plan, using the Delphi technique [25]. The German and Danish Governments were reported also to have employed such methods [26, 27]. A workshop member from Czechoslovakia said that that country's Economic Institute utilized technology forecasting and input/output models to establish the five year economic plans.

Articles have now appeared which evaluate the accuracy of technology forecasting (cf. Dalkey [28], Murray [29], and Martino [30]). Professor Roberts of MIT has compared various forecasting methods as to reliability and capability [31] and this whole topic continues to receive much attention and research. *Technology Forecasting – an International Journal* is a new journal serving as a communication medium in this field.

Fig. 2 also suggested the use of economic and market forecast models as part of the "futures generator". Many of the major schools of economics around the world maintain large digital computer forecast models which they regularly apply and continually improve. One such, for example, is the Wharton School model [32].

Market forecasting or market analysis and projection is different from an economic forecast model. It involves collection of inputs from sales personnel, and/or much interviewing of prospective customers and then exponential smoothing. This is difficult if not impossible in new technology areas as it involves asking persons how much they would use or pay for something they have never seen or had. Nevertheless, a number of models have been built for this purpose [33].

We turn now to the interaction model. This is used to evaluate the consistent combinations of scenarios, technology forecasts, and economic or market projections supplied by the "futures generator". We find that again, some work has been done (table 2). In workshop discussions it was found that the models were quite different in character depending on whether they pertained to interaction at the regional, national, or world level or whether they were interaction models at the level of the business firm or the mission-oriented agency. For example, models of the firm have been built that interacted market activity with production activity, with inventory levels, etc., to give a consistent view of the dynamic response of the firm to changing market conditions. An example is the well-known industrial dynamics model of Professor Forrester [19]. Other company-scale models have been built that estimate market share, evaluate product mix, analyze product-group trends, etc. [34–36].

For regional, national, and world levels, large models have also appeared. Many at the conference claimed that these models are premature and that they do more harm than good. Consensus was, however, that although these models are embryonic and should not be used for prediction nor relied on too firmly at this time, the concept of beginning to model these world-level activities in a feedback interaction model (such as that in fig. 2) is what is important and is what has been achieved. In time, the quality of the models will be improved as we gain experience. These models are found in refs. [15–17, 37]. Still another interaction model approach, more characteristic of the economist, is the input/output model [14].

To return to the output vector and its evaluation, the most important preference values for many persons are entirely qualitative and therefore extremely difficult to present in any valid quantitative manner. Two classes of "human goals" were identified, however, as directly related to "quality of life":

(1) goals of the human being with respect to the physical environment such as adequate food, water, space, housing, clean environment, etc., and

(2) goals of the human being with respect to his free spirit and his interfaces with other human beings as in minimizing group conflicts, job security, cultural stimulation, personal freedoms, etc.

Little is known about how to measure these factors, how people value them relatively, and how they will trade off some factors for others.

Establishing preference quantitatively is a basic stumbling block to any science of decision making, such as OR. Much research remains to be done in the analysis and understanding of utility theory, value theory, and preferential choice. Perhaps the best that can be done is the investigation of "if—then" cases. Mr. G. Traversa indicated that in Italy interesting human factors experiments in communication, in group dynamics, and in relationships within a plant work force are beginning. These may lend us insight into the evaluation of outputs (see section 8).

6. Managing technological development, given goals

Once the goals of technology have been established and the timing and resources identified, the next major task is to manage the technology development program efficiently to attain the goals within the constraints. The decision problems in the management of a complex R&D program that come to mind are:

(1) Project selection;

(2) Project operation after selection: stimulation of creativity, communication of ideas, resource allocation and budgeting, scheduling, make-or-buy for R&D, monitoring performance, the role of organization in successful project performance, lab verification, prototype testing, field trials, and project completion to patent, prototype, use, etc.

(3) Assessment (cost/benefit) analysis of projects.

In the above areas, a number of OR models have been developed to help characterize and structure the problems. However, as remarked earlier, little use is currently made of them. An international journal, *Research Management* [38], has now appeared aimed at fostering improved efficiency and high standards in managing industrial research. Books have also been written covering modern practice in all R&D management areas above, but again, the author knows of few successful formal quantitative methods that have been developed and are in use. (See Gerstenfeld [39].)

6.1. Project selection

In the entire R&D process this problem is one of the most amenable to expression as a formal optimization problem. The usual formulation is to maximize Z, the total "benefits" as follows:

$$Z_0 = \max_{\{\bar{x}\}} Z = \sum_{i=1}^{n} p_i b_i x_i,$$

where $x_i = 1$ or 0, according to whether the ith R&D project is funded or not; p_i is the probability of project success given funding; and b_i is the "benefit" if the ith project is successfully completed. Constraint inequations would involve limitations of budget, manpower, laboratory space, etc., as, for example,

$$\sum_{i=1}^{n} c_i x_i \leqslant C \text{ (budget)}, \sum_{i=1}^{n} m_i x_i \leqslant M \text{ (manpower)}, \sum_{i=1}^{n} s_i x_i \leqslant S \text{ (space)}.$$

Examples of this type of model are found in refs. [40,41].

Such a model is quite flexible in that it can respond to the desire that some minimum threshold of resources be allocated to keep expertise at a critical mass in certain R&D functional departments. This means merely one more constraint relationship. For example, for the Electrical Engineering Dept.,

$$\sum_{i=1}^{n} e_i x_i \geqslant E ,$$

where e_i is the number of electrical engineers required for the ith project, would guarantee that that department maintains a critical size of E.

The major difficulty that has been experienced with this model, however, is that the inputs required are virtually impossible to estimate with precision. Also, little data on probability of success and "benefits" have been kept. Other difficulties are:

(1) Not all companies can take the same R&D risks, nor sustain a particular R&D effort until success occurs;

(2) The model does not place a premium on early cash flows from completion of some projects that become available to help support others (although this might be included by another formulation as is done in investment models);

(3) The model does not recognize the differences from project to project as regards market readiness, manufacturing constraints, financing levels, impact on labor force, etc.

As a result of the foregoing, there has been little formal use of such models, although the viewpoint provided by the model is a good one. The workshop group concluded that IFORS should take steps to collect data on project success for use in such models, and should encourage publication of case histories in applying models. This would help. The September, 1972 issue of *Research Management* journal mentioned above contained just such a helpful case history paper, *Two successful experiments in project selection,* by W. Souder, P. Maher and A. Rubenstein. However, the OR modeler may not in the end have the detailed knowledge of the particular industry requisite to constructing a useful model unless he invests much personal time in acquiring such experience.

As a converse to project selection it was noted that one subject about which virtually nothing has been written is the optimal time to *terminate lagging R&D projects,* a very important problem. Approaches should be formulated using game theory or a gambling model in order to display the basic risk tradeoffs of stopping versus further investment.

6.2. Project operation

The aspects of optimal operation of R&D projects (once they have been selected for funding) have been the subject of numerous system studies and OR approaches. For example, Gerstenfeld [39] included a chapter on the proper climate for R&D *creativity.* Tom Allen and others at MIT have studied the *communication of ideas* within R&D labs and projects. They found that word-of-mouth transfer (people carriers) was a more effective mode for idea diffusion than formal data banks, information systems, or written reports.

Cost analysis, scheduling, budget allocation, and performance monitoring of R&D projects are areas in which PERT and other network modeling techniques *have* been rather widely applied. In the USA, for the most part, these methods have been introduced into R&D project management as government R&D contract management requirements. Examples of government sponsored development of such project management tools are the programs funded by the US Army Materiel Command at Case Western Reserve University [42, 43].

Apparently the role of organization structure in the success of R&D projects is a profound one. To achieve project success within schedule and cost requirements, many organizations have found it necessary to go to a pure project form or at least to a matrix form of organization.

In the project form, an interdisciplinary team is assembled under a strong leader who has full authority to "get the job done". Pure project activity, however, is often hard for the functional-discipline-oriented scientist to accept. He must operate away from his discipline-oriented home base and may be called upon for work that neither furthers his understanding of his field nor enhances his reputation among his peers.

In the matrix organizational structure, on the other hand, persons can retain their functional department homes but are likely to have responsibilities to more than one project. Concerning such multiple assignments, analyses have shown that busy persons assigned to several projects are more productive of innovative ideas than those assigned to only one project [44].

Simulation as a tool for studying the working of a laboratory has been tried at MIT, and is of some value in studying the inception, logistics, and close-out of projects. Such studies are reported in ref. [3].

This workshop concluded that formal models to assist quantitatively in tailoring R&D organizations to project need are not generally available, although some work has been done at MIT [39] and at Case [45]. OR workers ought to try to measure organizational dynamics in R&D. IFORS should encourage publication of case-history papers on this subject also. It should be particularly meaningful to study this problem in "rapid-change" industries such as Aerospace.

6.3. Assessment of project success, cost/benefit analysis

In recent years several after-the-fact analyses have been performed to trace the historic line of success in key technological developments. *Project Hindsight* [46] conducted by the US Government, which traced the key technology break-throughs involved in 20 weapon systems, was one of these. More of these studies would be useful for understanding and building valid models of the R&D process.

Some agencies and companies in the United States now require that proposed major R&D projects be subjected to a cost/benefit analysis to gauge whether projected benefits will be worth the cost. These studies also provide a basis for management decision to stop a project if intermediate milestone progress significantly lags anticipated results. Also, such analysis leads to the projection of costs and schedules for all phases of the project (conception,

lab-proof-of-principle, pilot plant, manufacturing tool-up, and market pene-
tration); it also enables all those involved (the R&D team, the R&D management, and the sponsors of the R&D) to be more realistic about technical rate
of progress, costs, and schedules. However well documented, it still comes as
a surprise to many that up to 90% of project cost occurs *after* the conceptual
or basic research phase, as was indicated in table 1. This is surely an area
where the broad OR systems approach can be helpful to R&D management.

7. The technology transfer and applications process, given the development

There are many difficulties, some little understood, in the transfer and
application of new technology. This is the most expensive and risky aspect of
the entire R&D process; ultimate market acceptance of a product or public
acceptance of a change is difficult to predict. For new products, market
analysis studies of demand can be terribly misleading, as witness the classic
market failure of Ford Company's Edsel motor car. It must also be remem-
bered that an R&D improvement in a manufacturing process is initially the
enemy of manufacturing management, for change usually means disruption
and operational trouble. Labor is also often against innovations for it may
mean a smaller work force or a change in work habits. It is not surprising,
therefore, that the mortality rate is high on application of R&D results.

The transfer and application process has several stages as listed in fig. 3.

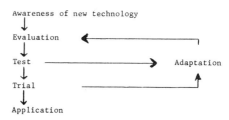

Fig. 3. Applications process for new technology.

Systems studies have shown (fig. 4) that acceptance of new products or ideas
can be accelerated by finding the opinion leaders in a given field and convincing them of its value. (Here is an opportunity for quantitative OR modeling.) Perhaps the use of simulation models would be effective in paving the
way for change. Models can help convince potential users of the value and
best use of the innovation. They may show labor, for example, that a change
in some cases may result in more employment, not less.

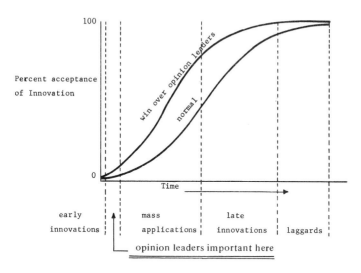

Fig. 4. Percent acceptance of innovation vs. time.

Thus far we have been talking about introducing new products or other innovation into established product lines of the firm or organization. What happens to unexpected or by-product R&D results, i.e., those innovations that fit neither the goals nor product lines of the sponsoring organization but nevertheless appear to have value in their own right? The rate of occurrence of these innovations has been studied in some detail by the author in [9].

Some companies have formed separate Departments of New Business Development for fruitfully disposing of these new ideas. General Electric Company has such an organization. It issues a subscription publication which advertises innovative ideas from GE and from the laboratories of other cooperating companies [47]. NASA established Regional Dissemination Centers at key points in the USA in order to make space age technological development available to industry [48]. Reference [9] also identifies several *modes* of exploiting by-product R&D results. These include sale, license, joint venture, acquiring a small subsidiary and injecting the new technology, and forming a new product line or subsidiary of the parent firm. Various OR models have been developed in [9, 49, 50] for analyzing these alternatives and for selecting one on the basis of risk, return on investment, and other such factors.

In the United States, the federal government has been very active in supporting the study of the technology transfer process. For example, in September 1969, the University of Denver under contract to the National Aeronautics and Space Administration (NASA) convened a conference of R&D management authorities to study environment and action in technology transfer [51]. The tenor of the conference was the frustration and difficulty of technology transfer. All was not going well; fundamental problems of transfer were not well understood.

Another University of Denver contract reported on technology transfer that has taken place from major, mission-oriented NASA R&D into the general consumer products field [52]. Specifically, NASA advancement of major developments in 12 fields (such as high temperature ceramics, high temperature metals, cryogenics, integrated circuits, etc.), was carefully traced through interviews, phone calls, literature searches and lab visits. The NASA contribution seemed to be broader, more complex, and more indirect than has been realized to date.

In a similar study, a team from NASA and the Departments of Defense and Transportation traced the effects of various R&D contributions to aviation progress [53]. The team found, for example, that the technical lineage of one of every four American-built jet airliners can be traced directly to innovations incorporated on a single military bomber model.

The USA National Science Foundation and the National Bureau of Standards are now entering experimental programs to determine the kinds of incentives to universities and industries that will accelerate the technology application process. There is a curious contradiction of national policies in this activity which influences the success of the technology transfer process. On the one hand, these incentive programs seek to accelerate technology transfer by providing various forms of cost-sharing of technological risk with industry. That is indeed encouraging to industry and can help the nation by stimulating technology and raising productivity. On the other hand, in an effort to be conscientious in the distribution of public funds, these same government incentive grants require that patent rights (even some background patent rights) in the field of endeavor revert to the government, thereby destroying the very incentive for any firm to apply its men and money to the risky technology development program in question. The dilemma is how to encourage technology development for the public good without giving undue advantage to a few private interests.

This entire matter of understanding (and, ultimately, predicting) technology transfers and successful application is a great challenge to OR modeling and is of great economic and social importance. In general, the area is little understood.

8. Human aspects of the technological development process

The human aspects of developing new technology are felt by two groups: those who make the innovation and those who must deal with it.

In the former group are the scientist, the engineer, the inventor, and the entrepreneur. It is important to note that these four types of R&D personnel are quite distinct as regards motives, work habits, fulfillment, and professional recognition. Generally, the engineer most easily fits into the industrial technology development milieu because his training and his career objectives have prepared him for the industrial system. With the scientist a real "identification" problem exists. Scientists have a difficult time orienting their careers to the industrial or mission-oriented goals of technology development. The problem is not, as many would claim, merely an ego problem. The roots lie deep in the basic concept of the growth of fundamental scientific fields as a sequence of "puzzles" to be solved vs. the technical development in applied fields as a series of (interdisciplinary) projects or "problems" to be solved.

Justin Wallace of Trinity College, Dublin, provided the workshop with fig. 5 as a portrayal of the dichotomy facing the scientist as he tries to leave the academic world and enter the world of application. Some of the problems pinpointed by this model of social interactions are:

(1) For the industrial organization:

How does one convert an academic scientist seeking peer group approval into an industrial scientist working to mangament objectives?

How can a scientist be helped to move outside "puzzle" definitions (usually arising within a single discipline) to "problem" definitions (crossing the boundaries of several disciplines)?

(2) For the community at large:

Assuming that "high fliers" approach industrial research via the Ph.D. route (academic research), how appropriate is this training?

Since puzzle definitions arise within scientific peer groups, and since a "puzzle" is usually not clearly formulated until the materials are available for its solution, how does one ensure that "problems" are not neglected?

Background reading in this fascinating area includes: for an introduction to the notion of science as puzzle solving see [54]; for a discussion of the mechanisms of social control in science (academic) see [55]; for a discussion of the interactions of scientists and organization in the industrial setting see [56].

The entrepreneur is little understood or abided in most organizations because he appears to be a nonconformist. He also causes the more traditional and structured employees a good deal of apparent trouble because they need

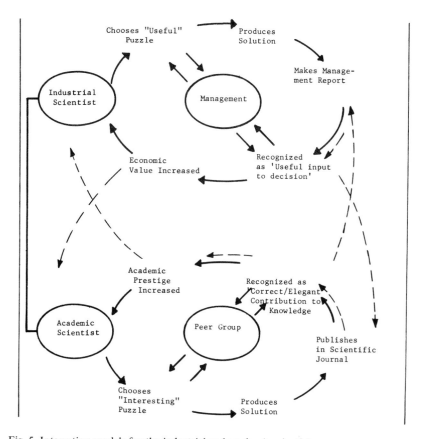

Fig. 5. Interaction models for the industrial and academic scientists.

Within each discipline exists a *pool of scientists*. Members are trained puzzle solvers with some basic training using the same concepts, techniques, apparatus etc.

Science "Universe" contains areas with a defined set of puzzles. In addition, contains unstructured areas of inquiry.

to cope with the procedural changes which his creativity sets into motion. Some studies have begun to shed light on this human relations aspect of R&D [57]. Professor Ed Roberts of MIT has written about "The care and feeding of entrepreneurs" and "What it takes to be an entrepreneur — and to hang on to one" [58].

A few deliberate case studies have begun to shed light on the character of the innovative entrepreneur. Project SAPPHO was a joint international project between Britain and the United States based upon case histories in the chemical and scientific instrumentation industries. In this particular study, fifty "pairs" of similar innovators were selected, each consisting of a "success" and a "failure". Some conclusions were:

Understanding – Successful innovators have a much better understanding of user needs. They may acquire this superiority in a variety of different ways. Some may collaborate closely with potential customers; others may do thorough market research or themselves have the necessary experience of user requirements. But, however acquired, this imaginative understanding is the "hallmark of success".

Marketing – Successful innovators pay much greater attention to marketing. Failures were sometimes characterized by neglect of market research, publicity, user education and customer problems.

Careful development – Successful innovators perform their development work more efficiently than failures, but not necessarily more quickly. They get the bugs out of the product or process before it is launched, not after the user complains. They usually employ a larger development team on the project and spend more money on it. This applies even when the successful firm is smaller than the failure.

Outside help – Successful innovators make more effective use of outside technology and scientific advice, even though they perform more of the work in-house. They have better contacts with the scientific community in the specific area concerned, although not necessarily in general.

Power structure – The responsible individuals in the successful attempts are usually more senior, and have greater authority than their counterparts who fail. In the instrument industry, they have more diverse experience, including experience abroad. The greater organizational power of the successful innovators enabled them to provide a properly scaled effort and to concentrate on the integration of R&D and marketing.

Turning now to the second group, namely, those whose lives are impacted by the technological development, we find: the manager who may fail while trying to incorporate the innovation into his business, the worker who may suffer job loss, and the general public who may suffer environmental deterioration or cultural impact due to the innovation. On the other hand, the new technology may bring great rewards to these same persons. How they feel about technology depends on whether they feel that their environment has been impersonalized and brutalized by its application.

Assuming that the physical wants of a human being are met, what makes him feel that his work is socially satisfying? Mr. Traversa of Italy suggested to the workshop that the technical complex must be designed so as to make the human being feel that he is a member of a social body. The system must

Table 3
Human interaction aspects of the technological development process

Effects	Group					
	Manager	Worker	Public	Scientiest/ engineer	Inventor	Entre- preneur
Information flow						
Training		Training simulation model				
Risk & sensitivity	Model of operation					Decision theory simulation
Technique of technology transfer						
Evaluation of conse- quences	Utility theory	Learning model				
Motivation and reward						
Technology, development, Environment						

allow and encourage reaction and stimulation between the person and the social body. The system must encourage: (1) communication exchange, (2) common goals among the group members, and (3) a critical responsible participation of each member in the group activities.

The experiments in Italy referred to earlier included studies of the human aspects of (1), (2) and (3) when a computer installation was made in a factory; the results of audio connections between private automobiles on the highways; and computerized teaching strategies where opninions were exchanged between students and teachers [59].

The interactions of the technology development process with individuals thus includes information flow, training, risk and sensitivity to the change, mechanisms for effecting the technology transfer, evaluation of consequences, motivations and rewards, and environmental impact. Table 3 portrays a matrix of these possible interactions or effects on all the persons involved in technological development or its consequences.

It is important to the improvement of the R&D process that we seek to identify and understand the phenomena in each row and column combination of table 3 and that we devise guidelines and policies for technological development to promote favorable human experiences in each case. Often this has not been true. For example, the starving inventor whose work benefits society after his death is not entirely a fiction. Moreover, technological developments that initially are successful always have by-product consequences, many unforeseen and undesirable, for the general public. Pollution from automobiles needs hardly be mentioned and it is interesting to note that when automobiles were first introduced they were thought to be a solution to the urban problem of too much manure on the streets due to the use of horses.

In a way project SAPPHO is an OR analysis of the results and mechanisms at work in those entries of table 3 having to do with successful technological development and the human characteristics of inventors and entrepreneurs. The challenge is unmistakable here for good, factual data-based OR, namely, fill in the rest of table 3.

9. Summary

(1) The overall importance of making *comprehensive* technology development decisions is increasing as increased populations place greater demands on resources. Correspondingly, the importance of having R&D goals in consonance with society's goals is increasing.

(2) The technology development process is not yet well understood and the first task is to perform studies based upon inquiries as to how the process works, using real data.

(3) Because of the complexity of the process, the lack of basic understanding of it, and the lack of input data, it is perhaps premature to try to model the process and to apply the models directly. At any rate, OR models are not being used now in this field, but rather, experienced and seasoned management makes its decisions and takes its risks.

(4) OR models can definitely be helpful in some of the project management areas of technology development provided the OR analyst immerses himself in the real details of the process. Whether it can be directly useful in the goal setting and human aspects is closely related to the ability to better understand human preference and value systems.

Acknowledgement

The author wishes to thank the Deputy Chairman Mr. A. Butterworth, the captains and secretaries of subgroups A, B, C and D, and the members of the workshop III for their splendid support and cooperation and for sharing their interesting ideas and experiences in the technology development process.

References

[1] A. Toffler, Future shock (Bantam Books, New York, 1970).
[2] H. Kahn and A.J. Wiener, The year 2000 (Macmillan, New York, 1967).
[3] Second annual research program on the management of science and technology 1965–1967, Sloan School of Mgmt. Sci., MIT, Cambridge (1967).
[4] B.V. Dean, New developments in industrial R and D management, Dept. Opns. Res., Case Western Reserve Univ., Cleveland, Tech. Mem. No. 34 (1956).
[5] Technological innovation: its environment and management, US Dept. of Commerce, Washington (1967).
[6] L. Laporte, R&D: its make-up, management, and measurement; managing the moderate sized company, Nat. Ind. Conf. Board, New York, Rept. No. 11 (1969).
[7] J. Milliken and E.J. Morrison, Aerospace management techniques, commercial and governmental applications, Univ. of Denver, Denver Res. Inst. (1971) (NASA contract).
[8] S. Myers and D.G. Marquis, Successful industrial innovations; A study of factors underlying innovation in selected firms, Nat. Sci. Found., Washington, NSF 69–17 (May 1969).
[9] G.W. Morgenthaler, Decision model and analysis of corporate utilization of by-product R&D; Thesis in Sloan School of Mgmt. Sci., MIT, Cambridge (1970); summarized in: Innovation 20 (1971).
[10] J.H. Hollomon and A.E. Harger, The technological dilemma of the United States, IEEE Spectrum (Oct. 1971) 55.
[11] J.H. Hollomon, Technology in the United States: the options before us, Center for Study of Policy Alternatives, School of Eng., MIT, Cambridge, Technol. Rev. (June and July/August 1972).
[12] Toward balanced growth: quantity versus quality; A report of the Natl. Goals Res. Staff (US Govt. Printing Office, Washington, 1970).
[13] Technological causes for change in the modern world, Intern. Federation of Automatic Control, and Yugoslavia Committee for ETAN, Dubrovnik (1971).
[14] Input/output economics; A compilation of 5 articles by the editors of Scientific American covering the period October 1951 to April 1966 (Freeman, San Francisco, 1966).
[15] J. Forrester, World dynamics (MIT Press, Cambridge, 1971).
[16] J. Forrester, Urban dynamics (MIT Press, Cambridge, 1969).
[17] B. Fuller, The world game, Study Group Southern Illinois Univ. Carbondale (1969).
[18] R. Felix, Weyerhauser ROI model; Internal company document, Manager Opns. Res. Group, Tacoma.

[19] J. Forrester, Industrial dynamics (MIT Press, Cambridge, 1961).

[20] Approaches to long range forecasting; A Symposium held at Alamogordo, New Mexico (April 1969) (US Govt. Printing Office, Washington, 1969).

[21] J.R. Bright, Technological forecasting for industry and government (Prentice–Hall, Englewood Cliffs, 1968).

[22] J.R. Bright, the following unpublished papers are presumably available upon request to the author: (1) An outline introduction to technology forecasting, (2) Some insights from the analysis of past forecasts, and (3) Technological forecasting by trend extrapolation (with R.C. Lenz, Jr.).

[23] J.R. Bright, Research development and technological innovation (Irwin Co., Homewood, 1964).

[24] H.Q. North and D.L. Pyke, "Probes" of the technological future, Harvard Business Rev. 47, No. 3 (1969) 68.

[25] Dutch Central Planning Bureau, 10 year plan using Delphi technique, among others.

[26] H. Bonus, Ph.D. Thesis on growth curves with parameters being functions of other variables, Univ. of Bonn (1969).

[27] Danish 15 year trend forecast for national development (1971).

[28] N.C. Dalkey, The Delphi method: an experimental study of group opinion, Rand Corp., Santa Monica, RM-5888-PR (1969).

[29] J.V. Murray, The development and test of a concept for long range forecasting, Doctoral Dissertation, Univ. of Colorado (1967); Univ. Microfilm 68–12, 318, Ann Arbor.

[30] J.P. Martino, An experiment with the Delphi procedure for long-range forecasting, IEEE Trans. on Eng. Mgmt. (Sept. 1968) 138.

[31] E.P. Roberts, Exploratory and normative technological forecasting: a critical appraisal, Technol. Forecasting – an Intern. J. 1, No. 2 (1969) 113.

[32] Wharton School economic forecasting model, Univ. of Pennsylvania, Philadelphia.

[33] C. Jones, Market Facts Inc., 100 So. Wacker Drive, Chicago, private communication.

[34] Investition und Liquidität, Wiesbaden, 1962.

[35] Das Optimale Investitionsbudget bei Unsicherheit, Zfb, August, 1967.

[36] H. Has, Investitionstheorie, Würzburg, 1972.

[37] D. Meadows et al., The limits to growth (Universe Books, New York, 1972).

[38] Research Management, a bi-monthly journal published by the Industrial Res. Inst., New York.

[39] A. Gerstenfeld, Effective management of research and development (Addison–Wesley, Reading, 1970).

[40] M.F. Shoeman, Resource allocation to related R&D activities, Dept. of Opns. Res., Case Western Reserve Univ., Cleveland, Tech. Mem. No. 109 (1968).

[41] B.D. Corwin, Multiple R&D project scheduling with limited resources, Dept. of Opns. Res., Case Western Reserve Univ., Cleveland, Tech. Mem. No. 122 (1968).

[42] W. Bahnsky, D. Friedel, M. Brown and M. Shoeman, R&D budget allocation for new product development, Dept. of Opns. Res., Case Western Reserve Univ., Cleveland, Tech. Mem. No. 110 (1968).

[43] B.V. Dean, S.J. Mantel, Jr., L.A. Roepcke, M. Green and J. Svestka, Research project cost distributions and budget forecasting, Dept. of Opns. Res., Case Western Reserve Univ., Cleveland, Tech. Mem. No. 107 (1968).

[44] D.C. Pelz and F.M. Andrews, Diversity in research, in: The R&D game, ed. D. Allison (MIT Press, Cambridge, 1969).

[45] B.V. Dean and L. Roepcke, Cost-effectiveness in R&D organizational resource allocation, Dept. of Opns. Res., Case Western Reserve Univ., Cleveland, Techn. Mem. No. 146 (1969).

[46] Project Hindsight, Office of the Director of Defense Res. and Eng., Science (1967) 1571.

[47] New business opportunities, Business Opportunities Service, General Electric Co., Schenectady.

[48] J. Geise, The role of regional dissemination centers in NASA's technology utilization program, Governmental Affairs Inst. for NASA, Washington, NASA CR-1763 (1971).

[49] T.E. Henry and S. Levine, Leasell program, a program for new product financial forecasting, Advanced Planning Dept., Bunker-Ramo Corp., Trumbull, Conn. (1970).

[50] I.J. Jaszlics, Improved decision-making techniques for new business ventures, New Product Development Business Analysis Report No. 1, Martin Marietta Corp., Denver (1971).

[51] The environment and the action in technology transfer 1970–1980; Conf. sponsored by Denver Res. Inst., Univ. of Denver, Denver (Sept. 1969).

[52] M.D. Robbins, J.A. Kelley and L. Elliott, Mission oriented R&D and the advancement of technology – the impact of NASA contributions, Vols. 1 and 2, Denver Res. Inst., Univ. of Denver, Denver (1972).

[53] R&D contributions to aviation progress (RADCAP); Executive summary, joint DOD–NASA–DOT study (1972), available from Nat. Tech. Inform. Serv.

[54] T.S. Kuhn, The structure of scientific revolution (Univ. of Chicago Press, Chicago, 1970).

[55] W.J. Mulkay, The social process of innovation (Macmillan, New York, 1972).

[56] S. Cotgrove and S. Box, Science, industry and society (Allan and Unwin, London, 1970).

[57] D. Allison, The R&D game – technical men, technical managers and research productivity, 2nd Ed. (MIT Press, Cambridge, 1969).

[58] E.P. Roberts, What it takes to be an entrepreneur – and to hang on to one, Innovation 7 (1970).

[59] G. Traversa, About a definition and a measure of social cost, Univ. of Aquila, Italy,

M. Ross, ed., OR '72. North-Holland Publishing Company (1973)

62

OPERATIONS RESEARCH, AGRICULTURAL RESEARCH AND AGRICULTURAL PRACTICE

*La recherche opérationnelle, la recherche agricole
et la pratique agricole*

J.B. DENT and R.A. PEARSE *
Department of Agriculture and Horticulture, University of Nottingham,
Nottingham, England

1. Introduction

The term "agricultural research" was given a broad interpretation by members of the workshop to include problems of the economics of the farm business and organisation of the agricultural sector as well as its traditional meaning in technical and scientific research. Whilst it is indisputable that most agricultural research funds are directed towards technical problems, it is within the field of agricultural economics that operations research techniques have been most widely applied. Although the two areas of research compete for funds they are not independent: farm business research relies on agricultural research for technical data – a major end product of technical research – and a reverse dependency is required so that new technology (the other major end product of technical research) may be properly assessed prior to its implementation. The end product of agricultural business research is the provision of a framework for improved decision making on individual farms. OR methods have also been applied to study locational problems within the agricultural sector to improve the overall performance of this branch of the economy.

The workshop decided to consider three main problem areas:

(1) planning problems on the individual farm,

* On leave from the Department of Agricultural Economics and Business Management, University of New England, N.S.W., Australia.

(2) regional planning problems in agriculture,
(3) planning problems in agricultural research.

2. Planning problems on the individual farm

2.1. OR and farm business research

Research in farm business planning has been concerned with the development of planning procedures which will incorporate the essential dynamic processes of the farm and the stochastic elements which make up the farm environment. These objectives have led to the study of how sophisticated OR techniques such as linear and non-linear programming, inventory theory, Markov chains, dynamic programming, utility theory and Bayesian statistics, game theory and simulation may be adapted for application within agriculture. To gain widespread field acceptance and practical application the OR techniques must be presented in such a manner that the cost of data collection, computation, interpretation and application are within the means of a business with an annual turnover measured in hundreds or thousands rather than in tens of thousands of pounds. The workshop identified three areas of decision process within the farm business particularly suited to the use of OR methods:

(1) Decisions relating to medium- and long-term investment opportunities;

(2) Decisions relating to the organisation of the farm, i.e., those decisions concerned with the deployment of major resources and the choice and combination of farm enterprises; and

(3) Decisions relating to the day-to-day operation of the farm business, for example, fodder conservation and livestock feeding related to seasonal factors, allocation of labour, timing of competing operations.

The workshop briefly examined the nature of the problem of applying OR methods to research in these three decision areas.

Investment planning is perhaps the most difficult decision area; the value of any investment clearly is dependent upon the changes in the economic climate, the rate of technological development during the life span of the new asset as well as the inherent variability of the yield of biological processes. Furthermore, the investment problem is one which frequently requires an integer solution from a whole range of mutually exclusive alternatives, for example two tractors or two or four bullocks. A technique which has come to be known as Monte Carlo programming has been developed by farm business research workers which takes account of the latter two requirements [1].

Although this technique can be operated in a quasi-dynamic mode [2] it has not yet been applied to stochastic situations nor has much advantage been taken of its non-linear properties which in theory could be easily adapted for this purpose.

The problem of organisation of the farm resources is the one that has received most attention from OR workers. A wide range of model types have been applied. Undoubtedly, the most generally applied model is linear programming which has been used to determine the static-deterministic optimum combination of enterprises relative to some criterion of profit. This approach has been adapted by McInerney [3] to a static-stochastic mode using a minimax criterion which, although an interesting OR development, is somewhat limiting conceptually and demanding on data. Rae [4], among others, developed a static stochastic linear programming routine but such models are very demanding of computer time and "memory" capacity. The dynamic-deterministic type of model has been represented by multi-period linear programming models in which several time periods are modelled simultaneously leading to a solution which, over the several periods involved, maximises some terminal criterion. This approach has been found particularly useful in examining changes in enterprise selection over time and can conveniently take such factors as tax payments into account [5]. Such models have usually been formulated over a period of years during which time circumstances change with the result that the deterministic mode can be somewhat restricting. Also for this type of model computer time can be excessive as convergence to an optimum solution can be slow if there are numerous activities with fairly similar objectives but dissimilar demands for capital or other limiting resources.

Since all agricultural production processes are intrinsically dynamic [6] and universally stochastic, models which adequately account for both these elements are desirable but involve the greatest modelling difficulties. Simulation has recently occupied a great deal of research thought in this respect and the range of problems that have been examined is large (see for example, refs. [7,8]). Most research of this type has been aimed at the organisation of a particular enterprise and by way of experimentation with a model has attempted to provide guide lines for improved policy decisions.

Operational decisions generally have not attracted as much research effort as those concerned with business organisation but in spite of this a number of major studies have been made. Bellman's [9] principal of optimally has been employed in problems mainly concerned with replacement. For example, phasing of wheat and fallow combinations in a crop rotation has been dealt with by Burt and Allison [10] and optimal replacement times for laying chickens have been examined by Low and Brookhouse [11]. Other recent work has been concerned with the operation of crop harvesting systems [12, 13]. The simulation models involved had as their objective the determination of bottlenecks in present machine complements under varying climatic conditions. Work study and CPA have also been applied to scheduling and phasing operations in intensive livestock buildings and glasshouses though little attention has yet been paid to crop phasing in more than mono-cropping conditions.

2.2. Practical farm management and OR methods

In spite of the considerable research effort that has been expended in applying OR methods to hypothetical agricultural problems, OR in fact has made little impact on the management of farm business. There are clearly special problems which inhibit widespread application of the kind of approaches that have been examined in research. First, the farm is a complex organisation involving biological as well as physical, sociological and economic factors. The biological factors associated with farming systems are unique to the industry and cause difficulties in both planning and control. Secondly, farming is traditionally a small scale business based on the family unit. The potential for improvement in profit for such a business is constrained not only by the important biological factors but also by strong social elements (the very survival of the family may depend on the year's outcome) and by the fact that this form of business structure cannot always gain ready access to credit. Further, farm managers have had, in general, less formal education than their counterparts in other industries. Also, it must be recognised, that in addition to their managerial function, farm managers form a large part of the agricultural labouring work force and such men cannot be expected to be well informed about the benefits of OR or even very sympathetic to the application of such theoretical models.

The workshop briefly reviewed those OR methods which have found their way into general agricultural practice and on a reasonably large scale. Such applications turned out to be extremely few in number. Linear programming has been widely applied in many countries to two distinct types of problem, first, to the selection of the least-cost combination of feed ingredients to meet certain nutrient constraints for livestock, and secondly, to the selection of optimum enterprise combinations relative to a profit criterion. Computer programmes developed for such applications are available in quite sophisticated packages. These normally give a number of alternative solutions and can be used in parametric form to study variations in both the level of resources and the range of prices. The packages with the greatest success are those with extensive report writing facilities and matrix generators, which greatly ease the problem of data collection, computation and interpretation of the results. In the United Kingdom this is exemplified by the MASCOT system [14].

Simple deterministic simulation models have been applied on a fairly wide scale particularly in the milk production enterprise. The models involved are of a very general nature but are made specific to each farm by accepting individual data for that farm at regular intervals. The models are used to forecast milk production for individual cows and to give a herd total on a monthly basis. Actual total milk yield for the month can be compared with that forecast and the possible causes of any deviation between the two can be explored. The basic concept is of a control model and although present application is relatively simple the approach is worthy of considerable development [15].

Although a number of other OR models have been applied to practical farm decision-making problems the workshop considered that they were not sufficiently extensively used to be included in this discussion.

2.3. Practical OR for the farm business

The workshop considered that there are two levels at which OR can be usefully applied in farm business planning:

(a) in relation to the whole farm business, and

(b) in relation to the individual enterprise.

Both levels have a common problem in that OR methods are relatively expensive in agriculture because it is necessary to deal with many and widely dispersed farms all with slightly different constraints on their business activity and different performance potentials. Management consultant time in this context becomes an expensive item. The workshop considered a new approach at each of the levels of application without considering these approaches to be either exclusive or universal.

Interest in whole farm planning in the past has centred on the selection of an optimal mix and level of activity from the enterprises generally feasible on a single farm. It was considered in the workshop that it would be desirable and effective to offer blueprint plans in this respect that could apply widely to all farms conforming to certain group characteristics. These plans, perhaps based on mathematical programming solutions, would refer to the typical farm in the group. It was considered that the situation on most farms is robust enough to permit this approach particularly as it is becoming clear that even on individually planned farms managers considerably adapted mathematical programming solutions before application, possibly because of inadequate representation of risk in most mathematical models. The problem that emerged was the difficulty of making an appropriate classification of farms into groups; indeed in the determination of acceptable classification criteria. Given more research into this particular problem the workshop considered the approach to have wide and general application in agriculture.

At the enterprise management level interest in the workshop centred on forms of agricultural production which are capital intensive, have high running costs and have complex biological and financial management features, e.g. broilers, pigs, lot fed cattle, milk, horticulture. A manager of such a unit, it was considered, would have two major requirements; first, to be able to determine with reasonable accuracy the impact of different policies, either of a tactical or development nature and secondly, to have ready access to a mechanism for both financial and biological control. Discussion centred on the concept of an entirely general simulation model to represent the basic logic of the enterprise structure. Such a model would form the basis of a computer system in which every farm in the scheme would be alloted on line computer memory space. The set up data for the individual farm would initially be provided in conjunction with a farm management consultant, but thereafter it would be updated at frequent intervals without such expensive aids [16]. At the end of each period each farmer in the scheme would receive a detailed forecast of business performance for the following twelve months and actual and forecast performance to date would be provided. An important element of such a scheme would be the incorporation of a diagnostic routine to indicate causes of any deviation between planned and actual performance. A valuable feature would be the possibility that a farmer have access to his own data file so that it is possible for him to "experiment" with his own unit either to examine the cost-benefit of correcting deviation from planned performance or to evaluate alternative development policies. The approach was considered to be again quite general to livestock units of different types and the workshop was informed that such a system was under active development for both pigs and milk cows in the United Kingdom.

3. Regional planning problems in agriculture

3.1. General statement of problems

The workshop recognised that specific regions had planning problems which were more complex than that of adjusting a commercial farm unit to the vagaries of changing prices and technology, although it was recognised that calamitous changes in either or both these factors could cause severe problems where a region was dependent upon the production of one commodity. However, of greatest moment were those regions characterised by a small farm problem, with a community which has a specific sub-culture which it was considered should not be destroyed but where small, and frequently fragmented, holdings are no longer viable given the changing values and economic structures of the twentieth century. Additional problems in creating a viable unit frequently include for example, an ageing population, ill-educated if not illiterate, with little national or regional economic growth, especially of local industry, to absorb those who might become displaced from the land. Whilst emphasis was laid upon the problems of Irish farmers in the Western counties it was recognised that similar problems existed in Europe, e.g., the highlands of Scotland and Wales, in Brittany and Southern Italy, and, though with varying degrees of emphasis on the given causal factors, in Africa, Asia and North and South America.

The nature of possible solutions was affected by the countries of origin of the disccusants. Those from a Western culture were prepared to consider the cost of subsidising subcultures and the debate was concerned with the political/economic problems of who should bear the costs of subsidies, whilst those from "under-developed" countries were striving for appropriate channels of distribution of inputs and outputs, to ensure a livelihood for the current population rather than assessing the structural problems which may be created for the next generation.

3.2. Specific adjustment problems

Members of the workshop outlined in detail adjustment problems in Australia, India and Ireland. In the Australian economy adjustment has become a major concern due to fluctuations in prices and demand for commodities such as wool, wheat and dairy products. Previously there had been a small hardcore adjustment problem associated with such factors as small farms, old age, infirmities, etc. Whilst there is a prosperous national economy, which offers employment prospects for those who wish to leave the land, farms have to be sold at depressed prices which might yield insufficient returns to buy an urban home after meeting debt obligations; it is, of course, necessary to leave the rural area to obtain alternative employment; farmers' skills, temperament and training suit them to little alternative employment, and they face a major fall in the social scale. Further the drift from the land, together with reduced farm incomes, creates small town business failures, which exacerbate the problem of 70 per cent of the Australian population being concentrated in six conurbations on the Australian coast line. Thus regional adjustment for agriculture includes the economic problems of decentralisation of industry as well as those of assisting the adjustment to farmers whose holdings, at current world prices for their commodities, are not economically viable.

The Western Irish regional problem is of long standing [17]. It has been complicated by problems of land ownership (which can create difficulties in obtaining security for loans), by the fact that farmers are frequently in their forties and fifties before they gain possession of the farm and can afford to marry and raise a family, (which creates extension problems as these people are fixed in their ways, as well as frequently possessing little formal education) by small farm size and fragmented holdings, by the fact that young, energetic and well educated youth leave the land and migrate because they see little future in waiting until middle age before they gain economic independence, by the high proportion (over 50 per cent) of the labour force in agriculture and by inadequate credit facilities. The combination of all these factors produce a low morale which further aggravates the situation. There is rarely alternative local employment available, partly due to lack of growth in the economy as a whole, partly due to the poor distribution of non-rural employment which is itself related to the departure of the energetic and well-educated young. Thus an attack on the problem again includes the need to consider the whole structure of the economy, to consider the change in social fabric as the proportion of the work force engaged in agriculture falls, and to accept that many farmers' sons will need to seek alternative employment as farm size grows and reduces the possibility of ownership. Modern farming methods and the consolidation of fragmented holdings will reduce the total demand for farm labour.

The Indian problem specified was that of how to organise the resettlement of a region in Bengal where water storage in dams is not practical but both ground and river water are available. The population of the region is five million. Farm size has been fixed at 18.5 acres to ration land to the "landless", but farm systems, allocation and distribution of seeds, water, fertiliser and insecticides have all to be determined, and infrastructures of transport and distribution to be created.

3.3. Applications of OR techniques in regional development

The workshop considered that in terms of existing knowledge the Bengal problem was most amenable to the application of OR techniques. In fact it seemed that existing techniques, such as dynamic programming (water allocation), transportation (decision on location of distribution points), and linear programming (allocation of scarce resource inputs and farm systems) could be applied directly to the problem. It was recognised that there would be difficulty in harmonising the results of the programmes — not simply because the output of one would form the input of another, but because of the interdependency of the programmes. Certainly, such techniques have been applied in other areas of India by such agencies as AID and FAO. Further, given that the political will to solve the problem and make decisions exists, progress would be far more probable than in a situation where perhaps the major output of an OR programme might be to provide impetus for political decisions to be made. An excellent example of regional development involving industry and agriculture and with political support is that of the Tennessee Valley Authority in the USA.

The workshop considered that one of the major problems in applying OR in regional planning was that rarely is there a clear and explicit objective. Words such as "decentralisation" sound well on the politician's tongue but may become very difficult to quantify when the issues have to be specified for a decision. Thus, if the Western Region of Ireland was to become a viable and productive community — itself a political question — then older farmers must be persuaded to retire, fragmented holdings must be aggregated and enlarged, possibly farm financing problems eased by the development of a landlord/tenant rather than an owner/occupier system; and transfer of ownership of holdings must occur at an earlier age. However, these are social, as much or more than economic questions and the influence which would cause the desired social action are as yet unquantified and not even fully understood. An attempt to formulate an OR plan of action foundered amongst these imponderables. Nevertheless, the workshop agreed that a model could be developed which would give a valuable analysis of the economic and social costs and benefits which might arise from alternative political decisions and actions.

4. Planning agricultural research programmes *

4.1. The background and structure of research in agriculture

The workshop recognised that in many countries the organisational structure of the technical agricultural research has been established relative to the farm gate being the end-point of production activity. Today this is no longer realistic for the whole chain of farm organisation, food marketing and food consumption is becoming totally integrated. The problems of agriculture, it was felt, must be recognised as those of a complex of industries servicing agriculture on both input and output sides. They include also the problems of a way of life not only for individuals but for peoples.

A peculiar characteristic of agricultural research is that it is largely financed from government funds, possibly supplemented by commodity levies. Publicly supported research and development can only be justified if it is assumed that private sources would develop research in a less socially desirable manner or would carry out less research than is socially desirable. Government participation implies that in many countries the social returns from research generally exceed the private returns to people who might finance it. If Government is to play an intelligent part in guiding the agricultural research effort (i.e., if centralised control is to be accepted) it is essential to be able to *measure* marginal social returns to alternative research proposals. The workshop considered measurement to be a key element and that if it was possible to measure adequately the value of research cost/benefit analysis would lead to optimum allocation of funds. The calculations would be extensive but then the kind of approach offered by Pasternak and Passy [18] in this conference may well be applicable. Any method developed along these lines would, however, need to take into account the severe infrastructural constraints involved; the high capital investment in buildings, equipment and personnel, all of which are purpose-built, specially-designed or specialist-trained as the case may be. Given this situation any direction of research effort in a broad sense can be nothing but sluggish.

4.2. Decision making areas

The workshop suggested five general levels at which direction of research

---

* This section of the workshop's deliberations was greatly aided by an incisive introductory paper by Dr. P. Ryan, Deputy Director, An Foras Taluntais and the report here reflects his contribution.

by allocation of funds can take place; five levels which, in fact, form a hierarchy of decisions:

(1) allocation of total funds to different sectors of the economy (i.e., into agriculture, health, education, etc.),

(2) allocation within sectors to major areas (i.e., within-agriculture into research and development, extension, veterinary control, etc.),

(3) allocation of research and development funds to specific fields or programmes, often at the commodity level (i.e., to meat, milk, cereal, etc. research). This will usually determine the allocation of funds to different institutions and research organisations,

(4) allocation of funds to different programme areas by individual institutions,

(5) allocation of funds on a project or activity basis.

Clearly, in this hierarchy, if evaluation at the national level is inadequate, procedures all down the line will be sub-optimal. Evaluation decisions at the national level should depend as little as possible on subjective judgement and political pressures. It was suggested that the allocation of funds to research in a particular sector should be related to the importance of the particular activity and its economic and social goals.

As far down as level 4 in the hierarchy the workshop had difficulty to decide on relevant precise criteria by which to judge alternative strategies and found problems in conceptualising adequate models. What is needed are models that can indicate the impact of alternative research direction policies relative to the technical excellence of the industry, the well-being of the rural population, the economic development of the agricultural sector and the general national policies. We suspect that present research and development policies in agriculture are biased towards the already larger and more efficient units enabling them to become even further ahead of the average farmer. A greater research effort directed at the average farmer could well have a greater social and economic pay-off [19]. This research would not only be technical in nature but also be involved with the problems of dissemination of knowledge and therefore also be sociological in character.

At the institute level, Pasternak and Passy [18] have indicated a possible OR approach to the selection of alternative projects but the type of criteria involved are possibly restrictive. Other institutes still operate on an intuitive basis in the evaluation of projects often, as at An Foras Taluntais, guided by a formal set of procedures that take into account several criteria of assessment (technological content, scientific merit, social and economic implications, and personal satisfaction of the individual research worker).

The workshop considered that the most immediate application of OR could be at the point where decisions about allocation of funds to projects had to be made because of the clearer criteria that can be stated in assessing the value of alternative proposals. Simulation models of farm systems could be developed with existing biological and physical data [8]. The model could be then used to rank areas of lack of knowledge by sensitivity analysis relative to the profit of the system rather in the way suggested by Naylor [20] at this conference. It was agreed that cost/benefit analysis for research in these areas of ignorance would be complex but not impossible. Benefits accruing to research are of course most difficult to assess in agriculture for it is necessary to determine the expected uptake of any new method or information on the many farms to which it is relevant as well as estimating the likely increase in revenue.

References

[1] S. Thompson, An approach to Monte Carlo programming, Dept. of Agriculture, Univ. of Reading, Study No. 3 (1967).

[2] J.B. Dent and P.F. Byrne, Investment planning by Monte Carlo simulation, Rev. Marketing Agr. Econ. 37 (1969) 104.

[3] J.P. McInerney, Linear programming and game theory models: some extensions, J. Agr. Econ. 20, No. 2 (1969) 269.

[4] A.N. Rae, An empirical application and evaluation of discrete stochastic programming in farm management, Am. J. Agr. Econ. 53 (1971) 625.

[5] R.A. Pearse, Capital taxation and farm development, Univ. of New England, Armindale, Farm Mgmt. Bull. No. 2 (1969).

[6] J.L. Dillon, Analysis of response in crop and livestock production (Pergamon, London, 1968).

[7] J.B. Dent and J.R. Anderson, Systems analysis in agriculture (Wiley, New York, 1971).

[8] G.W. Jones, The use of models in agricultural and biological research, Grassland Res. Inst., Hurley (1969).

[9] R. Bellman, Dynamic programming (Princeton Univ. Press, Princeton, 1957).

[10] O.R. Burt and J.R. Allison, Farm management decisions with dynamic programming, J. Farm Econ. 45 (1963) 121.

[11] E.M. Low and J.K. Brookhouse, Dynamic programming and the selection of replacement policies in commercial egg production, J. Agr. Econ. 18, No. 3 (1965) 339.

[12] G.E. Dalton, Simulation models for the specification of farm investment plans, J. Agr. Econ. 22, No. 2 (1971) 131.

[13] J.H. van Kampen, Farm machinery selection and weather uncertainty, in: Systems analysis in agricultural adjustment, eds. J.B. Dent and J.R. Anderson (Wiley, New York, 1971).

[14] R. Bond, P.G. Carter and J.F. Crozier, Computerised farm planning: MASCOT, Farm Mgmt. 1, No. 9 (1970) 17.

[15] R.A. Pearse and P.R. Street, Developments in business planning and control technique, J. Agr. Econ., in press.

[16] M.J. Blackie and J.B. Dent, Budgetary control: review and reconstruction, Farm Mgmt., in press.

[17] J.J. Scully, Agricultural adjustment in Ireland, in: Irish agriculture in a changing world, eds. I.F. Baillie and S.J. Sheehy (Oliver and Boyd, Edinburgh, 1971).

[18] H. Pasternak and U. Passy, Annual activity planning with bicriterion functions, in: Proc. 6th Intern. Conf. on Operational Research, ed. M. Ross (North-Holland, Amsterdam, 1973).

[19] J.L. Dillon, Agricultural education research and extension, School of Agriculture, Univ. of Nottingham, Fourteenth Heath Memorial Lecture (1971).

[20] T.H. Naylor, Simulation and validation, in: Proc. 6th Intern. Conf. on Operational Research, ed. M. Ross (North-Holland, Amsterdam, 1973).

M. Ross, ed., OR '72. North-Holland Publishing Company (1973)

63

HEALTH AND WELFARE SYSTEMS *

Systèmes de securité sociale

RACHEL ROSSER

Maudsley Hospital, London, England

and

VINCENT WATTS

Arthur Andersen & Co., London, England

1. Introduction

This workshop was attended by 30 participants from 11 countries of whom about 20 participants from 9 countries attended the majority of the sessions. The workshop started by defining the subjects for discussion since it had not proved possible to contact the participants before we assembled in Dublin. Before this first session the chairman's opening statement had suggested that the themes for discussion might include:

(1) population policy and the health service,

(2) measurement of the benefits achieved by health and welfare services,

(3) planning services for a region,

(4) recent national developments in the institutional framework and their consequences for health and welfare OR, and

(5) specific applications with particular emphasis on implementation.

The workshop fairly quickly defined its interest in the measurement of both benefits and efficiency. This was also the common thread running through the six papers presented by participants at the workshop which are

---

* This paper reports the main content of the discussions. Comments on the value of the workshop as part of the IFORS conference and suggestions for improving its productivity have been made separately to the organisers of the conference. Those comments were summarised from an evaluation form designed specifically for the workshop.

described in section 3. Accordingly the majority of seminars were devoted to this theme which also forms the main subject of this report. In addition one seminar was used to discuss recent national developments. *

2. The measurement of benefits and effectiveness in the health and welfare services

The discussion of the six studies, presented by participants, focussed upon a few major areas which are fundamental to OR methodology but which present peculiar difficulties when applied to the health and welfare area.

2.1. Definition of goals and boundaries

The six studies showed that a very careful choice can overcome the well-known difficulties of obtaining a clear statement of goals and boundaries of systems in the health and welfare services. The limited scope permitted useful analysis to be performed but introduced the attendant dangers of sub-optimisation.

2.2. The definition of operational objectives

Next the goals must be translated into a set of operational objectives which permit progress towards them to be quantified. Although all studies were able to develop satisfactory objectives, interestingly enough, none of them developed the same set of operational objectives and only infrequently were similar operational objectives used. This suggests that measures of perform-ance in the health and welfare services are at present most productively developed within a particular context. Perhaps, when a greater number of successful studies have been completed, the operational objectives developed from each study may be seen within a common theoretical framework. How-ever, such a framework did not emerge from our discussion.

The definition of operational objectives brings up two major questions; firstly, how to value the achievements of different operational objectives and

---

* Workshop seminars were not held at the time of the presentation of the papers by F. Fagnani and B. Lenehan on their work in ambulance services in France and Ireland, respectively, nor at the time of the paper by G. Torrance on the cost-effectiveness studies he had performed in Canada. The majority of workshop participants attended these presentations and hence these papers also formed part of the material discussed.

secondly, how to estimate the effectiveness of different programmes in achieving these objectives.

2.3. The valuation of the achievement of operational objectives

Interestingly, all studies found it totally unacceptable to their clients to express the achievement of health service objectives in monetary terms. Instead four of the studies adopted a form of utility measurement. Another, described by Langston, presented its client with a vector of performance and in this way it had forced the valuation onto the decision maker. The remaining study, described by Watts, obtained from the client a statement of alternative programmes which were judged to be equivalent. This produced a set of programmes whose actions could be assumed to lie within a region of indifference. In this way the problem of assigning values to the outcomes of the programmes was avoided and analysis could concentrate on effectiveness.

Those studies which adopted utility measurement had successfully used one or more of a variety of psychometric techniques. The validity of such methods was discussed at some length without a really satisfactory criterion of validity being found.

One way of generating evidence for the validity of the psychometric approach was to seek to identify the value judgements implicit in behaviour. One study, described by Rosser, analysed the awards made by the courts to the victims of personal injury to produce a ratio scale. Currently this scale is being compared with an equivalent one obtained psychometically.

2.4. Estimation of the effectiveness of different programmes in achieving operational objectives

The studies which required estimates of the effectiveness of *new programmes* or *modifications to existing programmes* relied largely, or entirely, on the informed judgements of experienced personnel aided in some cases by modelling. Some had estimated the effectiveness of *existing programmes* by new field studies (Langham, Rosser) but otherwise judgements of experienced personnel supported by existing data was used.

Using the product of judgements about effectiveness or value as a basis for reviewing allocation decisions was recognised to be unsatisfactory. The uncertainties in the judgement process make it questionable whether the product of these uncertainties is likely to provide useful information to the client. This point is appreciated in all six studies and is exhibited in the way the results are used. For example Trinkl and Fischer used their results to provide a rank ordering of a set of defined alternatives. Reisman and Service presented both the judgements on value and effectiveness as elements in a vector on which the client could perform his own subjective transformations.

Discussion focussed on the prospect of replacing these judgements about effectiveness with estimates based on measurement. Whilst in theory this might be done, in practice the resources and the time scale required implied that most studies would continue to rely on such judgements. However, the validity of these judgements could be tested by experiment from which general guidelines for improving the accuracy of such judgements might be developed.

2.5. Decision levels

It is important to distinguish between the different decision levels at which these issues arise in the health and welfare services. These levels stretch from the planning and allocation of a national or regional budget spanning all the social services, through the evaluation of the output of a social system or health programme, to the assessment in detail of the performance of a particular institution. Very different operational objectives may be required at these different levels. The relationships between the achievement of a particular objective at one level and the contribution this makes to the achievement of operational objectives at another level have not yet been defined. As a result suboptimisation is unavoidable at present.

Furthermore, analysts and decision makers at the aggregate level may make incorrect assumptions about the operation of the micro-systems. For example, the value sets of those operating the system may be ignored and hence assumptions about their behaviour under new operating conditions may prove incorrect. Formulating these values for use in micro-analyses will expose the main issues in the conflict and in the process may change its nature and help to resolve it. This problem may be more important in the social services than in other systems because management of social programmes is generally more diffuse and more dependent on the dedication and personal commitment of the manager.

2.6. Welfare services and health services

Distinction between the two services was not generally needed. An important distinction is between services which are aimed at individuals and those aimed at communities. For example, it is much easier to assess a service which is aimed at helping a sick person than one aimed at helping an ill-defined sub-section of a community which is judged to be deprived.

3. The studies presented on the subject of measurement

3.1. Bundeswehr hospital study – Dietrich Fischer *

Study background. The German military medical service has been considering using civilian hospitals to provide some of the hospital care required by military personnel.

Study method. The first part of the study dealing with the problem of assessing the attractiveness, or utility, of alternative hospital structures has been completed and is described here. The second part will involve determining the costs associated with various structures.

In close co-operation with the Medical Services seven different hospital structures were defined in addition to the present structure. These varied in organization, functions and degree of integration with the civilian hospital system and ranged from a purely military hospital system at one extreme to a fully civilian hospital system at the other.

The 57 objectives, defined for the future hospital system were grouped into 16 categories, such as patients, organization, hospital operation, etc. Then the decision maker representing the Medical Services Command was asked to assign weights to the various categories and the objectives within each category, and to assess the utility of structure alternatives by the extent to which they were felt to fulfill the objectives. The weighting of objective categories was left to the superior command levels. In a first meeting the participants were asked to arrive at an ordinal ranking of objective categories by two by two comparison. A second meeting served to determine the cardinal ranking by relating each objective category to the most preferred one.

The same procedure was followed in ranking the objectives within each category, with the medical officers responsible for the subject matter (ca. 10 in each case) taking part in the session. The final objective weight was achieved by multiplying its initial weight by the relative weight of the category to which it belonged. Whilst in the weighting process the participants were asked to arrive at an unanimous assessment, the participants were asked to assess the utility of the alternatives with respect to the various objectives independently. On the assumptions that these assessments were distributed normally it was then possible to determine the "time" utility values.

Summing up the products of weights and utility values resulted in a measure of the overall utility of the alternatives. After normalizing the latter values it was demonstrated to the decision maker by what percentage the

* IABG, 8012 Ottobrunn, Einsteinstrasse, West Germany.

utility of the various alternative hospital structures appeared to be higher or lower than that of the present structure according to the assessments of the decision maker reflecting his preference scale. Computerization of the evaluation process allowed for some sensitivity analysis to be made by changing specifically the weights assigned to various objectives by the decision maker.

The assessment exercise with the decision maker turned out to be extremely helpful, as it required him to (1) define precisely the alternatives, (2) make the objectives explicit, (3) come to an agreement with respect to the weight of the objectives, allowing everybody in the decision line to take part in the decision process, and (4) assess explicitly the value of the alternatives with respect to the objectives. It made the decision process transparent, reproducible and allowed for sensitivity analysis.

3.2. Evaluation of neighbourhood health centres – Joanne Langston *

Study background. The office of Economic Opportunity has developed a programme for the delivery of clinical medical care and social care to families with incomes of less than $3500 p.a. The goals of the programme were: (1) to reach the target population, (2) to satisfy the patients treated, (3) to provide a comprehensive health and social service, (4) to provide preventive care, and (5) to treat the family as a single unit.

Study objective. Five years after the start of the programme an evaluation was made on a sample of 21 neighbourhood programmes across the USA. The evaluation study team developed a number of measures which were designed to reflect achievement against the programme goals.

To measure utilisation, statistics were collected about the proportion of the target population reached by the service and, for those using the service, the proportion of their needs for health and social services which were met from the same source. Estimates were made of the extent to which the service provided was used appropriately.

The satisfaction of patients with the service was estimated using specially developed satisfaction scales. In addition the convenience of the service and its technical quality were estimated. The comprehensiveness of the service was examined in terms of the extent of implementation, the spectrum of services provided and the continuity of care.

The results of these measurements were presented to the client in terms of the individual dimensions. No attempt was made to externalise the judge-

* Geoment Inc., 50 Monroe St., Rockville, Maryland, USA.

ments which would be made about the relative values of performance along
the different dimensions.

3.3. Measurement model for planning and budgeting – Arnold Reisman and Allan Service *

Study backgrounds. Since the fall of 1968, the Jewish Community Federation of Cleveland has been engaged in an ambitious attempt ** to apply the
techniques of OR and systems analysis to its social welfare planning and
budgeting processes.

Study objective. The major purpose of the project was to design and
implement a *measurement model* which could be used to assess the services
offered by the component agencies of the federation system and to specify
the output of that system in a way that would permit meaningful comparisons. Early efforts focused on obtaining a generalized statement of system
goals and delineating a fundamental structural unit; namely, the service-
client-agency package. A crucial part of this latter task was the construction
of meaningful categories for the service and client dimensions.

Given this structuring of the system, attention turned to constructing the
model, i.e., to defining a set of concepts sufficient to measure the "output"
associated with each service-client-agency package. Operationalizing these
concepts required the development of an information system geared to producing not only objective data but also subjective information: attitudes,
perceptions, and opinions. In fact, the judicious blending of these two types
of information is one of the distinguishing characteristics of this work.

The model itself has three major components. One block of information is
concerned with the *throughput* of the system: the number of clients served in
each package and the duration of the service they received. A second component quantifies the *value* associated with each package. This step makes explicit the subjective priority system that defines the importance of each package to the Jewish community. A simple scaling technique, used in conjunction with a variant of the Delphi method, was sufficient to elicit this information from a succession of the panels selected to be representative of the larger
community.

* Case Western Reserve Univ., Cleveland, Ohio, USA.
** This effort has involved members of the Federation's staff and a multi-disciplinary
team of faculty and graduate students from the Dept. of Operations Research and the
School of Applied Social Sciences at Case Western Reserve Univ., Cleveland, Ohio,
and the School of Business Administration at the Univ. of Cincinnati, Ohio. Financial
support was provided by the Cleveland Associated Foundations.

The final component of the model, the "quality" of service, is, in fact, a set of six criteria. Two, *effectiveness* (data obtained via sampling of clients, staff and neutrals) and *efficiency* (data obtained from service statistics), relate directly to individual service-client-agency packages. Two others, *capability* (waiting line information) and accessibility (data obtained from a panel of intra-system referral agents), measure the extent to which expressed needs for service are met by the system. Finally, two criteria, *interrelationship* (service statistics related to cooperative efforts) and *system contribution* (service statistics on volunteer usage and data obtain from several panels), measure the extent of agency efforts in the system maintenance area. These criteria were also assigned relative weights by a panel of laymen and scores standardized via the definition of a set of utility trade-off curves, a step carried out by a panel of agency executives.

Taken together, this body of information provides a comprehensive qualitative portrait of the state of the federated system. The model is currently being computerized and incorporated in the planning and budgeting procedures of the Federation.

3.4. The measurement of hospital output – Rachel Rosser *

Study background. A general hospital (300 beds) was used as a site in which to develop a general measure of health outcome.

Study method. A theoretical model was developed which expressed the effect of the hospital on the health of its patients. Since much of the data required for this model was not available three outcome measures were derived from the model by using simplifying assumptions: sanative output (the effect of the hospital on the immediate health of its patients), long term output (the effect of the hospital on the health of its patients one or more years after discharge), and mortality, including the morbidity state on admission of those who died. These measures required the following to demonstrate that they were operational:

(1) a classification of morbidity which can be used for all specialities,

(2) a method of assigning a value to the transition from one morbidity state to another, and

(3) a pilot study to show that the measures were acceptable to clinicians and could be used under normal hospital condition.

The morbidity classification, which was developed through a number of pilot studies carried out in another hospital, used two main dimensions:

* Maudsley Hospital, Denmark Hill, Londen S.E.5, UK.

disability and distress, and contained 29 possible morbidity states. The method used to assign disutilities to the morbidity states was based on the awards made in the courts to the victims of personal injury and industrial disease. The descriptions of the plaintiffs were classified using the morbidity classification and a ratio scale was developed using that portion of the award which was specified by the court as being made to compensate the victim for the disability and distress which he suffered.

The morbidity classification was used for one month by all the clinicians in the hospital (48 individuals) to classify all patients on admission, on discharge and at subsequent out-patient visits, (over 2000 classifications). Tests conducted during the study showed an acceptable level of reliability. Furthermore, the classification was quick to use and acceptable to clinicians in all specialities. By weighting the observed transitions using the scale developed it was possible to obtain a measure of the output of the hospital for the months of the study.

The next stage of this study will include a more fundamental derivation of the morbidity classification, the assignment of disutilities to the states using a psychometric method (so that some evidence may provide for the validity of the scale) and further field studies to examine the sensitivity of the output measure obtained to known changes in the hospital studied and to differences between hospitals.

3.5. A Markovian analysis of programs for the mentally retarded – Frank Trinkl *

Study background. The State of Hawaii programmes for providing services to mentally retarded adults were used to provide a framework for developing a method of policy evaluation.

Programme goals. To provide patterns and conditions of everyday life which are as close as possible to the norms and patterns of the mainstream of society. In defining operational objectives two dimensions were chosen: the living environment and the work environment, viz:

Living environment states:

(A) Independent – living alone or with roommate or spouse with no direct supervision over daily activities;

(B) Moderate supervision – living in a situation in which a non-retarded person helps with certain daily activities;

* Univ. of California, Berkeley, California, USA.

(C) Constant supervision – living in a situation in which a non-retarded person helps with daily activities almost all of the time;

(D) Intensive care/treatment – living in a situation in which all personal and physical needs are provided by others.

Work environment states:

(1) Self-sufficient – full-time employment at minimum wage or above;

(2) Productive non-self-sufficient – part-time employment at minimum wage or full-time employment earning 1/2 of minimum wage to minimum wage;

(3) Marginally productive – work with earnings from 1/5 minimum wage to 1/2 minimum wage;

(4) Unproductive/active – structured learning or activity with or without pay but less than 1/5 minimum wage;

(5) Unproductive/idle – no structured training, work, or activity.

Study method. If one considers representing "living environment" simultaneously with the conditions representing "work environment", then the resulting joint conditions characterize the potential distribution of mentally retarded adults. The matrix structure suggests that programmes concerned with living and work situations of mentally retarded adults have as their purpose the positioning of persons in appropriate states; moreover, movements of persons over time can be expected to occur. It also becomes apparent that operationally meaningful objectives articulated in terms of movement (both progressive and regressive) can be related to the broadly stated goals. These viewpoints suggested that suitably modified, the concepts underlying a Markovian model could prove useful.

A matrix was set up in which the cells were the probability of moving from one of these joint living environment/working environment states in a two year period. The transition probabilities for each programme alternative were estimated by the programme managers. The value (or utility) of making each possible transition was elicited from three different groups of people concerned with policy making by using a specially designed questionnaire. The structure underlying the questionnaire is a tree relating a statement of goal to broad objectives to specific objectives describing the possible types of movements. Respondents were asked to distribute 100 points among each of the tree branches emitting from a specific tree node. The values presented in each of the questionnaires were combined so that the totality of value points among the nine types of movements summed to 100 points. Value assignments by members of the same group were averaged and were considered to represent a composite judgement of the group. The ranking of five alternative programmes was carried out for each of the three value sets.

The rankings obtained over different time periods and for the three value sets were similar and hence the "best-bet" alternative was identified.

3.6. National planning study – Vincent Watts *

Study background. The Department of Health and Social Security in England has recently mounted a major strategic OR study to help improve the planning of all health service resources. Although a large number of different studies contribute towards this general aim, they have taken a common approach to the question of the measurement of medical output.

Study method. A wide range of alternative ways of delivering the same type of health exists in England and an even wider range is considered by planners. For any pair of alternatives there is, in general, a set of patients who, in medical terms, are equivalently well served by either alternative. Thus, if the characteristics of this set of patients are described and the range of conditions are defined for which these alternatives are medically equivalent, then an analysis of the cost and convenience of each alternative provides useful information to the planner in deciding how much of each alternative to provide. For example with X-ray services, there is a group of patients who can have adequate X-ray pictures taken either at small clinics remote from hospital or in large clinics attached to hospitals. For this group of patients the decision as to whether or not to provide clinics can be reasonably based on an analysis of the staffing and building requirements and the advantages to the patients in terms of convenience. By building up a set of medically equivalent alternatives for the majority of the health care systems it then becomes possible, by using suitable models, to take account of the interactions between the various systems both in terms of the advantages to the patient and in terms of their competition for shared resources.

This approach avoids the difficulty of quantifying the output of each sub-system by having the policy maker define alternatives which have effectively the same utility to him along certain dimensions. By limiting the scope of the analysis in this way one is able to produce results quickly which make a useful contribution to the planning process. This is an important advantage in relation to the political time scale. This advantage is paid for by a parallel limitation on the nature of the questions which can be illuminated by the analysis. However, the difficulties encountered by the various study teams in obtaining reliable information on the operating characteristics of existing systems suggest that this limitation on scope is more of a blessing than a disadvantage in the short term. As more reliable information systems are installed the quantification of output will probably assume a greater importance in the extensions to these studies.

* Arthur Andersen and Co., 2 Fore Street, London, UK.

4. Conclusions

One of the most important conclusions to emerge from these discussions is that OR scientists no longer need to shy away from the problem of the measurement of output in the health and welfare services. This problem has now been tackled successfully by a number of different groups and, whilst there are many unresolved issues, it is likely that acceptable measures of performance can be defined for most specific situations. It is crucial for success to have a very clear understanding of the scope of the study and of the limitations of the particular method of measurement adopted.

The studies described by the participants in the workshop demonstrate that the development of new ways of measuring output is the most active area of OR in health and welfare. The main approach adopted is that of estimating the disutility of various states of sickness or social deprivation and also the estimation of the utilities of the alternative programmes which are designed to operate on such states. The major questions requiring research attention are the following:

4.1. The classification of sick or deprived people

So far the classifications developed have been arbitrary and different for each study. Any practical classification must be simple with relatively few states. Since it must classify complicated conditions of sickness or deprivation, some way must be developed for reducing the many dimensions of the classified object into the few dimensions of the classification. Is there a better way of doing this than the arbitrary decisions made at present and is there a set of criteria which can be used to distinguish good classifications from bad ones? Alternatively, is there some other way of avoiding the proliferation of classifications so that the results of different studies can be made comparable?

4.2. The validity of the estimates of utility

One of the main problems in getting the results of a study which relies on utility measurement accepted is that of the validity of the utility estimates. Do the numbers obtained really express the way in which the evaluators feel about the entities which were rated? Do these measured feelings really relate to the actions that the evaluators would take if faced by a real situation rather than a hypothetical one?

These and other related questions could be the subjects for future research. In particular a research study could estimate the utilities of a group and then analyse the past and/or future behaviour of this group to see whether a decision model can be developed which predicts this behaviour on the basis of the measured utilities.

4.3. Methods of improving the accuracy of the judgements made about factual material

Most of the studies rely on estimates of the size of entities which could in theory be measured using carefully designed experiments. In general there will be neither time nor resources for such experiments and judgements about the likely outcome of such experiments are needed to estimate the values of model parameters (e.g., the values of the transition probabilities). A variety of methods exist for helping experienced administrators or experts make these judgements. Research is required to establish which of these methods is likely to provide the most accurate estimates and also to provide an indication of the likely errors in these estimates to guide the sensitivity analysis.

4.4. Relationship between operational objectives at different levels in the decision framework

OR studies carried out at different organisational levels have developed different sets of operational objectives. No clear picture has been developed of the relationship between these operational objectives, and the way in which objectives attained at one level contribute to those of a higher level.

In developing operational objectives for a study it would be valuable to have a map of the main operational objectives developed at different levels and the nature of the relationship between them. Such a map would help to show the relative importance of the objectives at each level, and hence reduce the amount of sub-optimisation. This is closely related to the next issue.

4.5. Allowing for the values of the system managers

Studies made at one level in an organisation may make assumptions about the behaviour of managers at a lower level which turn out to be incorrect. In particular the system managers may have objectives which they see as important but which have been ignored at the higher level of analysis. If this is not perceived it may result in acrimonious disputes which could be avoided by a deeper understanding of the value sets used at the different levels in the organisation. More effective analysis would be possible at the aggregate level if some way were to be developed of formulating the systems manager's value so that behavioural models could be developed.

5. Other discussion topics

The workshop devoted a session to national developments. We record below those topics which the workshop thought suitable for further international discussion by similar workshops but for which time was not available at IFORS.

5.1. The best form of incentives for the medical profession to balance costs of care with quality

The systems used to pay the medical profession in different countries vary from a fee for service at one end of the spectrum to a salaried profession at the other. Within this range some very complicated payment structures have been developed. Each solution adopted has had to compromise between providing high quality care at unacceptably high cost and providing relatively cheap care with an unacceptably low quality. The discussion suggested that the problem was similar in different countries and that by structuring this problem it should be possible to develop a model which would permit predictions to be made of the likely consequences for health services for different methods of payment.

5.2. The dominant effect of geography on health service planning

This was brought out most clearly by the paper presented by B. Lenehan in which the response time of the ambulance service to an incident was shown to be largely independent of the size of the population serviced but to depend mainly on the geography of the area and the number of ambulances provided. The results of such a study could be transferred to other countries without much need for modification. It is likely that similar considerations apply to many other studies, e.g., the location and size of hospitals.

5.3. The movement towards forging closer links between hospitals and their communities

This is happening in most of the countries represented at the workshop. There seem to be few models to describe or to optimise this process or if they exist they are poorly publicised.

5.4. The development of models to help with facilities planning

The centralisation of services to gain economies of scale takes the services away from where people live. How does one develop services which are accessible and yet also gain the main economies of scale?

5.5. The relationship between population and the policies adopted for caring for elderly people

The investment in acute medical care is keeping more people alive until they suffer the diseases and deprivation of old age. What is the best balance of investment between providing facilities for providing medical and social care to the elderly and providing the acute facilities which ensure that a greater proportion of the population becomes elderly? How can one model the process and its implications for population policy?

Acknowledgement

We are very grateful for the dedication shown by the members of the workshop which made the discussions so productive. We are especially grateful to those who described the studies mentioned in this report. They did so with little or no notice and under difficult conditions. Charles Flagle and George Torrance ably chaired some of the sessions and F.J. Elliott from the Eastern Health Board in Dublin provided the workshop with many valuable practical insights.

M. Ross, ed., OR '72. North-Holland Publishing Company (1973)

64

CRIME PREVENTION AND CONTROL

Contrôle et prévention des délits

R. GORDON CASSIDY
Ministry of State for Urban Affairs, Ottawa, Canada

1. Introduction

This paper is a summary of the discussion on criminal justice during the crime prevention and control workshop. The intention of the workshop was exploratory, that is, it was an attempt to structure crime prevention and control so that the system problems will be more clearly elucidated and to stress ways in which operations research can be used to improve this system. In this context we specified a basic goal which we hoped to attain during the sessions.

The goal of the workshop was to define the criminal justice system, including prevention, police, courts and corrections, cross-nationally. This definition first was used to facilitate an explanation of the problems of the administration and management of the criminal justice system and to then define the areas and problems which were amenable to OR analysis. The methodology which we used to obtain this goal was to first describe the basic structure of the problem which we were analysing and then to relate this structure to existing models, techniques and methodologies existing in OR. Naturally there are very few direct applications of OR techniques; however, with suitable hedges it is possible to show that many problems and parts of the criminal justice system are very amenable to analysis with methodologies which are presently available.

In describing the criminal justice system as a system the workshop found

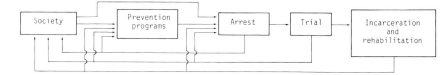

Fig. 1. Basic criminal justice system.

it useful to define initially the blocks or stages and the possible interrelation-ships of these stages. Thus the workshop viewed the criminal justice system as the basic social system described in fig. 1. This flow diagram describes the processing stages within the criminal justice system (which we shall refer to as subsystems), as well as the intermediate flows between these stages. Thus we will not simply be concerned with describing the problems and possible appli-cations of analysis to subsystems of the criminal justice system, such as the police, but rather with the analysis of the total criminal justice system and its effect on society.* The emphasis of the workshop was then to structure the criminal justice system so as to facilitate further research, rather than try to solve its multiplicity of problems here directly.

Initially we treated the criminal justice system in terms of strategic prob-lems which may arise affecting the system as a whole. This may include not only total system problems but also problems arising in one particular sub-system which has substantial impact on other subsystems. There were two types of problems defined: (1) effectiveness problems (which are problems where effectiveness is to be maximized subject to certain cost considerations), and (2) efficiency problems (where a minimum cost solution is desired subject to given levels of effectiveness). Obviously these two dimensions of effective-ness and cost interact and a best solution for the system would be one which was pareto optimal in both dimensions. The effectiveness types of problems have been traditionally treated (albeit more recently) by OR analyses. Exam-ples of effectiveness problems would be better manpower allocations in the court subsystem or police subsystem, subject to a budget constraint which has already been allocated to the subsystem. Only in the last few years problems of efficiency have been treated for the system as a whole using quantita-tive or analytic techniques, such as planned programmed budgeting systems (PPBS) in order to minimize system costs. The problems of efficiency and effectiveness naturally depend upon being able to develop output measures

---

* For more detail on a social system's approach to the criminal justice system see [1–3].

for the various parts of the system so that effectiveness can be well defined. The analysis presented in the following section will treat the system generally and provide an initial description of its problems.

The third section will describe in detail the problems which the workshop found which were peculiar to certain subsystems of the criminal justice system. Again there will be a division between two types of problems: (1) strategic or macro level problems of the subsystem itself (this includes both efficiency and effectiveness), and (2) micro or tactical problems within that subsystem dealing primarily with resource allocation and micro efficiency questions for the subsystem. Because of a lack of space and time it will be impossible to treat all of the subsystems articulated in fig. 1, rather we will deal specifically with the police subsystem, but making obvious analogies to the other subsystems so that the methodology presented here can easily be applied to them.

In order to define any of the above problems with any level of sophistication it is necessary to have a comprehensive and complete data base for the system. In the fourth section we will discuss the problems of producing such a data system compatible with all the subsystems for the criminal justice system and more importantly the problems in producing a decision-making data base or information system for it. The final section of this summary will deal with what the workshop felt was the most important phase of any type of analysis: implementation. It is here, particularly in public service systems, that the OR analyst may have to expand his horizons and deal not only with the solution of the particular problem presented, but also with quantitative methods of evaluating alternative implementation schemes. A detailed discussion is given and some conclusions are drawn about the types of methodology presented here and the usefulness of further types of research in criminal justice.

2. Criminal justice system

In order to obtain any measures of efficiency or evaluate the operation of the criminal justice system the workshop felt it was necessary to first define the objectives of that system and of its subsystems. By doing so we can define output measures which relate to these objectives and have measurable quantities for use in efficiency or effectiveness types of problems.

The workshop felt that a first approximation to this objective would be one of minimizing the total social cost, both psychic and economic, of crime to society, subject to certain qualitative and quantitative constraints introduced by the societal preference.* These qualitative and quantitative constraints include budgetary restrictions on the various subsystems of the criminal justice system, as well as constraints by society dictating that an individual has a right to "due process" of the law, is innocent until proven guilty, and so on. In particular the justice system itself has a qualitative constraint of guaranteeing an individual a right to "due process", that is, he is accorded certain rights as he is processed through the criminal justice system. In this context it is useful to view the justice system as a satisficing type of system which guarantees (or maximizes the probability that) a certain level of treatment for those who are being processed by the system. It is here that satisficing models in a very general form may be usefully applied to modelling the correct level of both the quantitative and qualitative constraints to be established for the criminal justice system and to evaluate alternate strategies for achieving these levels. To determine the best benefit/cost ratio for the system would be an almost impossible task; however, it is possible to detail the above objective for each of the subsystems and thereby examine the efficiency of their operation within themselves and perhaps as they relate to the whole justice system. This will be further explored in the following section.

While this objective and constraints for the justice system are very general, it nevertheless brings to light several points which have not been included in the traditional description of a criminal justice system. This objective is not very similar to the most commonly accepted concept of the criminal justice system, since it is usually viewed as a basic punishment system for people who violated certain societal constraints. As such it is generally thought of as primarily concerned with the detection of offences, the processing of accused, and the administration of punishment to the accused with the objective of deterring further crime. If, instead of taking this generally accepted notion of the criminal justice system, we accept the objective of minimizing total social cost, we are able to articulate many different strategies which have not been employed until recently. Thus minimizing social cost may include such strategies as prevention programs, which decrease the cost of crime. This is quite different from the cost of crime control which has normally been viewed as the real cost of the criminal justice system. Thus, the workshop felt that by focussing on the more general objective for the criminal justice system it would be possible to articulate these more diverse strategies for possible cost minimization in that system.

Perhaps one of the major benefits of an international workshop on crime

---

* For further discussion of possible objectives see [4] and "The economic impact of crime" in ref. [5].

prevention and control was the ability to compare the criminal justice systems of several different nations. This cross-national comparison identifies possible alternative strategies and provides a basis for assessing the differences in performance in different criminal justice systems. It is not to be implied, however, that criminal justice systems have necessarily planned to arrive at the particular form of the criminal justice system which they now have. Obviously a large proportion of the form of the systems is by historical development which may be the consequence of particular philosophical principles or simply of ad hoc decisions for change made by administrators in those systems. However, the consideration of these different systems enables analysts and administrators to examine possibilities which perhaps heretofore would not have been examined. By taking into account the difference in those systems and in the basic society they can then examine the possible application of some of those strategies to their own criminal justice system.

One interesting cross-national difference which the workshop noted was in the availability of bail in different nations. In North America, bail has traditionally not been available to a large sub-set of people who have been charged with offences. This has resulted in a number of people being detained in prisons before trial for long periods of time (see for example [6]) in some cases. In Ireland, however, bail is available to almost all people who are charged with crimes, but because of the delay in trial a proportion of the people who are out on bail commit further offences [7]. In fact, approximately 300 people last year in Ireland were charged with 1200 offences while they were out on bail. The analysis of these alternatives for a country considering alternate bail systems should be examined not only in terms of the costs of the options and the problem of detaining innocent people, but also in terms of the interdependency of bail with other parts of the system. By viewing the problem in this way possible solutions, such as better scheduling in the courts (using queuing or programming models), might be used to eliminate many of the problems which occur in this part of the system at present. Thus, by shortening waiting periods to trial most persons could be set free and would not have the opportunity to commit further offences.*

The bail problem is also affected then by the utilization of both the police and judiciary personnel since, for example, in France, investigations are carried out under the direction of the judge rather than by detectives. The possible redefinition of a judge's duties to include investigations might be able to

---

* It should be noted that it may be necessary to devise an interim solution such as better screening systems for awarding bail, until, for example, scheduling in the courts improves.

alleviate some of the stochastic problems involved in court scheduling at the present time. That is, by looking at both the bail question and the investigation question simultaneously it may be possible to propose an allocation of duties together with a better scheduling algorithm to reduce the amount of time which people are out on bail, thereby reducing the probability of being able to commit further offences as well as giving them their rights under "due process" of the law. The idea of this solution is not to try and over-load the court system or propose a type of bail reform system; rather the workshop used this particular case as an example of first, the type of modelling possible to examine alternative bail system, and, second, to show the extreme interdependency of parts of the criminal justice system and the ways in which changes in court scheduling could affect what type of bail reform is implemented.

A further difference between systems which the workshop felt it should articulate was in the general administration of the criminal justice system. In particular, the police subsystem is administered either nationally by a central agency or nationally and locally as in North America, including both federal police and local or state police (as well as possibly another level of municipal or city police). The best type of administration may be a subject of further study in trying to determine the hierarchical organization which, first of all, gives the particular subsystem best communication with policy-making bodies, and secondly, allows them an amount of independence such that they can operate efficiently without undue political intervention. It is here that structural models used in organization theory and lately designed for manpower and internal labor market usage can become extremely useful in examining the existence of communication links and their possible utilization by persons in the system. Determining the most effective method of administration of the police force in some general context as to efficiency of operation including economics of scale can be at least begun by OR analysts even though detailed mathematical techniques have not been developed for evaluating these alternatives.* The articulation of these problems and tradeoffs of administration is obviously an important output which management scientists can have in analysing most subsystems of the criminal justice system. Again detailed quantification of these areas may be far in the future but OR can provide directions for the analysis at present.

The usefulness of these types of cross-national comparisons to the workshop was two-fold. First, OR analysts can better evaluate possible effects of a

---

* However, there have been some initial forays into these areas with qualified results. See
  for example [8].

change in a justice system by looking at this change and its effects on some other country. Second, the existence of such a change in another criminal justice system makes the possibility of modifying a present justice system with these changes much more possible, particularly in the face of a conservative administration. In fact, the existence of these changes may well, together with an evaluation of its impact, convince an administrator of the necessity and the benefits of such a change in a criminal justice system. It should be emphasized, however, that cross-national data can only be used to show the direction of possible changes in a criminal justice system and not to evaluate these changes, since the basic socio-economic status of the country, as well as many environmental and demographic variables will obviously be different for different countries.

If indeed it is impossible to obtain data on an alternative strategy in a criminal justice system in another country, it may be necessary for the OR analyst to perform a multi-variant statistical analysis of the present change or to develop a pilot project.* That is, if there is no cross-national data existing such that one can determine comparative control groups in another country so as to evaluate the "real" effect of the program treatment it may be necessary simply to introduce the program and either a priori select the participants at random, or a postiori to generate a control group. One method which has been examined recently for generating a control group after the beginning of an experiment is to use a discriminate analysis to characterize the group being treated and then select another group which has similar characteristics to this group. It is then possible to examine the real effects of treatment on the individuals rather than the compounded effect of the treatment and the self selection of the participants into the program.

The workshop felt that not only in terms of comparatively examining alternate criminal justice systems, but also in the generation of new alternatives the cross-national comparisons were very useful. Criminal justice administrators are often forced not only to define new strategies, such as prevention programs, but also must make ad hoc decisions of what the probable impact of the program will be. This is as opposed to OR professionals defining these strategies either from cross-national data or an analytic approach to the system, and doing at least an elementary quantitative evaluation of alternate strategies. While it is recognized that there are no directly applicable statistical techniques at this present time to analyse these problems, the development of these techniques and their applications to this policy level analyses within the

---

* Normally, the analyst will have no opportunity to develop a pilot project but will have to rely on a postiori analysis of the effect.

subsystems is an important new area for the applications of OR.

At a more macro level the workshop also examined models which have recently been developed in OR for the examination of the systemwide impact of changes. These models are what might be called system planning models and include simple Markovian kinds of models which view the stages in fig. 1 as states and the transition between them as transition probabilities (see for example [9, 10] and "Science and technology" in ref. [5]). The models which have existed presently serve two primary purposes. First, they are very useful in predicting the future resource usage and occupancy of the criminal justice system. Secondly, they are being a useful interactive tool for acquainting criminal justice administrators from the various subsystems with the system wide impact of many of the changes which they implement. The models thus far which were examined by the workshop have been relatively simple process or simulation types of modelling. It was felt that the emphasis in the future should not only include these kinds of models which have the dual purpose mentioned above, but also more general analytic models which may be able to suggest better policy changes at a more macro level in a criminal justice system. This would include not only programming models (where it should be noted functional relationships relating present behavior to possible future behavior are hard to obtain) but also satisficing types of models and perhaps regulatory models reflecting the basic objective of the justice system to regulate societal behavior.

At a macro level of planning and analysis OR then can be used not only for the evaluation of alternative strategies (which are articulated either by cross-national comparisons or simply by needs within the system itself) but also in the stimulation of new strategies which would make the operation of the criminal justice system more effective. By performing these planning analyses of the criminal justice system it will be possible to detect subsystems which are operating very inefficiently and perhaps make suggestions for changes which would increase substantially their efficiency.*

It should be emphasized that OR activity need not be constrained to dealing merely with macro efficiency issues in the analysis of the criminal justice system. In many of the problems which the workshop addressed the cost allocations and methods for budgetting obviously needed substantial revision. In fact, perhaps one of the more critical issues is how monies in justice departments should be divided among the various subsystems [12]. In order to allocate these monies better we need methods of measuring the real output of these systems. In the following section the workshop examined some output

---

* A statistical analysis of different rehabilitation programs is given in [11].

measures for parts of the police subsystem. It felt these analyses should be pursued further in the future, not only in the sense of better analytic techniques (such as the inclusion of more sophisticated planned program budgeting system techniques) but also in beginning to delineate the types of data and information needed to make real evaluations of the output of the subsystems and their objectives.

3. Subsystem analysis

In detailing the objectives and consequent output measures of the subsystems of the criminal justice system, it would obviously be impossible in this short a space to treat all subsystems, their interactive effect and their effect on the total criminal justice system. For this reason we will concentrate on analyzing only the police subsystem of the criminal justice system. This subsystem obviously interacts heavily with all other parts of the criminal justice system, particularly prevention and the courts. Here two levels of analyses should be distinguished.

The first level is that of policy or strategy level analyses similar to that of the previous section, which defines and describes the probable impact of new alternatives in the subsystem (with possible spillover to other subsystems). Some possible strategies which might be used would include new fingerprinting capabilities for the police or a better dispatching system. Several planning models have been developed in the US in order to describe present operation of the system and allow analysis of the impact of future policy changes. It is important that OR become involved in this level of analyses since it is here that the macro decisions are made about the justice system and specifically about its subsystems.

The second level of analyses within the subsystems is that of resource allocation. There has been some recent activity both in North America and in Europe in the last five to ten years in the resource allocation within certain subsystems, particularly police. This has included reports which are available on patrol assignments, the optimal distribution of a patrol's activities, the analyses of an alternative strategies for the deployment and dispatching of cars and so on [13–16]. The types of resource allocation problems which have been dealt with in North America have been concerned first with the effectiveness type of problems where a certain budget allocation has been made. The problem is then to maximize coverage of police patrols or more generally police efficiency. Secondly it has included efficiency types of problems where the effectiveness has been established in terms of a minimum response time and the problem is to develop a dispatching strategy which will minimize cost while bringing response time within the predefined limit. There are several reasonably comprehensive bibliographies available on research which has been done in this area as well as some initial work in the planning area [17, 18].

Although a number of studies have been done on resource allocation within subsystems (not just the police subsystems but also courts and corrections), one of the points which was articulated strongly by management and administration attending the workshop was that much more research was needed in these areas, particularly research which is oriented directly towards a particular criminal justice system and its problems. Too often models have been concocted which had major modelling benefits rather than benefits in determining optimal or even better resource allocation within a subsystem.

4. Information and data systems

For OR analysts to perform strategy evaluations and analysis of resource allocation (both efficiency and effectiveness problems), the workshop deemed it fundamental to define a common data base for all parts of the system, both for offender flows through it as well as for costs and workloads of the subsystems. This data base is obviously necessary to facilitate the planning which is done mostly on an ad hoc basis in the criminal justice system at the present time. Currently there are no criminal justice systems of which we are aware which have statistics or data collected with the view to a functional use for examining alternative strategies and evaluating their impact on the system.* The statistics gathered (including the very extensive statistics in the US) seem to be a function of what is available, rather than of what is needed.

This lack of any common data base existing in criminal justice systems results from many factors. First, there has not been much analysis of the criminal justice system so that the statisticians could, even if they had the necessary manpower and monetary resources, decide what statistics should be kept and aggregated. Second, planning or research branches of criminal justice systems have traditionally been concerned with the evaluation of equipment and short-range evaluation, both because of a traditional orientation and a lack of long-range resources. Neither of these has helped in devel-

---

* This included examination of the Uniform Crime Reports (UCR) and related data in the US statistics, data on crime prevention and control in Canada, and Garda Headquarters Police Reports in Ireland.

oping the basic planning data base for the criminal justice system. The planning models developed by OR professionals should begin to articulate the data needs on a reasonable scale in order that statistics can start to be gathered with a view to the long-range planning analyses which are necessary for that system. In addition, the short-range resource allocation problems will obviously also be better served by developing this kind of data availability.

The basic data systems generated by these models will include not only flow and cost data on the criminal justice system being examined, but information system data on that particular system. That is, in addition to aggregating statistics which already exist, it is necessary for OR to provide evaluative information on possible effects of alternative programs so that the decision-maker will be able to make more well-informed decisions on alternative actions in the criminal justice system. For example, analysis is needed to determine the real effect of a new dispatch centre in terms of reducing arrival times of police at incidents. This could be assessed through an analytic modelling effort including queuing models or location-allocation models together with benefit-cost analysis of the actual introduction of the centre versus the present dispatching method. It should be emphasized that the actual decision is not made by the OR professional but requires the unique capabilities of the criminal justice administrator who recognizes many of the qualitative (including public and political) constraints on a new project. Rather the OR professional can provide information more completely and in a form which is more readily understandable to the criminal justice administrator. It is hoped that the provision of this information system will increase substantially the efficiency of criminal justice systems operating in many countries.

5. Implementation and conclusions

The workshop was critical of many of the analysis which have thus far been made of the criminal justice system. With some exceptions a large proportion of these analyses are oriented towards academic needs for research rather than system needs for quantitative assistance. Ideally research, which is directly oriented towards improving the efficiency or effectiveness (both flows and costs) of various parts of the criminal justice system, will provide a basis for developing new mathematical or OR theories, with a more general application to other systems (particularly social systems). For example, the discriminate analysis [19] previously described for the evaluation of a rehabilitation program would have a more general usefulness in generating control groups for any type of social program evaluation, not simply programs administered within the criminal justice system.

In implementing analyses within the criminal justice system the analyst should recognize that public service systems are fundamentally different from private enterprise. The top management of the system, normally being elected officials, have at least partially political objectives in the operation of that particular public service system. The actual administration within the system itself, however, has the objective of increased efficiency, or minimal cost for that system. These conflicting objectives make the problem of implementation many times more difficult than with private agencies, since a possible change within the system must not only be more efficient but also more advantageous in the political environment. The difficulty arises since many changes may have substantial long-run benefits, but the immediate returns may be very small (such as in a rehabilitation program where the real change in recidivism may not be detected for a five year period). One important area where OR workers could become more involved in their analysis in the criminal justice system is in actually trying to improve implementation methods for projects and analyses. The use of quantitative analysis for describing alternative implementation plans and their possible success is obviously an important phase in such analyses.

In the future the workshop hoped that OR will become increasingly involved in analysis of the criminal justice system, both in the articulation of macro strategies for planning and their evaluation and in the development of new models and methods for better resource allocation within the subsystems. Obviously the use of cross-national data, multi-variate statistical techniques and optimization and simulation models needs to be further explored in accomplishing these ends, both in terms of articulating the strategies and in their evaluation. The problems within the criminal justice system are many and there is an ideal opportunity for better analysis of that system in the coming years. The workshop felt that good quantitative analysis together with well defined implementation strategies will have a substantial effect on the criminal justice systems of many countries.

Acknowledgements

Professor Alfred Blumstein, Director, Urban Systems Institute, School of Urban and Public Affairs, Carnegie Mellon University, Pittsburgh, USA, gave generously of his time and expertise in helping to prepare this report.

I would also like to express my appreciation to the participants of the workshop. In particular, I would like to thank the members of the Irish Police

Force, Chief Superintendent E.J. Doherty, Superintendent Stephen Fanning, and Detective Inspector James Enright for their participation in the workshop. In addition the many OR professionals attending the workshop, including Madame E. Benejam, Mr. Brian Lenehan, Professor Paul Gray and Mr. Yus Tanguy, contributed a great deal of time and effort to this document.

The views expressed are those of the author and do not necessarily reflect those of the Ministry of State for Urban Affairs.

References

[1] A. Blumstein and R. Larson, Models of a total criminal justice system, Inst. for Defence Analyses, Arlington (1970).

[2] J. Belkin and A. Blumstein, Methodology for the analysis of total criminal justice systems, Carnegie Mellon Univ., Pittsburgh, Urban Systems Inst. (1970).

[3] A. Drake et al., Analysis of public systems (MIT Press, Cambridge, 1972).

[4] L.C. Thurow and C. Rapport, Law enforcement and cost-benefit analysis, Public Finance 24, No. 1 (1969).

[5] President's Comm. on Law Enforcement and Crime and its impact, Task Force Report, Admin. of Justice (US Gov. Printing Office, Washington, 1967).

[6] K. Fields, M. Lettre and R. Stafford, A description of the Alleghery Co. criminal justice system, Carnegie Mellon Univ., Pittsburgh, Urban Systems Inst. Working Paper (1972).

[7] Police crime statistics, Garda Headquarters, Phoenix Park, Dublin.

[8] H.J. Kiesling, Designing a public service in a metropolitan area: police, paper prepared for 28th Congr. of the Intern. Inst. of Public Finance, New York (Sept. 1972).

[9] J. Belkin, A. Blumstein and W. Glass, JUSSIM: An interactive computer program for the analysis of criminal justice systems, Carnegie Mellon Univ., Pittsburgh, Urban Systems Inst. (1971).

[10] A. Blumstein and R. Larson, Models of a total criminal justice system, Opns. Res. 17, No. 2 (1969) 199.

[11] J. Robison and G. Smith, The effectiveness of correctional programs, Crime and Delinquency (Jan. 1971) 67.

[12] J. Belkin, R. Brunner and R.G. Cassidy, A programming approach to the criminal justice system, presented at the CORS meeting in Toronto (1972).

[13] R.C. Larson, On quantitative approaches to urban police patrol problems, Crime and Delinquency (July 1970) 157.

[14] N.B. Heller, Operations research at the St. Louis Metropolitan Police Department, St-Louis, Missouri, Centre of Police Patrol Res., Metropol. Police Dept., St. Louis, Missouri.

[15] J.M. Chaiken and R.C. Larson, Methods for allocating urban emergency units, New York City Rand Inst., R-680-HUD/NSF (1971).

[16] R.C. Larson, Urban police patrol analysis (MIT Press, Cambridge, 1972).

[17] K. Lindby, Bibliography, some economics of crime and crime control, in: The cost of crime in crime control, Proc. 2nd Intern. Symp. in Comparative Criminology, Ste. Marguerite (1970) to be published by the Solicitor General of Canada.

[18] R.S. Sullivan, Bibliography on the economics of crime and law enforcement, Dept. of Econ., Carleton University, Ottawa, Working Paper.

[19] A. Blumstein, B. Pahl, R. Shankar and D. Teichmuller, Analysis of the Allegheny Com. College prison program, Carnegie Mellon Univ., Pittsburgh, Urban Systems Inst., Working Paper.

M. Ross, ed., OR '72. North-Holland Publishing Company (1973)

65

ENVIRONMENTAL POLLUTION

Pollution des environs

DONALD J. CLOUGH

University of Waterloo, Waterloo, Canada

1. Introduction

The workshop was considered to be an experiment in group dynamics. The primary purpose of the workshop was to provide an opportunity for interested conference participants to discuss problems of environmental pollution and the part that OR professionals might play in solving such problems. A secondary purpose was to reach some conclusions, if possible, and to report the conclusions in plenary session.

The primary purpose was satisfied to a degree that none of us would have predicted at the beginning. Considering that only 13 or 14 hours were available for the workshop, over a period of 3 days, and that preparation was minimal, the productivity of the group was beyond all expectations. As a matter of fact, the accumulated knowledge and the energy of the experts participating in the workshop were somewhat overwhelming.

The workshop group had a stable size of about 14 or 15 people during the entire session. The group was truly interdisciplinary, including several engineers with different backgrounds, a couple of economists, a biologist, a chemist, and a meteorologist, all of whom were OR professionals working directly with pollution problems or interested in pollution problems. There were also 3 consultants to the workshop from the Republic of Ireland. Unfortunately, there were no lawyers, architects, or working politicians in the group. An important characteristic of the group's behaviour was the respect shown for one another's points of view, even in the face of strong argument about controversial matters. There were difficulties of communication, arising out of the mis-matching of technical vocabularies of the various people, and a good deal of the total time was spent simply in trying to understand one another's terms. Because of the time constraints, the communication difficulties were not overcome, and the output of the group was less than it might have been if there had been time to reach agreement on some of the more controversial issues. In spite of all the difficulties, there was an apparent tolerance of new ideas, new theories, and new models.

The social benefits of the workshop were great. Surprisingly strong friendships were formed, considering the short time. There was an element of surprise in the information presented and discussed, so that the learning process was rather exciting.

The secondary purpose of the workshop was also satisfied to a surprising degree. A number of general issues were discussed in the context of several specific case studies in environmental pollution related to energy production, northern oil transportation, solid waste disposal, and water pollution. Both micro and macro problems were considered, and both local and international problems were discussed. A number of observations and conclusions were made concerning the state of the art of modelling and measurement, the decision processes involved in pollution control, and on the contributions that OR professionals can make. These observations and conclusions are discussed in the following sections.

2. Workshop chairman's opening statement

In his address in the opening plenary session of the conference, Sir Charles Goodeve talked about the need for an "urgency index" of important environmental problems. He used the recent increase of atmospheric carbon dioxide (CO_2) as an example of a problem that is, in his opinion, not very urgent. There exist differences of opinion about whether the CO_2 level will continue to increase or decrease and what the future effects will be, and we cannot be so sure that Sir Charles' assertions are correct. Whether or not he is right about CO_2, there are other problems such as global DDT pollution that cannot be so easily dismissed.

In his address in the opening plenary session, Charles Hitch referred to pollution control as "a game against nature" and suggested that the problems are therefore quite amenable to modelling and analysis by OR professionals. However, one could argue that pollution control is in fact a multi-person non-zero-sum game with scientists, politicians, laymen and indeed entire nations as players, in addition to "nature".

In this workshop we shall hopefully consider some examples of pollution problems to which Sir Charles Goodeve's "urgency index" might be applied. But we must face the fact that all the problems have not been identified. In fact, there is much more unknown than known about pollution effects. We do not know (for example), but we suspect that the time constants for detection of some new kinds of pollution may be longer than the life cycles of animal species that may be rendered extinct by the pollution.

2.1. Global versus local pollution problems

It is convenient to divide environmental pollution problems into those that have global effects and those that have any local (or regional) effects that are important enough to demand specific remedial actions. For purposes of discussion, the terms *global* and *local* will not be defined precisely. It is sufficient at this time to obtain some general agreement based on common usage of language. Because of communication difficulties, we propose to use common layman's language and avoid excessive use of technical terms, insofar as possible in a short report.

A global pollution problem may involve any or all of three main parts of the planet: the earth's atmosphere, the earth's oceans and seas, and the earth's biosphere. Roughly speaking, the biosphere consists of all living matter and its supporting dead organic matter, whether on the land surface, in the atmosphere, or in the oceans and seas.

A global pollutant is one which may originate at one or more sources and may be transported by one or more routes to various parts of the planet. It is global in the sense that its effects are distributed over the entire planet — for example, as gases or particles in the atmosphere or as pesticide residues deposited in the oceans by rainfall.

A local pollutant is one which may have one or more sources and one or more routes, but it is deposited locally — for example, heavy sediments at the mouth of a river.

2.2. Some global pollution problems

First of all, it is important to re-emphasize that much more is unknown than is known about specific global effects of specific pollutants and their interactions. Methods of monitoring and standards of measurement are lacking, statistical data are lacking, and models describing ecological, climatological and economic effects are either very primitive or non-existent. In spite of these gaps in knowledge and methodology, it is evident that certain pollutants have the potential to produce undesirable effects – perhaps disastrous effects – that are not easily reversed. Some of the more important global effects, and recommendations concerning their control, have been cited in [1] (hereafter called the SCEP report). The main effects are related to climate, ecology and industrial and agricultural production. Implicit in all considerations is a recognition of the need to maintain a global equilibrium (e.g., balance of natural predators, balance of energy exchanges) or at least a cautious approach to disturbing the equilibrium by human activities. Remedial actions themselves may have unpredictable side effects and much more is unknown than known about the effects of some of the remedial actions that have been proposed.

The workshop chairman outlined some of the conclusions and recommendations of the SCEP report under the following main headings:

(1) Climatic effects of global pollution: atmospheric carbon dioxide and world temperature, atmospheric interaction of gases and particles, atmospheric water and world climate, pollution effects of tropospheric and stratospheric jet aircraft, thermal pollution (not a global problem), atmospheric oxygen (not a global problem), man-made surface changes (potentially a global problem).

(2) Ecological effects of global pollution: concentration through the food chain, persistent pesticides (DDT, airborne and waterborne), toxic heavy metals, oil in oceans, nutrients in coastal waters, agricultural, industrial and domestic pollutants.

(3) Problems of remedial action: political priorities of developed and underdeveloped countries, economic feasibility of environmental control.

The chairman recommended the SCEP report as a fairly comprehensive but concise source volume for OR analysts interested in global environmental pollution problems.

2.3. Local pollution problems

Global pollution affects all people on the plant to some extent, and global environmental control poses special problems of international cooperation. Regional pollution may involve two or more countries and also poses problems of international cooperation. Local pollution, on the other hand, is defined as pollution which directly affects only local sub-populations within a single nation. It poses problems of economic analysis, local jurisdiction and government control of a different kind than those of global pollution.

In the case of local pollution, the costs of pollution are not borne equally by the polluters and those who suffer the effects of pollution, and the costs and benefits of remedial actions are not borne equally. Any economic analysis of costs and benefits has to take account of distributional effects (between states, provinces, municipalities, etc.) as well as allocative (total) effects. Local pollution problems may involve various agencies and levels of government, as well as groups of citizens having vested interests and property rights. The questions of who benefits? who pays? who decides? who controls? are typically very difficult to answer.

Workshop papers by Drs. Ahmed, Bernhardt, Kirby and Law deal essentially with local pollution problems, while the one by Drs. Matthews and Gupta deals with international (UN) cooperation to deal with global problems. The bias toward local problems reflects the fact that most OR analysis of environmental pollution deals with local problems.

3. Report of workshop analysis and conclusions

According to definitions proposed by Professor I. Bernhardt, environmental pollution is a product of human activities. Pollution occurs when (1) a byproduct of some human activity is dumped into a part of the environment which is used in common with one or more other persons, and (2) the dumped byproduct reduces the value of the part of the environment for at least one other person. In every activity causing pollution, both a benefit (from the activity itself) and a cost (from the pollution) are involved. Further, the benefit and the cost accrue to different individuals or groups. Finally, since pollution involves some environmental resources such as air or water, as "property" that is used in common, the "property rights" of various persons are subject to definition and government regulation.

The identification and measurement of pollution is seldom easy. Pollutants may have complex chemical, mechanical and biological characteristics. The modes of interaction, transformation and transportation through the environment are usually difficult to analyze. Some of the products of natural phenomena are almost identical to some of the pollutants produced by human activity, and differentiating the two may be very difficult if not impossible in many cases. The chain of events from original production to the final effects which reduce the value of the environment to humans may be long, and the final effects may be very large (e.g., as in the biological concentration of pollutants through the plant and animal food chain). The problems of modelling and measurement of pollution seem endless.

The workshop agreed that it was useful to classify the perception and measurement of environmental pollution at three different levels, as proposed by Professor Bernhardt:

(1) as physical volumes of pollutant measured at the source, or sometimes on a route from the source to some destination;

(2) as environmental effects measured on the land, in the atmosphere, in the oceans, and in biological organisms including man himself; and

(3) as the economic values of all direct and indirect effects on humans.

The state of the art of modelling and measurement of pollution at these three levels is not well advanced.

At the first level of consideration, the physical measurement of *volumes* of some pollutants *at the source* is fairly well done at the present time. However, the measurement of physical volumes on various routes from source to destination is not done effectively in most cases. In fact, many pollutants remain unidentified and unclassified. Their ultimate destinations are not known, and the necessary measuring instruments have not been developed. In some cases, simple transport phenomena are well understood in principle by engineers and physical scientists. Yet the complexities of real transport phenomena, coupled with the transformation of pollutants from one form to another, complicate the problem of modelling flows of pollutants through the atmosphere, in the oceans, and through biological food chains. Throughout the workshop, many specific examples were cited to illustrate the problems of measuring pollution and dealing with unknown factors. One of the factors most frequently cited as unknown is the time interval from the release of a pollutant to its perceived effect in the environment. By the time an effect is perceived, and the cause recognized as a pollutant and traced back to its sources, irreversible ecological damage may have occurred.

At the second level of consideration, the *environmental effects* of pollution are poorly understood, particularly the interaction effects involving chemical, biological, material, and energy transfer phenomena. As an example, biological effects of pollutants on living organisms, including man, are poorly understood, and as yet scarcely measurable in most cases. Useful biological theories and models are lacking. For example, the synergistic effects of air, gases, and various pollutants in the lungs of man are not well understood. We are frequently surprised by newly recognized pollution effects from past human activities – for instance, DDT and mercury damage. It seems safe to say that we will continue to be surprised by belated perceptions of effects yet unknown. This ignorance of effects is not surprising – as yet, we do not even know where most pollutants go! We do not even know the ambient background conditions against which to try to classify and measure pollutants – the *before* to compare with the *after*.

At the third level of consideration, measurement of the *value* of pollution effects on humans in economic terms is well beyond the present state of the art of economic modelling. The processes are too complex, and the physical and biological models required as an underpinning for economic models are lacking. There is also a paucity of raw scientific and economic data. In spite of the difficulties, however, economists are beginning to develop some theories. The simple consideration of pollutants as measurable outputs of production processes, in the sense of a Leontief input/output model for example, is a step forward. Models for the analysis of economically efficient pollution abatement measures, at least on a local (closed system) scale, are beginning to appear in the literature. Economists are beginning to model the processes of compensation payments, or tax and subsidy policies, required to implement economically efficient pollution abatement measures.

These initial questions of pollution measurements and modelling were introduced by Professors Clough and Bernhardt. In particular, two position papers by Professor Bernhardt — on "What is pollution?" and "Modelling the control of pollution" — helped in the organization of a framework for looking at the problems of pollution in a more coherent fashion. Professor Bernhardt's two papers represented a professional economist's view of pollution, and the difficulties of dealing with it at a conceptual level. He covered some of the matters outlined above, and added an example of a very simple abstract mathematical formulation of a general static equilibrium model of two regions which can export "products" but not "environment". This example helped illustrate how the models of economists can provide insights into pollution problems. Professor Bernhardt succeeded in provoking a good deal of controversial discussion by contrasting the difference between the economist's view of economic values to human beings, and the "natural philosopher's" view of the "intrinsic value" of nature (independent of its use by human beings).

Two position papers — "International environmental problems: systems approach to identify scientific and political perceptions and responses" by Professors W.H. Matthews and S.K. Gupte, and "An index of environmental impact" by Professor S.B. Ahmed — focussed attention on the basic problems of classifying information about pollution and organizing it to permit easier access and quicker preliminary evaluations of local, regional and global pollution conditions.

The paper read by Professor Gupta described the difficulties in classifying and indexing materials presented to the 1972 UN Stockholm conference on the human environment. The Stockholm conference produced twelve thousand pages of widely varying technical, political and legal material on pollution,prepared by delegates of 70 countries, representing the first global survey of issues and concerns. Professors Matthews and Gupta described a design for multi-dimensional content analysis of the Stockholm papers, as a means to make the material accessible to those wishing information on a very wide variety of possible dimensions – for example, information on types of pollutants, regional distribution of pollution, legal and political jurisdictional problems, state of pollution control technology, and state of development of proposals for specific action on pollution in various regions.

Indirectly, Professors Matthews and Gupta also provided evidence concerning the over-riding importance of political concerns that were expressed at the Stockholm conference. For example, control of DDT pollution may have high national priority in a developed industrial country which can afford it. But it may have low national priority in a relatively less developed agricultural country or a tropical country faced with continuing tropical disease and pest control problems. (Such political concerns, stressed by Professor Clough in his opening remarks to the plenary session, were discussed at length in the workshop and are amplified below.)

The paper read by Professor Ahmed dealt with the specific problem of measuring the impact of pollution from both nuclear and conventional thermal power plants. In addition to the usual engineering design criteria of efficiency, safety and cost, Professor Ahmed proposed that pollution criteria also be considered. As a proxy for a large number of factors, he proposed the use of an "index of environmental impact", based largely on the opinions of experts.

The main problems inherent in Professor Ahmed's approach involved the classification of different kinds of environmental effects, the definition of scales of value on which to measure these effects, and the definition of a set of weighting factors to aggregate these values into a single index number. He defined about 20 classes of effects, such as "transmission line construction effects on land" and "chemical effluent effects on surface waters". For each class of effects he proposed an arbitrary scale of measurement on which to score experts' opinions about the environmental impact of each power plant in each location. As an index of environmental impact for each plant in each location, he defined a linear combination (weighted sum) of the values for the 20 classes of effects.

Professor Ahmed suggested that with this scheme a "danger threshold" could be specified with respect to each class of effects. Such a threshold would be essentially a pollution control *standard*. He also suggested that the overall index of environmental impact could be used as a basis for the comparison of alternative plant designs or alternative plant locations.

Many of the members of the workshop had their doubts that such an index of environmental impact, based on a complex reduction of experts' opinions and so far removed from raw data, could be justified in the light of the difficulties in measurement and modelling of pollution outlined earlier. They feared that the index gave an appearance of reliability that would be difficult to support in a scientific forum or a court of law. The compounding of two levels of judgment – first in the subjective estimation of the value of each class of effects, and second in the weighting of each class of effects – caused some concern. Although the exercise was deemed worthwhile as a framework for considering crucial factors, the consensus of the workshop group was that the apparent reduction of uncertainty would be an illusion. A multitude of experts' opinions should not be hidden in a single index number.

Along the same lines, the workshop consensus was that an "urgency index" of important environmental problems, such as was proposed by Sir Charles Goodeve in his adddress at the opening plenary session of the conference, would have the same shortcomings as Ahmed's index of environmental impact and would involve reductions of information that would be subject to controversy. The problems of organizing information about global and regional pollution, and reconciling different scales of value and standards of control, would be immense, as indicated by Professor Gupta in his discussion of the Stockholm conference.

Two position papers were presented which dealt with problems of OR modelling in specific applications – "Solid waste disposal in a rural setting" by Dr. M. Kirby, and "Railroad alternative to Alaska and Northern Canada oil pipelines" by Professor C.E. Law. Dr. Kirby's model, which is now in widespread use in the USA, dealt chiefly with the selection of garbage collection routes, disposal sites and vehicle schedules in park systems and other rural areas. The objective is to maximize some measure of efficiency or to minimize cost, subject to constraints that describe a specified level of service and various physical restrictions. It is typical of OR models in which major policies and standards are given as constraints to be met, and the chief criterion is efficiency.

Professor Law's paper dealt with analysis of a proposed Arctic railroad transporation system to carry Prudhoe Bay (Alaska) oil through Canada to markets in the USA. The railroad was proposed as an alternative to (1) a pipeline across Alaska and super tanker transport along the Pacific coast of Canada to Seattle, and (2) a pipeline from Prudhoe Bay across Canada to link up with mid-western US pipelines. Professor Law analyzed the economic factors and estimated that the railroad would compare favourably with the other alternatives in terms of long-run costs. He also provided evidence that the railroad would be superior to the other alternatives, in terms of environmental pollution hazards. For example, earthquake maps of Alaska show that the proposed Alaska pipeline would cross several highly vulnerable areas, including the Yukon River which supports the world's largest remaining salmon runs. Oil tankers would be vulnerable to earthquake damage while at anchor in Alaska, and to various sea hazards off the Canadian coast, particularly approaching Seattle through the Juan de Fuca Straits. Professor Law pointed out that environmental effects are difficult to quantify, but he provided evidence that the expected damages of oil spills caused by train derailments would be much less than those caused by pipeline ruptures. (In the Arctic permafrost regions the pipelines would be on "stilts" above ground.)

The two papers of Dr. Kirby and Professor Law contrasted two extremes of OR modelling and cost-benefit analysis as they relate to environmental pollution problems. Dr. Kirby's model dealt with *optimal efficiency,* assuming that certain major policy questions about solid waste pollution control had already been answered. As a point of departure for his model, it must be assumed that questions of public need for pollution abatement, type of service, scale of service, and specific cost or efficiency criteria have already been answered. In other w)rds, the objective function and the constraints are pre-specified. Then the optimal solution is given in terms of such variables as the routing of trucks, the frequency of collection, and the number of trucks and men required.

Professor Law's approach, on the other hand, focussed on *feasibility,* assuming that certain major policy questions had not yet been answered. As a point of departure for his analysis, it must be assumed that major questions have not yet been answered about the public priorities for Arctic environmental protection and petroleum production, feasible technological alternatives for distribution, constraints on private enterprise, property rights, environmental monitoring and control, and methods of measuring costs and benefits. In other words, neither an objective function nor a complete set of constraints are pre-specified. The task of OR analysis in this case is to provide information to policy-makers about feasible alternatives and the range of possible environmental and economic effects of each feasible alternative. Although some formal OR modelling is involved (e.g., pipeline network models), the emphasis is on presentation of quantitative data and qualitative information about environmental, technological, economic, political and legal factors.

All but one of the position papers mentioned above, and the ensuing discussions, gave heavy weight to the presence of political concerns of many kinds. (The exception, Dr. Kirby's paper, discussed a model that applies after major political decisions have already been made.) Major decisions involving the control of environmental pollution typically involve many people, many agencies, even many nations – all of whom may have conflicting interests. Adversaries may include the polluters versus the pollutees, the government versus industry, the state or provincial government versus the federal government, the developed country versus the underdeveloped country, the naturalists versus the economists, the free enterprisers versus the socialists in a variety of associations, the taxed versus the subsidized, and a multitude of private and public pressure groups working against one another in the pursuit of competing objectives. Regions of pollution do not coincide with political boundaries, so that problems of legal jurisdiction arise frequently. Given these realities, mathematical models and systems analyses based on the implicit assumption of a single central decision-making authority playing against nature are generally inappropriate. Yet theories and models of the bargaining and informal voting processes involved in multi-organization decision making are not well developed at the present time.

A view of the OR practitioner as a politically neutral scientist above the battles is equally inappropriate. In the prevailing technical, political and legal adversary proceedings, all scientists are not neutral; all systems analysts are not neutral. The typical situation in which an OR practitioner is asked to create a model has been precipitated by previous political conflict. For example, the UN is trying to begin coordination on a global level to cope with global environmental problems; and as a part of this activity Professor Gupta is asked to help organize the information so that it is accessible. As another example, an electric power company is challenged by both government and private citizens' groups to incorporate new environmental considerations in its investment decisions; and in response to this Professor Ahmed is asked to help devise measures of environmental impact and to defend the decisions reached. As another example, the interactions of US and Canadian governments, the State of Alaska, several multi-national corporations, spokesmen for Alaskan native peoples, citizen conservation groups, and a variety of public and private agencies, create political chaos out of the Alaskan oil issue; and Professor Law is sponsored by a group of interveners to investigate the feasibility of an alternative oil transportation technology.

The typical practitioner is, like Professors Gupta, Ahmed and Law, hired by one of many conflicting groups. He is expected to be an advocate for the point of view of his client. He typically makes a multitude of value judgments when he structures his model and selects parameter values. He participates with his client in the adversary processes, whether they be within a government department, between governments, between a corporation and a control agency, between litigants in a court case, etc.

It was emphasized in the workshop discussions that the OR practitioner should be well aware of all these things if he is to be useful to his client. According to the experience of almost everyone who entered the discussions, the OR analyst should be completely aware of the "political" conditions that may limit what he can accomplish effectively. Even more than "awareness", a certain kind of "preparedness" may be required. Many cases which involve expenditures of public or private funds on environmental control lead to complex legal proceedings and litigation. Expert witnesses, including scientists and OR practitioners, appear as adversaries. If the arena is the courtroom, the ultimate test of the "validity" of the analysis is the judgment of the court. In other situations, "validity" may be provided by the passage of a law, the setting up of an agency, the adoption of a set of rules by an agency, the beginning of intergovernmental cooperation, the approval of an investment, the compromising of conflicting aims. Again, to be useful, the practitioner must become sensitive to these differing requirements. Most decisions concerning environmental control are essentially political and not centralized.

OR workers and OR models, as distinct from economists and economic models, have usually dealt with problems of an employer organization — attempting specific helps for specific situations. Typically, models have dealt with smaller isolated economic units such as a production line or a single company. Most formal OR models in such fields as energy production, transportation, manufacturing, etc. have not included pollution parameters. Where such parameters have been dealt with, they have often been considered a side-issue to be handled informally, outside the formal structure of the model. Heavy reliance has been placed on the use of source volumes of pollutants as proxies for environmental effects that cannot be measured directly. Heavy reliance has also been placed on qualitiative description of pollution effects, in narrative form.

Our earlier conclusions on the current state of measuring and modelling make it clear why this is so, and equally clear that this less-than-satisfactory state of affairs will continue for some time. However, OR models for the analysis and management of pollution must inevitably incorporate inputs from other scientific sources and from political sources. Not only must the OR analyst learn to integrate these inputs, but he must also learn to investigate and make judgments about their quality. The burden is a heavy one, and it is not yet clear that the traditional organization of research and modelling efforts will be successful.

Export opinion is often divided on the effects of pollution and the social values associated with such effects. The models in economics and OR often reflect specialized schools of thought. Political controversy is unavoidable, and so is scientific controversy. Although there is nothing new about scientifc controversy, there may be something new in the way political decision-making processes are using the inputs of scientists in adversary situations. Examples include the political and scientific controversies over supersonic transport aircraft, the scholarly and non-scholarly controversies about the growth models of Forrester and Meadows, and the mixtures of fact and value judgment employed by the ecologists Barry Commoner and Paul Ehrlich in their recent running battle over the population control issue. These scientific and non-scientific controversies suggest that some reasonable caution should be exercised in the application of large systems models of ecological effects, particularly when the required underpinning theories in the biological, physical, and social sciences may not yet exist.

Let us reiterate: the underpinnings for analysis either do not exist or have not yet won the widespread acceptance of the scientific community. This report cannot deal with all of the shortcomings of analysis, modelling and measurement that were covered in the workshop discussions. One brief example, of one of the better studied areas, must suffice: that of the instrumental monitoring of pollution.

Monitoring has not been carried out long enough in most cases to determine the stability and trends in ambient background conditions against which man-made pollution must be measured. Instruments are not yet available for the measurement of many currently recognized major pollutants. The logistics of global monitoring of pollution are complex and costly. In general, sensing of pollution *in situ* (sometimes called immersion sensing) is very costly. Remote sensing, from aircraft and satellites, may ultimately prove to be more effective and less costly than immersion sensing in some applications. However, the state of the art of remote sensing, particularly from satellites, is still quite primitive. Although a great deal of research and development work is presently being carried out, with the aim of developing sensors, sensor platforms, and data communication and imaging techniques, there is a strangling development bottleneck at the data interpretation end of the processes. We have not yet learned how to interpret remotely sensed data and derived information, or how to use it in decision-making in most fields of resource management and environmental control. In the long run, probably a combination of remote sensing and *in situ* sensing will prove the most effective and the most economical for most global environmental monitoring applications.

Within the time and manpower constraints of the workshop, many of the significant problems of OR workers in the area of pollution were mentioned briefly rather than discussed fully. It may be useful to list a few of them:

The problems of environmental pollution control are obviously multi-disciplinary. No single discipline can provide an appropriate framework alone for structuring analysis of the problems. Further, the decision making processes require a coalition of experts from various disciplines. The workshop dealt in some detail with the relationship between the contributions of economists and the contributions of operations researchers, but did little more than recognize the importance of coordinating inputs from engineers and scientists on the one hand or from political and legal experts on the other. Yet developing appropriate coordinating frameworks for analysis and for decision making may be very rewarding.

Workshop participants frequently mentioned the importance of cultural and legal standards and of political organization, but detailed consideration was not possible. The problem of assigning environmental property rights was mentioned, for example, and it was pointed out that dramatic cultural and legal changes are occurring. One change is from a situation in which property rights to dispose wastes in a common environmental resource (air, water) have been assumed willy-nilly, to a situation in which the property rights are controlled and granted by government agencies.

It was also mentioned that multi-national environmental pollution problems require that the systems analyst have a sensitivity to the value systems and political processes of many countries. Ethical, religious, cultural, and other factors are involved, and conflict resolution is a major aim of analysis.

It was also said that "societies are becoming more sophisticated". This seems to be true in the following sense. Formerly, societies delegated the setting of standards in such fields as engineering and medicine to the professionals in those fields (e.g., boiler codes, building codes, health standards). In most countries, the delegation of such powers has been accomplished by legislation and licensing. Usually, standards for environmental pollution control have been left implicitly in the hands of groups of professional engineers and medical doctors. The engineers have been concerned chiefly about design criteria for public safety and economic design, and have been forced by convention to neglect the problems of environmental pollution. Medical doctors have been concerned about pollution only at the threshold levels at which pollution becomes an obvious health hazard. Now, however, society is challenging the standards themselves, and the delegation of powers to specialized professional groups. Society (students, newsmen, citizens, Ralph Nader) is asking for an explanation of the values of the professionals and the qualifications of the experts who set the standards. The implications for systems analysts, who must include pollution control standards as parameters in their models, are obvious.

There was a consensus among the workshop participants that, in spite of all the difficulties involved in the multi-agency decision processes, the systems analyst can play a key role. In the face of uncertainties about objectives, alternative courses of action, modelling, measurement, and lack of data, analysts can help immensely by describing strategic alternatives and their costs, even though they may not be able to specify criteria for the selection of a "best" alternative.

There was also a prevailing view in the workshop that OR modelling, and the consequent delineation of pollution information requirements, may form a basis for the structuring of organizations to monitor and control the environment. For example, the organizational structure for a government agency concerned about a single energy source (e.g. coal) would be different from the organizational structure for an agency concerned about a mixture of many energy sources (e.g., coal, petroleum, atomic energy). The models and methods of analysis would be different, the controls would be different, and the organizational structures to implement government policies would be different.

4. Implications for operations research

OR analysts will be increasingly involved with problems of environmental pollution and its control, as will engineers. They will be involved in the problems of identifying pollution conditions, developing better methods of monitoring and measuring, and estimating pollution costs. They will be involved in devising methods for pollution control, incentives to assure that self-regulation occurs, and standards of performance to be pursued. They will participate with economists in benefit-cost analyses of large-scale environmental control schemes. They will appear as expert witnesses. And they will assist in the development of fundamental theories and complex models of the social and economic processes of environmental control.

Reference

[1] Man's impact on the global environment, the Report of a Study of Critical Environmental Problems (SCEP), M.I.T. Press (1970).

PART VIII

DISCUSSION FORUM

Forum de discussion

R.H.W. JOHNSTON

Introductory note

Group 1. Application of traditional OR techniques.

Group 2. Internal OR politics.

Group 3. Planning models involving judgement and the human element.

Group 4. Social and environmental problems.

Group 5. Development areas.

M. Ross, ed., OR '72. North-Holland Publishing Company (1973)

66

REPORT ON THE DISCUSSION FORUM

Rapport sur le forum de discussion

R.H.W. JOHNSTON

Trinity College, Dublin, Ireland

1. Introductory note

On behalf of the programme committee I wish to thank those who participated in the forum and accepted it in the experimental spirit with which it
was offered.

I cannot guarantee that the attendance figures given are accurate or that
they reflect any meaningful measure. It is, however, interesting to analyse
them. The attendance figure is given in brackets after the name of the contri-
butor. In some cases an alpha character is substituted. The meaning of these
is as follows:

x Author was registered at conference but was unable to be present;

y Location of meeting was changed from the forum to a lecture-room
elsewhere, leaving us with no attendance record. We can surmise that it was
large;

z We have no record of the attendance due to negligence of the duty
officer.

Some authors submitted abstracts in advance, were scheduled, but then
did not turn up. In one case, that of the late Dr. J. Walsh, it must be recorded
with regret and some shock that he died during the course of the conference.
In other, less forgivable, cases the scheduled authors were not even registered
at the conference; one was present but refused to register. Where people
turned up for an absent author, we have passed on (out of sheer goodwill; we

were under no obligation to do so) the names and addresses of enquirers to whatever contact-point we had.

We would like to place on record for future conference organisers that we think this practice reprehensible, as it makes the avoidance of schedule conflict more difficult by increasing the event-density, and generally increases the "noise-level" in the conference management system. Thus, if a prospective participant is uncertain as to his coming, he should make use of the real-time scheduling facility, to allow for which the forum was designed.

Finally, the grouping presented here is my own; it seemed worthwhile to look at the phenomena of OR fashionability. I am impressed by the high level of interest in models involving judgement and the human element; I am not surprised at the relatively poor support for applications of traditional techniques; I am pleased at the suggestion of a keen interest in social and environmental problems (although the numerical data in this case seems to say otherwise, there were two "y" papers, and the "zero" was a late submission, so I am inclined to give it little weight). I am surprised and disappointed at the poor support for the "development areas" group: most of this was clearly an effort to build bridges into disciplines where the relevance of OR is hitherto unrecognised. There is scope for more interaction with the civil and electrical engineers, and other such disciplines with long and distinguished numerate traditions; many OR techniques in fact have independent and parallel histories without the OR label.

2. Application of traditional OR techniques

Authors:
Boase, Brant, Ciriani, Haessig, Hansen/van Oudheusen, Saksena, Saleeb.
Mean attendance: 4.7
maximum: 10
minimum: 1

2.1. R.L. Boase (3); 6238 Mercedes, Dallas, Texas, USA

A method for validation of multivariate simulations whereby statistical tests are applied to a pair of data sets, (one real, one simulated) which need not be continuous, random or independent but must possess joint null distribution symmetry.

2.2. Major K.E. Brant, USAF (1); Aeronautical Systems Division, (ASD/SDMC) Wright–Patterson AFB, Ohio 45433, USA

Military applications of Bayesian statistics.

2.3. T.A. Ciriani (x); Pisa Scientific Centre, Pisa, Italy

Post-optimal analysis of linear-programming problems by free parametric variation of the coefficients.

2.4. Kurt Haessig (2); Inst. für Operations Research, Univ. Zürich, Zürich, Switzerland

A system of linear equalities or inequalities, including linear programmes, is applied to problems in banking and in multi-commodity flow.

2.5. Pierre Hansen; Inst. d'Economie Scientific et de Gestions, Lille, France, and Dirk van Oudheusen (10); Univ. of Brussels, Brussels, Belgium.

An implicit enumeration algorithm is proposed for batch processing of jobs on a production line where the latter can exist in several states with different costs, and where sequence-dependent costs associated with changes in state can also be incurred.

2.6. C.P. Saksena (6); Computing Lab., Univ. of St. Andrews, St. Andrews, Scotland, UK

A modification of the bounding hyperplane method of linear programming is developed which uses the equality constraints to obtain an efficient optimum.

2.7. Shafik I. Saleeb (6); Inst. of Statistical Studies, Cairo Univ., Ghiza, Egypt, UAR

A simulation technique, enabling distributions of CPU time, I/O events, core requirements etc. to be determined for a computer, has been used to improve the operation, and plan the expansion, of the Cairo University system.

3. Internal OR politics

Authors:
Abrams, Norden.
Mean attendance: 9
maximum: 12
minimum: 6

*3.1. J. Abrams (6); Inst. for the History and Philosophy
    of Science and Technology, Univ. of Toronto,
    Toronto 2B, Ontario, Canada*

The implementation of operations research in Canada.

*3.2. P.V. Norden (12); Data Processing Div., Columbia Univ.,
    White Plains, New York 10604, USA*

It is suggested that the communication gap between management science
and top management may be bridged by an Internship Programme sponsored
by TIMS.

4. Planning models involving judgement and the human element

Authors:
Buttimer, Muller-Malek/de Cock, Rasmusen, Sutton.
Mean attendance: 16.3
maximum: 22
minimum: 13

*4.1. A. Buttimer (22); Princeton 1, Ardilea, Roebuck,
    Dublin 14, Ireland*

A low-storage computational system utilising both empirical and exponential smoothing terms, suitable for short-term planning and forecasting, has
been developed which in the application proved 35% better than best known
alternative.

4.2. H. Muller-Malek and J. de Cock (14);
Fac. of Economic Sciences, Univ. of Ghent, 9000 Ghent, Belgium

The behaviour of a known decision-maker with regard to an operational repetitive task in an industrial environment was simulated on a computer; results were compared with the output from a mathematical programming model of the same problem. Satisficing behaviour, it is suggested, should not be considered as a deficiency in human behaviour, rather as an efficient way to deal with compromises.

4.3. H.J. Rasmusen (13); Inst. of Mathematical Statistics and
Operations Research, Tech. Univ. of Denmark, 2880 Lyngby, Denmark

A corporate planning model is proposed in which each decision-maker within the organisation has his own sub-model; it is suggested that by this means conflicting objectives might be exposed, and internal communications improved.

4.4. A.M. Sutton (16); Atkins Planning,
Woodcote Grove, Epsom, Surrey, UK

The use of modelling systems in budgeting, variance analysis and capital investment analysis.

5. Social and environmental problems

Authors:
Ahmed, Bruckhardt, Francis, Goodeve/Hitch, Langston, Trinkl.
Mean attendance: 6.7
maximum: 12
minimum: 0

We have no record of the attendance of three out of the six meetings; two of these were held elsewhere suggesting that space in the forum was a problem.

5.1. S. Basheer Ahmed (4); Univ. of Western Kentucky,
Bowling Green, Kentucky, USA

A common numerical measure is suggested for environmental effects on water, air and land, relating the quality of human life.

5.2. Werner Burckhardt (2); Systemberatung Fides Düsseldorf, Düsseldorf, Germany

A model for planning teacher supply is proposed which allows for demand, university capacity, retirement and sabbatical years; the discrete maximum principle of Pontryagin is used.

5.3. N.D. Francis (0); Dept. of Computer Science, Trinity College, Dublin, Ireland

An educational system is modelled by a linear matrix differential equation; control-theoretic concepts enable a dynamic programming approach to be developed, whereby inputs of student, staff and space are optimised to achieve a long-term educational target.

5.4. Sir G. Goodeve; Tavistock Inst. of Human Relations, London, England; and C.J. Hitch (12); Univ. of California, Berkeley, California, USA

An informal discussion took place arising out of two of the "Highlights" papers.

6. Development areas

Authors:
Cirina, Dyrberg, Manias, Milch, Riley.
Mean attendance: 2.0
maximum: 6
minimum: 0

One paper was heavily supported by the Dublin Press and got good coverage in at least one national daily paper. Perhaps the pressmen got into the count.

6.1. M. Cirina (0); Inst. Matematico Polytechnico, 10129 Turin, Italy

A dynamic programming technique is used to generate a pressure law which minimises reaction time in an industrial chemical process taking place in a discontinuous reactor.

6.2. J.H. Langston (4); Social Systems Program, GEOMET (Inc.),
  Rockville, Maryland 20850, USA

A neighbourhood health centre is studied; the effective use by target population, the degree of satisfaction and the service-level are determined; organisational and functional characteristics of the centre are related to its effective performance.

6.3. Frank H. Trinkl (8); Graduate School of Public Policy,
  Univ. of California, Berkeley, California 94720, USA

Resource allocation in social programmes is modelled in a manner permitting consistent decisions within a hierarchy and using consensus methods when judgements concerning value and effectiveness differ.

6.4. Christian Dyrberg (1); Inst. of Mathematical Statistics and
  Operational Research, Tech. Univ. of Denmark, 2800 Lyngby, Denmark

Renewal theory and other stochastic processes were used to determine risk profiles for various alternative methods of constructing a harbour.

6.5. T.N. Manias (6); Research Inst. of Ancient Knowledge,
  c/o D. Xirokostas, 24 Armatolon and Klefton Street,
  Athens T.T. 704, Greece

It is suggested that the proportions of the pyramid of Cheops may be related to some mathematical properties of sums of series of prime numbers, and that its absolute scale may be determined by reference to certain distances between centres of importance in Greek antiquity; a prior Greek influence is therefore suggested.

6.6. Paul R. Milch (1); Naval Post Graduate School,
  Monterey, California 93940, USA

A need is suggested for development of queue theory to cater for cases where a finite number of customers (say less than 20) form a queue for a relatively short time: in this case the queue length distribution is of no interest but the total system lifetime and the mean customer-in-system time are important.

6.7. W. Riley (4); MIS/DP Unit, ILO,
Geneva 22, Switzerland

Survey statistics and personal experiences from selected developing countries in Asia, Eastern Europe and Africa indicate a near crisis situation in respect to the application of computer technology contributing to national development. The alarming rate of increase in computer hardware acquisition, doubling the number of installations every two years, matched with inadequate or non-existent training for management and computer specialists is resulting in underutilization of the available computer capacity on non-significant user-applications. The background information supporting these conclusions are presented, in order to promote the exchange of experiences by others, leading to a discussion of possible steps to alleviate the obstacles faced by developing countries in utilizing computer technology for their national development.

PART IX

SUMMING UP

Récapitulation

HEINER MÜLLER-MERBACH

1. The application of Operations Research to problems of social interest.

2. The requirement of marketing Operations Research.

3. Model of the development of Operations Research on a national basis.

4. "Managerial puzzles" as a means to approach managers.

M. Ross, ed., OR '72. North-Holland Publishing Company

67

SUMMING UP

Récapitulation

HEINER MÜLLER-MERBACH

Technische Universität Darmstadt, West Germany

1. The application of Operations Research to problems of social interest

During this conference many papers and most of the workshops were concerned with subjects of *social interest*. This fact seems to indicate a new direction of the applications of Operations Research.

A rather simplified view of the history of Operations Research would count *three major epochs* in connection with the new fields of applications. In the *first epoch,* during the World War II, the name of OR was created, and *military problems* were the main focus of this unique new approach. In the *second epoch,* after the war, OR entered the huge field of *industrial* and *managerial applications* while continuing with military applications. The *third epoch* began more recently, roughly speaking in the late sixties, when an increasing number of operations researchers started to treat *problems of social interest* like educational planning, urban planning, health and welfare systems, crime prevention and control, environmental pollution, etc. Indeed, the many current and unsolved problems in these areas seem to have an urgent need of the OR approach.

The fact that many operations researchers know the means by which problems from these areas can be solved better than before is *not at all* sufficient for the real and effective use of OR. In addition to the knowledge of the operations researchers, it is necessary that the *decision makers*, i.e. the politicians and managers at the international, national, regional and local level, become convinced that OR can be a very helpful tool. This requires that OR be positively marketed.

2. The requirement of marketing Operations Research

There is no doubt that there exists quite a lot of experience from the military and industrial areas on how OR could be marketed and how it should *not* be marketed. I do not think I would be exaggerating when I say that 90 per cent of the experience reads: "Progress has been slow. Each individual operations researcher has done his best (or what he thinks to be best) on his own. Neither the national OR society nor any other institution have developed concrete concepts and explicit guidelines to work with to ensure more rapid advances".

OR has not only to be marketed to politicians, managers of local authorities, industrial managers, military leaders, etc. but also to teachers at different levels and different sciences.

In order to develop a strategy or a concept by which to market OR at the national level, an OR-model seems to be the appropriate tool. The structure of one model which serves this purpose will be briefly outlined in section 3. There exist many different ways of approaching those politicians, managers, professors etc. who are potential users or teachers of OR. Some of these ways will be mentioned in section 4.

The following statements are particularly dedicated to those countries which are *"developing countries"* from the OR point of view. This expression needs a definition and has to be distinguished from *developed* and *underdeveloped countries*. A simple formula is the following:

A *developed country* from the OR point of view is a country in which one *cannot earn money any more* by lectures like "OR — A new tool for management".

A *developing country* is a country in which one *can still earn money* by such lectures.

An *underdeveloped country* is one in which one *cannot as yet earn money* by such lectures.

I am going to consider the "developing countries" because my personal experience is mostly based on the German situation of OR and that Germany belongs to this group. A second reason for my decision is that it is still not too late to develop and/or modify strategies of marketing OR in these countries.

3. Model of the development of Operations Research on a national basis

A typical situation in many countries is that OR is integrated only in a *few* academic disciplines. In Germany e.g., OR is now being taught in most of the business schools. Also some mathematical departments at German universities have OR courses in their curricula. But very little OR is adopted by the engineering schools.

As I learned, the contrary is true in Japan. The Japanese engineering schools are the promoters of OR in Japan, but very few OR activities are going on in the Japanese business schools.

More countries could be mentioned in which the development and applications of OR depend more or less on one or two scientific disciplines and not on those 3, 4, ..., *n* disciplines which could contribute to OR or are potential users of OR. In particular, I know very few universities in which the curricula of social and political sciences include OR.

From these observations one may conclude that the development of OR depends to some extent on a random process, at least in several countries.

In order to gain some control over this process in Germany, some of my research fellows and I chose to experiment with a multi-period Linear Programming model though I can imagine that in other cases System Dynamics models might have been preferred.

Four types of *variables* were used in our model: the number of *teaching staff*, the number of *students*, the number of *problem solvers* in the sense of applied operations researchers, and the number of *decision makers*. The groups of teaching staff and students were subdivided according to the university departments, and the groups of problem solvers and decision makers were subdivided according to the areas of application. Since it was a multi-period model, for each time period (of one to five years) a separate set of variables was defined.

Four types of *constraints* (equations and inequalities) were formulated. In the *first group* of constraints, the *flow of manpower* between the four groups was put on record. The major streams came from the group of students who, after passing their examinations, may join the groups of teaching staff, problem solvers or (junior) decision makers. Also streams between the other three groups were taken into consideration.

The *second group* of constraints dealt with the various ways in which the different groups of OR teachers, students and professionals *influence* each other in their activities. The teaching staff certainly influence the students to use OR techniques and to become OR experts. The communication between universities and business may also affect decision makers to take advantage of new OR results. The problem solvers may win the decision makers over to OR by successful applications of OR methods. The fruitful implementation of OR in practice may give new impulses to research work and may motivate the students. Finally, managers, who benefitted from OR, may convince other decision makers, etc.

In the *third group* of constraints the *limited time capacity* of the teaching staff and of the problem solvers was taken into consideration.

The *demand for operations researchers* was considered in the *fourth group* of constraints. It was assumed that the demand for problem solvers comes mainly from the decision makers. Also demand functions for OR teaching staff were constructed. Equilibrium equations between demand and supply were also taken into consideration.

Several *objective functions* were discussed. In one case, an "ideal" number of the different types of decision makers and problem solvers were fixed, and the total sum of deficit was to be minimized.

There is no doubt that most of the *data* used in our model were rather weak. We knew this in advance. Nevertheless, we played around with the model which became rather large but had a nice structure.

Some of the results from playing around with the model were obvious. One result was that the effort of marketing OR was much too low in Germany. Another obvious result was that we need quite a few social scientists and political scientists, etc. who are familiar with OR.

The main advantage of this model (besides the more obvious results) was that the interdependence between the various groups of people became much clearer than before and that we *became aware* of these interdependencies.

We knew all the time that the model had to remain incomplete and unprecise (e.g. the quality of teaching OR could not be measured). Nevertheless, the experience from the experiments with the model gave us so much insight into the problem that we will now try to develop a concept of promoting OR in Germany more efficiently than before.

4. "Managerial puzzles" as a means to approach managers

A very important factor for marketing OR is the knowledge of the *media* and *means* by which the decision makers and other potential customers can be approached. One may think of *books* (primers for managers), *articles* in manager journals and newspapers (where case-studies, interviews and reports on OR-conferences are published), *pamphlets* (edited by the OR-societies), introductory *lectures, meetings* and *discussions* etc. Most of these media have the disadvantage that the potential customer has to be motivated in advance. Otherwise he would not read a book or article nor attend lectures and discussions. Therefore, the *motivation* is much more important than actual teaching OR in the first phase of learning about the use and techniques of OR.

In order to motivate the potential users of OR, we started a series of "*Managerial puzzles*" in German management journals. Our argument was the following: Reading is a more or less *passive* activity. After having read several articles in a journal (e.g. on a journey) one will become tired and wants to do something active. The reader may turn his interest to a "Managerial puzzle" in the same journal and try to solve it. This puzzle may be a more or less funny problem which can be solved by OR. It must be *simple enough* to motivate the reader to try and find a solution. On the other hand, it must be *difficult enough* to give him the impression that a *systematic approach* would be much more promising. The single puzzles may of course be of a standard problem type as if they were taken from an OR textbook, only funnier.

One example (published in Manager-Magazin, Hamburg, March 1972) reads as follows. A company plans to assign five new sales managers to five sales districts. Due to the different skills and personalities of the five candidates, it is expected that they gain different total sales in the single districts. The estimations on the total sales (in 10^6 DM) are given in the following table.

	Districts				
	Wholesalers south	Wholesalers north	Department stores	Industry south	Industry north
Herr Ackermann	15	21*	10	16	25
Herr Berger	19*	20	11	17	25
Herr Cramer	10	16	9	13*	19
Herr Dietz	12	19	9	13	24*
Herr Eichler	9	14	7*	10	16

The company seeks to assign managers to districts so that total sales are maximised.

The solution (marked with asterisks) of this simply classical assignment problem may, hopefully, be surprising for the non-specialists of OR because the fields with $25 \cdot 10^6$ DM (maximum!) are not in the optimal solution, but the field with $7 \cdot 10^6$ DM (minimum!) has been chosen.

The aim of this type of puzzles is to cause "breakthroughs" like: "Isn't this the very type of problem we have to solve?", or "How come Herr Eichler is assigned to the department stores? This combination is the very one with the smallest sales!", or "How come I try for more than 30 minutes and get a second class solution while OR people claim that they need only 5 minutes for the optimum?". If the reader asks these questions, he may be motivated enough to spend more time for becoming informed about the principles of OR.

I am convinced that the *slow progress* of OR in several countries, at least in Germany, is due to the *lack of a general concept* of how to market and promote OR. A *model* seems to be very useful in developing such a concept even if most of the data of the model are only approximations. The success of a general promotion concept based on such a model depends very much upon the *means* by which the potential customers are approached and by the *quality* of these approaches. Managerial puzzles are only one means among many. It cannot as yet be judged how successful our managerial puzzles will be.

AUTHOR INDEX

SUBJECT INDEX